GOOD GUIDE TO
DOG
FRIENDLY
PUBS, HOTELS
AND B&Bs

4TH EDITION

D0588446

Please send reports on dog friendly pubs, hotels and B&Bs to:

Dogs

FREEPOST TN1569

WADHURST

TN5 7BR

or email us at dogs@goodguides.com

GOOD GUIDE TO

DOG

FRIENDLY
PUBS, HOTELS
AND B&Bs

4TH EDITION

Edited by Alisdair Aird and Fiona Stapley

Managing Editor Karen Fick

Walks Consultant Tim Locke

Additional Research Fiona Wright

EBURY
PRESS

5 7 9 10 8 6 4

Good Guide publications are available at special discounts for bulk purchases or for sales promotions and premiums. Special editions, including personalised covers, excerpts of existing Guides and corporate imprints, can be created in large quantities for special needs. Enquiries should be sent to the Sales Development Department, Random House, 20 Vauxhall Bridge Road, London SW1V 2SA (020 7840 8400).

Published in 2009 by Ebury Press, an imprint of Ebury Publishing

A Random House Group Company

The Random House Group Limited Reg. No. 954009

Addresses for companies within the Random House Group can be found at www.randomhouse.co.uk

A CIP catalogue record for this book is available from the British Library.

The Random House Group Limited supports The Forest Stewardship Council (FSC), the leading international forest certification organisation. All our titles that are printed on Greenpeace approved FSC certified paper carry the FSC logo. Our paper procurement policy can be found at www.rbooks.co.uk/environment

Mixed Sources
Product group from well-managed forests and other controlled sources
www.fsc.org   Cert no. TT-COC-2139
© 1996 Forest Stewardship Council
FSC

Designed and set by seagulls.net

Printed in the UK by CPI Cox & Wyman, Reading, RG1 8EX

ISBN 9780091926922

To buy books by your favourite authors and register for offers visit www.rbooks.co.uk

Contents

Introduction

Most of the staff who put this *Guide* together own dogs and like going away with them. So we're rather well placed to know what places suit dog owners best – but we could never have put this book together without the help of the many thousands of reports we have had over the years from readers of our companion guides.

We have chosen places with a real welcome for dogs and their owners. These are all places that we would have no hesitation in including in a 'non-dog' guide book – indeed, many of them are distinguished entries in one of our sister publications. They span a tremendous range of styles, from simple B&Bs or farmhouses through cheery pubs and venerable inns to luxurious hotels. We have put special effort into tracking down places with plenty of good walks nearby.

Information in this *Guide* was correct when it was researched towards the end of 2008. Unfortunately, over the years, we have found that establishments can change their policy on welcoming dogs. One bad experience with a dog guest can be enough to cause a place to completely rescind their dog welcome. It is therefore possible that by the time you come to make a reservation, a handful of places included in the *Guide* will no longer welcome dogs.

Do please help us by telling us about places you have visited with your dog. Simply send an e-mail to dogs@goodguides.com, write to Dogs, FREEPOST TN1569, WADHURST, TN5 7BR – no stamp needed if you post in the UK, or use the pre-printed forms at the back of the book.

Ten tips for top dog holidays

Making sure your dog enjoys a break as much as you do boils down mainly to common sense and a little forethought. And do think of other people – a little consideration for staff and other visitors goes a long way.

1 Always phone the establishment to discuss with the owners or manager what their rules are regarding dogs BEFORE you book a room. If you turn up with two large rottweilers without pre-booking, you might not get the warm reception you were hoping for. Many places set aside bedrooms that are particularly suitable for dogs, such as ground floor rooms or rooms with access to the outside. And often, there is a charge for dogs – check this when booking.

2 Check your pet insurance to see that it covers personal liability – knocking over furniture, tripping people up, and so forth.

3 Check which areas your dog is allowed into, as some places will only allow them in bedrooms.

4 Most establishments will not allow dogs to be left alone in bedrooms as they could become unhappy, anxious or bored and then might howl endlessly or even end up chewing the room to pieces.

5 Make sure you take your dog's own bedding, a towel for drying muddy paws, and any favourite toys. Some places do provide bowls and food but often it's best to stick to regular mealtimes and the bowls and food they are used to.

6 Hairy dogs need a really thorough brushing beforehand, to minimise errant hairs.

7 Obviously, you wouldn't want to take a really unsociable dog away. Many proprietors have dogs and other animals of their own (and children of course), and therefore will not want a visiting pet that is difficult with them – or with other guests.

8 Do remember to keep your dog under control all the time – we find that it's more relaxing to keep even the best-behaved dogs on leads.

9 Make sure when you leave that there is no evidence that your dog has been there – either inside or out.

10 If you are hoping to explore the area, most proprietors will be able to point you in the direction of good nearby walks, and some attractions have facilities where you can leave your dog in special kennels; it is worth checking this beforehand.

In the countryside with your dog

Many dogs appreciate the countryside as much as their owners do. Whether your dog likes the hills, open heaths or coastal landscapes, there is plenty of choice across Britain. However, there's by no means unlimited access, and the law requires you to keep your dog under control and put it on a lead when crossing fields with livestock in. A farmer actually has the right to shoot dogs that are worrying his farm animals: though this not a common occurrence, it does happen from time to time. If your dog is on a lead and you find it and yourself being chased by a farm animal, it is generally safer to let the dog off the lead than to risk injury to yourself.

It's also considerate to carry plastic bags to clean up your dog's own mess, and to make sure your dog keeps well away from birds' nests (bear in mind that some birds lay their eggs on the ground) and other wildlife.

Places you can generally walk your dog in England and Wales are:

- **Public roads**, though they're obviously not always ideal.
- Most **beaches**. Some popular beaches ban dogs in the summer, and – even more than anywhere else – it is always considerate to clean up after your dog on beaches (as it is everywhere).
- Paths and tracks on **National Trust land** (apart from National Trust gardens and house estates, where you need a ticket to get in, though some of these welcome dogs on leads) that are dedicated as public land and have free access: these include areas of coast, woodlands and open land.
- **Canal towpaths** unless there's a sign to the contrary.
- Paths and tracks in areas of forest owned by the **Forestry Commission**, though these may be temporarily closed during felling operations.
- Areas designated as **country parks**. Many of these are owned by local authorities, and you are allowed to wander where you like within them.
- Anywhere along a **public footpath**, **public bridleway** or **public byway** (the three together are also known generically as **public rights of way**). Bridleways are also open to horse-riders and

cyclists, and byways are open to all traffic, so unless these have a paved surface they can be a lot more muddy in wet weather. Public rights of way are normally signposted from roads, and once you're on them there may be **waymark arrows** (red for byways, blue for bridleways and yellow for footpaths). There are also paths where the landowner allows access as '**permissive paths**' or '**licensed paths**' but which aren't formally public rights of way; here the landowner has the right to close the path at any time.

- **Access land** in uncultivated countryside, where you have a '**right to roam**' under recent legislation (the Countryside and Rights of Way Act) that is now in effect across England and Wales.
- **Scotland** has a quite different law about access to the country-side. There are some legal rights of way, but not many, and they aren't shown as such on OS maps. Generally things get by on an informal basis: there's a general tolerance towards walkers, who can effectively go anywhere on moorland and mountains outside the grouse-shooting and deer-stalking seasons. Dogs may not be welcome on moorland because of nesting game birds; look out for notices, or check locally at tourist information centres.

What the right to roam means

You have access on foot to many areas of moors, mountains, downland, heaths and registered commons that have been designated as **access land**. Here you have the right to walk wherever you like and don't have to stick to paths, although in places vegetation and the lie of the land won't make it universally possible to go absolutely everywhere. Not all uncultivated land is access land – just the bits that have been designated and mapped (some of it may have been open informally for years). And it doesn't cover farmland, woods, coast or parkland; even in areas of open-looking hills such as the South Downs, the access areas are quite confined.

Since the law set up these access areas in 2004, a large number of new gates and stiles have been erected to allow you to get in to access land, and at key points there are brown and white circular pictograms depicting a walker wandering through lumpy terrain. Once you are inside the access area there may only be one exit.

OS Explorer 1:25,000 scale maps (see below) show where these access areas are.

Do note the restrictions: you must keep dogs on a short lead if near livestock, and at all times during March to July; dogs may also, at any time, be banned temporarily or permanently from some areas of land such as places where birds tend to nest. You also aren't allowed to ride a horse, cycle, light fires, camp or feed livestock; if you do, you lose your right to roam for 72 hours. There may also be local restrictions on night-time access.

Getting information

- **OS maps** Wherever you are in England and Wales, the first point of reference is the local Ordnance Survey (OS) map: both the purple-covered Landranger series (at a scale of 1:50,000, or about one and a quarter inches to the mile) and the orange-covered Explorer series (at a scale of 1:25,000, or about two and a half inches to the mile) show rights of way (green crosses for byways, long green dashes for bridleways and short green dashes for footpaths; sometimes these are partly overprinted with green diamonds denoting long-distance routes like the Cotswold Way); on Landranger maps it's the same set of symbols, but with red instead of green. Access land is shown with a yellow wash and a dark orange border, on Explorer maps only; they also show with an *i* in an orange circle the points of 'primary access', where there's an information board and a way in to the access land; but other gates and stiles giving you access on to the land aren't shown. Areas of other land that are always open as access land (National Trust, National Trust for Scotland and Forestry Commission) are shown on Explorer and Landranger maps with purple boundaries.
- **Dog stiles and gates** Bridleways and byways use gates rather than stiles, which makes things much easier for dog walking, as some stiles are baffling for dogs. But you usually need local knowledge to find out whether a particular public footpath is going to be suitable for your dog in its provision of stiles and gates. Some councils and landowners are increasingly installing easily climbed stiles, or gates rather than stiles, or excellent

stiles with dog gates built into them – and there's now a legal requirement for councils to take into account the needs of the less mobile when stiles or gates are installed. In the meantime, finding out if a certain path has dog-friendly stiles or gates isn't straightforward. Some local tourist information centres stock leaflets showing stile-free walks suitable for dogs.

- **Dogs on trains** are carried free of charge. Obviously you need to have the dog on a lead. For journey planners by rail, see **www.nationalrail.co.uk**. For buses, **see www.traveline.org.uk**.

- **Guided walks** are run by all sorts of organisations. The largest of these is the Ramblers' Association, which has local clubs across the entire country. Leaders may or may not allow dogs, so it's always worth checking first. For details of group walks and other events, as well as a wide array of information about where to walk, rights of access and walking gear, **see www.ramblers.org**. You can try a walk for free, but are expected to join the Rambler's Association if you go on several. There's also the splendid Butcher's Great North Dog Walk (**www.cooksondogwalk.co.uk**), held each June in North-East England. A major fund-raising event, it has made it into the *Guinness Book of Records* as the largest dog walk ever held, with numbers each time now well in excess of 6,000 dogs.

- Finally, although it's not really connected to dog walking, if you're into cycling and want to take your dog along with you, there are **dog cycle trailers** that hitch on to the back of your bike, allowing your dog to enjoy the ride. A search on www.google.co.uk for dog+ "cycle trailers" comes up with some useful results.

How the *Guide* Works

Each chapter is divided into two sections – Dog Friendly Pubs, followed by Dog Friendly Hotels, Inns, B&Bs and Farms (not all types of accommodation are recommended in each area).

The maps will help you locate places that have accommodation – pubs that have bedrooms are indicated on the map with a ⦿. Other places that have bedrooms are marked with a ⊡.

Dog Friendly Pubs

- We show opening hours for pubs and note any days that places are closed altogether, whether they have a restaurant, and if they offer bar food.

- Standard food service times in pubs is 12-2, 7-9 Monday to Saturday (food service often stops a bit earlier on Sundays). If food times are significantly different to this, we list the times. We note days when we know pubs do not serve food, but suggest you check first before planning an expedition that depends on getting a meal there.

- Bedroom prices normally include full english breakfasts, VAT and any automatic service charge that we know about. If we give just one price, it is the total price for two people sharing a double or twin-bedded room for one night. Otherwise, prices before the / are for single occupancy, prices after it for double. A capital B against the price means that it includes a private bathroom, a capital S a private shower.

Dog Friendly Hotels, Inns, B&Bs and Farms

- The price we give in each entry in this section of the *Guide* is the total for two people sharing a double or twin-bedded room with its own bathroom for one night. It includes a full english breakfast, VAT and any automatic service charge that we know about. We say if dinner is included in this total price, which it may be at some of the more remote places.

- A price at the end of an entry tells you how much a place charges for your dog to stay.

- Many hotels have very good value short break prices, especially out of season, so it's always worth asking.

- If we know that the back rooms are the quietest or the front ones have the best views or the ones in the new extension are more spacious, then we say so.

- We always mention a restaurant if we know there is one and we commend food if we have information supporting a positive recommendation. Many B&Bs will recommend nearby pubs for evening meals if they do not offer dinner.

Let's Go for a Walk

Many of the places listed in this *Guide* are in particularly lovely countryside and some of them have great walks right on their doorsteps. This listing gives just a handful of pubs that are perfectly sited for a walk, a drink and a meal with your canine friend. We've only provided an outline to the actual walk, so you will need an OS map (1:25,000 scale Explorer sheets are the best) to help you plan and follow your precise route, though in some instances you might not need a map where the walks follow obvious physical features like coastline or canals, and in London an *A-Z* will work.

BEDFORDSHIRE
Prince of Wales at Ampthill (page 29)

There's free access in Ampthill Park – a surprisingly wild expanse just north-west of Ampthill, with woodland and grassland – once a hunting ground of Henry VIII. Car parks are on the south side, off the B530, and the park is crossed by the Greensand Ridge Walk. You can extend the stroll by walking north from the church to the ruins of Houghton House.

BERKSHIRE
Crown & Garter at Inkpen (page 35)

A few minutes' walk north-east along Great Common Road from the pub leads to Inkpen Common Nature Reserve, a patch of ancient heathland, with three types of heather and a variety of birdlife; kissing gates rather than stiles make it easy for most dogs. In total contrast, a mile south up the lane gets you to car parks at the top of the downs either side of Walbury Hill, a really bracing place in the wind, and with huge views north. The easy chalk track along the top of the escarpment west leads past the macabre landmark of Coombe Gibbet.

BUCKINGHAMSHIRE
White Horse at Hedgerley (page 42)

Around Hedgerley are some splendid broad-leafed woodlands, laced with paths and with plenty of potential for walks, at their most spectacular when carpets of bluebells appear in spring or when the leaves turn in autumn (autumn colours are especially famed at Burnham Beeches to the south-west). Almost next to the White Horse is the entrance to Church Wood RSPB Reserve (they request that you keep your dog on a lead, especially during the April to June nesting season), known for its woodland birds, including great spotted woodpeckers, nuthatches and tree creepers.

CHESHIRE
Ship at Wincle (page 60)

Just down the road from the Ship is the River Dane, and the start of some super woodland and hill walks for dogs who can cope with stiles and gradients – along the Dane Valley eastwards towards Gradbach, and up into Forest Wood (where you can search out the hidden chasm known as Lud's Church – not a church at all, but thought to have been a secret meeting place of religious dissenters), and back over the top and past Hangingstone Farm. A road corner at Bearstone Rock, to the east, is another possible objective with its sweeping views across the valley.

CORNWALL
Pandora near Mylor Bridge (page 65)

You can walk 2 miles (3.2km) around the coast south-east from the Pandora, past Weir Point and round to Mylor Creek, getting terrific views across the busy boating waters of Carrick Roads. The path eventually ends at Mylor Bridge, from where you can either take the road back to the pub or pick up a path and then a lane back to Weir Point.

CUMBRIA
Old Dungeon Ghyll at Langdale (page 91)

Some wonderful low-level walking from here is along a bridleway section of the Cumbria Way, with easily managed gates. West of Old Dungeon Ghyll is an easily managed track along the valley of Mickleden Beck, with formidable peaks rising ahead and on either side: you can walk for about 2 miles (3.2km) before the terrain steepens appreciably. Eastwards, the Cumbria Way heads to the Dungeon Ghyll New Hotel, from which it's a steep, rocky climb up to Stickle Tarn, marvellously placed under the Langdale Pikes summits. Southwards is Blea Tarn (one of several Blea Tarns in the Lake District, but the most scenic), with its own car park nearby; it's also within reach from the pub via a steep path that starts from the campsite.

Langstrath at Stonethwaite (page 86)

You can enjoy very satisfying views of Borrowdale by an easy level 2-mile (3.2km) circular walk from Stonethwaite – over Stonethwaite Bridge, then left along Stonethwaite Beck to the next hamlet, Rosthwaite, where you cross over and take the lane on the far side of the B5289, then left on the path by the River Derwent, over the next bridge and back on the lane to Stonethwaite.

DERBYSHIRE

Monsal Head Hotel at Monsal Head (page 98)

The view from here lures you down to the Monsal Trail, which goes over the old railway viaduct you can see below, and along a railway-track bed. It's easy going for dogs, and if you'd rather not take in the steep path from the hotel to the trail, you can start from a car park and picnic site on the A6 at the valley floor level. Either direction is beautiful: westwards extends a mile (1.6km) until you are diverted away from a tunnel entrance and past the old textile mill at Cressbrook and into Miller's Dale.

DEVON

Rock Inn at Haytor Vale (page 124)

One of the best viewpoints in Dartmoor is nearby: drive up to the car park at Haytor Rocks, and use the rock groups, the abandoned quarries and track beds of defunct tramways to guide you round the moor.

Rugglestone at Widecombe (page 118)

Good, breezy moorland strolls include eastwards up to Rugglestone Rock and the Logan Stone, and from Widecombe village to the wide ridge of Hamel Down – the latter reached by following the lane towards Natsworthy then branching up a steadily rising track, alongside a wall on the right. It can be boggy on the moor in places, but that is more than compensated by the wonderful feeling of space.

DORSET

Square & Compass at Worth Matravers (page 136)

Several routes lead out to the cliffs from here: the easiest, and least interesting, is along the road west to Renscombe Farm, then left on the lane down to the atmospherically unadorned ancient clifftop chapel on St Aldhelm's Head (1.5miles/2.4km total); it's more fun, but much more challenging to keep west on a path from Renscombe Farm to join the switchback coast path above Chapman's Pool. The coast path is wonderful in either direction, but it's not for vertigo sufferers, and there are stiles on the way. Eastwards you can edge round the coast and return to Worth Matravers along the valley floor of Winspit Bottom.

ESSEX

Sun at Dedham (page 141)

On the north side of the village, Dedham Mill is a starting point for walks along the River Stour at the heart of the landscapes associated with John Constable – the most famous section starts half a mile (1km) or so east, through unspoilt meadows that continue past Flatford Mill, the scene of his most-reproduced paintings. You can extend the walk into a 7-mile (11km) circuit by carrying on past Manningtree rail station and following the Essex Way back to Dedham.

GLOUCESTERSHIRE

Bell at Sapperton (page 156)

Beneath the church, a stroll down through the meadows and into trees brings you to the ornate tunnel entrance to the overgrown, derelict Thames and Severn Canal. The locks have gone and the canal has reverted into a rather beautiful wilderness, all easily enjoyed via the canal towpath, which makes a pleasant walk to Daneway. There's more good strolling ground just north of the village, where a lane to the right of the church dips to the valley floor and you can continue on a path through woods that have a memorably heady whiff of wild garlic in early summer.

HAMPSHIRE

Royal Oak at Fritham (page 166)

You can wander at will through much of the New Forest, but beware that ponies and deer may be at large, the presence of which might either frighten your dog or encourage it to give chase. Finding a path isn't difficult; more of a problem is losing your way, as there is a huge network of paths. From the end of the public road near the Royal Oak you can step straight into the wilds of the area, which here vary pleasantly between planted forest and open heathland.

HEREFORDSHIRE

Riverside Inn at Aymestrey (page 176)

A short distance east close to Croft Castle, Bircher Common has plenty of space for dogs to run around. You can park here and walk through forest up Fishpool Valley to Croft Ambrey, a grassy-topped Iron-Age fort with plenty of dips and ramparts, and choice views into Shropshire.

HERTFORDSHIRE

Greyhound at Aldbury (page 183)

Adjacent to Aldbury, the glorious forests of the Ashridge Estate make ideal dog-walking terrain, with tracks that go long distances without meeting a road. Just east of the Greyhound, a track leads from the road up into the woodlands and to the Bridgewater Monument (a tall column to the canal-building third Duke of Bridgewater), the major landmark hereabouts. If you prefer more open ground, head to Ivinghoe Beacon – a knob of chalk escarpment jutting out over a vast plain; it's a walk of 3.5 miles (5.6km) from Aldbury and you can avoid the road virtually all the way, or you can park near the Beacon.

ISLE OF WIGHT
Sun at Hulverstone (page 188)

The views from this pub might well tempt you out for a walk with your dog, and there are several possibilities. The best direction is downhill on a path towards the sea (you'll need to turn right after Downton Cottage to Brook to avoid reaching the A3055 with no continuation on the other side). In a few minutes, you reach the A3055 and then the coast path (about 1 mile/1.6km from the pub): beware the low cliffs which are very crumbly on this part of the coastline.

Inland, a path opposite the Sun climbs up fairly steeply to woodland and you can continue to the prehistoric Long Stone or up to the next ridge, which has two grassy summits either side of the B3399 – both with extensive views.

KENT
Chaser at Shipbourne (page 198)

Shipbourne has a patch of open common, through which runs the waymarked Greensand Way. Paths hereabouts are plentiful and easily followed, although an OS map is, as ever, handy for working out the best routes: by avoiding the busy A227 and using smaller lanes as link sections, you can use the Greensand Way and other paths to take in Ightham Mote and a nicely varied escarpment leading west from there towards One Tree Hill, or explore the country towards Ivy Hatch, Fairlawne Park and Plaxtol.

NORFOLK
Kings Arms at Blakeney (page 217)

All of the Norfolk Coast Path here is gloriously straightforward dog-walking terrain – easy to find, easy underfoot and plenty to enjoy looking at. From Blakeney, and many other places along the coast, the route follows the top of a grassy dyke around the marshes. Eastwards it loops around past the remains of Blakeney Chapel to Cley next the Sea (the frequent CoastHopper bus service is a useful means of getting back between Cley, Blakeney and other points on the coast; they don't charge for dogs, and will take them provided they're not a risk to other passengers; for details phone 01553 776980). Westwards, the coast path heads on the landward side of the marshes to Morston, from where there's a seasonal boat service to the long coastal spit of Blakeney Point.

SOMERSET

Crown at Churchill (page 256)

The Crown is well positioned for one of the very best walks in the Mendips, around Dolebury Warren and towards Burrington Combe. From the pub, head along The Batch southwards, then fork left to cross the A38, where you'll find a lane leading past a small car park: from there it's an easily managed valley-floor track with gates: it's worth continuing for 1 mile (1.6km) to a junction of tracks where you can return by turning left up over Dolebury Warren – an open hill with lots of space for dogs – with far-reaching views from the Iron-Age hill fort at the western end. You can extend the walk further east to take in the moorland above the limestone gorge of Burrington Combe; the road on the floor of the gorge is unfenced and pleasant to walk along.

Exmoor Forest Inn at Simonsbath (page 261)

This is delightfully quiet countryside: from Simonsbath, there's a stile-free, farm-yard-free walk parallel to the north bank of the River Barle, on an easily followed bridleway. About 2 miles (3.2km) of walking takes you past the site of Wheal Eliza mine to Cow Castle, as rustic as it sounds – a grassy hillock with traces of an Iron-Age hill fort on it. From there it's best to return the same way.

STAFFORDSHIRE

George at Alstonefield (page 269)

You'll need to keep your dog on a lead for much of this walk, but it is a most satisfying way of sneaking in through the back door to the spectacular natural wonders of Dove Dale, with its stone arches and other limestone formations. The popular way into Dove Dale is from the southern end, where you almost have to queue to get in at busy weekends: from Alstonefield you can either follow the lane down to Milldale (at Dove Dale's northern end) and then head downstream or walk across fields to Stanshope and down Hall Dale to join the main (broad and level) path in Dove Dale at a footbridge near Ilam Rock.

SUFFOLK

Lord Nelson at Southwold (page 275)

Plenty of space on the beach and some lovely areas of common give plenty of possibilities for dog walkers. Southwold has a long beach and a spacious common: dogs are allowed on the Denes (the southern stretch of the beach) but barred from certain areas near the pier during the holiday season. From there, you can continue round to the mouth of the canalised River Blyth, where a summer ferry sometimes operates to Walberswick (giving scope for carrying on along Dunwich River and towards Walberswick Nature Reserve); follow the river upstream to the bridge, then go right up to Southwold Common and back into the town to complete a very uncomplicated 2.5 miles (4km).

SURREY

Donkey at Charleshill (page 282)

Unproblematic stile-free routes head through the forest on either side of the road from Charleshill. Northwards, you can head along the lane (a bridleway only) towards Crooksbury Comon, an access area of heathland and woodland, where you can go where you please.

Three Horseshoes at Thursley (page 286)

Reached by taking the Greensand Way north from Thursley is Thursley Common, one of the best Surrey heaths for walking, with sandy paths and tracks running between large expanses of heather and patches of woodland. Several ponds make attractive points to head for, and the Moat car park just off the road to Elstead is another useful starting point.

SUSSEX

Bull at Ditchling (page 289)

There's plenty of space and a complete absence of stiles along the South Downs Way above Ditchling: you can drive up to the car park on Ditchling Beacon, or walk up by a combination of tracks and paths, parallel to and east of the Ditchling Beacon road. Once at the top, the South Downs Way has the best of the views, and any diversions involve dropping some way, often into bottoms of secluded dry valleys: objectives to the west include the Jack and Jill windmills, and (off the South Downs Way, but well waymarked) the Chattri Indian War Memorial.

Giants Rest at Wilmington (page 295)

Heading up Wilmington's village street from the Giants Rest, you reach the church: a track opposite heads east to Folkington, easy to follow but the mud gets impossibly sticky after rain. Alternatively, continue past the car park at Wilmington Priory, from where a path runs beside and just above the road towards the Long Man of Wilmington: by turning left along the base of the slope, you can find a path that climbs up the steep slope and to the top (if that is too steep for you or your dog, turn right to reach a junction with the South Downs Way, on which turn left uphill). Once up, there's appreciable space for dogs to run around – on the South Downs Way or on the bridleway leading south-west to Winchester's Pond – and you're well out of earshot of traffic and other intrusions.

WILTSHIRE

Bear at Devizes (page 307)

A few minutes' stroll leads to the Kennet and Avon Canal, where the towpath westwards encounters the Caen locks (29 in total) – the longest flight of locks in Britain. Unusually, there are pounds at the side of 15 of the locks for storing the water. It's best to return the same way, as other paths aren't that useful.

WORCESTER
Nags Head at Malvern (page 319)

From the top of the long Malverns ridge, there are terrific views across the Midlands and into the Welsh borders, and an almost bewildering number of paths to get you up to the top. It's all very dog friendly and somewhat more easily managed and municipal than you might expect for a range of hills that looks formidably Alpine from the hazy distance, with benches sited every few paces on amiable grassy terrain. Worcestershire Beacon, the highest point, is close to the town centre of Malvern and is easily reached by walking past St Ann's Well.

YORKSHIRE
Charles Bathurst at Langthwaite (page 334)

The higher-level walks hereabouts tend to involve less in the way of fiddly field crossing, and once you get up above the east side of Langthwaite you get some exhilarating views into Arkegarthdale – for instance along past intriguingly named Booze and along Fremington Edge. At valley level, a bridleway from Langthwaite's bridge leads along the river for 0.5 mile (1km) or so before rising past Strothwaite Hall.

Lion at Blakey Ridge (page 323)

Either side of the road from here are splendid level walks through the moor, on former railway tracks that once served the ironstone quarries. On the east side, the track loops around lazily, giving effortless views over Farndale.

White Lion at Cray (page 332)

There's a particularly wonderful 4.5 mile (7km) circular walk through Cray, which you can start from Buckden and follow the bridleway (a well-marked track) to Cray, then a path around through fields and along a level section beneath limestone scars, with grandstand views down Wharfedale, before dropping to Hubberholme. The final section follows the road and then the river path to Buckden.

SCOTLAND
George at Inveraray (page 348)

Good tracks through the forests west of Inveraray and the loch give some possibilities to take the dog for a walk from the George. In particular, the road past Inveraray Castle leads to the base of Dunchuach, a wooded hill where a path laces up to a sham ruined tower, giving terrific views of Loch Fyne, Ben Vorlich and more.

Border at Kirk Yetholm (page 350)

As Kirk Yetholm is at the very end of the long-distance Pennine Way, you might like to follow it in reverse for a distance and greet walkers who have nearly made it to the end. The first stretch is along a surfaced, but virtually traffic-free, farm road. After the last building, the route climbs appreciably up on to the high moors of the Cheviots, reaching a saddle between The Curr and Black Hag – a total distance from Kirk Yetholm of about 4 miles (6.5km).

WALES

Royal Oak at Gladestry (page 369)

Hergest Ridge is the hill to go up here: from the centre of Gladestry, the Offa's Dyke signs point you up a steadily rising track that very soon gets you up among the bracken and close-nibbled turf. There's a tremendous amount of space, though you need to keep the lead handy in case sheep or horses are at large. It's very easy going underfoot – almost carpet-like – and views take in Shropshire, the Malverns, the Black Mountains and the Brecon Beacons.

St Brides Inn at Little Haven (page 369)

The coastal position here may tempt you to sample some of the coast path, which is better in the westwards direction. There are no stiles on the 5 miles (8km) between here and St Brides, although there are one or two short, steep sections and several gates. From Strawberry Hill to St Brides is virtually level.

Pen-y-Gwryd at Llanberis (page 370)

There's really nothing here along the level, but energetic dogs may like the walk up from here following the Miners Track northwards to the saddle between Glyder Fach and Y Foel Goch. If you choose not to continue up either of these summits, you can just enjoy the superlative view ahead of Tryfan.

LONDON

Dove (page 341)

The entire walk from Putney Bridge, over Hammersmith Bridge and along Lower Mall and Upper Mall is full of interest, and free from traffic, with plenty of archi-tecture, riverside gardens and river scenery to enjoy as you continue into Chiswick Mall. It's worth going on as far as the Church of St Nicholas at the end of Chiswick Mall, and seeking out Hogarth's tomb.

Spaniards Inn (page 344)

A London *A-Z* is surprisingly handy for guiding you round Hampstead Heath – what is effectively a country walk through woodland and across the grass; it's all nicely complicated and feels much larger than it is – big enough to get lost in. There's a huge number of paths ideal for directionless ambling, but you might like to build in some landmarks – Kenwood House, Highate Ponds and the view-point at Parliament Hill are good targets to aim for.

Calendar of Dog Events

We've searched the country to locate some fun events that you and your dog can attend together and enjoy some sort of doggy attraction when you get there – anything from working dog displays to a waggiest tail competition. As the *Guide* is published biennially, we have given you the month of the event but in instances where the event always takes place on the same day of the year we've given the rule. As we went to press, organisers told us that well behaved dogs are welcome on a fixed length lead but it's worth checking that the dog welcome policy hasn't changed since we researched this information, and of course checking the date of the event before you leave home.

BEDFORDSHIRE
July
Old Warden
Bedfordshire County Show at the English School of Falconry with dog shows and working dog displays (01767) 627288; second weekend in July
September
Old Warden
Bedfordshire Steam and Country Fair at the Shuttleworth Collection: working dog demonstrations, steam tractors, heavy horses, working crafts, motor show (01462) 851711; third weekend after the August bank holiday weekend

CAMBRIDGESHIRE
October
Peterborough
Autumn Show: trade stands, rare breeds, heavy horses, pony club, have-a-go dog agility and dog show at the East of England Showground (01733) 234451

CHESHIRE
June
Tabley
Cheshire County Show: livestock, dog show (over 100 classes), horses, flowers, food hall with live demonstrations, crafts, country pursuits, hundreds of trade stands and main ring events (01565) 650200

August

Knutsford
Country Show at Tatton Park: gundog display, have-a-go fun scurry, sheepdog handling, lurcher and terrier shows, flyball racing, scurry driving, country trade, craft village (01283) 820548

Knutsford
Fun Dog Show at Tatton Park: turn up and take part – ten novelty classes including saddest eyes, waggiest tail and scruffiest dog, also fun agility course (01625) 534400; second Saturday in August

October

Tabley
Game and Country Show at the Cheshire Show Ground: gundog display, have-a-go fun scurry, flyball racing, sheepdog handling, lurcher and terrier shows, scurry driving, country trades, craft village (01283) 820548

CORNWALL

June

Wadebridge
Royal Cornwall Show: huge show with main arena, motor and steam fair, lots of animals and major dog show (01208) 812183

CUMBRIA

June

Ravenglass
West Lakes Country Fair: gundog display, have-a-go fun scurry, sheepdog handling, lurcher and terrier shows, scurry driving, country trade stands (01229) 717614

July

Carlisle
Cumberland County Show: main arena, lots of animals, countryside area, food hall and dog show at Rickerby Park (01697) 747397; first Saturday in July

August

Patterdale
Dog Day: sheepdog trials, sheep show, foxhound show, terrier show, children's pet dog show, gundog show, show of sticks and crooks, adults and children's fell race, trail hound races with bookmaker, crafts tent, trade stands, beer tent and refreshments (017684)82434; August bank holiday Saturday

Threlkeld
Sheepdog Trials: hound show and working terriers (017687) 79032

September

Crooklands
Westmorland County Show at the Westmorland County Showfield: over 350 trade stands, Kennel Club dog show, hound and terrier show and terrier racing (015395) 67804

DERBYSHIRE

August

Hope

Show and Sheepdog Trials with vintage tractors and engines, classic cars and gundogs (01433) 620507; August bank holiday Monday

September

Chatsworth

Country Fair at Chatsworth Park: dog agility, terrier racing and show, fun dog show, lurcher racing, sheepdog and gundog trials, grand ring, hot air balloons, trade and craft stands (01328) 821821; Friday to Sunday following August bank holiday weekend

Hayfield

Sheepdog Trials and Country Show at Spray House Farm: fun dog show, dog agility and terrier show (01663) 746580; third Friday to Sunday in September

DEVON

May

Clyst St Mary

County Show at Westpoint Arena: lots to see inc dog show every day (01392) 446000

July

Totnes

Totnes and District Show at Berry Pomeroy: terrier racing, family dog show, livestock, donkeys, rabbits, craft tent, over 100 trade stands, show jumping and main ring entertainment (01548) 821070

September

Powderham

South Western Game and Country Fair at Powderham Castle: gundog display, have-a-go fun scurry, sheepdog handling, lurcher and terrier shows, scurry driving, country trade stands (01626) 890243

DORSET

May

Sherborne

Country Fair at Sherborne Castle: dog scurries, dog show, dog agility displays, gundogs and a retriever event. Also falconry, craft stalls and demonstrations of country crafts and skills, main ring attractions, rural and leisure pursuits demonstrations and heavy horses and rare breeds show (01935) 813182; spring bank holiday Monday

ESSEX

August

Ongar

Essex Game and Country Fair at Blake Hall: gundog display, have-a-go fun scurry, sheepdog handling, lurcher and terrier shows, scurry driving, country trade stands (01277) 362502

September
Billericay
Essex Country Show: monster trucks, animal displays, steam engines, vintage cars and dog demonstrations (01268) 290228

GLOUCESTERSHIRE
September
Frampton on Severn
Country Fair at Frampton Court Park: gundogs, dog agility, companion dog show, lurchers and terriers, rural skills, agricultural breeds, main and lake rings (01452) 740267

HAMPSHIRE
May
Romsey
Hampshire Country Fair at Broadlands: gundog display, have-a-go fun scurry, sheepdog handling, lurcher and terrier shows, country trade, craft village (01283) 820548
Highclere
Country Fair at Highclere Castle: sheepdogs, gundogs, terriers and lurchers, shooting, trade shows, main arena demonstrations (01889) 563232 or 0845 2305175; spring bank holiday Sunday and Monday
July
Brockenhurst
New Forest and County Show: large agricultural and equestrian event with international showjumping, terrier racing, working hounds, horses, livestock, flower show, crafts, forestry, ring displays and 600 trade stands (01590) 622400; last Tuesday to Thursday in July

HERTFORDSHIRE
May
Redbourn
County Show: Hertfordshire flyball team, gundogs display, motorbike display, Devils Horsemen, livestock and country crafts (01582) 792626
August
Hatfield
Country Show at Hatfield House: rural crafts, dog agility, terrier racing, polo, heavy horse driving, falconry, children's farm (01707) 287010
October
Knebworth
Game and Country Show at Knebworth House: gundog display, have-a-go fun scurry, sheepdog handling, lurcher and terrier shows, scurry driving, country trade, craft village (01438) 812661

ISLE OF WIGHT
April
Binstead
Canine Show at Brickfields Horse Country (01983) 566801

KENT
March
Detling
Kent Game and Country Festival at the Kent Showground: gundog scurries, two arenas, countryside demonstrations, vintage tractor and machinery area and trade stands (01884) 250230
July
Detling
Kent Show: agricultural show with food, wine, rural crafts, game fair, equestrian events, terrier racing, sheepdogs, police dogs, gundogs, 600 trade stands and countryside and forestry area (01622) 630975

LANCASHIRE
August
Garstang
Agricultural Show: livestock, horses, a variety of entertainment inc vintage machinery displays, dog show, 100 stands, food hall and a parade of vintage and modern tractors (01253) 799119; first Saturday in August

LINCOLNSHIRE
May
Stamford
Game, Country and Angling Fair at Burghley House: gundog display, have-a-go fun scurry, sheepdog handling, lurcher and terrier shows, scurry driving, country trade stands (01780) 752451

NORFOLK
April
Norwich
Game and Country Fair in New Costessey: sheepdog and duck display, gundog displays, lurcher display, dog agility and have-a-go dog agility, pet dog show, hound parade, forestry displays, lots of animals from goats to reindeer, falconry, 300 trade stands and craft hall (01263) 735828
June
Norwich
Royal Norfolk Show: livestock, dog shows, trade stands, arena displays, gardeners show, arts and crafts (01603) 748931; last Wednesday and Thursday in June
July
Holkham
Biennial Country Fair at Holkham Hall: dog agility, terrier racing and show, fun dog show, lurcher racing, gundog trials, grand ring, hot air balloons, trade and craft stands (01328) 821821; alternate years, next in 2009

September

Sandringham

Game and Country Fair at Sandringham House: gundog display, have-a-go fun scurry, sheepdog handling, lurcher and terrier shows, scurry driving, country trade, craft village, steam engines (01283) 820548

NORTHAMPTONSHIRE

April

Kelmarsh

Country Fair at Kelmarsh Hall: working dogs, terriers and lurchers, main arena demonstrations, crafts (01889) 563232 or 0845 2305175

June

Rockingham

People, Pets and Family day at Rockingham Castle Park (01536) 770240

July

Kelmarsh

Festival of History at Kelmarsh Hall: huge event with around 50 re-enactments a day and possibly including a 'dogs in history' show (01604) 686543

Castle Ashby

Country Fair at Castle Ashby: gundogs, terrier and lurcher shows, Kennel Club dog show, main ring, classic cars, trade stands, equestrian events, craft tent and falconry (01604) 696521

August

Rockingham

Steam and Country Fair at Rockingham Castle Park: steam engines, vintage & classical vehicles, military vehicles, traditional fun fair, wild west show, shire horses and family dog show with obedience, agility classes, best-looking dog event and many more classes. All visitors with a dog are welcome to take part (01536) 770240

October

Rockingham

Game Fair at Rockingham Castle Park: gundogs, hounds and lurchers (01536) 770240

NORTHUMBRIA

June

Bishop Auckland

Game and Country Fair at Witton Castle: gundog display, have-a-go fun scurry, sheepdog handling, lurcher and terrier shows, scurry driving, country trade stands (01283) 820548

NOTTINGHAMSHIRE

May

Newark

Newark and Nottinghamshire County Show at Newark Showground: gundog display, parade of hounds, stunt riders, classic and vintage cars, equestrian events (0870) 2241035

October
Newark
Game and Country Show at the Newark Showground: dog scurries, sheep show, fun fair and jousting (01702) 549623

OXFORDSHIRE
April
Thame
Thame Game and Country Show: gundog display, have-a-go fun scurry, sheep-dog handling, lurcher and terrier shows, scurry driving, country trade stands (01283) 820548

SHROPSHIRE
May
Newport
British Falconry, Raptor Fair and Country Fair at Chetwynd Park: gundog events, terrier and lurcher shows, beagle and terrier shows, dog agility, sheepdog displays, continuous arena events, falconry displays, craft fair, sporting and wildlife artists, antique and collectors fair, trade stands (01983) 822490

August
Newport
Game and Country Fair at Chetwynd Park: novelty dog shows, dog agility, gundog competitions, falconry, equestrian displays, trade stands, antiques and crafts marquees (01983) 822490; August bank holiday Sunday and Monday

SOMERSET
March
Shepton Mallet
West Country Game Fair at the Royal Bath and West Showground: equine events, gundog training, lurcher display team, racing terriers and turn up and enter dog shows (01884) 250230

STAFFORDSHIRE
September
Weston-under-Lizard
Midland Game and Country Fair: countryside events, working dog competition, sheepdogs, gundogs, terriers and lurchers, shooting, trade stands, main arena demonstrations (01889) 563232

SURREY
May
Guildford
County Show at Stoke Park: lots of livestock, main arena, stunt teams, working and gundogs, equestrian events (01483) 890810

SUSSEX
June
Pulborough
Sussex Country Fair at Parham Park: sheepdogs, gundogs, terriers and lurchers, trade stands and main arena demonstrations (01889) 563232; third weekend in June

WARWICKSHIRE
August
Stoneleigh
Town and Country Festival at Stoneleigh Park, dogs welcome on a lead: top dog ring events, fun dog shows, canine makeovers, discover breeds, dog scurry (test your dog's speed against the clock) and international flyball (024) 7669 6969; August bank holiday Saturday to Monday
Alcester
Game and Country Fair at Ragley Hall: novelty dog shows, dog agility, gundog competitions, falconry, equestrian displays, trade stands, antiques and crafts marquees (01789) 762090; Saturday and Sunday before the August bank holiday weekend

SCOTLAND
January
Aviemore
Sled Dog Rally in Glenmore Forest Park: the biggest event in the British husky calendar (0871) 277 6783
June
Ingliston
Royal Highland Show: four-day show with gundogs, sheepdogs and terrier racing, children's farm, countryside arena and music (0131) 335 6200

WALES
April
Monmouth
Game and Country Show: gundog display, have-a-go fun scurry, sheepdog handling, lurcher and terrier shows, scurry driving and country trade stands (01283) 820548
June
Usk
Wales and Borders Game and Country Fair: gundog demonstrations, hounds, dog agility, terrier and lurcher shows and racing, 150 trade stands antique and collectors fair (01983) 822490
Bodelwyddan
Country Fair at Bodelwyddan Castle: as above and well worth a visit as this is the only time of year that dogs are allowed in the grounds (01983) 822490
Monmouth
Monmouthshire Show at Vauxhall Fields: biggest one-day agricultural show in Wales with a variety of main and countryside ring attractions, horses, live-stock, big dog show (over 1,000 dogs), craft marquee, shopping mall and trade stands (01291) 691160; last Thursday in August

Dog Quiz

Here is a fun quiz for you to try in the car on your way to your dog friendly destination. The answers are on page 387.

1   How many miles a year does the average dog owner walk with their dog? **a** 132   **b** 365   **c** 676   **d** 1142

2   What unique doggy claim to fame has the little Somerset church of St Mary at Orchardleigh?

3   Who is the owner of the labrador that won the CLA field trials trophy no fewer than four times (and, for a bonus point, what is the name of the dog)?

4   Who left between $5 billion and $8 billion for the care and welfare of dogs?

5   What was the name and breed of the pet dog that in 2008 became the first to be cloned successfully for a commercial fee?

6   What is the name of the starring beagle in the film *Year of the Dog*?

7   Which is the second-most popular dog breed in the UK?

8   In which breed do about one in 25 dogs suffer from the inherited disorder 'exercise-induced collapse', when vigorous activity makes them lose control over their back legs?

9   Which famous greyhound racecourse closed in 2008?

10 And how quickly can greyhounds or salukis (the fastest dogs) run?

11 What is the second line of the 1950s song that starts 'How much is that doggie in the window'?

11a And, for bonus points, what did the singer *not* want to buy for her boyfriend?

11b And why didn't she want the last of these?

12 When did the hospice high on the Great St Bernard Pass in the Swiss alps, which gave the dogs their name, stop keeping st bernards?

13 Who wrote the rap song *D.o.g's Get Lonely 2*?

14 What is the origin of the expression 'dog in the manger', describing someone too selfish to let people use or enjoy things that they themselves have no use for?

15 Which one of these ten breeds is shown by DNA analysis to be the least closely related to dogs' ancestor, the wolf: afghan hound, akita, alaskan malamute, basenji, chinese shar-pei, chow chow, german shepherd, saluki, shiba inu or siberian husky?

16 What is the name of the dog narrator in Rudyard Kipling's *Thy Servant a Dog*?

17 And the name of Hagrid's mastiff in the Harry Potter books and films?

18 What is Frazier's father's jack russell called, in the *Frazier* TV series?

19 How many people have been provided with guide dogs by the Guide Dogs for the Blind Association since it started in the early 1930s: about 800, 1,500, 4,500 or 21,000?

20 Central heating can make dogs moult more than this, but how often is it natural for most dogs to moult?

21 Many dogs such as terriers, spaniels and poodles have traditionally had their tails shortened by 'docking'. Does this still happen?

Bedfordshire

DOG FRIENDLY PUBS

AMPTHILL

Prince of Wales

Bedford Street (B540 N from central crossroads); MK45 2NB

Civilised lunch pub with contemporary décor and menu

This open-plan L-shaped bar-brasserie has big leather deco-style armchairs and sofas on wood strip flooring as you come in, then angles around past a slightly sunken flagstoned bit, with a brick fireplace, to a comfortable partly ply-panelled dining area with sturdy pine tables. They have Wells & Youngs Bombardier and Eagle on handpump, good coffee, and brisk helpful service; good lighting, nicely framed modern prints on mainly cream walls (dark green and maroon accents at either end), quite well reproduced piped music. There's a lunchtime snack menu and imaginative specials. There are picnic-sets out on a nicely planted two-level lawn, and a terrace by the car park.

Charles Wells ~ Tenants Richard and Neia Heathorn ~ Real ale ~ Bar food (12-2.30(3 Sun), 7-9.30) ~ Restaurant ~ (01525) 840504 ~ Children welcome ~ Dogs welcome ~ Open 12-3, 6-11; 12-midnight Fri, Sat; 12-4 Sun; closed Sun evening ~ Bedrooms: £55S/£70S

BIDDENHAM

Three Tuns

Village signposted from A428 just W of Bedford; MK40 4BD

Extended thatched village pub with fairly priced straightforward food, and good children's play area in big garden

The traditional pleasant low-beamed lounge here has wheelback chairs round dark wood tables, window seats and pews on a red turkey carpet, and country paintings. The green-carpeted oak panelled public bar has photographs of the local football team, darts, skittles, cards and dominoes; piped music. On handpump, Greene King Abbot is well kept alongside a guest such as Ruddles. Enjoyable pubby food, including sandwiches, ploughman's and steak and kidney pie is served in generous helpings. There are seats in the attractively sheltered spacious garden, lots of picnic-sets on a big decked terrace, and swings and a climbing frame.

Greene King ~ Lease Kevin Bolwell ~ Real ale ~ Bar food (not Sun evening) ~ Restaurant ~ (01234) 354847 ~ Children in dining room ~ Dogs allowed in bar ~ Open 11.30-2.30, 6-11; 12-3, 7-10.30 Sun

BROOM

Cock

High Street; from A1 opposite northernmost Biggleswade turn-off follow Old
Warden 3, Aerodrome 2 signpost, and take first left signposted Broom; SG18 9NA

Friendly traditional village green pub with straightforward tasty food, beers
tapped straight from the cask; garden, and caravanning and camping facilities

Readers enjoy the unspoilt simplicity of this little old-fashioned house. There's no
bar counter, so the Greene King IPA, Abbot and Ruddles County are tapped straight
from casks by the cellar steps off a central corridor. Original latch doors lead from
one quietly cosy little room to the next (four in all). You'll find warming winter
fires, low ochre ceilings, stripped panelling, and farmhouse tables and chairs on
antique tiles. Well liked generously served bar food runs from ploughman's to filled
yorkshire puddings; piped (perhaps classical) music, darts and board games. There
are picnic-sets and flower tubs on the terrace by the back lawn.

Greene King ~ Tenants Gerry and Jean Lant ~ Real ale ~ Bar food ~ Restaurant
~ (01767) 314411 ~ Children welcome ~ Dogs allowed in bar ~ Open 12-3
(4 Sat, Sun), 6-11; closed Sun evening

NORTHILL

Crown

Ickwell Road; village signposted from B658 W of Biggleswade; SG18 9AA

Prettily situated village pub with nice old interior, warmly relaxed atmosphere,
enjoyable food, and big child-friendly garden

The cosy little bar at this thoughtfully run place is snugly traditional with a big
open fire, flagstones, heavy low beams and comfortable bay window seats. Greene
King IPA and Abbot and a couple of guests from brewers such as Bath and Hydes
are served on handpump from the copper-topped counter. On the left is a small
dining area, while on the right, the light walled main dining room has elegantly
laid tables on bare boards, with steps up to a smaller more intimate side room.
The atmosphere throughout is warm and relaxed with friendly service and fairly
unobtrusive piped music. The bar menu is nicely traditional, from sandwiches up.
This attractive old building is situated just across from the church, in a green and
peaceful village, and has big tables under cocktail parasols out in front looking
over the village pond. A sheltered side terrace (with picnic-sets) opens up into a
very large back garden with widely spaced canopied tables, plenty of trees and
shrubs, a good play area, and masses of room for children to run around.

Greene King ~ Tenant Kevin Blois ~ Real ale ~ Bar food (12-2.30, 6.30-9.30;
12-9 Sun) ~ Restaurant ~ (01767) 627337 ~ Children welcome away from main
bar ~ Dogs allowed in bar ~ Open 11.30-3, 6-11; 11.30-midnight Fri, Sat in
summer; 12-11 Sun

OLD WARDEN

Hare & Hounds

Village signposted off A600 S of Bedford and B658 W of Biggleswade; SG18 9HQ

Popular but comfortably elegant dining pub with emphasis on good food served by thoughtful well turned out staff; lovely gardens

Four beautifully kept beamed rooms, with dark standing timbers, work their way round the central servery here. Cleverly blending contemporary styling with the attractive old structure, décor is in cosy reds and creams, with upholstered armchairs and sofas on stripped flooring, light wood tables and coffee tables, a woodburning stove in an inglenook fireplace and fresh flowers on the bar. Prints and photographs displayed on the walls depict historic aircraft in the famous Shuttleworth Collection just up the road. Wells & Youngs Eagle and Bombardier are on handpump, with eight or so wines by the glass including some from a local vineyard; piped music. Food here is imaginative and beautifully prepared and presented. They make an effort to use local and even organic ingredients (such as pork from the Shuttleworth Estate), the breads and ice-cream are home made, and they sell a small range of home-made larder goods. The village and pub form part of the Shuttleworth Estate which was built about 200 years ago in a swiss style, and the glorious sloping garden (with tables on a terrace) which stretches up to pine woods behind the pub dates back to the same period, and was designed in the same style. Though there's an ample car park, you may need to use the village hall parking as an overflow. There are some substantial walks nearby.

Charles Wells ~ Lease Jane Hasler ~ Real ale ~ Bar food (12-2(3 Sun), 6.30-9; not Sun evening) ~ (01767) 627225 ~ Children welcome in family room ~ Dogs allowed in bar ~ Open 12-3, 6-11; 12-10.30 Sun; closed Mon except bank hols

RISELEY

Fox & Hounds

High Street; village signposted off A6 and B660 N of Bedford; MK44 1DT

Cheery bustling old pub with decent food including good steaks; pleasant garden

The longstanding licensees here run a sound and welcoming establishment. Traditional pub furniture is spread among timber uprights under heavy low beams, and a relaxing clubby lounge area has comfortable leather chesterfields, low tables and wing chairs; unobtrusive piped classical or big band piped music. A decent range of drinks takes in Wells & Youngs Eagle and Bombardier with a guest such as Hook Norton Old Hooky on handpump, bin-end wines and a range of malts and cognacs. Service is normally very attentive and friendly, but it does get busy; they don't take bookings on Saturday night so you may have to wait for your table and food. The speciality here is steaks, you choose your own piece, pay by weight and you can watch it being cooked on an open grill. Other good food includes pubby dishes alongside some more adventurous items. An attractively decked terrace with wooden tables and chairs has outside heating, and the pleasant garden has shrubs and a pergola.

Charles Wells ~ Lease Jan and Lynne Zielinski ~ Real ale ~ Bar food (11.30-1.45, 6.30-9.30(10 Sat); 12-2, 7-9 Sun) ~ Restaurant ~ (01234) 708240 ~ Children welcome ~ Dogs allowed in bar ~ Open 11.30-2.30, 6.30-11; 12-3, 7-10.30 Sun

DOG FRIENDLY HOTELS, INNS, B&Bs AND FARMS

ASPLEY GUISE
Moore Place
The Square, Aspley Guise, Milton Keynes, Buckinghamshire MK17 8DW
(01908) 282000

£109; 63 well equipped, pretty rms. Elegantly restored Georgian house in attractive gardens, with bar and lounge, enjoyable food and nice breakfasts in light and airy Victorian-style conservatory restaurant, and friendly, helpful staff; 5 mins from Woburn Abbey and Safari Park; disabled access; dogs in bedrooms; plenty of nearby walks

FLITWICK
Flitwick Manor

Church Road, Flitwick, Bedford, Bedfordshire MK45 1AE (01525) 712242

£160; 18 thoughtfully decorated rms with antiques and period pieces. Georgian country house surrounded by acres of rolling gardens and wooded parkland, with log fire in entrance hall, comfortable tranquil lounge and library, and smart restaurant with fine french wines and imaginative food using home-grown and local produce; tennis and croquet; disabled access; dogs in downstairs bedrooms; £20

HOUGHTON CONQUEST
Knife & Cleaver
The Grove, Houghton Conquest, Bedford, Bedfordshire MK45 3LA (01234) 740387

£74; 9 stylish rms. Comfortably civilised and attractive 17th-c dining pub with cosy, clubby bar, lovely dark panelling, maps, drawings and old documents on the walls, open winter fires, real ales, two dozen good wines by the glass, imaginative modern cooking in airy white-walled conservatory, family room, and tables on terrace alongside neatly kept garden; dogs welcome in bedrooms

MARSTON MORETEYNE
White Cottage
Marston Hill, Marston Moreteyne, Cranfield, Bedfordshire MK43 0QJ
(01234) 751766

£58; 6 comfortable rms. Neatly kept, white painted cottage with fine views across the gardens and countryside, residents' lounge, super breakfasts in attractive dining room (good evening meals weekdays only), and a friendly, relaxed atmosphere; nearby country walks; dogs in annexe rooms only; £5

SANDY
Highfield Farm

Tempsford Road, Sandy, Bedfordshire SG19 2AQ (off A1 S-bound carriageway just S of Tempsford flyover) (01767) 682332

£82.25; 11 well equipped rms with hospitality trays and home-made biscuits. Neatly kept whitewashed house and beautifully converted barns set well away from A1, with walks in own grounds (dogs must be on leads) and surrounded by attractive arable farmland; warmly friendly, helpful owner, open fire in comfortable sitting room, and breakfasts in very attractive light and airy dining room; farm cats (not allowed inside); disabled access; dogs in some bedrooms; £10

DOG FRIENDLY PUBS

ALDWORTH

Bell

A329 Reading—Wallingford; left on to B4009 at Streatley; RG8 9SE

Exceptional unspoilt pub, super value snacks, very well kept beers, good quality house wines, lovely friendly atmosphere, and nice garden; can be busy

'One of the best pubs I've been to' and 'still the benchmark' are just a couple of the delighted comments readers have sent us about this unpretentious gem of a pub. It's been run by the same family for over 250 years and remains a favourite with the wide mix of customers who love the fact that mobile phones, piped music and games machines are banned. Quite unspoilt and unchanging, the rooms have benches around the panelled walls, an ancient one-handed clock, beams in the shiny ochre ceiling, and a woodburning stove. Rather than a bar counter for service, there's a glass-panelled hatch from which they serve the very well kept Arkells BBB and Kingsdown, local West Berkshire Old Tyler and Mild and a monthly guest from West Berkshire; also Upton farm cider, good house wines and spiced porter at Christmas; no draught lager. As you might expect, the pub games here are traditional: darts, shove-ha'penny and dominoes. Excellent value bar food is limited to filled hot crusty rolls and a variety of ploughman's; in winter they also do home-made soup. The quiet, old-fashioned cottagey garden is by the village cricket ground, and behind the pub there's a paddock with farm animals. In summer there may be occasional morris dancers, while at Christmas local mummers perform in the road by the ancient well-head (the shaft is sunk 365 feet through the chalk). It tends to get very busy at weekends; dogs must be kept on leads.

Free house ~ Licensee H E Macaulay ~ Real ale ~ Bar food (11-2.45, 6-9.30; 12-2.45, 7-9 Sun) ~ No credit cards ~ (01635) 578272 ~ Children welcome ~ Dogs welcome ~ Open 11-3, 6-11; 12-3, 7-10.30 Sun; closed Mon and Mon bank hol evenings

HOLYPORT

Belgian Arms

Handy for M4 junction 8/9, via A308(M) and A330; SL6 2JR

Popular dining pub with friendly staff, good food and waterside garden terrace

The low-ceilinged bar at this bustling place has well spaced tables and chairs on a stripped wooden floor, interesting cricketing memorabilia on the walls, a china cupboard in one corner, a log fire and a discreetly placed TV; piped music. The old cellar room is now a dining area, and a spacious conservatory opens onto a terrace with good quality wooden furniture and views overlooking the village pond. Friendly, humorous staff serve Brakspears Bitter and a guest beer on hand-pump, and there are quite a few wines by the glass. The well balanced menu includes a good range of dishes for most tastes, including a catch of the day.

Brakspears ~ Tenant Jamie Sears ~ Real ale ~ Bar food (12-2.30(3.30 Sun), 7-9) ~ Restaurant ~ (01628) 634468 ~ Children welcome ~ Dogs allowed in bar ~ Open 11-3, 5.30-11; 11-11 Fri, Sat; 12-10.30 Sun

INKPEN

Crown & Garter

Inkpen Common: Inkpen signposted with Kintbury off A4; in Kintbury turn left into Inkpen Road, then keep on into Inkpen Common; RG17 9QR

Remote-feeling pub with appealing layout, lovely garden and nearby walks, local ales and tasty food in nicely lit bars, and friendly licensee

This attractive old 16th-c brick pub is run by a welcoming landlady, and is surpris-ingly substantial for somewhere so remote-feeling. The appealing low-ceilinged and relaxed panelled bar keeps West Berkshire Mr Chubbs Lunchtime Bitter and Good Old Boy and Timothy Taylors Landlord plus a guest such as Arkells Moonlight on handpump, decent wines by the glass and several malt whiskies. Three areas radiate from here; our pick is the parquet-floored part by the raised log fire – it has a couple of substantial old tables and a huge old-fashioned slightly curved settle. Other parts are slate and wood with a good mix of well spaced tables and chairs, and nice lighting; piped music. Bar food is well liked with something to suit most tastes. There's a front terrace for outside eating, a lovely long side garden with picnic-sets, and plenty of good downland walks nearby. James II is reputed to have used the pub on his way to visit his mistress locally.

Free house ~ Licensee Gill Hern ~ Real ale ~ Bar food (not Sun evening) ~ Restaurant ~ (01488) 668325 ~ Children over 7 evenings and in bedrooms ~ Dogs allowed in bar ~ Open 12-3, 5.30-11; 12-5, 7-10.30 Sun; closed Mon and Tues lunchtimes

REMENHAM

Little Angel

A4130, just over bridge E of Henley; RG9 2LS

Relaxed linked contemporary areas plus attractive conservatory, good modern bar food, helpful service, and a dozen wines by the glass

The interior of this attractive pub has been cleverly opened up so you can feel tucked away in your own individually charactered area, but still feel part of the buzzy atmosphere. There are well spaced seats and tables on the bare boards or ochre tiles, and soft furnishings are mainly in pale fabrics or suede, running from comfortable bar seats through tub chairs to deep sofas, with new artwork on the walls. In one corner a case of art books and the like help to set the tone; conservatory. The attractive curved bar counter has a good choice of a dozen wines by the glass (plus champagne), smoothies and cocktails, and Brakspears Bitter and a guest on handpump; board games, unobtrusive piped music, TV, and friendly and efficient young staff. Using local estate game and organic fruit and vegetables, the chefs here add a gently enjoyable contemporary spin to traditional dishes, from interesting sandwiches up. A sheltered floodlit back terrace has tables under cocktail parasols, looking over to the local cricket ground.

Brakspears ~ Lease Douglas Green ~ Real ale ~ Bar food (12-3, 7-10; 12-4, 7-9 Sun) ~ Restaurant ~ (01491) 411008 ~ Well behaved children welcome, some restrictions on buggies etc ~ Dogs allowed in bar ~ Open 11-12; 11-12 Sat; 12-11 Sun

RUSCOMBE

Royal Oak

Ruscombe Lane (B3024 just E of Twyford); RG10 9JN

Wide choice of popular food at welcoming pub with interesting furnishings and paintings and adjoining antique and collectables shop

It's the genuine personal touches that lend such a welcoming atmosphere to this bustling village pub. The open plan carpeted interior is well laid out so that each bit is fairly snug, yet it keeps the overall feel of a lot of people enjoying themselves. A good variety of furniture runs from dark oak tables to big chunky pine ones, with mixed seating to match – the two sofas facing one another are popular. Contrasting with the old exposed ceiling joists, mostly unframed modern paintings and prints decorate the walls – mainly dark terracotta over a panelled dado. Drinks include Brakspears Bitter, Fullers London Pride and maybe a guest on handpump, and half a dozen nicely chosen wines including a local vintage. If there's nothing on the fairly extensive menu that takes your fancy, they also offer a good range of daily specials. Picnic-sets are ranged around a venerable central hawthorn in the garden behind (where there are ducks and chickens); summer barbecues. A pleasing new distraction is the landlady's antique and collectables shop, which is open during pub hours.

Enterprise ~ Lease Jenny and Stefano Buratta ~ Real ale ~ Bar food (12-2.30, 6.30-9.30; 12-3 Sun) ~ Restaurant ~ (0118) 934 5190 ~ Children welcome ~ Dogs welcome ~ Open 12-3, 6-11; 12-4 Sun; closed Sun, and Mon evenings

STANFORD DINGLEY

Old Boot

Off A340 via Bradfield, coming from A4 just W of M4 junction 12; RG7 6LT

Neat pub with emphasis on imaginative food; country furnishings and rural garden views

Good food is very much the draw at this stylish 18th-c pub – not surprising given that the kitchen is staffed by a team of well trained French chefs. As well as tasty standards such as filled baguettes and cod and chips, they offer more elaborate dishes such as seared scallops, gressingham duck breast with blackcurrant sauce. Most tables are laid for dining and to be sure of a place you must book in advance, especially at weekends. The beamed bar has two welcoming fires (one in an inglenook), fine old pews, settles, old country chairs, and polished tables. There are some striking pictures and hunting prints, boot ornaments in various sizes, and fresh flowers. Three real ales might include West Berkshire Good Old Boy, Batemans and Fullers London Pride on handpump and around half a dozen wines by the glass. There are seats in the quiet sloping back garden or on the terrace, and pleasant rural views; more tables out in front.

Free house ~ Licensees John and Jeannie Haley ~ Real ale ~ Bar food ~ Restaurant ~ (0118) 974 4292 ~ Children welcome ~ Dogs allowed in bar ~ Open 11(12 Sun)-3, 6-11

WINTERBOURNE

Winterbourne Arms

3.7 miles from M4 junction 13; at A34 turn into Chievley Services and follow Donnington signs to Arlington Lane, then follow Winterbourne signs; RG20 8BB

Charming country pub with enjoyable bar food, lots of wines by the glass and large landscaped garden

You can be sure of a warm welcome and rather good meal at this pretty black and white village house. The nicely varied menu includes a good range from filled baguettes and ploughman's up to wild boar terrine and grilled bass on crushed citrus potatoes with walnut and garlic butter; popular Sunday lunch. There's a good wine list with 20 offered by the glass (served in elegant glasses and including sparkling and sweet wines), and Fullers London Pride, Ramsbury Gold and Winterbourne Whistle Wetter on handpump. The traditional bars have stools along the counter, a collection of old irons around the big fireplace (log fire), and early prints and old photographs of the village on very pale washed pink, or exposed stone, walls; piped music. Big windows take in peaceful views over rolling fields – the surrounding countryside here is lovely, with nearby walks to Snelsmore Common and Donnington Castle, and there are seats outside in the large landscaped side garden and pretty flowering tubs and hanging baskets.

Free house ~ Licensee Frank Adams ~ Real ale ~ Bar food (12-2.30, 6-9.30; 12-3.30, 6-9 Sun) ~ (01635) 248200 ~ Children welcome ~ Dogs allowed in bar ~ Open 12-3, 6-11; 12-10.30 Sun

DOG FRIENDLY HOTELS, B&Bs AND FARMS

CHIEVELEY

Crab at Chieveley

Wantage Road, Chieveley, Berkshire RG20 8UE (01635) 247550

£150; 14 boldly furnished rms named after famous hotels, some with hot tub on private terrace. Former pub, now a restaurant-with-rooms, with interesting décor based on equestrian and maritime themes, friendly staff, and excellent food in brasserie area and more formal restaurant based on fresh fish and home-grown vegetables; seats outside under large parasols; dogs in hot tub bedrooms only

HUNGERFORD
Bear Hotel

41 Charnham Street, Hungerford, Berkshire RG17 OEL (01488) 682512

£125; 39 stylish, well equipped rms, some with views over the river. Civilised and carefully restored 13th-c hotel with open fires, a contemporary bar, cosy and relaxing snug with sofas and newspapers, good food in attractive beamed brasserie, and courtyard and riverside terrace; disabled access; dog biscuits and maybe treats and doggy stockings at Christmas; walks by canal or on common 2 mins away; dogs welcome in bedrooms

MAIDENHEAD
Sheephouse Manor

Sheephouse Road, Maidenhead, Berkshire SL6 8HJ (01628) 776902

£85; 3 individually decorated rms. 16th-c former farmhouse with original beams, timber floors and antique pine doors, open fireplaces, english breakfasts, and two acres of gardens with children's playground; river path and footpaths nearby for walks; plenty of pubs and restaurants nearby for evening meals; self-catering also; disabled access; dogs in cottages only; bedding available; £5

STREATLEY
Swan at Streatley

High Street, Streatley, Reading, Berkshire RG8 9HR (01491) 878800

£135; 45 individually styled rms, many overlooking the water. Well run, friendly riverside hotel with comfortable, relaxed lounges, bar with open fire and sofas, consistently good food in attractive restaurant, popular spa with indoor pool, restored Magdalen College Barge, and flower-filled gardens where dogs may walk – other walks nearby; disabled access; dogs in bedrooms and most public areas (not dining room); £15

Buckinghamshire

DOG FRIENDLY PUBS

BOVINGDON GREEN

Royal Oak

0.75 miles N of Marlow, on back road to Frieth signposted off West Street (A4155) in centre; SL7 2JF

Fantastic choice of european wines by glass and popular food in civilised and attractively decorated pub

This is an extremely well run and civilised old pub with a genuinely warm welcome for all and a really good mix of customers. Several attractively decorated areas open off the central bar, the half-panelled walls variously painted in pale blue, green or cream: the cosiest part is the low-beamed room closest to the car park, with three small tables, a woodburner in an exposed brick fireplace, and a big pile of logs. Throughout there's a mix of church chairs, stripped wooden tables and chunky wall seats, with rugs on the partly wooden, partly flagstoned floors, co-ordinated cushions and curtains, and a very bright, airy feel; thoughtful extra touches set the tone, with a big, square bowl of olives on the bar, carefully laid out newspapers and fresh flowers or candles on the tables. Brakspears Bitter, Fullers London Pride, and local Rebellion IPA on handpump, 19 wines and nine pudding wines by the glass and quick, helpful service; board games, and piped music. If you're planning to eat it's worth booking ahead (especially on Sundays) as a good few tables may have reserved signs. Food is very good and is successfully prepared in genuinely innovative ways. To give just one example, you might find pork belly faggot with calvados jus. A terrace with good solid tables leads to an appealing garden with plenty more, and there's a smaller garden at the side as well.

Salisbury Pubs ~ Lease Trasna Cryer ~ Real ale ~ Bar food (12-2.30(3 Sat, 4 Sun), 7-10) ~ Restaurant ~ (01628) 488611 ~ Children welcome ~ Dogs allowed in bar ~ Open 11-11; 12-10.30 Sun; closed 25 and 26 Dec

CHALFONT ST GILES

White Hart

Three Households (main street, W); HP8 4LP

Bustling place with quite an emphasis on food, modern but comfortable furnishings, neatly dressed staff

It's the imaginative award-winning modern cooking that draws customers to this civilised dining pub though they do keep Greene King IPA, Morlands Original, Old Speckled Hen and a guest beer on handpump. The bar has chocolate leather seats and sofas and contemporary artwork on the mushroom coloured walls. The extended, spreading dining room (similarly furnished to the bar) is mainly bare boards – the bright acoustics make for a lively medley of chatter – and it can be on the noisy side when very busy. Several wines by the glass, broadsheet daily papers, piped music, and neatly dressed young staff. A sheltered back terrace has squarish picnic-sets under cocktail parasols, with more beyond in the garden. Bedrooms are comfortable and modern.

Greene King ~ Lease Scott MacRae ~ Real ale ~ Bar food (12-2(2.30 Sat and Sun), 6.30-9.30) ~ Restaurant ~ (01494) 872441 ~ Well behaved children allowed in bar and restaurant ~ Dogs allowed in bar and bedrooms ~ Open 11.30-2.30, 5.30-11(11.30 Sat); 12-10.30 Sun ~ Bedrooms: £77.50S/£97.50S

CHENIES

Red Lion

2 miles from M25 junction 18; A404 towards Amersham, then village signposted on right; Chesham Road; WD3 6ED

Traditional pub with long-serving licensees, a bustling atmosphere, and very well liked food

By adding a small extension to this much loved village pub, the long-serving and friendly licensees will be able to create extra seating space where they will take bookings (a first for them). They were also hoping, as we went to press, to redecorate the whole pub. The bustling, unpretentious L-shaped bar has comfortable built-in wall benches by the front windows, other traditional seats and tables, and original photographs of the village and traction engines; there's also a small back snug. Well kept Rebellion Lion Pride (brewed for the pub), Vale Best Bitter, Wadworths 6X, and a guest beer on handpump, several wines by the glass and some nice malt whiskies. As well as lunchtime filled baps, baguettes and baked potatoes, the very reasonably priced and tasty bar food includes their incredibly popular lamb pie, as well as bangers with a surprise mash, and they've home-made puddings. The hanging baskets and window boxes are pretty in summer, and there are picnic-sets on a small side terrace. No children, games machines or piped music.

Free house ~ Licensee Mike Norris ~ Real ale ~ Bar food (12-2, 7-10(9.30 Sun) ~ Restaurant ~ (01923) 282722 ~ Dogs allowed in bar ~ Open 11-2.30, 5.30-11; 12-3, 6.30-10.30 Sun; closed 25 Dec

DENHAM

Swan

0.75 miles from M40 junction 1 or M25 junction 16; follow Denham Village signs; UB9 5BH

So popular, it's best to book in advance – civilised dining pub with a fine choice of wines and interesting food

In May when the wisteria is flowering, this civilised dining pub and the other old tiled village buildings here are a very pretty sight. The rooms are stylishly furnished with a nice mix of antique and old-fashioned chairs and solid tables, individually chosen pictures on the cream and warm green walls, rich heavily draped curtains, inviting open fires, newspapers to read, and fresh flowers. A smashing choice of 19 european wines plus nine pudding wines by two sizes of glass, and Courage Best, Rebellion IPA, and Wadworths 6X on handpump; piped music. Impressive bar food takes in all sorts of unusual combinations, anything from crayfish and cornish crab vol au vent with bloody mary jelly to coriander marinated halloumi burger with roast tomato and pumpkin seed pesto. The extensive garden is floodlit at night, and leads from a sheltered terrace with tables to a more spacious lawn. It can get busy at weekends, and parking may be difficult. The pub is part of a little group which comprises the Royal Oak, Bovingdon Green and the Old Queens Head in Penn (also in Buckinghamshire) and the Alford Arms in Frithsden (which is in Hertfordshire).

Salisbury Pubs ~ Lease Mark Littlewood ~ Real ale ~ Bar food (12-2.30(3 Sat, 4 Sun), 7-10) ~ Restaurant ~ (01895) 832085 ~ Children welcome ~ Dogs allowed in bar ~ Open 11-11; 12-10.30 Sun; closed 25 and 26 Dec

DORNEY
Pineapple

2.4 miles from M4 junction 7; turn left on to A4, then left on B3026 (or take first left off A4 at traffic lights, into Huntercombe Lane S, then left at T junction on main road – shorter but slower); Lake End Road; SL4 6QS

Fantastic choice of interesting sandwiches in unpretentious pub

Even when really busy – which this nicely old-fashioned and unpretentious pub usually is – the staff remain pleasant and helpful. There are low shiny Anaglypta ceilings, black-panelled dados and sturdy country tables – one very long, another in a big bow window. There is a woodburning stove at one end, a pretty little fireplace in a second room and china pineapples join the decorations on a set of shelves in one of three cottagey carpeted linked rooms on the left. It's bare boards on the right where the bar counter has Black Sheep Bitter, Fullers London Pride and Wells & Youngs Bombardier on handpump and several wines by the glass; friendly staff and piped music. A remarkable choice of up to 1,000 varieties of sandwiches in five different fresh breads come on their own, or with your choice of hearty vegetable soup, salad or chips. They also serve an enjoyable Sunday roast. A roadside verandah has some rustic tables, and there are plenty of round picnic-sets out in the garden, some on fairy-lit decking under an oak tree; the nearby motorway makes itself heard out here.

Punch ~ Lease Stuart Jones ~ Real ale ~ Bar food (12-9) ~ (01628) 662353 ~ Children welcome ~ Dogs welcome ~ Open 11-11; 12-10.30 Sun

FINGEST
Chequers

Village signposted off B482 Marlow—Stokenchurch; RG9 6QD

Friendly, spotlessly kept old pub with big garden, good food and sunny dining extension

Although there is a smart back dining extension, the licensees are keen to emphasise that this 15th-c place is a proper pub with a warm and friendly atmosphere and an unaffected public bar with real rural charm. Several spotless old-fashioned rooms have pewter tankards, horsebrasses and pub team photographs on the walls, large open fires, Brakspears Bitter and Oxford Gold and Wychwood Hobgoblin and Mad Hatter on handpump, a dozen wines by the glass, jugs of Pimms and several malt whiskies; helpful, welcoming service. Board games. Food is honest and enjoyable and you can buy fresh local eggs for sale over the bar counter. French doors from the dining extension open out on to the terrace where there are plenty of picnic-sets and this leads on to the big garden with fine views over the Hambleden valley; beyond here, quiet pastures slope up to beech woods. Over the road is a unique Norman twin-roofed church tower – probably the nave of the original church.

Brakspears ~ Tenants Ray Connelly and Christian Taubert ~ Real ale ~ Bar food (not Mon evening or winter Sun evening) ~ Restaurant ~ (01491) 638335 ~ Children welcome ~ Dogs allowed in bar ~ Open 12-3, 6-11; 12-10.30 Sun; closed winter Sun evening

HAWRIDGE COMMON
Full Moon

Hawridge Common; left fork off A416 N of Chesham, then follow for 3.5 miles towards Cholesbury; HP5 2UH

Attractive country pub with outside heaters and awning, six real ales, and enjoyable food; plenty of nearby walks

This is a nice pub with a good welcome. The low-beamed rambling bar is the heart of the building, with oak built-in floor-to-ceiling settles, ancient flagstones and flooring tiles, hunting prints and an inglenook fireplace. They keep half a dozen real ales on handpump such as Adnams Best, Bass, Brakspears Bitter, Fullers London Pride, Timothy Taylors Landlord, and a changing guest like Hopback GFB and there are several wines by the glass; pleasant service. Popular bar food is nicely varied, maybe including steak and kidney pudding or citrus-crusted bass fillet with a white wine and dill cream sauce; Sunday roasts. On fine days, you can sit outside in the garden or on the heated and covered terrace and gaze over the fields or windmill behind, and there are lots of walks over the common.

Enterprise ~ Lease Peter and Annie Alberto ~ Real ale ~ Bar food ~ Restaurant ~ (01494) 758959 ~ Well supervised children welcome ~ Dogs welcome ~ Open 12-11; 12-10.30 Sun; closed 25 Dec

HEDGERLEY
White Horse

2.4 miles from M40 junction 2; at exit roundabout take Slough turn-off then take Hedgerley Lane (immediate left) following alongside M40; after 1.5 miles turn right at T junction into Village Lane; SL2 3UY

Old-fashioned drinkers' pub with lots of beers, regular beer festivals and a jolly mix of customers

'Just what a village pub ought to be' is how one reader describes this unchanging country local. The cottagey main bar has plenty of character, with lots of beams, brasses and exposed brickwork, low wooden tables, some standing timbers, jugs, ballcocks and other bric-a-brac, a log fire, and a good few leaflets and notices about future village events. There is a little flagstoned public bar on the left. Tapped from the cask in a room behind the tiny hatch counter, there's Greene King IPA and Rebellion IPA and at least five daily changing guests from anywhere in the country, with good farm cider and perry, and belgian beers as well. Lunchtime bar food includes sandwiches, ploughman's, cold meats and quiches, and a handful of straightforward hot dishes. On the way out to the garden, which has tables and occasional barbecues, they have a canopy extension to help during busy periods. The atmosphere is cheerful with warmly friendly service from the chatty staff. In front are lots of hanging baskets and a couple more tables overlooking the quiet road. There are good walks nearby, and the pub is handy for the Church Wood RSPB reserve. It can get crowded at weekends.

Free house ~ Licensees Doris Hobbs and Kevin Brooker ~ Real ale ~ Bar food (lunchtime only) ~ (01753) 643225 ~ Children in canopy extension area ~ Dogs allowed in bar ~ Open 11-2.30, 5-11; 11-11 Sat; 12-10.30 Sun

PRESTWOOD
Polecat
170 Wycombe Road (A4128 N of High Wycombe); HP16 0HJ

Enjoyable food in several smallish civilised rooms, chatty atmosphere, and attractive sizeable garden

The atmosphere here is always very congenial and with its slightly chintzy appearance, rather civilised too. Opening off the low-ceilinged bar are several smallish rooms with an assortment of tables and chairs, various stuffed birds as well as the stuffed white polecats in one big cabinet, small country pictures, rugs on bare boards or red tiles, and a couple of antique housekeeper's chairs by a good open fire. Brakspears Bitter, Flowers IPA, Greene King Old Speckled Hen and Marstons Pedigree on handpump, quite a few wines by the glass, and 20 malt whiskies; piped music. The carefully prepared food here is jolly good, running from traditional dishes up to some more imaginative old favourites such as waldorf salad with toasted walnut bread. The garden is most attractive with lots of spring bulbs and colourful summer hanging baskets, tubs, and herbaceous plants; quite a few picnic-sets under parasols on neat grass out in front beneath a big fairy-lit pear tree, with more on a big well kept back lawn; in good weather these seats get snapped up fast.

Free house ~ Licensee John Gamble ~ Real ale ~ Bar food (not Sun evening) ~ (01494) 862253 ~ Children in Gallery Room and Drovers Bar only ~ Dogs allowed in bar ~ Open 11.30-2.30, 6-11; 12-3 Sun; closed Sun evening, evenings 24 and 31 Dec, all day 25 and 26 Dec and 1 Jan

SKIRMETT

Frog

From A4155 NE of Henley take Hambleden turn and keep on; or from B482 Stokenchurch—Marlow take Turville turn and keep on; RG9 6TG

Bustling, brightly decorated pub with a good mix of locals and visitors, modern cooking and wide choice of drinks; lovely garden and nearby walks

You can be sure of a friendly welcome from both the licensees and their staff at this well run country pub. The neatly kept beamed bar area has a mix of comfortable furnishings, a striking hooded fireplace with a bench around the edge (and a pile of logs sitting beside it), big rugs on the wooden floors and sporting and local prints around the salmon painted walls. The function room leading off is sometimes used as a dining overflow. Although brightly modernised, there is still something of a local feel with leaflets and posters near the door advertising raffles and so forth; piped music. Lodden Hoppit, Rebellion IPA and Sharps Doom Bar on handpump, 16 wines by the glass (including champagne), and 24 malt whiskies. Cooking definitely pushes the boundaries – you might even find roast fillet of pork in port with banana crème sauce on the menu here. A side gate leads to a lovely garden with a large tree in the middle, and the unusual five-sided tables are well placed for attractive valley views. Plenty of nearby hikes, Henley is close by, and just down the road is the delightful Ibstone windmill.

Free house ~ Licensees Jim Crowe and Noelle Greene ~ Real ale ~ Bar food (12-2.30, 6.30-9.30; not winter Sun evening) ~ Restaurant ~ (01491) 638996 ~ Children welcome ~ Dogs allowed in bar ~ Occasional live entertainment ~ Open 11-3, 6-11; 12-4, 6-10.30 Sun; closed Sun evening Oct-May

TURVILLE

Bull & Butcher

Off A4155 Henley—Marlow via Hambleden and Skirmett; RG9 6QU

Timbered pub, a handy all-day stop in this lovely village

Enjoyed by a very wide mix of customers, this remains a well run pub that can get packed at weekends. There are two low-ceilinged, oak-beamed rooms both with inglenook fireplaces, and the bar, with cushioned wall settles and a tiled floor, has a deep well incorporated into a glass-topped table. Brakspears Bitter, Oxford Gold and a seasonal guest, and Hook Norton Hooky Dark on handpump, Addlestone's cider and 16 wines by the glass; piped music and TV. There are seats on the lawn by fruit trees in the attractive garden, and plenty of walks in the lovely Chilterns valley. Bar food tends to be pretty traditional. The village is popular with television and film companies; *The Vicar of Dibley*, *Midsomer Murders* and *Chitty Chitty Bang Bang* were all filmed here.

Brakspears ~ Tenant Lydia Botha ~ Real ale ~ Bar food (12-2.30(4 Sat), 6.30-9.30; 12-4, 7-9 Sun and bank hol Mon; no food winter Sun evening) ~ (01491) 638283 ~ Children allowed but away from bar ~ Dogs allowed in bar ~ Live music monthly ~ Open 11-11(12 Sat); 12-10.30 Sun

DOG FRIENDLY HOTELS, INNS, B&Bs AND FARMS

AYLESBURY

Hartwell House

Oxford Road, Aylesbury, Buckinghamshire HP17 8NL (1.4 miles from A41, via A418 Oxford Road) (01296) 747444

£240; 46 rms, some large and well equipped, others with four-posters and fine panelling, inc ten secluded suites in restored 18th-c stables with private garden and statues. Elegant Grade I listed building with Jacobean and Georgian façades, wonderful decorative plasterwork and panelling, fine paintings and antiques, a marvellous Gothic central staircase, splendid morning room, and library, exceptional service, and excellent food and wine; 90 acres of parkland with ruined church, lake and statues, and spa with indoor swimming pool, saunas, gym and beauty rooms, and informal buttery and bar; tennis, croquet and fishing; two resident black labradors, and dog walking in grounds and on nearby footpaths; children over 8; good disabled access; dogs in Hartwell Court suites only

MARLOW

Compleat Angler

Bisham Road, Marlow, Buckinghamshire SL7 1RG (01628) 484444

£270; 64 pretty, stylish rms named after fishing flies and some overlooking garden or river. Famous Thames-side hotel with oak-panelled, 400-year-old cocktail bar, comfortable lounge, spacious beamed restaurant and conservatory-style brasserie with riverside terrace, imaginative food, and prompt service; coarse fishing and two boats for hire, walks in nearby park and along river; disabled access; dogs in bedrooms with treats; £10

TAPLOW

Cliveden

Taplow, Maidenhead, Berkshire SL6 0JF (01628) 668561

£240 (plus £7 per person paid to National Trust); 39 superb, luxurious rms. Superb Grade I listed stately home with gracious, comfortable public rooms, fine paintings, tapestries and armour, and a surprisingly unstuffy atmosphere; lovely views over the magnificent NT Thames-side parkland and formal gardens (open to the public); imaginative food in two restaurants with lighter meals in the conservatory, super buffet breakfasts, and impeccable staff; Pavilion Spa with indoor and heated outdoor swimming pools, gym, etc, tennis, squash, croquet, and boats for river trips; dogs can walk in most parts of the grounds; disabled access; dogs everywhere except dining rooms and Spa; beds, bowls and special menu

WESTBURY

Mill Farmhouse

Westbury, Brackley, Northamptonshire NN13 5JS (01280) 704843

£70; 3 pretty rms. Carefully restored miller's house on large farm with big, colourful garden and swimming pool; plenty of original features and open fire in comfortable sitting/dining room, oak furniture and lots of hunting prints, charming owners; good light suppers can be ordered; two self-contained flats; footpaths and bridleways to walk along; disabled access; dogs in bedrooms by arrangement

WINSLOW

Bell

Market Square, Winslow, Buckingham, Buckinghamshire MK18 3AB (01296) 714091

£82; 41 traditional rms. Carefully furnished and elegant black and white timbered inn overlooking the market square, with attractive beamed bars, comfortable lounges, open fires, enjoyable bar food, and good lunchtime and evening carvery in restaurant; disabled access; dogs; £10

Cambridgeshire

MAP 5

DOG FRIENDLY PUBS

BARNACK

Millstone

Off B1443 SE of Stamford, via School Lane into Millstone Lane; PE9 3ET

Stone-built pub in a picturesque village with good range of drinks and pubby food

This pub is built of the same local stone as most of Cambridge University and Ely Cathedral. There are welcoming fires and cosy corners in the timbered bar, some bold oil paintings by local artists and a clean, contemporary feel. Adnams Bitter, Greene King Old Speckled Hen, and Everards Tiger and Original on hand-pump and several wines by the glass. The menu includes traditional pubby dishes. There's a lovely enclosed courtyard for outside dining. Burghley House, home of the famous horse trials, is nearby.

Everards ~ Tenants Luke Marsh and Lauren Mackintosh ~ Real ale ~ Bar food (12-2.30(3 Sun), 6.30-9.30) ~ Restaurant ~ (01780) 740296 ~ Children welcome ~ Dogs allowed in bar ~ Open 12-3, 5.30-11; 12-midnight Sun and Sat; closed evenings 25 and 26 Dec and 1 Jan

CAMBRIDGE

Free Press

Prospect Row; CB1 1DU

Calm and unchanging with some interesting local décor, and good value food

The quiet, unspoilt atmosphere in this little pub is undisturbed by mobile phones, piped music or games machines and you can sit peacefully reading a paper by the warm log fire. In a nod to the building's history as home to a local newspaper, the walls of its characterful bare-board rooms are hung with old newspaper pages and printing memorabilia, as well as old printing trays that local customers are encouraged to top up with little items. Greene King IPA, Abbot and Mild and a guest or two such as Bath Ales Gem or Hydes Jekyll Gold on handpump, around 20 malt whiskies and up to nine wines by the glass; quite a few assorted board games. The short pubby menu changes monthly, and they offer good value lunch and evening set menus Monday and Tuesday. In fine weather, there are seats in the suntrap sheltered and paved back garden.

Greene King ~ Tenant Craig Bickley ~ Real ale ~ Bar food (12-2(2.30 Sat and Sun), 6-9; not Sun evening) ~ (01223) 368337 ~ Children welcome ~ Dogs welcome ~ Open 12-2.30, 6-11; 12-11 Sat; 12-3, 7-10.30 Sun

Live & Let Live

40 Mawson Road; off Mill Road SE of centre; CB1 2EA

Fine real ales in popular local, a relaxed atmosphere, and pubby food

The eight real ales on handpump or tapped from the cask in this busy old local are the main draw here: Everards Tiger, Nethergate Umbel Magna, and five changing guests that might include B&T Black Dragon Mild, Buntingford Robin Hood, and Tring Brock Bitter. There are also 40 Belgian bottled beers, a guest draught, and local ciders. The atmosphere is relaxed and friendly, and the heavily timbered brickwork rooms have sturdy varnished pine tables with pale wood chairs on bare boards, and sometimes, real gas lighting. An assortment of collectables takes in lots of interesting old country bric-a-brac and some steam railway and brewery memorabilia, and posters advertise local forthcoming events; cribbage and dominoes. The handful of very pubby dishes on offer here is very reasonably priced.

Burlison Inns ~ Lease Peter Wiffin ~ Real ale ~ Bar food ~ (01223) 460261 ~ Children welcome ~ Dogs welcome ~ Open 11.30-2.30, 5.30(6 Sat)-11; 12-3, 7-11 Sun

ELTON

Black Horse

B671 off A605 W of Peterborough and A1(M); Overend; PE8 6RU

Well run dining pub with country furnishings and super views from big garden

Regulars do still drop into this handsome honey-brick dining pub for a chat and a pint of Adnams Bitter, Black Sheep, Digfield Barnwell Bitter or Everards Tiger on handpump, but many people are here to eat. There are roaring log fires, hop-strung beams, a homely and comfortable mix of furniture (no two tables and chairs seem the same), antique prints, and lots of ornaments and bric-a-brac including an intriguing ancient radio set. Dining areas at each end of the bar have parquet flooring and tiles, and the stripped stone back lounge towards the restaurant has an interesting fireplace; 15 wines by the glass. They do offer some bar snacks (including sandwiches and a pie of the day) but most of the not particularly cheap dishes are more restauranty. The big garden has super views across to Elton Hall park and the village church, there are seats on the terrace, and a couple of acres of grass where children can play.

Free house ~ Licensee John Clennell ~ Real ale ~ Bar food (12-2, 6-9; all day April-Oct) ~ Restaurant ~ (01832) 280240 ~ Children welcome ~ Dogs allowed in bar ~ Open 12-11(midnight Sat)

ELY

Fountain

Corner of Barton Square and Silver Street; CB7 4JF

Happily escaping tourists but close to cathedral

Simple yet genteel, this 19th-c corner pub is very neatly kept and has no music, fruit machines or even food. There's a good mix of chatty customers, old cartoons, local photographs, regional maps and mementoes of the neighbouring King's School on the elegant dark pink walls, and tied-back curtains hanging from gold colour rails above the big windows. Above one fireplace is a stuffed pike in a case, and there are a few antlers dotted about. An extension at the back provides much needed additional seating. Adnams Bitter and Broadside, Woodfordes Wherry and a guest such as Fullers London Pride on handpump. Note the limited opening times below. No food served.

Free house ~ Licensees John and Judith Borland ~ Real ale ~ No credit cards ~ (01353) 663122 ~ Children welcome away from bar until 8pm ~ Dogs welcome ~ Open 5-11; 12-2, 6-11.30 Sat; 12-2, 7-10.30 Sun; closed weekday lunchtimes

FEN DITTON

Ancient Shepherds

Off B1047 at Green End, The River signpost, just NE of Cambridge; CB5 8ST

Beamed and comfortable with coal fires and homely food

Although many customers come to this solidly beamed old pub to enjoy the generously served food, the friendly staff will make you just as welcome if you only want a pint and a chat. Perhaps the nicest room is the softly lit central lounge where you can't fail to be comfortable on one of the big fat dark red button-back leather settees or armchairs, which are grouped round low dark wood tables. The warm coal fire and heavy drapes around the window seat with its big scatter cushions add to the cosiness. Above a black dado, the walls (and ceiling) are dark pink, and decorated with comic fox and policeman prints and little steeplechasing and equestrian ones. On the right the smallish more pubby bar, with its coal fire, serves Adnams Bitter and Greene King IPA and Old Speckled Hen on handpump. The licensee's west highland terrier, Billie, might be around outside food service times. As well as lunchtime filled baguettes, the well liked bar food is tasty, with some interesting specials.

Punch ~ Tenant J M Harrington ~ Real ale ~ Bar food (12-2(2.30 Sun), 6-9; not Sun or Mon evenings) ~ Restaurant ~ (01223) 293280 ~ Children allowed until 9pm ~ Dogs allowed in bar ~ Open 12-2.30, 6-11; 12-5 Sun; closed Sun and Mon evenings; 1 Jan

HELPSTON

Blue Bell

Woodgate; off B1443; PE6 7ED

Bustling and friendly, fine choice of beers, and tasty food

Particularly well run by a knowledgeable, hard-working landlord and his cheerful staff, this bustling, friendly pub remains as popular as ever. Comfortable cushioned chairs and settles, plenty of pictures, ornaments, mementoes and cart-wheel displays give a homely atmosphere to the lounge, parlour and snug. Food here is popular, particularly their very good value two-course lunch (not Sunday). Grainstore Cooking Bitter, Ten Fifty and (exclusive to this pub) John Clare, and a quickly changing guest such as Black Dog Mild, Exmoor Gold or Tydd

Steam Swedish Blond on handpump and Weston's cider in summer; pool and TV. A sheltered and heated terrace has plastic seats and garden tables and an awning; pretty hanging baskets and wheelchair access.

Free house ~ Licensee Aubrey Sinclair Ball ~ Real ale ~ Bar food (12-2, 6.30-9; 12-4 Sun) ~ Restaurant ~ (01733) 252394 ~ Children in snug and dining areas but no under-16s after 9pm ~ Dogs allowed in bar ~ Open 11.30-2.30, 5(6 Sat)-11; 12-6 Sun; closed 1 Jan

HEYDON

King William IV

Off A505 W of M11 junction 10; SG8 8PW

Rambling rooms with fascinating rustic jumble, good vegetarian menu, and pretty garden

The beamed rooms in this neatly kept dining pub are warmed by a winter log fire and filled with ploughshares, yokes and iron tools, cowbells, beer steins, samovars, brass or black wrought-iron lamps, copper-bound casks and milk ewers, harness, horsebrasses, and smith's bellows – as well as decorative plates, cut-glass and china ornaments. Including several imaginative vegetarian dishes, food here is jolly decent. Adnams Best, Fullers London Pride, Greene King IPA and Timothy Taylors Landlord on handpump and helpful staff; piped music. There are teak seats and tables and outdoor heaters on the terrace as well as more seats in the pretty garden.

Free house ~ Licensee Elizabeth Nicholls ~ Real ale ~ Bar food (12-2 (2.15 Sun), 6.30-9.30) ~ Restaurant ~ (01763) 838773 ~ Children over 12 in restaurant ~ Dogs allowed in bar ~ Open 12-3, 6(7 Sun)-11

HINXTON

Red Lion

2 miles off M11 junction 9 northbound; take first exit off A11, A1301 N, then left turn into village – High Street; a little further from junction 10, via A505 E and A1301 S; CB10 1QY

Pink-washed and handy for Duxford and M11; friendly staff, and neat, big garden

With its twin gables and pink-washed walls, this carefully extended 16th-c inn is most attractive. The mainly open-plan beamed bar is bustling and convivial and has leather chesterfields on wooden floors, an old wall clock, a dark green fireplace, and Adnams Bitter, Greene King IPA, Woodfordes Wherry and a guest such as Nethergate Augustinian Ale on handpump, 12 wines by the glass, and Aspall's cider; there are some unusual foreign insects in glass cases. Food is gently imaginative, and if you're a dessert fan it's worth finding out which night of the week the Pudding Club meets here. The neatly kept big garden has a pleasant terrace with picnic-sets, a dovecote and views of the village church. By the time this book is published they hope to have opened eight bedrooms.

Free house ~ Licensee Alex Clarke ~ Real ale ~ Bar food (12-2, 6.45-9; 12-2.30, 6.45-9.30 Fri and Sat; 12-2.30, 7-9 Sun) ~ Restaurant ~ (01799) 530601 ~

Well behaved children welcome ~ Dogs allowed in bar ~ Open 11-3, 6-11;
12-4, 7-10.30 Sun; closed evenings 25 and 26 Dec and 1 Jan

KEYSTON
Pheasant

Just off A14 SE of Thrapston; village loop road, off B663; PE28 0RE

Essentially a restaurant but dogs are welcome in the relaxed bar, highly thought-of modern food and excellent range of drinks

This most attractive long, low thatched dining pub is just the place for an excellent meal out but they do keep four real ales on handpump from breweries such as Adnams, Cottage, Grainstore and Nethergate. The immaculately kept spacious oak-beamed bar has a comfortably civilised atmosphere, open fires, simple wooden tables and chairs and country paintings on the pale walls. The very delicious thoughtfully prepared food here ranges from little bowls of tasty bar nibbles up to some really imaginative out of the ordinary dishes. The menu has helpful notes about some of their ingredients and lists their preferred suppliers. 16 wines by the glass (plus eight sweet wines and two champagnes), and fine port and sherry; very good service. There are seats out in front of the building and on a back terrace.

Free house ~ Licensee Taffeta Scrimshaw ~ Real ale ~ Bar food (12-2.30, 6.30-9.30) ~ Restaurant ~ (01832) 710241 ~ Children welcome ~ Dogs allowed in bar ~ Open 12-11(till 6 on Sun); closed Sun evening and all day Mon

LITTLE WILBRAHAM
Hole in the Wall

Taking Stow cum Quy turn off A14, turn off A1303 Newmarket Road at The Wilbrahams signpost, then right at Little Wilbraham signpost; High Street; CB1 5JY

Charming tucked-away dining pub – quite a find

This interesting place scores highly in every way. Whatever your drinks tastes, you'll be pleased: well kept Woodfordes Wherry and Nelsons Revenge and a changing guest like Isle of Ely Fenland Rabbit Poacher on handpump, a good choice of wines by the glass, unusual soft drinks such as pomegranate and elderflower pressé. Service is friendly and unfailingly helpful. The carpeted ochre-walled bar on the right is a cosy place for a robust no-nonsense pub lunch, with its logs burning in the big brick fireplace, 15th-c beams and timbers, snug little window seats and other mixed seating around scrubbed kitchen tables. For more of an occasion, the similar middle room or the plusher dining room (both with fires) fit the bill well. From a modern menu, the beautifully presented food ranges from basic lunchtime specials to more refined dishes like asparagus with poached organic salmon. The neat side garden has good teak furniture, and a little verandah. It's a very quiet hamlet, with an interesting walk to nearby unspoilt Little Wilbraham Fen.

Free house ~ Licensees Stephen Bull, Jenny Chapman and Chris Leeton ~ Real ale ~ Bar food ~ (01223) 812282 ~ Well behaved children welcome ~ Dogs allowed in bar ~ Open 11.30-3, 6.30-11; closed Sun evening, all day Mon

PETERBOROUGH

Brewery Tap

Opposite Queensgate car park; PE1 2AA

Fantastic range of real ales including its own brews and popular thai food in huge conversion of old labour exchange

There's a vast two-storey-high glass wall in this striking modern conversion of an old labour exchange that divides the bar and the brewery, giving fascinating views of the massive copper-banded stainless brewing vessels. From here they produce their own Oakham beers (Bishops Farewell, JHB, and White Dwarf) but also keep nine guests from thoughtfully chosen countrywide brewers as well; also, a good number of bottled belgian beers and quite a few wines by the glass. The thai food served here is very good and extremely popular, running from snacks such as chicken satay or tempura vegetables to curries and stir fries. There's an easy-going relaxed feel to the open-plan contemporary interior, with an expanse of light wood and stone floors for drinkers and blue-painted iron pillars holding up a steel-corded mezzanine level. It's stylishly lit by a giant suspended steel ring with bulbs running around the rim, and steel-meshed wall lights. A band of chequered floor tiles traces the path of the long sculpted light wood bar counter, which is boldly backed by an impressive display of bottles in a ceiling-high wall of wooden cubes. A sofa seating area downstairs provides a comfortable corner for a surprisingly mixed bunch of customers from young to old; there's a big screen TV for sporting events, piped music and games machines and DJs or live bands at the weekends. It gets very busy in the evening.

Own brew ~ Licensee Jessica Loock ~ Real ale ~ Bar food (12-2.30, 6-9.30; 12-10.30 Fri, Sat) ~ Restaurant ~ (01733) 358500 ~ Children welcome until 9pm ~ Dogs allowed in bar ~ Two live bands per month ~ Open 12-11(till 2am, Fri and Sat); closed 25 and 26 Dec, 1 Jan

REACH

Dyke's End

From B1102 E of A14/A1103 junction, follow signpost to Swaffham Prior and Upware – keep on through Swaffham Prior (Reach signposted from there); Fair Green; CB5 0JD

Candle-lit rooms in former farmhouse, enjoyable food, and own-brewed beer

Built around a 17th-c farmhouse, this popular pub is next to the church and the charming village green. A high-backed winged settle screens off the door and the simply decorated ochre-walled bar has stripped heavy pine tables and pale kitchen chairs on dark boards and one or two rugs. In a panelled section on the left are a few rather smarter dining tables, and on the right there's a step down to a red-carpeted part with the small red-walled servery and sensibly placed darts at the back. All the tables have lit candles in earthenware bottles, and there may be a big bowl of lilies to brighten up the serving counter. As well as their own-brewed Devils Dyke Bitter, No 7 Pale Ale and No 8 Ale, they keep a couple of guests such as Adnams Bitter and Milton Pegasus on handpump alongside a decent wine list, and Old Rosie cider. The tasty food here is mostly traditional, and it's best to book at the weekends. There are picnic-sets under big green canvas parasols out in front on the grass and Banger and Butter, the dachshunds, may have pride of place on a rug spread on the lawn. The very close relationship which the pub has with the village does mean that when it's busy with cheerful regulars at the weekend, outsiders may feel a little left out.

Free house ~ Licensee Simon Owers ~ Real ale ~ Bar food (not Sun evening or Mon lunchtime) ~ Restaurant ~ (01638) 743816 ~ Children allowed but no small children after 7.30pm ~ Dogs allowed in bar ~ Folk first and third Sun ~ Open 12-2.30, 6-11; 12-11(10.30 Sun) Sat; closed Mon lunchtime

DOG FRIENDLY HOTELS, INNS AND B&Bs

BUCKDEN

George

High Street, Buckden, St Neots, Cambridgeshire PE19 5XA (01480) 812300

£100; 12 charming rms, all named after a famous George. Handsome Georgian-faced former coaching inn stylishly and elegantly refurbished with contemporary furnishings but making the most of medieval origins; beamed bar with log fire, real ales, 20 wines by glass, bustling brasserie with first-rate modern cooking and pretty foliage arrangements, and seats under large parasols on sheltered terrace; dogs in bedrooms

ELY

Lamb

2 Lynn Road, Ely, Cambridgeshire CB7 4EJ (01353) 663574

£100; 31 comfortable rms. Pleasant, neatly kept 15th-c coaching inn near cathedral, with two smart bars, enjoyable food in attractive restaurant, very friendly staff, and limited car parking; walking in nearby park; dogs in bedrooms, £10

HUNTINGDON

Old Bridge

1 High Street, Huntingdon, Cambridgeshire PE29 3TQ; just off A14
(01480) 451591

£135; 24 excellent, individually decorated rms. Civilised, creeper-covered Georgian hotel with pretty lounge, log fire and comfortable sofas in panelled bar, imaginative british cooking and extensive wine list in light, lively and informal restaurant and in second, more formal restaurant, too; quick courteous service, riverside gardens and terraces, and walks behind the hotel; partial disabled access; dogs in bedrooms, bar, and lounge

SIX MILE BOTTOM

Swynford Paddocks

Six Mile Bottom, Newmarket, Cambridgeshire CB8 0UE (1 mile from A11, via A1304) (01638) 570234

£135; 15 spacious, elegant rms with good bthrms. 17th-c country house in five acres of grounds overlooking stud paddocks; carefully furnished rooms with fresh flowers and log fires, lively bar decorated with Brigadier memorabilia (a tribute to the great racehorse who is buried in the hotel grounds), good food in conservatory-styled brasserie, relaxed atmosphere, and friendly service; tennis, putting and croquet; dog walking in close-by recreation ground and surrounding fields or on Newmarket heath and gallops (after midday); disabled access; dogs welcome in bedrooms

WANSFORD

Haycock

London Road, Wansford, Peterborough, Cambridgeshire PE8 6JA (just off A1, highly visibly just S of A47) (01780) 782223

£125; 48 individually decorated rms. 17th-c golden stone inn with relaxed, comfortable and carefully furnished lounges, pubby bar, pretty lunchtime café, smart restaurant with good food and excellent wines, and efficient friendly service; garden with pétanque, fishing and cricket; dogs can walk in the grounds and there are lots of nearby country walks too; disabled access. The little village it dominates is attractive, with a fine bridge over the Nene, and a good antiques shop; dogs in some bedrooms

DOG FRIENDLY PUBS

ALDFORD

Grosvenor Arms

B5130 Chester—Wrexham; CH3 6HJ

Spacious place with buoyantly chatty atmosphere, impressive range of drinks, well balanced sensibly imaginative menu, good service; lovely big terrace and gardens

Cream-painted areas are sectioned by big knocked-through arches and a variety of wood, quarry tile, flagstone and black and white tiled floor finishes – some nice richly coloured turkey rugs look well against these natural materials. Good solid pieces of traditional furniture, plenty of interesting pictures and attractive lighting keep it all intimate enough. A big panelled library room has tall book-shelves lining one wall, and lots of substantial tables well spaced on its hand-somely boarded floor. Lovely on summer evenings, the airy terracotta-floored conservatory has lots of gigantic low hanging flowering baskets and chunky pale wood garden furniture. This opens out to a large elegant suntrap terrace, and a neat lawn with picnic-sets, young trees and an old tractor. The rather fine look-ing bar counter stocks a comprehensive range of drinks including around 16 wines (all served by the glass), an impressive range of whiskies (including 100 malts, 30 bourbons, and 30 irish whiskeys) as well as Caledonian Deuchars IPA, Weetwood Eastgate, Thwaites and three interesting guests from brewers such as Beartown, Station House and Osset. Food is interesting and very good, service is attentive, friendly and reliable, and they keep a good selection of board games.

Brunning & Price ~ Manager Tracey Varley ~ Real ale ~ Bar food (12-9.30) ~ (01244) 620228 ~ Children welcome till 7pm ~ Dogs allowed in bar ~ Open 11.30-11; 12-10.30 Sun

ASTON

Bhurtpore

Off A530 SW of Nantwich; in village follow Wrenbury signpost; CW5 8DQ

Fantastic range of drinks (especially real ales) and tasty curries in warm-hearted pub with some unusual artefacts; big garden

With its full complement of 11 real ales, you're likely to find beers from anywhere in the country at this very enthusiastically run red-brick free house, though they do try to give preferential treatment to local brews. Other than Salopian Shropshire Gold, which tends to be on most of the time, they usually get through over 1,000 different superbly kept real ales in a year. They also stock dozens of unusual bottled beers and fruit beers, a great many bottled ciders and perries, over 100 different whiskies, carefully selected soft drinks, and have a good wine list. If you're a very keen real ale enthusiast, it's worth going during their summer beer festival. The food is enjoyable including five different curries. The pub takes its unusual name from the town in India, where a local landowner, Lord Combermere, won a battle; it also explains why a collection of exotic artefacts in the carpeted lounge bar has an indian influence – look out for the turbaned statue behind the counter, proudly sporting any sunglasses left behind by customers; also good local period photographs, and some attractive furniture. Tables in the comfortable public bar are reserved for people not eating; darts, dominoes, cribbage, pool, TV and games machine. At lunchtime and early weekday evenings the atmosphere is cosy and civilised, and on week-ends, when it gets packed, the cheery staff cope superbly.

Free house ~ Licensee Simon George ~ Real ale ~ Bar food (12-9 Sun) ~ Restaurant ~ (01270) 780917 ~ Children welcome ~ Dogs allowed in bar ~ Open 12-2.30(3 Sat), 6.30-11.30(midnight Sat); 12-11 Sun

BARTHOMLEY

White Lion

A mile from M6 junction 16; from exit roundabout take B5078 N towards Alsager, then Barthomley signposted on left; CW2 5PG

Charming 17th-c thatched village tavern with classic period interior and good value straightforward tasty lunchtime food

Unchanging and forever warmly welcoming, the main bar here has a timelessly informal feel, with its blazing open fire, heavy low oak beams (dating back to Stuart times), attractively moulded black panelling, cheshire history and prints on the walls, latticed windows and thick wobbly old tables. Up some steps, a second room has another welcoming open fire, more oak panelling, a high-backed winged settle, a paraffin lamp hinged to the wall, and shove-ha'penny, cribbage and dominoes; local societies make good use of a third room, and look out for the slightly mad cat. Five real ales include Marstons Bitter and Pedigree and Mansfield and a couple of guests – usually Jennings Cocker Hoop and Snecklifter – and nice food from a short traditional menu. Outside, seats and picnic-sets on the cobbles have a charming view of the attractive village, and the lovely early 15th-c red sandstone church of St Bertiline across the road, where you can learn about the Barthomley massacre, is well worth a visit.

Marstons ~ Tenant Laura Condliffe ~ Real ale ~ Bar food (lunchtime only) ~ (01270) 882242 ~ Children welcome away from bar until 9pm ~ Dogs welcome ~ Open 11.30-11; 12-10.30 Sun

BUNBURY

Dysart Arms

Bowes Gate Road; village signposted off A51 NW of Nantwich; and from A49 S of Tarporley – coming this way, coming in on northernmost village access road, bear left in village centre; CW6 9PH

Civilised chatty dining pub attractively filled with good furniture in thoughtfully laid out rooms; very enjoyable food, lovely garden with pretty views.

The meandering series of knocked-through rooms at this well run country pub give rise to an intimate and homely but still very social feeling atmosphere. They are immaculately kept and ramble gently around the pleasantly lit central bar. Cream walls keep it light, clean and airy, with deep venetian red ceilings adding cosiness, and each room (some with good winter fires) is cleverly furnished with an appealing variety of well spaced sturdy wooden tables and chairs, a couple of tall filled bookcases and just the right amount of carefully chosen bric-a-brac, properly lit pictures and plants. Flooring ranges from red and black tiles, to stripped boards and some carpet. Service is efficient and friendly, and the food is attractively presented and tasty. Thwaites and Weetwood Eastgate and a couple of guests such as Spitting Feathers Farmhouse Ale and Youngs Special are very well kept on handpump, alongside a good selection of 16 wines by the glass, just over 20 malts and fresh apple juice. Sturdy wooden tables on the terrace and picnic sets on the lawn in the neatly kept slightly elevated garden are lovely in summer, with views of the splendid church at the end of the pretty village, and the distant Peckforton Hills beyond.

Brunning & Price ~ Manager Greg Williams ~ Real ale ~ Bar food (12-9.30(9 Sun)) ~ (01829) 260183 ~ Children welcome ~ Dogs allowed in bar ~ Open 11.30-11; 12-10.30 Sun

BURWARDSLEY

Pheasant

Higher Burwardsley; signposted from Tattenhall (which itself is signposted off A41 S of Chester) and from Harthill (reached by turning off A534 Nantwich—Holt at the Copper Mine); follow pub's signpost on up hill from Post Office; OS Sheet 117 map reference 523566; CH3 9PF

Fantastic views, local beer and good range of very enjoyable food at heavily beamed and spaciously fresh conversion of old inn

The nicely beamed interior of this half-timbered sandstone 17th-c pub has an airy modern feel, with wooden floors and well spaced furniture, including comfy leather armchairs and some nice old chairs. They say the see-through fireplace houses the largest log fire in the county, and there's a pleasant restaurant. Three local Weetwood beers and a guest from a brewer such as Beartown are served on handpump alongside a selection of bottled beers, nine wines by the glass and around 20 malts; the food from a changing menu is modern and interesting. Piped music, daily newspapers. On a clear day the telescope on the terrace (with nice hardwood furniture) lets you make out the pier head and cathedrals in Liverpool, while from inside you can see right across the Cheshire plain. A big side lawn has picnic-sets, and on summer weekends they sometimes have barbecues. Popular with walkers, the pub is well placed for the Sandstone Trail along the Peckforton Hills.

Free house ~ Licensee Andrew Nelson ~ Real ale ~ Bar food (12-3, 6-9.30 Mon; 12-9.30 (10 Fri, Sat, 8.30 Sun)) ~ (01829) 770434 ~ Children welcome till 6pm ~ Dogs welcome ~ Open 12-11 ~ Bedrooms: £65B/£85B

CHESTER

Albion

Albion Street; CH1 1RQ

Strongly traditional pub with comfortable Edwardian décor and captivating World War I memorabilia; hearty food and good drinks

Tucked away on a quiet street corner in the shadow of the Roman Wall, this unspoilt Victorian pub is said to be the last surviving place in the city in its original layout. Uniquely, its homely interior is entirely dedicated to the Great War of 1914-18, and most unusually it's the officially listed site of four war memorials to soldiers from the Cheshire Regiment. Throughout its tranquil rooms (no games machines or children here) you'll find an absorbing collection of World War I memorabilia, from big engravings of men leaving for war, and similarly moving prints of wounded veterans, to flags, advertisements and so on. The post-Edwardian décor is appealingly muted, with dark floral William Morris wallpaper (designed on the first day of World War I), a cast-iron fireplace, appropriate lamps, leatherette and hoop-backed chairs, a period piano and cast-iron-framed tables; there's an attractive side dining room too, and the wholesome bar food is generously served. Service is friendly, though this is a firmly run place (the landlord has been here 37 years now): groups of race-goers are discouraged (opening times may be limited during meets), and they don't like people rushing in just before closing time. Beers come from Batemans, Black Sheep and Timothy Taylor, with a guest such as Coach House Cheshire Gold. They also stock new world wines, fresh orange juice, over 25 malt whiskies and a good selection of rums and gins.

Punch ~ Lease Michael Edward Mercer ~ Real ale ~ Bar food (12-2, 5-8(6-8.30 Sat); not Sun evening) ~ Restaurant ~ No credit cards ~ (01244) 340345 ~ Dogs allowed in bar ~ Open 12-3, 5(6 Sat, 7 Sun)-11(10.30 Sun)

LANGLEY

Hanging Gate

Meg Lane, Higher Sutton; follow Langley signpost from A54 beside Fourways Motel, and that road passes the pub; from Macclesfield, heading S from centre on A523 turn left into Byrons Lane at Langley, Wincle signpost; in Sutton (0.5 miles after going under canal bridge, ie before Langley) fork right at Church House Inn, following Wildboarclough signpost, then 2 miles later turning sharp right at steep hairpin bend; OS Sheet 118 map reference 952696; SK11 0NG

Remotely set old place with fires in traditional cosy rooms, helpful licensees, lovely views from airy extension and terrace

Clinging to the top of a Peak District ridge, this welcoming old drover's inn commands panoramic views across the Cheshire plains and beyond. Still in their original layout, its three cosy little low-beamed rooms are simply furnished. The tiny little snug bar, at its pubbiest at lunchtime, has a welcoming log fire in a big brick fireplace, a single table, plain chairs and cushioned wall seats (though there's barely room in here to sit), and a few old pub pictures and seasonal photographs on its creamy walls. Beers served in here include well kept Hydes Original, Jekylls Gold and a Hydes and a guest such as Saddleworth St George on handpump, quite a few malt whiskies and ten wines by the glass. The second room, with a section of bar counter in the corner, has only five tables, and a third appealing little oak beamed blue room has a little chaise longue. Food from the changing specials board is pubby. Seats out on the crazy-paved terrace have great views; piped music. It does get busy so it's best to book on weekends.

Hydes ~ Tenants Ian and Luda Rottenbury ~ Real ale ~ Bar food (12-2.30 (4 Sun), 6.30(6 Sun)-9.30) ~ Restaurant ~ (01260) 252238 ~ Children welcome with restrictions ~ Dogs welcome ~ Open 11.30-3, 5-10.30; 11-11 Sat; 12-10.30 Sun

MARBURY

Swan

NNE of Whitchurch; OS Sheet 117 map reference 562457; SY13 4LS

Charmingly set proper country pub with good value food and drinks

This prettily set village-green pub is in the good hands of a welcoming publican (with his new wife and chocolate labrador Cally) who takes as much care of its warm-hearted atmosphere as he does of its beers. These he calls 'my lads'; Adnams and a couple of changing guests such as Weetwoods Cheshire Cat (from nearby Wrenbury) and Woodlands Bees Knees. All 16 wines of the reasonably priced wines on the list are available by the glass. The roomy partly panelled lounge has upholstered easy chairs and other country furniture, a copper-canopied fireplace with a good winter log fire (masses of greenery in summer), daily papers, board games, quiet piped music and discreet lighting. Their very popular two-course lunch deals (a handful of pubby dishes) are incredibly good value. The evening menu is more elaborate. The garden is good-sized, with well spaced picnic-sets and big shrubs. Rebuilt in 1884, the pub is in a quiet and attractive village, a half-mile's country walk from the Llangollen Canal, Bridges 23 and 24. Showing a lovely generosity of spirit, the licensees are quite happy for you to use their car park if walking, even if you aren't popping in for a drink. The nearby lakeside church dates from the 1400s.

Oxford Hotels ~ Lease Rob and Clarissa Adam ~ Real ale ~ Bar food (12-2, 6.30-9) ~ (01948) 662220 ~ Children welcome ~ Dogs allowed in bar ~ Open 12-3, 6.30-11; 12-11 Sat, Sun in summer; closed Mon except bank hols

PEOVER HEATH

Dog

Off A50 N of Holmes Chapel at the Whipping Stocks, keep on past Parkgate into Wellbank Lane; OS Sheet 118 map reference 794735; note that this village is called Peover Heath on the OS map and shown under that name on many road maps, but the pub is often listed under Over Peover instead; WA16 8UP

Homely pub with interesting range of beers and generous traditional food

The neatly kept bar here is gently old fashioned with a comfortably cottagey feel. Neat tied back floral curtains hang at its little windows, a curved cushioned banquette is built into a bay window and mixed furnshings, mostly traditional dark wheelbacks, are arranged on a patterned carpet. A coal fire, copper pieces and pot plants dotted around add to the homely feel; games machine, darts, pool, dominoes, board games, TV and piped music. Decent standard bar food and the five reasonably priced and very well kept real ales here will probably be Copper Dragon Scotts 1816, Hydes Bitter and Dark Mild, Weetwood and a guest. They also have Addlestone's cider, 35 different malt whiskies and eight wines by the glass. There are picnic-sets beneath colourful hanging baskets on the peaceful lane, and more out in a pretty back garden. It's a pleasant walk from here to the Jodrell Bank Centre and Arboretum.

Free house ~ Licensee Steven Wrigley ~ Real ale ~ Bar food (12-2.30, 6-9; 12-8.30 Sun) ~ Restaurant ~ (01625) 861421 ~ Dogs allowed in bar ~ Live music monthly Fri, also Weds and Fri in Dec ~ Open 11.30-3, 4.30-11; 11.10-11 Sat; 12-10.30 Sun

WINCLE
Ship

Village signposted off A54 Congleton—Buxton; SK11 0QE

Popular sandstone 16th-c village pub in good walking country, thoughtful staff, Lees beers, good inventive food, and little garden

Durable flagstone floors and a warming coal fire in two simple little tap rooms make this thick stone walled pub the perfect refreshment stop after a walk in the lovely surrounding countryside – they even sell their own book of local walks, £3. The carpeted and gently lit lounge bar and restaurant provide a comfier alternative, and the sympathetically designed extension into the old stables, with flagstone floors, beams and wood burning stove, helps ease the weekend bustle. Interesting sandwiches and more substantial meals, and the three or four real ales come from the J W Lees portfolio; they've a few foreign bottled beers, too. A small garden has wooden tables.

Lees ~ Tenant Christopher Peter Knights ~ Real ale ~ Bar food (12-2.30(3 Sat, Sun), 6.30-9) ~ Restaurant ~ (01260) 227217 ~ Children welcome but not in bar after 8pm ~ Dogs allowed in bar ~ Open 12-3, 6.30(5 Fri)-11; 5-11 Mon; 12-11 Sat; 12-10.30 Sun; closed Mon lunchtime

WRENBURY
Dusty Miller

Village signposted from A530 Nantwich—Whitchurch; Cholmondeley Road; CW5 8HG

Generous food and views of busy canal from bars and terrace of big mill conversion

Sitting right next to the Shropshire Union Canal, this substantial brick pub is a neatly converted 19th-c corn mill – you can still see the old lift hoist up under the rafters. The River Weaver runs in an aqueduct under the canal at this point, and it was the river that once powered the millrace. These days a constant stream of boats slipping through the striking counter-weighted canal drawbridge outside provides entertainment, if you're sitting at picnic-sets among rose bushes on the gravel terrace, or at one of the tables inside by a series of tall glazed arches. The atmosphere is low-key restauranty, with some emphasis on the generously served food (which changes monthly), though drinkers are welcome, and in summer the balance may even tip. The very spacious modern feeling main bar area is comfortably furnished with a mixture of seats (including tapestried banquettes, oak settles and wheelback chairs) round rustic tables. Further in, a quarry-tiled part by the bar counter has an oak settle and refectory table. Friendly staff serve three well kept Robinsons beers on handpump; eclectic piped music.

Robinsons ~ Tenant Mark Sumner ~ Real ale ~ Bar food (12-2(2.30 Sun), 6.30-9.30(7-9 Sun)) ~ Restaurant ~ (01270) 780537 ~ Children welcome ~ Dogs allowed in bar ~ Folk last Fri of the month ~ Open 12-3, 6.30(7 Sun)-11; closed Mon lunchtime in winter

DOG FRIENDLY HOTELS, INNS AND B&Bs

BEESTON
Wild Boar Hotel
Whitchurch Road, Beeston, Tarporley, Cheshire CW6 9NW (01829) 260309

£90; 37 recently refurbished rms. Timbered 17th-c former hunting lodge, much extended over the years, with relaxed, comfortable bars and lounges, enjoyable meals in beamed, brasserie-style restaurant and in the Steakhouse, and friendly, professional service; lots of nearby walks; disabled access; dogs in ground-floor bedrooms only; £10

BICKLEY MOSS
Cholmondeley Arms
Cholmondeley, Malpas, Cheshire SY14 8HN (01829) 720300

£80; 6 rms. Airy converted Victorian schoolhouse close to castle and gardens, with lots of atmosphere, very friendly staff, interesting furnishings, open fire, imaginative bar food, and very good choice of wines; garden for dogs to walk and nearby walks, too; resident cat; disabled access; dogs welcome in bedrooms

FULLERS MOOR
Frogg Manor
Nantwich Road, Broxton, Chester CH3 9JH (A534 just E of A41 junction)
(01829) 782629

£98; 8 lavishly decorated rms with thoughtful extras – one is in a tree house in the garden. Enjoyably eccentric Georgian manor house full of ornamental frogs and antique furniture, open fires and ornate dried-flower arrangements; restful upstairs sitting room, cosy little bar, a large collection of 30s/40s records (and a discreet small dance floor), and good English cooking in elegant dining room which leads to conservatory overlooking the gardens; resident mini yorkshire terrier; tennis; disabled access; dogs welcome away from residents' lounge and restaurant

KNUTSFORD

Longview

51-55 Manchester Road, Knutsford, Cheshire WA16 OLX (01565) 632119

£94; 32 individually decorated rms – the suites have their own sitting room and garden. Friendly, family-run Victorian hotel with attractive period and reproduction furnishings, open fires in original fireplaces, cosy cellar bar, elegant restaurant, and good mediterranean cooking; cl Christmas and New Year; dogs can walk on the heath directly opposite hotel; dogs in bedrooms; £10

MOBBERLEY

Laburnum Cottage

Knutsford Road, Mobberley, Knutsford, Cheshire WA16 7PU (01565) 872464

£61; 5 pretty rms. Neatly kept and friendly country guest house in an acre of landscaped garden; relaxed atmosphere in comfortable residents' lounge with books, a sunny conservatory, and very good food; resident cat; dogs can walk in the grounds and in nearby fields; dogs by arrangement in annexe; £5

POTT SHRIGLEY

Shrigley Hall

Shrigley Park, Pott Shrigley, Macclesfield, Cheshire SK10 5SB (2.5 miles off A523, in Adlington just N of Macclesfield)(01625) 575757

£159; 149 light and airy traditional rms. In over 260 acres of parkland, this impressive country house has a splendid entrance hall with several elegant rooms leading off, a bustling bar, enjoyable food in the stylish restaurant overlooking the grounds, and good service from friendly staff; spa with swimming pool, beauty rooms, and gym, 18-hole championship golf course, fishing, tennis, and leisure centre in former church building; resident cat; dogs can walk in grounds and in Lyme Park; plenty to do nearby; partial disabled access; dogs in bedrooms; £15

TARPORLEY

Swan

50 High Street, Tarporley, Cheshire CW6 OAG (01829) 733838

£96.50; 16 rms. Well managed Georgian inn with good mix of individual tables and chairs in attractive bay-windowed bar, coal fires, real ales, decent wines, and quite a few malt whiskies; good food from an extensive menu in connecting beamed and panelled dining rooms, nice breakfasts, and friendly staff; cl one week Nov; limited disabled access; dogs in coach house annexe bedrooms

DOG FRIENDLY PUBS

BLISLAND

Blisland Inn

Village signposted off A30 and B3266 NE of Bodmin; PL30 4JF

Super choice of real ales and beer-related memorabilia in welcoming local; home-made food, and cheerful service

In a pretty village, this chatty local is a friendly place with a cheerful atmosphere and one reader even told us that a dog is virtually a requirement for visiting here! Every inch of the beams and ceiling is covered with beer badges (or their particularly wide-ranging collection of mugs), and the walls are similarly filled with beer-related posters and memorabilia. Up to eight real ales are kept at any one time, tapped from the cask or on handpump. Two are brewed for the pub by Sharps – Blisland Special and Bulldog – and there's Exmoor Ale and four constantly changing guests from all over the country. They also have a changing farm cider, fruit wines, and real apple juice; good service. The carpeted lounge has a number of barometers on the walls, a rack of daily newspapers for sale, and a few standing timbers, and the family room has pool, table skittles, euchre, cribbage and dominoes; piped music. Food here is very traditional and tasty. Plenty of picnic-sets outside. The popular Camel Trail cycle path is close by – though the hill up to Blisland is pretty steep. As with many pubs in this area, it's hard to approach without negotiating several single-track roads.

Free house ~ Licensees Gary and Margaret Marshall ~ Real ale ~ Bar food ~ (01208) 850739 ~ Children in family room only ~ Dogs welcome ~ Live music Sat evening ~ Open 11.30-11; 12-10.30 Sun

CADGWITH

Cadgwith Cove Inn

Down very narrow lane off A3083 S of Helston; no nearby parking; TR12 7JX

Fine walks in either direction from old-fashioned inn at the bottom of fishing cove

This is a genuine community local but friendly to visitors too. It's in a fishing cove setting at the bottom of a charming village and whilst it's best to park at the top and meander down through the thatched cottages, it is quite a steep hike back up again. The two snugly dark front rooms have plain pub furnishings on their mainly parquet flooring, a log fire in one stripped stone end wall, lots of local photographs including gig races, cases of naval hat ribands and of fancy knot-work and a couple of compass binnacles. Some of the dark beams have ships' shields and others have spliced blue rope hand-holds. Flowers IPA, Sharps Doom Bar, Skinners Betty Stogs and a guest beer on handpump. A back bar has a huge and colourful fish mural and the left-hand room has a games machine and piped music. Bar food includes sandwiches (the crab ones are well liked), seasonal lobster and other decent specials; best to check food times in winter. There are green-painted picnic-sets on the good-sized front terrace, some under a fairy-lit awning, looking down to the fish sheds by the bay. Fine coastal walks in either direction.

Punch ~ Lease David and Lynda Trivett ~ Real ale ~ Bar food ~ (01326) 290513 ~ Well supervised children welcome away from main bar ~ Dogs welcome ~ Live folk Tues evening, cornish singers Fri evening ~ Open 12-3, 6-11.30; midday-1am Sat; 12-10.30 Sun ~ Bedrooms: £30.25(£47.50S)/£60.50(£82.50S)

LANLIVERY

Crown

Signposted off A390 Lostwithiel—St Austell (tricky to find from other directions); PL30 5BT

Chatty atmosphere in nice old pub, old-fashioned rooms, and well liked food and drink; the Eden Project is close by

There have been quite a few changes and substantial restorations at this fine old pub. A woodburning stove has been installed into the opened-up fireplace of the main bar, there are now flagstones throughout the bars, the terrace has been extended and improved and they have bedrooms in a granite outbuilding; a huge old well was found beneath the porch and this has been topped with a glass lid and lit. The pub dates from the 12th c and has quite a bit of real character – our readers enjoy their visits very much. The small public bar has heavy beams and a mix of tables and chairs, and a lighter room leads off, with beams in the white boarded ceiling, cushioned black settles, and a little fireplace with an old-fashioned fire; another little room is similarly furnished. Sharps Doom Bar and Skinners Betty Stogs and Ginger Tosser on handpump, nine wines by the glass, and local cider; board games. Enjoyable food is prepared with thought – they list their local suppliers on the menu. The Eden Project is only ten minutes away.

Wagtail Inns ~ Licensee Andrew Brotheridge ~ Real ale ~ Bar food (12-2.30(3 summer), 6.30-9(9.30 summer); not 25 Dec) ~ Restaurant ~ (01208) 872707 ~ Children welcome but must be away from bar ~ Dogs allowed in bar and bedrooms ~ Occasional live music Sun ~ Open 12-11(10.30 Sun) ~ Bedrooms: /£79.95S

MITHIAN

Miners Arms

Just off B3285 E of St Agnes; TR5 0QF

Cosy pub with open fires in several smallish rooms and friendly staff

In its 400 years, this old pub has been a court, a chapel and a smuggler's lair. Several cosy little rooms and passages are warmed by winter open fires, and the small back bar has an irregular beam and plank ceiling, a wood block floor and bulging squint walls (one with a fine old wall painting of Elizabeth I). Another small room has a decorative low ceiling, lots of books and quite a few interesting ornaments. Sharps Doom Bar and a guest beer on handpump served by cheerful staff; piped music and darts. There are seats outside on the back terrace with more on the sheltered front cobbled forecourt. Bar food, which includes lunchtime sandwiches, is very pubby.

Punch ~ Lease Anouska House ~ Real ale ~ Bar food (12-2, 6-9) ~ Restaurant ~ (01872) 552375 ~ Children allowed away from bar ~ Dogs allowed in bar ~ Pub quiz every third Thurs ~ Open 12-midnight

MYLOR BRIDGE

Pandora

Restronguet Passage: from A39 in Penryn, take turning signposted Mylor Church, Mylor Bridge, Flushing and go straight through Mylor Bridge following Restronguet Passage signs; or from A39 further N, at or near Perranarworthal, take turning signposted Mylor, Restronguet, then follow Restronguet Weir signs, but turn left down hill at Restronguet Passage sign; TR11 5ST

Beautifully placed waterside inn with seats on long floating pontoon, lots of atmosphere in beamed and flagstoned rooms, and some sort of food all day

On a fine day particularly, this is an idyllic spot. You can sit at picnic-seats on the long floating pontoon in front of this lovely medieval thatched pub and watch children crabbing and visiting dinghies pottering about in the sheltered waterfront. Inside is special too: several rambling, interconnecting rooms have low wooden ceilings (mind your head on some of the beams), beautifully polished big flagstones, cosy alcoves with leatherette benches built into the walls, old race posters, model boats in glass cabinets, and three large log fires in high hearths (to protect them against tidal floods). St Austell HSD, Tinners and Tribute and a guest such as Bass on handpump, and a dozen wines by the glass. The menu is fairly pubby at lunchtime (good crab sandwiches) but tends to be a bit more elaborate in the evening and food is well liked. The pub does get very crowded and parking is difficult at peak times.

St Austell ~ Tenant John Milan ~ Real ale ~ Bar food (all day; sandwiches and afternoon tea between 3-6) ~ Restaurant ~ (01326) 372678 ~ Children welcome away from bar area ~ Dogs allowed in bar ~ Open 10.30am-midnight (11 in winter)

PERRANWELL

Royal Oak

Village signposted off A393 Redruth—Falmouth and A39 Falmouth—Truro; TR3 7PX

Welcoming and relaxed with quite an emphasis on well presented food, and thoughtful wines

A back decking area should have been added at this pretty and quietly set village pub by the time this *Guide* is published; you will be able to enjoy tapas and drinks while watching the sun going down. The roomy, carpeted bar has a gently upmarket atmosphere, horsebrasses and pewter and china mugs on its black beams and joists, plates and country pictures on the cream-painted stone walls, and cosy wall and other seats around candlelit tables. It rambles around beyond a big stone fireplace (with a good log fire in winter) into a snug little nook of a room behind, with just a couple more tables. Food plays quite a big role here. It's attractively presented, with something for most tastes, and is rather good. Skinners Betty Stogs and Greene King Old Speckled Hen on hand-pump from the small serving counter, good wines by the glass, scrumpy cider, summer sangria and winter mulled wine; piped music and board games. We heard that the pub was up for sale as we went to press.

Free house ~ Licensee Richard Rudland ~ Real ale ~ Bar food (12-2.30, 7-9.30) ~ Restaurant ~ (01872) 863175 ~ Children in dining areas only ~ Dogs allowed in bar ~ Open 11-3, 6-midnight; 12-4, 6-11 Sun

PORTHLEVEN
Ship

Village on B3304 SW of Helston; pub perched on edge of harbour; TR13 9JS

Fisherman's pub built into cliffs, fine harbour views from seats on terrace, and tasty bar food

On a stormy night, this friendly old fisherman's pub is just the place to sit in snug warmth and watch the boats and birds blowing across the harbour. In kinder weather, there are tables in the terraced garden that make the most of the sea view, and the harbour is interestingly floodlit. The knocked-through bar has a relaxed atmosphere, welcoming log fires in big stone fireplaces and some genuine individuality. The family room is a conversion of an old smithy with logs burning in a huge open fireplace; the candlelit dining room also looks over the sea. Good bar food runs from sandwiches and toasties up to minted leg of lamb casserole in rosemary and red wine sauce. Courage Best and Sharps Doom Bar and a couple of summer guests on handpump; piped music and board games.

Free house ~ Licensee Colin Oakden ~ Real ale ~ Bar food ~ (01326) 564204 ~ Children in family room only ~ Dogs allowed in bar ~ Open 11.30-11; 12-10.30 Sun

PORTHTOWAN
Blue

Beach Road, East Cliff; use the car park (fee in season), not the slippy sand; TR4 8AW

Informal, busy bar – not a traditional pub – right by wonderful beach, lively staff and customers

Certainly not a traditional pub (but it does now serve real ale which they tell us is incredibly popular), this light and airy bar, with its easy, informal atmosphere, is usually packed. Right by a fantastic beach – huge picture windows look across the terrace to the huge expanse of sand and sea – there's a genuinely interesting range of customers (and dogs) of all ages. The front bays have built-in pine seats and throughout are chrome and wicker chairs around plain wooden tables on the stripped wood floor, quite a few high-legged chrome and wooden bar stools, and plenty of standing space around the bar counter; powder blue painted walls, ceiling fans, some big ferny plants, two large TVs showing silent surfing videos, and fairly quiet piped music; pool table. Good modern bar food (though they do serve lunchtime filled baps too) is prepared using local, seasonal produce where possible. Several wines by the glass, cocktails and shots, and giant cups of coffee; perky, helpful young staff.

Free house ~ Licensees Tara Roberts, Luke Morris and Alexandra George ~ Real ale ~ Bar food (12-9; limited menu in afternoon) ~ (01209) 890329 ~ Children welcome ~ Dogs welcome ~ Live bands Sat evening (and Fri also, in summer) ~ Open 10am-11pm(midnight Sat); 10am-10.30pm Sun; closed two weeks Jan

RUAN LANIHORNE
Kings Head
Off A3078; TR2 5NX

Friendly country pub with good popular food and beer, and welcoming licensees

In a little hamlet down country lanes and just a stroll from an interesting church, this attractive, neatly kept pub is run by friendly licensees and their helpful staff. The main bar has high bar chairs, comfortable sofas and seats around a low table, a winter log fire, and locals enjoying a chat and a pint of Skinners Betty Stogs, Cornish Knocker and a beer named for the pub on hand-pump; several malt whiskies and wines by the glass, and farm cider. Off to the right are two dining rooms with lots of china cups hanging from ceiling joists, plenty of copper and brass, built-in planked seats with attractive cushions and pubby tables and chairs; piped music. The enjoyable menu includes lovely crab sandwiches and other tasty dishes. Across the road is a sunken terrace with seats and tables under trees, and outdoor heaters.

Free house ~ Licensees Andrew and Niki Law ~ Real ale ~ Bar food (12.30-2, 6.30-9; not winter Sun evening or Mon) ~ Restaurant ~ (01872) 501263 ~ Well behaved children welcome in dining areas only ~ Dogs allowed in bar ~ Open 12-2.30, 6-11(10.30 Sun); closed Mon in winter

WATERGATE BAY
Beach Hut
B3276 coast road N of Newquay; TR8 4AA

Bustling, informal beach bar with cheerful young staff, good mix of customers, decent drinks and popular food

Right on the beach and a short walk down from the public car park, this is one of those new breeds of beach bars. It's modern and relaxed, with a cheerful, bustling atmosphere, a good mix of customers of all ages, and friendly, helpful young staff. Big new windows and doors open out on to a new glass-fronted decking area and look across the sand to the sea which on our visit had a lone kite boarder battling with huge waves in a storm – quite extraordinary to watch. To set the scene, inside there are surfing photographs on the planked walls, a large surfboard above a sizeable leatherette wall seat by one big table, and another above the bar counter. Wicker and cane armchairs with blue or pink cushions around green and orange painted tables sit on the nicely weathered stripped wooden floor, there's plenty of mushroom and cream paintwork, orange blinds, and an unusual sloping bleached-board ceiling. Generous helpings of popular bistro-style food include clam chowder and local mussels. Decent wines by the glass, lots of coffees and teas and hot chocolate; piped soft rock music. An end room is slightly simpler, and outside on decking are some picnic-sets. They also run an extreme sports academy.

Free house ~ Licensee Mark Williams ~ Bar food (all day) ~ (01637) 860877 ~ Children welcome ~ Dogs welcome ~ Open 8.30am-11pm; 10.30-dusk in winter

WIDEMOUTH

Bay View

Village signposted (with Bude Coastal Route) off A39 N of Pounstock; Marine Drive; EX23 0AW

Sizeable hotel, wonderful views of Widemouth Bay, real ales and bistro food, and relaxed atmosphere

Contemporary picnic-sets on decking in front of this sizeable, family-run hotel looks across the road and dunes to a magnificent stretch of sand; the sunsets can be lovely. Inside are several spreading, interestingly decorated areas, and on our visit a good mix of customers. As well as some modern seaside paintings and large sea and sunset photographs, there are rugs on stripped wooden floors, some flag-stones, comfortable leather sofas with cushions, low chunky tables with lit church candles, and several fireplaces with log-effect gas fires or decorative pebbles. A front part has pale wooden tables and chairs and a dresser with little wooden beach huts and china plates. Sharps Doom Bar, Skinners Betty Stogs and a beer named for them on handpump, some unusual bottled beers, several wines by the glass (and a notice for a 'fun and free wine tasting quiz'), and cheerful young staff; piped pop. The menu includes traditional and bistro-style food and they may offer a late afternoon bargain dish of the day and cream teas. Outside, there's an equipped children's play area with good, solid picnic-sets on grass beside it.

Free house ~ Licensees Dave and Cherylyn Keene ~ Real ale ~ Bar food (12-2.30, 6-9; 12-8 Sun) ~ Restaurant ~ (01288) 361273 ~ Children welcome ~ Dogs allowed in bar ~ Open 10am-midnight(1am Sat); closed evening 25

ZENNOR

Tinners Arms

B3306 W of St Ives; TR26 3BY

Good mix of customers, friendly atmosphere, and tasty food

Our readers enjoy this well run and popular pub and there's always a good mix of locals and visitors. It's a friendly old place with low wooden-ceilings, cushioned settles, benches, and a mix of chairs around wooden tables on the stone floor, antique prints on the stripped plank panelling, and a log fire in cool weather. Sharps Own and a beer named for the pub, and St Austell Tinners on handpump. There are some fine nearby coastal walks and in good weather you can sit on benches in the sheltered front courtyard or at tables on a bigger side terrace. At lunchtime the menu here is fairly short and pubby but in the evening they offer more imaginative dishes, maybe roasted pigeon with parsley and capers. The pub was built in 1271 to house the masons who constructed St Senara's Church.

Free house ~ Licensees Grahame Edwards and Richard Motley ~ Real ale ~ Bar food (12-2.30, 6.30-9) ~ (01736) 796927 ~ Children welcome away from main bar ~ Dogs welcome ~ Maybe live music Thurs evening ~ Open 11-11; 12-10.30 Sun; 11.30-3.30, 6.30-11 in winter ~ Bedrooms: £45/£80S

DOG FRIENDLY HOTELS, INNS AND B&Bs

BODINNICK

Old Ferry

Bodinnick, Fowey, Cornwall PL23 1LX (01726) 870237

£80; 12 comfortable and spacious rms, most with river views. 400-year-old inn in lovely situation overlooking Fowey estuary; back flagstoned bar partly cut into the rock, real ales, comfortable residents' lounge with french windows opening on to a terrace, and decent food in both bar and little evening restaurant; quiet out of season; resident old english sheepdog and a collie; walks nearby; cl 25 Dec; dogs everywhere except restaurant; £3.50

BRYHER

Hell Bay

Bryher, Isles of Scilly TR23 0PR (01720) 422947

£460 inc dinner; 25 rms and suites, many with stunning sea views. Relaxed and peaceful hotel on the western tip of the island's rugged coastline and in extensive private grounds with outdoor heated swimming pool, golf, and boules; light, airy contemporary décor and original sculptures and paintings from the owners' private collections, residents' lounge, and sea-view restaurant with plenty of local fish and shellfish; boat trips, fishing, diving, and water sports; resident dog; cl Nov-Feb; disabled access; dogs in bedrooms; £12

CARNE BEACH

Nare Hotel

Carne Beach, Veryan, Truro, Cornwall TR2 5PF (01872) 501279

£316; 40 lovely rms to suit all tastes – some stylish ones overlook garden and out to sea. Attractively decorated and furnished hotel in magnificent clifftop position with secluded gardens, outdoor and indoor swimming pools, a new hot tub overlooking the beach, tennis, sailboarding, and fishing; antiques, fresh flowers and log fires in the airy, spacious day rooms, very good food in two restaurants (one with a more relaxed atmosphere), wonderful breakfasts, and run by staff who really care; ideal for quiet family holidays, with safe sandy beach below; miles of NT land for walks; resident dog; disabled access; dogs welcome from £15 inc daily meal

CONSTANTINE BAY

Treglos Hotel

Constantine Bay, Padstow, Cornwall PL28 8JH (01841) 520727

£176; 42 light rms, some with coastal views. Quiet and relaxed hotel close to good sandy beach, and which has been in the same family for over 30 years; comfortable traditional furnishings in light and airy lounges and bar, open fires, good food in attractive restaurant, friendly helpful staff, sheltered garden plus playground and adventure equipment, indoor swimming pool, table tennis, table football and pool table, and children's playroom; self-catering apartments; resident dog; lovely surrounding walks; cl Nov-end Feb; children over 7 in evening restaurant; disabled access; dogs allowed away from public areas; £8.50

CRANTOCK

Crantock Bay Hotel

West Pentire, Crantock, Newquay, Cornwall TR8 5SE (01637) 830229

£174; 33 comfortable rms, most with fine sea views. In a lovely setting on the West Pentire headland, facing the Atlantic and a huge sheltered sandy beach, this relaxed and informal hotel has been run by the same friendly family for over 50 years; four acres of grounds, indoor swimming pool, toddlers' pool, spa, sauna and exercise room, all-weather tennis court, putting course and children's play area; two lounges, bar, and restaurant, enjoyable food using local produce, and nice afternoon teas; wonderful surrounding walks; cl Nov-mid Feb; families most welcome; lots to do nearby; disabled access and facilities; dogs in bedrooms; meals, bowl, blanket provided; £5

FALMOUTH

Penmere Manor

Mongleath Road, Falmouth, Cornwall TR11 4PN (01326) 211411

£144; 37 spacious rms. Quietly set and newly refurbished Georgian manor with five acres of subtropical gardens and woodland, heated outdoor swimming pool, croquet, and leisure centre with indoor swimming pool, gym, and sauna; particularly helpful friendly staff, a convivial and informal bar, and elegant restaurant (live pianist several nights a week) with imaginative modern cooking; disabled access; dogs in some bedrooms only; £8

FALMOUTH

Rosemary

22 Gyllyngvase Terrace, Falmouth, Cornwall TR11 4DL (01326) 314669

£72; 8 airy and pretty rms. Family-run Victorian house with sea views, helpful, welcoming owners, comfortable lounge with books and magazines, small, cosy bar, enjoyable hearty breakfasts, and seats on sundeck in pretty little garden; resident black labrador; fine nearby walks; cl Nov-Jan; well behaved dogs in some bedrooms

FOWEY

Fowey Hall

Fowey, Cornwall PL23 1ET (01726) 833866

£245 inc dinner; 36 rms inc 12 suites, many with estuary views. Fine Gothic-style mansion in five acres of grounds overlooking the harbour and run as a luxury family hotel; marble fireplaces, baroque plasterwork, panelling, antiques, big potted plants, deeply comfortable lounge with open log fire, two enjoyable restaurants, library, marvellous facilities for children inc supervised nursery, and covered swimming pool, new spa, croquet and badminton; young resident dog; plenty of fine walks in grounds, surrounding coastline and beach (dogs are not allowed on beaches during the summer); disabled access; dogs in courtyard bedrooms; bowls and blanket provided; £7

FOWEY

Marina Villa Hotel

17 Esplanade, Fowey, Cornwall PL23 1HY (01726) 833315

£204; 17 individually furnished rms, several with lovely views and some with balcony. Friendly Georgian hotel in fine position overlooking Fowey River and open sea (private access from secluded walled garden); comfortable lounge/reading room, contemporary stylish bar area, light and airy attractive dining room overlooking the water, excellent food (super fresh fish and shellfish), and helpful service; nearby beach for walks; dogs in bedrooms

LOOE

Talland Bay Hotel

Porthallow, Looe, Cornwall PL13 2JB (01503) 272667

£135; 23 charming rms with sea or country views. Down a little lane between Looe and Polperro, this restful partly 16th-c country house has lovely subtropical gardens just above the sea; comfortable drawing room with log fire, smaller lounge with library, fresh flowers, courteous service, good food in pretty oak-panelled dining room, and pleasant afternoon teas; heated outdoor swimming pool, putting, croquet; cl Jan; children over 5 in evening restaurant (high tea for younger ones); resident labrador; endless surrounding walks; dogs in some bedrooms; bedding and treats; £7.50

MAWNAN SMITH

Meudon Hotel

Mawnan Smith, Falmouth, Cornwall TR11 5HT (01326) 250541

£192 inc dinner, plus special breaks; 29 well equipped comfortable rms in modern wing. Run by the same caring family for 42 years, this is a victorian stone mansion with a newer wing set in beautiful subtropical gardens laid out 200 years ago by R W Fox; fine views from dining room, comfortable lounge with log fire and fresh flowers, good English cooking, and old-fashioned standards of service; resident cat; walks in own grounds and along coastal footpath at bottom of garden; hotel yacht available for skippered charter; cl Jan; disabled access; dogs in bedrooms; £9.50

MITHIAN

Rose-in-Vale Country House Hotel

Mithian, St Agnes, Cornwall TR5 0QD (3.5 miles from A30: A3075, then left on B3284, bearing left to village) (01872) 552202

£155; 19 pretty rms. Secluded and quietly set Georgian house in ten acres of neatly kept grounds, with comfortable, spacious day rooms, friendly atmosphere, helpful, long-standing local staff, and good food in enlarged dining room; ducks on ponds, trout stream, outdoor swimming pool, badminton and croquet, plus sauna and solarium; resident black labrador; children over 12; cl 2 wks Jan; disabled access; dogs in bedrooms; £5

MULLION

Polurrian Hotel

Mullion, Helston, Cornwall TR12 7EN (01326) 240421

£156; 39 rms, some with memorable sea view. Clifftop hotel in lovely gardens with path down to sheltered private cove below; a restful atmosphere in three comfortable lounges, convivial bar area, good food using fresh local ingredients in all day restaurant (stunning sea views), and enjoyable breakfasts; leisure club with heated swimming pool, and outdoor pool, tennis, mini-golf, and squash; 12 acres of grounds and coastal path for walks; particularly good for families; self-catering bungalows, too; cl Jan; limited disabled access; dogs in bedrooms; £8

PADSTOW

St Petroc's Hotel & Bistro

4 New Street, Padstow, Cornwall PL28 8EA (01841) 532700

£135; 10 comfortable little rms. Attractive Georgian hotel (under the same ownership as the Seafood Restaurant) with stylish lounge, quiet reading room, airy dining room, good quickly served food from short bistro-type menu (plenty of fish), sensible wine list, and friendly atmosphere; small courtyard garden; nearby fields for walks; cl 24 and 25 Dec; disabled access; dogs in bedrooms; bowl and big fleece blanket; £15 (£5 for additional nights)

PENZANCE

Abbey Hotel

Abbey Street, Penzance, Cornwall TR18 4AR (01736) 366906

£190; 8 charming rms. Stylish little 17th-c house close to harbour with marvellous views, a relaxed atmosphere in comfortable drawing room full of flowers, fine paintings and antiques, and breakfasts in oak-panelled room (the Abbey Restaurant next door is not connected); pretty garden and park nearby for walks and beaches (out of season); dogs welcome everywhere

PORT ISAAC

Port Gaverne Hotel

Port Gaverne, Port Isaac, Cornwall PL29 3SQ (01208) 880244

£105; 15 comfortable rms. Lovely place to stay and an excellent base for the area (dramatic coves, super clifftop walks and lots of birds); big log fires in well kept bars, relaxed lounges, decent bar food, good restaurant meals, and fine wines; also, restored 18th-c self-catering cottages; children over 7 in restaurant; dogs welcome away from dining room; £3.50

PORTSCATHO

Rosevine

Porthcurnick Beach, Portscatho, Cornwall TR2 5EW (01872) 580206

£150; 15 apartments and suites with self-catering facilities and hotel-style facilities. Imposing house set above a fine beach with two acres of attractive gardens and lovely views; comfortable and elegant grown-ups, drawing room, well-equipped playroom, enjoyable food in attractive, contemporary restaurant, friendly staff, and indoor swimming pool; walks on beach and along coastal paths; cl Jan; disabled access; dogs in three bedrooms; bowls and treats; £10

SENNEN

Lands End Hotel

Sennen, Penzance, Cornwall TR19 7AA (01736) 871844

£150; 32 elegant airy rms named after local landscape features and many with splendid sea views. Comfortable hotel right on the clifftop with fine sea views, good food in attractive conservatory-style restaurant, elegant seating areas, informal bar with lots of malt whiskies, and helpful staff; lots to do nearby and lovely cliff walks; dogs welcome away from bar and restaurant; £20

ST MARTIN'S

St Martin's on the Isle

Lower Town, St Martin's, Isles of Scilly TR25 0QW (01720) 422092

£332 inc dinner, plus special breaks; 30 attractively decorated rms, most with fine sea views. Welcomed by the manager as you step off the boat, you find this stone-built hotel set idyllically on a white sand beach, with stunning sunsets; comfortable, light and airy split-level bar-lounge with doors opening on to the terrace, lovely flower arrangements, genuinely friendly professional staff, sophisticated food in main restaurant (lighter lunches in the bar), and fine wine list; they are particularly kind to children, with buckets and spades to borrow, videos, and high tea (they must be over 9 in evening restaurant); fine walks (the island is car free), launch trips to other islands, and good bird-watching; small indoor swimming pool; cl end Oct-Easter; disabled access; dogs in bedrooms; £15

ST MAWES

Rising Sun

The Square, St Mawes, Truro, Cornwall TR2 5DJ (01326) 270233

£170; 8 rms. Small, attractive old inn in popular picturesque waterside village; bustling airy lounge with lively bar area and end conservatory, newly decorated restaurant, modern english food, simpler bar meals and well liked breakfasts; seats outside on terrace looking across road to harbour; dogs in bedrooms and bar

Tresanton

Lower Castle Road, St Mawes, Truro, Cornwall TR2 5DR (01326) 270055

£275; 29 rms all with individual furnishings and sea views. Hidden away behind a discreet entrance, with elegant terraces (heating for cool weather), charming little bottom bar, steps up to the main building and its stylish lounge with deeply comfortable sofas and armchairs, big bowls of flowers, log fire, daily papers and sophisticated but relaxed atmosphere; excellent food, fine wine list and friendly informal service; can hire speedboat and beautiful 48-ft yacht *Pinuccia*; cl two weeks Jan; children over 6 in evening restaurant; disabled access; dogs in two bedrooms (Room 1 is super); bowls, baskets and blankets; £20

TREVAUNANCE COVE

Driftwood Spars

Trevaunance Cove, St Agnes, Cornwall TR5 0RT (01872) 552428

£98; 13 attractive, comfortable rms, some with sea views, 8 in separate building. Friendly hotel dating from the 17th c and just up road from beach and dramatic cove; woodburner in comfortable lounge, main bar with large open fire, upstairs gallery, beamed ceilings, local real ales, helpful staff and enjoyable food in informal restaurant; live music wknds; coastal footpath passes the door, 3 rms have own garden and 5 rms have access to cliff garden; disabled access; dogs everywhere except seafood restaurant; £2

TRURO

Alverton Manor

Tregolls Road, Truro, Cornwall TR1 1ZQ (01872) 276633

£130; 32 antique-filled, individually decorated rms. Elegant sandstone hotel, formerly a convent, in six acres of pretty grounds and close to city centre; comfortable public rooms including a Great Hall, Library and former chapel, proper old-fashioned values and friendly service, and imaginative British cooking in smart restaurant, using local, seasonal produce and their own beef and honey; dogs in bedrooms; £5

DOG FRIENDLY PUBS

AMBLESIDE

Golden Rule

Smithy Brow; follow Kirkstone Pass signpost from A591 on N side of town; LA22 9AS

Simple town local with cosy, relaxed atmosphere, and real ales

Popular locally and with walkers and dogs, this is a no frills and quite unchanging town pub. The bar area has built-in wall seats around cast-iron-framed tables (one with a local map set into its top), horsebrasses on the black beams, assorted pictures on the walls, a welcoming winter fire, and a relaxed atmosphere. Robinsons Cumbria Way, Double Hop, Hartleys XB, Hatters, Unicorn, and a seasonal ale on handpump. A brass measuring rule hangs above the bar. There's also a back room with TV (not much used), a left-hand room with darts and a games machine, and a further room down a couple of steps on the right with lots of seating. You may be able to get a snack here, such as pork pies, jumbo scotch eggs and (at weekends) filled rolls, but don't count on it. The back yard has benches and a covered heated area, and the window boxes are especially colourful.

Robinsons ~ Tenant John Lockley ~ Real ale ~ Bar food ~ No credit cards ~ (015394) 32257 ~ Children welcome away from bar until 9pm ~ Dogs welcome ~ Open 11am-midnight; 12-midnight Sun

ARMATHWAITE

Dukes Head

Off A6 S of Carlisle; CA4 9PB

Interesting food in comfortable lounge, heated outside area and day fishing tickets; good value bedrooms

Not only is this an enjoyable place to stay with hearty breakfasts, but it is good value too. The comfortable lounge bar has oak settles and little armchairs among more upright seats, oak and mahogany tables, antique hunting and other prints, and some brass and copper powder-flasks above the open fire. Black Sheep and Jennings Cumberland on handpump and sometimes home-made lemonade and ginger beer; the separate public bar has darts, table skittles and board games. The thoughtfully constructed menu here is nicely varied, with lots of tasty dishes to choose from. There are seats on a heated area outside with more on the lawn behind; boules. Day tickets for fishing are available.

Punch ~ Tenant Henry Lynch ~ Real ale ~ Bar food ~ Restaurant ~ (016974) 72226 ~ Children welcome ~ Dogs allowed in bar and bedrooms ~ Open 11.30am-11.30pm; closed 25 Dec ~ Bedrooms: £38.50S/£62.50S

BAMPTON

Mardale

7.1 miles from M6, J39. A6 through Shap, then left at Post Office, signed to
Bampton. After 3.5m cross river in Bampton Grange then next right. In Bampton
turn left over bridge by Post Office; CA10 2RQ

Appealing country dining pub, with relaxed welcoming feel and spotless up-to-date furnishings

Formerly the St Patrick's Well, this pretty and attractively placed beamed pub has been completely reworked for its friendly and helpful new landlord. The décor is clean-cut and contemporary, with chunky modern country tables and chairs on newly laid flagstones, one or two big Lakeland prints and a modicum of rustic bygones on pastel walls (and in one big brick fireplace), and a log fire in a second stylish raised fireplace. Coniston Bluebird, Hesket Newmarket Sca Fell Blonde, Timothy Taylors Landlord and maybe a summer guest on handpump, and 40 european bottled beers. Dogs will find a water bowl (and maybe even a biscuit) in the nicely lit bar, which is welcoming to walkers and has comfortable backed stools. Using local produce, food is pubby at lunchtime and a little more imaginative in the evening. There are good walks straight from the door, for example to the nearby Haweswater nature reserve.

Free house ~ Licensee Sebastian Hindley ~ Real ale ~ Bar food (12-2, 6-9) ~ (01931) 713244 ~ Well behaved children welcome ~ Dogs welcome ~ Open 11-11(10.30 Sun) ~ Bedrooms: £45S/£70S

BASSENTHWAITE LAKE

Pheasant

Follow Pheasant Inn sign at N end of dual carriageway stretch of A66 by
Bassenthwaite Lake; CA13 9YE

Charming, old-fashioned bar in smart hotel with enjoyable bar food and fine range of drinks; excellent restaurant, and attractive surrounding woodlands; comfortable bedrooms

Much loved by many of our readers, this is a particularly well run, civilised hotel with comfortable bedrooms and excellent restaurant food. So it comes as a surprise to find a pubby and pleasantly old-fashioned little bar that has remained quite unchanged over many years. It's just the place to enjoy a quiet pint or informal lunch and the staff are friendly and knowledgeable staff. There are mellow polished walls, cushioned oak settles, rush-seat chairs and library seats, hunting prints and photographs, and Bass, Jennings Cumberland and Theakstons Best on handpump; 12 good wines by the glass and over 60 malt whiskies. Several comfortable lounges have log fires, beautiful flower arrangements, fine parquet flooring, antiques, and plants. Very good food is imaginative and carefully prepared – they even make their own bread. Dogs are allowed in some bedrooms (breakfasts are excellent), the residents' lounge at lunchtime and they do let them into the bar during the day too, unless people are eating. There are seats in the garden, attractive woodland surroundings, and plenty of walks in all directions.

Free house ~ Licensee Matthew Wylie ~ Real ale ~ Bar food (not in evening – restaurant only then) ~ Restaurant ~ (017687) 76234 ~ Children in eating area of bar if over 8 ~ Dogs allowed in bar and bedrooms ~ Open 11.30-2.30, 5.30-10.30(11 Sat); 12-2.30, 6-10.30 Sun; closed 25 Dec ~ Bedrooms: £85B/£160B

BROUGHTON MILLS

Blacksmiths Arms

Off A593 N of Broughton-in-Furness; LA20 6AX

Good food, local beers and open fires in charming small pub liked by walkers

The walks surrounding this charming little pub are superb – and the warm log fires in the bars very welcome. The staff are cheerful and friendly, and three of the four simply but attractively decorated small rooms have straightforward chairs and tables on ancient slate floors, Dent Aviator, Jennings Cumberland, and Tirril Thomas Slee's Academy Ale on handpump, eight wines by the glass, and summer farm cider. Using local produce, the good, often interesting bar food works its way up from sandwiches (lunchtimes only) to more elaborate dishes such as fillets of bass with fennel, orange, beetroot and green bean salad with a mustard dressing; darts, board games, dominoes and cribbage. The hanging baskets and tubs of flowers in front of the building are pretty in summer.

Free house ~ Licensees Mike and Sophie Lane ~ Real ale ~ Bar food (12-2, 6-9; not Mon lunchtime) ~ Restaurant ~ (01229) 716824 ~ Children welcome ~ Dogs welcome ~ Open 12-11(5-11 Mon); 12-10.30 Sun; 12-2.30, 5-11 Tues-Fri in winter; closed Mon lunchtime

CARTMEL

Kings Arms

The Square, off Causeway; LA11 6QB

Timbered pub in ancient village with seats facing lovely village square

Seats outside this little black and white pub look over the lovely village square and there's a fine medieval stone gatehouse nearby. Inside, the neatly kept, rambling bar has a friendly atmosphere and is liked by both drinkers and diners. There are small antique prints on the walls, a mixture of seats including old country chairs, settles and wall banquettes, fresh flowers on the tables, and tankards hanging over the bar counter. Barngates Cat Nap, Bass, Hawkshead Red, and Marstons Pedigree on handpump and ten wines by the glass. Bar food is traditional and well liked; good service, piped music.

Enterprise ~ Lease Richard Grimmer ~ Real ale ~ Bar food (12-2.30(3 Sat and Sun), 5.30-8.30(8.45 Fri and Sat)) ~ Restaurant ~ (01539) 536220 ~ Children welcome ~ Dogs allowed in bar ~ Open 11-11(10.30 Sun); closed 25 Dec

CHAPEL STILE
Wainwrights
B5343; LA22 9JH

Fine choice of beers, lovely views, and surrounding walks

The fine range of seven real ales in this white-rendered Lakeland house is quite a draw after enjoying one of the good surrounding walks. On handpump there might be Black Sheep Best Bitter, Dent Ramsbottom Strong Ale, Moorhouses Black Cat and Blond Witch, Thwaites Lancaster Bomber, York Stonewall, and a beer named for the pub; quick, friendly service. They also have 16 wines by the glass and some malt whiskies. The slate-floored bar has plenty of room and it is here that walkers and their dogs are welcomed. There's a relaxed atmosphere, an old kitchen range, cushioned settles and piped music, TV and games machine. The pubby food is quickly served and reasonably priced. Picnic-table sets out on the terrace have fine views.

Free house ~ Licensee Mrs C Darbyshire ~ Real ale ~ Bar food (12-2(2.30 Sun), 6-9) ~ (015394) 38088 ~ Children welcome ~ Dogs welcome ~ Open 11.30-11; 12-11 Sun

CROSTHWAITE
Punch Bowl
Village signposted off A5074 SE of Windermere; LA8 8HR

Stylish dining pub, fine choice of drinks, impressive food, good wines and real ales, and seats on terrace overlooking valley; lovely bedrooms

Food served by attentive and friendly staff at this stylish place is very good – they've got a fair range of real ales too, and enough life to still call it a pub. Barngates Cracker, Tag Lag and Westmorland Gold (brewed at their sister pub, the Drunken Duck near Hawkshead), and Coniston Bluebird on handpump, 16 wines by the glass and a dozen malt whiskies. The raftered and hop-hung bar has a couple of eye-catching rugs on flagstones and bar stools by the slate-topped counter, and this opens on the right into two linked carpeted and beamed rooms with well spaced country pine furnishings of varying sizes, including a big refectory table. The walls, painted in restrained neutral tones, have an attractive assortment of prints, with some copper objects, and there's a dresser with china and glass; winter log fire and daily papers. Throughout, the pub feels relaxing and nicely uncluttered. Terrific food from the innovative menu tends to be more unusual in the evening (maybe braised pig's trotter with seared scallops and quail egg) and puddings are particularly tempting. There are some tables on a terrace stepped into the hillside, overlooking the lovely Lyth Valley.

Free house ~ Licensee Paul Spencer ~ Real ale ~ Bar food (12-3, 6-9.30) ~ Restaurant ~ (015395) 68237 ~ Children welcome ~ Dogs allowed in bar ~ Open 12-11(10.30 Sun)

GREAT SALKELD
Highland Drove
B6412, off A686 NE of Penrith; CA11 9NA

Bustling place with a cheerful mix of customers, good food, fair choice of drinks, and fine views from upstairs verandah

Neatly kept and genuinely friendly, this is a well run country pub liked by both drinkers and diners. The chatty main bar has sandstone flooring, stone walls, cushioned wheelback chairs around a mix of tables and an open fire in a raised stone fireplace. Theakstons Black Bull and a couple of guests such as Batemans Maypole Dancer and Hesket Newmarket Haystacks Refreshing Ale on handpump, several wines by the glass and around 25 malt whiskies. Piped music, TV, juke box, darts, pool, games machine and board games. On the whole, food here sticks to traditional favourites, but it's prepared to a very high standard and is very enjoyable. The lovely views over the Eden Valley and the Pennines are best enjoyed from seats on the upstairs verandah. There are more seats on the back terrace.

Free house ~ Licensees Donald and Paul Newton ~ Real ale ~ Bar food (12-2, 6-9; not Mon lunchtime except bank hols) ~ Restaurant ~ (01768) 898349 ~ Children welcome ~ Dogs allowed in bar ~ Open 12-3, 6-midnight; 12-midnight Sat; 12-3, 6-midnight Sun in winter; closed Mon lunchtime except bank hols; 25 Dec

HAWKSHEAD
Drunken Duck
Barngates; the hamlet is signposted from B5286 Hawkshead—Ambleside, opposite the Outgate Inn; or it may be quicker to take the first right from B5286, after the wooded caravan site; OS Sheet 90 map reference 350013; LA22 0NG

Stylish small bar, own-brewed beers and bar meals; stunning views

There's no doubt that this civilised inn is at its most pubby during the day when walkers drop in for a pint of the own-brewed beers and a sandwich or bar meal. The small, smart bar has seating for around 30 on leather-topped bar stools by the slate-topped bar counter and leather club chairs, beams and oak floorboards, photographs, coaching prints and hunting pictures on the walls, and some kentish hop bines. From their Barngates brewery, there might be Cat Nap, Cracker, Moth Bag, Pride of Westmorland, and Westmorland Gold on handpump as well as 18 wines plus three pudding wines by the glass, a fine choice of spirits, and belgian and german draught beers. Good bar food (up till 4pm) includes sandwiches (which you can take away as well) and there's also an interesting two- and three-course set lunch menu, and afternoon tea. In the evening, the emphasis is on the imaginative (and pricey) food in the three restaurant areas. Outside, wooden tables and benches on the grass bank opposite the building offer spectacular views across the fells, and there are thousands of spring and summer bulbs.

Own brew ~ Licensee Steph Barton ~ Real ale ~ Bar food (12-4(2.30 restaurant), 6-9.30) ~ Restaurant ~ (015394) 36347 ~ Children allowed until 7pm ~ Dogs allowed in bar ~ Open 11.30-11; 12-10.30 Sun

Kings Arms

The Square; LA22 0NZ

Some fine original features in 16th-c inn, decent drinks, pubby food, and free fishing permits for residents

If you want to bag a table on the terrace and enjoy the view over the central square of this lovely Elizabethan village, you must get here early. Inside this busy 16th-c inn there are some fine original features, traditional pubby furnishings, and an open log fire; Coniston Bluebird, Hawkshead Bitter and Red, and Moorhouses Pride of Pendle on handpump, 50 malt whiskies, a decent wine list, and summer farm cider. The bar food is traditional, working its way up from lunchtime sandwiches to steak and ale pie. Piped music, games machine, and board games. As well as bedrooms, they offer self-catering cottages.

Free house ~ Licensee Edward Johnson ~ Real ale ~ Bar food (12-2.30, 6-9.30) ~ Restaurant ~ (015394) 36372 ~ Children welcome ~ Dogs allowed in bar and bedrooms ~ Live music third Thurs in month ~ Open 11am-midnight; closed evening 25 Dec ~ Bedrooms: £47S/£84S

INGS

Watermill

Just off A591 E of Windermere; LA8 9PY

Busy, cleverly converted pub with fantastic range of real ales including own brew

With a fantastic range of 16 real ales on handpump, it's not surprising that this chatty place is so popular. As well as their own-brewed Watermill Collie Wobbles, A Bit'er Ruff and W'Ruff Night (and maybe their guests such as Blackbeard and Dog'th Vader), there might be Coniston Bluebird, Hambleton Giddy Up, Hawkshead Bitter, Jennings Cumberland, Keswick Thirst Flight, Phoenix White Monk, Saltaire Pale Bitter, Theakstons Old Peculier, Ulverston Laughing Gravy, York Guzzler, and Youngs Special. Also, 60 foreign bottled beers and over 50 whiskies. The building has plenty of character and is cleverly converted from a wood mill and joiner's shop and the bars have a friendly, bustling atmosphere, a happy mix of chairs, padded benches and solid oak tables, bar counters made from old church wood, open fires and interesting photographs and amusing cartoons by a local artist. The spacious lounge bar, in much the same traditional style as the other rooms, has rocking chairs and a big open fire. Darts and board games. Served all day, bar food is very traditional. Seats in the gardens, and lots to do nearby. Dogs may get biscuits and water.

Free house ~ Licensee Brian Coulthwaite ~ Real ale ~ Bar food (12-9) ~ (01539) 821309 ~ Children welcome ~ Dogs allowed in bar and bedrooms ~ Storytelling first Tues of month, folk third Tues ~ Open 11.45-11; 12-10.30 Sun; closed 25 Dec ~ Bedrooms: £42S/£78S

KIRKBY LONSDALE

Sun

Market Street (B6254); LA6 2AU

Nice contrast between mellow bar and stylish contemporary restaurant, good interesting food and several real ales; comfortable bedrooms

With a cheerful landlord and genuinely friendly, helpful staff, this 17th-c inn is an enjoyable place. The attractive rambling bar has a two log fires, and seats of some character, from cosy window seats and pews to armchairs; also, beams, flagstones and stripped oak boards, nice lighting, and big landscapes and country pictures on the cream walls above its handsome panelled dado. There's a back lounge with a leather sofa and comfortable chairs, too. Jennings Cumberland Ale, Hawkshead Bitter, Marstons Pedigree, Timothy Taylors Landlord, and guest beers on hand-pump, eleven wines by the glass (plus some organic ones) and plenty of malt whiskies; piped music and board games. The back dining room is very up to date: comfortable tall-backed seats and tables on woodstrip flooring, a clean-cut cream and red décor with a modicum of stripped stone, and attractive plain modern crockery. Traditional pub dishes and more imaginative meals are thoughtfully prepared using carefully sourced ingredients. It's an interesting looking building with its upper floors supported by three sturdy pillars above the pavement and a modest front door.

Free house ~ Licensee Mark Fuller ~ Real ale ~ Bar food ~ Restaurant ~ (015242) 71965 ~ Children welcome ~ Dogs allowed in bar and bedrooms ~ Open 10am-11pm ~ Bedrooms: /£90S(£110B)

LEVENS

Strickland Arms

4 miles from M6 junction 36, via A590; just off A590, by Sizergh Castle gates; LA8 8DZ

Friendly, open plan place, popular for home-made food and local ales

The staff here are always friendly and obliging – and the food is very good. The very traditional menu includes lunchtime sandwiches, fish night is every Thursday and there's a well thought-of two-course set lunch menu during the week. It's a largely open plan dining pub with a light and airy modern feel, and the bar on the right has oriental rugs on the flagstones, a log fire, Thwaites Original and Lancaster Bomber and a couple of guests such as Coniston Bluebird and Dent Aviator on handpump, 30 malt whiskies and 11 wines by the glass. On the left are polished boards and another log fire and throughout there's a nice mix of sturdy country furniture, candles on tables, hunting scenes and other old prints on the walls, heavy fabric for the curtains and some staffordshire china ornaments; there's a further dining room upstairs, piped music and board games, and seats out in front on a flagstone terrace. The Castle, in fact a lovely partly medieval house with beautiful gardens, is open in the afternoon (not Friday and Saturday) from April to October. They have disabled access and facilities. The pub is owned by the National Trust.

Free house ~ Licensees Kerry Parsons and Martin Ainscough ~ Real ale ~ Bar food

(12-2(2.30 Sat), 6-9; all day Sun) ~ (015395) 61010 ~ Children welcome ~ Dogs welcome ~ Open 11.30-11(10.30 Sun); 11.30-3, 5.30-11 weekdays in winter

LITTLE LANGDALE
Three Shires

From A593 3 miles W of Ambleside take small road signposted The Langdales, Wrynose Pass; then bear left at first fork; LA22 9NZ

Friendly inn with valley views from seats on terrace, good lunchtime bar food with more elaborate evening meals

Mr and Mrs Stephenson have been running this friendly, stone-built inn for 25 years now. There's a good mix of customers and a genuine welcome for walkers, and with warm winter fires and lovely views from seats on the terrace over the valley to the partly wooded hills below Tilberthwaite Fells, it's popular all year round; there are more seats on a well kept lawn behind the car park, backed by a small oak wood. Inside, the comfortably extended back bar has a mix of green lakeland stone and homely red patterned wallpaper (which works rather well), stripped timbers and a beam-and-joist stripped ceiling, antique oak carved settles, country kitchen chairs and stools on its big dark slate flagstones, and lakeland photographs. An arch leads through to a small, additional area and there's a front dining room. Black Sheep Best and Jennings Cumberland and a couple of guests like Coniston Old Man and Hawkshead Red on handpump, over 50 malt whiskies and a decent wine list; darts and board games. At lunchtime the menu is very pubby, becoming a much more elaborate affair in the evening. The three shires are the historical counties Cumberland, Westmorland and Lancashire, which meet at the top of the nearby Wrynose Pass. The award-winning summer hanging baskets are very pretty.

Free house ~ Licensee Ian Stephenson ~ Real ale ~ Bar food (12-2, 6-8.45; not 24 or 25 Dec) ~ Restaurant ~ (015394) 37215 ~ Children welcome until 9pm ~ Dogs allowed in bar ~ Open 11-10.30(11 Fri and Sat); 12-10.30 Sun; 11-3, 6-10.30 in winter; closed 24 and 25 Dec

LOWESWATER
Kirkstile Inn

From B5289 follow signs to Loweswater Lake; OS Sheet 89 map reference 140210; CA13 0RU

Busy bar in popular inn surrounded by stunning peaks and fells; own-brewed beers and tasty food

As this friendly 16th-c inn is situated between Loweswater and Crummock Water, it's not surprising that many of its customers are walkers. The fine view can be enjoyed from picnic-sets on the lawn, from the very attractive covered verandah in front of the building and from the bow windows in one of the rooms off the bar. The bustling main bar is low-beamed and carpeted, with a good mix of customers, a roaring log fire, comfortably cushioned small settles and pews and partly stripped stone walls; there's a slate shove-ha'penny board. As well as their own-brewed Loweswater Grasmere Dark Ale, Kirkstile Gold and Melbreak Bitter on handpump, they keep a couple of guest beers, too; ten wines by the glass. The bar food includes something for most tastes.

Own brew ~ Licensee Roger Humphreys ~ Real ale ~ Bar food (12-2, 6-9) ~ (01900) 85219 ~ Children welcome ~ Dogs allowed in bar ~ Occasional jazz ~ Open 11-11(10.30 Sun); closed 25 Dec

MUNGRISDALE

Mill Inn

Off A66 Penrith—Keswick, 1 mile W of A5091 Ullswater turn-off; CA11 0XR

Bustling pub in fine setting with marvellous surrounding walks, real ales, and interesting food and bedrooms

An amiable irish chef/landlord has taken over this partly 16th-c inn and early reports from our readers are very warm and enthusiastic. The neatly kept bar has a wooden bar counter with an old millstone built into it, traditional dark wooden furnishings, hunting pictures on the walls, an open log fire in the stone fireplace, Robinsons Cumbria Way, Dizzy Blonde, Hartleys XB, and Top Tipple on handpump, and up to 30 malt whiskies; good service, even when busy. Piped music, winter pool and darts, and an active dominoes team. Mr Carroll sources his local ingredients carefully and the imaginative food is enjoyable. In the lee of the Blencathra fell range, the pub is surrounded by stunning scenery and spectacular walks, and there are seats in the garden by the little river. Please note that there's a quite separate Mill Hotel here.

Robinsons ~ Tenant Adrian Carroll ~ Real ale ~ Bar food (12-2, 6-9) ~ Restaurant ~ (017687) 79632 ~ Children welcome ~ Dogs welcome ~ Open 11-11 ~ Bedrooms: £47.50S/£75S

NEAR SAWREY

Tower Bank Arms

B5285 towards the Windermere ferry; LA22 0LF

Backing on to Beatrix Potter's farm with a good range of ales; bedrooms

Many illustrations in the Beatrix Potter books can be traced back to their origins in this village, including this little country pub, which features in *The Tale of Jemima Puddleduck*. The low-beamed main bar has plenty of rustic charm, seats on the rough slate floor, game and fowl pictures, a grandfather clock, a wood-burning stove, and fresh flowers. Barngates Cat Nap, Hawkshead Bitter and Brodie's Prime, Keswick Thirst Blossom, and Hesket Newmarket Sca Fell Blonde on handpump (in winter the choice may be smaller); board games. The simple lunchtime bar menu becomes more extensive and imaginative in the evening. There are pleasant views of the wooded Claife Heights from seats in the garden.

Free house ~ Licensee Anthony Hutton ~ Real ale ~ Bar food (12-2, 6-9(8 Sun and bank hols) ~ Restaurant ~ (015394) 36334 ~ Children welcome until 9pm ~ Dogs allowed in bar and bedrooms ~ Open 11-11; 12-10.30 Sun; 11(12 Sun)-3, 5.30-11(10.30 Sun) in winter; closed one week Jan ~ Bedrooms: £50B/£80B

SANDFORD

Sandford Arms

Village and pub signposted just off A66 W of Brough; CA16 6NR

Neat little former farmhouse in tucked-away village with enjoyable food and ale

The L-shaped carpeted main bar at this neat and friendly little inn has stripped beams and stonework, a collection of Royal Doulton character jugs and some Dickens ware, Black Sheep Best Bitter and a beer from Hesket Newmarket and Tirril on handpump. The compact and comfortable dining area is on a slightly raised balustraded platform at one end, and a second bar area has broad flagstones, charming heavy-horse prints, and an end log fire; piped music, darts, TV, and board games. Outside there is a garden in front and a courtyard with covered seating. The sensible imaginative bar food is cooked by the landlord using local produce.

Free house ~ Licensee Steven Porter ~ Real ale ~ Bar food (all day weekends; not winter Tues) ~ Restaurant ~ (017683) 51121 ~ Children welcome ~ Dogs allowed in bar ~ Open 11-3, 6-11; 11(12 Sun)-11 Sat; closed Tues in winter

SANTON BRIDGE

Bridge Inn

Off A595 at Holmrook or Gosforth; CA19 1UX

Cheerful atmosphere, and plenty of surrounding walks

This bustling and friendly black and white hotel is nicely placed in a quiet riverside spot with fell views. The turkey-carpeted bar is popular with locals and has stripped beams, joists and standing timbers, a coal and log fire, and three rather unusual timbered booths around big stripped tables along its outer wall. Bar stools line the long concave bar counter, which has Jennings Bitter, Cocker Hoop, Cumberland Ale, and Sneck Lifter and a couple of guest beers like Marstons Pedigree and York Guzzler on handpump; good big pots of tea, speciality coffees, and six wines by the glass. Piped music, games machine, darts and board games. A small reception hall has a rack of daily papers and the hotelish lounge on the left is comfortable. Well liked bar food includes baguettes and a curry of the day. There are seats out in front by the quiet road and plenty of surrounding walks.

Marstons ~ Lease John Morrow and Lesley Rhodes ~ Real ale ~ Bar food (12-2.30, 5.30-9) ~ Restaurant ~ (01946) 726221 ~ Children welcome ~ Dogs allowed in bar and bedrooms ~ Open 11-11(midnight Sat) ~ Bedrooms: £65B/£85B

SEATHWAITE

Newfield Inn

Duddon Valley, near Ulpha (ie not Seathwaite in Borrowdale); LA20 6ED

Climbers' and walkers' cottagey inn with genuine local feel and hearty food

The good value homely food here is usefully served all day for the walkers and climbers who crowd into this cottagey 16th-c inn – but there's still a relaxed and genuinely local atmosphere. The slate-floored bar has wooden tables and chairs, some interesting pictures and Jennings Cumberland Ale and Snecklifter and Tirril Thomas Slee's Academy Ale on handpump; several malt whiskies. There's a comfortable side room and a games room with board games. Tables outside in the nice garden have good hill views. The pub owns and lets the next-door self-catering flats and there's a large area for children to play and fine walks from the doorstep.

Free house ~ Licensee Paul Batten ~ Real ale ~ Bar food (12-9; not 25 Dec) ~ Restaurant ~ (01229) 716208 ~ Children welcome ~ Dogs allowed in bar ~ Open 11-11; closed evenings 25 and 26 Dec

STONETHWAITE
Langstrath
Off B5289 S of Derwent Water; CA12 5XG

Civilised little place in lovely spot with interesting food and drink

The neat and simple bar (at its pubbiest at lunchtime) has a welcoming coal and log fire in a big stone fireplace, just a handful of cast-iron-framed tables, plain chairs and cushioned wall seats, and on its textured white walls maybe quite a few walking cartoons and attractive lakeland mountain photographs. Black Sheep and Jennings Bitter and a couple of guests such as Hawkshead Bitter and Hesket Newmarket Doris's 90th Birthday Ale on handpump, 30 malt whiskies and eight wines by the glass; quite a few customers also drop in for tea and coffee. Board games. A little oak-boarded room on the left is a bit like a doll's house living room in style – this is actually the original cottage built around 1590. They pay attention to detail when it comes to the food, which is imaginative and good. Outside, a big sycamore shelters a few picnic-sets and there are fine surrounding walks as the pub is in a lovely spot in the heart of Borrowdale and en route for the Cumbrian Way and the Coast to Coast Walk. Please note, if they are very busy with diners in the evening, they may not serve those only wanting a drink – probably best to phone beforehand.

Free house ~ Licensees Sara and Mike Hodgson ~ Real ale ~ Bar food (12-2.15, 6-9; not Mon, winter Sun and Tues, or Dec and Jan) ~ Restaurant ~ (017687) 77239 ~ Children allowed lunchtime only; no children under 6 in bedrooms ~ Dogs allowed in bar ~ Open 12.30-10.30(10 Sun); closed Mon all year and winter Sun and Tues; all Dec and Jan

THRELKELD
Horse & Farrier
A66 Penrith—Keswick; CA12 4SQ

Well run 17th-c fell-foot dining pub with good food and drinks; bedrooms

A happy mix of locals and tourists can be found in this civilised Lakeland inn, enjoying the real ales and hearty food. The neatly fitted out, mainly carpeted bar has sturdy farmhouse and other nice tables, and seats from comfortably padded ones to pubby chairs and from stools to bigger housekeeper's chairs and wall settles, with country pictures on its white walls, one or two stripped beams, and some flagstones. Jennings Bitter, Cumberland, and Sneck Lifter, and a couple of seasonal guests, a good range of wines by the glass, and winter open fires; efficient service. The partly stripped stone restaurant is smart and more formal, with quite close-set tables. Bar food ranges from traditional dishes to more elaborate choices. They have good disabled access and facilities, and a few picnic-sets outside, with inspiring views up to Blease and Gategill Fells behind the pretty white-painted inn, or over to Clough Head behind the houses opposite; good walks straight from this attractive village.

Jennings (Marstons) ~ Lease Ian Court ~ Real ale ~ Bar food (12-3, 5.30-9; all day weekends) ~ Restaurant ~ (017687) 79688 ~ Children welcome ~ Dogs allowed in bar and bedrooms ~ Open 11am-midnight ~ Bedrooms: £35B/£70B

ULVERSTON

Bay Horse

Canal Foot signposted off A590 and then you wend your way past the huge Glaxo factory; LA12 9EL

Civilised waterside hotel at its most relaxed at lunchtime, with super food, wine and beer, and a nice, smart place to stay

Once a staging post for coaches crossing the sands of Morecambe Bay to Lancaster, this smart and civilised hotel is at its most informal at lunchtime. The bar has a relaxed atmosphere despite its smart furnishings: attractive wooden armchairs, some pale green plush built-in wall banquettes, glossy hardwood traditional tables, blue plates on a delft shelf, a huge stone horse's head and black beams and props with lots of horsebrasses. Magazines are dotted about, there's an open fire in the handsomely marbled green granite fireplace, and decently reproduced piped music; board games, TV, and cards. Jennings Cumberland, Marstons Pedigree and Wadworths 6X on handpump, a dozen wines by the glass (champagne, too) from a carefully chosen and interesting wine list, and several malt whiskies. Cakes with tea and coffee are served here all day, and meals from an innovative menu are very good indeed. The conservatory restaurant has fine views over Morecambe Bay (as do the bedrooms) and there are some seats out on the terrace.

Free house ~ Licensee Robert Lyons ~ Real ale ~ Bar food (12-6 (2 in conservatory restaurant, 4 Mon), 7.30-9) ~ Restaurant ~ (01229) 583972 ~ Children in eating area of bar but must be over 9 in evening ~ Dogs allowed in bar and bedrooms ~ Open 11-11; 12-10.30 Sun; closed 3 and 4 Jan ~ Bedrooms: £80B/£120B

DOG FRIENDLY HOTELS, INNS, B&Bs AND FARMS

ALSTON

Lovelady Shield Country House

Nenthead Road, Alston, Cumbria CA9 3LF (01434) 381203

£200 inc dinner; 13 rms. In a lovely setting with River Nent running along bottom of garden, this handsome Georgian country house has a tranquil atmosphere, cosy cocktail bar, library and lounge with log fires, courteous staff, and very good, imaginative food in elegant dining room; luxury self-catering cottages; children over 7 in evening restaurant; dogs in bedrooms only; £10

AMBLESIDE

Regent by the Lake

Waterhead Bay, Ambleside, Cumbria LA22 OES (015394) 32254

£150; 30 well equipped, contemporary rms, 10 in courtyard, 5 in garden. Family run hotel opposite slipway on to Lake Windermere, with pretty gardens, lounges, bar and split-level restaurant in warm colours of browns and cream, good, brasserie-style food, marvellous breakfasts served till midday (you can even have breakfast in bed), and helpful staff; indoor heated pool; lots to do nearby; cl Christmas; disabled access; dogs in courtyard bedrooms; £6.00

BARBON

Barbon Inn

Barbon, Carnforth, Cumbria LA6 2LJ (015242) 76233

£70; 10 simple but comfortable rms. Small friendly 17th-c village inn in quiet spot below fells, with relaxing bar, traditional lounge, good meals in candlelit dining room, and helpful service; resident black labrador and jack russell; lots of good tracks and paths all around; cl 25 and 26 Dec; dogs in bar and bedrooms; £10

BASSENTHWAITE LAKE

Armathwaite Hall Hotel

Bassenthwaite Lake, Keswick, Cumbria CA12 4RE (017687) 76551

£210; 42 rms. Turreted 17th-c mansion in 400 acres of deerpark and woodland; handsome public rooms with lovely fireplaces, fine panelling, antiques, paintings and fresh flowers, good french and english cooking using local seasonal produce, a super wine list, and helpful staff; snooker room, croquet, pitch-and-putt, tennis court, spa with swimming pool, sauna, steam room, gym and beauty salon, fishing, archery and clay pigeon shooting, jogging and mountain-bike tracks, and children's country club; resident black labrador and two belgian shepherds; disabled access; dogs in bedrooms; bed and treats; £15

BOUTH

White Hart

Bouth, Ulverston, Cumbria LA12 8JB (01229) 861229

£70; 5 characterful rms, two with country views. Cheerful Lakeland inn with plenty of bric-a-brac, woodburning stoves and sloping ceilings and floors in bustling bars, fine range of well kept real ales, tasty bar food, and good surrounding walks; cl Mon and Tues lunchtimes, live music second Sun April-Dec; dogs in bedrooms; £5

BRAMPTON

Farlam Hall

Hallbankgate, Brampton, Cumbria CA8 2NG (1.8 miles off A69, via A689)
(016977) 46234

£290 inc dinner; 12 smart and comfortable rms. Very civilised, mainly 19th-c country house with log fires in ornately victorian lounges, excellent attentive service, good four-course dinner using fine china and silver in friendly but formal restaurant, marvellous breakfasts, and peaceful, spacious grounds with croquet lawn and small pretty lake; plenty of fine nearby walks; cl 24-30 Dec; children over 5; partial disabled access; dogs welcome away from restaurant

CARTMEL

Uplands

Haggs Lane, Cartmel, Grange-over-sands, Cumbria LA11 6HD (01539) 536248

£110; 5 pretty rms overlooking estuary or gardens. Comfortable Edwardian house in two acres of grounds (plenty of wildlife) with views over to Morecambe Bay; large, attractively decorated lounge, welcoming owners, an informal atmosphere, very good modern food cooked by the owner, and super breakfasts; children over 8; walks from the front door; dogs welcome away from public rooms

CROOK

Wild Boar

Crook, Windermere, Cumbria LA23 3NF (015394) 45225

£106; 36 rms. Comfortable well run former coaching inn in 72 acres of woodland and plenty of walks; period furnishings and log fires in ancient core, real ales in sociable bar, good food in heavily beamed and candlelit dining room, and attentive service; dogs in bedrooms; £25

CROSBY ON EDEN

Crosby Lodge

High Crosby, Crosby on Eden, Carlisle, Cumbria CA6 4QZ (4.7 miles from M6 junction 44 (A7/A74 terminal roundabout), via A689 eastbound; High Crosby) (01228) 573618

£160; 11 spacious rms (2 in stable conversion). Imposing and carefully converted country house in the same family for nearly 40 years and surrounded by attractive mature grounds; comfortable and appealing individual furnishings, enjoyable home-made food using local produce in richly decorated restaurant, and plenty of walks in grounds and nearby countryside; resident dog; cl Christmas-New Year; limited disabled access; dogs in courtyard bedrooms; £5

DERWENT WATER
Lodore Falls

Borrowdale, Keswick, Cumbria CA12 5UX (017687) 77285

£142; 71 attractive rms with lakeside or fell views. Long-standing, imposing hotel set in 40 acres of lakeside gardens and woodlands with comfortable day rooms, good modern cooking in elegant restaurant and lounge bar, indoor swimming pool, spa and beauty salon; tennis and squash, outdoor swimming pool, and games room; self-catering house too; marvellous walks all round; dogs in bedrooms; £10

ELTERWATER
Britannia Inn

Elterwater, Ambleside, Cumbria LA22 9HP (015394) 37210

£94; 9 rms. Simple charmingly traditional pub in fine surroundings opposite village green, with a happy friendly atmosphere (it does get very busy at peak times), hearty home cooking inc superb breakfast, coal fires in the small, cosy bars, a comfortable residents' lounge, and real ales; walks of every length and gradient from front door; dogs welcome away from residents' lounge and dining room

EMBLETON
Highside Farmhouse

Embleton, Cockermouth, Cumbria CA13 9TN (01768) 776893

£64; 2 rms with lovely views. 17th-c farmhouse with spacious garden looking across the Solway and Scottish uplands, private guest entrance and own homely sitting/dining room with open fire, helpful owners, and hearty breakfasts with their own eggs and home-made bread and marmalade; resident collie and two cats; children over 10; dogs in bedrooms and on lead in public areas; £2.00

ENNERDALE BRIDGE
Shepherds Arms

Ennerdale, Cleator, Cumbria CA23 3AR (01946) 861249

£77; 8 rms, most with own bthrm. Set on popular Coast-to-Coast path and with wonderful surrounding walks, this is a welcoming inn with convivial bar, wood-burning stove, carpeted main bar with coal fire and homely variety of comfortable seats, and conservatory; cheerful and obliging service, substantial bar food using local fresh produce, well kept real ales, and good choice of wines by the glass; resident collie; walks around Ennerdale Lake a mile away; dogs welcome away from dining room; £5

FAR SAWREY

Sawrey

Far Sawrey, Ambleside, Cumbria LA22 0LQ (015394) 43425

£70; 19 rms. Friendly hotel well placed at the foot of Claife Heights, with simple pubby and smarter bars, friendly staff, good straightforward food, and seats on pleasant lawn; resident dog; cl Christmas; kind to children; partial disabled access; dogs in bedrooms as long as not left alone; £3.50

GRASMERE

Swan

Keswick Road, Grasmere, Ambleside, Cumbria LA22 9RF (015394) 35551

£150; 38 rms, most with fine views. Smart and friendly 17th-c hotel in beautiful fell-foot surroundings, with several comfortable, beamed lounges, a walkers' bar and drying room, log fires in inglenook fireplaces, traditional and modern cooking in elegant dining room, and attractive sheltered garden; lovely walks; partial disabled access; dogs in some bedrooms; £15

IREBY

Overwater Hall

Ireby, Carlisle, Cumbria CA5 1HH (017687) 76566

£170; 11 individually decorated rms. Partly castellated family-run hotel in 18 acres of gardens and woodland, with a relaxed, friendly atmosphere, log fire in traditionally furnished, comfortable drawing room, good imaginative food in cosy dining room, hearty breakfasts, and lots of walks; two resident black labradors; cl two weeks early Jan; children over 5 in evening restaurant; partial disabled access; dogs in bedrooms, bar and one lounge

LANGDALE

Old Dungeon Ghyll

Great Langdale, Ambleside, Cumbria LA22 9JY (015394) 37272

£110; 13 rms, some with shared bthrm. Friendly, simple and cosy walkers' and climbers' inn dramatically surrounded by fells, wonderful views and terrific walks straight from the front door; cosy residents' lounge and popular food in dining room – best to book for dinner if not a resident; cl Christmas; dogs in bedrooms

MAULDS MEABURN

Meaburn Hill Farmhouse

Maulds Meaburn, Penrith, Cumbria CA10 3HN (01931) 715168

£80; 3 attractive and characterful rms. Comfortable 16th-c farmhouse with genuinely caring and friendly owners, homely knick-knacks, books, TV and music in library and dining room/lounge, Aga-cooked breakfasts and suppers and packed lunches by arrangement using home-grown and local produce; bring your own wine; two resident jack russells and a cat; self-catering cottage; cl 2 Jan-2 Feb; two-acre garden and lots of surrounding walks; dogs welcome away from dining room; £5.00

NEWBIGGIN-ON-LUNE

Brownber Hall Country House

Newbiggin-on-Lune, Kirkby Stephen, Cumbria CA17 4NX (01539) 623208

£120; 10 comfortable rms. Victorian country house in mature grounds with marvellous spreading views, a relaxing atmosphere, many original features in two traditionally furnished sitting rooms, good breakfasts, and evening meals on request (bring your own wine); seats on terrace; disabled access; dogs welcome in bedrooms

RAVENSTONEDALE

Black Swan

Ravenstonedale, Cumbria CA17 4NG (015396) 23204

£70; 10 lovely rms, 3 on ground floor. Family-run Victorian inn, recently refurbished throughout, with a thriving stripped stone bar area, log fire, two restaurants with a nice mix of dining chairs and wooden tables, real ales, extensive range of enjoyable food, and tables in charming tree-sheltered stream-side garden; good serious walking country; dogs in bar and bedrooms

RYDAL WATER

White Moss House

White Moss, Ambleside, Cumbria LA22 9SE (015394) 35295

£104; 5 thoughtfully furnished and comfortable little rms in main house plus separate cottage let as one unit with 2 rms. Bought by Wordsworth for his son, this attractive stripped-stone country house – set in charming mature grounds overlooking the lake – is a marvellously relaxing place to stay, with owners who have been there for over 20 years; comfortable lounge, excellent fixed-price five-course meals in pretty dining room, fine wine list, and exemplary service; free fishing and free use of local leisure club; cl Dec-Jan; no toddlers; dogs in cottage

SCALES

Scales Farm

Scales, Threlkeld, Cumbria CA12 4SY (01768) 779660

£60; 6 comfortable, well equipped rms, 3 with ground-floor access. Converted 17th-c farmhouse with wide stretching views, friendly owners, woodburning stove and wide screen TV in homely beamed lounge, traditional english breakfasts in large dining room (good pub next door for evening meals), and packed lunches on request; fine walks all around; three resident dogs and a cat; cl Nov-Mar; disabled access; dogs in bedrooms and lounge; £3

SEATOLLER

Seatoller House

Borrowdale, Keswick, Cumbria CA12 5XN (017687) 77218

£116 inc dinner; 10 spotless, comfortable rms. Friendly house-party atmosphere in 17th-c house that has been a guesthouse for over 100 years, with self-service drinks and board games in comfortable lounges (no TV), and good no-choice fixed-time hearty dinner (not Tues) served at two big oak tables; packed lunches; two acres of grounds and many walks from doorstep (house is at the foot of Honister Pass); resident husky; cl Dec-Feb; children over 5 in dining room; dogs welcome away from public rooms

SKELWITH BRIDGE

Skelwith Bridge Hotel

Skelwith Bridge, Ambleside, Cumbria LA22 9NJ (015394) 32115

£80; 28 attractive rms with fine views. Carefully extended 17th-c farm in quiet countryside (only 2 miles to Ambleside) with beams and other original features, open fire in comfortable sitting room, antiques and fresh flowers, oak-panelled library bar and convivial little Talbot bar, and enjoyable food in restaurant overlooking gardens and river; self-catering cottage; lots of surrounding walks; disabled access; dogs welcome away from dining areas; £5.00

TIRRIL

Queens Head

Tirril, Penrith, Cumbria CA10 2JF (01768) 863219

£80; 7 lovely rms. Bustling inn with flagstones and bare boards in the bar, spacious back restaurant, low beams, black panelling, inglenook fireplace and old-fashioned settles in older part, good interesting food inc snacks and OAP specials, and well kept real ales; two resident dogs; nearby walks; dogs in bedrooms and bars; £5

WASDALE HEAD

Wasdale Head Hotel

Wasdale Head, Seascale, Cumbria CA20 1EX (019467) 26229

£108; 9 simple but warmly comfortable pine-clad rms, with 3 more luxurious ones in farmhouse annexe. Old flagstoned and gabled walkers' and climbers' inn in magnificent setting surrounded by steep fells and wonderful walks; micro-brewery (tours welcome), civilised day rooms, resident lounge with books and games, popular home cooking, good wine list, huge breakfasts, and cheerfully busy public bar; self-catering cottages; three resident collies; partial disabled access; dogs in bedrooms; £5

WATERMILLOCK

Rampsbeck Country House

Watermillock, Penrith, Cumbria CA11 0LP (017684) 86442

£140; 19 attractive, traditional rms, many with stunning views. Fine Victorian hotel in wonderful lakeside setting with 18 acres of formal gardens and parkland; open fire in cosy sitting room, french windows into garden from plush, comfortable lounge, friendly attentive staff, and carefully prepared food in attractive dining room; croquet; lots to do nearby; cl Jan; children over 7 in dining room; dogs in some bedrooms and hall lounge; £10

WINDERMERE

Langdale Chase Hotel

Windermere, Cumbria LA23 1LW (on A591 N towards Ambleside) (015394) 32201

£150; 29 rms, many with marvellous lake view. Welcoming family-run hotel in lovely position on the edge of Lake Windermere with bathing from the hotel jetty; croquet, putting, afternoon tea on the terraces, gracious oak-panelled rooms with antiques, paintings, fresh flowers, open fires, very good food (huge breakfasts, too), and friendly service; resident boxer; dogs may walk in grounds on a lead but plenty of good walks all around; disabled access; dogs welcome away from eating areas; £3

DOG FRIENDLY PUBS

ALDERWASLEY

Bear

Village signposted with Breanfield off B5035 E of Wirksworth at Malt Shovel; inn 0.5 miles SW of village, on Ambergate—Wirksworth high back road; DE56 2RD

Country inn with plenty of character in low-beamed cottagey rooms; five real ales and peaceful garden

With warming open fires in winter, the dark, low-beamed rooms at this lovely old place have a cheerful miscellany of antique furniture including high-backed settles and locally made antique oak chairs with derbyshire motifs. Other characterful décor includes Staffordshire china ornaments, old paintings and engravings, and a trio of grandfather clocks. One little room is filled right to its built-in wall seats by a single vast table. Bass, Greene King Old Speckled Hen, Timothy Taylors Landlord, Whim Hartington Bitter and a guest such as Black Sheep are on handpump, with several wines by the glass. There's a large choice of food and you must book to be sure of a table. Well spaced picnic-sets out on the side grass have peaceful country views. There's no obvious front door – you get in through the plain back entrance by the car park.

Free house ~ Licensee Pete Buller ~ Real ale ~ Bar food (12-9.30) ~ Restaurant ~ (01629) 822585 ~ Children welcome in designated areas ~ Dogs allowed in bar ~ Open 12-midnight

BRASSINGTON

Olde Gate

Village signposted off B5056 and B5035 NE of Ashbourne; DE4 4HJ

Lovely old interior, candlelit at night, country garden

After a good number of years under the same licensee this ancient tavern has changed hands. It's a listed building so we are sure that the recent opening up of an unused Georgian panelled room will be a gentle improvement. It's still full of lovely old furnishings and features, from a fine ancient wall clock to rush-seated old chairs and antique settles, including one ancient black solid oak one. Log fires blaze away, gleaming copper pots sit on a 17th-c kitchen range, pewter mugs hang from a beam, and a side shelf boasts a collection of embossed Doulton stoneware flagons. To the left of a small hatch-served lobby, another cosy beamed room has stripped panelled settles, scrubbed-top tables, and a blazing fire under a huge mantelbeam. Marstons Pedigree and a couple of guests from brewers such as Hook Norton and Jennings are on handpump, and they keep a good selection of malt whiskies; board games. Bar food is gently imaginative. Stone-mullioned windows look out across lots of tables in the pleasant garden to idyllic little silvery-walled pastures, and there are some benches in the small front yard; maybe Sunday evening boules in summer and Friday evening bell-ringers. Carsington Water is a few minutes' drive away.

Marstons ~ Lease Peter Scragg ~ Real ale ~ Bar food (not Mon) ~ (01629) 540448 ~ Children over 10 welcome ~ Dogs welcome ~ Open 12-2.45(3.30 Sat), 6(6.30 Sun, 7 Sun in winter)-11

DERBY

Brunswick

Railway Terrace; close to Derby Midland station; DE1 2RU

One of Britain's oldest railwaymen's pubs, now something of a treasure trove of real ales, with its own microbrewery adjacent

Seven or eight of the 16 or so beers on handpump or tapped straight from the cask at this Victorian pub come their own purpose-built microbrewery – if you're interested you can do a tour for £7.50 (price includes a meal and a pint). As well as a couple of beers from Everards, changing guests might be from Burton Bridge, Oakham, Sharpes and Timothy Taylors. The welcoming high-ceilinged bar has heavy well padded leather seats, whisky-water jugs above the dado, and a dark blue ceiling and upper wall with squared dark panelling below. Another room is decorated with little old-fashioned prints and swan's neck lamps, and has a high-backed wall settle and a coal fire; behind a curved glazed partition wall is a chatty family parlour narrowing to the apex of the triangular building. Informative wall displays tell you about the history and restoration of the building, and there are interesting old train photographs; TV, games machines and darts. Straightforward lunchtime bar food includes toasties and home-made beef stew and is limited to filled baguettes on Sunday and Monday. There are two outdoor seating areas, including a terrace behind. They'll gladly give dogs a bowl of water.

Everards ~ Tenant Graham Yates ~ Real ale ~ Bar food (11.30-2.30 Mon-Thurs; 11.30-5 Fri and Sat) ~ No credit cards ~ (01332) 290677 ~ Children in family parlour ~ Dogs welcome ~ Open 11-11; 12-10.30 Sun

FOOLOW

Bulls Head

Village signposted off A623 Baslow—Tideswell; S32 5QR

A cheerfully run inn by a village green, with well kept ales and decent food

'Dogs, muddy boots and children on leads' are all welcome at this friendly village pub. It's in an enjoyable area for a good country walk – from here you can follow paths out over rolling pasture enclosed by dry-stone walls, and the plague village of Eyam is not far away, or you can just stroll round the green and duck pond. The simply furnished flagstoned bar has interesting photographs including a good collection of Edwardian naughties, and well kept Adnams, Black Sheep, Peak Ale Swift Nick and a guest beer from a brewer such as Caledonian on handpump and they've just over two dozen malts; piped music, board games and darts. A step or two takes you down into what may once have been a stables with its high ceiling joists, stripped stone and woodburning stove. On the other side, a sedate partly panelled dining room has more polished tables and plates arranged around on delft shelves. Tasty bar food is fairly traditional at lunchtime, with more restauranty dishes in the evening. They do a good value OAP two-course lunch menu during the week, and on Tuesday and Wednesday nights good value steak and chicken deals. The west highland terriers are called Holly and Jack. Picnic-sets at the side have nice views.

Free house ~ Licensee William Leslie Bond ~ Real ale ~ Bar food (12-2, 6.30-9(5-8 Sun)) ~ Restaurant ~ (01433) 630873 ~ Children welcome ~ Dogs allowed in bar and bedrooms ~ Live music Fri evening ~ Open 12-3, 6.30-11; 12-10.30 Sun; closed Mon except bank hols ~ Bedrooms: £50S/£70S

HOLBROOK

Dead Poets

Village signposted off A6 S of Belper; Chapel Street; DE56 0TQ

Reassuringly pubby and unchanged, with an excellent range of real ales and simple cottagey décor

Readers enjoy the unpretentious and cheerfully chatty atmosphere at this unspoilt place. Although there's a range of basic snacks, beer is the thing, with eight well kept real ales on handpump or served in jugs from the cellar: Greene King Abbot and Marstons Pedigree with guests from breweries such as Abbeydale, Caledonian, Exmoor, Hartington, Hop Back and Theakstons. They also serve Old Rosie farm cider and country wines. Alongside cobs (nothing else on Sundays), bar food is limited to a few good value hearty dishes such as home-made soup and chilli con carne or casserole. It's quite a dark interior with low black beams in the ochre ceiling, stripped stone walls and broad flagstones, although there is a lighter conservatory at the back. There are candles on scrubbed tables, a big log fire in the end stone fireplace, high-backed winged settles forming snug cubicles along one wall, and pews and a variety of chairs in other intimate corners and hideaways. The décor makes a few nods to the pub's present name (it used to be the Cross Keys) including a photo of W B Yeats and a poem dedicated to the pub by Les Baynton, and there are old prints of Derby; piped music. Behind is a sort of verandah room with lanterns, heaters, fairy lights and a few plants, and more seats out in the yard.

Everards ~ Tenant William Holmes ~ Real ale ~ Bar food (12-2 only) ~ No credit cards ~ (01332) 780301 ~ Children welcome in conservatory till 8pm ~ Dogs welcome ~ Open 12-2.30, 5-12; 12-midnight Fri, Sat; 12-11 Sun

HOPE

Cheshire Cheese

Off A6187, towards Edale; S33 6ZF

Cosy up-and-down old stone pub in attractive Peak District village

The three very snug oak-beamed rooms at this 16th-c pub are arranged on different levels, each with its own coal fire. It's a very popular place, with a true local following and at certain times plenty of tourists, so as parking is limited it might be worth arriving on foot: there is a glorious range of local walks, taking in the summits of Lose Hill and Win Hill, or the cave district of the Castleton area, and the village of Hope itself is worth strolling around. Black Sheep Bitter and Whim Hartington plus guests from brewers such as Adnams and Timothy Taylor and Peak Ales are on handpump, and they've a good range of spirits and several wines by the glass; piped music. The pub was recently taken over by Enterprise so we're very much keeping our fingers crossed for its unspoilt atmosphere. Bar food, from sandwiches up, is fairly straightforward.

Enterprise ~ Lease Craig Oxley ~ Real ale ~ Bar food (12-2(3.30 Sat), 6.30-9; 12-5 Sun) ~ Restaurant ~ (01433) 620381 ~ Dogs allowed in bar ~ Open 12-3, 6.30-11; 12-11.30 Sat; 12-7 Sun; closed Sun evening

LITTON
Red Lion

Village signposted off A623, between B6465 and B6049 junctions; also signposted off B6049; SK17 8QU

Convivial all-rounder with unspoilt charm, prettily placed by village green

The landlady at this 18th-c village pub caringly oversees a particularly welcoming and enjoyable establishment. The two homely linked front rooms have low beams and some panelling, and blazing log fires. There's a bigger back room with good-sized tables, and large antique prints on its stripped stone walls. The small bar counter has very well kept Oakwell Barnsley and a couple of guests such as Abbeydale Absolution and Whim Hartington, with a good choice of decent wines and several malt whiskies; darts, board games and piped music. Bar food is well liked and traditional. Outdoor seating is on the pretty village green, which is covered in daffodils in early spring. A particularly interesting time to visit this village is during the annual well-dressing carnival (usually the last weekend in June), when locals create a picture from flower petals, moss and other natural materials.

Enterprise ~ Lease Suzy Turner ~ Real ale ~ Bar food (12-2, 6-8; 12-8.30 Thurs-Sun) ~ (01298) 871458 ~ Children over 6 welcome ~ Dogs allowed in bar ~ Open 12-11(midnight Fri, Sat); 12-10.30 Sun

MONSAL HEAD
Monsal Head Hotel

B6465; DE45 1NL

Popular hilltop inn with good food, beer and friendly staff; worth seeking out for the view alone

You'll find the best selection of real ales and most relaxing atmosphere (and maybe muddy walkers and their dogs) in the cosy stable bar. In days gone by the stables here gave shelter to the horses that used to pull guests and their luggage up from the station at the other end of the steep valley – stripped timber horse-stalls, harness and brassware, and lamps from the disused station itself, all hint at those days. There are cushioned oak pews around the tables on the flagstone floor, and the big warming open fire is quite a feature. Lloyds Monsal Bitter and Theakstons Best are kept alongside four guests from local brewers such as Thornbridge or Whim, a good choice of german bottled beers and at least a dozen wines by the glass; board games. Bar food includes lunchtime sandwiches and can be a little ambitious. One of Derbyshire's most classic views is from this very spot, looking down to a bend in steep-sided Monsal Dale with its huge railway viaduct, which is now crossed by the Monsal Trail. The best places to admire this terrific view are from the big windows in the smarter lounge and the extensive garden.

Free house ~ Licensee Sarah Belfield ~ Real ale ~ Bar food (12-9.30(9 Sun)) ~ Restaurant ~ (01629) 640250 ~ Children welcome ~ Dogs allowed in bar ~ Open 11.30-midnight

MONYASH
Bulls Head
B5055 W of Bakewell; DE45 1JH

Unpretentious local with very tasty home cooking

Good traditional food is served at this very friendly village inn. It's high-ceilinged rooms are quite simple with a good log fire, straightforward furnish-ings, horse pictures and a shelf of china. A small back bar room has darts, games machine, juke box and pool; may be quiet piped music. Burton Ale, John Smiths and a guest such as Bradfield Farmers Blonde are on handpump. The menu includes a handful of sensibly priced pubby dishes. A gate from the pub's garden leads into a nice new village play area, and this is fine walking country.

Free house ~ Licensee Sharon Barber ~ Real ale ~ Bar food (12-2.30, 6.30-9; 12-9 Sun) ~ (01629) 812372 ~ Children welcome ~ Dogs welcome ~ Live music alt Sats ~ Open 12-3, 6(6.30 winter)-midnight; 12-1am Fri, Sat; 11.30-midnight Sun ~ Bedrooms: £25/£45

OVER HADDON
Lathkil
Village and inn signposted from B5055 just SW of Bakewell; DE45 1JE

Traditional pub well placed for Lathkill Dale with super views, good range of beers and decent food

Little changes from year to year at this well liked country inn where Robert Grigor-Taylor has been licensee for more than a quarter of a century. It's popular with a varied clientele, from day trippers to hikers (dogs are welcome but muddy boots must be left in the lobby) and can get very busy. The walled garden is a good place to sit and soak in the views over the bewitchingly secretive surround-ings of Lathkill Dale, and there are great views from the pub windows too. The airy room on the right as you go in has a nice fire in the attractively carved fire-place, old-fashioned settles with upholstered cushions and chairs, black beams, a delft shelf of blue and white plates, original prints and photographs, and big windows. Bar food includes a lunchtime buffet-style menu. They keep Everards Tiger and Whim Hartington, three guests from brewers such as Bradfield, Cottage and Peak Ales on handpump, a reasonable range of wines and a decent selection of soft drinks; piped music, darts, shove-ha'penny and dominoes.

Free house ~ Licensee Robert Grigor-Taylor ~ Real ale ~ Bar food (12-2(2.30 Sat, Sun), 6(7 Fri, Sat)-8) ~ Restaurant ~ (01629) 812501 ~ Children welcome ~ Dogs welcome ~ Open 11.30(11 Sat)-11; 12-10.30 Sun; 11.30-3, 6-11 Mon-Fri in winter ~ Bedrooms: £45B/£65S(£80B)

SHELDON
Cock & Pullet

Village signposted off A6 just W of Ashford; DE45 1QS

Well run village local with an appealingly unpretentious atmosphere

A collection of 30 clocks, various representations of poultry (including some stuffed) and a cheerful assembly of deliberately mismatched furnishings greets you from the cosy little rooms at this family-run pub. With its low beams, exposed stonework, flagstones, scrubbed oak tables, pews and open fire it looks like it's been a pub for hundreds of years, but surprisingly it was only converted some dozen years ago. A plainer public bar has pool, darts, dominoes, board games and a TV; piped music. Black Sheep and Timothy Taylors Landlord are on handpump with one guest. The good value pubby menu includes sandwiches and a curry of the day. At the back a pleasant little terrace has tables and a water feature, and as this pretty village is just off the Limestone Way this is a popular all year round stop with walkers.

Free house ~ Licensees David and Kath Melland ~ Real ale ~ Bar food (12-2.30, 6-9) ~ No credit cards ~ (01629) 814292 ~ Children welcome ~ Dogs welcome ~ Open 11-11; 12-10.30 Sun ~ Bedrooms: /£60B

DOG FRIENDLY HOTELS, INNS, B&Bs AND FARMS

ASHBOURNE
Callow Hall

Mappleton Road, Ashbourne, Derbyshire DE6 2AA (Union Street; 0.5 miles off A515; Mappleton Road, off B5035) (01335) 300900

£150; 27 rms, many with marvellous lake view. Welcoming family-run hotel in lovely position surrounded by 44 acres on edge of Lake Windermere with bathing from the hotel jetty; croquet, putting, afternoon tea on the terraces, gracious oak-panelled rooms with antiques, paintings, fresh flowers, open fires, very good food (huge breakfasts, too), and friendly service; two resident dogs; dogs may walk in grounds on a lead but plenty of good walks all around; disabled access; dogs in bedrooms but must sleep in own basket in bathroom

Mercaston Hall

Mercaston, Ashbourne, Derbyshire DE6 3BL (01335) 360263

£66; 3 comfortable rms. Quietly set and handsome 17th-c farmhouse on working sheep with friendly owners, comfortable and homely beamed lounge with woodburning stove, hearty breakfasts, and tennis court; cl Christmas; good surrounding walks; dogs in bedrooms but must not be left alone; £2

BAKEWELL

Hassop Hall

Hassop, Bakewell, Derbyshire DE45 1NS (2.7 miles from A6 in Bakewell via A619 and B6001) (01629) 640488

£114; 13 gracious rms. Mentioned in the Domesday Book and in lovely parkland surrounded by fine scenery, this handsome hotel has antiques and oil paintings, an elegant drawing room, cosy oak-panelled bar, good food and friendly service; tennis; partial disabled access; dogs in bedrooms but must not be left alone

BEELEY

Devonshire Arms

The Beeches, Beeley, Matlock, Derbyshire DE4 2NR (01629) 733259

£145; 8 chic, comfortable rms. Handsome old stone building in pretty village within strolling distance of Chatsworth and its huge park; light, brightly coloured modern furnishings in beamed and flagstoned bars, cheerful log fires and fresh flowers, interesting, delicious food using produce from kitchen gardens on Chatsworth Estate in two dining areas, five local beers, good wine list

BIGGIN-BY-HARTINGTON

Biggin Hall

Biggin-by-Hartington, Buxton, Derbyshire SK17 0DH (0.8 miles off A515, just S of Hartington) (01298) 84451

£84; 20 spacious rms with antiques, some in converted 18th-c stone building and in bothy. Cheerfully run 17th-c house in 8 acres of quiet grounds with very relaxed atmosphere, two comfortable sitting rooms, one with a library, the other with a woodburning stove in inglenook fireplace, and attractive dining room serving traditional country house home cooking using local and free-range wholefoods; plenty of trails and dales to walk; resident dogs and geese; children over 12; limited disabled access; dogs in annexe bedrooms only

DOVE DALE

Peveril of the Peak

Thorpe, Ashbourne, Derbyshire DE6 2AW (08704) 008109

£135; 45 rms, many with lovely views. Relaxing hotel in pretty village amidst some of the finest scenery in the Peak District and with 6 acres of grounds; comfortable sofas and log fire in spacious lounge bar, friendly staff, and good english cooking in attractive restaurant overlooking the garden; wonderful walking nearby; dogs welcome away from restaurant; bowls and treats; £15

GRINDLEFORD

The Maynard

Main Road, Nether Padley, Grindleford, Hope Valley, Derbyshire S32 2HE (2 miles off A623, via B6001; Nether Padley) (01433) 630321

£115; 10 rms. Comfortable hotel with log fire and good Peak District views from the first-floor lounge, smart welcoming bar, good choice of food, popular evening restaurant, and particularly attentive service; good walks in garden and nearby; disabled access; dogs in bedrooms and bar; bedding, bowls, meals, treats; £10

HOPE

Round Meadow Barn

Parsons Lane, Hope, Derbyshire S33 6RB (01433) 621347

£50; 3 characterful rms, two with own bthrm. Neatly and attractively converted barn in several acres of grounds at the foot of Win Hill with wonderful views, original stone walls, big timbers, and hearty breakfasts taken around one big table in family kitchen; resident jack russell and cat; lovely walks and lots to do nearby; dogs in bedrooms; £3

Underleigh House

Edale Road, Hope, Castleton, Derbyshire S33 6RF (01433) 621372

£80; 5 thoughtfully decorated rms. In unspoilt countryside, this spotlessly kept converted barn has fine views from the comfortable sitting room, hearty breakfasts with good home-made preserves enjoyed around communal table in flagstoned dining room, friendly cheerful owners, and attractive gardens; packed lunches can be arranged; resident border terrier and cat; terrific walks on doorstep; cl Christmas, New Year, and Jan; children over 12; partial disabled access; dogs in ground floor bedrooms only (not in any public areas) and by prior arrangement

KIRK IRETON

Barley Mow

Kirk Ireton, Ashbourne, Derbyshire DE6 3JP (01335) 370306

£55; 5 rms. Tall, Jacobean, walkers' inn with lots of woodwork in series of inter-connecting bar rooms, a solid-fuel stove in beamed residents' sitting room, and well kept real ales; close to Carsington Reservoir so lots of walks; cl Christmas and New Year; dogs in one ground-floor bedroom and in bar

MATLOCK

Riber Hall

Matlock, Derbyshire DE4 5JU (01629) 582795

£145; 14 lovely beamed rms. Elizabethan manor house in pretty grounds surrounded by peaceful countryside, with antique-filled heavily beamed rooms, log fires, airy conservatory, fresh flowers, elegant restaurant with enjoyable food and fine wines, and tennis and croquet; walks in grounds and nearby fields; dogs in some bedrooms

MONSAL HEAD

Monsal Head Hotel

Monsal Head, Buxton, Derbyshire DE45 1NL (1.6 miles off A6 in Ashford, via B6465) (01629) 640250

£90; 7 very good rms, some with outstanding views. Comfortable and enjoyable small hotel in marvellous setting high above the River Wye, with horsey theme in bar (converted from old stables), freshly prepared enjoyable food using seasonal produce, well kept real ales, and good service; resident dog; lots of trails and walks from the hotel; dogs in bedrooms and much of pub but not dining room; £5

ROWSLEY

Peacock

Rowsley, Matlock, Derbyshire DE4 2EB (on A6)(01629) 733518

£175 16 comfortable rms. Smart 17th-c country house hotel by River Derwent (private fishing in season), with well kept gardens, friendly staff, interesting and pleasant old-fashioned inner bar, spacious and comfortable lounge, and very popular restaurant; no accommodation at Christmas; children over 10; dogs may walk in garden, on moors and at Chatsworth Park; dogs in bedrooms; £10

DOG FRIENDLY PUBS

BEESANDS

Cricket

About 3 miles S of A379, from Chillington; in village turn right along foreshore road; TQ7 2EN

Welcoming small pub by beach with enjoyable food (especially fish) and beer

Just over the sea wall in front of this friendly little pub is Start Bay beach; there are picnic-sets by the wall and the pub is popular with South Devon Coastal Path walkers. Inside, it's neatly kept and open-plan with dark traditional pubby furniture (carpeted in the dining part and with a stripped wooden floor in the bar area), some nice, well captioned photographs of local fisherpeople, knots and fishing gear on the walls and a couple of small fireplaces. Fullers London Pride and Otter Bitter on handpump, a dozen wines by the glass and local cider; piped music. The cheerful black labrador is called Brewster. As well as very good fresh local fish and shellfish, the well liked bar food includes traditional pubby dishes and tasty specials.

Heavitree ~ Tenant Nigel Heath ~ Real ale ~ Bar food ~ Restaurant ~ (01548) 580215 ~ Children welcome ~ Dogs allowed in bar ~ Open 11-11; 11-3, 6-11 in winter

BRANSCOMBE

Masons Arms

Main Street; signed off A3052 Sidmouth—Seaton, then bear left into village; EX12 3DJ

Rambling low-beamed rooms, woodburning stoves, good choice of real ales and wines, popular food, and seats in quiet terrace and garden; bedrooms

The heart of this 14th-c longhouse is the rambling main bar with its ancient ships' beams, massive central hearth in front of the roaring log fire (where spit-roasts are held) and comfortable seats and chairs on slate floors. The Old Worthies bar also has a slate floor, a fireplace with a two-sided woodburning stove and woodwork that has been stripped back to the original pine. Bar food from a tempting list of imaginative dishes is very good. Branscombe Vale Branoc and Summa That, Otter Bitter, St Austell Tribute, and a guest such as Timothy Taylors Landlord on handpump, 14 wines by the glass and 33 malt whiskies; darts, shove-ha'penny, cribbage, and dominoes. Outside, the quiet flower-filled front terrace, which has tables with little thatched roofs, extends into a side garden. You may have to leave your credit card behind the bar.

Free house ~ Licensees Colin and Carol Slaney ~ Real ale ~ Bar food ~
Restaurant ~ (01297) 680300 ~ Children in bar with parents but not in
restaurant ~ Dogs allowed in bar and bedrooms ~ Open 11-11; 12-10.30 Sun;
11-3, 6-11 weekdays in winter ~ Bedrooms: /£80S(£85B)

BUCKLAND BREWER

Coach & Horses

*Village signposted off A388 S of Monkleigh; OS Sheet 190 map reference
423206; EX39 5LU*

**Friendly old village pub with a mix of customers, open fires, and real ales; good
nearby walks**

Handy after a visit to the RHS garden Rosemoor, this friendly old thatched
village pub is liked by regulars as well as visitors. The heavily beamed bar has
comfortable seats (including a handsome antique settle) and a woodburning
stove in the inglenook – there's also a good log fire in the big stone inglenook
of the cosy lounge. A small back room has darts and pool; several cats. Cotleigh
Golden Seahawk, Shepherd Neame Spitfire, and Skinners Betty Stogs on handpump, and around eight wines by the glass; games machine, skittle alley (that
doubles as a function room), piped music, and occasional TV for sports. Bar food
includes sandwiches, filled baguettes and baked potatoes, pasties, burgers and
daily specials. There are picnic-sets on a front terrace and in the side garden,
and walks on the nearby moorland and along the beaches of Westward Ho!

Free house ~ Licensees Oliver Wolfe and Nicola Barrass ~ Real ale ~ Bar food ~
Restaurant ~ (01237) 451395 ~ Well behaved children welcome ~ Dogs allowed
in bar ~ Open 12-3, 5.30(6 Sun)-midnight

BUCKLAND MONACHORUM

Drake Manor

Off A386 via Crapstone, just S of Yelverton roundabout; PL20 7NA

**Nice little village pub with snug rooms, popular food, quite a choice of drinks,
and pretty back garden**

The upstairs here has been converted into a very attractive self-catering apart-
ment which is proving very popular with customers. It's a charming, friendly little
pub and the long-serving landlady offers a warm welcome to both locals and
visitors – she is keen that this should remain a proper village pub whilst offering good food, too. The heavily beamed public bar on the left has brocade-
cushioned wall seats, prints of the village from 1905 onwards, some horse tack
and a few ship badges on the wall, and a really big stone fireplace with a woodburning stove; a small door leads to a low-beamed cubbyhole. The snug Drakes
Bar has beams hung with tiny cups and big brass keys, a woodburning stove in
an old stone fireplace, horsebrasses and stirrups, a fine stripped pine high-backed
settle with a hood, and a mix of other seats around just four tables (the oval one
is rather nice). On the right is a small, beamed dining room with settles and
tables on the flagstoned floor. Shove-ha'penny, darts, games machine and euchre.
Courage Best, Greene King Abbot and Sharps Doom Bar on handpump, around 30

malt whiskies, and 11 wines by the glass. Some interesting daily specials are served alongside quite a few traditional items from the menu – food here is well liked. The sheltered back garden – where there are picnic-sets – is prettily planted, and the floral displays in front are very attractive all year round.

Punch ~ Lease Mandy Robinson ~ Real ale ~ Bar food (12-2, 7-10(9.30 Sun)) ~ Restaurant ~ (01822) 853892 ~ Children in restaurant and cellar bar if eating ~ Dogs allowed in bar ~ Open 11.30-2.30(3 Sat), 6.30-11(11.30 Fri and Sat); 12-10.30 Sun

CADELEIGH

Cadeleigh Arms

Village signposted off A3072 just W of junction with A396 Tiverton—Exeter in Bickleigh; EX16 8HP

Attractively refurbished and civilised pub in rolling countryside, carefully chosen wines, high quality food, and relaxed atmosphere

This is a well run and civilised pub in a farming community surrounded by rolling hills. It's been attractively refurbished by its present owners, who have placed quite an emphasis on the innovative cooking in relaxed surroundings. To the left of the door are high-backed farmhouse, church and blond chairs around wooden tables (one is a barrel table) on the grey carpet, a bay window seat, an ornamental stove in the stone fireplace, and rather striking hound paintings; darts. This part leads to a flagstoned room with a high-backed settle to one side of the log fire in its big standstone fireplace, and similar chairs and tables. Otter Bitter on handpump, farm cider, a carefully chosen little wine list; friendly, efficient service; and unobtrusive piped music. The high quality food is attractively presented and very good. On a gravel terrace are some picnic-sets, with more on a sloping lawn.

Free house ~ Licensee Jane Dreyer ~ Real ale ~ Bar food (not winter Sun evening or Mon) ~ Restaurant ~ (01884) 855238 ~ Children welcome ~ Dogs allowed in bar ~ Open 12-2.30-ish, 6-11; 12-3.30-ish, 7-10.30 Sun; closed winter Sun evening, all day Mon; 25 Dec

CHERITON BISHOP

Old Thatch Inn

Village signposted from A30; EX6 6JH

Welcoming old pub, handy for the A30 with good food and beer, and a pretty garden

Our readers enjoy their visits to this old-fashioned, thatched place very much. There's a happy, bustling atmosphere and the warmly welcoming licensees are very hands-on, cheerful and chatty. The traditionally furnished lounge and rambling beamed bar are separated by a large open stone fireplace (lit in the cooler months) and they keep O'Hanlons Royal Oak and Yellowhammer, Otter Ale, Sharps Doom Bar and a changing guest on handpump, and ten wines by the glass. The sheltered garden has lots of pretty flowering baskets and tubs. Good bar food includes lunchtime sandwiches and many imaginative dishes such as seared pigeon breast on steamed fennel with a raspberry balsamic dressing.

Free house ~ Licensees David and Serena London ~ Real ale ~ Bar food (12-2(2.30 Fri and Sat), 6.30-9(9.30 Fri and Sat); 12-3, 7-9 Sun) ~ Restaurant ~ (01647) 24204 ~ Children welcome away from bar area ~ Dogs allowed in bar ~ Open 11.30-3, 6-11; 12-4 Sun; closed Sun evening; 25 and 26 Dec

CLAYHIDON

Merry Harriers

3 miles from M5 junction 26: head towards Wellington; turn left at first roundabout signposted Ford Street and Hemyock, then after a mile turn left signposted Ford Street; at hilltop T junction, turn left towards Chard – pub is 1.5 miles on right; EX15 3TR

Bustling dining pub with imaginative food, several real ales and quite a few wines by the glass; sizeable garden

Run by a friendly landlord, this is a popular dining pub with a fair choice of drinks, too. There are several small linked green-carpeted areas with comfortably cushioned pews and farmhouse chairs, candles in bottles, a woodburning stove with a sofa beside it and plenty of horsey and hunting prints and local wildlife pictures. Two dining areas have a brighter feel with quarry tiles and lightly timbered white walls. Using very carefully sourced local and even organic ingredients (they name all their suppliers on a special sheet), food is interesting and very good. Cotleigh Harrier Lite and Otter Head and a guest like Exmoor Fox or Yeovil Stargazer on handpump, 14 wines by the glass, two local ciders, 25 malt whiskies and a good range of spirits. There are picnic-sets on a small terrace, with more in a sizeable garden (which they hope to extend) sheltered by shrubs and the skittle alley; this is a good walking area. As we went to press, we heard that the Gatlings may be thinking of a change of scene, but they've made no decisions yet.

Free house ~ Licensees Peter and Angela Gatling ~ Real ale ~ Bar food (not Sun evening or Mon) ~ Restaurant ~ (01823) 421270 ~ Children welcome ~ Dogs allowed in bar ~ Open 12-3, 6.30-11; 12-3.30 Sun; closed Sun evening, all day Mon; 25 and 26 Dec

COCKWOOD

Anchor

Off, but visible from, A379 Exeter—Torbay; EX6 8RA

Extremely popular dining pub specialising in seafood (other choices available), with six real ales too

A new quirky extension has been added to this extremely popular place, which will provide much needed extra dining space. It's been constructed using mainly reclaimed timber and decorated with over 300 ship emblems, brass and copper lamps and nautical knick-knacks. The other small, low-ceilinged, rambling rooms have black panelling, good-sized tables in various alcoves, and a cheerful winter coal fire in the snug – and despite the emphasis on food, there's still a pubby atmosphere. Fantastic fish dishes include 27 different ways of serving River Exe mussels, nine ways of serving local scallops and five ways of serving oysters, as well as crab and brandy soup, and various platters to share. Non-fishy dishes feature as well. The six real ales on handpump might include Adnams Broadside, Bass, Fullers London Pride, Greene King Abbot, Otter Ale, and Timothy Taylors Landlord, and there's a fine wine list of 300 (bin ends and reserves and 12 by the glass), 20 brandies and 20 ports, and 130 malt whiskies; lots of liqueur coffees too. Piped music and games machine. From the tables on the sheltered verandah you can look across the road to the inlet. There's often a queue to get in but they do two sittings in the restaurant on winter weekends and every evening in summer to cope with the crowds.

Heavitree ~ Tenants Mr Morgan and Miss Sanders ~ Real ale ~ Bar food (all day) ~ Restaurant ~ (01626) 890203 ~ Children welcome if seated and away from bar ~ Dogs allowed in bar ~ Jam session last Thurs in month and themed nights monthly ~ Open 11-11; 12-10.30 Sun; closed evening 25 Dec

COLEFORD
New Inn
Just off A377 Crediton—Barnstaple; EX17 5BZ

Thatched 13th-c inn with interestingly furnished areas, inventive food and real ales

The licensees at this 600-year-old inn have lots of enthusiasm and as we went to press, had many plans for subtle improvements. It's an L-shaped building with the servery in the 'angle', and interestingly furnished areas leading off it: ancient and modern settles, cushioned stone wall seats, some character tables – a pheasant worked into the grain of one – and carved dressers and chests; also, paraffin lamps, antique prints and old guns on the white walls and landscape plates on one of the beams, with pewter tankards on another. Captain, the chatty parrot, has stayed on and will greet you with a 'hello' or even a 'good-bye'. The imaginative menu makes very tempting reading and dishes are prepared using good local produce. Greene King IPA, and Otter Ale with a couple of guests such as Gales HSB and Skinners Heligan Honey on handpump, local cider and ten wines by the glass; good, cheerful service, piped music, games machine, darts, and board games. There are chairs and tables on decking under the willow tree by the babbling stream and more on the terrace and lawn.

Free house ~ Licensees Carole and George Cowie ~ Real ale ~ Bar food ~ Restaurant ~ (01363) 84242 ~ Children welcome ~ Dogs allowed in bar ~ Open 12-3, 6-11; 12-3, 7-10.30 Sun; closed 25 and 26 Dec

CULMSTOCK
Culm Valley
B3391, off A38 E of M5 junction 27; EX15 3JJ

Quirky dining pub with imaginative food, quite a few real ales, a fantastic wine list, and outside seats overlooking River Culm

'Determinedly free-spirited' is a rather nice way to describe this idiosyncratic and even scruffy pub and it's certainly not the place for those who like every-thing neat and tidy. But the lively atmosphere and the cheerful and friendly, slightly off-beat landlord are part of the appeal to most customers. The salmon-coloured bar has a hotch-potch of modern and unrenovated furnishings, a big fireplace with some china above it, newspapers, and a long elm bar counter; further along is a dining room with a chalkboard menu, a small front conservatory, and leading off here, a little oak-floored room with views into the kitchen. A larger back room has paintings by local artists for sale. Board games and a small portable TV for occasional rugby, rowing and racing events. Very good food, prepared using as much free-range and organic local produce as possible, includes home-made sausages, a popular selection of tapas and other inventive dishes. The landlord and his brother import wines from smaller french vineyards, so you can count on a few of those (they offer 40 wines by the glass), as well as some unusual french fruit liqueurs, somerset cider brandies, vintage rum, good sherries and madeira, local farm ciders, and real ales such as Bath Ales Gem Bitter, Blackawton Saltash Sunrise, Box Steam Dark and Handsome, Downton Chimera Dark Delight, Otter Bright, and Stonehenge Danish Dynamite tapped from the cask; they may hold a beer festival over the late spring bank holiday weekend. Outside, tables are very attractively positioned overlooking the bridge and the River Culm. The gents' is in an outside yard.

Free house ~ Licensee Richard Hartley ~ Real ale ~ Bar food (not Sun evening) ~ Restaurant ~ No credit cards ~ (01884) 840354 ~ Children allowed away from main bar ~ Dogs welcome ~ Live impromptu piano every two weeks or so ~ Open 12-3, 6-11; 11-11 Sat; 12-10.30 Sun ~ Bedrooms: £35B/£60B

DREWSTEIGNTON
Drewe Arms
off A30 NW of Moretonhampstead; EX6 6QN

Pretty thatched village pub, warmly welcoming, proper basic bar plus dining rooms, well liked food and real ales; bedrooms and bunk house (for walkers)

Although there have been quite a few changes to this thatched and friendly village pub over the last few years, the small room on the left remains as unspoilt as ever with its serving hatch and basic wooden wall benches, stools and tables. There are three dining areas now, Mabel's Kitchen with its original raeburn and a history of Aunt Mable (Britain's longest serving and oldest landlady, whom both editors of this *Guide* remember well), the Card Room which has a woodburning stove, and the back Dartmoor Room which is ideal for a private party: high-backed, wooden slatted dining chairs around a mix of wooden tables, lots of prints and pictures on the walls, and an array of copper saucepans. Otter Ale, Bright and Druid Ale (made by Otter exclusively for the pub) and Dartmoor Brewery Jail Ale tapped from casks in the original tap room; skittle alley. Tasty food includes traditional standards and some more interesting specials. There are seats under umbrellas along the front terrace surrounded by lovely flowering tubs and hanging baskets, with more in the terraced garden. The bedrooms have been refurbished and they've also converted some stables into bunk rooms which are ideal for walkers. The inn is handy for Castle Drogo.

Enterprise ~ Lease Fiona Newton ~ Real ale ~ Bar food (all day in summer; 12-2.30, 6-9.30 in winter) ~ Restaurant ~ (01647) 281224 ~ Children welcome ~ Dogs allowed in bar and bedrooms ~ Live music in Long Room every two weeks ~ Open 11-midnight; 11-3, 6-midnight Mon-Fri in winter ~ Bedrooms: /£80B

EXMINSTER

Turf Hotel

Follow the signs to the Swan's Nest, signposted from A379 S of village, then continue to end of track, by gates; park, and walk right along canal towpath – nearly a mile; there's a fine seaview out to the mudflats at low tide; EX6 8EE

Remote but very popular waterside pub with fine choice of drinks, super summer barbecues and lots of space in big garden

This place is great fun and extremely popular, especially on a sunny day when you must arrive early to be sure of a seat (the tables in the bay windows are much prized). You can't get here by car – you must either walk (which takes about 20 minutes along the ship canal) or cycle or catch a 60-seater boat which brings people down the Exe estuary from Topsham quay (15-minute trip, adult £4, child £2); there's also a canal boat from Countess Wear Swing Bridge every lunchtime. Best to phone the pub for all sailing times. For those arriving in their own boat, there is a large pontoon as well as several moorings. Inside, the end room has a slate floor, pine walls, built-in seats, lots of photographs of the pub, and a woodburning stove; along a corridor (with an eating room to one side) is a simply furnished room with wood-plank seats around tables on the stripped wooden floor. Otter Ale and Bitter, O'Hanlons Yellowhammer and Royal Oak, and Topsham & Exminster Ferryman on handpump, local Green Valley cider, local juices, 20 wines by the glass (and local wine too), and jugs of Pimms. The outdoor barbecue is much used in good weather (as are the cook-your-own barbecues), and there are plenty of picnic-sets spread around the big garden. The children's play area was built using a lifeboat from a liner that sank off the Scilly Isles around 100 years ago; it was rebuilt last winter. Although the pub and garden do get packed in good weather and there are inevitable queues, the staff remain friendly and efficient. The sea and estuary birds are fun to watch at low tide. Interesting bar food uses organic and local produce.

Free house ~ Licensees Clive and Ginny Redfern ~ Real ale ~ Bar food (12-2(3 Fri-Sun), 7-9(9.30 Fri and Sat); not Sun evening) ~ (01392) 833128 ~ Children welcome ~ Dogs welcome ~ Open 11-11(10.30 Sun); only open weekends Oct, Nov, March; closed Dec-Feb

HOLNE

Church House

Signed off B3357 W of Ashburton; TQ13 7SJ

Medieval inn on Dartmoor, plenty of surrounding walks, log fires, real ales, and tasty bar food

Surrounded by fine walks and with open moorland just ten minutes away, this medieval inn is popular with walkers – especially at lunchtime – though there are plenty of cheerful locals, too. A hard-working new landlord has taken over and has refurbished throughout, adding fresh flowers and lit candles. The lower bar has stripped pine panelling and an 18th-c curved elm settle, and is separated from the lounge bar by a 16th-c heavy oak partition; open log fires in both rooms. Well liked bar food includes pasties and a popular seafood platter.

Butcombe Bitter and Teignworthy Reel Ale with a guest like Otter Ale on hand-pump, and several good wines by the glass; darts, dominoes and board games. Charles Kingsley (of *Water Babies* fame) was born in the village. The church is well worth a visit.

Free house ~ Licensee Steve Ashworth ~ Real ale ~ Bar food (12-2.30, 7-8.30-ish) ~ Restaurant ~ (01364) 631208 ~ Children welcome ~ Dogs welcome ~ Open 12-3, 6-11(midnight Fri and Sat, 10.30 Sun); evening opening Mon-Sat 7pm, Sun 9pm in winter ~ Bedrooms: £35S/£70S

HORNDON

Elephants Nest

If coming from Okehampton on A386 turn left at Mary Tavy Inn, then left after about ½ mile; pub signposted beside Mary Tavy Inn, then Horndon signposted; on the Ordnance Survey Outdoor Leisure Map it's named as the New Inn; PL19 9NQ

Isolated old inn surrounded by Dartmoor walks, some interesting original features, real ales, and popular food

Surrounded by walks, this 400-year-old inn has plenty of picnic-sets under umbrellas in the spreading, attractive garden, and from here you look over dry-stone walls to the pastures of Dartmoor's lower slopes and the rougher moorland above. Inside, the main bar has lots of beer pump clips on the beams, high bar chairs by the bar counter, and Palmers IPA, Dartmoor Brewery Jail Ale, Sharps Doom Bar, and a guest like O'Hanlons Yellowhammer on handpump, farm cider and several wines by the glass. There are two other newly refurbished rooms with nice modern dark wood dining chairs around a mix of tables, and throughout there are bare stone walls, flagstones, and three woodburning stoves; darts and maybe piped music. Bar food, with anything from lunchtime filled baguettes up to chinese-style pork belly with pak choi and rice noodles, is good.

Free house ~ Licensee Hugh Cook ~ Real ale ~ Bar food ~ (01822) 810273 ~ Children welcome ~ Dogs welcome ~ Open 12-3, 6.30-11 ~ Bedrooms: £65B/£75B

IDDESLEIGH

Duke of York

B3217 Exbourne—Dolton; EX19 8BG

Unfussy and exceptionally friendly pub with simply furnished bars, popular food and fair choice of drinks

'Everything a country pub should be' say several readers to describe this friendly, informal inn. It's run by a hospitable, genuinely welcoming landlord and there may well be chatty locals in their wellies (with maybe a dog or two) sitting around a roaring log fire, and flower posies on the tables. The enjoyably unspoilt bar has a lot of homely character: rocking chairs, cushioned wall benches built into the wall's black-painted wooden dado, stripped tables and other simple country furnishings, and well kept Adnams Broadside, Cotleigh Tawny, and

Sharps IPA tapped from the cask, and quite a few wines by the glass. It does get pretty cramped at peak times; darts. Food is good, honest and fairly priced and some dishes include the landlord's own rare-breed beef. Through a small coach arch is a little back garden with some picnic-sets.

Free house ~ Licensees Jamie Stuart and Pippa Hutchinson ~ Real ale ~ Bar food (all day) ~ Restaurant ~ (01837) 810253 ~ Children welcome ~ Dogs welcome ~ Open 10am-11pm; 12-10.30 Sun ~ Bedrooms: £40B/£70B

MARLDON

Church House

Just off A380 NW of Paignton; TQ3 1SL

Spreading bar plus several other rooms in pleasant inn, well liked drinks and bar food, and seats on three terraces

This is an attractive inn with friendly, efficient staff and well liked food and drink. The spreading bar has several different areas that radiate off the big semi-circular bar counter with interesting windows, some beams, dark pine chairs around solid tables on the turkey carpet, and yellow leather bar chairs. Leading off here is a cosy little candlelit room with just four tables on the bare-board floor, a dark wood dado and stone fireplace. Bar food is good and gently imaginative – maybe loin of pork with cider sauce and glazed pear. Bass, Bays Gold, Fullers London Pride, and St Austell Dartmoor Best on handpump, and ten wines by the glass; piped music. There are picnic-sets on three carefully maintained grassy terraces behind the pub.

Enterprise ~ Lease Julian Cook ~ Real ale ~ Bar food ~ Restaurant ~ (01803) 558279 ~ Children welcome ~ Dogs allowed in bar ~ Open 11-2.30, 5-11(11.30 Sat); 12-3, 5.30-10.30 Sun

MEAVY

Royal Oak

Off B3212 E of Yelverton; PL20 6PJ

Pleasant old pub with country furnishings

Friendly licensees have taken over this partly 15th-c pub, but apart from some re-painting, thankfully little has changed. The heavy-beamed L-shaped bar has pews from the church, red plush banquettes, and old agricultural prints and church pictures on the walls; a smaller bar – where the locals like to gather – has flagstones, a big open hearth fireplace and side bread oven. Dartmoor Brewery Jail Ale and IPA, and Sharps Doom Bar, with a guest such as St Austell Tribute or Skinners Betty Stogs on handpump. Decent bar food is traditional, from lunchtime sandwiches up. This is a pretty Dartmoor-edge village and the pub has seats on the green in front and by the building itself. The ancient oak from which the pub gets its name is just close by.

Free house ~ Licensee Steve Earp ~ Real ale ~ Bar food ~ Restaurant ~ (01822) 852944 ~ Children in lounge bar only ~ Dogs allowed in bar ~ Open 11-3, 6-11; 11-midnight Sat; 11-11 Sun

MOLLAND

London

Village signposted off B3227 E of South Molton, down narrow lanes; EX36 3NG

A proper Exmoor inn with customers and their dogs to match, a warm welcome, honest food, farm cider and real ales

This old-fashioned inn carries on as it has always been – a traditional Exmoor pub with the local farmers and gamekeepers (and their working dogs) being very much the focal part of things. The two small linked rooms by the old-fashioned central servery have hardly changed in 50 years and have local stag-hunting pictures, tough carpeting or rugs on flagstones, cushioned benches and plain chairs around rough stripped trestle tables, a table of shooting and other country magazines, ancient stag and otter trophies, and darts and board games. On the left an attractive beamed room has accounts of the rescued stag which lived a long life at the pub many years ago. A small hall with stuffed birds and animals and lots of overhead baskets has a box of toys. Cotleigh Tawny and Exmoor Ale, farm cider, and several wines by the glass; winter mulled wine and cider. Using local, seasonal produce, bar food includes snacks such as pork crackling, beef dripping on toast, pork pies and so forth and traditional british dishes like steak and kidney suet pudding and rabbit pie. The low-ceilinged lavatories are worth a look, with their Victorian mahogany and tiling (and in the gents' a testament to the prodigious thirst of the village cricket team). The garden is to be spruced up and they hope to use another garden opposite the pub for extra outdoor seating space. Don't miss the next-door church, with its untouched early 18th-c box pews – and in spring, a carpet of tenby daffodils in the graveyard.

Free house ~ Licensees Deborah See and Toby Bennett ~ Real ale ~ Bar food (not winter Sun evening) ~ Restaurant ~ No credit cards ~ (01769) 550269 ~ Children welcome ~ Dogs allowed in bar ~ Open 12-3, 6-11; 12-11 Sun and Sat

NEWTON FERRERS

Dolphin

Riverside Road East – follow Harbour dead end signs; PL8 1AE

Terraces looking down over the River Yealm, a simply furnished bar and local ales

From the two terraces across the lane from this 18th-c pub, there's a grandstand view of the boating action on the busy tidal River Yealm. Inside, the L-shaped bar has a few low black beams, slate floors, some white-painted plank panelling, and simple pub furnishings including cushioned wall benches and small winged settles. It can get packed in summer. Traditional pubby bar food includes chunky sandwiches and beer-battered fish. Badger Tanglefoot, First Gold and a seasonal beer on handpump and ten wines by the glass; euchre Monday evenings and winter Tuesday evening quiz nights. Parking by the pub is very limited, with more chance of a space either below or above. You can walk along the waterfront to the west end of the village.

Badger ~ Tenants Jackie Cosens and Adrian Jenkins ~ Real ale ~ Bar food (12-2.30, 6-9; cream teas all day) ~ (01752) 872007 ~ Children welcome as long as seated and with adults ~ Dogs welcome ~ Open 10am-11pm(10.30pm Sun); 10-2.30, 6-11 Mon-Thurs in winter; closed winter Sun evening

NOMANSLAND

Mount Pleasant

B3137 Tiverton—South Molton; EX16 8NN

Three fireplaces and a mix of furnishings in long bar, fair choice of drinks, and friendly service

Informal and friendly, this is a pleasant place for a drink or meal. The long bar is divided into three with huge fireplaces each end, one with a woodburning stove under a low dark ochre black-beamed ceiling, the other with a big log fire, and there are tables in a sizeable bay window extension. A nice mix of furniture on the patterned carpet includes an old sofa with a throw, old-fashioned leather dining chairs, pale country kitchen chairs and tables all with candles in attractive metal holders; country prints and local photographs including shooting parties, and magazines and daily papers to read. The public bar, with plenty of bar stools, has Cotleigh Tawny and Sharps Doom Bar on handpump, several wines by the glass and Weston's Old Rosie cider. Decent bar food is fairly straightforward. Piped music, darts and board games. There are some picnic-sets in the neat back garden and some in front of the building.

Free house ~ Licensees Anne, Karen and Sarah Butler ~ Real ale ~ Bar food (all day) ~ Restaurant ~ (01884) 860271 ~ Well behaved children welcome ~ Dogs allowed in bar ~ Open 11.30-11; 12-10.30 Sun; closed 25 and 26 Dec, 1 Jan

NOSS MAYO

Ship

Off A379 via B3186, E of Plymouth; PL8 1EW

Busy pub, seats overlooking inlet and visiting boats, thick-walled bars with log fires, west country beers and friendly atmosphere

The front terrace here is extremely popular in fine weather – you can sit at the octagonal wooden tables under parasols and look over the inlet, and visiting boats can tie up alongside (with prior permission); there are outdoor heaters for cooler evenings. Inside, it's very attractively furnished and the two thick-walled bars have a happy mix of dining chairs and tables on the wooden floors, log fires, bookcases, dozens of local pictures, newspapers and magazines to read, and a chatty atmosphere; board games, dominoes and cards. Comprising traditional dishes alongside one or two more imaginative items, bar food here is well liked and popular. Dartmoor Brewery IPA, Summerskills Tamar and a changing guest on handpump, lots of malt whiskies, and quite a few wines by the glass. Parking is restricted at high tide.

Free house ~ Licensees Charlie and Lisa Bullock ~ Real ale ~ Bar food (all day) ~ Restaurant ~ (01752) 872387 ~ Children welcome ~ Dogs allowed in bar ~ Open 11-11; 12-10.30 Sun

PETER TAVY

Peter Tavy Inn

Off A386 near Mary Tavy, N of Tavistock; PL19 9NN

Old stone inn with pretty garden, bustling bar with beams and big log fire, and good choice of food and drink

This is a very well run and friendly pub with an enjoyably bustling atmosphere and helpful, efficient staff. The low-beamed bar has high-backed settles on the black flagstones by the big stone fireplace (a fine log fire on cold days), smaller settles in stone-mullioned windows, and Blackawton Original Bitter, Dartmoor Brewery Jail Ale, Sharps Doom Bar and maybe Cotleigh 25 on handpump; local cider, 30 malt whiskies and several wines by the glass. The good evening menu tends to be a little more imaginative than the popular lunchtime one. There's also a snug dining area and restaurant; maybe piped music. From the picnic-sets in the pretty garden, there are peaceful views of the moor rising above nearby pastures.

Free house ~ Licensees Chris and Joanne Wordingham ~ Real ale ~ Bar food (not 25 Dec, evenings 24-26 Dec and 1 Jan) ~ (01822) 810348 ~ Children welcome ~ Dogs welcome ~ Open 12-3, 6-11(10.30 Sun)

POSTBRIDGE

Warren House

B3212 0.75 miles NE of Postbridge; PL20 6TA

Straightforward old pub, relaxing for a drink or snack after a Dartmoor hike

Friendly and with plenty of atmosphere, this straightforward place is most welcome after a hike on Dartmoor. One of the fireplaces in the cosy bar is said to have been kept alight almost continuously since 1845, and there are simple furnishings like easy chairs and settles under the beamed ochre ceiling, old pictures of the inn on the partly panelled stone walls, and dim lighting (fuelled by the pub's own generator); a family room also. Decent hearty food meets most walkers' needs. Otter Ale, Ringwood Old Thumper, St Austell Tribute and a guest beer on handpump, local farm cider and malt whiskies; piped music, darts and pool. The picnic-sets on both sides of the road have moorland views.

Free house ~ Licensee Peter Parsons ~ Real ale ~ Bar food (all day but more restricted winter Mon and Tues) ~ (01822) 880208 ~ Children in family room ~ Dogs allowed in bar ~ Open 11-11; 12-10.30 Sun; 11-5 Mon and Tues during Nov-Feb

POUNDSGATE

Tavistock Inn

B3357 continuation; TQ13 7NY

Friendly old pub with some original features; lovely scenery and plenty of walkers

There are plenty of moorland hikes that start and finish, or pass, this family-run and picturesque old pub, so many customers are walkers (often with their dogs).

There are tables on the front terrace and pretty flowers in stone troughs, hanging baskets and window boxes and more seats (and ducks) in the quiet back garden; lovely scenery. Inside, some original features include a narrow-stepped granite spiral staircase, original flagstones, ancient log fireplaces, and beams, and there's a friendly atmosphere and a good mix of locals and visitors. Food runs to a short handful of pubby dishes. Courage Best, Otter Ale, and Wychwood Hobgoblin Best on handpump, and several malt whiskies.

Punch ~ Lease Peter and Jean Hamill ~ Real ale ~ Bar food (all day in summer) ~ Restaurant ~ (01364) 631251 ~ Children welcome away from bar ~ Dogs allowed in bar ~ Open 11-11; 12-10.30 Sun; 11-3, 6-11 winter

RATTERY

Church House

Village signposted from A385 W of Totnes, and A38 S of Buckfastleigh; TQ10 9LD

One of Britain's oldest pubs with some fine original features and peaceful views

As this is one of Britain's oldest pubs, it's worth a visit to see some of the fine original features – notably the spiral stone steps behind a little stone doorway on your left as you come in that date from about 1030. There are massive oak beams and standing timbers in the homely open-plan bar, large fireplaces (one with a little cosy nook partitioned off around it), windsor armchairs, comfortable seats and window seats, and prints on the plain white walls; the dining room is separated from this room by heavy curtains and there's also a lounge area too. Otter Ale, Dartmoor Brewery Jail Ale, St Austell Dartmoor Best, and a guest such as Teignworthy Reel Ale on handpump, quite a few malt whiskies and several wines by the glass. The menu is pretty traditional, it includes a fry-up and battered cod. The garden has picnic-sets on the large hedged-in lawn, and peaceful views of the partly wooded surrounding hills.

Free house ~ Licensee Ray Hardy ~ Real ale ~ Bar food ~ Restaurant ~ (01364) 642220 ~ Children welcome ~ Dogs allowed in bar ~ Open 11-2.30, 6-11; 12-2.30, 6-10.30 Sun

SANDY PARK

Sandy Park Inn

A382 Whiddon Down—Moretonhampstead; TQ13 8JW

Busy little thatched inn with snug bars and attractive bedrooms

With no intrusions from machines or music, the atmosphere in this little thatched inn is relaxed and chatty. The small bar on the right has rugs on the black-painted composition floor, black beams in the cream ceiling, varnished built-in wall settles forming separate areas around nice tables, and high stools by the chatty bar counter with Otter Ale, St Austell Tribute and guests such as Exe Valley Bitter and O'Hanlons Yellowhammer on handpump, and a decent choice of wines by the glass. The back snug has one big table that a dozen people could just squeeze around, stripped stone walls, and a cream-painted bright-cushioned built-in wall bench. Food is gently imaginative, enjoyable and atttractively presented. There are seats by outdoor heaters in the large garden with fine views.

Free house ~ Licensee Nic Rout ~ Real ale ~ Bar food (12-2.30(4 Sun), 6.30-9) ~ Restaurant ~ (01647) 433267 ~ Children welcome ~ Dogs allowed in bar and bedrooms ~ Open 11(12 Sun)-11 ~ Bedrooms: £55B/£96B

SIDBURY

Hare & Hounds

3 miles N of Sidbury, at Putts Corner; A375 towards Honiton, crossroads with B3174; EX10 0QQ

Large well run roadside pub with log fires, beams and attractive layout, popular daily carvery, efficient staff, and big garden

This extremely popular and very well run roadside pub serves food all day though the carvery is at mealtimes only (except Sunday when it's all day). It's much bigger inside than you could have guessed from outside and there are two good log fires (and rather unusual wood-framed leather sofas complete with pouffes), heavy beams and fresh flowers throughout, some oak panelling, plenty of tables with red leatherette or red plush-cushioned dining chairs, window seats and well used bar stools, too; it's mostly carpeted, with some bare boards and stripped stone walls. At the opposite end, on the left, another big dining area has huge windows looking out over the garden. Branscombe Best Bitter and Otter Bitter and Ale tapped from the cask, local farm cider and several wines by the glass; a side room has a big-screen sports TV and games machine. The big garden, giving nice valley views, has picnic-sets, a children's play area and a marquee, and there may be a small strolling flock of peafowl.

Free house ~ Licensees Graham Cole and Lindsey Chun ~ Real ale ~ Bar food (all day) ~ Restaurant ~ (01404) 41760 ~ Children welcome ~ Dogs allowed in bar ~ Open 10am-11pm; 12-10.30 Sun

TORBRYAN

Old Church House

Most easily reached from A381 Newton Abbot—Totnes via Ipplepen; TQ12 5UR

Ancient inn with lovely original features, neat rooms, friendly service and well liked tasty food

Much enjoyed by both locals and visitors, this is a cheerfully run old pub with bags of atmosphere. The particularly attractive bar on the right of the door is neatly kept and bustling and has benches built into the fine old panelling as well as a cushioned high-backed settle and leather-backed small seats around its big log fire. On the left there is a series of comfortable and discreetly lit lounges, one with a splendid deep Tudor inglenook fireplace with a side bread oven; piped music. Skinners Betty Stogs and Cornish Knocker on handpump, 30 malt whiskies, and several wines by the glass. Friendly staff serve generous helpings of good pubby food; friendly service. Plenty of nearby walks.

Free house ~ Licensees Kane and Carolynne Clarke ~ Real ale ~ Bar food ~

Restaurant ~ (01803) 812372 ~ Children welcome ~ Dogs allowed in bar and
bedrooms ~ Live music Sun evenings ~ Open 11-11 ~ Bedrooms: £54B/£79B

TUCKENHAY

Maltsters Arms

*Take Ashprington road out of Totnes (signed left off A381 on outskirts), keeping
on past Watermans Arms; TQ9 7EQ*

**Lovely spot by wooded creek with tables by the water, a good choice of drinks
and varied food**

In fine weather, you can really appreciate this pub's lovely position by a peaceful wooded creek; there are tables by the water, summer barbecues and regular
live music concerts on the quayside. Inside, the long, narrow bar links two other
rooms – a small snug one with an open fire and plenty of bric-a-brac and another
with red-painted vertical seats and kitchen chairs on the wooden floor; there are
nautical charts and local photographs on the walls. The menu is thoughtfully put
together, with platters of meats, cheeses, and a range of dishes such as sausage
and mash or smoked chicken and duck pâté with elderberry and apple jelly.
Adnams Explorer, Batemans XB Bitter, Dartmoor Brewery IPA and maybe a guest
beer on handpump, 20 wines by the glass, seven kinds of kir, and local farm
cider and perry; they keep several varieties of snuff. Darts, board games and
maybe TV for sports.

Free house ~ Licensees Denise and Quentin Thwaites ~ Real ale ~ Bar food
(12-3, 7-9.30) ~ Restaurant ~ (01803) 732350 ~ Children welcome (not in bar
or main part of restaurant) ~ Dogs welcome ~ Open 11-11; closed evening
25 Dec ~ Bedrooms: /£75S(£95B)

WIDECOMBE

Rugglestone

*Village at end of B3387; pub just S – turn left at church and NT church house,
OS Sheet 191 map reference 720765; TQ13 7TF*

**Unspoilt local near busy tourist village with just a couple of bars, cheerful
customers and homely food**

The small bar in this unspoilt local has a strong country atmosphere and plenty
of cheerful customers. There are just four tables, a few window and wall seats,
a one-person pew built into the corner by the nice old stone fireplace, and a
rudimentary bar counter dispensing Bays Gold, Butcombe Bitter, St Austell
Dartmoor Best, and a guest beer tapped from the cask; local farm cider and a
decent little wine list. The room on the right is a bit bigger and lighter-feeling
with another stone fireplace, beamed ceiling, stripped pine tables, and a built-
in wall bench. Well liked bar food is traditional and tasty. The pub is in rural
surroundings – though just up the road from the bustling tourist village – and
if you sit outside in the field, across the little moorland stream, where there are
lots of picnic-sets, you might be joined by some wild dartmoor ponies. Tables
and chairs in the garden, too. They now have a holiday cottage for rent.

Free house ~ Licensees Richard Palmer and Vicky Moore ~ Real ale ~ Bar food ~ (01364) 621327 ~ Children allowed but must be away from bar area ~ Dogs welcome ~ Open 11.30-3, 6-midnight; 11.30am-midnight Sat; 12-11 Sun

WINKLEIGH

Kings Arms

Village signposted off B3220 Crediton—Torrington; Fore Street; EX19 8HQ

Friendly pub with woodburning stoves in beamed bar

On the edge of the little village square, this is a friendly thatched pub with a happy mix of customers. The attractive beamed main bar has some old-fashioned built-in wall settles, scrubbed pine tables and benches on the flagstones and a woodburning stove in a cavernous fireplace; another woodburning stove separates the bar from the dining rooms (one has military memorabilia and a mine shaft). Their popular pubby food and cream teas are served all day. Butcombe Bitter and Sharps Cornish Coaster and Doom Bar on handpump, local cider and several wines by the glass; darts and board games. There are seats out in the garden.

Enterprise ~ Lease Chris Guy and Julia Franklin ~ Real ale ~ Bar food (all day) ~ Restaurant ~ (01837) 83384 ~ Children welcome ~ Dogs allowed in bar ~ Open 11-11; 12-10.30 Sun

YEALMPTON

Rose & Crown

A379 Kingsbridge—Plymouth; PL8 2EB

Smart modern place, plenty of dark wood and heavy brass, neat staff, enjoyable bar food

Whether you are after a meal or just a drink, this is a civilised and stylish place for either. The big central bar counter, all dark wood and heavy brass with good solid leather-seated bar stools, has Otter Ale, St Austell Tribute and Sharps Doom Bar on handpump, quite a few wines by the glass and a fine choice of other drinks too; quick, friendly service by neatly aproned black-dressed staff. There's an attractive mix of tables and old dining chairs, good lighting, and some leather sofas down on the left. With its stripped wood floor and absence of curtains and other soft furnishings, the open-plan bar's acoustics are lively; beige carpeting keeps the two dining areas on the right rather quieter and here smart leather high-backed dining chairs, flowers on the tablecloths and framed 1930s high-life posters take you a notch or two upscale. Food from two menus – one quite pubby and the other more elaborate – is very well prepared, and they do a good value two- and three-course set menu (not Sunday lunch or Friday or Saturday evenings).

Enterprise ~ Lease Simon Warner ~ Real ale ~ Bar food ~ Restaurant ~ (01752) 880223 ~ Children welcome ~ Dogs allowed in bar ~ Open 12-3, 6.30-11; 12-10.30 Sun

DOG FRIENDLY HOTELS, INNS, B&Bs AND FARMS

APPLEDORE

West Farm

Irsha Street, Appledore, Bideford, Devon EX39 1RY (01237) 425269

£94; 3 lovely rms. 17th-c townhouse, just 20 paces from the sea, with antiques and fresh flowers in homely sitting room and elegant dining room, open fires, very friendly, helpful owners, super breakfasts, and nearby pubs and restaurants for evening meals; dogs in one bedroom with door to garden

ASHBURTON

Roborough House

85 East Street, Ashburton, Devon TQ13 7AL (01364) 654614

£68; 3 individually furnished rms. Handsome listed townhouse with welcoming staff, a relaxed, informal atmosphere and particularly good west country breakfasts using as much organic produce as possible; large romantic garden with small Victorian knot maze, large lawned area plus a safe children's garden which has a bouncy castle; lots of places in village for evening meals; resident golden retriever; dogs in bedrooms

ASHWATER

Blagdon Manor

Ashwater, Beaworthy, Devon EX21 5DF (01409) 211224

£135; 8 pretty rms. Standing in rolling countryside, this carefully restored and tranquil 17th-c manor has 20 acres of grounds including three acres of gardens; beams and flagstones, log fires and fresh flowers in the bar and lounge, comfortable library, delicious food cooked by the owner using the best local produce and some from their own garden, big breakfasts in airy conservatory, and genuinely warm welcome; two resident chocolate labradors; cl Jan, one week autumn; children over 12; dogs welcome away from restaurant; treats, own blanket, towel and bowl; £7.50

BAMPTON

Bark House

Oakford Bridge, Bampton, Devon EX16 9HZ (01398) 351236

£97; 6 cottagey rms. Charming hotel with lovely rural views, garden, and plenty of surrounding walks; caring, hospitable owners, open fires and low beams in comfortable homely sitting and dining rooms, delicious food using local produce, a thoughtful wine list, and super breakfasts; two resident dogs; dogs in bedrooms; £4

BIGBURY-ON-SEA

Henley

Folly Hill, Bigbury-on-Sea, Kingsbridge, Devon TQ7 4AR (01548) 810240

£96; 5 compact rms. Renovated Edwardian cottage with fine views of Avon estuary, Burgh Island, and beyond; lounge and conservatory dining room with magnificent sea views, deep wicker chairs and polished furniture, binoculars and books, good, enjoyable food from small menu, super breakfasts, and steep, private path down the cliff to a sandy bay where dogs may walk; cl end Oct–mid-Mar; resident dog; children over 12; dogs in bedrooms only; £4

BOLBERRY

Port Light

Bolberry, Salcombe, Devon TQ7 3DY (01548) 561384

£100; 6 pleasant rms with lovely sea views. Clifftop former RAF radar station (an easy walk from Hope Cove) with a warmly friendly welcome, good home-made food (super fresh fish) in attractive bar and restaurant, woodburner, and good outdoor children's play area; 20 acre NT field borders the garden; cl Jan; dogs welcome

BOVEY TRACEY

Edgemoor Hotel

Haytor Road, Bovey Tracey, Newton Abbot, Devon TQ13 9LE (3.3 miles off A38; B3344 from Chudleigh Knighton, then keep on into B3387) (01626) 832466

£140; 16 charming rms. Ivy-covered country house (about to change hands as we went to press) in neatly kept gardens on the edge of Dartmoor; comfortable lounge and bar, log fires, good modern english cooking in elegant restaurant; resident dogs; walks in grounds and on Dartmoor; no children; limited disabled access; dogs in Woodland Wing bedrooms with back door leading to private patio

BRADWORTHY

Lake Villa

Bradworthy, Devon EX22 7SQ (01409) 241962

£56; 2 rms with garden or country views. 300-year-old farmhouse offering a warm welcome from the friendly owners to well-behaved pets (and their owners); gardens, tennis court and barbecue equipment, and nearby common for dog exercise; walking holidays arranged, and self-catering also; resident springer spaniel and cocker spaniel; cl Christmas; dogs in bedrooms

BUDLEIGH SALTERTON

Downderry House

10 Exmouth Road, Budleigh Salterton, Devon EX9 6AQ (01395) 442663

£89; 5 lovely carefully furnished rms. Neatly kept and most attractive 1920s house close to seafront, with an acre of garden, and plenty of nearby walks; restful drawing room with honesty bar, afternoon tea on arrival, very good breakfasts, supper tray on request, and light and airy dining room overlooking gardens; resident beagle and cat; children over 10; disabled access; dogs in ground floor bedroom only; £5

CHAGFORD

Easton Court

Sandy Park, Chagford, Newton Abbot, Devon TQ13 8JN (01647) 433469

£80; 5 comfortable rms. Extended Tudor thatched longhouse in four acres of gardens and paddocks, with a relaxed and informal atmosphere, hearty breakfasts in guest lounge/breakfast room, helpful, friendly owners, and lots to do nearby; two resident dogs; nearby restaurants and plenty of surrounding pubs; children over 10; partial disabled access; dogs in some bedrooms; £2.50

Gidleigh Park

Chagford, Newton Abbot, Devon TQ13 8HH (01647) 432367

£310; 25 opulent and individual rms (recently refurbished) with flowers and fruit. Exceptional and luxurious Dartmoor-edge mock Tudor hotel with deeply comfortable panelled drawing room, wonderful flowers, conservatory overlooking the fine grounds (54 acres, with walks straight up on to the moor), log fires, exceptional food and a marvellous wine list, and caring staff; children over 8 in restaurant; disabled access; dogs in some bedrooms only

CLAWTON

Court Barn Hotel

Clawton, Holsworthy, Devon EX22 6PS (01409) 271219

£90; 7 individually furnished rms. Charming country house in three acres of pretty gardens with croquet, nine-hole putting green, small chip-and-putt course, and tennis and badminton courts; comfortable lounges, log fires, library/TV room, bar, good service, imaginative food and super wines (and teas), and a quiet relaxed atmosphere; walks in grounds and surrounding country lanes; they are kind to families; cl 2-10 Jan; dogs in bedrooms only with bowls and treats; £4

COUNTISBURY

Blue Ball Inn

Countisbury, Lynton, Devon EX35 6NE (01598) 741263

£70; 16 rms. 13th-c inn surrounded by fine scenery and many walks with five fireplaces in comfortable low ceilinged lounge areas and bar, enjoyable food using fresh local produce, local beers, and a warm welcome; two resident dogs; dogs welcome

DARTMOUTH

Knocklayd

Redoubt Hill, Kingswear, Dartmouth, Devon TQ6 0DA (01803) 752873

£90; 3 comfortable rms. Friendly and very homely small guest house with panoramic views over Dartmouth and the river; hospitable owners, open fire in sitting room, garden room with french windows on to the lawn, and dinner party-style meals and good breakfasts in separate dining room; one sociable resident dog; dogs welcome

Royal Castle

11 The Quay, Dartmouth, Devon TQ6 9PS (01803) 833033

£155; 25 individually furnished, charming rms. Well restored mainly Georgian hotel (part 16th c) overlooking the inner harbour – great views from most rooms; lively and interesting public bar with open fires and beams, quiet library/lounge with antiques, drawing room overlooking the quayside, winter spit-roasts in lounge bar, elegant upstairs river view restaurant, decent bar food, and friendly staff; walks in nearby park and more beyond; resident dog; dogs in some bedrooms and bars; bedding and treats; £10

EXETER

Barcelona Hotel

Magdalen Street, Exeter, Devon EX2 4HY (01392) 281000

£140; 46 beautifully furnished rms with CD-player and video, and lovely bthrms. Stylishly modern, converted Victorian eye hospital filled with bright posters and paintings, a bar with 1950s-style furniture and fashionable cocktails, a smart but informal restaurant overlooking the big walled garden, good contemporary food, a nightclub, and very helpful staff; walks in nearby park; disabled access; dogs in bedrooms (not to be left unattended) and on lead in hotel; £15

Edwardian Hotel

30-32 Heavitree Road, Exeter, Devon EX1 2LQ (01392) 276102

£75; 13 individually furnished rms, 2 with four-posters. Popular guesthouse close to cathedral and city centre, with pretty lounge, enjoyable breakfasts in attractive dining rooms, and warm and friendly resident owners; plenty of places nearby for evening meals; park opposite for dog walking; resident dog; partial disabled access; dogs in bedrooms (not to be left unattended); £10

GITTISHAM

Combe House

Gittisham, Honiton, Devon EX14 3AD (2 miles off A30 at W end of Honiton bypass) (01404) 540400

£170; 15 individually decorated pretty rms with lovely views, plus cottage with private walled garden. Peaceful, Grade I listed, Elizabethan country hotel in gardens with spectacular views and walks around the 3,500-acre estate; grand public rooms with fine panelling, antiques, portraits, log fires and fresh flowers, a happy relaxed atmosphere, very good food, super breakfasts, and fine wines; resident cat; dogs in some bedrooms and public rooms (not restaurant); bedding; £8

GULWORTHY

Horn of Plenty

Gulworthy, Tavistock, Devon PL19 8JD (3 miles off A386, via A390 from Tavistock) (01822) 832528

£195; 10 lovely rms with personal touches, 6 in Garden House annexe with french windows to walled gardens. Luxury restaurant-with-rooms in five acres of gardens and orchards with wonderful views; drawing room with log fires and fresh flowers, separate lounge, delicious modern cooking (and super breakfasts) in glass-fronted restaurant using their own organic vegetables and fruit, and friendly, relaxed atmosphere; cookery courses; cl Christmas; disabled access; dogs in Garden Rooms; £10

HAWKCHURCH

Fairwater Head Country House

Hawkchurch, Axminster, Devon EX13 5TX (01297) 678349

£120; 16 rms most with country views. Edwardian hotel in quiet, flower-filled gardens with genuinely friendly, attentive owners and staff, open fire in comfortable lounge hall, drawing room, sitting room and sunny morning room, well stocked bar and wine cellar, and enjoyable food; resident spring/cocker spaniel; walks in garden and surrounding countryside; cl Jan; disabled access; dogs welcome away from restaurant

HAYTOR VALE

Rock Inn

Haytor Vale, Newton Abbot, Devon TQ13 9XP (01364) 661305

£88; 9 individual rms. Civilised old coaching inn on edge of Dartmoor National Park, with very good lunchtime and evening food, nice mix of visitors and locals in the two rooms of panelled bar, open fires, courteous service, and big garden;

walking on moor, fishing, riding and golf nearby; cl 25 and 26 Dec; disabled access; dogs in some bedrooms; £5.50

HEXWORTHY
Forest Inn

Hexworthy, Princetown, Yelverton, Devon PL20 6SD (01364) 631211

£75; 10 cosy, comfortable rms. Country inn in fine Dartmoor setting, popular with walkers and anglers; varied menu in both bar and restaurant, local ales, good choice of wines, log fire in lounge area, and welcoming staff; two resident dogs; cl 25 and 26 Dec; dogs welcome (but must be on lead); treats

ILFRACOMBE
Strathmore

57 St Brannock's Road, Ilfracombe, Devon EX34 8EQ (01271) 862248

£65; 8 pretty rms. Victorian hotel close to the town centre and beach with comfortable, well stocked lounge bar, hearty breakfasts in attractive dining room, welcoming owners and staff, and terraced garden; resident sheltie; plenty of nearby walks; cl Christmas-end Jan; dogs in bedrooms; own personal letter and big breakfasts of bacon/sausage; £5

LEWDOWN
Lewtrenchard Manor

Lewdown, Okehampton, Devon EX20 4PN (01566) 783256

£195; 14 well equipped rms with fresh flowers and period furniture. Lovely Elizabethan manor house in garden with fine dovecote and surrounded by peaceful estate with shooting, fishing and croquet – and walks; dark panelling, ornate ceilings, antiques, fresh flowers, and log fires, friendly welcome, relaxed atmosphere, and candlelit restaurant with very good imaginative food (cooked by the chef/patron) using produce from their walled garden; resident dog; children over 8 in evening restaurant; partial disabled access; dogs in bedrooms (must not be left alone); £10

LIFTON
Arundell Arms

Fore Street, Lifton, Devon PL16 0AA (a mile off A30, at A388 turn-off)
(01566) 784666

£170; 21 well equipped rms. Carefully renovated old coaching inn with 20 miles of its own waters – salmon and trout fishing and long-established fly-fishing school; comfortable sitting room, log fires, super food in both bar and elegant restaurant, carefully chosen wines, and kind service from staff; attractive terraced garden (where dogs may walk) and walks in nearby playing fields; cl three nights over Christmas; dogs welcome away from restaurant; bowls and food on request; £5

MALBOROUGH

Soar Mill Cove Hotel

Malborough, Salcombe, Devon TQ7 3DS (01548) 561566

£238; 21 comfortable rms that open on to garden. Neatly kept single-storey hotel in idyllic spot by peaceful and very beautiful cove on NT coast with lovely views, ten acres of grounds, tennis/putting, and warm indoor pool; well trained, kind staff, imaginative meals in restaurant with stunning view, coffee shop, bars and lounge and they are kind to children of all ages; excellent walks all around and also a dog walk map; cl Jan; two resident dogs; disabled access; dogs in bedrooms and coffee shop; sausage at breakfast

MEMBURY

Lea Hill

Membury, Axminster, Devon EX13 7AQ (01404) 881881

£75; individually furnished rms. Thatched 14th-c longhouse in 8 acres of secluded grounds and lovely views; comfortable and cosy guest lounge with books and helpful information, beamed dining room with woodburning stove, relaxed and friendly owners, good breakfasts, and light suppers by arrangement; resident dog and cat; self-catering, too; footpaths from the grounds for walks; dogs in bedrooms and guest lounge (if other guests are agreeable); £5

MORETONHAMPSTEAD

Great Sloncombe Farm

Moretonhampstead, Newton Abbot, Devon TQ13 8QF (01647) 440595

£70; 3 rms – the big double is the favourite. Lovely 13th-c farmhouse on working stock farm, with friendly owners, carefully polished old-fashioned furniture in oak-beamed lounge with woodburning stove in inglenook; games and books, hearty breakfasts, relaxed atmosphere, and good nearby walking and bird-watching; children over 8; dogs welcome in bedrooms

NORTH BOVEY

Gate House

North Bovey, Newton Abbot, Devon TQ13 8RB (01647) 440479

£76; 3 charming rms. 15th-c thatched and beamed cottage in picturesque village, with huge granite fireplace in attractive sitting room, breakfasts and candlelit evening meals in dining room, tea with home-made cakes, friendly owners, and outdoor swimming pool in peaceful garden; plenty to do nearby and walks down to the river; cl Christmas; no children; dogs in bedrooms only; must be fed outside

NORTHAM

Yeoldon House

Durrant Lane, Northam, Bideford, Devon EX39 2RL (01237) 474400

£115; 10 individually decorated rms. Quietly set hotel in two acres of grounds by the River Torridge, with warmly friendly and relaxed atmosphere, comfortable lounge, good food using local produce in attractive dining room, and helpful service; resident dog; plenty of walks; lots to do nearby; cl Christmas; dogs in bedrooms (not to be left unattended); £5

PARKHAM

Penhaven

Rectory Lane, Parkham, Bideford, Devon EX39 5PL (01237) 451711

£110; 12 spacious rms. Former rectory in ten acres of lovely grounds with plenty of wildlife – the local badgers come on to the lawn at night; friendly, peaceful atmosphere, big fire in the lounge, and good seasonal food using local produce in the dining room that overlooks the wood and garden; walks in grounds; self-catering cottages; two resident dogs; dogs in bedrooms only; £7

POSTBRIDGE

Lydgate House

Postbridge, Yelverton, Devon PL20 6TJ (01822) 880209

£126; 7 rms. Friendly and relaxed Victorian country house in secluded wild Dartmoor valley spot (lots of wildlife and own 36 acres), with log fire in comfortable sitting room, enjoyable homely cooking in candlelit conservatory dining room, and fine breakfasts (light lunches and picnics are available); good walks from the door; resident dog; no children; dogs in bedrooms and guest lounge; £5

SALCOMBE

Tides Reach

Cliff Road, South Sands, Salcombe, Devon TQ8 8LJ (01548) 843466

£250 inc dinner; 35 rms, many with estuary views. Unusually individual resort hotel run by long-serving owners in pretty wooded cove by the sea, with airy, spreading day rooms, cocktail bar, good restaurant food using fresh local produce, friendly efficient service, and leisure complex, health area, and big heated pool; windsurfing etc, beach over lane, and lots of coast walks; resident dog; cl Dec-Jan; children over 8; disabled access; dogs in bedrooms; £8.50

SANDY PARK

Mill End

Sandy Park, Chagford, Newton Abbot, Devon TQ13 8JN (3.5 miles off A30, via A382) (01647) 432282

£150; 14 attractive rms with fine bthrms and views. Quietly set former flour mill with waterwheel in 15 acres of neatly kept grounds below Dartmoor and 600 yards of private salmon and trout fishing, access to miles of game fishing and still-water fishing on local lakes; comfortable lounges, carefully prepared interesting food, fine breakfasts, cream teas on the lawn, and good service; two resident dogs and one cat; plenty of surrounding walks (they provide a map); cl two weeks Jan; children over 12 in restaurant; partial disabled access; dogs in bedrooms; treats, towels, leads, bowls and so forth; £10

SHEEPWASH

Half Moon

Sheepwash, Beaworthy, Devon EX21 5NE (01409) 231376

£90; 11 newly refurbished rms inc some in converted stables. Civilised heart-of-Devon hideaway in colourful village square with 10 miles of private salmon, sea trout and brown trout fishing on the Torridge (rod room and drying facilities) and plenty of surrounding walks; neatly kept friendly bar, solid old furnishings and big log fire, attractive separate dining room, good food and wine, and real ales; two resident cats; limited disabled access; dogs welcome away from dining room; £5

SIDFORD

Salty Monk

Church Street, Sidford, Exeter, Devon EX10 9QP (01395) 513174

£110; 5 attractive rms, some with spa baths. Very popular 16th-c former salt house (where monks trading in salt stayed on their way to Exeter) with leather armchairs in comfortable lounge, imaginative food using local produce cooked by chef/patron, and quiet garden; two resident water spaniels; nearby walks; cl Jan, two weeks Nov; disabled access; dogs in bedrooms (though not to be left unattended); doggy welcome pack; £20

SOUTH ZEAL

Oxenham Arms

South Zeal, Okehampton, Devon EX20 2JT (01837) 840244

£110; 7 rms. Grandly atmospheric old inn dating back to 12th c and first licensed in 1477 (a neolithic standing stone still forms part of the wall in the back bar); elegant beamed and panelled bar with chatty relaxed atmosphere and open fire, popular food, and charming ex-monastery small garden; walks nearby; resident dogs; dogs welcome away from dining room; £5

STAVERTON

Sea Trout

Staverton, Totnes, Devon TQ9 6PA (1.9 miles off A384; village signed from just W of Dartington) (01803) 762274

£92; 10 cottagey rms. Comfortable pub – recent change of management – in quiet hamlet near River Dart with two relaxed beamed bars, log fires, well liked food in lounge and airy dining conservatory, real ales, and terraced garden; plenty of surrounding walks; dogs in bedrooms; £3.50

STOCKLAND

Kings Arms

Stockland, Honiton, Devon EX14 9BS (2.4 miles off A30 in Yarcombe; village signposted) (01404) 881361

£75; 3 rms. Cream-faced thatched pub with elegant rooms, open fires, first-class food in bar and evening restaurant, and interesting wine list; skittle alley; plenty of walks from front door; dogs in bedrooms and bar

THURLESTONE

Thurlestone Hotel

Thurlestone, Kingsbridge, Devon TQ7 3NN (01548) 560382

£206; 64 comfortable rms, many with sea or country views. Owned by the same family since 1896, this well run hotel is in lovely grounds with marvellous views over the coast; tennis and squash courts, badminton court, swimming pool, golf course, and super play area for children; stylish and spacious public rooms, relaxing cocktail bar, imaginative food in attractive restaurant, and courteous helpful staff; marvellous nearby beaches and walks, and fishing, riding, and sailing on request; disabled access; dogs in some bedrooms; £6

TORQUAY

Orestone Manor

Rockhouse Lane, Maidencombe, Torquay, Devon TQ14SX (01803) 328098

£135; 12 individually decorated rms, most with sea views. Elegant country house in fine setting surrounded by mature gardens and overlooking Lyme Bay; colonial-style, comfortable public rooms, a relaxed atmosphere, attentive staff, and excellent contemporary british cooking using home-grown produce and local seafood; outdoor swimming pool; dogs in bedrooms; £5

TWO BRIDGES

Prince Hall

Two Bridges, Yelverton, Devon PL20 6SA (01822) 890403

£160; 9 attractive spacious rms. Surrounded by Dartmoor National Park, this tranquil 18th-c country house is run by caring friendly owners and their helpful staff; lovely views from convivial bar, comfortable sitting room, and cosy dining room, open fires, very good evening meals and enjoyable breakfasts, and lots of fine walks in 45 acres of grounds; two resident dogs; cl Jan; no children; dogs welcome away from restaurant; treats from reception

DOG FRIENDLY PUBS

MIDDLEMARSH

Hunters Moon

A352 Sherborne—Dorchester; DT9 5QN

Plenty of bric-a-brac in several linked areas, reasonably priced food, and a good choice of drinks

Readers continue to enjoy this cosy pub, which has remained largely unchanged since the present licensee took over in autumn 2007. The comfortably welcoming interior rambles around in several linked areas, with a great variety of tables and chairs, plenty of bric-a-brac from decorative teacups, china ornaments and glasses through horse tack and brassware, to quite a collection of miniature spirit bottles. Beams, some panelling, soft lighting from converted oil lamps, three log fires (one in an inglenook), and the way that some attractively cushioned settles form booths all combine to give a cosy relaxed feel. Bar food is pubby and includes some 'smaller appetite meals'. Butcombe Bitter and a couple of guests such as Greene King Old Speckled Hen and Ringwood Fortyniner on handpump; faint piped music; children's books, colouring pads and puzzles; board games. A neat lawn has circular picnic-sets as well as the more usual ones, and the en-suite bedrooms are in what was formerly a skittle alley and stable block.

Enterprise ~ Lease Dean and Emma Mortimer ~ Real ale ~ Bar food (12-2, 6-9.30(9 Sun)) ~ (01963) 210966 ~ Children welcome ~ Dogs welcome ~ Open 11.30-3, 6-11; closed 25 and 26 Dec ~ Bedrooms: £55S/£65S

MUDEFORD

Ship in Distress

Stanpit; off B3059 at roundabout; BH23 3NA

Wide choice of fish dishes, nautical décor, and friendly staff in cheerful cottage

A splendidly quirky and welcoming place, this former smugglers' haunt is well worth the effort of finding, whether to sample the real ales or for a meal. Adnams, Ringwood Best Bitter are served on handpump alongside a couple of guests such as Brains Bread of Heaven and Daleside Old Legover and that change about three times a week; 12 wines by the glass. It is crammed with nautical bric-a-brac from rope fancywork and brassware through lanterns, oars and ceiling nets and ensigns, to an aquarium, boat models (we particularly like the Mississippi steamboat), and the odd piratical figure; darts, games machine, board games, a couple of TV sets and piped music. Besides a good few boat pictures, the room on the right has masses of snapshots of locals caught up in various waterside japes, under its glass tabletops. Enjoyable fresh local fish and seafood is the thing here, and they've more expensive à la carte offerings (which you can eat in the bar or in the restaurant). There are tables out on the suntrap back terrace.

Punch ~ Tenants Colin Pond and Maggie Wheeler ~ Real ale ~ Bar food ~ Restaurant ~ (01202) 485123 ~ Children welcome ~ Dogs allowed in bar ~ Open 10am-midnight; 11-11 Sun

NETTLECOMBE
Marquis of Lorne
Off A3066 Bridport—Beaminster, via W Milton; DT6 3SY

Tasty food and beer in welcoming country pub in beautiful countryside, with large, mature garden

The bars and dining rooms in this friendly 16th-c former farmhouse are named after local hills, one after Eggardon Hill, the site of one of Dorset's most spectacular Iron-Age hill forts, which is within walking distance. The comfortable bustling main bar has a log fire, mahogany panelling and old prints and photographs around its neatly matching chairs and tables; two dining areas lead off, the smaller of which has another log fire. The wooden-floored snug (liked by locals) has cribbage, dominoes, board games and table skittles. In addition to tasty sandwiches and winter ploughman's, the menu includes fillet steaks from a local farm and other very pubby dishes. Three real ales from Palmers are well kept on handpump, with Copper, IPA and 200, and Tally Ho in winter, a decent wine list with several by the glass. The maturing big garden is full of pretty herbaceous borders, and has a rustic-style play area among the picnic-sets under its apple trees.

Palmers ~ Tenants David and Julie Woodroffe ~ Real ale ~ Bar food (12-2.30, 7-9.30(9 winter)) ~ Restaurant ~ (01308) 485236 ~ No children under 10 in bedrooms ~ Dogs allowed in bar ~ Open 11-11

OSMINGTON MILLS
Smugglers
off A353 NE of Weymouth; DT3 6HF

Centuries-old inn useful for the coastal path; copes well with the peak-time crowds

Open all day, this family-friendly inn is very efficiently run, even when crowded in summer, when the garden really comes into its own. There are picnic sets out on crazy paving by a little stream, with a thatched summer bar (which offers Pimms and plates of smoked salmon) and a good play area (including a little assault course) beneath a steep lawn. Inside, woodwork divides the spacious bar into cosy, welcoming areas, with logs burning in two open stoves and old local pictures scattered about, and various quotes and words of wisdom painted on the wall ('a day without wine is a day without sunshine'). Some seats are tucked into alcoves and window embrasures. The games machines are kept sensibly out of the way; piped music. Pubby bar food is handily served all day, and they will do smaller helpings for children. Three ales from Badger feature Tanglefoot and a seasonal brew like Fursty Ferret on handpump.

Badger ~ Manager Sonia Henderson ~ Real ale ~ Bar food (12-10(9 winter)) ~ (01305) 833125 ~ Children welcome ~ Dogs allowed in bar ~ Open 11-11; 12-10.30 Sun

PAMPHILL

Vine

Off B3082 on NW edge of Wimborne: turn on to Cowgrove Hill at Cowgrove signpost, then turn right up Vine Hill; BH21 4EE

Charming and unchanging, run by the same family for three generations

This well-cared-for little place will delight those who take pleasure in individual, simple country pubs. Frequented by locals but also welcoming to visitors, it's been run by the same family for three generations but is actually owned by the National Trust as part of the Kingston Lacy estate. Of its two tiny bars one, with a warm coal-effect gas fire, has only three tables, the other just half a dozen or so seats on its lino floor, some of them huddling under the stairs that lead up via narrow wooden steps to an upstairs games room; darts and board games. Local photographs (look out for the one of the regular with his giant pumpkin) and notices decorate the painted panelling; quiet piped music. Two real ales include one on handpump and one served from the cask, from brewers such as Fullers, Goddards or Ringwood; farm cider. Bar food is limited to lunchtime bar snacks such as good, fresh sandwiches and ploughman's. There are picnic-sets and benches out on a sheltered gravel terrace and more share a fairy-lit, heated verandah with a grapevine. Round the back a patch of grass has a climbing frame; outside lavatories. The National Trust estate includes Kingston Lacy house and the huge Badbury Rings Iron-Age hill fort (itself good for wild flowers), and there are many paths. They don't accept credit cards or cheques.

Free house ~ Licensee Mrs Sweatland ~ Real ale ~ Bar food (11(12 Sun)-2; not evenings) ~ No credit cards ~ (01202) 882259 ~ Well behaved children in upper room (not evenings) ~ Dogs welcome ~ Open 11(12 Sun)-3, 7-10.30(11 Sat)

PIDDLETRENTHIDE

European

B3143 N of Dorchester; DT2 7QT

Mellow, civilised and intimate dining pub with a fresh rustic look, caring staff and thoughtfully presented food

This modest-looking inn has recently been completely transformed. The two opened-up linked beamed rooms are attractively furnished with quite a mix of dining chairs, lit church candles on all sorts of wooden tables, little country cushions on the comfortable, mushroom-coloured built-in wall seats, pretty window blinds, and nicely worn rugs on terracotta tiles. The yellow walls are hung with duck and hunting prints, fishy plates and a couple of fox masks, and there are interesting fresh flower arrangements, hand-made walking sticks for sale, newspapers to read and maybe one or more of the pub dogs on a cushion in front of the woodburning stove in the sandstone fireplace. Very good food, imaginative but by no means over elaborate, is carefully prepared using some produce from their own farm and game from local estate. Butcombe, Palmers Copper and a guest from a brewer such as Hidden Brewery on handpump, good wines by the glass, home-made elderflower cordial in season, and they have their own damson vodka and sloe gin, too. The atmosphere is chatty and relaxed. There are a few picnic-sets in front and at the back, with an outdoor heater. The two new bedrooms have good views.

Free house ~ Licensees Mark and Emily Hammick ~ Bar food ~ (01300) 348308 ~ Children welcome ~ Dogs welcome ~ Open 11.30-3, 6-11; closed two weeks end of Jan-early Feb winter; closed Sun evening and all day Mon except bank hols ~ Bedrooms: £55B/£80B

POWERSTOCK
Three Horseshoes
Off A3066 Beaminster—Bridport via W Milton; DT6 3TF

Friendly inn in fine countryside with imaginative food and a fair choice of drinks; walks nearby

Part of the pleasure of visiting this secluded Victorian village inn is arriving there, tucked away as it is among steep valleys and in tempting terrain for walkers. Inside, the L-shaped bar has good log fires, magazines and newspapers to read, stripped panelling, country furniture including settles, Palmers IPA and Copper on handpump, and several wines by the glass served by friendly staff. There are local paintings for sale in the dining room; piped music and board games. The enterprising food is prepared using home-grown vegetables, fruit and herbs, and is cooked by the landlord/chef. Smart teak seats and tables under large parasols on the back terrace (steps down to it) have a lovely uninterrupted view towards the sea and there's a big sloping garden. Two of the bedrooms have fine valley views.

Palmers ~ Tenant Andy Preece ~ Real ale ~ Bar food (12-3, 7-9.30; Sun 12-4, 7-8.30) ~ Restaurant ~ (01308) 485328 ~ Children welcome ~ Dogs allowed in bar and bedrooms ~ Open 11-3, 6.30-11.30(midnight Sat); 11-4, 6.30-11 Sun ~ Bedrooms: /£80S

SHAVE CROSS
Shave Cross Inn
On back lane Bridport—Marshwood, signposted locally; OS Sheet 193 map reference 415980; DT6 6HW

Caribbean touches to food and drink in 14th-c pub; carefully tended garden

It's well worth a pilgrimage to this out-of-the-way flint and thatch inn, named because travelling monks once lodged here, and got their heads shaved in preparation for the final stage of their journey to the shrine of St Wita at Whitchurch. The original timbered bar is a lovely flagstoned room, surprisingly roomy and full of character, with country antiques, two armchairs either side of a warming fire in an enormous inglenook fireplace and hops round the bar – a scene little altered from the last century. Branscombe Vale Branoc, their own-label 4Ms and a guest on handpump, alongside half a dozen wines by the glass, farm cider, several vintage rums and a caribbean beer; piped music (jazz or caribbean). Pool, darts and a juke box (a real rarity now) are in the skittle alley. With some caribbean influence, bar food (as well as more traditional dishes) might include caribbean chicken curry and caribbean vegetable bake. Lovingly tended, the sheltered flower-filled garden with its thatched wishing-well, carp pool and children's play area is very pretty.

Free house ~ Licensee Mel Warburton ~ Real ale ~ Bar food (12-3, 7-9) ~ Restaurant (7-9.30) ~ (01308) 868358 ~ Children welcome ~ Dogs allowed in bar ~ Open 11-3, 6-11; 12-3, 7-11 Sun; 11-3, 6-1am Sat and 12-3, 7-1am Sun in winter; closed Mon except bank hols

SHERBORNE
Digby Tap
Cooks Lane; park in Digby Road and walk round corner; DT9 3NS

Regularly changing ales in simple tavern, usefully open all day; close to abbey

Refreshingly no-nonsense and no frills, this alehouse has a constantly changing array of interesting and reasonably priced beers, with one cornish ale among Sharps Cornish Coaster, St Austell Dartmoor or Tinners, and three others such as Moles Landlords Choice, Northumberland Legends of the Tyne and Scattor Rock Teign Valley Tipple. Its simple flagstoned bar is chatty and full of character. A little games room has pool and a quiz machine, and there's a TV room. Served lunchtimes only, the straightforward bar is good value. There are some seats outside and the pub is only a couple of minutes' walk from the famous abbey.

Free house ~ Licensees Oliver Wilson and Nick Whigham ~ Real ale ~ Bar food (12-1.45, not Sun) ~ No credit cards ~ (01935) 813148 ~ Children welcome until 6pm ~ Dogs welcome ~ Open 11-11; 12-11 Sun

SYDLING ST NICHOLAS
Greyhound
Off A37 N of Dorchester; High Street; DT2 9PD

Genuinely welcoming staff, attractively presented food, good range of drinks, and country décor in beamed rooms

In a peaceful streamside village, this supremely well run inn continues to hit top form consistently. Sydling Bitter brewed for the pub by St Austell is on handpump along with a couple of guests such as Fullers London Pride and Greene King Old Speckled Hen, and a dozen wines are sold by the glass; several malt whiskies; fairly unobtrusive piped music and board games. The beamed and flagstoned serving area is airy and alluring with a big bowl of lemons and limes, a backdrop of gleaming bottles and copper pans, and plenty of bar stools, with more opposite ranging against a drinking shelf. On one side, a turkey-carpeted area with a warm coal fire in a handsome portland stone fireplace has a comfortable mix of straightforward tables and chairs and country decorations such as a stuffed fox eyeing a collection of china chickens and a few farm tools. Extremely accomplished, if not cheap, bar food features meat reared in Dorset and a range of fish including shellfish from Lyme Bay; vegetables here are extra. A garden room has succulents and other plants on its sills and simple modern café furniture. The small front garden has a wooden climber and slide alongside its picnic-sets.

Free house ~ Licensees John Ford, Karen Trimby, Ron Hobson, Cherry Ball ~ Real ale ~ Bar food (12-2(3 Sun), 6.30-9; not Sun evening) ~ Restaurant ~ (01300) 341303 ~ Children welcome ~ Dogs allowed in bar ~ Open 11-2.30, 6-11; 12-3.30 Sun; closed Sun evening

WEST BAY

West Bay

Station Road; DT6 4EW

Restauranty seaside inn with an emphasis on seafood

Looking out to sea and within strolling distance of the little harbour at West Bay, this dining pub is largely set out for eating, but you could just pop in for a drink; several local teams meet to play in the pub's skittles alley. An island servery separates the fairly simple bare-boards front part, with its coal-effect gas fire and mix of sea and nostalgic prints, from a cosier carpeted dining area with more of a country kitchen feel; piped music. Though its spaciousness means it never feels crowded, booking is virtually essential in season. Palmers 200, Copper Ale and IPA are served on handpump alongside good house wines (with eight by the glass); several malt whiskies. Very enjoyable food (not cheap) focuses mostly on fish and shellfish but also includes lunchtime ploughman's and sandwiches. There are tables in the small side garden, with more in a large garden; plenty of parking.

Palmers ~ Tenants Richard and Lorraine Barnard ~ Real ale ~ Bar food (12-2(3 Sun); 6.30-9.30) ~ Restaurant ~ (01308) 422157 ~ Children welcome ~ Dogs allowed in bar ~ Open 12-3, 6-11; closed Sun evening Oct-Jun

WORTH MATRAVERS

Square & Compass

At fork of both roads signposted to village from B3069; BH19 3LF

Unchanging country tavern, masses of character, in the same family for many years; lovely sea views and fine nearby walks

A firm favourite among readers, who treasure its marvellously individual character, this pub has been in the hands of the Newman family for 100 years now and to this day there's no bar counter. Ringwood Best and guests like Clearwater Olivers Nectar and Palmers Dorset Gold as well as up to 13 ciders, including one made on the premises, are tapped from a row of casks and passed to you in a drinking corridor through two serving hatches; several malt whiskies. A couple of basic unspoilt rooms have simple furniture on the flagstones, a woodburning stove and a loyal crowd of friendly locals; darts, cribbage, board games, shove-ha'penny and table skittles; a table tennis championship is held here twice a year. Bar food is limited to tasty home-made pasties, served till they run out. From benches out in front there's a fantastic view down over the village rooftops to the sea around St Aldhelm's Head; there may be free-roaming hens, chickens and other birds clucking around your feet. A little museum (free) exhibits local fossils and artefacts, mostly collected by the current friendly landlord and his father; mind your head on the way out. There are wonderful walks from here to some exciting switchback sections of the coast path above St Aldhelm's Head and Chapman's Pool; you will need to park in the public car park 100 yards along the Corfe Castle road (which has a £1 honesty box).

Free house ~ Licensee Charlie Newman ~ Real ale ~ Bar food (all day) ~ No credit cards ~ (01929) 439229 ~ Children welcome ~ Dogs welcome ~ Live music most Sats and some lunchtimes Fri and Sun ~ Open 12-11; closed weekdays 3-6 in winter

DOG FRIENDLY HOTELS, INNS, B&Bs AND FARMS

BEAMINSTER
Bridge House
3 Prout Bridge, Beaminster, Dorset DT8 3AY (01308) 862200

£128; 13 newly decorated rms. 13th-c priest's house, family owned, with open fire in sitting room, cosy bar, breakfast room overlooking the attractive walled garden (where dogs may walk), good food using local produce in new brasserie, friendly service, and an informal, relaxed atmosphere; disabled access; dogs in coach house bedrooms; £15

BOURNEMOUTH
Langtry Manor
26 Derby Road, Eastcliff, Bournemouth, Dorset BH1 3QB (01202) 290550

£97; 25 pretty rms, some in the manor, some in the lodge. Built by Edward VII for Lillie Langtry and with lots of memorabilia, this popular hotel has relaxed public rooms, helpful friendly staff, and good food inc Edwardian banquet every Sat evening; walks for dogs in grounds and some fine walks in the area and on beach (Oct-Apr); resident boxer; disabled access; dogs in bedrooms

White Topps
Southbourne, Bournemouth, Dorset BH6 4BB (01202) 428868

£139; 6 rms, shared bthrms. Edwardian house that is 100% dog oriented and all guests bring at least one dog; two lounges, one with a bar and one with a fridge for guests (used for storing dog food), traditional meals (and vegetarian choices) in dining room, and lots of doggy pictures and ornaments; six resident pets; walks on nearby beach; cl Nov-Mar; no children; dogs welcome everywhere and ground floor rms for elderly or disabled dogs

BRIDPORT

Britmead House

West Bay Road, Bridport, Dorset DT6 4EG (0.5 miles off A35; take West Bar Road from B3157 roundabout) (01308) 422941

£70; 8 rms. Extended Edwardian guest house with lots to do nearby, comfortable lounge overlooking garden, attractive dining room, good breakfasts, and kind helpful service; fields at back of grounds to walk dogs and nearby beach; cl Christmas; disabled access; dogs in bedrooms (must not be unattended)

DORCHESTER

Maiden Castle Farm

Dorchester, Dorset DT2 9PR (0.5 miles off A35; first turn right off A354) (01305) 262356

£68; 4 rms. Victorian farmhouse in 2 acres of gardens in the heart of Hardy country and set beneath the prehistoric earthworks from which the farm takes its name; views of the hill fort and countryside, nice breakfasts, afternoon tea with home-made cakes, and comfortable traditionally furnished sitting room which overlooks the garden; walks around 1,200 acre farm; resident jack russell; dogs in bedrooms; £5

EAST KNIGHTON

Countryman

East Knighton, Dorchester, Dorset DT2 8LL (01305) 852666

£85; 6 rms. Attractively converted and much liked pair of old cottages with open fires and plenty of character in the main bar which opens into several smaller areas; family room, half a dozen real ales, generously served food inc nice breakfasts, country-style restaurant, and courteous staff; walks in garden and nearby; dogs in bedrooms

EVERSHOT

Summer Lodge

Evershot, Dorchester, Dorset DT2 0JR (01935) 83424

£225; 24 big, individually decorated rms. Beautifully kept, peacefully set former dower house with lovely flowers in comfortable and elegantly furnished day rooms, excellent food using the best local produce in pretty restaurant overlooking pretty garden, carefully chosen wines, delicious breakfasts and afternoon tea, and personal caring service; indoor swimming pool, tennis and croquet; dogs on lead in garden, walks nearby; resident cat; partial disabled access; dogs in some bedrooms; bedding and bowls; £20

FARNHAM

Museum Inn

Farnham, Blandford Forum, Dorset DT11 8DE (1.5 miles off A354) (01725) 516261

£95; 8 rms. Odd-looking thatched building with various civilised areas such as flagstoned bar with big inglenook fireplace, light beams and good comfortably cushioned furnishings, dining room with cosy hunt theme, and what feels rather like a contemporary version of a baronial hall, soaring up to a high glass ceiling, with dozens of antlers and a stag's head looking down on to a long wooden table and church-style pews; excellent food, several real ales, decent wines, and good attentive service; walks in surrounding fields; children over 8; disabled access; dogs welcome away from restaurant; doggie treats

KINGSTON

Kingston Country Courtyard

West Street, Kingston, Corfe Castle, Wareham, Dorset BH20 5LH (01929) 481066

£80; 20 rms in most attractive farm building conversion. A collection of stylish suites and apartments in beautifully decorated houses keeping much original character and charm, and with wonderful views over Corfe Castle, Arne peninsula, and the Isle of Wight; enjoyable full english or continental breakfasts in Old Cart Shed dining room; self-catering too; two german shepherds and two labradors; plenty of surrounding walks and lots to do nearby; cl Jan; good disabled access; dogs in bedrooms (not to be left unattended); £10

LOWER BOCKHAMPTON

Yalbury Cottage

Lower Bockhampton, Dorchester, Dorset DT2 8PZ (1.3 miles off A35, E of Dorchester) (01305) 262382

£110; 8 rms overlooking garden or fields. Very attractive 300-year-old thatched house, refurbished under newish owners, with relaxed friendly atmosphere, low beams and inglenook fireplaces in comfortable lounge, classical french cooking using the best seasonal produce in beamed and stone-walled dining room, good wines, enjoyable breakfasts, and attractive mature garden; cl one week Nov; partial disabled access; dogs in bedrooms; £6

SHIPTON GORGE

Innsacre Farmhouse

Shipton Lane, Shipton Gorge, Bridport, Dorset DT6 4LJ (01308) 456137

£80; 4 rms. 17th-c farmhouse in 22 acres of lawns, woodland and nature trails and tucked away in little valley; french country-style furnishings, a simple and comfortable lounge with woodburning stove in big inglenook, super continental breakfasts in beamed dining room, and an informal, friendly atmosphere; several pets; children over 9; dogs in bedrooms (must not be left unattended); £10

STUDLAND

Knoll House

Studland, Swanage, Dorset BH19 3AH (01929) 450450

£270 inc lunch and dinner; 80 comfortable rms. Spacious, very well run hotel owned by the same family for over 45 years and set in 100 acres with marvellous views of Studland Bay and direct access to the fine 3-mile beach; relaxed friendly atmosphere, particularly helpful staff, super food in dining room overlooking gardens, cocktail bar, TV lounge, and excellent facilities for families; table tennis, pool and table football, heated outdoor pool and health spa, tennis courts, small private golf course, marvellous adventure playground, and nearby sea fishing, riding, walking, sailing and windsurfing; resident dogs; cl end Nov-Mar; children over 8 in evening dining room; disabled access; dogs welcome away from dining rooms, pool and spa; £5 inc food

Manor House Hotel

Studland, Dorset BH19 3AU (01929) 450288

£103; 21 rms, many with sea views; 19th-c hotel in 20 acres of grounds overlooking Studland Bay, and walks along coastal path; log fires, oak panelled bar, freshly prepared meals using plenty of local fish in dining room with conservatory extension, and attentive, friendly service; resident german shepherd; tennis and nearby golf and riding; children over 5; dogs in bedrooms; £5

STURMINSTER NEWTON

Plumber Manor

Hazelbury Bryan Road, Plumber, Sturminster Newton, Dorset DT10 2AF
(01258) 472507

£145; 16 very comfortable rms, some in nearby period buildings and many in the house itself overlook the peaceful, pretty garden and down the stream with herons and maybe egrets. Handsome 17th-c, family-run house in quiet countryside, with warm fires, convivial well stocked bar, attractive writing room/lounge, good interesting food in three dining rooms, nice breakfasts, a relaxed atmosphere, and exceptionally friendly helpful service; tennis; two resident labradors; cl Feb; disabled access; dogs in two bedrooms

WINTERBORNE ZELSTON

Huish Manor

Winterborne Zelston, Blandford Forum, Dorset DT11 9ES (01929) 459065

£90; 2 large comfortable rms overlooking grounds. Handsome 18th-c manor house with pretty walled garden, large lawn, orchard and paddocks; antiques and marine paintings in drawing room, log fire in elegant dining room, super evening meals and breakfasts, and charming hosts; cl Christmas, New Year and Easter

DOG FRIENDLY PUBS

DEDHAM

Sun

High Street (B2109); CO7 6DF

Popular stylish inn in Constable country, with elegant seasonal italian-biased food and an impressive wine selection

This fine old coaching inn is a lovely building and beautifully furnished. High carved beams, squared panelling, wall timbers and big log fires in splendid fireplaces provide a setting for high settles, sofas with sorbet-coloured cushions and other good quality wooden tables and chairs. A charming little window seat in the bar looks across to the church, which is at least glimpsed in several of Constable's paintings. Relaxed and friendly but efficient young staff serve Adnams Broadside and Crouch Vale Brewers Gold and a couple of guests from brewers such as Earl Soham and Whitstable, a very good selection of more than 70 wines (20 by the glass) and some interesting soft drinks; piped music and board games. Food is not cheap but prices do reflect the quality of the ingredients used in an imaginative contemporary menu which places much emphasis on seasonal game, fish, fruit and vegetables. On the way out to picnic-sets on the quiet attractive back lawn, notice the unusual covered back staircase with what used to be a dovecote on top, and if you have time, beautiful walks into the heart of Constable country lead out of the village, over water meadows towards Flatford Mill; an archway annexe houses their fruit and vegetable shop.

Free house ~ Licensee Piers Baker ~ Real ale ~ Bar food (12-2.30(3 Sat, Sun), 6.30-9.30 (10 Fri, Sat)) ~ Restaurant ~ (01206) 323351 ~ Children welcome ~ Dogs allowed in bar ~ Open 12-11

HORNDON-ON-THE-HILL

Bell

M25 junction 30 into A13, then left into B1007 after 7 miles, village signposted from here; SS17 8LD

Very popular ancient pub with mostly restauranty food and very good range of drinks

A curious collection of ossified hot cross buns hangs along a beam in the saloon bar at this lovely old Tudor inn. The first was put there some 90 years ago to mark the day that the licensee Jack Turnell took over the Bell – it was a Good Friday. Now the oldest person in the village (or at least the oldest available on the day) hangs the bun. During the war a concrete bun was hung, bearing witness to the shortage of food. Although emphasis is on the imaginative real food, the heavily beamed bar does maintain an unchanging pubby appearance with some antique high-backed settles and benches and rugs on the flagstones or highly polished oak floorboards. As well as a short bar menu, their menu includes some tempting daily specials. They keep an impressive range of drinks, including Bass (tapped straight from the cask), Greene King IPA, five guests from brewers such as Crouch Vale and over a hundred well chosen wines from all over the world (16 by the glass). You do need or get here early or book as tables are often all taken soon after opening time.

Free house ~ Licensee John Vereker ~ Real ale ~ Bar food (12-2, 6.30(7 Sun)-9.45; not bank hol Mon) ~ Restaurant ~ (01375) 642463 ~ Children in eating area of bar and restaurant ~ Dogs allowed in bar and bedrooms ~ Open 11-2.30, 5.30-11; 11-3, 6-11 Sat; 12-4, 7-10.30 Sun ~ Bedrooms: £44.50B/£49B

LITTLE BRAXTED

Green Man

Kelvedon Road; village signposted off B1389 by NE end of A12 Witham bypass – keep on patiently; OS Sheet 168 map reference 848133; CM8 3LB

Prettily traditional brick-built pub with a garden and reasonably priced food

Picnic-sets in the pleasant sheltered garden behind this tucked away house are a good place to while away an hour or two, and in winter, the traditional little lounge is especially appealing with its warming open fire. Horsebrasses seem to be disappearing from pubs these days so the 200 or so here form quite an unusual collection. There's also some harness, mugs hanging from a beam, a lovely copper urn and other interesting bric-a-brac. The tiled public bar has books, darts, cribbage and dominoes; three Greene King beers and nine wines by the glass. Bar food is traditional.

Greene King ~ Tenant Matthew Ruffle ~ Real ale ~ Bar food (12-2.30, 6-9; 12-6 Sun) ~ Restaurant ~ (01621) 891659 ~ Children until 8pm ~ Dogs welcome ~ Open 11.30-3.30, 5-11.30(midnight Sat); 12-11 Sun

LITTLE WALDEN

Crown

B1052 N of Saffron Walden; CB10 1XA

Bustling 18th-c cottage with a warming log fire and hearty food

This homely low-ceilinged pub has bookroom-red walls, flowery curtains and a mix of bare boards and navy carpeting. A higgledy-piggledy mix of chairs ranges from high-backed pews to little cushioned armchairs spaced around a good variety of closely arranged tables, mostly big, some stripped. The small red-tiled room on the right has two little tables. They light a fire in one of the three fireplaces, though not in the unusual walk-through one! The fairly traditional bar food is popular, so you may need to book at weekends. Four or five beers are tapped straight from casks racked up behind the bar, normally Adnams, City of Cambridge Boathouse and Greene King Abbot with a guest or two such as Woodfordes Wherry; piped light music (one reader found it obtrusive); disabled access. Tables out on the terrace take in views of surrounding tranquil countryside.

Free house ~ Licensee Colin Hayling ~ Real ale ~ Bar food (not Sun and Mon evenings) ~ Restaurant ~ (01799) 522475 ~ Dogs welcome ~ Trad jazz Weds evening ~ Open 11.30-2.30, 6-11; 12-10 Sun ~ Bedrooms: £55B/£70B

MARGARETTING TYE
White Hart

From B1002 (just S of A12/A414 junction) follow Maldon Road for 1.3 miles, then turn right immediately after river bridge, into Swan Lane, keeping on for 0.7 miles; The Tye; CM4 9JX

Fine choice of ales in cheery country pub with good family garden

Besides well kept Adnams Best and Broadside and a beer from Mighty Oak on handpump, they bring on a constant stream of unusual guest beers from all over the country – on our visit they had Archers Around The Maypole, Oxfordshire Marshmallow and Slaters Monkey Magic, with others due to take over later that same day. They do take-aways and have interesting bottled beers, too, and run a popular beer festival around midsummer. It's open-plan and unpretentious, with plenty of mixed seating, from comfortably worn wall banquettes to a group of housekeeper's chairs around a low table with country magazines. There are cosier areas on the left, and a neat dark-tiled back conservatory on the right, with John Ireland brewing cartoons; the front lobby has a charity paperback table; darts, quiz machine, skittles, board games and piped music. Food here is pubby and, as the chef is vegetarian, the vegetarian dishes should be good. There are plenty of picnic-sets out on grass and terracing around the pub, with a sturdy play area, a safely fenced duck pond, an aviary with noisy cockatiels (they don't quite drown the larks), and pens of rabbits, guinea-pigs and a pygmy goat.

Free house ~ Licensee Elizabeth Haines ~ Real ale ~ Bar food (12-2, 6-9.30, 12-4.30, 6.30-8.30 Sun; not Mon evening) ~ (01277) 840478 ~ Children welcome away from main bar ~ Dogs allowed in bar ~ Open 11.30-3, 6-12; 12-12(11 Sun) Sat

STAPLEFORD TAWNEY
Mole Trap

Tawney Common, which is a couple of miles away from Stapleford Tawney and is signposted off A113 just N of M25 overpass – keep on; OS Sheet 167 map reference 500013; CM16 7PU

Tucked away but humming with customers; interesting selection of guest beers

Quirky as ever, this isolated little country pub is run with considerable individuality – it's the sort of place to fall into easy chat with the locals who prop themselves along the counter. The smallish carpeted bar (mind your head as you go in) has black dado, beams and joists, brocaded wall seats, library chairs and bentwood elbow chairs around plain pub tables, and steps down through a partly knocked-out timber stud wall to a similar area. There are a few small pictures, 3-D decorative plates, some dried-flower arrangements and (on the sloping ceiling formed by a staircase beyond) some regulars' snapshots, with a few dozen beermats stuck up around the serving bar, and warming fires; quiet piped radio. As well as Fullers London Pride on handpump, they have three constantly changing guests from smaller brewers such as Country Life, Crouch Vale and Sharps. The pub fills up quickly at lunchtimes, so it's worth getting here early if you want to eat. Besides sandwiches and popular Sunday roasts, bar food is very traditional. Outside are some plastic tables and chairs and a picnic-set, and a happy tribe of resident animals, many rescued, including friendly cats, rabbits, a couple of dogs, hens, geese, a sheep, goats and horses. Do make sure children behave well, and note that food service stops very promptly, sometimes even before the allotted time.

Free house ~ Licensees Mr and Mrs Kirtley ~ Real ale ~ Bar food (not Sun and Mon evenings) ~ No credit cards ~ (01992) 522394 ~ Dogs welcome ~ Open 11.30-2.30, 6-11; 12-3.30, 7-10.30 Sun

DOG FRIENDLY HOTELS, INNS AND B&Bs

BURNHAM-ON-CROUCH
White Harte
The Quay, Burnham-on-Crouch, Essex CM0 8AS (01621) 782106

£84; 11 rms. Old-fashioned 17th-c yachting inn on quay overlooking the River Crouch with its own jetty; high ceilings, oak tables on polished parquet flooring, sea pictures, panelling, residents' lounge, and decent food in bar and restaurant; resident border collie; walks by the river; dogs welcome away from dining room; £3

GREAT CHESTERFORD
Crown House
Great Chesterford, Saffron Walden, Essex CB10 1NY (01799) 530515

£96.50; 22 rms, some in restored stable block. Carefully restored, imposing Georgian coach house in lovely gardens with plenty of original features, open fire and brown leather chairs in attractive lounge bar, airy conservatory with avocado tree, good, interesting food in panelled restaurant, and pleasant, efficient staff; dogs in bedrooms; £5

HOWLETT END
Beeholme House
Howlett End, Wimbish, Saffron Walden, Essex CB10 2XP (01799) 599458

£90; 2 beautifully decorated little bedrooms. Lovely thatched house with neat country garden (the charming and friendly owners are very keen gardeners), antiques, flowers, and large fireplaces in comfortable beamed rooms, super breakfasts and afternoon teas, and surrounding fields for dog walks; good nearby pubs and restaurants for evening meals; dogs allowed in bedrooms if small and very well behaved

MISTLEY

Mistley Thorn

High Street, Mistley, Manningtree, Essex CO11 1HE (01206) 392821

£80; 5 cream-coloured, uncluttered rms. 18th-c inn, now a restaurant-with-rooms with views of the Stour estuary; friendly, relaxed atmosphere, modern artwork. small sitting area, good breakfasts and very popular seafood and brasserie-style dishes in bustling contemporary restaurant; cookery school; dogs in bedrooms; £5

Gloucestershire

DOG FRIENDLY PUBS

BARNSLEY

Village Pub

B4425 Cirencester—Burford; GL7 5EF

Good mix of customers in civilised communicating rooms, newspapers and candles, and enjoyable food

Although most customers come to this smart, civilised country pub to enjoy the very good contemporary food (the menu is modern with some unusual dishes), those popping in for a drink and chat (with or without their dogs) are made just as welcome. There's a good mix of customers, and the low-ceilinged communicating rooms have flagstones and oak floorboards, oil paintings, plush chairs, stools, and window settles around polished candlelit tables, three open fireplaces and country magazines and newspapers to read. Butcombe Bitter, Hook Norton Old Hooky, and St Austells Tribute on handpump, and an extensive wine list with over a dozen by the glass. The sheltered back courtyard has plenty of good solid wooden furniture under umbrellas, outdoor heaters and its own outside servery.

Free house ~ Licensees Tim Haigh and Rupert Pendered ~ Real ale ~ Bar food (12-2.30(3 Fri-Sun), 7-9.30(10 Fri and Sat)) ~ Restaurant ~ (01285) 740421 ~ Well behaved children welcome ~ Dogs welcome ~ Open 11-3, 6-11.30; 11-11.30 Sat; 11-10.30 Sun ~ Bedrooms: £75S/£110B

BLAISDON

Red Hart

Village signposted off A4136 just SW of junction with A40 W of Gloucester; OS Sheet 162 map reference 703169; GL17 0AH

Relaxed and friendly, some interesting bric-a-brac in attractive rooms, and several real ales

This is a bustling and friendly pub in a quiet, tucked away village with a fair choice of real ales on handpump: Fullers London Pride, Harviestoun Bitter & Twisted, Hook Norton Hooky Bitter, RCH Pitchfork, and Shepherd Neame Spitfire. The flagstoned main bar has cushioned wall and window seats, traditional pub tables, a big sailing-ship painting above the log fire and a thoroughly relaxing atmosphere – helped along by well reproduced piped bluesy music and maybe Spotty the jack russell (who is now 12). On the right, there's an attractive, beamed restaurant with some interesting prints and bric-a-brac, and on the left, you'll find additional dining space for families; board games and table skittles. Bar food includes a few interesting specials. There are some picnic-sets in the garden and a children's play area, and at the back of the building is a terrace for barbecues. The little church above the village is worth a visit.

Free house ~ Licensee Guy Wilkins ~ Real ale ~ Bar food ~ Restaurant ~ (01452) 830477 ~ Children allowed but must be well behaved ~ Dogs welcome ~ Open 12-3, 6(7 Sun)-11

BLEDINGTON
Kings Head
B4450; OX7 6XQ

Beams and atmospheric furnishings in rather smart old place, super wines by the glass, interesting food

Although there is quite an emphasis on the interesting food and comfortable bedrooms in this rather smart 500-year-old inn, it's still popular with villagers popping in for a drink. The main bar is full of ancient beams and other atmospheric furnishings (high-backed wooden settles, gateleg or pedestal tables) and there's a warming log fire in the stone inglenook where there are bellows and a big black kettle; sporting memorabilia of rugby, racing, cricket and hunting. To the left of the bar, a drinking space for locals has benches on the wooden floor and a woodburning stove. Hook Norton Best and guests such as Ballards Trotton Bitter, Hook Norton Best, Purity Pure Ubu and Wye Valley Bitter on handpump, an excellent wine list with ten by the glass, 20 malt whiskies and interesting bottled ciders; piped music and darts. As well as lunchtime sandwiches and ploughman's, food is very rewarding. There are seats at the front and in the back courtyard garden, and the pub is set back from the village green where there are usually ducks pottering about.

Free house ~ Licensees Nicola and Archie Orr-Ewing ~ Real ale ~ Bar food ~ Restaurant ~ (01608) 658365 ~ Children allowed but away from bar area ~ Dogs allowed in bar ~ Open 11.30-3, 6-11; 11.30-11 Sat; 12-11 Sun; closed 25 and 26 Dec ~ Bedrooms: £55B/£70B

BRIMPSFIELD
Golden Heart
Nettleton Bottom (not shown on road maps, so we list the pub instead under the name of the nearby village); on A417 N of the Brimpsfield turning northbound; GL4 8LA

Nice old-fashioned furnishings in several cosy areas, big log fire and fair choice of food and drink; suntrap terrace and nearby walks

'A timeless little gem' and 'probably my favourite local' are just a couple of the enthusiastic comments from regular visitors to this bustling roadside pub. It's a place of some genuine character and run by friendly, helpful licensees. The main low-ceilinged bar is divided into five cosily distinct areas; there's a roaring log fire in the huge stone inglenook fireplace in one, traditional built-in settles and other old-fashioned furnishings throughout, and quite a few brass items, typewriters, exposed stone and wood panelling. Newspapers to read. A comfortable parlour on the right has another decorative fireplace, and leads into a further room that opens on to the terrace. Archers Best Bitter, Festival Gold, Otter Bitter and Youngs Special on handpump, some rare ciders, and a few wines by the glass. Well liked bar food is very traditional. From the tables and chairs under parasols on the suntrap terrace, there are pleasant views down over a valley; nearby walks. The bedrooms are at the back of the pub and so escape any road noise.

Free house ~ Licensee Catherine Stevens ~ Real ale ~ Bar food (12-3, 6-10; all day Fri, Sat and Sun) ~ Restaurant ~ (01242) 870261 ~ Children welcome ~ Dogs welcome ~ Open 11-3, 5.30-11; 11-11 Sat; 12-10.30 Sun ~ Bedrooms: £35S/£55S

CHEDWORTH
Seven Tuns

Village signposted off A429 NE of Cirencester; then take second signposted right turn and bear left towards church; GL54 4AE

Handy for nearby Roman villa and with several open fires, lots of wines by the glass, good bar food, and plenty of seats outside

Delightful inside and out, this little 17th-c pub has exceptionally nice staff who offer a friendly welcome to all. The small snug lounge on the right has comfortable seats and decent tables, sizeable antique prints, tankards hanging from the beam over the serving bar, a partly boarded ceiling, and a good winter log fire in a big stone fireplace. Down a couple of steps, the public bar on the left has an open fire and this opens into a dining room with another open fire. The food tends to be quite pubby at lunchtime with many more inventive dishes in the evening. Wells & Youngs Bombardier and Youngs Special and a seasonal guest on handpump, ten wines by the glass and 15 malt whiskies; darts, skittle alley, dominoes and piped music. One sunny terrace has a boules pitch and across the road there's another little walled raised terrace with a waterwheel and a stream; plenty of tables and seats. There are nice walks through the valley.

Youngs ~ Tenant Mr Davenport-Jones ~ Real ale ~ Bar food (12-2.30 (3 weekends), 6.30-9.30(10 weekends)) ~ Restaurant ~ (01285) 720242 ~ Children welcome ~ Dogs welcome ~ Open 12-midnight(2am Sat); 12-11 Sun; 12-3.30, 6-closing hours as above in winter

CHIPPING CAMPDEN
Eight Bells

Church Street (which is one way – entrance off B4035); GL55 6JG

Handsome inn with massive timbers and beams, log fires, well liked food, and seats in large terraced garden; handy for Cotswold Way

This handsome old inn has plenty of history. It was used, many hundreds of years ago, as a hostel for workmen building the nearby church and inset into the floor of the dining room is a glass inlet showing part of the passage from the church by which Roman Catholic priests could escape from the Roundheads. The bars have heavy oak beams, massive timber supports and stripped stone walls with cushioned pews, sofas and solid dark wood furniture on the broad flagstones, and log fires in up to three restored stone fireplaces; daily papers to read. North Cotswold Pig Brook and three guest beers such as Brains Bread of Heaven, Everards Sunchaser and Goffs Jouster on handpump from the fine oak bar counter, quite a few wines by the glass, Old Rosie cider and country wines. The rewarding choice of enjoyable food here is very popular. Piped music and board games. There's a large terraced garden with plenty of seats, and striking views of the almshouses and church. The pub is handy for the Cotswold Way walk to Bath.

Free house ~ Licensee Neil Hargreaves ~ Real ale ~ Bar food (12-2(2.30 Fri-Sun), 6.30(7 Sun)-9(9.30 Fri and Sat)) ~ Restaurant ~ (01386) 840371 ~ Children must be well behaved and supervised by parents ~ Dogs allowed in bar ~ Open 12-11(10.30 Sun); closed 25 Dec

COATES

Tunnel House

Follow Tarlton signs (right then left) from village, pub up rough track on right after railway bridge; OS Sheet 163 map ref 965005; GL7 6PW

Warm welcome for all at friendly, interestingly decorated pub, lots of character, popular food and drink, and seats in sizeable garden; guards derelict canal tunnel

With plenty of character and an informal and relaxed atmosphere, this rather eccentric bow-fronted stone house has impressive views from tables on the pleasant terrace and a big garden sloping down to the derelict entrance tunnel of the old Thames and Severn Canal (which is under slow restoration). Inside, there are rambling rooms with beams, flagstones, a happy mix of furnishings including massive rustic benches and seats built into the sunny windows, lots of enamel advertising signs, race tickets and air travel labels, a stuffed wild boar's head and stuffed owl, plenty of copper and brass and an upside-down card table complete with cards and drinks fixed to the beams; there's a nice log fire with sofas in front of it. The more conventional dining extension and back conservatory fill up quickly at mealtimes. Three changing real ales from breweries such as Hook Norton, Stroud, Uley and Wickwar on handpump, several wines by the glass, and two draught ciders; quick, friendly service. Piped music and juke box. The pubby lunchtime menu becomes a little more adventurous in the evening. There may be an amiable black labrador and almost certainly lots of students from the Agricultural College (especially on term-time weekend evenings). Good walks nearby.

Free house ~ Licensee Rupert Longsdon ~ Real ale ~ Bar food (12-2.15, 6.45-9.15) ~ (01285) 770280 ~ Children welcome ~ Dogs welcome ~ Open 11.30-3.30, 6-11.30; 11.30-11.30 Sun and Sat; closed 25 Dec

COWLEY

Green Dragon

Off A435 S of Cheltenham at Elkstone, Cockleford signpost; OS Sheet 163 map reference 970142; GL53 9NW

Cosy and old-fashioned bars with winter fires, good food, real ales, and terraces overlooking Cowley Lake; comfortable bedrooms

Extremely popular and exceptionally well run, this is a smashing country inn much loved by our readers. The two beamed bars have a cosy and genuinely old-fashioned feel with big flagstones and wooden boards, winter log fires in two stone fireplaces, candlelit tables, a woodburning stove and Butcombe Bitter, Courage Directors and Hook Norton on handpump. The furniture and the bar itself in the upper Mouse Bar were made by Robert Thompson, and little mice run over the hand-carved chairs, tables and mantelpiece; piped music. The menu here is very tempting, with dishes such as duck confit rillette with pink pepper-corns and shallots and a prune and apple jam, as well as traditional pub staples. Terraces outside overlook Cowley Lake and the River Churn, and the pub is a good centre for the local walks. The bedrooms are very comfortable and well equipped and the breakfasts are good.

Buccaneer Holdings ~ Licensees Simon and Nicky Haly ~ Real ale ~ Bar food (12-2.30(3.30 Sun), 6-10(9 Sun)) ~ Restaurant ~ (01242) 870271 ~ Children welcome ~ Dogs allowed in bar and bedrooms ~ Open 11(12 Sun)-11; closed evenings 25 and 26 Dec and 1 Jan ~ Bedrooms: £65B/£85B

CRANHAM

Black Horse

Village signposted off A46 and B4070 N of Stroud; look out for small sign up village side turning; GL4 8HP

Friendly, old-fashioned country inn with obliging staff, homely food and real ales

Surrounded by woodland, this old-fashioned and unassuming 17th-c inn is popular with walkers – the Cotswold Way is only a mile away. A cosy little lounge has just three or four tables, the main bar has window seats and other traditional furniture and a good log fire, and the atmosphere is friendly and convivial; there are a couple of upstairs dining rooms, too (they take bookings up here but not in the bar or lounge). Butcombe Bitter, Hancocks HB, Sharps Doom Bar, and a guest beer on handpump. The popular food is well priced and freshly cooked. Outside, there are tables to the side of the pub and some in front; the labradoo-dle is called Percy and the jack russell, Baxter. They have a successful pub cricket team and regular morris dancers.

Free house ~ Licensees David and Julie Job ~ Real ale ~ Bar food (not Sun evening or Mon) ~ Restaurant ~ (01452) 812217 ~ Children welcome if well behaved; no small children evenings ~ Dogs allowed in bar ~ Open 12-2.30(3 Sat), 6.30-11; 12-3.30, 8-11 Sun; closed Mon

DUNTISBOURNE ABBOTS

Five Mile House

Off A417 at Duntisbourne Abbots exit sign; then, coming from Gloucester, pass filling station and keep on parallel to main road for 200 yards; coming from Cirencester, take Duntisbourne Abbots services sign, then immediate right and take underpass below main road, then turn right at T junction; avoid going into Duntisbourne Abbots village; pub is on the old main road; GL7 7JR

A lively landlord and a favourite with many for its good food, beer and atmosphere; plenty of original character, open fires and newspapers; nice views from garden

Thankfully, this extremely well run and genuinely friendly village pub doesn't change from year to year – and many of our readers go considerably out of their way to come back here on a regular basis. The atmosphere is always buoyant and bustling but, no matter how busy it is, the cheerful Carriers make all their customers feel at home. There's plenty of original character and the front room has a companionable bare-boards drinking bar on the right (plenty of convivial banter from the locals), with wall seats around the big table in its bow window and just one other table. On the left is a flagstoned hallway tap room snug formed from two ancient high-backed settles by a stove in a tall carefully exposed old fireplace; newspapers to read. There's a small cellar bar, a back restaurant down steps and a family room on the far side; darts and board games. Donningtons BB, Timothy Taylors Landlord and Youngs Bitter on handpump (the cellar is temperature-controlled) and an interesting wine list (strong on new world ones). Cooked by the landlord and his team, bar food is very good with plenty of imaginative choices and they offer several dishes in smaller helpings too; the friendly pub dog is called Sacha. The gardens have nice country views; the country lane was once Ermine Street, the main Roman road from Wales to London.

Free house ~ Licensees Jo and Jon Carrier ~ Real ale ~ Bar food (12-2.30, 6 (7 summer Sun)-9.30; not winter Sun evening) ~ Restaurant ~ (01285) 821432 ~ Children welcome if well behaved ~ Dogs allowed in bar ~ Open 12-3, 6-11; 12-3, 7-10.30 Sun

EWEN

Wild Duck

Village signposted from A429 S of Cirencester; GL7 6BY

Bustling, civilised inn with open fires, a nice mix of furniture, and well liked food and drink; sheltered garden

Handy for Cirencester, this 16th-c inn is a fine old building on the edge of a peaceful village. The high-beamed main bar has a nice mix of comfortable armchairs and other seats, paintings on the red walls, crimson drapes, a winter open fire, and maybe candles on tables. The residents' lounge, which overlooks the garden, has a handsome Elizabethan fireplace and antique furnishings. Besides Duckpond Bitter (brewed especially for the pub), you'll find Butcombe Bitter, Theakstons Best and Old Peculier and Wells & Youngs Bombardier on handpump, 37 wines by the glass, several malts and local liqueurs; piped music and giant chess in the garden. Running from antipasti up, bar food here is very good and the menu displays just the right amount of invention. There are wooden seats and tables under parasols and outdoor heaters in the neatly kept and enclosed courtyard garden; if you eat out here, you will be asked to leave your credit card behind the bar (but not if you eat inside).

Free house ~ Licensees Tina and Dino Mussell ~ Real ale ~ Bar food (12-2, 6.45-10; 12-2, 2.30-10 Sat; 12-2.30, 3.30-6, 6.45-9.30 Sun) ~ Restaurant ~ (01285) 770310 ~ Children welcome ~ Dogs allowed in bar and bedrooms ~ Open 11-11(midnight Sat); 12-11 Sun ~ Bedrooms: £80B/£125B

GREAT RISSINGTON

Lamb

off A40 W of Burford, via Great Barrington; GL54 2LN

Well run, bustling inn, interesting, enjoyable bar food, fair choice of drinks and seats in sheltered garden; good surrounding walks

There's a really good balance between those popping in for a drink and a chat and customers hoping to enjoy the very good food in this warm and bright partly 17th-c inn – and the hard-working landlord and his friendly staff are sure to make everyone welcome. The rather civilised two-roomed bar has heritage red and stone coloured walls, fixed cushioned seating with fluted backs in a dark faux-aged suede, high-backed leather chairs grouped around polished tables, and a woodburning stove in the cotswold stone fireplace. Some interesting things to look out for are parts of a propeller, artefacts in display cases and pictures of the Canadian crew from the Wellington bomber that crashed in the garden in October 1943; also, photographs of the guide dogs that the staff, customers and owners have raised money to sponsor. The restaurant has another woodburning stove and various old agricultural tools on the walls. Hook Norton Old Hookey and Wye Valley Best Bitter on handpump, 11 wines by the glass from a comprehensive list and several malt whiskies; piped music, darts and TV for sports. Food is prepared using seasonal local produce and is quite a draw here. You can sit outside on the front terrace or in the sheltered, well kept hillside garden. There's a local circular walk which takes in part of the idyllic village, church, River Windrush and stunning countryside surrounding the pub.

Free house ~ Licensees Paul and Jacqueline Gabriel ~ Real ale ~ Bar food (12-2.30, 6.30-9.30; all day weekends) ~ Restaurant ~ (01451) 820388 ~ Children welcome ~ Dogs welcome ~ Open 12-11; closed evening 25 Dec ~ Bedrooms: £55B/£80B

GUITING POWER

Hollow Bottom

Village signposted off B4068 SW of Stow-on-the-Wold (still called A436 on many maps); GL54 5UX

Popular old inn with lots of racing memorabilia and a good bustling atmosphere

This snug old stone cottage is liked by a wide mix of customers – in particular, jockeys, owners and trainers. The comfortable beamed bar has plenty of atmosphere, lots of racing memorabilia including racing silks, tunics and photographs and a winter log fire in an unusual pillar-supported stone fireplace. The public bar has flagstones and stripped stone masonry and racing on TV; newspapers to read, darts, board games and piped music. Fullers London Pride, North Cotswold Shagweaver and a beer named for the pub (from Badger) on handpump, 18 malt whiskies and several wines (including champagne) by the glass. Obliging staff serve the traditional food. From the pleasant garden behind the pub are views towards the peaceful sloping fields; decent nearby walks.

Free house ~ Licensees Hugh Kelly and Charles Pettigrew ~ Real ale ~ Bar food (all day) ~ Restaurant ~ (01451) 850392 ~ Children welcome ~ Dogs allowed in bar and bedrooms ~ Live music during Cheltenham race meetings ~ Open 9am-12.30am ~ Bedrooms: £45B/£70B

LITTLE BARRINGTON

Inn For All Seasons

On the A40 3 miles W of Burford; OX18 4TN

Fish specials as well as other interesting food in creeper-covered old inn; fine wines, big log fire, and pleasant garden; very busy during Cheltenham Gold Cup Week

The Sharp family have now been running this handsome old coaching inn for over 20 years. They specialise in fresh fish with dishes such as irish rock oysters and seared scallops with crisp smoked bacon and coriander dressing. The non-fishy menu is equally tempting with plenty of mouthwatering combinations. The attractively decorated, mellow lounge bar has low beams, stripped stone and flagstones, old prints, leather-upholstered wing armchairs and other comfortable seats, country magazines to read, and a big log fire; the atmosphere is friendly and relaxed. 16 wines by the glass from a particularly good list, over 60 malt whiskies and a couple of real ales on handpump from breweries such as Bass, Sharps and Wadworths; friendly, kind service and newspapers to read. There's also a conservatory and restaurant. Cribbage, board games and piped music. The pleasant garden has tables, a play area, and aunt sally, and there are walks straight from the inn. It gets very busy during Cheltenham Gold Cup Week.

Free house ~ Licensees Matthew and Heather Sharp ~ Real ale ~ Bar food (11.30-2.30, 6.30-9.30; 12-2, 7-9 Sun) ~ (01451) 844324 ~ Children welcome ~ Dogs allowed in bar and bedrooms ~ Open 10-2.30, 6-11; 10a,-11pm Sat; 12-10.30 Sun ~ Bedrooms: £68B/£115B

LOWER ODDINGTON

Fox

Signposted off A436 between Stow and Chipping Norton; GL56 0UR

Popular dining inn with excellent food and wines, several real ales, and helpful staff

There's no doubt that this smart, busy inn places firm emphasis on the very good interesting modern food (served by neat, uniformed staff) but they do still offer Greene King Abbot, Hook Norton Bitter and a beer from Wickwar on handpump, and if you are lucky you might be able to sit at one of the bar stools in the small pubby bit by the bar counter; several wines by the glass. The simply furnished rooms have fresh flowers and flagstones, hunting scene figures above the mantelpiece, a display cabinet with pewter mugs and stone bottles, daily newspapers and an inglenook fireplace. The terrace has a custom-built awning and outdoor heaters, and the cottagey garden is pretty. A good eight-mile walk starts from here (though a stroll around the pretty village might be less taxing).

Free house ~ Licensees James Cathcart and Ian MacKenzie ~ Real ale ~ Bar food (12-2(3.30 Sun), 6.30-9.30(7-9 Sun)) ~ Restaurant ~ (01451) 870555 ~ Children welcome ~ Dogs allowed in bar ~ Open 12-midnight(11 Sun); closed 25 Dec

NAILSWORTH

Weighbridge

B4014 towards Tetbury; GL6 9AL

Super two-in-one pies served in cosy old-fashioned bar rooms, a fine choice of drinks, lots of black ironware hanging from beams, and sheltered landscaped garden

The hugely popular two-in-one pies here come in a large bowl, with half the bowl containing the filling of your choice whilst the other is full of home-made cauliflower cheese (or broccoli mornay or root vegetables), and it's all topped with pastry. You can also have mini versions or straightforward pies, and they do offer other dishes. This is a really good pub with genuinely welcoming, help-ful staff – it's the sort of place that customers happily return to again and again. The relaxed bar has three cosily old-fashioned rooms with stripped stone walls, antique settles and country chairs, window seats and open fires. The black beamed ceiling of the lounge bar is thickly festooned with black ironware – sheepshears, gin traps, lamps, and a large collection of keys, many from the old Longfords Mill opposite the pub. Upstairs is a raftered hayloft with an engaging mix of rustic tables. No noisy games machines or piped music. Well kept Uley Old Spot and Laurie Lee and Wadworths 6X on handpump, 15 wines (and cham-pagne) by the glass, Weston's cider and several malt whiskies. Behind the build-ing is a sheltered landscaped garden with picnic-sets under umbrellas. Good disabled access and facilities.

Free house ~ Licensee Howard Parker ~ Real ale ~ Bar food (all day) ~ Restaurant ~ (01453) 832520 ~ Children allowed away from the bars until 9pm ~ Dogs welcome ~ Open 12-11(10.30 Sun); closed 25 Dec and ten days in Jan

NETHER WESTCOTE

Westcote Inn

Pub signposted off A424 Burford—Stow; OX7 6SD

Contemporary and stylish with fine food and drink and a friendly atmosphere

This very light and airy place is popular with the racing fraternity – some of the best racehorse trainers live in the area. The main bar, the Tack Room, has stripped stone walls, beams, dark wooden tables and chairs and high bar stools on nice flagstones and lots of racing memorabilia such as Cheltenham Festival Tickets, passes, jockey colours and so forth. The pub even supports its own race horse, Westcote, which is syndicated by enthusiasts from the village. There's a smart Champagne Bar with comfortable leather seats on the wood-strip floor, an open fire and a high vaulted ceiling, a coffee lounge and a rather chic restau-rant. Food here is jolly good and includes top notch takes on traditional pub favourites, and some more inventive dishes. Hook Norton Hooky Bitter and a couple of changing guest beers such as Flowers IPA and Timothy Taylors Landlord on handpump and over 20 wines (including champagne) by the glass from a carefully chosen list; piped music, TV, darts, and board games. There are seats on the terrace and in the garden and lovely views across the Evenlode Valley; spit-roasts and barbecues out here in summer.

Free house ~ Licensee Julia Reed ~ Real ale ~ Bar food (12-2.30, 7-9.30) ~
Restaurant ~ (01993) 830888 ~ Children welcome ~ Dogs allowed in bar and
bedrooms ~ Open 8am-1am ~ Bedrooms: £85(£95B)/£110B

NEWLAND

Ostrich

*Off B4228 in Coleford; or can be reached from the A466 in Redbrook, by the
turning off at the England-Wales border – keep bearing right; GL16 8NP*

**Liked by walkers and their dogs with a friendly feel in spacious bar, super choice
of beers, open fire, daily papers, and popular food**

You can be sure of a genuinely friendly welcome from the cheerful landlady in
this relaxed old pub, parts of which date back to the 13th c. The low-ceilinged
bar is spacious but cosily traditional, refreshed by some light refurbishment in
2008. There are creaky floors, uneven walls with miners' lamps, window shutters,
candles in bottles on the tables, and comfortable furnishings such as cushioned
window seats, wall settles and rod-backed country-kitchen chairs. There's a fine
big fireplace, newspapers to read, perhaps quiet piped jazz, and board games.
The pub lurcher is called Alfie – and children who manage to tire him out with
his rubber ball get an ice-cream for their efforts. A marvellous choice of up to
eight well kept real ales on handpump might include Adnams Bitter, Fullers
London Pride, Hook Norton Old Hooky, Greene King Abbot, Hop Back Summer
Lightning, RCH Pitchfork, Timothy Taylors Landlord and Wye Valley Butty Bach.
Food here, including home-made bread, chutneys and so on, is pubby and well
liked. There are picnic-sets in a walled garden behind and out in front; the
church, known as the Cathedral of the Forest, is well worth a visit, and this is a
charmingly picturesque village.

Free house ~ Licensee Kathryn Horton ~ Real ale ~ Bar food (12-2.30, 6.30(6
Sat)-9.30) ~ Restaurant ~ (01594) 833260 ~ Children welcome ~ Dogs allowed
in bar ~ May have live jazz on summer evenings in garden ~ Open 12-3, 6.30-
11; 12-3, 6-midnight Sat; 12-4, 6.30-10.30 Sun

NORTH NIBLEY

New Inn

E of village itself; Waterley Bottom – OS Sheet 162 map ref 758963; GL11 6EF

**Good choice of real ales and draught ciders in friendly country pub, tasty food
and seats in garden**

Peacefully tucked away in lovely south cotswold countryside, this bustling pub
has a range of interesting real ales from antique beer pumps and holds two beer
festivals a year (best to phone for dates): Cotleigh Tawny, Goffs Jouster,
Matthews Brassknocker, and Wye Valley Butty Bach. Also, five draught ciders and
an August cider festival. The lounge bar has cushioned windsor chairs and high-
backed settles against the partly stripped stone walls and the simple, cosy
public bar has darts. Bar food is enjoyable and includes several thoughtfully put-
together dishes. There are lots of tables on the lawn with more on a covered
decked area (where there is an outdoor pool table).

Free house ~ Licensee Les Smitherman ~ Real ale ~ Bar food (not Mon) ~
Restaurant ~ (01453) 543659 ~ Children welcome ~ Dogs welcome ~ Open
12-2.30, 6-11; 12-11 Sat; 12-10.30 Sun; closed Mon lunchtime; 2-15 Feb ~
Bedrooms: £40S/£60S

OLDBURY-ON-SEVERN

Anchor

Village signposted from B4061; BS35 1QA

Bustling country pub with well liked food, a fine choice of drinks, and pretty garden and hanging baskets

Well priced for the area and kept on handpump in very good condition, the real
ales in this popular and friendly pub continue to be quite a draw: Bass,
Butcombe Bitter, Otter Bitter, Theakstons Old Peculier and Wickwar Spring Ale.
They also have a fine range of 75 malt whiskies and 14 wines by the glass. Good,
reasonably priced bar food is on the whole fairly traditional with a few interesting specials, and there's also a good value two-course weekday lunch menu. The
neatly kept lounge has an easy-going atmosphere, modern beams and stone, a
mix of tables including an attractive oval oak gateleg, cushioned window seats,
winged seats against the wall, oil paintings by a local artist and a big winter
log fire. Diners can eat in the lounge or bar area or in the dining room at the
back of the building (good for larger groups) and the menu is the same in all
rooms. In summer, you can eat in the pretty garden and the hanging baskets
and window boxes are lovely then; boules. They have wheelchair access and a
disabled lavatory. Plenty of walks to the River Severn and along the many footpaths and bridleways, and St Arilda's Church nearby is interesting, on its odd
little knoll with wild flowers among the gravestones (the primroses and daffodils
in spring are quite a show).

Free house ~ Licensees Michael Dowdeswell and Mark Sorrell ~ Real ale ~ Bar
food (12-2, 6(6.30 winter weekdays)-9) ~ Restaurant ~ (01454) 413331 ~
Children in dining room only ~ Dogs allowed in bar ~ Open 11.30-3,
6-midnight; 11.30-1am(midnight Sun) Sat; noon opening Sun and 6.30
evening opening all week in winter

SAPPERTON

Bell

*Village signposted from A419 Stroud—Cirencester; OS Sheet 163 map reference
948033; GL7 6LE*

**Super pub with beamed cosy rooms, a really good mix of customers, delicious
food, local ales, and very pretty courtyard**

This is a delightful pub run with great care by the hard-working licensees and
their staff. There is quite an emphasis on the excellent food but drinkers are
most welcome too. The menu kicks off with a lunchtime daily pub classic dish
such as beef and dumpling casserole and works its way up to some very thoughtfully put-together up-to-date combinations – maybe crispy belly of gloucester
old spot pork with a pork samosa and sage and parmesan polenta – all of which

are highly enjoyable. They keep four real ales on handpump: Bath Ales Gem and Wild Hare, Otter Bitter and Uley Old Spot. Also, 16 wines by the glass or half litre carafe from a large and diverse wine list with very helpful notes, Ashton Press cider, 20 malt whiskies, several armagnacs and cognacs and local soft drinks. Harry's Bar (named after their sociable springer spaniel) has big cushion-strewn sofas, benches and armchairs where you can read the daily papers with a pint in front of the woodburning stove – or simply have a pre-dinner drink. The two other cosy rooms have stripped beams, a nice mix of wooden tables and chairs, country prints and modern art on stripped stone walls, one or two attractive rugs on the flagstones, fresh flowers and open fires. The gents' has schoolboy humour cartoons on the walls. There are tables out on a small front lawn and in a partly covered and very pretty courtyard, for eating outside. Horses have their own tethering rail (and bucket of water).

Free house ~ Licensees Paul Davidson and Pat LeJeune ~ Real ale ~ Bar food ~ (01285) 760298 ~ Children allowed but must be over 10 in evenings ~ Dogs welcome ~ Open 11-2.30, 6.30-11; 12-3, 7-10.30 Sun; closed 25 Dec

SHEEPSCOMBE

Butchers Arms

Off B4070 NE of Stroud; GL6 7RH

Fine views, real ales and pubby food and friendly young licensees

The views from this 17th-c cotswold stone pub over the lovely surrounding steep beech wood valley are terrific. It is thought that this area was once the royal hunting ground for King Henry VIII. Inside, the bustling lounge bar has a good mix of locals and visitors, beams, wheelback chairs and cushioned stools around simple wooden tables, built-in cushioned seats in the big bay windows, interesting oddments like assorted blow lamps, irons and plates, and a woodburning stove; friendly service. Butcombe Bitter, Wye Valley Butty Bach and a guest like St Austells Tribute on handpump, several wines by the glass and Weston's cider; darts, chess and cribbage. As well as lunchtime sandwiches, food is pubby, with one or two interesting specials. There are seats outside.

Free house ~ Licensee Mark Tallents ~ Real ale ~ Bar food (12-2.30, 6.30(7 winter)-9.30; all day weekends) ~ (01452) 812113 ~ Children welcome ~ Dogs allowed in bar ~ Open 11.30-3, 6-11; 11.30am-midnight Sat; 12-10.30 Sun; weekday evening opening 6.30 in winter

TETBURY

Snooty Fox

Market Place; small residents' car park, nearby pay & display; free car park some way down hill; GL8 8DD

Upmarket hotel with unstuffy bar, real ales, lots of wines by glass, and popular food

Although this is a smart hotel, the bar here is unpretentious and friendly and has a good mix of chatty locals (often with their dogs) and visitors. It's a high-ceilinged, carpeted room with stripped stone, like much of the rest of the ground floor, comfortable sturdy leather-armed chairs around cast-iron tripod tables, a big log fireplace flanked by an imposing pair of brass flambeaux, brass ceiling fans, and Ronald Searle pony-club cartoons. Three real ales on hand-pump from breweries such as Otter, Nailsworth and Wickwar, lots of wines by the glass and a fine collection of armagnac, cognac, calvados and port; good service from neat young staff and unobtrusive piped music. Behind the main bar is a similar room with a colourful rug on bare boards and a leather sofa among other seats. On the right, a smaller quieter room has church candles on the dining tables and subdued lighting. Lunchtime snacks and pubby standards are replaced in the evening by more substantial dishes such as roast rabbit loin with sausage and a haricot bean and wild mushroom stew. Outside, there's a sheltered entryway with teak tables and chairs facing the ancient central covered market. Comfortable, well equipped bedrooms and good breakfasts.

Free house ~ Licensee Marc Gibbons ~ Real ale ~ Bar food ~ Restaurant ~ (01666) 502436 ~ Children welcome ~ Dogs allowed in bar and bedrooms ~ Open 11-11; 12-10.30 Sun ~ Bedrooms: £79B/£103B

Trouble House

A433 towards Cirencester, near Cherington turn; GL8 8SG

Smart and friendly bars with customers to match, an ambitious menu, good drinks, and attentive service

There's no doubt that most emphasis in this rather smart place is on the restaurant-style cooking although they do keep (in the small saggy-beamed middle room) Wadworths IPA and 6X on handpump and a dozen wines by the glass (including champagne). The interesting bar food is prepared using carefully sourced local produce and they make all their own ice-creams and bread. Furnishings are mainly close-set stripped pine or oak tables with chapel, wheelback and other chairs, and there are attractive mainly modern country prints on the cream or butter-coloured walls. On the left is a parquet-floored room with a big stone fireplace, a hop-girt mantelpiece and some big black beams; piped music and attentive service. You can also sit out at picnic-sets on the gravel courtyard behind.

Wadworths ~ Tenants Martin & Neringa Caws ~ Real ale ~ Bar food (not Sun evening or Mon) ~ (01666) 502206 ~ Children allowed away from bar area; must be over 10 in evening ~ Dogs welcome ~ Open 11.30-3, 6.30(7 winter)-11; 12-3 Sun; closed Sun evening, all day Mon; two weeks in Jan

DOG FRIENDLY HOTELS, INNS, B&Bs AND FARMS

BIBURY

Bibury Court

Bibury, Cirencester, Gloucestershire GL7 5NT (01285) 740337

£180; 18 individual rms, some overlooking garden. Lovely peaceful mansion dating from Tudor times set in six acres of beautiful gardens (where dogs may walk), with an informal friendly atmosphere, panelled rooms, antiques, huge log fires, conservatory, a fine choice of breakfasts, and good interesting evening meals; dogs in bedrooms (but must not be left unattended); £5

Swan

Bibury, Cirencester, Gloucestershire GL7 5NW (01285) 740695

£165; 21 very pretty individually decorated rms. Handsome creeper-covered hotel on the River Coln, with private fishing and attractive formal garden (where dogs may walk); lovely flowers and log fires in carefully furnished comfortable lounges, stylish bar with real ales, informal lunches in bustling brasserie, good food in romantic dining room decorated with oil paintings, nice breakfasts, and attentive staff; disabled access; dogs in bedrooms; £10

CHELTENHAM

Alias Hotel Kandinsky

Bayshill Road, Cheltenham, Gloucestershire GL50 3AS (3.5 miles off M5 junction 11; A40 into town; turn left into Montpellier Street, bearing left into Parabola Road; turn right into Bayshill Road) (01242) 527788

£125; 48 large, stylish and well equipped rms. White-painted Regency hotel with an interesting mix of old and new furnishings, antiques and modern paintings, big pot plants, lots of mirrors, log fire in comfortable drawing room, and a relaxed, informal atmosphere; enjoyable modern food in bustling Café Paradiso, popular afternoon tea, friendly bar, willing young staff, downstairs cocktail bar, and seats out on decked terrace; they are kind to families; resident cat; disabled access; dogs in bedrooms; if cleaning is needed, £15

CHIPPING CAMPDEN

Cotswold House

The Square, Chipping Campden, Gloucestershire GL55 6AN (01386) 840330

£200; 29 comfortable, contemporary rms. Imposing Regency house in lovely town, with fine central staircase, relaxing drawing room with log fire, good modern cooking in brasserie or restaurant, a cosseting atmosphere, sunny terraces, and formal garden; plenty to see nearby; disabled access; dogs welcome in bedrooms

CLEARWELL

Tudor Farmhouse

Clearwell, Coleford, Gloucestershire GL16 8JS (01594) 833046

£115; 20 cottagey, well equipped rms. Carefully restored Tudor farmhouse and stone cottages with landscaped gardens and surrounding fields (walks for dogs); lots of beams and panelling, oak doors and sloping floors, inglenook fireplaces, enjoyable food in candlelit restaurant, and friendly staff; two resident cats; cl Christmas; disabled access; dogs in bedrooms; £5

CORSE LAWN

Corse Lawn House

Corse Lawn, Gloucester, Gloucestershire GL19 4LZ (01452) 780771

£150; 19 pretty, individually furnished rms. Handsome Queen Anne building with two comfortable drawing rooms, imaginative, refined food in smart restaurant, lighter meals in brightly decorated bistro, excellent wines, warmly friendly staff, and a relaxed atmosphere; indoor swimming pool, new leisure spa, tennis court, croquet, and horses in 12 acres of surrounding gardens and fields, and plenty of walks in grounds and nearby common and forest; two resident black labradors; cl three days over Christmas; disabled access; dogs welcome away from restaurant (must be on lead in public rooms)

ENGLISH BICKNOR

Dryslade Farm

English Bicknor, Coleford, Gloucestershire GL16 7PA (01594) 860259

£60; 3 homely bdrms. 18th-c farmhouse owned by same family for 100 years and part of a working farm; friendly and relaxed atmosphere, cosy guest lounge with log fire, and traditional breakfast in light and airy conservatory (bring in or order takeaway food for evening meals); two resident spaniels; endless surrounding walks; disabled access; dogs welcome in bedrooms

GUITING POWER

Guiting Guest House

Post Office Lane, Guiting Power, Cheltenham, Gloucestershire GL54 5TZ (01451) 850470

£85; 7 pretty rms with thoughtful extras. 16th-c cotswold stone guesthouse with inglenook fireplaces, beams, and rugs on flagstones, two sitting rooms, enjoyable evening meals by candlelight, four-course breakfasts, attentive owners, and a very relaxed atmosphere; dogs in bedrooms

LOWER SLAUGHTER

Washbourne Court

Lower Slaughter, Cheltenham, Gloucestershire GL54 2HS (01451) 822143

£165; 30 individually decorated rms, some in cottage suites. Honey-coloured stone hotel (recently redecorated) by the River Eye in 4 acres of neat grounds where dogs may walk (nearby local walks, too); comfortable and charming lounges, beams, open fires and persian rugs on polished parquet floors, stone mullioned windows, and delicious modern cooking in light airy restaurant; children must be over 12 in restaurant; disabled access; dogs in bedrooms; £20

NORTH CERNEY

Bathurst Arms

North Cerney, Cirencester, Gloucestershire GL7 7BZ (2.6 miles off A417, exit at NW end of Cirencester bypass heading N of main road and across to turn left on to A435) (01285) 831281

£75; 6 pleasant rms. Handsome 17th-c pink-washed inn with lots of atmosphere, a nice mix of old tables and nicely faded chairs in beamed and panelled bar with fireplace at each end, enjoyable food in carefully renovated dining room, quite a few well chosen wines by the glass, well kept real ales, and an attractive garden running down to the River Churn; lots of surrounding walks; dogs in some bedrooms and bar; treat and dog bowl

PARKEND

Edale House

Folly Road, Parkend, Lydney, Gloucestershire GL15 4JF (01594) 562835

£64; 6 rms, most with own bthrm. Georgian house opposite cricket green and backing on to Nagshead Nature Reserve; comfortable, homely sitting room, honesty bar, very good food in attractive dining room, and relaxed atmosphere; resident cat; walks nearby; children over 12; disabled access; dogs in bedrooms and lounge; £3

STOW-ON-THE-WOLD

Grapevine

Sheep Street, Stow-on-the-Wold, Cheltenham, Gloucestershire GL54 1AU (0.2 miles off A429; Sheep Street (A436)) (01451) 830344

£140; 22 individually decorated, attractive rms. Warm, friendly and very well run 17th-c hotel with antiques, comfortable chairs and relaxed atmosphere in the lounge, imaginative food in attractive, fairy and candlelit conservatory restaurant with its 70-year-old trailing vine, and bistro food in both brasserie and beamed bar (real ales, too); partial disabled access; dogs in bedrooms (if small and well behaved)

Old Stocks

The Square, Stow-on-the-Wold, Cheltenham, Gloucestershire GL54 1AF (0.1 miles off A429; Market Square, best entered from N end of town) (01451) 830666

£90; 18 rms. Well run 16th/17th-c cotswold stone hotel overlooking the Market Square with cosy welcoming small bar, old beams and open fire, comfortable residents' lounge, good food in restaurant, friendly staff, and three-terraced garden; cl Christmas; partial disabled access; dogs in bedrooms and some public rooms but not restaurant; £5

THORNBURY

Thornbury Castle

Castle Street, Thornbury, Bristol BS35 1HH (01454) 281182

£155; 25 opulent rms, some with big Tudor fireplaces or fine oriel windows. Impressive and luxuriously renovated early 16th-c castle with tapestries, antiques, huge fireplaces and mullioned windows in the baronial public rooms, three dining rooms (one in the base of a tower), fine cooking, extensive wine list (inc wine from their own vineyard), thoughtful friendly service, and vast grounds inc the oldest Tudor gardens in England; partial disabled access; dogs in bedrooms only; £10

DOG FRIENDLY PUBS

BENTWORTH

Sun

Sun Hill; from the A339 coming from Alton the first turning takes you there direct; or in village follow Shalden 2¼, Alton 4¼ signpost; GU34 5JT

Marvellous choice of real ales and welcoming landlady in popular country pub; nearby walks

To be sure of a table in this bustling and charming 17th-c country pub, you must book ahead as it's always busy. Food is fairly traditional and clearly popular, though despite plenty of customers, service remains efficient and friendly and the welcoming landlady is very hands-on. There's a fine choice of seven real ales on handpump such as Badger Hopping Hare, Fullers London Pride, Gales HSB, Ringwood Best and Old Thumper, Stonehenge Pigswill, and Timothy Taylors Landlord; several malt whiskies. The two little traditional communicating rooms have high-backed antique settles, pews and schoolroom chairs, olde-worlde prints and blacksmith's tools on the walls, and bare boards and scrubbed deal tables on the left; big fireplaces (one with an open fire) make it especially snug in winter; an arch leads to a brick-floored room with another open fire. There are seats out in front and in the back garden and pleasant nearby walks.

Free house ~ Licensee Mary Holmes ~ Real ale ~ Bar food ~ (01420) 562338 ~ Children welcome ~ Dogs welcome ~ Open 12-3, 6-11; 12-10 Sun

BRAISHFIELD

Wheatsheaf

Village signposted off A3090 on NW edge of Romsey, pub just S of village on Braishfield Road; SO51 0QE

Cheerful pub with interesting and unusual décor, good choice of wines, and food using some their own produce; nearby walks

All very friendly and laid-back, this rambling place has quite a mish-mash of idio-syncratic décor, but it does work well. There are all sorts of tables from elegant little oak ovals through handsome Regency-style drum tables to sturdy more rustic ones, with a similarly wide variety of chairs, and on the stripped brick or deep pink-painted walls a profusion of things to look at, from Spy caricatures and antique prints through staffordshire dogs and other decorative china to a leg in a fishnet stocking kicking out from the wall and a jokey 'Malteser grader' (a giant copper skimmer). Traditional and some gently imaginative dishes are prepared using local meat, their own rare breed pigs (they make their own sausages and black puddings) and local game – the landlord can often be found plucking and preparing pheasants, rabbits and so forth. They do gourmet burgers on Wednesday evenings and run a Ladies Night on Thursdays. Ringwood Best and a couple of guests like Bowmans Wallops Wood and Hampshire Pride of Romsey on handpump, and 18 wines by the glass; daily papers, several reference books, piped music and board games. Disabled access and facilities. Unusually, the chairs, tables and picnic-sets out on the terrace are painted in greek blue; boules. There are woodland walks nearby and the pub is handy for the Sir Harold Hillier Arboretum.

Enterprise ~ Lease Peter and Jenny Jones ~ Real ale ~ Bar food (12-2.30, 6.30-9.30; all day Sun) ~ Restaurant ~ (01794) 368372 ~ Children welcome away from bar ~ Dogs welcome ~ Open 12-11.30

DUNBRIDGE
Mill Arms

Barley Hill, just by station on Portsmouth—Cardiff line; SO51 0LF

Extended coaching house with plenty of space, several real ales, bistro-style food and pretty garden

In fine Test Valley countryside where there are plenty of walks (and dogs on leads are welcome), this is an attractively extended 18th-c building. There's a relaxed, friendly atmosphere in the high-ceilinged rooms with scrubbed pine tables and farmhouse chairs on the oak or flagstone floors, a couple of log fires, several sofas, and Ringwood Best with guests such as Brains SA, Caledonian XPA, Gales (Fullers) HSB, and Wychwood Hobgoblin on handpump; several wines by the glass, enjoyable food, and prompt service. There's a skittle alley and piped music. The large, pretty garden has picnic-sets. Dunbridge railway station is opposite.

Enterprise ~ Lease Mr I Bentall ~ Real ale ~ Bar food (12-2.30, 6-9.30; 12-9.30 Sat(9 Sun)) ~ Restaurant ~ (01794) 340401 ~ Children welcome ~ Dogs allowed in bar ~ Open 12-11(10.30 Sun)

DUNDRIDGE
Hampshire Bowman

Off B3035 towards Droxford, Swanmore, then right at Bishops W signpost; SO32 1GD

Friendly country pub with quickly changing real ales, unpretentious food and peaceful garden with children's play equipment

Extremely popular with a good mix of customers, this extended country tavern has a friendly and relaxed atmosphere and a good range of real ales tapped from the cask: Archers Jackass, Bowman Swift One, Hop Back Summer Lightning, Ringwood Fortyniner, and Stonehenge Pigswill. There's a smart stable bar that sits comfortably alongside the cosy unassuming original bar, some colourful paintings, several wines by the glass, local apple juice, and cider (from April-October). Board games, puzzles and Daisy the pub dog. The homely bar food, supplemented by a handful of imaginative specials, is much enjoyed. There are picnic-sets on the attractive lawn, a giant umbrella with lighting and heating on the terrace (where you can enjoy the lovely sunsets), and new children's play equipment; peaceful nearby downland walks.

Free house ~ Licensee Heather Seymour ~ Bar food (12-2, 6.30-9; all day Fri-Sun) ~ (01489) 892940 ~ Children welcome until 9pm ~ Dogs welcome ~ Open 12-11(10.30 Sun)

EAST TYTHERLEY

Star

Off B3084 N of Romsey; SO51 0LW

Warm welcome for drinkers and diners in pretty pub, inventive food, real ales, and comfortable bedrooms

The friendly, hard-working licensees in this pretty country pub have encouraged drinkers by creating more room for them in the main bar – they want to be, first and foremost, a village inn. The bar has comfortable sofas and tub armchairs, pub dining tables and chairs, bar stools and chairs, an overflowing bookcase to one side of the log fire, and rich red walls. Ringwood Best Bitter and a guest plus Hidden Quest on handpump, several wines by the glass and malt whiskies and a range of apple juices; piped music and board games. Cooked by the licensees' son, food is inventive and attractively presented; there's also a good value two-course set lunch menu. There are picnic-set sets in front and tables and chairs on the back terrace by a giant chessboard. The bedrooms overlook the cricket pitch and the breakfasts are particularly good; nearby walks.

Free house ~ Licensees Alan and Lesley Newitt ~ Real ale ~ Bar food ~ Restaurant ~ (01794) 340225 ~ Children welcome ~ Dogs allowed in bar and bedrooms ~ Open 11-3, 6-10.30; 11-4 Sun; closed Sun evening, Mon ~ Bedrooms: £55S/£80S

EASTON

Chestnut Horse

3.6 miles from M3 junction 9: A33 towards Kings Worthy, then B3047 towards Itchen Abbas; Easton then signposted on right – bear left in village; SO21 1EG

Cosy dining pub with log fires, fresh flowers and candles, deservedly popular food and friendly staff; Itchen Valley walks nearby

Cosy and well run, this is a busy dining pub with friendly, helpful staff. The inventive food is good and carefully cooked. It's not cheap, but there is a good value, seasonally changing two-course menu (not available weekend evenings or Sunday lunchtime). The open-plan interior manages to have a pleasantly rustic and intimate feel with a series of cosily separate areas and the snug décor takes in candles and fresh flowers on the tables, log fires in cottagey fireplaces and comfortable furnishings. The black beams and joists are hung with all sorts of jugs, mugs and chamber-pots, and there are lots of attractive pictures of wildlife and the local area. Badger K&B Sussex Bitter and Hopping Hare on handpump, several wines by the glass and 30 malt whiskies; piped music. There are good tables out on a smallish sheltered decked area with colourful flower tubs and baskets, and plenty of nearby walks in the Itchen Valley.

Badger ~ Tenant Karen Wells ~ Real ale ~ Bar food ~ Restaurant ~ (01962) 779257 ~ Children welcome ~ Dogs allowed in bar ~ Open 11-3, 5.30-11.30; 11am-11.30pm Sat; 12-10.30 Sun; 12-6 Sun in winter; closed winter Sun evening

FRITHAM
Royal Oak

Village signed from exit roundabout, M27 junction 1; quickest via B3078, then left and straight through village; head for Eyeworth Pond; SO43 7HJ

Rural New Forest spot and part of a working farm; traditional rooms, log fires, seven real ales and simple lunchtime food

One nostalgic reader remembers this pub nearly 50 years ago when 'opening hours were whimsical and late night drinking guaranteed'. This is still a lovely, simple country tavern with plenty of chatty locals (almost invariably with a dog in tow), a genuinely warm welcome from the friendly staff and really enjoyable, good quality unfussy food. Three neatly kept black beamed rooms are straightforward but full of proper traditional character, with prints and pictures involving local characters on the white walls, restored panelling, antique wheelback, spindleback and other old chairs and stools with colourful seats around solid tables on new oak flooring, and two roaring log fires. The back bar has quite a few books. Half a dozen real ales are tapped from the cask: Hop Back Summer Lightning, Ringwood Best and Fortyniner and changing guests from brewers such as Bowman and Keysone. Also, a dozen wines by the glass (mulled wine in winter) and a September beer festival; darts. Summer barbecues are put on in the neatly kept big garden which has a marquee for poor weather and pétanque. Using eggs from their free-range hens and pork from their own pigs, the much liked simple lunchtime food is limited to winter soups, ploughman's, pies and quiches, sausages and pork pie, and smoked chicken breast wrapped in bacon. The pub is part of a working farm so there are ponies and pigs out on the green and plenty of livestock nearby.

Free house ~ Licensees Neil and Pauline McCulloch ~ Real ale ~ Bar food (lunchtime only (till 3pm weekends)) ~ No credit cards ~ (023) 8081 2606 ~ Children welcome if well behaved ~ Dogs welcome ~ Open 11-11; 11-11 Sat; 12-10.30 Sun; 11-3, 6-22 weekdays in winter

HAWKLEY
Hawkley Inn

Take first right turn off B3006, heading towards Liss 0.75 miles from its junction with A3; then after nearly 2 miles take first left turn into Hawkley village – Pococks Lane; OS Sheet 186 map reference 746292; GU33 6NE

Nine real ales in friendly country pub with home-cooked food

The fine range of nine real ales on handpump here come from breweries such as Bowman, Dark Star, FFF, Hogs Back, Hop Back, Ringwood, and Suthwyk. There are also a dozen malt whiskies and local cider. This is still a proper country pub with walking boots, wellies, horses, and bikes, and the unchanging front rooms have open fires, board games and piped music. The back rooms have been knocked through, effectively creating a central bar so you can now walk all round the pub. The menu is short and pubby with a few daily specials. There are seats on the terrace and in the garden. The pub is on the Hangers Way Path, and at weekends there are plenty of walkers (and it does tend to be crowded then).

Free house ~ Licensee Jean Jamieson ~ Real ale ~ Bar food (12-2(2.30 Sat), 7-9.30) ~ (01730) 827205 ~ Children welcome until 8pm ~ Dogs allowed in bar ~ Open 12-3, 5.30-11; 12-11(10.30 Sun) Sat

HOUGHTON

Boot

Village signposted off A30 in Stockbridge; SO20 6LH

Riverside pub with good generous food either in cheerful locals' bar or in roomy more decorous lounge/dining room

On a sunny day, this is an enchanting spot for lunch with the long sheltered back lawn runing down to a lovely tranquil stretch of the River Test (unfenced and quick-flowing here); you may be able to arrange fishing with the pub – though one monster trout in the bar's generous assortment of stuffed creatures was actually taken on the Itchen. This nice country bar is bustling and pubby, with a good log fire, plenty of regulars both at the counter and around the various tables, and perhaps one or two dogs making themselves at home (visiting dogs may get a chew). Service is efficient and natural – treating people good-naturedly as individuals without being artificially over-friendly. Ringwood Best and Seventy Eight on handpump; faint piped music. The tasty food is inventive and served in generous helpings. On the left is a much more extensive part with cream and green décor and attractive high-backed, modern dining chairs around good solid tables. The Test Way cycle path is on the far side of the river.

Free house ~ Licensees Richard and Tessa Affleck ~ Real ale ~ Bar food ~ (01794) 388310 ~ Children welcome if well behaved ~ Dogs allowed in bar ~ Open 12-2.30, 6-11; 12-2.30, 7-10.30 Sun

LOWER WIELD

Yew Tree

Turn off A339 NW of Alton at Medstead, Bentworth 1 signpost, then follow village signposts; or off B3046 S of Basingstoke, signposted from Preston Candover; SO24 9RX

Relaxed atmosphere, super choice of wines and popular bar food in pleasant country pub; sizeable garden and nearby walks

This is the sort of place that once found, you'll want to come back to. It's a tile-hung country pub with an attractively informal atmosphere and a genuinely friendly and enthusiastic landlord. There's a small flagstoned bar area on the left with pictures above its stripped brick dado, a steadily ticking clock and log fire. Around to the right of the serving counter – which has a couple of stylish wrought-iron bar chairs – it's carpeted, with a few flower pictures; throughout there is a mix of tables, including some quite small ones for two, and miscellaneous chairs. 13 wines by the glass from a well chosen list which may include Louis Jadot burgundies from a shipper based just along the lane and summer rosé. Hammerpot Meteor and a beer from fff named after the pub on handpump. Bar food, with pub standards such as shoulder of lamb with red wine and rosemary jus, is well liked. There are solid tables and chunky seats out on the front terrace, picnic-sets in a sizeable side garden, pleasant views, and a cricket field just across the quiet lane. Nearby walks.

Free house ~ Licensee Tim Gray ~ Real ale ~ Bar food ~ (01256) 389224 ~ Children welcome ~ Dogs allowed in bar ~ Open 12-3, 6-11; 12-10.30 Sun; closed Mon; ten days in early Jan

LYMINGTON
Kings Head

Quay Hill; pedestrian alley at bottom of High Street; you can park down on quay and walk up from Quay Street; SO41 3AR

Rambling beamed and timbered pub with nice mix of old-fashioned seating, several ales, and newspapers to read

A handsome sight at the top of a steep cobbled lane of smart small shops, this 17th-c pub is a popular place for a drink: Adnams Bitter, Gales HSB, Greene King Old Speckled Hen and a beer from Fullers and Ringwood on handpump, and several wines by the glass. The mainly bare-boarded rooms ramble up and down steps and through timber dividers with tankards hanging from great rough beams. There's a nice old-fashioned variety of seating at a great mix of tables from an elegant gateleg to a huge chunk of elm, and the local pictures include good classic yacht photographs. A cosy upper corner past the serving counter has a log fire in a big fireplace, its mantelpiece a shrine to all sorts of drinking paraphernalia from beer tankards to port and champagne cases; an interesting clock, too. Daily papers in a rack and piped pop music; standard bar food.

Enterprise ~ Lease Paul Stratton ~ Real ale ~ Bar food (11-2.30(3 Fri, 3.30 weekends), 6-10) ~ (01590) 672709 ~ Children welcome ~ Dogs welcome ~ Open 11.30-3, 6-midnight; 11-midnight Sat; 12-midnight Sun; closed 25 and 26 Dec

OVINGTON
Bush

Village signposted from A31 on Winchester side of Alresford; SO24 0RE

Cottagey pub with seats in waterside back garden and several peaceful rooms

Especially busy at weekends, this tucked away pub is in a charming spot with picnic-sets by the River Itchen. It's attractively cottagey inside and the low-ceilinged bar is furnished with cushioned high-backed settles, elm tables with pews and kitchen chairs, masses of old pictures in heavy gilt frames on the walls, and a roaring fire on one side with an antique solid fuel stove opposite.

Wadworths IPA, 6X, and Horizon on handpump, several wines by the glass and quite a few country wines. Bar food (not cheap) includes sandwiches and ploughman's. Look out for the sociable scottish springer spaniel, Paddy; board games. Please note that if you want to bring children it's best to book, as there are only a few tables set aside for families. Nice nearby walks.

Wadworths ~ Managers Nick and Cathy Young ~ Real ale ~ Bar food (12-4 Sun; not Sun evening) ~ (01962) 732764 ~ Children allowed but limited room for them ~ Dogs welcome ~ Open 11-3, 6-11(all day summer hols); 12-4, 7-10.30 Sun; closed 25 Dec

PETERSFIELD

Trooper

From B2070 in Petersfield follow Steep signposts past station, but keep on up past Steep, on old coach road; OS Sheet 186 map reference 726273; GU32 1BD

Charming landlord, popular food, decent drinks, and little persian knick-knacks and local artists' work

Mr Matini continues to offer a genuinely friendly welcome to all his customers and this is the sort of well run all-rounder that people come back to again and again. There's an island bar, blond chairs and a mix of tripod tables on bare boards or red tiles, tall stools by a broad ledge facing big windows that look across to rolling downland fields, old film star photos and paintings by local artists for sale, little persian knick-knacks here and there, quite a few ogival mirrors, lit candles all over the place, fresh flowers, and a well tended log fire in the stone fireplace; carefully chosen piped music, and newspapers and magazines to read. Arundel Sussex Gold, Bowmans Swift One, and Ringwood Best on handpump and several wines by the glass. The menu includes very enjoyable takes on quite a few traditional dishes, and more. There are lots of picnic-sets on an upper lawn and the horse rail in the car park ('horses and camels only before 8pm') does get used, though probably not often by camels.

Free house ~ Licensee Hassan Matini ~ Real ale ~ Bar food ~ Restaurant ~ (01730) 827293 ~ Children must be seated and supervised by an adult ~ Dogs allowed in bar ~ Open 12-3, 5-11; 12-11 Sat; 12-5 Sun; closed Sun evening and all day Mon (except for bank hols), 25 and 26 Dec, 1 Jan

ROWLAND'S CASTLE

Castle Inn

Village signposted off B2148/B2149 N of Havant; Finchdean Road, by junction with Redhill Road and Woodberry Lane; PO9 6DA

A cheerful feel and generous food served by smart staff in bustling pub; largish garden

Well run and cheerful, this popular pub has friendly hands-on licensees. There are two appealing little eating rooms on the left. The front one has rather nice simple mahogany chairs around sturdy scrubbed pine tables, rugs on flagstones, a big fireplace, and quite a lot of old local photographs on its ochre walls. The back one is similar, but with bare boards and local watercolour landscapes by Bob Payne for sale. There is a small separate public bar on the right with a good fire and Fullers London Pride, Gales Butser and HSB and a guest like Fullers Festival Mild on handpump. Served by smartly dressed staff, there's a pubby, fairly priced lunchtime menu and a more elaborate evening menu. The publicans' own ponies are in view from the largish garden, which is equipped with picnic-sets and a couple of swings; disabled access and facilities are good.

Gales (Fullers) ~ Lease Jan and Roger Burrell ~ Real ale ~ Bar food (12-3, 6-9; not Sun evening) ~ Restaurant ~ (023) 9241 2494 ~ Children welcome ~ Dogs allowed in bar ~ Open 10.30am-midnight; 12-midnight Sun

SPARSHOLT
Plough

Village signposted off B3049 (Winchester—Stockbridge), a little W of Winchester; SO21 2NW

Neat, well run dining pub with interesting furnishings, an extensive wine list, and popular bar food; garden with children's play fort

As well as four real ales, this bustling pub is very popular for its extremely good food. It's a neatly kept place and the main bar has an interesting mix of wooden tables and chairs with farm tools, scythes and pitchforks attached to the ceiling. Wadworths IPA, 6X, Horizon and a seasonal beer on handpump, and an extensive wine list with a fair selection by the glass, including champagne and pudding wine. Served by friendly, efficient staff, bar food is very tasty, particularly the steak, mushroom and ale pie. Disabled access and facilities; there's a children's play fort, and plenty of seats on the terrace and lawn.

Wadworths ~ Tenants Richard and Kathryn Crawford ~ Real ale ~ Bar food (12-2, 6-9(8.30 Sun)) ~ (01962) 776353 ~ Children welcome except in main bar area ~ Dogs welcome ~ Open 11-3, 6-11; 12-3, 6-10.30 Sun; closed 25 Dec

SWANMORE
Rising Sun

Village signposted off A32 N of Wickham and B2177 S of Bishops Waltham; pub E of village centre, at Hillpound on the Droxford Road; SO32 2PS

Friendly licensees make this proper country pub a warmly welcoming all-rounder

The hard-working, hands-on licensees in this bustling 17th-c coaching inn make all their customers comfortable and welcome, and their young staff are attentive and helpful, too. The low-beamed carpeted bar has some easy chairs and a sofa by its good log fire, and a few tables with pubby seats. Beyond the fireplace on the right is a pleasant much roomier dining area, with similarly unpretentious furnishings, running back in an L past the bar; one part of this has stripped brick barrel vaulting. Marstons Pedigree and Ringwood Best and guests such as Adnams and Greene King Old Speckled Hen on handpump, and a good range of a dozen or so wines by the glass; faint piped music. A fair choice of good value pubby food runs from sandwiches to a pie of the day. There are picnic-sets out on the side grass with a play area, and the Kings Way long distance path is close by – readers tell us it is best to head north where there is lovely downland country, plus fine views and interesting winding lanes.

Punch ~ Lease Mark and Sue Watts ~ Real ale ~ Bar food (12-2, 6-9) ~ Restaurant ~ (01489) 896663 ~ Children allowed but must be well behaved ~ Dogs allowed in bar ~ Open 11.30-3, 5.30-11; 12-3, 5.30-10.30 Sun

TICHBORNE
Tichborne Arms
Village signed off B3047; SO24 0NA

Traditional pub in rolling countryside and liked by walkers; big garden

This attractive thatched pub extends a cheery welcome and the traditional, very good food is totally home made (apart from the ice-creams) and uses seasonal produce. The comfortable square-panelled room on the right has wheelback chairs and settles (one very long), a stone fireplace and latticed windows. On the left is a larger, livelier, partly panelled room used for eating. Pictures and documents on the walls recall the bizarre Tichborne Case, in which a mystery man from Australia claimed fraudulently to be the heir to this estate. Bowmans Swift One, Goddards Ale of Wight, Ringwood Best, Sharps Doom Bar and a couple of guest beers are tapped from the cask, alongside seven wines by the glass, and farm cider. There are picnic-sets in the big, neat garden. The Wayfarers Walk and Itchen Way pass close by and the countryside around is attractively rolling.

Free house ~ Licensee Nicky Roper ~ Real ale ~ Bar food (12-2(3 Sat and Sun), 6.30-9.30) ~ (01962) 733760 ~ Children welcome ~ Dogs welcome ~ Open 11.30-3(4 Sat), 6.30-11(midnight Sat); 12-4, 7-11 Sun; closed evenings of 25 and 26 Dec and 1 Jan

UPHAM
Brushmakers Arms
Off Winchester—Bishops Waltham downs road; Shoe Lane; SO32 1JJ

Friendly old place with extensive displays of brushes, local beers, and nice unfussy food

This is an enjoyable old local with a friendly landlord, helpful staff, and a good mix of customers. Picking up on the pub's name, the walls in the L-shaped bar (divided in two by a central brick chimney with a woodburning stove) are hung with quite a collection of old and new brushes. A few beams in the low ceiling add to the cosiness, and there are comfortably cushioned settles and chairs and a variety of tables including some in country-style stripped wood; there's also a little back snug with fruit machine, dominoes and board games. Hampshire Ironside and Uncle Bob, Ringwood Best and changing guests on handpump; the pub cats are called Gilbert and Kera and the ghost is known as Mr Chickett (apparently seen as a shadowy figure searching the pub for his lost money and belongings). Well liked bar food is straightforwardly pubby. The big garden is well stocked with mature shrubs and trees and there are picnic-sets on a shel-tered back terrace amongst tubs of flowers, with more on the tidy tree-sheltered lawn. It's best to park by the duck pond; good walks nearby.

Free house ~ Licensee Keith Venton ~ Real ale ~ Bar food (12-2, 6(7 Sun)-9(9.30 Fri, Sat)) ~ (01489) 860231 ~ Children welcome ~ Dogs allowed in bar ~ Open 11-3, 5.45-11; 12-3, 7-10.30 Sun

WEST MEON

Thomas Lord

High Street; GU32 1LN

Friendly pub, cheerful licensees, lots of wooden furniture in several rooms, interesting food and fine choice of beers

This is an individually decorated pub with a lively, warm-hearted atmosphere. There's an interesting mix of wooden dining and pubby chairs around lots of different wooden tables (each with a candle on it – lit on a dark day), bare boards, some cricketing prints and memorabilia, various pictures and portraits above the wooden dados, and two blazing fires. The back room is lined with books which you can buy for 50p. The welcoming, chatty landlords keep a fine range of real ales tapped from the cask such as Ballards Best, Bowmans Swift One and Wallops Wood, Goddards Ale of Wight, Itchen Valley Winchester Ale, and Ringwood Best; also farm ciders, several wines by the glass and decent coffee. Enjoyable food using carefully sourced local produce includes inventive dishes such as home-cured duck with red cabbage coleslaw and chicken and ox tongue pie. The garden was being redesigned as we went to press and carpenters were hard at work designing new seats and tables; there's an outside oven here, too. Good walks to the west of the village.

Enterprise ~ Lease David Thomas and Richard Taylor ~ Real ale ~ Bar food (not Sun evening) ~ Restaurant ~ (01730) 829244 ~ Children welcome ~ Dogs welcome ~ Open 11-3, 6-midnight; 11-midnight Sat; 12-11 Sun

WHERWELL

Mayfly

Testcombe (over by Fullerton, and not in Wherwell itself); A3057 SE of Andover, between B3420 turn-off and Leckford where road crosses River Test; OS Sheet 185 map reference 382390; SO20 6AX

Extremely (and deservedly) popular pub with decking and conservatory seats overlooking the River Test, half a dozen ales, and wide range of enjoyable bar food, usefully served all day

Mr and Mrs Lane have been running this idyllically placed pub for over 20 years. It's on an island between the River Test and a smaller river to the back, and in good weather the tables on the decking area overlooking the water are extremely popular – best to get there early. Inside, the spacious, beamed and carpeted bar has fishing pictures and fishing equipment on the cream walls, rustic pub furnishings, and a woodburning stove. There's also a conservatory with riverside views; piped music. A fine choice of six real ales on handpump served by friendly staff might include Hop Back Summer Lightning, Palmers Gold, Ringwood Best, Wadworths 6X, Wychwood Hobgoblin, and a changing guest; 20 wines by the glass. Good, popular bar food is handily available all day and features a daily hot and cold buffet (at its largest in summer).

Enterprise ~ Manager Barry Lane ~ Real ale ~ Bar food (11.30-9) ~ (01264) 860283 ~ Children welcome if well behaved ~ Dogs welcome ~ Open 10am-11pm; 10am-10pm winter

DOG FRIENDLY HOTELS, INNS AND B&Bs

CHERITON

Flower Pots

Cheriton, Alresford, Hampshire SO24 0QQ (0.7 miles off A272; pub signed left off B3046 in village) (01962) 771318

£70; 4 rms. Unspoilt and quietly comfortable village local run by very friendly family, with two pleasant little bars, log fire, decent bar food (not Sun evening), super own-brew beers, and old-fashioned seats on the pretty lawns; no credit cards; no accommodation Christmas and New Year; two resident english springers; lots of walks nearby; no children; dogs in bedrooms and bars if well behaved and on a lead

HURSTBOURNE TARRANT

Esseborne Manor

Hurstbourne Tarrant, Andover, Hampshire SP11 0ER (01264) 736444

£125; 19 individually decorated rms. Small stylish Victorian manor with relaxed, friendly atmosphere, comfortable lounge and snug little bar, good modern cooking and log fires in elegant dining room, and courteous staff; three acres of neat gardens (where dogs may walk) with tennis and croquet; special arrangement with local golf club and health and leisure centre; disabled access; dogs welcome in bedrooms

LYMINGTON

Efford Cottage

Milford Road, Everton, Lymington, Hampshire SO41 0JD (01590) 642315

£60; 3 comfortable little rms. Spacious Georgian cottage in an acre of garden which has a special doggy area marked out; marvellous breakfasts with home-baked bread, home-made preserves and honey from their own bees served in charming dining room, and friendly, helpful owners; resident english springer spaniel; good parking; walks on nearby beach, footpaths and in New Forest; no children; dogs in bedrooms but must not be left unattended; £2

Stanwell House

High Street, Lymington, Hampshire SO41 9AA (01590) 677123

£150; 27 pretty rms. Handsome town house with comfortable attractively furnished lounge, cosy little bar, good food in both bistro and seafood restaurants, and pretty walled back garden; New Forest nearby for walks; dogs in bedrooms; bowl and treats; £15

MILFORD ON SEA

Westover Hall

Park Lane, Milford-on-Sea, Lymington, Hampshire SO41 0PT (01590) 643044

£280; 14 individually furnished rms, 6 with sea views. Victorian mansion in marvellous spot near peaceful beach, views of Christchurch Bay, Isle of Wight and the Needles rocks; impressive original features including dramatic stained glass, magnificent oak panelling and ornate ceilings, very good food using the best local produce in grand (but not stuffy) candlelit restaurant overlooking garden and sea, lighter lunches in lounge bar also with water views, sunny terrace, and helpful friendly staff; resident cat; plenty of fine nearby walks; disabled access; dogs in bedrooms and maybe lounge bar (if on a lead); £10

OWER

Ranvilles Farm House

Pauncefoot Hill, Romsey, Hampshire SO51 6AA (3.3 miles off M27 exit 2; after just under 2 miles on A31 towards Romsey, turn back into southbound carriageway – Ranvilles is next on left) (023) 80814481

£65; 4 attractively decorated rms with antique furniture. Dating from the 13th c when Richard de Ranville came from Normandy and settled with his family, this Grade II* listed house is in 3½ quiet acres of gardens and paddock, with warmly friendly owners and enjoyable breakfasts; no evening meals; resident labrador; walks in the grounds and in the New Forest; disabled access; dogs in bedrooms; bedding, bowls, treats; £3

PETERSFIELD

Langrish House

Langrish, Petersfield, Hampshire GU32 1RN (01730) 266941

£116; 13 pretty, themed rms with country views. Family home dating back to 17th-c family and set in lovely garden and 14 acres of grounds, with genuinely helpful and friendly staff, bar in candlelit vaults, and imaginative food in small, cosy restaurant with log fire; resident labrador and siamese cats; endless local footpaths for walking; cl two weeks in Jan; partial disabled access; dogs welcome away from restaurant; pet pack and welcome letter; £10

SPARSHOLT

Lainston House

Sparsholt, Winchester, Hampshire SO21 2LT (01962) 776088

£274; 50 spacious, individually decorated rms. Close to Winchester, this elegant William and Mary hotel stands in 63 acres of fine parkland, with tennis court, croquet, fishing, archery, and clay pigeon shooting; fresh flowers and paintings in relaxing and elegant lounge, panelled bar, creative modern cooking in smart restaurant, and fine wine list; gym; disabled access; dogs in bedrooms; special dog menu, bowls, etc; £50 (per stay)

STUCKTON

Three Lions

Stuckton, Fordingbridge, Hampshire SP6 2HF (0.8 miles off A338; village signed from A338/B3078 Fordingbridge roundabout) (01425) 652489

£105; 7 rms, 3 in newish courtyard block. Friendly family-run restaurant-with-rooms on edge of New Forest with small bar, comfortable little lounge, airy conservatory, particularly good food in cottagey restaurant, enjoyable breakfasts and attractive garden with hot tub and sauna; resident cat; cl two weeks in Feb; disabled access; dogs welcome away from restaurant; £10

WINCHESTER

Hotel du Vin

14 Southgate Street, Winchester, Hampshire SO23 9EF (3.2 miles off M3 junction 10, following B3335 into town; Southgate Street) (01962) 841414

£135; 24 stylish, well equipped rms. Engaging early 18th-c town house with lots of character in bustling Champagne Bar and comfortable lounge, attractively decorated and very popular bistro with imaginative brasserie-style food, exceptional wine list, cheerful, helpful staff, and lovely walled garden for summer dining; disabled access; dogs in bedrooms; £10

Wykeham Arms

75 Kingsgate Street, Winchester, Hampshire SO23 9PE (01962) 853834

£115; 14 well equipped attractive rms. Very well run, smart old town inn, close to cathedral, with interestingly furnished bustling bars, two small dining rooms serving excellent food (very good breakfasts, too), fine wines (lots by the glass), and prompt friendly service; walks along water meadows and more close by; cl 25 Dec; no children; dogs in one bedroom and in bar; £10

DOG FRIENDLY PUBS

AYMESTREY

Riverside Inn

A4110, at N end of village, W of Leominster; HR6 9ST

Lovely spot with seats making most of the view, and river fishing for residents; cosy, rambling rooms, open fires, enjoyable food, and warm welcome

In attractively folded wooded country, this half-timbered inn stands right by an ancient stone bridge over the River Lugg, and in warm weather the temptation to linger at picnic-sets in the tree-sheltered garden can be very strong. The rambling beamed bar has several cosy areas and the décor is drawn from a pleasant mix of periods and styles, with fine antique oak tables and chairs, stripped pine country kitchen tables, fresh flowers, hops strung from a ceiling wagon-wheel, horse tack and nice pictures. Warm log fires in winter, while in summer big overflowing flower pots frame the entrances; fairly quiet piped pop music. The service is both professional and friendly: the landlord really likes to talk to his customers. The very tasty bar food, from a sensibly put-together menu, is prepared using local specialist producers, and even fruit and vegetables grown by the licensees. Wye Valley Hereford Pale Ale and a guest such as Wye Valley Butty Bach on handpump, Brook Farm cider (pressed in the next village), and more than 20 malt whiskies. Residents can try fly-fishing.

Free house ~ Licensees Richard and Liz Gresko ~ Real ale ~ Bar food (12-2.15, 7-9.15) ~ Restaurant ~ (01568) 708440 ~ Children welcome ~ Dogs allowed in bar and bedrooms ~ Open 11-3, 6-11; 12-3, 6.30-10.30 Sun; closed lunchtime Mon and 26 Dec-1 Jan ~ Bedrooms: £45B/£70B

BRIMFIELD

Roebuck Inn

Village signposted just off A49 Shrewsbury—Leominster; SY8 4NE

Smartly refurbished dining pub with French owners and fine food

Readers appreciate the efforts made by the owners to update this pub. Its front lounge bar has dark brown and orange club chairs, sofas and an open fire in the impressive inglenook fireplace. The middle bar area also has an open fire but has kept more of a pubby feel, and what was the dining room is now more of a bistro with chunky cord seating in brown and apricot around contemporary wooden tables and modern art on deep-coloured walls. As you might expect, the contemporary menu here has a french bias though you'll also find lunchtime sandwiches and sausage and mash. Banks's and Marstons Pedigree on handpump, farm cider and several wines by the glass; and piped jazz. There are some seats outside on the heated and sheltered terrace.

Union Pub Company ~ Tenant Oliver Bossut ~ Real ale ~ Bar food (12-2.30, 6.30-9.30) ~ Restaurant ~ (01584) 711230 ~ Children welcome ~ Dogs allowed in bar ~ Open 11.30-3, 6-11(1am Sat); 11.30-4 Sun; closed Sun evening

BRINGSTY COMMON
Live & Let Live

Off A44 Knightwick—Bromyard 1.5 miles W of Whitbourne turn; take track southwards at black cat inn sign, bearing right at fork; WR6 5UW

Charmingly restored country tavern surrounded by rolling partly wooded common; enjoyable food and drink

This rustic 17th-c pub, beautifully restored and re-thatched, reopened in 2007 after more than ten years' closure. The restoration's been a long hard slog for its friendly local landlady, but her painstaking care has paid off well. The cosy bar has non-matching scrubbed or polished old tables on its flagstones, a very high-backed traditional winged settle by the log fire in the cavernous stone fireplace, and a variety of seats from comfortably cushioned little chairs to a long stripped pew. Earthenware jugs hang from the low stripped beams, with more bygones on the mantelshelf. The hop-hung bar counter, which has old casks built into its facing, has well kept Malvern Hills Black Pear on handpump, with a couple of guests, always local, such as Spinning Dog Herefordshire Owd Bull, and Oliver's cider and perry. They do a short choice of bar lunches from soup and sandwiches (choice of breads) to three or four simple hot dishes such as fish pie or lamb chops – the lamb is usually from the black welsh mountain flock which grazes on the common, and other meats come from local farmers. Outside the timbered cottage with its massive stone chimney, a glass-topped well and big wooden hogshead have been pressed into service as tables for the flagstoned terrace, which has a splendid leather-cushioned bench, and the grassy former orchard blends into the partly scrubby and partly wooded slopes of this high ancient-feeling common, with picnic-sets giving long peaceful views. You really do feel miles from anywhere here.

Free house ~ Licensee Sue Dovey ~ Real ale ~ Bar food (12-2(3 Sun) 6-9, not Sun evening or Mon) ~ Restaurant ~ No credit cards ~ (01886) 821462 ~ Children welcome ~ Dogs allowed in bar ~ Open 12-2.30, 5-11, 12-11 Fri-Sun; closed Mon lunchtime except bank hols

HOARWITHY
New Harp

Village signposted off A49 Hereford—Ross-on-Wye; HR2 6QH

Contemporary décor in busy country pub where walkers and dogs are welcome; plenty of outside seats, fair range of interesting drinks

You can take your pick from a terrific range of drinks here: as well as Spinning

Dog Hereford Owd Bull and ales from breweries such as Cottage, Freeminer and Malvern Hills on handpump, and herefordshire farm cider, there is a very extensive collection of unusual bottled beers – among them wheat beers, trappist ales, lesser-known lagers, fruit beers and a fair range of wines by the glass. Each item on the menu is paired with a drink or two that will complement it. Daily specials often include game from local shoots and Tuesday is fish night. Booking is advisable. The bars are decorated in a contemporary style with mainly crisp off-white paintwork, nicely lit modern artwork including cartoons and caricatures, brown leather tub armchairs in front of a woodburning stove, a mix of comfortable dining chairs around individual tables, stone floor tiling and some stripped masonry. The bar angles round to a cosy dining room and the atmosphere is relaxed throughout. Bow windows look up the hill to a remarkable italianate Victorian church with a tall tower, and the little stream which runs through the pretty tree-sheltered garden soon meets the nearby River Wye. The red labrador is called Foxy; piped music and board games. There are plenty of picnic-sets, some on decking in a sort of arbour, and in summer they have barbecues and erect a marquee. Service could be more welcoming at times.

Badger ~ Tenants Fleur and Andrew Cooper ~ Real ale ~ Bar food (12-2.30, 6-9.30) ~ (01432) 840900 ~ Children welcome ~ Dogs welcome ~ Open 12-11(10.30 Sun); 12-3, 6-11 Mon-Thurs in winter

SELLACK
Lough Pool

Back road Hoarwithy—Ross-on-Wye; HR9 6LX

Black and white cottage with individual furnishings in beamed bars, a good choice of food and drinks, lots of seats outside in pretty garden

Near the River Wye and Herefordshire Trail, this characterful, cottagey place is full of thoughtful touches, books and newspapers left out for customers, and crayons and paper for children, and dogs are made to feel welcome too. Outside are picnic-sets on an inviting front lawned area and a pretty array of hanging baskets. Its beamed central room has rustic chairs and cushioned window seats around wooden tables on the mainly flagstoned floor, sporting prints, bunches of dried flowers and fresh hop bines, and a log fire at one end with a woodburner at the other. Leading off are other rooms, gently brightened up with attractive individual furnishings and antique bottles, and nice touches such as the dresser of patterned plates. Food (not cheap) is prepared using home-grown herbs and rare-breed meat from nearby farms. John Smiths and Wye Valley Bitter and Butty Bach and a guest such as Butcombe Bitter on handpump, several malt whiskies, local farm ciders, perries and apple juices, and several wines by the glass from a thoughtful wine list.

Free house ~ Licensees David and Janice Birch ~ Real ale ~ Bar food ~ Restaurant ~ (01989) 730236 ~ Children welcome ~ Dogs allowed in bar ~ Open 11.30(12 Sun)-3, 6.30-11(10.30 Sun); 12-10.30 Sun; closed Sun evening and all day Mon in Nov, and mid Jan-Apr

ST OWEN'S CROSS

New Inn

Junction A4137 and B4521, W of Ross-on-Wye; HR2 8LQ

Huge inglenooks, beams and timbers, a friendly welcome, food served all day, and fine choice of drinks; big garden with views

From this half-timbered 16th-c inn, views extend to the Black Mountains, and in decent weather the spacious enclosed garden is particularly inviting. The friendly licensees have attractively refurbished the interior: lounge bar and restaurant have huge inglenook fireplaces, dark beams and timbers, various nooks and crannies, old pews and a mix of tables and chairs and lots of watercolours on warm red walls. Marstons Burton Bitter plus guests such as Hook Norton 303AD and Jennings Cocker Hoop on handpump, farm cider and perry, several malt whiskies and ten wines by the glass; piped music, table and outdoor games. Standard pub food is served all day. The hanging baskets are quite a sight.

Marstons ~ Lease Nigel Maud ~ Real ale ~ Bar food (12-9) ~ Restaurant ~ (01989) 730274 ~ Children welcome ~ Dogs allowed in bar ~ Open 11(9 Sat, Sun)-11

SYMONDS YAT

Saracens Head

Symonds Yat E, by ferry, ie over on the Gloucs bank; HR9 6JL

Lovely riverside spot, contemporary food and a fine range of drinks in friendly inn; waterside terraces

This idyllic inn far beneath the Symonds Yat viewpoint in the Wye gorge is a memorable place to arrive at on foot: a classic river walk crosses the Wye downstream by an entertainingly bouncy wire bridge at the Biblins and re-crosses here by the long-extant hand-hauled chain ferry that one of the pub staff operates. There are lots of picnic-sets out on the waterside terrace. Inside, it's warm and relaxed with cheerful staff who make you feel at home. The busy, basic flagstoned public bar has Greene King Old Speckled Hen, Theakstons Old Peculier and Wye Valley Butty Bach and Hereford Pale Ale plus a guest such as Butcombe Bitter on handpump, and several wines by the glass; piped music, TV, games machine and pool. As well as lunchtime sandwiches, ciabatta, bruschettas and ploughman's, food can be interesting and quite modern, such as mussels poached with honey and saffron. There's also a cosy lounge and a modernised bare-boards dining room.

Free house ~ Licensees P K and C J Rollinson ~ Real ale ~ Bar food (12-2.30, 6.30-9) ~ Restaurant ~ (01600) 890435 ~ Children welcome ~ Dogs allowed in bar ~ Open 11-11(10.30 Sun)

TITLEY

Stagg

B4355 N of Kington; HR5 3RL

Fantastic food using tip-top ingredients served in extensive dining rooms, a fine choice of drinks, two-acre garden, comfortable bedrooms

Consistently hitting the mark for many years as one of the top dining pubs in the country, this is a place for a special meal, and a lot of effort goes into creating an atmosphere that appeals to both visitors and locals. Readers also enjoy staying here, in bedrooms above the pub or in the additional rooms within a Georgian vicarage four minutes away, and the breakfasts are wonderful, too. The bar, though comfortable and hospitable, is not large, and the atmosphere is civilised rather than lively. Very good food, using their own-grown vegetables, pigs and free-range chickens includes bar snacks (not Saturday evenings or Sunday lunch) and a more elaborate menu. The british cheese board is stupendous, with 23 different ones, mostly from Herefordshire and Wales. Hobsons Best and a couple of guests such as Brains Rev James and Timothy Taylors Landlord on handpump, several wines by the glass including champagne and pudding wines from a carefully chosen 100-bin wine list, home-made sloe gin, local ciders, perry, apple juice and pressés. The two-acre garden has seats on the terrace and a croquet lawn.

Free house ~ Licensees Steve and Nicola Reynolds ~ Real ale ~ Bar food (12-2, 6.30-9; not Sun evening or Mon) ~ Restaurant ~ (01544) 230221 ~ Children welcome ~ Dogs allowed in bar and bedrooms ~ Open 12-3, 6.30-11; 12-3 Sun; closed Sun evening ~ Bedrooms: £70B/£85B

YARPOLE

Bell

Just off B4361 N of Leominster; HR6 0BD

Modern cooking using home-grown vegetables in black and white village pub, particularly good service, real ales and extensive gardens

Readers praise the service and food at this well run dining pub. In an ancient timbered ancient building extended into a former cider mill, it has a basic tap room, a comfortable beamed lounge bar with a log fire and a large, high-raftered restaurant featuring a cider press and mill wheel; a mix of traditional furniture, some modern art on the walls and brass taps embedded into the stone bar counter. Hook Norton Hooky Bitter, Timothy Taylors Landlord and Wye Valley Hereford Pale Ale on handpump and a short but interesting wine list; efficient service even when busy. Providing a balance of innovative dishes (such as fricassee of herefordshire snails with garlic and parsley) and cheaper, pubbier dishes, food is prepared using all home-grown vegetables. The golden labrador is called Marcus; piped music. There are picnic-sets under green parasols in the sunny flower-filled garden and the pub is very handy for Croft Castle.

Enterprise ~ Lease Claude Bosi ~ Real ale ~ Bar food (12-2.30, 6.30-9.30) ~ Restaurant ~ (01568) 780359 ~ Children welcome ~ Dogs allowed in bar ~ Open 12-3, 6.30-11(10.30 Sun); closed Sun evening in winter; closed Mon

DOG FRIENDLY HOTELS, INNS, B&Bs AND FARMS

GLEWSTONE

Glewstone Court

Glewstone, Ross-on-Wye, Herefordshire HR9 6AW (01989) 770367

£118; 8 well equipped rms. Elegant, partly Georgian and partly Regency country house set in glorious grounds with a fine cedar of Lebanon and views over Ross-on-Wye; long-standing, warmly welcoming owners and staff, comfortable and relaxing public rooms, and good food in antique-filled dining room; croquet; resident golden retrievers and long-haired miniature dachsie, and two farm cats; walks in the grounds and in surrounding countryside; cl Christmas; dogs in bedrooms; welcome note, blanket, dining mat; £10

LEDBURY

Feathers

25 High Street, Ledbury, Herefordshire HR8 1DS (just off A449; High Street) (01531) 635266

£115; 20 carefully decorated rms making the most of the old beams and timbers. Very striking, mainly 16th-c, black and white hotel with relaxed atmosphere, log fires, comfortable lounge hall with country antiques, beams and timbers, particularly enjoyable food and friendly service in hop-decked Fuggles bar, good wine list, and cheerful mix of locals and visitors; health and leisure spa with indoor swimming pool; disabled access; dogs in bedrooms if small and well behaved

ROSS-ON-WYE

Wilton Court

Wilton Lane, Ross-on-Wye, Herefordshire HR9 6AQ (01989) 562569

£115; 10 pretty, chintzy rms, some with garden views, some with river ones. 16th-c riverside building with friendly owners, lots of original features like leaded windows, heavy beams, and sloping floors, comfortable sitting room, bar with open fire and river views, lovely breakfasts and imaginative food in smart conservatory-style restaurant and two-acres of grounds; fishing; dogs in bedrooms; £10

SYMONDS YAT

Norton House

Whitchurch, Symonds Yat, Herefordshire HR9 6DJ (01600) 890046

£70; 3 attractive rms. 300-year-old farmhouse with plenty of original features, stripped pine shutters and doors, woodburning stoves, guest sitting room and homely lounge, fine breakfasts taken around antique mahogany table in beamed dining room with farmhouse dresser and evening meals (on request) served by candlelight and oil lamp; two resident standard poodles; self-catering cottages; lots of nearby walks; cl Christmas; children over 12; dogs in bedrooms and in public rooms on leads; welcome pack, dog shower, towels, bowl

WOOLHOPE

Butchers Arms

Woolhope, Hereford, Herefordshire HR1 4RF (01432) 860281

£50; 2 rms, shared bthrms. Friendly 14th-c inn tucked away down country lane, with welcoming staff, old-fashioned furnishings and hop-draped low beams in several bars, log fires, real ales, enjoyable bar food, good breakfasts, and inviting garden; fine nearby walks; dogs in bedrooms

DOG FRIENDLY PUBS

ALDBURY

Greyhound

Stocks Road; village signposted from A4251 Tring—Berkhamsted, and from B4506; HP23 5RT

Spacious yet cosy old dining pub with traditional furnishings, popular food, and courtyard

The beamed interior of this handsome virginia creeper-covered inn shows some signs of considerable age (around the copper-hooded inglenook, for example), with plenty of tables in the two traditionally furnished rooms off either side of the drinks and food serving areas. In winter the lovely warm fire and subtle lighting make it feel really cosy. Three beers on handpump are usually Badger First Gold and Tanglefoot and King & Barnes Sussex. The tasty food from a short but sensible menu does draw a crowd, but the friendly staff cope well and meals are served promptly. An airy oak floored restaurant at the back overlooks a sun-trap gravel courtyard, and benches outside face a picturesque village green complete with stocks and a duck pond lively with wildfowl.

Badger ~ Tenant Tim O'Gorman ~ Real ale ~ Bar food (12-2.30(4 Sun), 6.30-9.30; not Sun evenings) ~ Restaurant ~ (01442) 851228 ~ Children welcome away from bar ~ Dogs allowed in bar ~ Open 11-11; 12-10.30 Sun

ASHWELL

Three Tuns

Off A505 NE of Baldock; High Street; SG7 5NL

Comfortable gently old-fashioned hotel bars with generous helpings of tasty food, and substantial garden

As at all good pubs, there seems to be something for everyone at this well run hotel and pub – everything from boules in the shaded garden to breakfasts for non-residents. Wood panelling, relaxing chairs, big family tables, lots of pictures, stuffed pheasants and fish, piped light classical music and antiques lend an air of Victorian opulence to the cosy lounge. The recently refurbished public bar is more modern, with leather sofas on reclaimed oak flooring, and pool, cribbage, dominoes, a games machine and TV. They stock a good choice of wines (with 16 by the glass), as well as Greene King IPA, Abbot and a guest such as Bath Ales Gem on handpump. The pubby food is nicely presented. A big terrace has metal tables and chairs, while a large garden has picnic-sets under apple trees. The charming village is full of pleasant corners and is popular with walkers as the landscape around rolls enough to be rewarding.

Greene King ~ Tenants Claire and Darrell Stanley ~ Real ale ~ Bar food (12-2.30, 6.30-9.30; 12-9.30 Fri, Sat, Sun) ~ Restaurant ~ (01462) 742107 ~ Children welcome ~ Dogs allowed in bar ~ Open 11-11; 12-10.30 Sun

BATFORD

Gibraltar Castle

Lower Luton Road; B653, S of B652 junction; AL5 5AH

Pleasantly traditional pub with interesting militaria displays, some emphasis on food (booking advised); terrace

A most impressive collection of military paraphernalia, including rifles, swords, medals, uniforms and bullets (with plenty of captions to read) is packed into this neatly kept welcoming pub. The long carpeted bar has a pleasant old fireplace, comfortably cushioned wall benches, and a couple of snugly intimate window alcoves, one with a fine old clock. Pictures depict its namesake, and various moments in the Rock's history. In one area the low beams give way to soaring rafters. Several board games are piled on top of the piano, and they've piped music. Quickly served pubby food includes a good range of lunchtime sandwiches; booking is recommended for Sunday roast. They stock a thoughtful choice of wines by the glass and a good range of malt whiskies, and serve three Fullers beers on handpump. Hanging baskets and tubs dotted around lend colour to a decked back terrace, and there are a few more tables and chairs in front by the road.

Fullers ~ Lease Hamish Miller ~ Real ale ~ Bar food (12-2.30(4 Sun), 6-9; not Sun evening) ~ Restaurant ~ (01582) 460005 ~ Children welcome ~ Dogs allowed in bar ~ Live music Tues evenings from 9pm ~ Open 11.30-11; 12-11 Sun

CHAPMORE END

Woodman

Off B158 Wadesmill—Bengeo; 300 yards W of A602 roundabout keep eyes skinned for discreet green sign to pub pointing up otherwise unmarked narrow lane; OS Sheet 166 map reference 328164; SG12 0HF

Peaceful country local with down-to-earth interior, beers straight from the cask, lunchtime snacks (occasionally more), cheery staff, and garden with play area

The two straightforward little linked rooms at this early Victorian local have plain seats around stripped pub tables, flooring tiles or broad bare boards, log fires in period fireplaces, cheerful pictures (for sale), lots of local notices, and darts over to one side. Three very well kept Greene King beers are tapped straight from the cask, and they've several malt whiskies; chess, backgammon, shove ha'penny and cribbage. A minimal lunchtime menu includes sandwiches, soup and ploughman's. In winter they serve a Sunday lunchtime roast and in summer they have regular barbecues and tasty hog roasts.

Greene King ~ Tenant Tony Dawes ~ Real ale ~ Bar food (12-2 Tues-Sat; 1-3 Sun; not Mon lunchtime) ~ (01920) 463143 ~ Children welcome till 8pm ~ Dogs welcome ~ Open 12-2, 5.30-11; 12-11 Sat; closed Mon lunchtime

FLAUNDEN

Bricklayers Arms

Off A41; Hogpits Bottom; HP3 0PH

Cosy traditional country restaurant (drinkers welcome) with emphasis on beautifully prepared food (booking almost essential) and very good wine list

To experience exceptional food in a charming environment is likely to be your main reason for visiting this well refurbished, low brick and tiled 18th-c pub. Originally two cottages and now covered with virginia creeper, it's tucked away down a winding country lane. The low-beamed bar is snug and comfortable, with roaring winter log fires and dark brown wooden wall seats. Stubs of knocked-through oak-timbered walls keep some feeling of intimacy in the three areas that used to be separate rooms. They've a very good extensive wine list (with about 20 by the glass) as well as Fullers London Pride, Greene King IPA and Old Speckled Hen, Timothy Taylors and a guest such as Tring Jack o' Legs on handpump. On the whole, food (a fusion of anglo and gallic styles) is fairly elaborate and not cheap, but the French chef does take tremendous care over preparation and ingredients. Some of the herbs and vegetables come from the pub's garden, and they smoke their own meats and fish. This is a lovely peaceful spot in summer, when the beautifully kept old-fashioned garden with its foxgloves against sheltering hedges comes into its own. Just up the Belsize road there's a path on the left which goes through delightful woods to a forested area around Hollow Hedge.

Free house ~ Licensee Alvin Michaels ~ Real ale ~ Bar food (12-2.30(4 Sun); 6.30-9.30(8.30 Sun)) ~ Restaurant ~ (01442) 833322 ~ Dogs allowed in bar ~ Open 12-11.30(10.30 Sun)

FRITHSDEN

Alford Arms

From Berkhamsted take unmarked road towards Potten End, pass Potten End turn on right, then take next left towards Ashridge College; HP1 3DD

Attractively located thriving dining pub with chic interior, good food and thoughtful wine list

Buzzing with cheerful diners and friendly staff, this stylish place is one of the county's most popular dining pubs (though locals still pop in to sit at the bar). You will probably need to book and it's worth getting here early as parking is limited. The fashionably elegant but understated interior has simple prints on pale cream walls, with blocks picked out in rich Victorian green or dark red, and an appealing mix of good antique furniture (from Georgian chairs to old commode stands) on bare boards and patterned quarry tiles. It's all pulled together by luxurious opulently patterned curtains; darts and piped jazz. The seasonally changing menu is imaginative and food very rewarding. In order to reduce 'wine miles' all the wines on their list are european, with most of them available by the glass, and they've Brakspears, Flowers Original, Marstons Pedigree and Rebellion IPA on handpump. The pub stands by a village green and is surrounded by lovely National Trust woodland. There are plenty of tables outside.

Salisbury Pubs ~ Lease Richard Coletta ~ Real ale ~ Bar food (12-2.30(4 Sun),

7-10) ~ (01442) 864480 ~ Children welcome ~ Dogs allowed in bar ~ Open 11-11; 12-10.30 Sun

DOG FRIENDLY HOTELS AND B&Bs

BISHOP'S STORTFORD

Down Hall Country House

Matching Road, Hatfield Heath, Bishops Stortford, Hertfordshire CM22 7AS (01279) 731441

£150; 99 stylish, comfortable rms, some on ground floor with individual access. Fine italianate mansion dating from 14th c in 110 acres of gardens and grounds; comfortable lounges with ornate décor, log fires and afternoon teas, relaxing atmosphere, cocktail bar, imaginative cooking in modern bistro and smarter restaurant, snooker and indoor swimming pool; dogs in bedrooms; welcome doggy pack; £5

KNEBWORTH

Homewood

Park Lane, Old Knebworth, Knebworth, Hertfordshire SG3 6PP (3 miles off A1(M) junction 7; B187 right off A602, then on N edge of Knebworth (not before) turn right towards Knebworth House) (01438) 812105

£80; 3 rms. Lovely Lutyens-designed house in six beautiful acres of grounds; elegant rooms with antiques and tapestries and interestingly decorated by the owner, good breakfasts, nearby places for evening meals, and four resident cats and friendly dog; walks in the grounds and nearby woods; cl two weeks Christmas; dogs welcome in bedrooms

Isle of Wight

MAP 2

DOG FRIENDLY PUBS

BEMBRIDGE

Crab & Lobster

Foreland Fields Road, off Howgate Road (which is off B3395 via Hillway Road); PO35 5TR

Seafood speciality and prime location draw crowds

The Island offers few better places on a summer's day than the terrace outside this well positioned inn. It's perched on low cliffs within yards of the shore, with great views over the Solent. The dining area and some of the bedrooms share the same view. Inside it's roomier than you might expect (just as well as it does get busy) and it's done out in an almost parlourish style, with lots of yachting memorabilia, old local photographs, and a blazing fire in winter months; darts, dominoes and cribbage. As well as pubby meals, they do several seafood dishes including a mixed seafood grill and crab and lobster platters. Flowers Original, Goddards Fuggle-Dee-Dum and Greene King IPA are on handpump, with decent house wines, about 20 malt whiskies, farm cider and good coffee; piped music (even in the lavatories).

Enterprise ~ Lease Eric and Belinda Dewey and Caroline and Ian Quekett ~ Real ale ~ Bar food (12-2.30, 6-9(9.30 Fri, Sat)) ~ (01983) 872244 ~ Children welcome ~ Dogs allowed in bar ~ Open 11-11; 12-10.30 Sun; 11-3, 6-11 in winter

FRESHWATER

Red Lion

Church Place; from A3055 at E end of village by Freshwater Garage mini-roundabout follow Yarmouth signpost, then take first real right turn signed to Parish Church; PO40 9BP

Good mix of locals and visiting diners, reasonable range of drinks and decent food at understated tucked away pub

Though food is quite a draw, chatting locals occupying stools along the counter keep a pubby feel at this firmly run place. The not over-done but comfortably furnished open-plan bar has fires, low grey sofas and sturdy country-kitchen style furnishings on mainly flagstoned floors, and bare board flooring too. The well executed paintings hung round the walls (between photographs and china platters) are by the licensee's brother and are worth a look. Flowers Original, Shepherd Neame Spitfire, Wadworths 6X and a guest such as Goddards are kept under light blanket pressure, and the good choice of wines includes 16 by the glass. Fines on mobile phone users go to charity (they collect a lot for the RNLI); there's a games machine but no music. Pubby bar food is listed on blackboards behind the bar. There are tables on a carefully tended grass and gravel area at the back (some under cover), beside which is the kitchen's herb garden, and a couple of picnic-sets in a quiet square at the front have pleasant views of the church. The pub is virtually on the Freshwater Way footpath that connects Yarmouth with the southern coast at Freshwater Bay.

Enterprise ~ Lease Michael Mence ~ Real ale ~ Bar food (12-2, 6.30(7 Sun)-9) ~ (01983) 754925 ~ Children over 10 ~ Dogs welcome ~ Open 11.30-3, 5.30-11; 11.30-4, 6-11 Sat; 12-3, 7-10.30 Sun

HULVERSTONE

Sun

B3399; PO30 4EH

Lovely thatched building with terrific coastal views, down-to-earth old-world appeal and four quickly changing real ales

The unpretentiously traditional and low-ceilinged bar at this thatched whitewashed country pub is full of friendly chatter, has a blazing fire at one end (with horse-brasses and ironwork hung around the fireplace), a nice mix of old furniture on flagstones and floorboards, and brick stone and walls; piped music, darts and board games. Leading off from one end is the traditionally decorated more modern dining area, with large windows making the most of the view. Four quickly changing real ales come from quite a range of brewers; maybe Charles Wells, Shepherd Neame, Timothy Taylor and Wychwood. Friendly staff serve up bar food, and they do an 'all you can eat' curry night on Thursdays and Sunday roasts. The building is in a captivating setting, with views from its charmingly secluded cottagey garden (which has a terrace and several picnic-sets) down to a wild stretch of coast. It's very well positioned for some splendid walks along the cliffs, and up Mottistone Down to the prehistoric Long Stone.

Enterprise ~ Lease Chris and Kate Cole ~ Real ale ~ Bar food (12-9) ~ (01983) 741124 ~ Children welcome ~ Dogs allowed in bar ~ Open 11-11; 12-10.30 Sun

NITON

Buddle

St Catherine's Road, Undercliff; off A3055 just S of village, towards St Catherine's Point; PO38 2NE

Distinctive stone pub with good food and half a dozen real ales; nice clifftop garden

With a little imagination, the bar with its heavy black beams, big flagstones, broad stone fireplace and massive black oak mantelbeam does conjure up the time when this rambling old pub was the haunt of notorious local smugglers, though these days its most adventurous visitors are more likely to be cyclists and walkers with their dogs (it's handy for the coast path). Old-fashioned captain's chairs are arranged around solid wooden tables, and its walls are hung with pewter mugs and the like. Along one side of the lawn, and helping to shelter it, is what they call the Smugglers' Barn, which doubles as a family dining area. Six real ales will probably include Adnams Best, Hampshire Pride of Romsey, Ringwood Fortyniner, Shepherd Neame Spitfire and Yates. Food is tasty and pubby including a pie of the day. Service can slow down a little when it's busy, but the very helpful staff keep you well informed. You can look out over the cliffs from the well cared-for garden, with its tables spread over the sloping lawn and stone terraces, and there is a good walk to the nearby lighthouse – at night you may be able to see the beam of light sweeping the sea far below.

Enterprise ~ Lease Stephen Clayton ~ Real ale ~ Bar food (12-2.45, 6-9; 12-9 July, Aug) ~ (01983) 730243 ~ Children welcome ~ Dogs welcome ~ Open 11-11(12 Sat); 12-10.30 Sun

SHALFLEET
New Inn
A3054 Newport—Yarmouth; PO30 4NS

Cheerful old pub with great fresh seafood, good beers and wines too

The strengths of this 18th-c former fisherman's haunt lie equally in its cheery welcome, good seafood and well kept beer. It is popular so you will need to book – there may even be double sittings in summer. The partly panelled flagstoned public bar has yachting photographs and pictures, a boarded ceiling, scrubbed pine tables and a log fire in the big stone hearth. The carpeted beamed lounge bar has boating pictures and a coal fire, and the snug and gallery have slate floors, bric-a-brac and more scrubbed pine tables. A big draw here is their famous seafood platter and crab and lobster salads, which are served alongside a dozen or so other fish dishes, and they do pubby meals too. Goddards Fuggle-Dee-Dum and Ventnor Golden and a couple of guests such as Bass and Flowers Original are kept under a light blanket pressure, and they stock around 60 wines; piped music.

Enterprise ~ Lease Mr Bullock and Mr McDonald ~ Real ale ~ Bar food (12-2.30, 6-9.30) ~ (01983) 531314 ~ Children welcome ~ Dogs welcome ~ Open 12-11(10.30 Sun)

VENTNOR
Spyglass
Esplanade, SW end; road down very steep and twisty, and parking nearby can be difficult – best to use the pay-and-display (free in winter) about 100 yards up the road; PO38 1JX

Interesting waterside pub with appealing seafaring bric-a-brac, half a dozen very well kept beers and enjoyable food

No matter what the season, this cheery place always seems to be brimming with customers. It's in a super position, perched on the wall just above the beach, and tables outside on a terrace have lovely views over the sea. There are strolls westwards from here along the coast towards the Botanic Garden as well as heftier hikes up on to St Boniface Down and towards the eerie shell of Appuldurcombe House. Inside, a fascinating jumble of seafaring memorabilia fills the snug quarry-tiled interior – anything from wrecked rudders, ships' wheels, old local advertisements and rope-makers' tools to stuffed seagulls, an Admiral Benbow barometer and an old brass telescope; games machine and piped music. Ringwood Best and Fortyniner and Ventnor Gold are well kept alongside a couple of guests such as Marstons Pedigree and Goddards Special. Generous helpings of very tasty bar food are promptly served and they've several seasonal fish dishes and crab and lobster salad; they may ask to keep your credit card behind the bar.

Free house ~ Licensees Neil and Stephanie Gibbs ~ Real ale ~ Bar food (12-9.30) ~ (01983) 855338 ~ Children welcome away from main bar area, not in bedrooms ~ Dogs allowed in bar ~ Open 10.30-11

DOG FRIENDLY HOTELS

BONCHURCH
Lake Hotel
Bonchurch, Ventnor, Isle of Wight PO38 1RF (01983) 852613

£88; 20 rms. Early 19th-c country house run by same family for over 40 years and set in two acres of pretty gardens, 400 metres from beach; lots of flowers and plants in three light and airy lounges (one is an attractive conservatory), a well stocked bar, and good food in comfortable restaurant; walks in part of the grounds and on the beach; cl Nov-Feb; partial disabled access; dogs in bedrooms and one lounge area; £5

SEAVIEW
Priory Bay Hotel
Priory Croft, Priory Road, Seaview, Isle of Wight PO34 5BU (01983) 613146

£180; 18 individually furnished rms with 10 more in cottages. Former Tudor farmhouse with Georgian and more recent additions in grounds leading to a fine sandy private beach with a beach bar (good for lunch); lovely day rooms with comfortable sofas, books and magazines on coffee tables, pretty flower arrangements, imaginative food in restaurants with charming Georgian murals and elaborate plasterwork, and an informal, relaxed atmosphere; outdoor swimming pool, tennis, croquet, and a nine-hole par three golf course; resident dog; plenty of walks; disabled access; dogs in cottages in grounds; £15

Seaview Hotel
High Street, Seaview, Isle of Wight PO34 5EX (01983) 612711

£120; 24 attractively decorated rms, some with sea views and private drawing rooms. Small, friendly and spotlessly kept hotel with fine ship photographs in the chatty and relaxed front dining bar, an interesting old-fashioned back bar, and good imaginative food; cl three days over Christmas; partial disabled access; dogs in some bedrooms

TOTLAND

Sentry Mead Hotel

Totland Bay, Isle of Wight PO39 0BJ (01983) 753212

£100; 12 pretty rms. Victorian country house hotel in flower-filled gardens overlooking the Solent and 100 yards from the beach; traditionally furnished rooms, open fire in lounge, bar area and airy conservatory, caring, attentive staff, and good food in stylish restaurant; dogs welcome by arrangement, if well behaved

YARMOUTH

George Hotel

Quay Street, Yarmouth, Isle of Wight PO41 0PE (01983) 760331

£190; 18 comfortable rms. 17th-c house by the harbour, with gardens leading to little private beach; fine flagstoned hall, fresh flowers and open fires, convivial bar and attractive residents' sitting room with marvellously relaxing atmosphere, imaginative enjoyable food in recently refurbished brasserie and smart restaurant, hearty breakfasts, and prompt courteous service; motor yacht for hire; dogs in bedrooms; £7.50

DOG FRIENDLY PUBS

BIDDENDEN
Three Chimneys

A262, 1 mile W of village; TN27 8LW

Pubby beamed rooms of considerable individuality, log fires, imaginative food and pretty garden

This is a particularly well run pub and much enjoyed by our readers. It's a pretty, old-fashioned cottage with a series of low-beamed, very traditional little rooms with plain wooden furniture and old settles on flagstones and coir matting, some harness and sporting prints on the stripped brick walls and good log fires. The atmosphere is civilised and relaxed and service is friendly and efficient. Adnams Best, a seasonal beer from Harveys and a changing guest tapped straight from casks racked behind the counter, several wines by the glass, local cider and apple juice and ten malt whiskies. The simple public bar has darts, dominoes and cribbage. Food is extremely good and imaginative (if not cheap). The garden (ploughman's only out here) has picnic-sets in dappled shade, and the smart terrace area has tables and outdoor heaters. Sissinghurst Gardens are nearby.

Free house ~ Licensee Craig Smith ~ Real ale ~ Bar food ~ Restaurant ~ (01580) 291472 ~ Dogs welcome ~ Open 11.30-3, 6-11; 12-3.30, 6.30-10.30 Sun; closed 25 and 31 Dec

BODSHAM
Timber Batts

Following Bodsham, Wye sign off B2068 keep right at unsigned fork after about 1½ miles; TN25 5JQ

Lovely french food (bar snacks too) and charming French owner in cottagey old country pub, good real ales, enjoyable wines and fine views

The charming French landlord in this 15th-c former farmhouse remains keen to keep a proper pubby feel and local drinkers in the public bar – despite a strong emphasis on the extremely good french food. The little heavy-beamed cottagey area to the right has a couple of comfortable armchairs and two wicker chairs each with a small table, an open fire in the brick fireplace with photographs of the pub above it, some hunting horns and a few high bar chairs; down a little step is more of a drinking part with a mix of cushioned dining chairs, a wall settle, two long tables and several bar stools. There are various froggy cushions and knick-knacks on the window sills (the pub is known locally as Froggies at the Timber Batts). Cooked by the landlord's son, the delicious french food (specials are listed in French on a blackboard) is prepared using top local produce or good french ingredients (the cheese is lovely). They also do a handful of traditional pub meals, such as ham and eggs. Adnams Bitter, Fullers London Pride and Woodfordes Wherry on handpump and very good french wines by the glass (some from Mr Gross's cousin's vineyard). This hilltop pub is tucked away in lovely country with fine valley views from straightforward seats and tables in the back garden.

Free house ~ Licensee Joel Gross ~ Real ale ~ Bar food (12-2.30, 7-9.30(9 Sun)) ~ Restaurant ~ (01233) 750237 ~ Children welcome ~ Dogs welcome ~ Open 12-3, 6.30-11; 12-3, 7-10.30 Sun; closed 24 Dec-3 Jan

BOUGH BEECH
Wheatsheaf

B2027, S of reservoir; TN8 7NU

Ex-hunting lodge with lots to look at, fine range of local drinks, popular food and plenty of seats in appealing garden

There's a lot of history and masses of interesting things to look at in this warmly welcoming, bustling pub. The neat central bar and the long front bar (with an attractive old settle carved with wheatsheaves) have unusually high ceilings with lofty oak timbers, a screen of standing timbers and a revealed king post; dominoes and board games. Divided from the central bar by two more rows of standing timbers – one formerly an outside wall to the building – are the snug and another bar. Other similarly aged features include a piece of 1607 graffiti, 'Foxy Holamby', thought to have been a whimsical local squire. On the walls and above the massive stone fireplaces, there are quite a few horns and heads as well as a sword from Fiji, crocodiles, stuffed birds, swordfish spears and a matapee. Thoughtful touches include piles of smart magazines, tasty nibbles and winter chestnuts to roast. Harveys Best and from a village just three miles away, Westerham Brewery British Bulldog and Grasshopper Kentish Bitter on handpump, three farm ciders (one from nearby Biddenden), a decent wine list, several malt whiskies, summer Pimms and winter mulled wine. A wide range of well liked food includes light lunchtime snacks and they use Kent or Sussex reared meat. Outside is appealing too, with plenty of seats, flowerbeds and fruit trees in the sheltered side and back gardens. Shrubs help divide the garden into various areas, so it doesn't feel too crowded even when it's full.

Enterprise ~ Lease Liz and David Currie ~ Real ale ~ Bar food (12-10) ~ (01732) 700254 ~ Children welcome in one part of bar only ~ Dogs welcome ~ Open 11am-11.30pm(midnight Sat, 11pm Sun)

BOYDEN GATE
Gate Inn

Off A299 Herne Bay—Ramsgate – follow Chislet, Upstreet signpost opposite Roman Gallery; Chislet also signposted off A28 Canterbury—Margate at Upstreet – after turning right into Chislet main street keep right on to Boyden; the pub gives its address as Marshside, though Boyden Gate seems more usual on maps; CT3 4EB

Friendly, long-serving landlord in unchanging pub, well kept beers, simple food, and tame ducks and geese to feed

Right on the edge of the marshes, this unspoilt, traditional pub thankfully does not change at all from year to year. It's been run by the same landlord for 34 years now and you can be quite sure of a genuinely warm welcome – whether you are a regular or a visitor. The comfortably worn interior is properly pubby with an inglenook log fire serving both the well worn quarry-tiled rooms, flowery-cushioned pews around tables of considerable character, hop bines hanging from the beams and attractively etched windows. Shepherd Neame Master Brew, Spitfire and a seasonal ale are tapped from the cask and you can also get interesting bottled beers, and half a dozen wines by the glass; board games. Tasty bar food includes lots of different sandwiches and melts, soup, a big choice of baked potatoes and burgers, ploughman's, home-made vegetable flan, spicy hotpots and gammon and egg. The sheltered holly-hock flowered garden is bounded by two streams with tame ducks and geese (they sell bags of food, 10p), and on fine summer evenings you can hear the contented quacking of a multitude of ducks and geese, coots and moorhens out on the marshes.

Shepherd Neame ~ Tenant Chris Smith ~ Real ale ~ Bar food (12-2, 6(7 Sun)-9) ~ No credit cards ~ (01227) 860498 ~ Well behaved children in eating area of bar and family room ~ Dogs welcome ~ Open 11-2.30(3 Sat), 6-11; 12-4, 7-10.30 Sun

BROOKLAND

Woolpack

On A259 from Rye, about 1 mile before Brookland, take the first right turn signposted Midley where the main road bends sharp left, just after the expanse of Walland Marsh; OS Sheet 189 map reference 977244; TN29 9TJ

15th-c pub with simple furnishings, massive inglenook fireplace, tasty food and large garden

The award-winning hanging baskets in front of this pretty white pub are really quite a sight in summer and there are plenty of picnic-sets under parasols in the attractive garden with its barbecue area; it's all nicely lit up in the evenings. Inside, there's plenty of marshland character and a good, friendly bustling atmosphere. The ancient entrance lobby has an uneven brick floor and black-painted pine-panelled walls, and to the right, the simple quarry-tiled main bar has basic cushioned plank seats in the massive inglenook fireplace (with a lovely log fire on chilly days), a painted wood-effect bar counter hung with lots of water jugs and some very early ships' timbers (maybe 12th c) in the low-beamed ceiling; a long elm table has shove-ha'penny carved into one end and there are other old and newer wall benches, chairs at mixed tables with flowers and candles and photographs of locals on the walls. To the left of the lobby is a sparsely furnished little room and an open-plan family room; piped music. Bar food is good value, pubby and served in generous helpings. Shepherd Neame Master Brew, Spitfire and a seasonal brew on handpump; look out for the two pub cats, Liquorice and Charlie Girl.

Shepherd Neame ~ Tenant Barry Morgan ~ Real ale ~ Bar food (12-2.30, 6-9; all day weekends) ~ (01797) 344321 ~ Children in family room ~ Dogs welcome ~ Open 11-3, 6-11; 11-11 Sat; 12-11 Sun

GROOMBRIDGE

Crown

B2110; TN3 9QH

Charming village pub with quite a bit of bric-a-brac in snug, low-beamed rooms, and enjoyable food and drink

Part of a row of pretty tile-hung cottages, this friendly pub has picnic-sets out in front on a wonky but sunny brick terrace that overlooks the steep village green. Inside, the snug left-hand room has old tables on worn flagstones and a big brick inglenook with a cosy winter log fire – arrive early for a table in here. The other low-beamed rooms have roughly plastered walls, some squared panelling and timbering, and a quite a bit of bric-a-brac, from old teapots and pewter tankards to antique bottles. Walls are decorated with small topographical, game and sporting prints and there's a circular large-scale map with the pub at its centre. The end dining room has fairly close-spaced tables with a variety of good solid chairs, and a log-effect gas fire in a big fireplace. Three ales from Harveys, Larkins and Pilgrims on handpump and up to ten wines by the glass. Lunchtime food is fairly pubby, with more elaborate evening dishes. There's a back car park and pub garden. A public footpath across the road beside the small chapel leads through a field to Groombridge Place Gardens.

Free house ~ Licensee Peter Kilshaw ~ Real ale ~ Bar food (12-2.30(3 Sat and Sun), 6.30-9(9.30 Sat); not Sun evening) ~ (01892) 864742 ~ Children welcome ~ Dogs allowed in bar ~ Open 11-3, 6-11; 11-11 Sat; 12-10.30 Sun; 12-5 Sun in winter; closed winter Sun evening

HODSOLL STREET

Green Man

Hodsoll Street and pub signed off A227 S of Meopham; turn right in village; TN15 7LE

Bustling pub by village green, friendly atmosphere, lots of food specials, real ales and seats in garden

You can be sure of a friendly welcome from the hard-working licensees in this popular pub. There are big airy carpeted rooms that work their way around a hop-draped central bar, traditional neat tables and chairs spaced tidily around the walls, interesting old local photographs and antique plates on the walls, and a warm winter log fire; piped music. Greene King Old Speckled Hen, Harveys Best, Timothy Taylors Landlord and a changing guest on handpump and decent wines. As well as generous pubby meals they offer a popular two-course weekday lunch menu and hold themed food evenings. The summer tubs and hanging baskets are pretty and there are seats on the well tended lawn; maybe summer morris dancers. The nearby North Downs have plenty of walks.

Enterprise ~ Lease John, Jean and David Haywood ~ Real ale ~ Bar food (12-2.30(3 weekends), 6.30-9.30) ~ (01732) 823575 ~ Children welcome ~ Dogs welcome ~ Live music second Thurs of month ~ Open 11-2.30, 6-11; 11-11 Sat; 12-10.30 Sun

LANGTON GREEN

Hare

A264 W of Tunbridge Wells; TN3 0JA

Interestingly decorated Edwardian pub with a fine choice of drinks and popular food

Chatty and relaxed, this Edwardian roadside pub offers a good choice of food and drink. The front bar tends to be where drinkers gather and the knocked-through interior has big windows and high ceilings that give a spacious feel. Décor, more or less in period with the building, runs from dark-painted dados below light walls, 1930s oak furniture, and turkish-style carpets on stained wooden floors to old romantic pastels, and a huge collection of chamber-pots hanging from one beam. Interesting old books, pictures and two huge mahogany mirror-backed display cabinets crowd the walls of the big room at the back, which has lots of large tables (one big enough for at least a dozen) on a light brown carpet. Food is well liked, sensibly imaginative and served in generous helpings. Greene King IPA, Abbot and Old Speckled Hen and a couple of guests such as Bath Ales Gem Bitter and Hardys & Hansons Olde Tripe on handpump, over 100 whiskies, 20 vodkas, 18 wines by the glass and farm ciders; board games. French windows open on to a big terrace with picnic-sets and pleasant views of the tree-ringed village green. Parking is limited.

Brunning & Price ~ Lease Christopher Little ~ Real ale ~ Bar food (12-9.30(10 Fri and Sat) ~ (01892) 862419 ~ Children allowed away from bar until 7pm ~ Dogs allowed in bar ~ Open 11-11; 11-midnight Sat; 12-10.30 Sun

OARE

Shipwrights Arms

S shore of Oare Creek, E of village; coming from Faversham on the Oare road, turn right into Ham Road opposite Davington School; or off A2 on B2045, go into Oare village, then turn right towards Faversham, and then left into Ham Road opposite Davington School; OS Sheet 178 map reference 016635; ME13 7TU

Remote pub in marshland with lots of surrounding bird life and simple little bars

In the middle of marshland and almost alone by a boatyard, this unspoilt old tavern is actually three feet below sea level. The three simple little bars (redecorated this year) are dark, and separated by standing timbers and wood partitions or narrow door arches. A medley of seats runs from tapestry-cushioned stools and chairs to black wood-panelled built-in settles forming little booths, and there are pewter tankards over the bar counter, boating jumble and pictures, pottery boating figures, flags or boating pennants on the ceilings, several brick fireplaces and a good woodburning stove. Look out for the electronic wind gauge above the main door which takes its reading from the chimney. A beer from Goachers and Whitstable and maybe a couple of guests tapped from the cask and several wines by the glass; piped local radio. Bar food is traditional and the menu short. There are seats in the large garden and nearby walks.

Free house ~ Licensees Derek and Ruth Cole ~ Real ale ~ Bar food (12-2.30, 7-9; not Sun evening or Mon) ~ Restaurant ~ (01795) 590088 ~ Children welcome away from bar area ~ Dogs allowed in bar ~ Open 11-3(4 Sat), 6-11; 12-4, 6-10.30 Sun; closed Mon

PLUCKLEY

Dering Arms

Pluckley station, which is signposted from B2077; or follow Station Road (left turn off Smarden Road in centre of Pluckley) for about 1.3 miles S, through Pluckley Thorne; TN27 0RR

Fine fish dishes plus other good food in handsome building, stylish main bar, carefully chosen wines, and roaring log fire

This striking old building was originally built as a hunting lodge on the Dering Estate. The stylishly plain high-ceilinged main bar has a solid country feel with a variety of good wooden furniture on stone floors, a roaring log fire in the great fireplace, country prints and some fishing rods. The smaller half-panelled back bar has similar dark wood furnishings, and an extension to this area has a wood-burning stove, comfortable armchairs and sofas and a grand piano; board games. Fresh local fish is the speciality here but they offer other good food too; the fruits de mer platter needs 24 hours' notice. Goachers Gold Star and a beer named for the pub on handpump, a good wine list, local cider and quite a few malt whiskies. Classic car meetings (the long-serving landlord has a couple of cars) are held here on the second Sunday of the month.

Free house ~ Licensee James Buss ~ Real ale ~ Bar food (not Sun evening, not Mon) ~ Restaurant ~ (01233) 840371 ~ Children in Club Room bar ~ Dogs allowed in bar ~ Open 11.30-4, 6-11; 12-4 Sun; closed Sun evening, all Mon, 25-27 Dec, 1 Jan ~ Bedrooms: £40(£60S)/£50(£75S)

Mundy Bois

Mundy Bois – spelled Monday Boys on some maps – off Smarden Road SW of village centre; TN27 0ST

Friendly country pub with relaxing bars, traditional bar food and more elaborate restaurant menu, and play area in nice garden

With a friendly welcome for families and dogs, this quietly set pub has a vibrant, cheerful atmosphere. The informal main bar with its massive inglenook fireplace (favourite spot of Ted the pub labrador) leads on to a little pool room; TV, darts, games machine, juke box and piped music. The small snug bar has oak flooring, and chesterfield sofas beside a roaring log fire, and is also used as a pre and post drinking area for the restaurant. Shepherd Neame Master Brew and Youngs Bitter with Wadworths 6X in summer and at Christmas and maybe a guest beer on handpump and several wines by the glass. Using rare breed local meat and other local produce, bar food here is carefully cooked and quite pubby. You can also eat from the pricier and more elaborate restaurant menu in the bar. There are seats in the pretty garden, which has a good children's play area, and you can eat on the terrace which looks over to the hillside beyond.

Free house ~ Licensees Peter and Helen Teare ~ Real ale ~ Bar food (12-2, 6.30-9(9.30 Sat); 12-4 Sun; not Sun or Mon evenings) ~ Restaurant ~ (01233) 840048 ~ Children welcome ~ Dogs allowed in bar ~ Open 11.30-3, 6-11; 11.30-11 Sat; 12-5 Sun; closed Sun and Mon evenings; 25 Dec

SELLING

Rose & Crown

Signposted from exit roundabout of M2 junction 7: keep right on through village and follow Perry Wood signposts; or from A252 just W of junction with A28 at Chilham follow Shottenden signpost, then right turn signposted Selling, then right signposted Perry Wood; ME13 9RY

Nice summer garden, winter log fires, hop-covered beams and several real ales

Tucked away up a very quiet lane through ancient woodland, this country pub has pretty flowering tubs and hanging baskets in summer; the cottagey back garden is lovely then too, with picnic-sets and a children's play area. Inside, there are comfortably cushioned seats, winter log fires in two inglenook fireplaces, hop bines strung from the beams, and fresh flowers; steps lead down to another timbered area. Adnams Southwold, Goachers Mild, Harveys Sussex Best and a guest beer on handpump; piped music, cribbage, dominoes, cards and shut-the-box. Standard bar food includes filled rolls, ploughman's, steak and mushroom pudding and the like, and they hold a themed food evening on the last Thursday of the month. Good surrounding walks.

Free house ~ Licensees Tim Robinson and Vanessa Grove ~ Real ale ~ Bar food (not Mon evening) ~ Restaurant ~ (01227) 752214 ~ Children welcome ~ Dogs allowed in bar ~ Open 11.30-3(3.30 Sat), 6.30(6 Sat)-11; 12-3.30, 7-10.30 Sun; closed Mon evening and evenings 25 and 26 Dec and 1 Jan

SHIPBOURNE

Chaser

Stumble Hill (A227 N of Tonbridge); TN11 9PE

Comfortable, civilised country pub, log fires, popular food, quite a few wines by the glass, and covered and heated outside terrace

'A really good all-rounder' is how one reader describes this bustling pub – and others tend to agree with him. It's civilised and rather smart with a friendly atmosphere and helpful, welcoming staff. There are several open-plan areas that meander into each other, all converging on a large central island bar counter: stripped wooden floors, frame-to-frame pictures on deepest red and cream walls, stripped pine wainscoting, an eclectic mix of solid old wood tables (with candles) and chairs, shelves of books, and open fires. A striking school chapel-like restaurant, right at the back, has dark wood panelling and a high timber vaulted ceiling. Greene King IPA and Abbot and a couple of guest beers on handpump, quite a few wines by the glass and several malt whiskies; piped music and board games. The enjoyable range of food is tasty and served in very generous helpings. French windows open on to a covered and heated central courtyard with teak furniture and big green parasols, and a side garden, with the pretty church rising behind, is nicely enclosed by hedges and shrubs. There is a small car park at the back or you can park in the lane opposite by a delightful green; farmer's market on Thursday morning.

Whiting & Hammond ~ Lease Richard Barrett ~ Real ale ~ Bar food (all day) ~ (01732) 810360 ~ Children welcome ~ Dogs allowed in bar ~ Open 11-11(midnight Sat); 12-11 Sun

ST MARGARET'S BAY
Coastguard
Off A256 NE of Dover; keep on down through the village towards the bay, pub off on right; CT15 6DY

Bustling and friendly seaside place with terrific views, plenty of fish on menu, nautical décor, fine range of drinks, helpful uniformed staff

To make the best of the tremendous views in fine weather here, you must arrive early to bag one of the tables out on a prettily planted balcony that look across the Straits of Dover; there are more seats down by the beach below the National Trust cliffs. Inside, it's a cheerful and lively place and the warm, carpeted, wood-clad bar has some shipping memorabilia, three real ales from local Kentish breweries like Gadds or Goachers and from Scotland (they only use smaller breweries) on handpump, interesting continental beers, 40 malt whiskies, Weston's cider and a carefully chosen wine list including those from local vineyards; good service even when busy. Naturally the menu includes plenty of local fish and seafood (scallops with samphire and hot-devilled crab) but there are plenty of choices if you prefer something else; maybe piped music.

Free house ~ Licensee Nigel Wydymus ~ Real ale ~ Bar food (12.30-2.45, 6.30-8.45) ~ Restaurant ~ (01304) 853176 ~ Children allowed away from bar ~ Dogs allowed in bar ~ Open 11-11(10.30 Sun)

STAPLEHURST
Lord Raglan
About 1.5 miles from town centre towards Maidstone, turn right off A229 into Chart Hill Road opposite Chart Cars; OS Sheet 188 map reference 785472; TN12 0DE

Simple and relaxed with chatty locals, beams and hops, good value bar snacks, and nice little terrace

Deservedly busy, this is a well run country pub with friendly licensees and swift, efficient service. There's an enjoyably cheerful feel and the interior is cosy but compact, with a narrow bar – you walk in almost on top of the counter and chatting locals – widening slightly at one end to a small area with a big log fire in winter. In the other direction it works its way round to an intimate area at the back, with lots of wine bottles lined up on a low shelf. Low beams are covered with masses of hops, and the mixed collection of comfortably worn dark wood furniture on quite well used dark brown carpet tiles and nice old parquet flooring is mostly 1930s. Goachers Light, Harveys Best, and a guest like Westerham Brewery British Bulldog on handpump, a good wine list, local Double Vision farm cider and Weston's perry. Food is good value and enjoyable with one or two interesting specials. Small french windows lead out to an enticing little high-hedged terraced area with green plastic tables and chairs, and there are wooden picnic-sets in the side orchard; reasonable wheelchair access.

Free house ~ Licensees Andrew and Annie Hutchison ~ Real ale ~ Bar food (12-2.30, 7-9.30; not Sun) ~ (01622) 843747 ~ Children welcome ~ Dogs allowed in bar ~ Open 12-3, 6.30-11.30; closed Sun

STOWTING
Tiger

3.7 miles from M20 junction 11; B2068 N, then left at Stowting signpost, straight across crossroads, then fork left after 0.25 miles and pub is on right; coming from N, follow Brabourne, Wye, Ashford signpost to right at fork, then turn left towards Posting and Lyminge at T junction; TN25 6BA

Peaceful pub with friendly staff, interesting traditional furnishings and open fires; good walking country

This is a friendly country pub traditionally furnished with newly cushioned dark wooden pews on wooden floorboards and open fires at each end of the bar. There's an array of books meant to be read rather than left for decoration, candles in bottles, brewery memorabilia and paintings, lots of hops, and some faded rugs on the stone floor towards the back of the pub. Fullers London Pride and Shepherd Neame Master Brew and three guests like Harveys Best, Shepherd Neame Spitfire, and Theakstons Old Peculier on handpump, lots of malt whiskies, several wines by the glass and local cider. Bar food works its way up from simple lunchtime snacks to a few more evening dishes including fresh fish. There are seats out on the front terrace and an outside smokers' shelter with an environmentally friendly heater and stools made from tractor seats. Plenty of nearby walks along the Wye Downs or North Downs Way.

Free house ~ Licensees Emma Oliver and Benn Jarvis ~ Real ale ~ Bar food (all day; not Tues) ~ Restaurant ~ (01303) 862130 ~ Children welcome ~ Dogs allowed in bar ~ Jazz Mon evenings ~ Open 12-midnight; closed Tuesdays

TOYS HILL
Fox & Hounds

Off A25 in Brasted, via Brasted Chart and The Chart; TN16 1QG

Country pub in fine surroundings with well liked food and nice garden

Surrounded by good walks, this bustling pub is in lovely countryside, and as you approach it from the pretty village you will glimpse one of the most magnificent views in Kent. The appealing tree-sheltered garden has picnic-sets, and a covered and heated area. Inside, the small first room has a few plain tables and chairs on dark boards and a small woodburning stove in a knocked-through fire-place which lets it also heat the main bar. Although modernised (including an unobtrusive wide-screen TV and blackboards promoting evening events), this is fondly reminiscent of the former landlady's slightly eccentric regime. Under the shiny pinkish ceiling, which looks as old as the building itself, are a low leather sofa and easy chair by the coffee table in front of the woodburner, a mix of tables and chairs, hunting prints, illustrated plates, old photographs, pewter mugs and copper jugs, and a small coal fire at the end. A good range of enjoyable food includes something for most tastes. Greene King IPA, Abbot and Ruddles County on handpump and several wines by the glass; friendly helpful staff. Piped music and board games; no mobile phones. The pub is handy for Chartwell and Emmetts Garden.

Greene King ~ Tenants Tony and Shirley Hickmott ~ Real ale ~ Bar food (12-2(2.30 Sat, 3 Sun), 7-9; not Sun or Mon evenings) ~ Restaurant ~ (01732) 750328 ~ Children welcome away from bar ~ Dogs allowed in bar ~ Live music last Fri of month ~ Open 11-3, 6-11; 11-10.30 Sat; 11-11(till 8 winter Sun) Sun; closed Mon evening

DOG FRIENDLY HOTELS, INNS AND B&Bs

BOUGHTON LEES

Eastwell Manor

Eastwell Park, Boughton Lees, Ashford, Kent TN25 4HR (4.4 miles off M20 junction 9, via A28 towards Canterbury, forking left on A251) (01233) 219955

£190; 62 prettily decorated rms in hotel and 19 courtyard cottages (some cottages have their own garden and can also be booked on self-catering basis). Fine Jacobean-style manor (actually rebuilt in the 1920s) in 62 acres with croquet lawn, tennis court, two boules pitches and putting green; grand oak-panelled rooms, open fires, comfortable leather seating, antiques and fresh flowers, courteous helpful service, and extremely good food; health and fitness spa with 20-metre indoor pool and 15 treatment rooms; walks on the estate; disabled access; dogs in mews cottages only; £15

CANTERBURY

Cathedral Gate

36 Burgate, Canterbury, Kent CT1 2HA (01227) 464381

£116; 25 rms, 12 with own bthrm and some overlooking cathedral. 15th-c hotel that predates the adjoining sculpted cathedral gateway; bow windows, massive oak beams, sloping floors, antiques and fresh flowers, continental breakfast in little dining room or your own room, and a restful atmosphere; municipal car parks a few minutes away; dogs in bedrooms

DOVER

Hubert House

9 Castle Hill Road, Dover, Kent CT16 1QW (01304) 202253

£59.95; 6 pleasant rms. Fine Georgian building just beneath the castle and close to the beach and ferry; enjoyable breakfasts and home-baked croissants in smart coffee house (open all day) and friendly owners; two resident dogs; walking area nearby; forecourt parking; dogs in some bedrooms; treats, bedding, bowls; £7.50

THURNHAM

Black Horse

Pilgrims Way, Thurnham, Maidstone, Kent ME14 3LD (01622) 739170

£80; 16 pretty rms in separate annexe. Bustling dining pub with traditional bar and restaurant, beams, hops and open fires, real ales, friendly staff, wide choice of enjoyable food, and pleasant garden with partly covered back terrace, water features and nice views; resident dog; good nearby walks; disabled access; dogs in bedrooms; must be kept on lead elsewhere; £6

TUNBRIDGE WELLS

Hotel Du Vin

Crescent Road, Tunbridge Wells, Kent TN1 2LY (01892) 526455

£147; 34 well equipped, chic rms. Handsome sandstone building with relaxed atmosphere and comfortable sofas and chairs in two lounge rooms, good modern cooking in the airy, high-ceilinged and informally french-feeling restaurant, and particularly good wines; seats on the terrace; dog walking in nearby park; disabled access; dogs in bedrooms; bowls and beds available; £10

DOG FRIENDLY PUBS

BISPHAM GREEN
Eagle & Child

Maltkiln Lane (Parbold—Croston road, off B5246); L40 3SG

Well liked friendly pub with antiques in stylishly simple interior, interesting range of beers, very well prepared food, and nice garden

As well as an interesting range of changing real ales, there are some diversions here, with crown green bowling to try, and a wild garden that is home to crested newts and moorhens; the pub's dogs are called Betty and Doris. In the largely open-plan bar, attractively understated old furnishings include a mix of small oak chairs around tables in corners, an oak coffer, several handsomely carved antique oak settles (the finest apparently made partly from a 16th-c wedding bed-head), and old hunting prints and engravings. There's coir matting in the snug, and oriental rugs on flagstones in front of the fine old stone fireplaces. There's quite an emphasis on the well cooked very good food which includes pubby dishes alongside some gently imaginative ones; you do need to book. The range of five changing beers might typically include Three Bs Doff Cocker, Phoenix White Monk, Southport Golden Sands, Thwaites Original and Timothy Taylors Landlord, and they also keep a farm cider, decent wines and around 30 malt whiskies. They hold a popular beer festival over the first May bank holiday weekend. The handsome side barn was being converted into a deli as we went to press; smokers can retreat to the cart shed.

Free house ~ Licensee David Anderson ~ Real ale ~ Bar food (12-2, 5.30-8.30(9 Fri, Sat); 12-8.30 Sun) ~ (01257) 462297 ~ Children welcome ~ Dogs welcome ~ Open 12-3, 5.30-11; 12-10.30 Sun

GREAT MITTON
Three Fishes

Mitton Road (B6246, off A59 NW of Whalley); BB7 9PQ

Stylish modern conversion, tremendous attention to detail, excellent regional food with a contemporary twist, interesting drinks

Although on a large scale, this stylishly revamped dining pub does things very well even at the busiest of times (which are frequent), with friendly staff serving very accomplished and thoughtful regional cuisine. The interior stretches back much further than you'd initially expect. The areas closest to the bar are elegantly traditional with a couple of big stone fireplaces, rugs on polished floors, newly upholstered stools, and a good chatty feel; then there's a series of individually furnished and painted rooms with exposed stone walls and floors, careful spot-lighting, and wooden slatted blinds, ending with another impressive fireplace; facilities for the disabled. The long bar counter (with elaborate floral displays) serves Thwaites Lancaster Bomber and Wainwright, a guest from Bowland such as Golden Trough or Hen Harrier, cocktails, a good choice of wines by the glass and unusual soft drinks such as locally made sarsaparilla and dandelion and burdock. You order your meal at various food points dotted around. The emphasis is on traditional Lancastrian dishes with a modern twist. Products are carefully sourced from small local suppliers, many of whom are immortalised in black and white photographs on the walls, and located on a map on the back of the menu. Most dish descriptions indicate the origins of the main ingredient – the beef particu-larly is exclusive to here. Overlooking the Ribble Valley, the garden has tables and perhaps its own menu in summer. They don't take bookings (except for groups of eight or more), but write your name on a blackboard when you arrive, and find you when a table becomes free – the system works surprisingly well. This pub is under the same ownership as the Highwayman at Nether Burrow.

Free house ~ Licensees Nigel Haworth, Andy Morris ~ Real ale ~ Bar food (12-2, 6(5.30 Sat)-9; 12-8.30 Sun) ~ (01254) 826888 ~ Children welcome ~ Dogs welcome ~ Open 12-11(10.30 Sun)

NETHER BURROW
Highwayman

A683 S of Kirkby Lonsdale; LA6 2RJ

Substantial old stone house with country interior serving carefully sourced and prepared food; lovely gardens

This upmarket dining pub is especially popular for its cheerful service and food that uses locally sourced products. Although large, its flagstoned 17th-c inte-rior is nicely divided into nooks and corners, with a big log fire at one end; this, another smaller fire and the informal wooden furnishings give it a relaxed comfortable feel. Black and white wall prints (and placemats) show local farmers and producers from whom the pub sources its ingredients – clearly some of these are real characters, and this seems to work nicely through into their produce; the food is traditional Lancastrian but brought up to date a bit. Thwaites Lancaster Bomber and Original and a guest such as Thwaites Wainwrights are served on handpump, alongside good wines by the glass and about 20 whiskies. French windows open to a big terrace and lovely gardens. They don't take bookings except for groups of eight or more.

Free house ~ Licensee Andy Morris ~ Real ale ~ Bar food (12-2, 6(5.30 Sat)-9; 12-8.30 Sun) ~ (01254) 826888 ~ Children welcome ~ Dogs welcome ~ Open 12-11(10.30 Sun)

RABY

Wheatsheaf

Off A540 S of Heswall; Raby Mere Road; CH63 4JH

Small-windowed, cottagey village pub, decent bar food; eight real ales

The nicely chatty rambling rooms in this popular timbered and whitewashed country cottage (which is known simply as The Thatch) are simply furnished, with an old wall clock and homely black kitchen shelves in the cosy central bar, and a nice snug formed by antique settles built in around its fine old fireplace. A second, more spacious room has upholstered wall seats around the tables, small hunting prints on the cream walls, and a smaller coal fire. The spacious restaurant (Tuesdays to Saturday evening) is in a converted cowshed that leads into a larger conservatory; piped music is played in these areas only. Eight real ales are kept on handpump, with two guests like Elland Bargee and Hanby Golden Honey alongside half a dozen regular brews: Black Sheep, Brimstage Trappers Hat, Greene King Old Speckled Hen, Tetleys, Theakstons Best, Thwaites Original and Wells & Youngs Bombardier. Good straightforward lunchtime bar food includes a wide range of sandwiches and ploughman's, steak and ale pie and other pubby dishes. There are picnic-sets on the terrace and in the pleasant garden behind, with more seats out front.

Free house ~ Licensee Wes Charlesworth ~ Real ale ~ Bar food (12-2(3 Sun), 6-9.30; not Mon or Sun evenings) ~ Restaurant (evenings 6-9.30, Tues-Sat; not Sun and Mon) ~ (0151) 336 3416 ~ Children welcome in restaurant if supervised ~ Dogs allowed in bar ~ Open 11.30-11; 12-10.30 Sun

WADDINGTON

Lower Buck

Edisford Road; BB7 3HU

Popular village pub with reasonably priced, tasty food; five real ales

In a lovely village, this chatty local is handily placed for walks in the Ribble Valley. The friendly landlord keeps a range of five local ales, with Moorhouses Black Cat Mild and guests such as Bowland Hen Harrier and Odd Shaped Balls, Moorhouses Premier and Timothy Taylors Landlord. The décor is nicely sympathetic with cream-painted walls hung with pictures, a built-in dresser in the front bar, and a welcoming coal fire. Using meat reared at a farm nearby in the Longridge, and vegetables grown in Longridge too, the food is traditionally pubby and good. There is seating outside in the garden.

Free house ~ Licensee Andrew Warburton ~ Real ale ~ Bar food (12-2.30, 6-9; 12-9 Sat, Sun and bank hols) ~ Restaurant ~ (01200) 423342 ~ Children welcome ~ Dogs welcome ~ Open 11(12 Sun)-11(midnight Sat)

WHEATLEY LANE

Old Sparrow Hawk

Wheatley Lane Road; towards E end of village road which runs N of and parallel to A6068; one way of reaching it is to follow Fence, Newchurch 1¼ signpost, then turn off at Barrowford ¾ signpost; BB12 9QG

Comfortably civilised dining pub, with very well prepared food and five real ales

This pleasantly chatty place has a good range of beers, with Bass, Black Sheep, Moorhouses Blonde Witch and Premier Bitter, and Thwaites on handpump, and draught Fransizkaner wheat beer, in addition to good wines by the glass. Locals pop in for an early evening drink and there's a buoyant relaxed atmosphere. Attractively laid out in several distinct areas, some with carpet and some with red tiles, it's nicely characterful, with interesting furnishings, dark oak panelling and timbers, stripped stonework, lots of snug corners including a nice area with a fire, and a sofa under a domed stained-glass skylight; daily papers, piped music and board games. Fresh flowers cheer up the cushioned leatherette bar counter. Good fresh bar food runs from sandwiches and wraps to duck breast on bacon and lentil stew. Heavy wood tables out on a spacious and attractive front terrace (pretty flower beds and a water feature) have good views to the moors beyond Nelson and Colne.

Mitchells & Butlers ~ Lease Stephen Turner ~ Real ale ~ Bar food (12-2.30, 5-9; 12-9.30 Sat; 12-8 Sun) ~ Restaurant ~ (01282) 603034 ~ Children welcome ~ Dogs welcome ~ Live music at bank hols ~ Open 12-11(12 Sat, 10.30 Sun)

WHEELTON

Dressers Arms

2.1 miles from M61 junction 8; Briers Brow, off A674 Blackburn road from Wheelton bypass (towards Brinscall); 3.6 miles from M65 junction 3, also via A674; PR6 8HD

Good choice of beer and big helpings of food at invitingly traditional pub run by warm friendly licensees

This converted cottage row usually keeps eight real ales, including their own Milk of Amnesia and Mild (now brewed off the site), Black Sheep and Tetleys, plus five guests from brewers such as Bank Top, Phoenix and Thwaites; also 16 malt whiskies, and some well chosen wines, with several by the glass. The snug low-beamed rooms are full of traditional features, including a handsome old wood-burning stove in the flagstoned main bar; there are newspapers and magazines; piped music, juke box, pool table, games machine and TV. The generous helpings of food are pubby and they do a Sunday carvery, and an all-you-can-eat curry night on Thursdays. There are lots of picnic-sets, a large umbrella with lighting and heaters on a terrace in front of the pub. Their big car park is across the road.

Own brew ~ Licensees Steve and Trudie Turner ~ Real ale ~ Bar food (12-2.30, 5-9; 12-9 weekends and bank hols) ~ Restaurant ~ (01254) 830041 ~ Children welcome ~ Dogs welcome ~ Open 11-12.30am(1am Sat)

YEALAND CONYERS

New Inn

3 miles from M6 junction 35; village signposted off A6; LA5 9SJ

Good generous food all day and warm welcome at village pub near M6

In a very attractive setting, this much-liked 17th-c village pub stays open all day and has a sheltered lawn at the side with picnic-sets among colourful roses and flowering shrubs. Inside, the simply furnished little beamed bar on the left has a cosy village atmosphere, with its log fire in the big stone fireplace. On the right, two communicating shiny beamed dining rooms are filled with closely set dark blue furniture and an attractive kitchen range. Robinsons Hartleys XB and another of their beers are served on handpump alongside around 30 malt whiskies; piped music and very friendly service. Hearty helpings of decent bar food include sandwiches, baguettes and baked potatoes, all with interesting fillings, plus there are specials of the day. The pub is a useful objective if you're walking in the area or visiting Leighton Moss RSPB reserve.

Robinsons ~ Tenants Bill Tully and Charlotte Pinder ~ Real ale ~ Bar food (11.30(12 Sun)-9.30) ~ Restaurant ~ (01524) 732938 ~ Children welcome ~ Dogs allowed in bar ~ Open 11.30-11; 12-10.30 Sun

DOG FRIENDLY HOTELS, INNS, B&Bs AND FARMS

ASHWORTH VALLEY

Leaches Farm

Ashworth Road, Rochdale, Lancashire OL11 5UN (01706) 41117

£46; 3 rms, shared bthrm. Creeper-clad 17th-c hill farm with really wonderful views, massive stone walls, beams and log fires, and nice breakfasts in dining room; self-catering too; walks on farm but dogs must be on lead (especially at lambing time) plus unrestricted walking on nearby moorland; resident retriever and two cats; cl 22 Dec-2 Jan; children over 8; dogs in bedrooms by arrangement

BLACKPOOL

Imperial Hotel

North Promenade, Blackpool, Lancashire FY1 2HB (01253) 623971

£138; 180 well equipped rms, many with sea views. Fine Victorian hotel overlooking the sea, with spacious and comfortable day rooms, lots of period features, enjoyable food and fine wines, and a full health and leisure club with indoor swimming pool, gym, sauna and so forth; lots to do nearby; disabled access; dogs in bedrooms; £15

COWAN BRIDGE

Hipping Hall

Cowan Bridge, Kirkby Lonsdale, Carnforth, Lancashire LA6 2JJ (01524) 271187

£205; 9 pretty rms, some in main hotel and 2 cottage suites across courtyard (with self-catering facilities). Relaxed country-house atmosphere and elaborate modern british food in handsome and sensitively furnished small hotel, open fires, lovely beamed Great Hall with minstrels' gallery, and four acres of walled gardens; fine walks from front door; cl three weeks in Jan; children over 12; disabled access; dogs in one bedroom only

HURST GREEN

Shireburn Arms

Whalley Road, Hurst Green, Clitheroe, Lancashire BB7 9QJ (01254) 826518

£85; 22 rms. Lovely 17th-c country hotel with refined but friendly atmosphere, airy modernised bar with real ales, morning coffee and afternoon tea, comfortable lounge, open fires, well presented enjoyable food, good service, and fine view of the Ribble Valley from the conservatory; dogs in bedrooms if well behaved; £10

MANCHESTER

Malmaison

Piccadilly, Manchester M1 3AQ (0161) 278 1000

£160; 160 chic rms with CD player, in-house movies, smart bthrms, and really good beds. Stylishly modern hotel with comfortable contemporary furniture, exotic flower arrangements, bright paintings, very efficient service, french brasserie, generous breakfasts, and refurbished spa; good disabled access; dogs in bedrooms; bedding and bones available; £10

WHITEWELL

Inn at Whitewell

Whitewell, Clitheroe, Lancashire BB7 3AT (01200) 448222

£145; 23 rms, some with open peat fires. Civilised Forest of Bowland stone inn on the River Hodder, with seven miles of trout, salmon and sea trout fishing, and six acres of grounds with views down the valley; old-fashioned pubby main bar with sonorous clocks, antique furniture, roaring log fires, newspapers and magazines to read, well kept real ales, an exceptionally good wine list, particularly good food in bar and dining room, and courteous, friendly staff; lots of fine walks from the door; dogs in bedrooms and other areas but away from kitchen

Leicestershire and Rutland

DOG FRIENDLY PUBS

CLIPSHAM

Olive Branch

Take B668/Stretton exit off A1 N of Stamford; Clipsham signposted E from exit roundabout; LE15 7SH

A very special place for an exceptional meal in comfortable surroundings, fine choice of drinks and luxury bedrooms

'You are made to feel like a special guest' and 'a wonderful place' are just two of the enthusiastic comments from the many of our readers who love this civilised place. The various smallish attractive rambling rooms have a relaxed and friendly atmosphere, dark joists and beams, country furniture, an interesting mix of pictures (some by local artists), candles on tables, and there's a cosy log fire in the stone inglenook fireplace. Many of the books were bought at antiques fairs by one of the partners, so it's worth asking if you see something you like, as much is for sale; piped music. Food here is excellent, with both traditional and inventive dishes, all beautifully prepared with carefully sourced ingredients. A thoughtful range of drinks includes Grainstore Olive Oil and a guest beer on handpump, an enticing wine list (with a dozen by the glass), a fine choice of malt whiskies, armagnacs and cognacs, and quite a few different british and continental bottled beers; service is particularly good – friendly and attentive. Outside, there are tables, chairs and big plant pots on a pretty little terrace, with more on the neat lawn, sheltered in the L of its two low buildings. The bedrooms (in their Beech House which is just opposite) are lovely and the breakfasts are wonderful, too.

Free house ~ Licensees Sean Hope and Ben Jones ~ Real ale ~ Bar food (12-2(3 Sun), 7-9.30(9 Sun)) ~ (01780) 410355 ~ Children welcome ~ Dogs allowed in bar and bedrooms ~ Open 12-3.30, 6-11; 12-11(10.30 Sun) Sat; closed 26 Dec, 1 Jan ~ Bedrooms: £85S(£95B)/£100S(£110B)

EXTON

Fox & Hounds

Signposted off A606 Stamford—Oakham; LE15 8AP

Bustling and well run with italian emphasis on popular food, log fire in comfortable lounge and quiet garden

This splendid old coaching inn, facing the quiet village green, is handy for

Rutland Water and the gardens at Barnsdale. The comfortable high-ceilinged lounge bar is traditionally civilised with some dark red plush easy chairs, as well as wheelback seats around lots of pine tables, maps and hunting prints on the walls, fresh flowers and a winter log fire in a large stone fireplace. As the landlord is from Italy, the menu features quite a few italian dishes including lunchtime filled ciabattas and panini, a vast selection of handmade pizzas in almost every combination you could imagine (Monday-Saturday evenings only), italian sausage of the day and much more, as well as some traditional british standards. Adnams Bitter, Grainstore Ten Fifty and Greene King IPA on handpump and a good range of wines by the glass; helpful, friendly service, piped music. The sheltered walled garden has seats among large rose beds on the pleasant well kept back lawn that looks out over paddocks.

Free house ~ Licensees Valter and Sandra Floris ~ Real ale ~ Bar food (not Sun evening or Mon) ~ Restaurant ~ (01572) 812403 ~ Children welcome ~ Dogs allowed in bar and bedrooms ~ Open 11-2.30, 6-11; 11-3, 8-11 Sun; closed Mon ~ Bedrooms: £45B/£60(£70B)

NEWTON BURGOLAND

Belper Arms

Village signposted off B4116 S of Ashby or B586 W of Ibstock; LE67 2SE

Plenty of nooks and seating areas with original features in ancient pub, well liked food, changing ales and seats in rambling garden

Another new landlord for this bustling pub but readers have been quick to voice their warm enthusiasm, and bar food is now usefully served all day. There's a warm welcome for all and although the original building is very opened up, there are lots of ancient interior features such as the heavy beams, changing floor levels and varying old floor and wall materials that break the place up into enjoyable little nooks and seating areas. Parts are thought to date back to the 13th c and much of the exposed brickwork certainly looks at least three or four hundred years old. A big freestanding central chimney at the core of the building has a cottagey old black range on one side and open fire on the other, with chatty groups of nice old captain's chairs. And plenty to look at too, from a suit of old chain mail, to a collection of pewter teapots, some good antique furniture and, framed on the wall, the story of the pub ghost – Five to Four Fred. Black Sheep, Fullers London Pride, Greene King Abbot, Marstons Pedigree and Theakstons Old Peculier on handpump, 30 wines by the glass, quite a few malt whiskies and Stowford Press cider; piped music and dominoes. There are seats in the rambling garden and on the terrace.

Punch ~ Lease David Cordy ~ Real ale ~ Bar food (12-9) ~ Restaurant ~ (01530) 270530 ~ Children welcome ~ Dogs welcome ~ Open 12-12

OAKHAM

Grainstore

Station Road, off A606; LE15 6RE

Super own-brewed beers in converted grain rail warehouse, friendly staff, cheerful customers and pubby food

Laid back or lively, depending on the time of day, and with noises of the brewery workings above, the interior of this converted three-storey Victorian grain warehouse is plain and functional. There are wide well worn bare floorboards, bare ceiling boards above massive joists which are supported by red metal pillars, a long brick-built bar counter with cast-iron bar stools, tall cask tables and simple elm chairs. Their own-brewed beers are served both traditionally at the left end of the bar counter and through swan necks with sparklers on the right: Grainstore Cooking Bitter, Rutland Panther, Rutland Rouses, Silly Billy, Ten Fifty and Triple B. The friendly staff are happy to give you samples. Games machine, darts, board games, shove-ha'penny, giant Jenga and bottle-walking. In summer they pull back the huge glass doors that open on to a terrace with picnic-sets, and often stacked with barrels; disabled access. You can tour the brewery by arrangement, they do take-aways, and hold a real ale festival with over 65 real ales and lots of live music during the August bank holiday weekend. Decent unfussy pubby food includes sandwiches, soup, baguettes, baked potatoes, burgers, sausage and mash, chilli, and all day breakfast.

Own brew ~ Licensee Tony Davis ~ Real ale ~ Bar food (11-3; not Sun) ~ (01572) 770065 ~ Children welcome till 8pm ~ Dogs welcome ~ Live blues first Sun of month, jazz third and fourth Sun ~ Open 11-11(midnight Sat); 12-11 Sun

STATHERN

Red Lion

Off A52 W of Grantham via the brown-signed Belvoir road (keep on towards Harby – Stathern signposted on left); or off A606 Nottingham—Melton Mowbray via Long Clawson and Harby; LE14 4HS

Splendid range of drinks and imaginative food in civilised dining pub, open fires, good garden with play area; own shop too

Well run and rather civilised, this bustling place is under the same ownership as the Olive Branch in Clipsham and has the same high standards. There's a lot of emphasis on the excellent inventive food (maybe thai-style local pigeon with chilli and ginger dressing as well as sausage and mash) and a fine range of drinks but the atmosphere is relaxed and informal and the service very good indeed. The yellow room on the right has a country pub feel and the lounge bar has sofas, an open fire and a big table with books, newspapers and magazines; it leads off the smaller, more traditional flagstoned bar with terracotta walls, another fireplace with a pile of logs beside it, and lots of beams and hops. Dotted around are various oddities picked up by one of the licensees on visits to Newark Antiques Fair: some unusual lambing chairs for example and a collection of wooden spoons. A little room, with tables set for eating, leads to the long, narrow main dining room and out to a nicely arranged suntrap with good hardwood furnishings spread over its lawn and terrace. Brewsters Hophead, Fullers London Pride and Grainstore Olive Oil on handpump, alongside draught belgian beer and continental bottled beers, several ciders, a varied wine list with several by the glass, winter mulled wine and summer home-made lemonade. There's an unusually big play area behind the car park with swings, climbing frames and so on.

Free house ~ Licensees Sean Hope and Ben Jones ~ Real ale ~ Bar food (12-2(3 Sun), 7-9.30; not Sun evening or Mon) ~ Restaurant ~ (01949) 860868 ~

Children welcome ~ Dogs allowed in bar ~ Open 12-3, 6-11; 12-11 Sat; 12-6.30 Sun; closed Sun evening, all day Mon, 1 Jan

WOODHOUSE EAVES

Wheatsheaf

Brand Hill; turn right into Main Street, off B591 S of Loughborough; LE12 8SS

Bustling and friendly country pub with charming licensees, interesting things to look at, good bistro-type food and fair choice of drinks

Even when really busy, the staff in this rather smart country pub remain welcoming and helpful. It's open plan with beams, a log fire, newspapers to read, motor-racing memorabilia and pictures and artefacts to do with winter sports, a chatty bustling atmosphere, and Adnams Broadside, Greene King IPA, Shepherd Neame Spitfire, and Timothy Taylors Landlord on handpump with several wines including champagne by the glass from a thoughtful list. Bar food includes sandwiches, ploughman's and enjoyable bistro-style dishes. The floodlit, heated terrace has plenty of seating.

Free house ~ Licensees Richard and Bridget Dimblebee ~ Real ale ~ Bar food (12-2, 6.30-9.30; all day Sat; not Sun evening) ~ Restaurant ~ (01509) 890320 ~ Children welcome ~ Dogs allowed in bar ~ Open 11.30-3, 6-11; 11.30-11 Sat; 12-10.30 Sun; 11.30-3, 6-11 weekends in winter

DOG FRIENDLY HOTELS, INNS AND B&Bs

HALLATON

Old Rectory

Hallaton, Market Harborough, Leicestershire LE16 8TY (01858) 555350

£90; 3 lovely spacious rms overlooking grounds. Spotlessly kept 18th-c stone former rectory where guests are greeted with afternoon tea in antique-filled drawing room; comfortable lounge, welcoming hosts, breakfasts served in small dining room around a long trestle table (there may be suppers in large dining room using home-grown organic produce, too), and landscaped gardens; Rutland Water for walks, bird-watching and fishing, is nearby; children over 7; dogs in large downstairs cloakroom

MELTON MOWBRAY

Sysonby Knoll

Asfordby Road, Melton Mowbray, Leicestershire LE13 0HP (0.6 miles off A606/A607 junction; A6006 Asfordby Road) (01664) 563563

£82; 30 rms, most facing a central courtyard, and 6 in annexe. Family-run Edwardian brick house on the edge of bustling market town; reception and lounge areas furnished in period style, winter open fire, friendly owners and excellent service, generous helpings of imaginative food inc lots of puddings in airy restaurant, and 5 acres of gardens (where dogs may walk) leading down to the River Eye where guests can fish; footpaths from the door; two resident miniature dachsunds; cl Christmas-New Year; disabled access; dogs welcome away from restaurant

OAKHAM
Barnsdale Lodge Hotel
The Avenue, Oakham, Leicestershire LE15 8AH (01572) 724678

£110; 44 individually decorated rms with views over courtyard or countryside. Former farmhouse and in the same family since the 18th c and on north shore of Rutland Water; relaxed atmosphere, helpful staff, comfortable lounge and bar, carefully cooked, enjoyable, interesting food in conservatory and smart dining room, and seats under parasols on the terrace; dogs in bedrooms; £10

SOMERBY
Stilton Cheese
High Street, Somerby, Melton Mowbray, Leicestershire LE14 2QB (01664) 454394

£40; 3 rms, shared bthrms. 17th-c village pub with bustling, cheerful atmosphere in comfortable hop-strung beamed bar/lounge, chatty staff, decent bar food, local real ales, and seats on heated terrace; dogs in bedrooms

STAPLEFORD
Stapleford Park
Stapleford, Melton Mowbray, Leicestershire LE14 2EF (01572) 787522

£295; 55 individually designed rms inc cottages. Luxurious country house, recently carefully refurbished, in 500 acres of lovely large grounds with riding and stabling, tennis, croquet, putting green, 18-hole championship golf course, trout fishing, falconry, and clay pigeon shooting; lots of opulent furnishings, fine oil paintings and an impressive library, delicious food in restaurants, enthusiastic owner, and warmly welcoming staff; health spa and indoor swimming pool; walks around the grounds and in nearby Rutland Park; partial disabled access; dogs in bedrooms (not to be left unattended) and most public areas; welcome pack; £15

UPPINGHAM
Lake Isle
16 High Street East, Uppingham, Oakham, Rutland LE15 9PZ (01572) 822951

£75 (just off A6003; High Street East); 12 rms with home-made biscuits, sherry and fresh fruit, and three cottage suites. In charming market town, this 18th-c restaurant-with-rooms has an open fire in attractive lounge, comfortable bar, good, imaginative food and enjoyable breakfasts, carefully chosen wine list, and small and pretty garden; dogs in bedrooms if well behaved

Lincolnshire

MAP 8

DOG FRIENDLY PUBS

SOUTH WITHAM

Blue Cow

Village signposted just off A1 Stamford—Grantham (with brown sign for pub); NG33 5QB

Tap for its own Blue Cow real ales; traditional interior, pubby food, garden

No one can accuse this country pub of racking up real-ale miles as all the beer sold here (Blue Cow Best and Witham Wobbler) is brewed on site. Its two appealing rooms (completely separated by a big central open-plan counter) have a relaxed pubby atmosphere, cottagey little windows, plush blue banquettes around a mix of tables including some scrubbed pine ones), flowery carpets and floral upholstered stools along the counter. Dark low beams and standing timbers are set off against exposed stone walls – this is actually a much older building than a first glance at its exterior might suggest. Some areas have shiny flagstones, and there are cottagey pictures and a mantelpiece above the fireplace in one bar; piped music, darts and TV. Bar food is very traditional: sandwiches, fish and chips, pies, curries and steaks, and a popular Sunday roast. The attractive garden has tables on a pleasant terrace.

Own brew ~ Licensee Simon Crathorn ~ Real ale ~ Bar food (10.30-9.30 (not 3-6 Sun)) ~ Restaurant ~ (01572) 768432 ~ Chidren welcome away from counter ~ Dogs welcome ~ Open 10.30(12 Sat, Sun)-11(10.30 Sun) ~ Bedrooms: £45S/£55S

WOOLSTHORPE

Chequers

The one near Belvoir, signposted off A52 or A607 W of Grantham; NG32 1LU

Interesting food at comfortably relaxed inn with good drinks; appealing castle views from outside tables

'There was always a selection, even down to what gin to have with the tonic' is a reader's comment that gives a hint at the tremendous effort and attention to detail they put into making your visit at this excellent 17th-c coaching inn a satisfying one. Their fabulous range of drinks includes well kept Brewsters Marquis and a guest from a brewer such as Ridgeway on handpump, a selection of belgian beers, local fruit pressés, over 35 wines by the glass, over 20 champagnes and 50 malt whiskies. The heavy-beamed main bar has two big tables (one a massive oak construction), a comfortable mix of seating including some handsome leather chairs and leather banquettes, and a huge boar's head above a good log fire in the big brick fireplace. Among cartoons on the wall are some of the illustrated claret bottle labels from the series commissioned from famous artists, initiated by the late Baron Philippe de Rothschild. The lounge on the right has a deep red colour scheme, leather sofas and a big plasma TV, and on the left, there are more leather seats in a dining area in what was once the village bakery. Food ranges from pub classics (with inventive sandwiches such as red pepper, feta and rocket) to more imaginative specials, and is very rewarding. A corridor leads off to the light and airy main restaurant which has contemporary pictures and another bar; piped music. There are good quality teak tables, chairs and benches outside and beyond these, some picnic-sets on the edge of the pub's cricket field, with views of Belvoir Castle.

Free house ~ Licensee Justin Chad ~ Real ale ~ Bar food (12-2.30, 6-9.30; 12-4, 6-8.30 Sun) ~ Restaurant ~ (01476) 870701 ~ Children welcome ~ Dogs allowed in bar and bedrooms ~ Open 12-3, 5.30-11; 12-11 Sat; 12-10.30 Sun ~ Bedrooms: £49B/£59B

DOG FRIENDLY HOTELS, INNS AND B&Bs

STAMFORD
George of Stamford

71 St Martins, Stamford, Lincolnshire PE9 2LB (1.7 miles off A1 via B1081 from S end of Stamford bypass; St Martins, just S of bridge) (01780) 750700

£130; 47 individually decorated rms. Ancient former coaching inn with quietly civilised atmosphere, sturdy timbers, broad flagstones, heavy beams and massive stonework, and open log fires; good food in Garden Lounge, restaurant and summer courtyard, an excellent range of drinks inc very good value italian wines, and welcoming staff; well kept walled garden and sunken croquet lawn, and an area where dogs may walk; two resident cats; children over 10 in restaurant; disabled access; dogs in bedrooms (not left unattended); welcome pack

WINTERINGHAM
Winteringham Fields

1 Silver Street, Winteringham, Scunthorpe, Lincolnshire DN15 9ND (01724) 733096

£165; 10 pretty rms (3 off courtyard). Thoughtfully run restaurant-with-rooms in 16th-c manor house with comfortable and very attractive Victorian furnishings, beams and open fires, really excellent, inventive and beautifully presented food (inc a marvellous cheeseboard), fine breakfasts, exemplary service, and an admirable wine list; two resident labradors and a great dane; miles of walks close by; cl two weeks Dec/Jan, one week April, two weeks Aug, one week Oct; disabled access; dogs in bedrooms (not to be left unattended); welcome pack; £10

WOODHALL SPA

Petwood

Stixwould Road, Woodhall Spa, Lincolnshire LN10 6QF (01526) 352411

£145; 53 pleasant rms. Sizeable Edwardian house in 30 acres of mature woodland, lawns and gardens; many original features inc panelling and a fine main staircase, spacious public rooms decorated and furnished in keeping with the style of the hotel, smart restaurant, and snooker table, putting green and croquet lawn; dogs in bedrooms and public rooms (not restaurant); £15

DOG FRIENDLY PUBS

AYLSHAM

Black Boys

Market Place, just off B1145; NR11 6EH

Good value food with lots of fresh fish in nicely updated traditional market-place inn with a warm-hearted bar

The quite imposing Georgian façade fronts a building which dates back to 1650. It's been appealingly brought up to date inside, keeping the high dark beams in the ochre ceiling, stripping some walls back to the warm red brickwork, with a dark-panelled dado, neat new wood flooring, and comfortably old-fashioned chairs or built-in wall seats around good well spaced solid tables. Friendly helpful young staff jolly along the cheery thriving atmosphere in the bar and the adjoining dining area. Food from the wide-ranging menu (from snacks to lobster) is home made, served generously, and well priced for its quality; Sunday carvery. They usually have a very good range of fresh fish. Adnams Best and Woodfordes Wherry and a couple of guests like Adnams Broadside and Fullers London Pride are on handpump, and they've over a dozen decent wines by the glass. Neat modern tables and chairs out in front face the market place. The four bedrooms (there's a £5 charge for dogs if they stay) have been attractively refurbished.

Unique (Enterprise) ~ Lease Matthew Miller ~ Real ale ~ Bar food (12-2(6 Sun), 6.30-9(9.30 Fri Sat, 8.30 Sun)) ~ Restaurant ~ (01263) 732122 ~ Children welcome ~ Dogs allowed in bar and bedrooms ~ Open 11-12; 12-10.30 Sun ~ Bedrooms: £51.50B/£70.50B

BLAKENEY

Kings Arms

West Gate Street; NR25 7NQ

A stroll from the harbour, friendly and chatty, with home cooking and local ales; walled garden

Our readers enjoy their visits to this attractive white inn. It's a friendly place with a pleasant, welcoming atmosphere and courteous, helpful staff. The three simply furnished, knocked-through pubby rooms have a good mix of locals and visitors, low ceilings, some interesting photographs of the licensees' theatrical careers, other pictures including work by local artists, and what must be the smallest cartoon gallery in England – in a former telephone kiosk. Look out for the brass plaque on the wall that marks a flood level. There's an airy garden room, too; darts, games machine, and board games. The pubby bar food is very popular. Adnams Bitter and Woodfordes Nelsons Revenge and Wherry on handpump, and quite a few wines by the glass. The large garden has lots of tables and chairs; the harbour is a stroll away and the Norfolk Coast Path runs close by.

Free house ~ Licensees John Howard, Marjorie Davies and Nick Davies ~ Real ale ~ Bar food (all day) ~ (01263) 740341 ~ Children welcome ~ Dogs welcome ~ Open 11-11; 12-10.30 Sun ~ Bedrooms: £45S/£65S

BRANCASTER STAITHE

Jolly Sailors

Main Road (A149); PE31 8BJ

Own-brewed beers in cosy rooms, and plenty of seats in sizeable garden; great bird-watching nearby

This is an enjoyable little pub with a friendly, unpretentious atmosphere. The three simply furnished and cosy rooms have a good mix of pubby seats and tables, and an open fire. The dining area has been smartened up and now feels less cluttered. From their on-site microbrewery they produce Brancaster Staithe Brewery Old Les and IPA, and they keep a guest like Woodfordes Norfolk Nog on handpump. Sausages, on the enjoyably traditional menu, are made with their own beer. There's a sizeable garden with a big new play area and a covered terrace with plenty of picnic-sets. This is prime bird-watching territory and the pub is set on the edge of thousands of acres of National Trust dunes and salt flats; walkers are welcome.

Free house ~ Licensee Mr Boughton ~ Real ale ~ Bar food (12-9) ~ Restaurant ~ (01485) 210314 ~ Children welcome ~ Dogs allowed in bar ~ Open 11-11; 12-10.30 Sun

White Horse

A149 E of Hunstanton; PE31 8BY

Bustling, popular bar, big airy dining conservatory looking over tidal bird marshes, real ales and lovely food; comfortable bedrooms

They've cleverly managed to appeal to a very wide range of customers here and seem able to cater for most needs. It's a comfortable and enjoyable place to stay and the food in the bar and restaurant is particularly good. But what most appealed to one of our readers was the sign saying that they welcomed tired walkers and dogs, and he much appreciated sitting on the sun deck with a pint of beer looking out to Scolt Head across the salt marsh. The informal bar has plenty of locals dropping in, good photographs on the left, with bar billiards and maybe piped music, and on the right is a quieter group of cushioned wicker armchairs and sofas by a table with daily papers and local landscapes for sale; there are plenty of seats outside in front, some under cover and with heaters, for casual dining. The food includes delicious local fish and other tempting dishes, is very good indeed, and very fairly priced. The dining area and adjoining conservatory restaurant are at the back with well spaced furnishings in unvarnished country-style wood and some lighthearted seasidey decorations;

the wide tidal marsh views seen through the big glass windows are splendid. Adnams Bitter, Fullers London Pride, Woodfordes Wherry, and a guest like Timothy Taylors Landlord on handpump, several malt whiskies and about a dozen wines by the glass from an extensive and thoughtful wine list; friendly service. The coast path runs along the bottom of the garden.

Free house ~ Licensees Cliff Nye and Kevin Nobes ~ Real ale ~ Bar food (all day in bar and on outside terrace; 12-2, 6.30-9 restaurant) ~ Restaurant ~ (01485) 210262 ~ Children welcome ~ Dogs allowed in bar and bedrooms ~ Open 11-11; 12-10.30 Sun ~ Bedrooms: £89B/£128B

BURNHAM THORPE
Lord Nelson

Village signposted from B1155 and B1355, near Burnham Market; PE31 8HL

Interesting Nelson memorabilia, fine drinks including secret rum-based recipes, tasty food, and much character; play area in big garden

This spotlessly clean, 17th-c pub has plenty of memorabilia and pictures of Nelson (who was born in this sleepy village). The little bar has well waxed antique high-backed settles on the worn red flooring tiles and smoke ovens in the original fireplace, and there's a little snug leading off. The eating room has flagstones, an open fire and a history alongside more pictures of Nelson, and there's a separate dining room, too; board games. Greene King Abbot, Woodfordes Wherry and a guest like Fox Nelsons Blood tapped from the cask, a dozen wines by the glass and secret rum-based recipes called Nelson's Blood and Lady Hamilton's Nip; Nelson's Blood was first concocted in the 18th c and is passed down from landlord to landlord by word of mouth. As well as lunchtime open sandwiches and ploughman's and several more imaginative dishes, good bar food includes a surf and turf menu and a three-course set menu. There's a good-sized play area and pétanque in the very big garden (where there may be summer barbecues). They hold special Nelson events throughout the year.

Greene King ~ Lease Simon Alper ~ Real ale ~ Bar food (12-2(2.30 Sat), 7-9(9.30 Sat); not Sun evening or Mon except summer school holidays) ~ Restaurant ~ (01328) 738241 ~ Children welcome ~ Dogs allowed in bar ~ Live bands Thurs evenings ~ Open 12-3(3.30 Sat), 6-11 (open all day during summer school holidays); 12-3.30, 6.30-11 Sun; closed Mon (except half term and school holidays)

EDGEFIELD
Pigs

Norwich Road; B1149 S of Holt; NR24 2RL

Good enterprising food and good range of drinks in enthusiastically run pub – still keeping a proper bar

This splendid pub is a good all-rounder, and actually something of a front-runner on the food side. The carpeted central bar greets you with the reassuring sight of a good row of handpumps, with well kept Adnams Bitter and Broadside,

Woodfordes Wherry, and a couple of changing guests. They have continental beers on tap, and a good range of wines by the glass, in two glass sizes; they do coffee in two sizes, too. No crisps – instead they do their own pork scratching and interesting seed, bean and nut snacks with nibbly things like spiced almonds and salted broad beans. Service, under the very hands-on landlord, is uniformly cheerful and efficient. A games area has darts, dominoes, shove-ha'penny and bar billiards (Thursday is games night, and they have a Wednesday quiz night); there's a proper children's playroom, too. On the left, arches open through to a simply refurbished area with a mix of random dining chairs and built-in pews around the plain tables on broad stripped pine boards. From a cheerfully set out menu, the good interesting food includes some very well prepared deliciously inventive dishes, as well as sandwiches. Outside, a big covered terrace has sturdy rustic tables and benches on flagstones, and there is an adventure play area. Wheelchair access is easy.

Free house ~ Licensee Chloe Wasey ~ Real ale ~ Bar food (12-2.30(3 Sun), 6-9; not Sun evening or Mon (except bank hols)) ~ (01263) 587634 ~ Children welcome ~ Dogs allowed in bar ~ Open 11-3, 6-11; 12-4 Sun; closed Sun evening, Mon (except bank hols when they open 12-4)

ITTERINGHAM

Walpole Arms

Village signposted off B1354 NW of Aylsham; NR11 7AR

Ambitious food in popular dining pub, quietly chatty open-plan bar, decent drinks and good garden

New licensees have taken over this busy dining pub, but apart from the menu, little seems to have changed. Food, from a wide ranging menu, is now more inventive, with dishes such as slow-roast pork belly with chickpea and chorizo stew and rouille. The sizeable open-plan bar is rather civilised and has exposed beams, stripped brick walls, little windows, a mix of dining tables and a quietly chatty atmosphere. Adnams Bitter, Wolf Golden Jackal, and Woodfordes Wherry on handpump, quite a few wines by the glass, and Aspall's cider; friendly young manager and helpful staff. Behind the pub is a two-acre landscaped garden and there are seats on the vine-covered terrace.

Free house ~ Licensees Mr and Mrs Sayers ~ Real ale ~ Bar food (12-2(3 Sun), 7-9; not Sun evening) ~ Restaurant ~ (01263) 587258 ~ Children welcome ~ Dogs allowed in bar ~ Open 12-3, 6-11; 12-7 Sun; closed 25 Dec

MORSTON

Anchor

A149 Salthouse—Stiffkey; The Street; NR25 7AA

Quite a choice of rooms filled with bric-a-brac and prints, real ales, and well liked food

There's a good mix of varied interiors at this busy pub. The contemporary airy extension on the left has groups of deep leather sofas around low tables, grey-painted country dining furniture, fresh flowers and fish pictures. On the right are three more traditional rooms with pubby seating and tables on original wooden floors, coal fires, local 1950s beach photographs and lots of prints and bric-a-brac. The menu has been thoughtfully compiled, with sandwiches, oysters, well prepared versions of traditional dishes and a few more imaginative items. Greene King IPA, Old Speckled Hen and local Winters Golden on hand-pump, several decent wines including vintage champagne by the glass, oyster shots (a local oyster in a short bloody mary), and daily papers. There are tables and benches out in front of the building. You can book seal-spotting trips from here and the surrounding area is wonderful for bird-watching and walking.

Free house ~ Licensee Sam Handley ~ Real ale ~ Bar food (12-2.30, 6-9(9.30 Fri and Sat); 12-8 Sun) ~ Restaurant ~ (01263) 741392 ~ Children welcome ~ Dogs allowed in bar ~ Open 11-11(10.30 Sun)

SNETTISHAM

Rose & Crown

Village signposted from A149 King's Lynn—Hunstanton just N of Sandringham; coming in on the B1440 from the roundabout just N of village, take first left turn into Old Church Road; PE31 7LX

Constantly improving old pub, log fires and interesting furnishings, thoughtful food, fine range of drinks, and stylish seating on heated terrace; well equipped, popular bedrooms

Many of our readers very much enjoy staying overnight at this pretty white cottage, and the upgrading of the bedrooms continues – they now have a lovely four-poster room, too. It's a favourite with a lot of customers who enjoy the infor-mal and relaxed feel of the place, helped no doubt by the presence of locals who are always popping in for a pint and a chat. The smallest of the three bars has had a facelift this year and is now a mocha coffee colour with coir flooring but still with the old prints of King's Lynn and Sandringham. The other two bars each have a separate character: an old-fashioned beamed front bar with black settles on its tiled floor and a big log fire, and a back bar with another large log fire and the landlord's sporting trophies and old sports equipment. There's also the Garden Room with inviting wicker-based wooden chairs, careful lighting and a quote by Dr Johnson in old-fashioned rolling script on a huge wall board. The residents' lounge is popular with non-residents too and has squashy armchairs and sofas, rugs on the floor, newspapers, magazines, jigsaws and board games – this can sometimes be dragooned into action as another dining room. Usually very reward-ing, food includes antipasti and charcuterie platters, interesting dishes such pigeon breast with broad bean and chorizo salad and well composed staples such as steak burger with bacon, cheese and real tomato ketchup. Adnams Bitter, Bass, Fullers London Pride and Greene King IPA on handpump, quite a few wines by the glass, organic fruit juices and farm cider; friendly service. In the garden there are stylish café-style blue chairs and tables under cream parasols on the terrace, outdoor heaters, and colourful herbaceous borders. Two of the comfortable bedrooms are downstairs and there are disabled lavatories and wheelchair ramps.

Free house ~ Licensee Anthony Goodrich ~ Real ale ~ Bar food (12-2(2.30 weekends and school holidays), 6.30-9(9.30 Fri and Sat) ~ Restaurant ~

(01485) 541382 ~ Children welcome ~ Dogs welcome ~ Open 11-11; 12-10.30 Sun ~ Bedrooms: £70B/£90B

STIFFKEY
Red Lion

A149 Wells—Blakeney; NR23 1AJ

Bustling atmosphere and attractive layout and good food

This traditional pub is a bustling friendly place with a wide mix of customers. The oldest parts of the simple bars have a few beams, aged flooring tiles or bare floorboards, and big open fires. There's also a mix of pews, small settles and a couple of stripped high-backed settles, a nice old long deal table among quite a few others. Tasty bar food runs from well liked beer-battered cod to confit of duck with wilted spinach, jus and parsnip crisps. Woodfordes Nelsons Revenge and Wherry and a guest like Yetmans Blue on handpump, and nine wines by the glass; good service, board games. A back gravel terrace has proper tables and seats, with more on grass further up beyond; there are some pleasant walks nearby.

Free house ~ Licensee Stephen Franklin ~ Real ale ~ Bar food (12-3, 6-9; all day weekends; breakfast from 8am) ~ (01328) 830552 ~ Children welcome ~ Dogs welcome ~ Live music monthly Fri evening ~ Open 8am-11pm ~ Bedrooms: £80B/£100B

WELLS-NEXT-THE-SEA
Crown

The Buttlands; NR23 1EX

Smart coaching inn, friendly, informal bar, local ales, good, modern food, and stylish orangery; bedrooms

Although this is a rather smart 16th-c coaching inn, there's a bustling, cheerful atmosphere in the beamed bar and a good mix of both drinkers and diners. This bar has an informal mix of furnishings on the stripped wooden floor, local photographs on the red walls, a good selection of newspapers to read in front of the open fire, Adnams Bitter, Woodfordes Wherry and a guest like 3 Rivers IPA on handpump, quite a few wines by the glass and several whiskies and brandies; friendly, helpful staff. Piped music and board games. Award winning bar food is attractively presented, inventive and very good.

Free house ~ Licensees Chris and Jo Coubrough ~ Real ale ~ Bar food (12-2.30, 6.30-9.30) ~ Restaurant ~ (01328) 710209 ~ Children welcome ~ Dogs allowed in bar ~ Open 11-11

DOG FRIENDLY HOTELS, INNS, B&Bs AND FARMS

BLAKENEY

Blakeney Hotel

Blakeney, Holt, Norfolk NR25 7NE (01263) 740797

£172; 63 very comfortable rms, many with views over the salt marshes and some with own little terrace. Overlooking the harbour with fine views, this friendly hotel has two comfortable and appealing lounges (one with an open fire), good food in restaurant and bar, very pleasant staff, indoor swimming pool, saunas, spa bath, billiard room, and safe garden; very well organised for families, with plenty for them to do nearby; good disabled access; dogs in some bedrooms; £5

BURNHAM MARKET

Hoste Arms

Market Place, Burnham Market, King's Lynn, Norfolk PE31 8HD (01328) 738777

£125; 35 comfortable rms. Handsome inn on green of lovely Georgian village, with smart but relaxed atmosphere, convivial bar and friendly conservatory, some interesting period features, big log fires, stylish food using local produce (plus morning coffee and afternoon tea) in several restaurant areas, well kept real ales and good wines, and professional friendly staff; big awning covering a sizeable eating area in the garden; lovely beaches for walking nearby; partial disabled access; dogs welcome away from restaurant; £10

ERPINGHAM

Saracens Head

Wolterton, Norwich, Norfolk NR11 7LZ (2.3 miles off A140; keep straight on past Erpingham itself, then through Calthorpe to Wolterton) (01263) 768909

£85; 6 cottagey rms. Comfortably civilised inn with simple but stylish two-room bar, nice mix of seats, log fires and fresh flowers, excellent inventive food, very well kept real ales, interesting wines; charming old-fashioned gravel stableyard with picnic-sets; cl Mon, 25 Dec; limited disabled access; dogs in bedrooms

MORSTON

Morston Hall

The Street, Morston, Holt, Norfolk NR25 7AA (01263) 741041

£300 inc dinner; 7 comfortable rms with country views. Attractive 17th-c flint-walled house with lovely quiet gardens, two small lounges (one with an antique fireplace), conservatory, and hard-working friendly young owners; particularly fine modern english cooking (they also run cookery demonstrations and hold wine and food events), thoughtful small wine list, and super breakfasts; croquet;

coastal path for walks right outside; cl Jan; they are kind to families; partial disabled access; dogs in bedrooms; £5

MUNDFORD

Crown

Crown Street, Mundford, Thetford, Norfolk IP26 5HQ (0.2 miles off A134 roundabout; first fork left off A1065) (01842) 878233

£69.50; 32 good rms. Friendly village pub, originally a hunting inn and rebuilt in the 18th c, with an attractive choice of reasonably priced straightforward food, very welcoming staff, a happy atmosphere, well kept real ales, and nearby forest walks; disabled access; dogs in some bedrooms if well behaved; £10

NORTH WALSHAM

Beechwood

Cromer Road, North Walsham, Norfolk NR28 0HD (01692) 403231

£150 inc dinner; 17 charming, comfortable rms. Creeper-covered Georgian house, once Agatha Christie's Norfolk hideaway, with comfortable lounge, garden lounge and bar, charming owners and super staff, good, imaginative modern cooking in attractive dining room, nice breakfasts, and lovely garden where dogs may walk – there's also a park nearby; two resident dogs; children over 10; dogs in bedrooms; treats in bar; £8

OLD CATTON

Catton Old Hall

Lodge Lane, Old Catton, Norwich, Norfolk NR6 7HG (01603) 419379

£80; 7 comfortable rms. 17th-c former farmhouse with lots of original features such as oak timbers, flint walls, and inglenook fireplaces; cosy lounge, huge dresser in beamed dining room, small honesty bar, hearty breakfasts (evening meals by prior arrangement), and attentive, welcoming owners; plenty of country walks nearby; resident yorkshire terrier; cl Christmas and New Year; children over 12; dogs if small, in some bedrooms

SWAFFHAM

Strattons

Ash Close, Swaffham, Norfolk PE37 7NH (1.5 miles off A47; Ash Close, off Lynn Street nr centre) (01760) 723845

£150; 10 eclectic and individual rms. Environment-friendly Palladian-style villa with comfortable and boldly decorated rooms filled with sculptures, ornaments and original paintings, fresh flower arrangements, and log fires; imaginative food using local organic produce, good breakfasts using their own eggs and home-baked bread, and a carefully chosen wine list; two resident dogs, two cats, and roaming chickens; plenty of nearby walks; cl Christmas; dogs in bedrooms but must not be left unattended; welcome pack; £6.50

THORNHAM
Lifeboat
Ship Lane, Thornham, Hunstanton, Norfolk PE36 6LT (01485) 512236

£94; 14 pretty rms, most with sea view. Rambling old white-painted stone pub, well placed by coastal flats, with lots of character in the main bar – open fires, antique oil lamps, low settles and pews around carved oak tables, big oak beams hung with traps and yokes, and masses of guns, swords and antique farm tools; several rooms lead off; enjoyable popular food in bar and elegant restaurant, and well kept real ales; sunny conservatory with steps up to terrace; marvellous surrounding walks; disabled access; dogs in bedrooms and bars; £6

TITCHWELL
Titchwell Manor Hotel
Main Road, Titchwell, King's Lynn, Norfolk PE31 8BB (01485) 210221

£130; 27 light, pretty rms. Comfortable hotel, handy for nearby RSPB reserve, and with lots of walks and footpaths nearby; roaring log fire, magazines and good naturalists' records of the wildlife, cheerful bar, attractive brasserie restaurant (lots of seafood) with french windows on to lovely sheltered walled garden, good breakfasts, and particularly helpful licensees and staff; high tea for younger children; disabled access; dogs in ground-floor bedrooms; towel, bowl, walk map, biscuits; £8

WARHAM
Three Horseshoes
The Street, Warham, Wells-next-the-Sea, Norfolk NR23 1NL (01328) 710547

£60; 5 rms, one with own bthrm. Basic but cheerful local with marvellously unspoilt traditional atmosphere in three friendly gaslit rooms, simple furnishings, log fire, tasty generous bar food, decent wines, and well kept real ales; bedrooms are in Old Post Office adjoining the pub, with lots of beams and a residents' lounge dominated by inglenook fireplace; resident english bull terrier; plenty of surrounding walks; cl 25-26 Dec; no children; dogs in bedrooms

WINTERTON-ON-SEA
Fishermans Return
The Lane, Winterton-on-Sea, Great Yarmouth, Norfolk NR29 4BN (01493) 393305

£70; 3 rms reached by a tiny staircase. Traditional 300-year-old pub in quiet village, close to the beach (fine walking), with warmly welcoming and helpful owners, relaxed lounge bar with well kept real ales, open fire, good home-made food inc fresh fish (fine crabs in season), enjoyable breakfasts, and sheltered garden with children's play equipment; resident vizsla; dogs welcome; treats and water bowl

DOG FRIENDLY DOGS

CRICK

Red Lion

1 mile from M1 junction 18; in centre of village off A428; NN6 7TX

Nicely worn-in friendly coaching inn off M1 with good value straightforward lunchtime food and pricier more detailed evening menu

Not elaborate but very reliable, this old stone thatched pub is favoured by readers for its welcoming atmosphere and sensible prices. The cosy low-ceilinged bar is nice and traditional with lots of comfortable seating, some rare old horse-brasses, pictures of the pub in the days before it was surrounded by industrial estates, and a tiny log stove in a big inglenook. Four well kept beers on hand-pump include Wells & Youngs Bombardier, Greene King Old Speckled Hen, Theakstons Best and a guest from a brewer such as Sharpes. Homely lunchtime bar food includes sandwiches, ploughman's and pies – prices go up a little in the evening when they add a few more substantial dishes; bargain-price Sunday roast. There are a few picnic-sets under parasols on grass by the car park, and in summer you can eat on the terrace in the old coachyard which is sheltered by a Perspex roof and decorated with lots of pretty hanging baskets.

Wellington ~ Tenants Tom and Paul Marks ~ Real ale ~ Bar food (12-2, 6.30-9; not Sun evening) ~ (01788) 822342 ~ Children under 14 welcome lunchtimes only ~ Dogs welcome ~ Open 11-2.30, 6.15-11; 12-3, 7-10.30 Sun

EYDON

Royal Oak

Lime Avenue; village signed off A361 Daventry—Banbury, and from B4525; NN11 3PG

Enjoyable low-beamed old place with good lunchtime snacks and imaginative evening menu

This attractive 300-year-old ironstone inn retains plenty of original features, including fine flagstone floors and leaded windows. The room on the right has cushioned wooden benches built into alcoves, seats in a bow window, some cottagey pictures, and an open fire in an inglenook fireplace. The bar counter (with bar stools) runs down a long central flagstoned corridor room and links several other small characterful rooms. An attractive covered terrace with hardwood furniture is a lovely place for a meal in fine weather. The fairly pubby lunchtime menu moves up a notch in the evening, with dishes such as beef fillet with stilton soufflé and cumberland sauce. Friendly staff serve well kept Fullers

London Pride, Greene King IPA, Timothy Taylors Landlord and a guest, usually from Archers, on handpump; piped music and table skittles.

Free house ~ Licensee Justin Lefevre ~ Real ale ~ Bar food ~ (01327) 263167 ~ Children welcome ~ Dogs welcome ~ Open 12-2.30, 6-11; 12-3, 7-10.30 Sun; closed Mon lunchtime

FARTHINGSTONE

Kings Arms

Off A5 SE of Daventry; village signposted from Litchborough on former B4525 (now declassified); NN12 8EZ

Individual place serving carefully sourced regional foods, with cosy traditional interior and lovely gardens; note limited opening times

Given that they serve food just a couple of sessions a week, the friendly licensee couple at this quirky gargoyle-embellished stone 18th-c country pub must be having some success at keeping it at the heart of the local community – they run regular quiz nights and even the occasional debating evening. The timelessly intimate flagstoned bar has a huge log fire, comfortable homely sofas and armchairs near the entrance, whisky-water jugs hanging from oak beams, and lots of pictures and decorative plates on the walls. A games room at the far end has darts, dominoes, cribbage, table skittles and board games. Thwaites Original and Wells & Youngs are well kept on handpump alongside a guest such as St Austell Tinners, the short wine list is quite decent, and they have a few country wines. Look out for the interesting newspaper-influenced décor in the outside gents'. The tranquil terrace is charmingly decorated with hanging baskets, flower and herb pots and plant-filled painted tractor tyres. They grow their own salad vegetables and there's a cosy little terrace by the herb garden. Bar food might include soup, good filled baguettes, ploughman's, loch fyne fish platter and a british cheese platter, with a couple of main courses such as yorkshire pudding filled with steak and kidney and cumbrian wild boar sausage and mash.

Free house ~ Licensees Paul and Denise Egerton ~ Real ale ~ Bar food (12-2 Sat, Sun only) ~ No credit cards ~ (01327) 361604 ~ Children welcome ~ Dogs welcome ~ Open 7(6.30 Fri)-11; 12-3.30, 7-11.30 Sat; 12-4, 9-11 Sun; closed Mon, weekday lunchtimes and Weds evenings

FOTHERINGHAY

Falcon

Village signposted off A605 on Peterborough side of Oundle; PE8 5HZ

Upmarket dining pub, good food from snacks up, good range of drinks and attractive garden

The neatly kept little bar at this civilised pub is sedately furnished with cushioned slatback arm and bucket chairs, good winter log fires in a stone fireplace, and fresh flower arrangements. As well as imaginative sandwiches, thoughtful (if not cheap) bar food includes inventive dishes such as fried sea bream with cherry vine tomato and crab risotto. Though the main draw is dining, there is a thriving little locals' tap bar (and darts team) if you do just want a drink. The very good range of drinks includes three changing beers from brewers such as Digfield, Greene King IPA and Oakham on handpump, good wines (20 by the glass), organic cordials and fresh orange juice. The attractively planted garden is particularly enjoyable, the vast church behind is worth a visit, and the ruined Fotheringhay Castle, where Mary Queen of Scots was executed, is not far away.

Free house ~ Licensees Sally Facer and Jim Jeffries ~ Real ale ~ Bar food (12-2.15, 6.15-9.15; 12-3, 6.15-8.30 Sun) ~ Restaurant ~ (01832) 226254 ~ Children welcome ~ Dogs allowed in bar ~ Open 12-3, 6-11; 12-11 Sat; 12-10.30 Sun

GREAT BRINGTON

Fox & Hounds/Althorp Coaching Inn

Off A428 NW of Northampton, near Althorp Hall; NN7 4JA

Friendly golden stone thatched pub with great choice of real ales, tasty food, sheltered garden

'An olde worlde haven, often with a dog or two sprawled out' is the description one reader gives of the ancient bar at this cosy old coaching inn. It has all the features you'd expect of such a place, from old beams and saggy joists to an attractive mix of country chairs and tables (maybe with fresh flowers) on its broad flagstones and bare boards. There are also plenty of snug alcoves, nooks and crannies, some stripped pine shutters and panelling, two fine log fires, and an eclectic medley of bric-a-brac from farming implements to an old typewriter and country pictures. A cellarish games room down some steps has a view of the casks in the cellar. Food is hearty and very rewarding. Cheery staff serve the splendid range of nine real ales which include Greene King IPA, Abbot and Old Speckled Hen and Fullers London Pride, with up to five thoughtfully sourced guests from brewers such as Brewsters, Church End, Hoggleys (local to them), and they've about a dozen wines by the glass and a dozen malt whiskies; piped music. The coach entry from the road opens into a lovely little paved courtyard with sheltered tables and tubs of flowers, and there is more seating in the side garden.

Free house ~ Licensee Jacqui Ellard ~ Real ale ~ Bar food (12-2.30(3 Sat, Sun) 6.30-9.30) ~ Restaurant ~ (01604) 770164 ~ Dogs allowed in bar ~ Open 11-12; 12-10.30 Sun

SLIPTON

Samuel Pepys

Off A6116 at first roundabout N of A14 junction, towards Twywell and Slipton, bearing right to Slipton; the pub (in Slipton Lane) is well signed locally; NN14 3AR

Exemplary dining pub with prompt friendly service, good beers, nice surroundings and garden

Though popular for food (which is good value, well presented and tasty), there's still a properly pubby feel and good range of beers in the long back bar of this smartly reworked old stone pub. It's gently modern and airy with good lighting, very heavy low beams, a log fire in the stone chimney-breast's big raised hearth (with plenty of logs stacked around), and chapel chairs on a simple mauve carpet. At one side, beyond a great central pillar that looks as if it was once part of a ship's mast, is an area with squashy leather seats around low tables; piped music. The white painted bar counter stocks a good range of half a dozen real ales on handpump or tapped straight from the cask, including Greene King IPA, Hop Back Summer Lightning, John Smiths, Oakham JHB and Potbelly Aisling (from Kettering) and interesting changing guests from brewers such as Brewsters and Nethergate. They have an interesting choice of reasonably priced wines by the glass and bottle. Service is very friendly and helpful, and there is wheelchair access throughout. The sheltered garden is spacious and well laid out, with picnic-sets under cocktail parasols, and a terrace with heaters.

Mercury Inns ~ Manager Frazer Williams ~ Real ale ~ Bar food (12-3, 7-9.30) ~ Restaurant ~ (01832) 731739 ~ Children welcome ~ Dogs welcome ~ Open 12-3, 6-11.30; 12-11.30 Sat, Sun)

WADENHOE

Kings Head

Church Street; village signposted (in small print) off A605 S of Oundle; PE8 5ST

Country pub in idyllic riverside spot; decent range of beers, pubby food

Not to be missed in summer, this cheery stone-built 16th-c inn is in a wonderful spot with picnic-sets among willows and aspens on grass leading down to the River Nene – you can even arrive by boat and moor here. Inside, there's an uncluttered simplicity (maybe too much so for some) to the very welcoming partly stripped-stone main bar, which has pleasant old worn quarry-tiles, solid pale pine furniture with a couple of cushioned wall seats, and a leather-upholstered chair by the woodburning stove in the fine inglenook. The bare-boarded public bar has similar furnishings and another fire; steps lead up to a games room with dominoes and table skittles, and there's more of the pale pine furniture in an attractive little beamed dining room. Pubby bar food might include lunchtime sandwiches, ham, egg and chips, catch of the day and rib-eye steak. As well as either Digfield Barnwell or Digfield Kings Head, they have a guest or two, maybe from Grainstore or Ruddles, and a dozen wines by the glass.

Free house ~ Licensee Peter Hall ~ Real ale ~ Bar food (11.30-2.15(2.30 Sun), 6.30-9.15) ~ Restaurant ~ (01832) 720024 ~ Children welcome ~ Dogs allowed in bar ~ Open 11-11; 12-7.30 Sun

DOG FRIENDLY HOTELS, INNS, B&BS AND FARMS

BADBY

Windmill

Main Street, Badby, Daventry, Northamptonshire NN11 3AN (01327) 702363

£72.50; 10 rms. Carefully modernised and warmly welcoming thatched stone inn with beams, flagstones and huge inglenook fireplace in front bar, cosy comfortable lounge, relaxed and civilised atmosphere, good generously served bar and restaurant food, and decent wines; fine views of pretty village from car park and woods to walk in a mile away; disabled access; dogs welcome away from main restaurant

CRANFORD

Dairy Farm

12 St Andrews Lane, Cranford, Kettering, Northamptonshire NN14 4AQ (1.7 miles off A14 at A510 junction; turn right off High Street into Grafton Road, then next right into St Andrews Lane) (01536) 330273

£60; 3 comfortable rms. Charming 17th-c manor house of great character on an arable and sheep farm, with oak beams and inglenook fireplaces, good homely cooking using home-grown fruit and vegetables, kind, attentive owners, and garden with charming summer house and ancient dovecote; walks half a mile away; cl Christmas; dogs in annexe bedrooms; £5

DAVENTRY

Fawsley Hall

Fawsley, Daventry, Northamptonshire NN11 3BA (01327) 892000

£175; 52 classical rms with period furniture. Lovely Tudor hotel with Georgian and Victorian additions set in quiet gardens designed by Capability Brown and surrounded by 2,000 acres of parkland (where dogs may walk); smart, beautifully furnished antique-filled reception rooms with impressive décor, open fires, a Great Hall for afternoon tea, excellent food in elegant restaurant and more informal brasserie, and spa, fitness centre, jogging trail, and tennis courts; dogs in bedrooms but not to be left unattended

OLD

Wold Farm

Harrington Road, Old, Northampton, Northants NN6 9RJ (3.1 miles off A43 via Walgrave; handy too for A508 via Lamport; Harrington Road) (01604) 781258

£68; 5 rms. 18th-c farmhouse in quiet village with spacious interesting rooms, antiques and fine china, open log fire, hearty breakfasts in beamed dining room, attentive welcoming owners, snooker table, and two pretty gardens where dogs may walk; resident labrador; dogs in bedrooms; £2

DOG FRIENDLY PUBS

BLANCHLAND

Lord Crewe Arms

B6306 S of Hexham; DH8 9SP

Ancient, historic building with some unusual features; characterful bedrooms

Built by the Premonstratensians around 1235 as the abbot's lodging for their adjacent monastery – the lovely walled garden was formerly the cloisters – this comfortable hotel is a wonderful evocation of the past and is in a remote village beneath the moors. An ancient-feeling bar is housed in an unusual long and narrow stone barrel-vaulted crypt, its curving walls being up to eight feet thick in some places. Plush stools are lined along the bar counter on ancient flagstones and next to a narrow drinks shelf down the opposite wall; TV. Upstairs, the Derwent Room has low beams, old settles, and sepia photographs on its walls, and the Hilyard Room has a massive 13th-c fireplace once used as a hiding place by the Jacobite Tom Forster (part of the family who had owned the building before it was sold in 1704 to the formidable Lord Crewe, Bishop of Durham). Straightforward bar food includes filled rolls, generous ploughman's, cumberland sausage with black pudding and daily specials, as well as more elaborate restaurant food (available in the evening). Black Sheep Best Bitter and Ale on handpump, and a good selection of wines.

Free house ~ Licensees A Todd and Peter Gingell ~ Real ale ~ Bar food ~ Restaurant ~ (01434) 675251 ~ Children welcome ~ Dogs welcome ~ Open 11-11; 12-10.30 Sun ~ Bedrooms: £50B/£100B

CARTERWAY HEADS

Manor House Inn

A68 just N of B6278, near Derwent Reservoir; DH8 9LX

Popular inn with a good choice of drinks and nice views

With good bar food available all day, and views towards the Derwent Valley and reservoir, this country inn is an enjoyable place to eat. You can buy local produce, as well as chutneys, puddings and ice-cream made in the kitchens from their own little deli. The locals' bar has an original boarded ceiling, pine tables, chairs and stools, old oak pews, and a mahogany counter. The comfortable lounge bar, warmed by a woodburning stove, and restaurant have picture windows that make the most of the setting. Courage Directors, Theakstons Best, Wells & Youngs Bombardier and a guest from a brewery such as Consett Ale Works or Mordue on handpump, 70 malt whiskies and a dozen wines by the glass;

darts, dominoes, board games and piped music (only in the bar). There are rustic tables in the garden.

Free house ~ Licensees Moira and Chris Brown ~ Real ale ~ Bar food (12-9.30(9 Sun)) ~ Restaurant ~ (01207) 255268 ~ Well behaved children welcome away from bar ~ Dogs welcome ~ Open 11-11; 12-10.30 Sun ~ Bedrooms: £43S/£65S

HAYDON BRIDGE

General Havelock

A69 Cobridge—Haltwhistle; NE47 6ER

Civilised, chatty riverside dining pub with local beers and interesting food

This old stone terrace house has been imaginatively decorated, and the back dining room and terrace make the most of the riverside views over the South Tyne. The attractively lit L-shaped bar is in shades of green, and is at its best in the back part – stripped pine chest-of-drawers topped with bric-a-brac, colourful cushions on long pine benches and a sturdy stripped settle, interestingly shaped mahogany-topped tables, good wildlife photographs and a stuffed mountain hare. The food is well above average and helpings are generous, with home-made bread, local game and farm-assured meat. They have a very local brew from Allendale or High House alongside a guest such as Durham Definitive on handpump, good wines and a choice of apple juices; they have no machines or background music but they do have board games and boules. Haydon Bridge itself is a short and very pretty stroll downstream.

Free house ~ Licensees Gary and Joanna Thompson ~ Real ale ~ Bar food (12-2(4.30 Sun), 7-9; not Sun evening) ~ Restaurant ~ 01434 684376 ~ Children welcome in lounge ~ Dogs allowed in bar ~ Open 12-3, 7-midnight; 12-3, 8-11 Sun; closed Mon and first week of Jan

NEWTON-BY-THE-SEA

Ship

Village signposted off B1339 N of Alnwick; Low Newton – paid parking 200 metres up road on right, just before village (none in village); NE66 3EL

In charming square of fishermen's cottages by green sloping to sandy beach, good food; best to check winter opening times

They started brewing their beers here at their own Ship Inn Brewery in 2008: Dolly Daydream, Sandcastles at Dawn, Sea Wheat and Ship Hop are on handpump, with a guest beer at busier times. The coastal setting is quite enchanting: a row of converted fishermen's cottages and looking across a sloping village green to a sandy beach just beyond. The plainly furnished bare-boards bar on the right has nautical charts on its dark pink walls, beams and hop bines. Another simple room on the left has some bright modern pictures on stripped-stone walls, and a woodburning stove in its stone fireplace; darts, dominoes. It can get very busy indeed at lunchtimes (quieter at night and during the winter) and service can slow down then (although we've generally had glowing reports, a couple of readers have found service can leave a bit to be desired when the staff are under pressure); booking at busier times is strongly recommended. Bar food is prepared using local free-range and organic produce, working its way up from stotties and so forth at lunchtime to a wide evening choice. Out in the corner of the square are some tables among pots of flowers, with picnic-sets over on the grass. There's no nearby parking, but there's a car park up the hill.

Free house ~ Licensee Christine Forsyth ~ Real ale ~ Bar food (12-2.30, 7-8 (not winter evenings except Thurs-Sat)) ~ No credit cards ~ (01665) 576262 ~ Children welcome ~ Dogs welcome ~ Live folk/blues/jazz; phone for details ~ Open 11(12 Sun)-11; 11-4 Sun-Weds; 11-4, 8-11 Thurs, Fri; 11-11 Sat winter; closed Sun-Weds evenings in winter

WARK

Battlesteads

B6320 N of Hexham; NE48 3LS

Good local ales, fair value tasty food and relaxed atmosphere

In a village on a scenic road by the North Tyne River and close to Wark Forest, this friendly inn originated as an 18th-c farmstead and served for a period as a temperance hotel. The nicely restored carpeted bar has a woodburning stove with traditional oak surround, and on the low beams, comfortable seats including some low leather sofas, and old *Punch* country life cartoons on the off-white walls above its dark dado; this leads through to the restaurant and spacious conservatory. There's a relaxed unhurried atmosphere and good changing local ales such as Black Sheep Ale and Best Bitter, Durham Magus and a couple of guests such as Hadrian & Border Gladiator and Wylam Gold Tankard from hand-pumps on the heavily carved dark oak bar counter; good coffee, cheerful service. Good value bar food includes a northumbrian smoked platter and mussels with wild garlic leaves. There are tables on a terrace in the walled garden.

Free house ~ Licensees Richard and Dee Slade ~ Real ale ~ Bar food (12-3, 6.30-9.30) ~ Restaurant ~ (01434) 230209 ~ Children welcome ~ Dogs allowed in bar and bedrooms ~ Open 11-11; closed 3-6 Mon-Fri in winter ~ Bedrooms: £55S/£90B

DOG FRIENDLY HOTELS, INNS, B&Bs AND FARMS

CORNHILL-ON-TWEED

Tillmouth Park

Cornhill-on-Tweed, Northumberland TD12 4UU (3 miles off A697 via A698 towards Berwick) (01890) 882255

£135; 14 spacious, pretty rms with period furniture. Solid stone-built country house in 15 acres of parkland (where dogs may walk), with comfortable relaxing lounges, open fires, galleried hall, good food in bistro or restaurant, and carefully chosen wine list; two resident black labradors; nearby golf and shooting; lots to do locally; cl Jan-Mar; dogs in bedrooms and ground floor bar

CROOKHAM

Coach House

Crookham, Cornhill-on-Tweed, Northumberland TD12 4TD (A697 S of Cornhill)
(01890) 820293

£84; 10 individual rms with fresh flowers and nice views, 8 with own bthrm. 17th-c farm buildings around sunny courtyard, with helpful and friendly staff, airy beamed lounge with comfortable sofas and big arched windows, good breakfasts with home-made preserves (which you can also take home), afternoon tea, and enjoyable dinners using local vegetables; two resident dogs; paddocks for walking; lots to do nearby; cl end Nov-Feb; good disabled access; dogs in bedrooms; £2.50

GRETA BRIDGE

Morritt Arms

Greta Bridge, Barnard Castle, County Durham DL12 9SE (just off A66 on village loop) (01833) 627232

£110; 27 rms. Smart, old-fashioned coaching inn where Dickens stayed in 1838 to research for *Nicholas Nickleby* – one of the interesting bars has a colourful Dickensian mural; comfortable lounges, fresh flowers, good open fires, enjoyable modern food in bar and restaurant, and pleasant garden; lots of surrounding walks; coarse fishing; disabled access; dogs in some bedrooms; £5

HEADLAM

Headlam Hall

Headlam, Darlington, County Durham DL2 3HA (01325) 730238

£135; 40 pretty rms, in the main house and adjacent coach house. Peaceful Jacobean mansion in four acres of carefully kept gardens with little trout lake, tennis court, and croquet lawn; elegant rooms, fine carved oak fireplace in main hall, stylish food in four individually decorated restaurant rooms, and courteous staff; spa with swimming pool, sauna, gym and treatment rooms and nine-hole golf course, driving range and shop; walks in grounds and surrounding footpaths; cl 25 and 26 Dec; disabled access; dogs in mews bedrooms

LONGFRAMLINGTON

Embleton Hall

Longframlington, Morpeth, Northumberland NE65 8DT (on A697) (01665) 570249

£105; 13 comfortable, pretty and individually decorated rms. Charming hotel in lovely grounds surrounded by fine countryside, with genuinely friendly, relaxed atmosphere, and courteous staff; neat little bar, elegant lounge, log fires, excellent value bar meals, and very good food in the attractive dining room; resident welsh springer spaniel; dog walking field half a mile away; dogs in bedrooms and lounge

LONGHORSLEY
Macdonald Linden Hall

Longhorsley, Morpeth, Northumberland NE65 8XF (just off A697 N of Morpeth)
(01670) 516611

£135; 50 individually decorated neat rms. Georgian hotel in 450 acres of landscaped park with mountain biking (bike hire available), 18-hole golf course, pitch and putt, croquet, and lots of leisure facilities inc swimming pool, sauna, steam room and spa bath; its own pub (the Linden Tree), elegant drawing room, and imaginative, enjoyable food in attractive restaurant with views over unspoilt landscape; children in main restaurant early evening only; disabled access; dogs in two bedrooms only; £10

NEWCASTLE UPON TYNE
Malmaison

Quayside, Newcastle Upon Tyne, Tyne & Wear NE1 3DX (0191) 245 5000

£160; 122 individually decorated and well equipped rms. Stylish hotel in former Co-op warehouse overlooking river, with contemporary furniture and artwork, genuinely friendly staff, a buzzy bar, modern cooking in fashionable brasserie, and decent breakfasts; disabled access; dogs in bedrooms; bedding and bowls offered; £10

ROMALDKIRK
Rose & Crown

Romaldkirk, Barnard Castle, County Durham DL12 9EB (01833) 650213

£135; 12 rms, 5 in back courtyard. Smart and interesting old coaching inn by green of delightful Teesdale village, with Jacobean oak settle, log fire, old black and white photographs and lots of brass in beamed traditional bar; cosy residents' lounge, very good imaginative food in bar and fine oak-panelled restaurant, and well kept real ales and wines; walks along old railway line nearby; cl Christmas; disabled access; dogs in Courtyard rooms but not to be left unattended; £5

WELDON BRIDGE
Anglers Arms

Weldon Bridge, Longframlington, Morpeth, Northumberland NE65 8AX (just off A697 S of Longframlington, via B6344) (01665) 570271

£80; 7 attractive rms. Sizeable hotel with fishing rights along a mile of bank by River Coquet, nicely lit and interestingly furnished traditional bars, sofa in front of warm coal fire, some oak panelling and shiny black beams; real ales, lots of malt whiskies, generous helpings of bar food and more elaborate choice in restaurant (a former railway dining car), and tables in garden; dogs in bedrooms only

DOG FRIENDLY PUBS

CAUNTON

Caunton Beck

Newark Road; NG23 6AE

Civilised dining pub with very good (if not cheap) food all day from breakfasts first thing, good wine list, nice terrace

Warmly welcoming service contributes to making this lovely inn a memorable place. Surprisingly the building is almost new, but as it was reconstructed using original timbers and reclaimed oak, around the skeleton of the old Hole Arms, it seems old. Scrubbed pine tables, clever lighting, an open fire, country-kitchen chairs, low beams and rag-finished paintwork in a spacious interior create a comfortably relaxed atmosphere. You can get something to eat at most times of the day, from hearty english breakfasts (served until midday; 11.30 weekends and bank holidays) to delicious sandwiches and a fairly elaborate seasonally changing menu and specials list later on. Over two dozen of the wines on the very good wine list are available by the glass, and they've well kept Batemans Valiant, Marstons Pedigree and Tom Woods Farmers Blonde on handpump; also espresso coffee; daily papers and magazines, no music. With lots of flowers and plants in summer, the terrace is very pleasant when the weather is fine.

Free house ~ Licensee Julie Allwood ~ Real ale ~ Bar food (8am-11pm) ~ Restaurant ~ (01636) 636793 ~ Children welcome ~ Dogs allowed in bar ~ Open 8am-11pm

LAXTON

Dovecote

Signposted off A6075 E of Ollerton; NG22 0NU

Traditional village pub handy for A1; bar food and garden

The three dining areas at this red-brick free house are traditionally furnished with dark pubby tables and wheelback chairs on carpeted or wooden flooring. There's a coal-effect gas fire and a proper pool room with darts, fruit machine and dominoes; piped music. As well as a farm cider and around nine wines by the glass, their three changing beers on handpump might be Fullers London Pride, Milestone Black Pearl and Wadworths 6X. Served by friendly courteous staff, food is fairly priced and tasty. Wooden tables and chairs on a small front terrace and sloping garden have views towards the village church. Campers can stay in the orchard and field. Laxton is famously home to three huge medieval open fields – it's one of the few places in the country still farmed using this system. Every year, in the third week of June, all the grass is auctioned for haymaking, and anyone who lives in the parish is entitled to a bid and a drink. You can get more information about it all from the visitor centre behind the pub.

Free house ~ Licensees David and Linda Brown ~ Real ale ~ Bar food (12-2, 6.30-9; 12.30-6.30 Sun) ~ (01777) 871586 ~ Children welcome ~ Dogs allowed in bar ~ Open 11.30-3, 6.30(6 Sat)-11; 12-10.30 Sun

SCROOBY

Pilgrim Fathers

Great North Road (A638 S of Bawtry); DN10 6AT

Good enterprising food in spotless traditional pub

In the couple of years since the current licensees took over here, they've gently improved things at this spotless beamed pub. Its comfortably traditional interior remains unchanged (red patterned carpets, swirly white plastered walls, a leather wing armchair, panelled window seat and other traditional pub furniture) but the welcome and food are definitely up a notch. A separate simple public bar (Billy's bar) has traditional games and a TV. Cooked fresh to order, tasty bar food includes imaginative open sandwiches, traditional dishes and a handful of specials. Theakstons and a guest such as Adnams are well kept on handpump, they've decent wines and they do good coffee; unobtrusive piped music, daily papers and garden.

Enterprise ~ Lease Geoff and Neece Francess-Allen ~ Real ale ~ Bar food (12-2.30, 6-9.30; 12-7 Sun) ~ Restaurant ~ (01302) 710446 ~ Children welcome ~ Dogs allowed in bar ~ Open 12(4 Tues)-11

WINTHORPE

Lord Nelson

Handy for A1 Newark bypass, via A46 and A1133; Gainsborough Road; NG24 2NN

Smartly updated former watermill with reasonably priced imaginative food and good drinks choice

This recently reworked place greets you with relaxing leather sofas and easy chairs, and the seats around the chunky dining tables are very comfortable, too – dark leather, with well shaped high backs. There are beam and plank ceilings, flagstones and flooring bricks, a little stripped brickwork, prints on the cream or pastel walls, fresh flowers, a woodburning stove and an open fire. There are one or two slightly unusual Nelson mementoes; piped music and TV. They have well kept Black Sheep and up to three guests such as Gales HSB, Shepherd Neame Spitfire and Wadworths 6X on handpump, and eight wines by the glass. Lunchtime bar food is very pubby but evening dining here is a much more elaborate affair with complimentary canapés, pre-pudding sorbet and sophisticated specials. Service is good. There's a good-sized and attractive walled garden, sheltered by trees all around, and children like the shallow former mill race which runs along the side of the building.

Enterprise ~ Lease Stuart Bagley ~ Real ale ~ Bar food (12-2(2.30 Fri, Sat), 6.30-9(9.30 Fri, 10 Sat); 12-3.30, 6.30-8.30 Sun) ~ (01636) 703578 ~ Children welcome ~ Dogs allowed in bar ~ Open 12-2.30(3 Fri), 6-11; 11.30-11 Sat, Sun; closed Mon, Tues

DOG FRIENDLY HOTELS AND B&Bs

FARNSFIELD

Grange Cottage

Main Street, Farnsfield, Newark-on-Trent, Nottinghamshire NG22 8EA
(01623) 882259

£60; 3 pretty rms. 300-year-old house in two acres of mature gardens, with seats on terrace, helpful caring owners, fantastic, hearty breakfasts using local produce and taken around one big table in charming beamed dining room, and packed lunches and barbecues; self-catering too; resident pointer and bearded collie; dogs in bedrooms; £5

LANGAR

Langar Hall

Church Lane, Langar, Nottingham, Nottinghamshire NG13 9HG (3.5 miles off A52; heading E, first right turn into Tithby Road, keeping straight on into Bingham Road; in Langar, first right into Barnstone Road then Church Lane)
(01949) 860559

£185; 10 lovely, nicely old-fashioned rms, some in wing and courtyard as well. Fine country house in spacious grounds with family portraits in hall, friendly homely drawing room, library, small modern bar, pillared dining hall, antiques and fresh flowers, a relaxed informal atmosphere, lively, helpful owner and willing young staff, and very good food; resident cat; 30 acres of surrounding fields for walks; dogs in some bedrooms, if small; £20

NOTTINGHAM

Harts

Standard Hill, Park Row, Nottingham, Nottinghamshire NG1 6FN (0115) 988 1900

£147; 32 well appointed quiet rms with fine views. Smart, stylish purpose-built hotel in traffic-free cul-de-sac on site of city's medieval castle and adjacent to well known restaurant of same name; charming, friendly staff, lounge and snack bar, small exercise room, and private gardens (no dogs here but can go to park next door); disabled access; dogs in bedrooms (not to be left unattended); £5

Lace Market

29-31 High Pavement, Nottingham, Nottinghamshire NG1 1HE (0115) 852 3232

£149; 42 modern, comfortable rms. Georgian town house next to lovely church, with relaxed atmosphere, friendly young staff, convivial bar with daily papers, wood-strip floors and strong but subtle colours, good brasserie-style food in contemporary restaurant, and enjoyable breakfasts; dogs in bedrooms, if small; £16

SOUTHWELL

Old Forge

Burgage Lane, Southwell, Nottinghamshire NG25 0ER (1.7 miles off A617 from Hockerton via Hockerton Road, keeping straight on through Normanton into Burgage Lane) (01636) 812809

£78; 5 rms. 200-year-old former blacksmith's house in quiet but central spot with own parking; welcoming owner, interesting furnishings, super breakfasts in conservatory overlooking the Minster, and pretty terrace; two resident dogs; Southwell Trail half a mile away for walks; limited disabled access; dogs in bedrooms; £2

DOG FRIENDLY PUBS

COLESHILL

Radnor Arms

B4019 Faringdon–Highworth; village signposted off A417 in Faringdon and A361 in Highworth; SN6 7PR

Bustling pub with imaginative food, good choice of drinks and friendly service; small back garden and good nearby walks

The National Trust owns this pub – and the attractive village, too. It's a popular place for an imaginative meal, though there's often a couple of locals chatting over a pint of Ramsbury Bitter or Youngs Bitter tapped from casks behind the counter and the atmosphere is relaxed and informal. A good range of wines by the glass, a few malt whiskies and summer Pimms and home-made lemonade. This small bar has a couple of cushioned settles as well as comfortable plush carver chairs, and a woodburning stove; a back alcove has a few more tables. Steps take you down into the main dining area, once a blacksmith's forge: with a lofty beamed ceiling, this has kept its brick chimney stack angling up (with a log fire now) and its canary walls are decorated with dozens of forged tools and smith's gear. Using organic local produce where possible, the interesting bar food includes lunchtime sandwiches up to pork belly with sage and apple potato cake and calvados jus. A small garden up behind, with a big yew tree, has picnic-sets under cocktail parasols; plenty of good walking nearby.

Free house ~ Licensees Chris Green and Shelley Crowhurst ~ Real ale ~ Bar food (no food Sun evening or Mon) ~ Restaurant ~ (01793) 861575 ~ Children welcome ~ Dogs allowed in bar ~ Open 11.30-3, 6-11; 12-3, 7-10.30 Sun; closed Mon

CUXHAM

Half Moon

4 miles from M40 junction 6; S on B4009, then right on to B480 at Watlington; OX49 5NF

Lovely 16th-c country pub with relaxed atmosphere and delicious food cooked by friendly landlord

Well worth the detour from the motorway, this attractive 16th-c thatched pub is run by obliging young licensees. Both diners and drinkers are welcomed equally and there's a relaxed pubby atmosphere and cheerful service. The small red and black tiled bar has a brick fireplace and two main eating areas have old beams, Edwardian tables and chairs and Brakspears Bitter on handpump and several wines by the glass. Using home-grown vegetables and produce from their own cold smokehouse, the excellent food includes appetising takes on traditional meals and other inventive dishes. There are wooden-slatted chairs and tables in the good-sized garden and pretty window boxes. This is a sleepy hamlet surrounded by fine countryside.

Brakspears ~ Tenants Andrew Hill and Eilidh Ferguson ~ Real ale ~ Bar food (12-2(3 Sun), 6-9; not Sun evening) ~ (01491) 614151 ~ Children welcome ~ Dogs welcome ~ Open 12-3, 5.30-11; 12-11(10.30) Sat; closed Sun evening

HAILEY
King William IV

The Hailey near Ipsden, off A4074 or A4130 SE of Wallingford; OX10 6AD

Attractive old pub, wonderful views from seats in garden, friendly staff, well liked food and several real ales

There are outstanding, wide-ranging views from this 400-year-old pub looking across peaceful, rolling pastures. Inside, the thriving, beamed bar has some good, sturdy furniture on the tiles in front of the big winter log fire; three other cosy seating areas open off here. Brakspears Bitter and guest ales are tapped from the cask, there's an interesting wine list, and farm cider. Food is enjoyable and pubby; friendly service. The terrace and large garden have plenty of seats and tables. The pub is popular with walkers.

Brakspears ~ Tenant Neal Frankel ~ Real ale ~ Bar food ~ (01491) 681845 ~ Children allowed in two rooms off bar area ~ Dogs allowed in bar ~ Open 11.30-2.30, 6-11; 12-3, 6.30-10.30 Sun

HOOK NORTON
Gate Hangs High

Banbury Road; a mile N of village towards Sibford, at Banbury—Rollright crossroads; OX15 5DF

Friendly country pub with traditional bar, real ales, and pretty courtyard garden

The bar in this tucked-away country pub has joists in the long, low ceiling, assorted chairs and stools around traditional tables, a gleaming copper hood over the hearth in the inglenook fireplace and Hook Norton Best and Old Hooky and a guest such as Wadworths 6X on handpump, bottled beers and decent wines. You'll need to book for Saturday evening and Sunday lunch in the slightly chintzy side dining extension; piped music and dominoes.

Hook Norton ~ Tenant Stephen Coots-Williams ~ Real ale ~ Bar food (12-2.30, 6-9.30; all day Sat and Sun) ~ Restaurant ~ (01608) 737387 ~ Children welcome ~ Dogs allowed in bar and bedrooms ~ Open 12-2.30, 6-11; 12-11 (10.30 Sun) Sat ~ Bedrooms: £45B/£60B

LANGFORD

Bell

Village signposted off A361 N of Lechlade, then pub signed; GL7 3LF

Beams, flagstones, a good log fire, well chosen wines and beer and enjoyable bar food in civilised pub

This is a popular little dining pub and whilst Mr Wynne produces the consistently enjoyable food, Mrs Wynne offers a friendly welcome to all – dogs may even be offered a doggy treat. The simple low-key furnishings and décor add to the appeal here: the main bar has just six sanded and sealed mixed tables on grass matting, a variety of chairs, three nice cushioned window seats, an attractive carved oak settle, polished broad flagstones by a big stone inglenook fireplace with a good log fire, low beams and butter-coloured walls with two or three antique engravings. A second, even smaller, room on the right is similar in character; daily papers on a little corner table. Food here is sensibly inventive, bustly flavoured and well up to restaurant quality – maybe braised lamb shank with swede mash and red wine jus and chocolate panna cotta with berry coulis. Hook Norton Hooky Bitter, Timothy Taylors Landlord and Wells & Youngs Bombardier on handpump, farm cider and ten wines by the glass. The bearded collie is called Madison; piped music, board games and summer aunt sally. There are two or three picnic-sets out in a small garden with a play house. This is a quiet and charming village.

Free house ~ Licensees Paul and Jackie Wynne ~ Real ale ~ Bar food (not Sun evening or Mon) ~ Restaurant ~ (01367) 860249 ~ Children welcome but babies must leave before 7pm ~ Dogs welcome ~ Open 12-3, 7-11(midnight Fri, 11.30 Sat); 12-4 Sun; closed Sun evening, all day Mon

LEWKNOR

Olde Leathern Bottel

Under a mile from M40 junction 6; just off B4009 towards Watlington; OX49 5TH

Unchanging bustling country local with decent food and beer and seats in size-able garden

Happily unchanging, this friendly place has a good mix of customers; it does get busy at lunchtimes (being so close to the M40) so it's best to arrive early to be sure of a table. There are heavy beams and low ceilings in the two bar rooms as well as rustic furnishings, open fires, and an understated décor of old beer taps and the like; the family room is separated only by standing timbers, so you won't feel segregated from the rest of the pub. Brakspears Bitter and Wychwood Hobgoblin and Dirty Tackle on handpump, and all their wines are available by the glass. Food is fairly standard. The attractive sizeable garden has plenty of picnic-sets under parasols and a children's play area.

Brakspears ~ Tenant L S Gordon ~ Real ale ~ Bar food (12-2, 7-9.30) ~ (01844) 351482 ~ Children in restaurant and family room ~ Dogs welcome ~ Open 11-2.30(3 Sat), 6-11; 12-3, 7-10.30 Sun

LONGWORTH

Blue Boar

Off A420/A415; Tucks Lane off Cow Lane; OX13 5ET

Smashing old pub with a friendly welcome for all, good wines and beer and fairly priced good food; Thames-side walks nearby

With a good choice of food and drink, open fires, and a welcome to both locals and visitors, it's not surprising that this 17th-c thatched stone pub is so bustling and popular. The three low-beamed, characterful little rooms are warmly traditional with well worn fixtures and furnishings, and two blazing log fires, one beside a fine old settle. Brasses, hops and assorted knick-knacks like skis and an old clocking-in machine line the ceilings and walls, there are fresh flowers on the bar and scrubbed wooden tables, and faded rugs on the tiled floor; benches are firmly wooden rather than upholstered. The main eating area is the red-painted room at the end. The good, reasonably priced food, with something to please most, is listed on a huge chalkboard; quiet piped music. Brakspears, Fullers London Pride, and Timothy Taylors Landlord on handpump, 30 malt whiskies, 15 wines by the glass, summer Pimms and quite a few brandies and ports. The licensee has been here for 30 years, though his friendly young team are generally more in evidence. There are tables in front and on the back terrace, and the Thames is a short walk away.

Free house ~ Licensee Paul Dailey ~ Real ale ~ Bar food (12-2(2.30 Sat, 3 Sun), 7-10(9 Sun)) ~ Restaurant ~ (01865) 820494 ~ Children welcome ~ Dogs allowed in bar ~ Open 12-11(midnight Fri and Sat); closed 25 Dec, 1 Jan

SHIPLAKE

Baskerville Arms

Station Road, Lower Shiplake (off A4155 just S of Henley); RG9 3NY

Emphasis on imaginative food though proper public bar too, real ales, several wines by the glass, interesting sporting memorabilia and pretty garden

Locals do gather around the high bar chairs in the public bar of this neat brick pub for a pint and a chat and there are also blue armchairs, darts and piles of magazines – but mostly, it's laid out for eating. Apart from the wooden flooring around the bar, modern bar counter, it's all carpeted and there are a few beams, pale wooden furnishings (lit candles on all the tables), plush red banquettes around the windows, and a brick fireplace with plenty of logs next to it. A fair amount of sporting memorabilia and pictures, especially old rowing photos (the pub is very close to Henley) and signed rugby shirts and photographs (the pub runs its own rugby club), plus some maps of the Thames are hung on the red walls, and there are flowers and large houseplants dotted about. It all feels quite homely, but in a smart way, with some chintzy touches such as a shelf of china dogs. The lunchtime menu includes good pubby snacks and interesting specials, there's a more elaborate restauranty choice in the evening and they have a good value, two-course menu of the day. Loddon Hoppit and a couple of changing guests on hand-pump, 30 malt whiskies and ten wines by the glass. The pretty garden has a proper covered barbecue area and smart teak furniture under huge parasols.

Free house ~ Licensee Allan Hannah ~ Real ale ~ Bar food (12-2, 7-9.30(10 Fri
and Sat); not Sun evening) ~ Restaurant ~ (0118) 940 3332 ~ Children
welcome but no babies in evening restaurant ~ Dogs allowed in bar ~ Open
11.30-2.30, 6-11; 12-5 Sun; closed Sun evening

STANTON ST JOHN

Star

*Pub signposted off B4027, in Middle Lane; village is signposted off A40 heading
E of Oxford (heading W, you have to go to the Oxford ring-road roundabout and
take unclassified road signposted to Stanton St John, Forest Hill etc); OX33 1EX*

**Nice old village pub with interesting rooms, friendly landlord, fair value food
and Wadworths beers**

This is a friendly old place – chatty and relaxed and popular for its good value
food. It is appealingly arranged over two levels and the oldest parts are two
characterful little low-beamed rooms, one with ancient brick flooring tiles and
the other with quite close-set tables. Up some stairs is an attractive extension
on a level with the car park with old-fashioned dining chairs, an interesting mix
of dark oak and elm tables, rugs on flagstones, bookshelves on each side of an
attractive inglenook fireplace (good blazing fires in winter), shelves of good
pewter, terracotta-coloured walls with a portrait in oils, and a stuffed ermine.
Wadworths IPA and 6X on handpump and ten wines by the glass. A good choice
of bar food includes pubby staples and a handful of more interesting specials
such as bass in ginger, coriander and lime. There's a family room and conservatory, too; piped music, darts and board games. The walled garden has seats
among the flower beds; children's play equipment.

Wadworths ~ Tenant Michael Urwin ~ Real ale ~ Bar food ~ (01865) 351277 ~
Children welcome ~ Dogs welcome ~ Open 12-3, 6.30-11; 12-3, 7-10.30 Sun

SWINBROOK

Swan

Back road a mile N of A40, 2 miles E of Burford; OX18 4DY

**Civilised 17th-c pub with handsome oak garden room; nice, smart bars, local
beers and contemporary food**

Extremely well run, this is a smart, civilised and very popular 17th-c pub. Even
on a Monday lunchtime, there are lots of customers so it is advisable to book a
table in advance. There's a little bar with simple antique furnishings, settles and
benches, an open fire, and (in an alcove) a stuffed swan; locals do still drop in
here for a pint and a chat. The small dining room to the right of the entrance
opens into this room, and there's a green oak garden room with high-backed
beige and green dining chairs around pale wood tables and views over the
garden and orchard. As the pub is owned by the Duchess of Devonshire – the
last of the Mitford sisters who grew up in the village – there are lots of old
Mitford family photographs blown up on the walls. Bar food is very rewarding,
from a modern menu which runs from a good burger to slowly braised feather
blade of beef on truffle mash with wild mushrooms, and puddings such as

coconut and lemongrass crème brulée. Hook Norton Hooky Bitter, and a couple of guests from maybe Cottage Brewery or Sharps on handpump, 13 wines by the glass, Weston's organic cider, a proper bloody mary and local apple juice; piped music. This is a lovely spot by a bridge over the River Windrush and seats by the fuchsia hedge make the best of the view. The licensees also run the Kings Head at Bledington in Gloucestershire.

Free house ~ Licensees Archie and Nicola Orr-Ewing ~ Real ale ~ Bar food (12-2(3 Sun), 7-9(9.30 weekends)) ~ Restaurant ~ (01993) 823339 ~ Children welcome ~ Dogs allowed in bar ~ Live music monthly Sun ~ Open 11-3, 6-11; 12-11 Sun and Sat; closed Mon evenings; 25 Dec

TADPOLE BRIDGE
Trout

Back road Bampton—Buckland, 4 miles NE of Faringdon; SN7 8RF

Busy country inn with River Thames moorings, fine choice of drinks, particularly good restaurant-style food, lovely summer garden; super bedrooms

Having just refurbished this civilised and comfortable place, extensive flood damage meant they had to refurbish yet again, so the whole place is extremely smart now. It's in a peaceful spot by the Thames and the L-shaped bar has attractive pink and cream checked chairs around a mix of nice wooden tables, some rugs on the flagstones, a modern wooden bar counter with terracotta paintwork behind, fresh flowers, a woodburning stove and a large stuffed trout. The airy restaurant is appealingly candlelit in the evenings. Ramsbury Bitter, Wells & Youngs Bitter and guests like Arkells Moonlight and Butts Barbus Barbus on handpump, a dozen wines by the glass from a wide-ranging and carefully chosen list, some fine sherries and several malt whiskies; the hard-working licensees positively welcome locals who pop in for a pint and a chat. Cooking here is particularly inventive and dishes are attractively presented – maybe terrine of chicken and foie gras wrapped in prosciutto with fig chutney and melba toast or steamed beef and smoked oyster pudding. There are good quality teak chairs and tables under blue parasols in the lovely garden and six moorings for visiting boats; you can also hire punts with champagne hampers. The bedrooms are exceptionally well equipped and extremely attractive.

Free house ~ Licensees Gareth and Helen Pugh ~ Real ale ~ Bar food (not winter Sun evening) ~ Restaurant ~ (01367) 870382 ~ Children welcome ~ Dogs welcome ~ Open 11.30-3, 6-11; 12-3.30, 6.30-10.30 Sun; closed winter Sun evening ~ Bedrooms: £75B/£110B

WOOLSTONE
White Horse

Village signed off B4507; SN7 7QL

Gabled old pub with hard-working, friendly landlord, enjoyable food and drink, seats in front and back garden; bedrooms

Handy for White Horse and Ridgeway walkers, this partly thatched, 16th-c pub with steep Victorian gables, is just the place for a drink or meal. It's plushly refurbished, with two big open fires in the spacious and eclectically decorated beamed and part-panelled bar and has Arkells 2B, 3B and Moonlight Ale on handpump, decent wines and lots of whiskies; good coffee, too. There's an evening restaurant and the staff are friendly and helpful. Generous helpings of good bar food are prepared using produce from local suppliers and cornish fish. The well organised back garden has plenty of seats with more in the small front garden. The bedrooms are charming and they offer big breakfasts. This is a secluded and interesting village.

Arkells ~ Tenant Angus Tucker ~ Bar food (not Sunday evening) ~ Restaurant ~ (01367) 820726 ~ Children welcome ~ Dogs welcome ~ Open 11am-midnight ~ Bedrooms: £70B/£75B

DOG FRIENDLY HOTELS, INNS AND B&Bs

BURFORD

Lamb

Sheep Street, Burford, Oxfordshire OX18 4LR (0.4 miles off A40, via A361; Sheep Street, left off High Street) (01993) 823155

£145; 17 rms. Very attractive 500-year-old Cotswold inn with lovely restful atmosphere, spacious beamed, flagstoned and elegantly furnished lounge, and classic civilised public bar; bunches of flowers on good oak and elm tables, three winter log fires, antiques, enjoyable modern food in airy restaurant, and pretty little walled garden; nearby woodland for walks; disabled access; dogs in ground floor bedrooms

CLIFTON

Duke of Cumberlands Head

Clifton, Banbury, Oxfordshire OX15 0PE (01869) 338534

£75; 6 rms in sympathetic extension. Pretty thatched 17th-c golden stone inn with friendly atmosphere, low-beamed lounge with good log fire in vast stone fireplace and attractive paintings by landlord's grandmother on walls; tasty food in bar and stripped stone dining room, real ales, quite a few whiskies, and tables in garden; towpath and bridle paths for walking nearby; dogs in bedrooms and bar

KINGHAM

Mill House

Station Road, Kingham, Chipping Norton, Oxfordshire OX7 6UH (01608) 658188

£100; 23 good rms with country views. Family-owned and carefully converted stone mill house dating back to Domesday Book and set in ten acres of lawned gardens; comfortable spacious beamed lounges, open fires and fresh flowers, original features, excellent modern cooking in fine restaurant, lighter lunches in bar and on terrace, and an extensive wine cellar; resident labrador; disabled access; dogs welcome in bedrooms

KINGSTON BAGPUIZE

Fallowfields

Southmoor, Kingston Bagpuize, Abingdon, Oxfordshire OX13 5BH (0.9 miles off A420; A415 S, then first right on to Faringdon Road; Southmoor) (01865) 820416

£160; 10 rms, some with fine garden and countryside views. Delightful and very well kept Gothic-style manor house with elegant, relaxing sitting rooms, open fires, imaginative food using home-grown produce in attractive conservatory dining room, courteous helpful service, and 12 acres of pretty gardens and paddocks (where dogs may walk – countryside all around for longer walks); two resident cats; lots to see nearby; cl 24-27 Dec; dogs in bedrooms and lounge; £5

OXFORD

Old Parsonage

1 Banbury Road, Oxford OX2 6NN (01865) 310210

£170; 30 lovely rms. Handsome and civilised 17th-c parsonage with courteous staff, small lounge, open fires and fine paintings, good breakfasts and excellent light meals in cosy bar/restaurant, and pretty little garden; they provide picnics; walks in nearby parks; dogs welcome away from restaurant; bowls and basket on request

SHILLINGFORD

Shillingford Bridge Hotel

Shillingford Road, Shillingford, Wallingford, Oxfordshire OX10 8LZ (01865) 858567

£130; 40 rms. Riverside hotel with moorings, fishing, boat hire (from local boat-yards), and terraced gardens; friendly, relaxed atmosphere, spacious, comfortable bar and lounges, attractive airy restaurant (all with fine views), squash, outdoor heated swimming pool, and nearby golf; walks along the Thames; disabled access; dogs welcome away from restaurant; £7.50

SHIPTON-UNDER-WYCHWOOD

Shaven Crown

High Street, Shipton-under-Wychwood, Chipping Norton, Oxfordshire OX7 6BA (01993) 830330

£85; 8 comfortable rms. Densely beamed, ancient stone hospice built around striking medieval courtyard with seating by lily pool and roses; impressive medieval hall with magnificent lofty ceiling, sweeping stairway and old stone walls, open fire in bar with real ales, residents' lounge, candlelit restaurant, friendly service, and bowling green; lots of walks not far away; cl 25 and 26 Dec; dogs welcome away from restaurant

WOODSTOCK

Feathers

Market Street, Woodstock, Oxfordshire OX20 1SX (01993) 812291

£169; 20 individually decorated rms. Lovely old building with fine relaxing drawing room and study, open fires, first-class friendly staff, gentle atmosphere, daily changing imaginative food, and sunny courtyard with attractive tables and chairs; resident parrot; walks nearby; dogs welcome away from restaurant; bedding and bowls available; £10

DOG FRIENDLY PUBS

CHETWYND ASTON

Fox

Village signposted off A41 and A518 just S of Newport; TF10 9LQ

Civilised dining pub with generous food and interesting ales served by ever-attentive staff

This substantial dining pub goes from strength to strength, with readers enthusing about its delicious food and good range of ales, and friendly staff who keep up a high level of service even at busy times. The 1920s building was handsomely done up by Brunning & Price a few years ago – its style will be familiar to anyone who has tried their other pubs. A series of linked semi-separate areas, one with a broad arched ceiling, has plenty of tables in all shapes and sizes, some quite elegant, and a vaguely matching diversity of comfortable chairs, all laid out in a way that's fine for eating but serves equally well for just drinking and chatting. There are masses of attractive prints, three open fires, a few oriental rugs on polished parquet or boards, some attractive floor tiling; big windows and careful lighting help towards the relaxed and effortless atmosphere. The handsome bar counter, with a decent complement of bar stools, serves an excellent changing range of about a dozen wines by the glass, and Thwaites Original, Woods Shropshire Lad and three or four guests from brewers such as Batemans, Hanby and Woodlands are well kept on handpump. The staff, mainly young, are well trained, cheerful and attentive. Disabled access and facilities are good (no push chairs or baby buggies, though); there is a selection of board games. The spreading garden is quite lovely, with a sunny terrace, picnic-sets tucked into the shade of mature trees and extensive views across quiet country fields.

Brunning & Price ~ Manager Samantha Malloy ~ Real ale ~ Bar food (12-10(9.30 Sun)) ~ (01952) 815940 ~ Children welcome till 7pm ~ Dogs allowed in bar ~ Open 12-11(10.30 Sun)

GRINSHILL

Inn at Grinshill

Off A49 N of Shrewsbury; SY4 3BL

Looks after its customers admirably: a civilised place to stay or dine

This elegantly refurbished early Georgian country inn enjoys a good reputation for its excellent (though not cheap) food and welcoming staff. As well as deliciously imaginative dishes, they also do lunchtime sandwiches, and offer a good value lunchtime and early bird menu. Food is prepared with real care, and Hanby Drawwell and three guests from a brewer such as Greene King, John Smiths and Theakstons are on handpump, and they have over a dozen wines by the glass. The smartly comfortable 19th-c bar has an open log fire, while the spacious contemporary main restaurant has a view straight into the kitchen, and doors into the back garden, which is laid out with tables and chairs; TV, piped music, dominoes, and an evening pianist on Friday. Beautifully decorated bedrooms have wide-screen TV and broadband access. Though not at all high, the nearby hill of Grinshill has an astonishingly far-ranging view.

Free house ~ Licensees Kevin and Victoria Brazier ~ Real ale ~ Bar food (12-2.30(3 Sun), 6.30-9.30) ~ Restaurant ~ (01939) 220410 ~ Children welcome ~ Dogs welcome ~ Open 11-3, 6-11; 11-11 Sat; 12-4 Sun; closed Sun and bank hol evenings ~ Bedrooms: £60S/£120B

IRONBRIDGE

Malthouse

The Wharfage (bottom road alongside Severn); TF8 7NH

Right in the heart of the historic gorge, with pleasantly airy décor and tasty bar food

What with its position right down in the Gorge and hulking great structure, it's still fairly apparent that this imaginatively converted 18th-c building was originally constructed as a malthouse. Tucked down below, the spacious bar is broken up by white-painted iron pillars supporting heavy pine beams. A mix of scrubbed light wooden tables with candles, cream-painted banquettes and bright pictures keeps it feeling light; piped music and TV. Greene King IPA and Scottish Courage Directors are on handpump, and they've a wide choice of wines including several by the glass. The bistro-style food is appropriately informal and tasty. There are a few tables outside in front by the car park. Note that they may retain your credit card if you eat in the bar.

Free house ~ Licensees Alex and Andrea Nicoll ~ Real ale ~ Bar food (12-2.30, 6.30-9.30; 12-8 Sun) ~ Restaurant ~ (01952) 433712 ~ Children welcome ~ Dogs allowed in bar ~ Live music Weds, Sat evenings ~ Open 11-11.30(midnight Sat); 12-11 Sun

PICKLESCOTT

Bottle & Glass

Village signposted off A49 N of Church Stretton; SY6 6NR

Remote village pub with a charismatic and hospitable landlord who gets all the details right

This 16th-c pub has a lovely position 1,000 feet above sea level and near the Long Mynd. Remote but surprisingly busy, it's well worth the pilgrimage along tortuous country lanes. It's run by a charismatic, bow-tied landlord who makes things tick along with great aplomb. He works hard to make sure everyone is happy, easily running the bar and striking up conversations with customers –

ask him to tell you about the antics of the resident ghost of the former land-lord, Victor. Much to the delight surely of the two resident cats, Hello and Cookie, the fire rarely goes out in the small low-beamed and quarry-tiled cosy candlelit bar. The lounge, dining area and library area (for dining or sitting in) have open fires. The very good home-made bar food is promptly served, in hearty helpings. Beers brewed by Hobsons, Three Tuns and Woods are on handpump; unobtrusive piped classical music. There are picnic-sets in front.

Free house ~ Licensees Paul and Jo Stretton-Downes ~ Real ale ~ Bar food (not over the Christmas period) ~ Restaurant ~ (01694) 751345 ~ Children welcome ~ Dogs allowed in bar ~ Open 12-3, 6-midnight; closed Sun evening, Mon

DOG FRIENDLY HOTELS, INNS, B&Bs AND FARMS

BISHOP'S CASTLE
Castle Hotel
Market Square, Bishop's Castle, Shropshire SY9 5BN (01588) 638403

£90; 6 spacious rms with fine views. Enjoyable 17th/18th-c hotel on site of old castle keep, with good fires, relaxed and friendly atmosphere, lovely home-made food, well kept beers, and welcoming owners; crown bowling green at top of garden (available for residents); dogs in some bedrooms and bar but must be well behaved

CLUN
New House Farm
Clun, Craven Arms, Shropshire SY7 8NJ (01588) 638314

£80; 2 rms. Remote 18th-c farmhouse near the Welsh border with plenty of surrounding hillside walks; homely rooms, packed lunches, good breakfasts, plenty of books, country garden and peaceful farmland (which includes an Iron-Age hill fort), and helpful friendly owner; resident cats; cl end Oct-Easter; children over 10; dogs in bedrooms if well behaved; bring own bed, must be towelled down if wet; £5

HOPTON WAFERS
Crown
Hopton Wafers, Kidderminster, Worcestershire DY14 0NB (01299) 270372

£95; 11 charming rms. Attractive creeper-covered inn in pleasant countryside, with interestingly furnished bar, beams, stonework, and inglenook fireplace, enjoyable food, decent house wines and well kept real ales, friendly efficient service, and streamside garden; nearby walks; disabled access; dogs in bedrooms; £15

KNOCKIN

Top Farmhouse

Knockin, Oswestry, Shropshire SY10 8HN (2 miles W off A5 via B4396/B4397; turn left in village) (01691) 682582

£65; 3 pretty rms. Most attractive Grade I listed black and white timbered house dating back to the 16th c, with friendly owners, lots of timbers and beams, log fire in restful comfortable drawing room, good breakfasts in large dining room, and appealing garden; nearby walks; children over 12; dogs in bedrooms

LONGVILLE

Longville Arms

Longville, Much Wenlock, Shropshire TF13 6DT (01694) 771206

£60; 2 comfortable rms in converted stables, with showers. Warmly friendly inn with two spacious bars, well kept real ales, wide range of tasty food in restaurant or lounge bar, smashing breakfasts, and large terrace overlooking a large children's play area; fine surrounding walks; disabled access; dogs in bedrooms

LUDLOW

Bromley Court

Lower Broad Street, Ludlow, Shropshire SY8 1PH (01584) 876996

£115; 3 large, attractively decorated suites with sitting areas and kitchenette in renovated Georgian cottages with oak beams and inglenook fireplaces, generous continental breakfasts (taken in suites), and terraced garden; excellent restaurants close by

Dinham Hall

Dinham, Ludlow, Shropshire SY8 1EJ (1.7 miles off A49; Dinham, which is road to the Teme bridge below the Castle) (01584) 876464

£140; 13 individually decorated rms, 2 in cottage. Late 18th-c manor house in quiet walled gardens opposite ruins of Ludlow Castle, with restful lounges, open fires and period furnishings, friendly, helpful staff, and modern british cooking in elegant restaurant; children over 13 in dining hall; dogs in cottage bedrooms only; £15

NORTON

Hundred House

Bridgnorth Road, Norton, Shifnal, Shropshire TF11 9EE (on A442 S of Telford) (01952) 730353

£99; 10 cottagey rms with swing and lavender-scented sheets. Mainly Georgian inn with neatly kept bar, old quarry-tiled floors, beamed ceilings, oak panelling and handsome fireplaces, good food in bar and restaurant using inn's own herbs, nice breakfasts, and friendly service; delightful garden (dogs allowed here under owner's control) and walks at Ironbridge Gorge and the Severn Walking Trail; dogs in bedrooms if well behaved; £10

RHYDYCROESAU

Pen-y-Dyffryn Hall

Rhydycroesau, Oswestry, Shropshire SY10 7JD (01691) 653700

£124; 12 rms, 4 with terrace in coach house. Handsome Georgian stone-built rectory in five acres of grounds with lovely views of Shropshire and Welsh hills, and trout fishing, hill-walking and riding (shooting can be arranged); log fires in both elegant, comfortable lounges, convivial bar, especially good food using best local ingredients, helpful staff, and relaxed, friendly atmosphere; two resident dogs; lovely nearby woodland for walks; children over 3; dogs welcome, but not in public areas after 6pm

STREFFORD

Strefford Hall Farm

Strefford, Craven Arms, Shropshire SY7 8DE (0.2 miles off A49; minor road E, just under a mile N of A489 junction – farm is then on right) (01588) 672383

£70; 3 rms. Victorian stone-built farmhouse surrounded by 360 acres of working farm; woodburner in sitting room, good breakfasts in sunny dining room with home-made preserves and local honey (pubs and restaurants nearby for evening meals), and lots of walks; resident jack russells and several cats; self-catering and farm shop, too; cl end Oct-Mar; dogs in bedrooms if small and well behaved

WORFIELD

Old Vicarage

Hallon, Worfield, Bridgnorth, Shropshire WV15 5JZ (1.5 miles off A442, from Lower Alscot) (01746) 716497

£140; 14 very comfortable, pretty rms. Restful and carefully restored Edwardian rectory in two acres of grounds, with two conservatory-style lounges, delicious innovative food in Orangery Restaurant, fine wine list, cosseting atmosphere, and warmly friendly, helpful service; two resident dogs; cl Christmas; good disabled access; dogs in bedrooms; £10

WREKIN

Buckatree Hall

Wrekin, Telford, Shropshire TF6 5AL (1.4 miles off M54 junction 7; S on minor road towards The Wrekin, then first left) (01952) 641821

£95; 62 neatly decorated rms, several with own balconies and many with lake views. Comfortable former hunting lodge dating from 1820, in large wooded estate at the foot of the Wrekin; friendly, relaxed bar, enjoyable food in the Terrace Restaurant, and helpful attentive service; dogs in bedrooms; £10

Somerset

DOG FRIENDLY PUBS

ASHILL

Square & Compass

Windmill Hill; off A358 between Ilminster and Taunton; up Wood Road for a mile behind Stewley Cross service station; OS Sheet 193 map reference 310166; TA19 9NX

Friendly simple pub with local ales, tasty food and good regular live music in sound-proofed barn

Much enjoyed by our readers, this is a traditional pub with genuinely welcoming licensees and a nice mix of friendly customers. The sweeping views over the rolling pastures around Neroche Forest can be enjoyed from the upholstered window seats in the little bar, and there are other seats, an open winter fire – and perhaps the pub cat, Lilly. Exmoor Ale and Otter Bitter on handpump and good house wines by the glass. Good pubby food is served in generous helpings; Sunday roasts. The piped music is often classical. There's a garden with picnic-sets, a large glass-covered walled terrace, and good regular live music in their sound-proofed barn.

Free house ~ Licensees Chris, Janet and Beth Slow ~ Real ale ~ Bar food (not Tues, Weds or Thurs lunchtimes) ~ Restaurant ~ (01823) 480467 ~ Children welcome ~ Dogs welcome ~ Monthly live music in separate barn ~ Open 12-2.30, 6.30(7 Sun)-11; closed Tues, Weds and Thurs lunchtimes

BATCOMBE

Three Horseshoes

Village signposted off A359 Bruton—Frome; BA4 6HE

Well run, attractive dining pub with smart rooms, friendly staff, elaborate food and quite a choice of drinks; comfortable bedrooms

This 17th-c coaching inn is a neatly kept honey-coloured stone building with quite an emphasis on the brasserie-style food. There's a warm welcome from the friendly staff, and the long, rather narrow main room is smartly traditional: beams, local pictures on the lightly ragged dark pink walls, built-in cushioned window seats and solid chairs around a nice mix of old tables, and a woodburning stove at one end with a big open fire at the other. At the back on the left, the Gallery Bar has panelled walls, tiled floors and modern pictures for sale and there's also a pretty stripped stone dining room (no mobile phones); best to book to be sure of a table, especially at weekends. Butcombe Bitter, Palmers

IPA, and Bats in the Belfry (brewed for the pub) on handpump, eight wines by the glass, and farm cider. The imaginative menu changes seasonally and ranges from fresh beer-battered fish served in paper with tartare sauce to cassoulet of shellfish and white fish with rouille. There are picnic-sets on the heated back terrace with more on the grass and a pond with koi carp. The pub is on a quiet village lane by the church which has a very striking tower. The bedrooms are comfortable and the breakfasts are good.

Free house ~ Licensees Bob Wood and Shirley Greaves ~ Real ale ~ Bar food (not Sun evening or Mon) ~ Restaurant ~ (01749) 850359 ~ Children in eating areas but must be 13 in evening ~ Dogs allowed in bar and bedrooms ~ Live music some Thurs ~ Open 12-3, 6-11; 12-3, 8-11 Sun; closed Mon ~ Bedrooms: /£75B

BATH

King William

Thomas Street, corner with A4 London Road – may be no nearby parking; BA1 5NN

Simple bars in small corner pub with informally friendly service, interesting food and drink

It's quite a surprise to find such individual food in this little corner pub. Many customers are here for a drink and a chat, and the two plain, un-smart rooms have straightfoward seating and just three chunky old tables each on dark bare boards; big windows look out on the busy street. Bristol Beer Factory Sunrise, Newmans Red Stag Bitter, and Palmers Dorset Gold on handpump and a fine choice of good wines by the glass. Daily papers, a few lighted church candles, and perhaps a big bunch of flowers on the counter. Interesting bar food (such as braised brisket with bacon, sweet onions and horseradish cream) is thoughtfully prepared using free-range or organic meat.

Free house ~ Licensees Charlie and Amanda Digney ~ Real ale ~ Bar food (12-3, 6-10; not Sun evening) ~ Restaurant ~ (01225) 428096 ~ Well behaved children welcome until 9pm ~ Dogs allowed in bar ~ Open 12-3, 5-11.30(midnight Fri); 12-midnight(11pm Sun) Sat

Star

Vineyards; The Paragon (A4), junction with Guinea Lane; BA1 5NA

Quietly chatty and unchanging old town local, brewery tap for Abbey Ales; filled rolls only

As the brewery tap for Abbey Ales, this honest old town pub keeps Bellringer plus Bass, St Austell Tribute, Thwaites Lancaster Bomber, and a couple of guests on handpump; they hold a July weekend beer festival. The interior is quite unchanging and there's a quiet, chatty atmosphere not spoilt by noisy fruit machines or music. The four (well, more like three and a half) small linked rooms are served from a single bar, separated by panelling with glass inserts. They are furnished with traditional leatherette wall benches and the like – even one hard bench that the regulars call Death Row – and the lighting's dim, and not rudely interrupted by too much daylight. Friendly staff and customers; it does get busy at weekends. This place being all about they beer, they only do filled rolls and maybe bar nibbles Thursday evening.

Punch ~ Lease Paul Waters and Alan Morgan ~ Real ale ~ Bar food (see text) ~ (01225) 425072 ~ Children welcome ~ Dogs welcome ~ Open 12-2.30, 5.30-midnight (1am Fri); 12-1am Sat; 12-midnight Sun

CHURCHILL

Crown

The Batch; in village, turn off A368 into Skinners Lane at Nelson Arms, then bear right; BS25 5PP

Unspoilt and unchanging small cottage with friendly customers and staff, super range of real ales and homely lunchtime food

---

'As good as ever' has been the comment used by several of our readers to describe this much enjoyed and unpretentious little cottage. Little has changed over many years and the small and rather local-feeling stone-floored and cross-beamed room on the right has a wooden window seat, an unusually sturdy settle, built-in wall benches, and chatty, friendly customers; the left-hand room has a slate floor, and some steps past the big log fire in a big stone fireplace lead to more sitting space. No noise from music or games (except perhaps dominoes) and a fine range of real ales tapped from the cask: Bass, Butcombe Bitter, Cheddar Best Bitter, Cotleigh Batch, Palmers IPA and Tally Ho, RCH Hewish IPA and PG Steam, St Austells Tribute and Black Prince. Several wines by the glass and local ciders. Straightforward lunchtime bar food includes sandwiches (the rare roast beef is popular), ploughman's and beef casserole and puddings like fruit crumbles and treacle tart. Outside lavatories. There are garden tables at the front, a smallish back lawn and hill views; the Mendip Morris Men come in summer. Good walks nearby.

Free house ~ Licensee Tim Rogers ~ Real ale ~ Bar food (12-2.30; not evenings) ~ No credit cards ~ (01934) 852995 ~ Children welcome away from bar ~ Dogs welcome ~ Open 11-11(midnight Fri); 11-10.30 Sun

CONGRESBURY

White Hart

Wrington Road, off A370 Bristol—Weston; BS49 5AR

Friendly licensee, specialist gin menu, real ales, decent food and seats in size-able garden

---

You can be sure of a friendly welcome here. It's a companionable country pub with a few heavy black beams in the bowed ceiling of the L-shaped main bar, big stone inglenook fireplaces at each end, country kitchen furniture and Badger K&B Sussex Bitter, Tanglefoot and a seasonal beer on handpump; they specialise in gin, with 36 different types, and have several wines by the glass. Two areas lead off, and there's a big bright conservatory; piped music, table skittles and board games. Pubby food includes lunchtime filled baguettes and is prepared using fresh local produce where possible. Outside, there are picnic-sets under a back terrace arbour with more in the big garden. The hills you can see are the Mendips.

Badger ~ Tenant Murat Gumus ~ Real ale ~ Bar food (11.30-3, 6-9.30) ~ Restaurant ~ (01934) 833303 ~ Children welcome away from bar area ~ Dogs allowed in bar ~ Live turkish music and belly dancers monthly ~ Open 11-midnight

DULVERTON

Woods

Bank Square; TA22 9BU

Smartly informal place with exceptional wines and enjoyable food

You can order any of the 400 or so wines from an amazing wine list by the glass in this mildly upmarket place, and the landlord also keeps an unlisted collection of about 500 well aged new world wines which he will happily chat about. It's all comfortably relaxed and very Exmoor – plenty of good sporting prints on the salmon pink walls, some antlers, other hunting trophies and stuffed birds and a couple of salmon rods. There are bare boards on the left by the bar counter, which has well kept Exmoor Ale, Otter Head and St Austells Tribute tapped from the cask, a farm cider, many sherries, and some unusual spirits; daily papers to read. Its tables partly separated by stable-style timbering and masonry dividers, the bit on the right is carpeted and has a woodburning stove in the big fire-place set into its end wall, which has varnished plank panelling; maybe unobjectionable piped music. Bar food from a very inventive menu is extremely good, with dishes ranging from local wild boar sausages with spicy oriental sauce to gilthead bream with anchovy, samphire and fennel salad and caper nut brown butter – puddings are unusual, too. Big windows keep you in touch with what's going on out in the quiet town centre (or you can sit out on the pavement at a couple of metal tables). A small suntrap back courtyard has a few picnic-sets.

Free house ~ Licensee Patrick Groves ~ Real ale ~ Bar food (12-2(3 Sun), 6-9.30) ~ Restaurant ~ (01398) 324007 ~ Well behaved children welcome ~ Dogs welcome ~ Open 11-3, 6-midnight(1am Sat); 12-3, 7-11 Sun; closed evenings 25 and 26 Dec

HUISH EPISCOPI

Rose & Crown

Off A372 E of Langport; TA10 9QT

In the same family for over 140 years and a real throwback; local ciders and beers, simple food and friendly welcome

Very sadly as we went to press, we heard that the long-serving landlady, Eileen Pittard, had passed away. Her son and daughters (who were also born in the pub as Mrs Pittard was) will continue to run this determinedly unpretentious, unspoilt thatched tavern. There's no bar as such – to get a drink, you just walk into the central flagstoned still room and choose from the casks of Teignworthy Reel Ale and guests such as Branscombe Vale Summa That, Glastonbury Mystery Tor, and

Hopback Crop Circle; farm cider, too. This servery is the only thoroughfare between the casual little front parlours with their unusual pointed-arch windows – and genuinely friendly locals; good helpful service. Using some home-grown fruit and vegetables, the simple, cheap food includes generously filled sandwiches and other traditional pubby dishes. Shove-ha'penny, dominoes and cribbage, and a much more orthodox big back extension family room has pool, darts, games machine and juke box; skittle alley and popular quiz nights. There are tables in a garden and a second enclosed garden has a children's play area. Summer morris men, fine nearby walks and the site of the Battle of Langport (1645) is close by.

Free house ~ Licensee Stephen Pittard ~ Real ale ~ Bar food (12-2, 5.30-7.30; not Sun or Mon evenings) ~ No credit cards ~ (01458) 250494 ~ Children welcome ~ Dogs welcome ~ Singalongs every third Sat (Sept-May) and irish night last Thurs in month ~ Open 11.30-2.30, 5.30-11; 11.30-11 Fri and Sat; 12-10.30 Sun

LOVINGTON
Pilgrims
B3153 Castle Cary—Keinton Mandeville; BA7 7PT

Rather smart but relaxed dining pub with particularly good food, local beer and cider, and decked terrace

The emphasis in this civilised and rather upmarket dining pub is very much on the enjoyable food cooked by the landlord. But the bar is chatty and relaxed with a few stools by a corner counter, a rack of daily papers, 16 wines by the glass, local cider and cider brandy, and Cottage Champflower on handpump from the nearby brewery. A cosy little dark green inner area has sunny modern country and city prints, a couple of shelves of books and china, a cushioned pew, and some settees by the big fireplace. With flagstones throughout, this runs into the compact eating area, with candles on tables and some stripped stone. The very rewarding sensibly imaginative food is cooked by the landlord using the best local produce he can source, and the landlady's service is efficient and friendly. The enclosed garden has tables, chairs and umbrellas on a decked terrace. The car park exit has its own traffic lights – on your way out line your car up carefully or you may wait for ever for them to change.

Free house ~ Licensees Sally and Jools Mitchison ~ Real ale ~ Bar food (not Sun evening, Mon, Tues lunchtime) ~ Restaurant ~ (01963) 240597 ~ Children welcome ~ Dogs allowed in bar ~ Open 12-3, 7-11; closed Sun evening, Mon, Tues lunchtime

MONKSILVER
Notley Arms
B3188; TA4 4JB

Friendly, busy pub in lovely village with beamed rooms, a fair choice of drinks and well liked food; neat streamside garden

In fine weather, the immaculate garden of this bustling pub has plenty of tables, and there's a swift clear stream at the bottom. The beamed and L-shaped bar has small settles and kitchen chairs around the plain country wooden and candlelit tables, original paintings on the ochre-coloured walls, fresh flowers and a couple of woodburning stoves. The Tack Room is decorated with horse tack (saddles, bridles and so forth) and has some toys. Bath Ales Gem, Exmoor Ale and Wadworths 6X on handpump, farm ciders and several wines by the glass; piped classical music, and good service from the friendly staff. Bar food is pubby, with one or two interesting specials. This is a lovely village.

Unique (Enterprise) ~ Lease Russell and Jane Deary ~ Real ale ~ Bar food (not Mon lunchtime or winter Mon) ~ (01984) 656217 ~ Children are encouraged to be in family room with books and toys ~ Dogs welcome ~ Open 12-2.30, 6.30-10.30(11 Sat); 12-2.45, 7-10.30 Sun; closed Mon lunchtime (all day Mon in winter)

NORTON ST PHILIP

George

A366; BA2 7LH

Wonderful ancient building full of history and interest, with well liked food, pleasant service and fine spacious bedrooms

This exceptional place was built around 700 years ago to house merchants buying wool and cloth at the great August cloth market. The central Norton Room – the original bar – has really heavy beams, an oak panelled settle and solid dining chairs on the narrow strip wooden floor, a variety of 18th-c pictures and an open fire in the handsome stone fireplace. Wadworths IPA, 6X, Bishops Tipple and Horizon, and a changing guest beer on handpump from the low wooden bar, and pleasant service. As you enter the building, there's a room on the right with high dark beams, squared dark half-panelling, a broad carved stone fireplace with an old iron fireback and pewter plates on the mantelpiece, a big mullioned window with leaded lights, and a round oak 17th-c table reputed to have been used by the Duke of Monmouth who stayed here before the Battle of Sedgemoor – after their defeat, his men were imprisoned in what is now the Monmouth Bar. The Charterhouse Bar is mostly used by those enjoying a drink before a meal: a wonderful pitched ceiling with trusses and timbering, heraldic shields and standards, jousting lances, and swords on the walls, a fine old stone fireplace, high backed cushioned heraldic-fabric dining chairs on the big rug over the wood plank floor, and an oak dresser with some pewter. The dining room (a restored barn with original oak ceiling beams, a pleasant if haphazard mix of early 19th-c portraits and hunting prints, and the same mix of vaguely old-looking furnishings) has a good relaxing, chatty atmosphere. The menu includes well liked pubby dishes, such as beef in ale pie, and there's a more elaborate restaurant menu. Bedrooms are atmospheric and comfortable – some reached by an external Norman stone stair-turret, and some across the cobbled and flagstoned courtyard and up into a fine half-timbered upper gallery. A stroll over the meadow behind the pub (past the picnic-sets on the narrow grass pub garden) leads to an attractive churchyard around the medieval church whose bells struck Pepys (here on 12 June 1668) as 'mighty tuneable'.

Wadworths ~ Manager Mark Jenkinson ~ Real ale ~ Bar food (12-2, 6-9; all day

weekends) ~ Restaurant ~ (01373) 834224 ~ Well behaved children welcome ~
Dogs allowed in bar and bedrooms ~ Open 11.30-11; 12-10.30 Sun ~
Bedrooms: £70B/£90B

PITNEY

Halfway House

Just off B3153 W of Somerton; TA10 9AB

**Up to ten real ales, local ciders and continental bottled beers in bustling
friendly local; good simple food**

Warm and friendly with helpful, welcoming staff, this traditional village local
keeps a fine range of ten real ales tapped from the cask. Changing regularly,
these might include Bath Ales SPA, Branscombe Vale Branoc, Butcombe Bitter,
Exmoor Fox, Hop Back Crop Circle and Summer Lightning, Moor Peat Porter, Otter
Ale, RCH Pitchfork, and Teignworthy Reed Ale. They also have 20 or so continental bottled beers, three farm ciders, several wines by the glass, and 15 malt
whiskies; cribbage, dominoes and board games. There's a good mix of people
chatting at communal tables in the three old-fashioned rooms, all with roaring
log fires and a homely feel underlined by a profusion of books, maps and newspapers. Good simple filling food includes hot smoked foods from their own
garden smokery, sandwiches, ploughman's with home-made pickle, lamb stew
with dumplings and fish pie, and in the evening they do about half a dozen
home-made curries. There are tables outside.

Free house ~ Licensee Julian Lichfield ~ Real ale ~ Bar food (12-2.30, 7.30-9;
not Sun) ~ (01458) 252513 ~ Children welcome ~ Dogs welcome ~ Open 11.30-
3, 5.30-11(midnight Fri and Sat); 12-3, 7-11 Sun; closed evening 25 Dec

SHEPTON MONTAGUE

Montague Inn

Village signposted just off A359 Bruton—Castle Cary; BA9 8JW

**Friendly licensees in busy country pub with real ales, good bar food, and pretty,
heated terrace**

The pretty terrace behind this popular little country pub has smart new teak seats
and tables this year and the views from here are very pleasant; more seats in the
garden, too. Inside, there's a good welcome from the friendly landlord and the
rooms are simply but tastefully furnished with stripped wooden tables and kitchen
chairs, and there's a log fire in the attractive inglenook fireplace. French windows
in the restaurant lead to the terrace. Wadworths IPA and 6X and maybe Bath Ales
Gem tapped from the cask, local cider, several wines by the glass, and smiling,
helpful service. Food is tasty and varied, ranging from beer-battered fish up to
duckling with bacon, pine nuts and savoy cabbage with a shallot and lentil sauce.

Free house ~ Licensee Sean O'Callaghan ~ Real ale ~ Bar food (12-2(3 Sun and
bank hols), 7-9; not Sun evening or Mon) ~ Restaurant ~ (01749) 813213 ~
Well behaved children welcome ~ Dogs allowed in bar ~ Open 12-3, 6-11;
closed Sun evening and all day Mon (except bank hols)

SIMONSBATH

Exmoor Forest Inn

B3223/B3358; TA24 7SH

In lovely surroundings with plenty of fine walks, comfortable inn with enjoyable food, good range of drinks and friendly licensees

This popular inn is a friendly place and even on a wet, miserable day there are usually plenty of customers. The bar has a few red plush stools around little circular tables by the bar counter and steps up to a larger area with joists in the ceiling, cushioned settles, upholstered stools and mates chairs around a mix of dark tables, a woodburning stove with two shelves of stone flagons to one side and hunting prints, trophies and antlers on the walls. The walls of the Tack Room are covered in all sorts of horse tack, with similar tables and chairs as well as one nice long table for a bigger party. Otter Bright, Quantock Bitter and a couple of summer guests such as Cotleigh Honey Buzzard and St Austell Black Prince on handpump, local cider and local juices, 30 malt whiskies and several wines by the glass. There's a cosy little residents' lounge and an airy dining room. Piped music, board games, bar skittles, and skittle alley. Picnic-sets and wooden and metal benches around tables under parasols in the front garden. Interesting bar food is prepared using some home-grown vegetables, and produce from local suppliers. The dogs are Billy the lurcher, Noddy the collie and Pip the jack russell. The inn is in lovely surroundings and perfectly positioned for a first or last night's stay on the Two Moors Walk linking Exmoor to Dartmoor; they provide dog beds, bowls and towels.

Free house ~ Licensees Chris and Barry Kift ~ Real ale ~ Bar food ~ Restaurant ~ (01643) 831341 ~ Children welcome ~ Dogs allowed in bar and bedrooms ~ Open 12-3, 6.30-11(10.30 Sun); closed Mon lunchtime except bank hols; Sun evening and all day Mon Nov-March ~ Bedrooms: £45S/£85S

TARR

Tarr Farm

Tarr Steps – rather narrow road off B3223 N of Dulverton, very little nearby parking (paying car park quarter-mile up road); OS Sheet 181 map reference 868322 – as the inn is on the E bank, don't be tempted to approach by car from the W unless you can cope with a deep ford; TA22 9PY

Lovely Exmoor setting looking over Tarr Steps and lots to do nearby; popular food, a fine range of drinks, and friendly staff; bedrooms

Despite being in a remote – if glorious – setting, there are plenty of locals (and visitors) popping in and out of this busy inn throughout the day. It's set on an Exmoor hillside looking down on the famous Tarr Steps just below – that much-photographed clapper bridge of massive granite slabs for medieval packhorses crossing the River Barle as it winds through this lightly wooded combe. The pub part consists of a line of compact and unpretentious rooms, with plenty of good views, slabby rustic tables, stall seating, wall seats and pub chairs, a woodburning stove at one end, salmon pink walls, nice game bird pictures and a pair of stuffed pheasants. The serving bar up a step or two has Exmoor Ale and Gold on handpump, eight wines by the glass and a good choice of other drinks. Bar food is imaginative (though plenty of traditional dishes too) thoughtfully prepared and very rewarding, and this is a lovely place for a cream tea, served all day until 5pm. The residents' end has a smart little evening restaurant (you can eat from this menu in the bar), and a pleasant log-fire lounge with dark leather armchairs and sofas. Outside, lots of chaffinches hop around between slate-topped stone tables above the steep lawn.

Free house ~ Licensees Richard Benn and Judy Carless ~ Real ale ~ Bar food (11.30-2.30, 6.30-9.30) ~ Restaurant ~ (01643) 851507 ~ Children allowed if over 10 ~ Dogs allowed in bar and bedrooms ~ Open 11-11; closed 1-10 Feb ~ Bedrooms: £90B/£150B

WATERROW

Rock

A361 Wiveliscombe—Bampton; TA4 2AX

Friendly, family-run half-timbered inn, local ales and good food, and nice mix of customers; bedrooms

Civilised and friendly, this striking timbered inn – run by a mother and son partnership – is on the edge of Exmoor National Park. There's quite an emphasis on the imaginative food and attractive bedrooms, but locals do drop in for a pint and a chat. The bar area has a dark brown leather sofa and low table with newspapers and books in front of the stone fireplace with its log fire and big blackboard menus. There's a mix of dining chairs and wooden tables on the partly wood and partly red carpeted floor, a few high-backed bar chairs, hunting paintings and photographs, a couple of built-in cushioned window seats; Cotleigh Tawny, Exmoor Ale, and Otter Ale on handpump, Sheppy's cider, and 15 wines by the glass. A back room has a popular pool table; darts and piped music. Up some steps from the bar is the heavily beamed restaurant. Using local produce and beef from their own farm, food focuses on good quality european country dishes. The welsh collie is called Meg. There are a few seats outside under umbrellas by the road.

Free house ~ Licensees Matt Harvey and Joanna Oldman ~ Real ale ~ Bar food (12-2.30, 6-9.30) ~ Restaurant ~ (01984) 623293 ~ Children welcome ~ Dogs allowed in bar and bedrooms ~ Open 12-3, 6-11(10.30); closed 25 and 26 Dec ~ Bedrooms: £45S/£75S

WEST HATCH

Farmers

W of village, at Slough Green; from A358 head for RSPCA centre and keep on past; TA3 5RS

Attractively decorated rooms, civilised but relaxed atmosphere, bright young staff, a good choice of drinks, and interesting food

The four attractively decorated rooms in this spreading pub are linked by open doorways and decorated in pastels of magnolia, mushroom and green, with bits of stone wall here and there. There are nice stripped floorboards throughout, low ceilings with pale beams, good farmhouse and wheelback chairs around a mix of tables, wooden wall lamps, various large plants, and black and white photographs of teasels and old and modern prints; piped jazz. One fireplace is filled with hundreds of logs and another has a woodburning stove, with some brown leather sofas, little armchairs and a couple of low copper tables in front of it. The atmosphere is civilised and relaxing, and the neat young staff are helpful. Often inventive bistro-style bar food, including focaccia sandwiches, is prepared (where possible) using home-grown vegetables. Exmoor Ale and Otter Ale on handpump, several wines by the glass, home-made cider, and on our visit winter Pimms, hot toddy and whisky mac. The labrador is called Pickle. Smart picnicsets on the terrace, covered floodlit area and small neat lawn.

Free house ~ Licensees Debbie Cunliffe and Tom Warren ~ Real ale ~ Bar food (12-2(3 weekends), 7-9(9.30 weekends)) ~ Restaurant ~ (01823) 480480 ~ Well behaved children welcome away from bar area ~ Dogs allowed in bar ~ Open 12-2.30(3 weekends), 6(7 weekends)-11

DOG FRIENDLY HOTELS, INNS, B&Bs AND FARMS

ALLERFORD
West Lynch Farm

West Lynch, Allerford, Somerset TA24 8HJ (01643) 862816

£60; 3 rms. Listed 15th-c National Trust farmhouse in six acres of landscaped gardens and paddocks on the edge of Exmoor; lots of original features, antiques and persian rugs, homely lounge with woodburning stove, super breakfasts with their own honey and home-made marmalade, and lots of animals; falconry days, riding, and collection of owls and birds of prey; cl 25 Dec; children over 5; no walking in the grounds but lots in surrounding countryside; 6 resident dogs; dogs welcome but not around farm or falconry centre; £5

BABINGTON
Babington House

Babington, Frome, Somerset BA11 3RW (01373) 812266

£354; 28 individually decorated, well equipped contemporary rms, 12 in coach house, 5 in stable block, 3 in lodge. Georgian mansion in lovely grounds with walled garden, tennis courts, croquet, and cricket and football pitches; interestingly decorated and comfortable lounges, open fire in bar, library, pool room, wide range of good food in both Log Room restaurant and light and airy House Kitchen, a particularly relaxed, informal atmosphere, and helpful and welcoming young staff; free cinema with films five days a week, and lots for children to do; indoor and outdoor swimming pools, gym, sauna, steam and aroma rooms, and treatment cabins; disabled access; dogs in some ground floor bedrooms

BARWICK

Little Barwick House

Barwick, Yeovil, Somerset BA22 9TD (0.4 miles off A37 Keyford roundabout, via Church Lane E) (01935) 423902

£154; 6 attractive rms. Carefully run listed Georgian dower house (a restaurant-with-rooms) in 3½ acres of grounds, with lovely relaxed atmosphere, log fire in cosy lounge, excellent food using local produce, thoughtful wine list, super breakfasts, nice afternoon tea, and particularly good service; two resident dogs and two cats; walks in grounds and nearby; cl two weeks from Christmas; children over 5; dogs in bedrooms; £5

BATHFORD

Eagle House

23 Church Street, Bathford, Bath BA1 7RS (01225) 859946

£78; 8 rms, 2 in cottage with sitting room and kitchen. Friendly and relaxed Georgian house with homely furnishings and family mementoes, winter log fires, elegant drawing room, nice continental breakfasts (full english is extra), and two-acre gardens with tennis, croquet, treehouse and swings (dogs may walk here but public footpaths close by, too); resident dog and cat; plenty to do nearby; cl 10 Dec-6 Jan; dogs in bedrooms and public (not dining) rooms; £4

CHARD

Watermead

83 High Street, Chard, Somerset TA20 1QT (01460) 62834

£59; 10 comfortable rms, most with own bthrm. Smart, family-run Victorian house with original features, homely residents' lounge, generous breakfasts in sizeable dining room and pleasant spacious garden; resident labrador and cat; walks in nearby field; self-catering studio also; dogs in bedrooms; £5

EXFORD

Crown

Exford, Minehead, Somerset TA24 7PP (01643) 831554

£110; 16 rms. Comfortably upmarket coaching inn on village green in Exmoor National Park, with delightful back water garden – lovely summer spot with trout stream, gently sloping lawns, tall trees and plenty of tables; brightly furnished lounge with very relaxed feel, hunting prints on cream walls, old photographs of the area, and smart cushioned benches; real ales, good wine list, and enjoyable modern cooking in dining room with simpler meals in bar; good base for walking; resident patterdale terrier; dogs welcome away from restaurant; treats; £8

HATCH BEAUCHAMP

Farthings

Hatch Beauchamp, Taunton, Somerset TA3 6SG (0.5 miles off A358 SE of Taunton) (01823) 480664

£130; 11 pretty rms with thoughtful extras. Charming Georgian house in two acres of gardens, with open fires in comfortable lounge, convivial bar, and good varied food using fresh local produce in two elegant dining rooms; plenty of open countryside for walks; dogs in some bedrooms; must be well behaved

HOLFORD

Combe House

Holford, Bridgwater, Somerset TA5 1RZ (01278) 741382

£150; 16 rms. Warmly friendly former tannery (still has waterwheel) in pretty spot, with comfortable rooms, log fires, good home-made food, and relaxed atmosphere; heated indoor swimming pool and tennis court; two resident dogs plus two cats; walks on the Quantock Hills; disabled access; dogs in bedrooms and bar; £5

HUNSTRETE

Hunstrete House

Hunstrete, Pensford, Bristol BS39 4NS (1.5 miles off A37 from Chelwood via A368 E) (01761) 490490

£170; 25 individually decorated rms. Classically handsome, mainly 18th-c country-house hotel on edge of Mendips in 92 acres of grounds inc lovely Victorian walled garden and deer park (plenty of walks); comfortable and elegantly furnished day rooms with restful atmosphere, antiques, paintings, log fires and fresh garden flowers; excellent service, very good food using home-grown produce, and super breakfasts; croquet lawn, heated outdoor swimming pool, all-weather tennis court, and nearby riding; limited disabled access; dogs in bedrooms; £10

LANGFORD BUDVILLE

Bindon Country House

Langford Budville, Wellington, Somerset TA21 0RU (01823) 400070

£145; 12 attractive rms. Tranquil 17th-c house designed as bavarian hunting lodge and set in seven acres of formal and woodland gardens; comfortable, elegant drawing room, panelled bar, open log fires, and enjoyable modern cooking and thoughtful wine list in intimate restaurant; outdoor swimming pool, tennis, boules, and croquet; dogs in some bedrooms

LUXBOROUGH
Royal Oak

Luxborough, Watchet, Somerset TA23 0SH (01984) 640319

£65; 12 neat, recently refurbished rms. Unspoilt and interesting old country pub in idyllic spot, marvellous for exploring Exmoor; convivial locals' bar with beams, flagstones and log fire in inglenook fireplace, several cosy dining rooms with interesting furnishings, a thriving atmosphere throughout, real ales, good food, and helpful, friendly staff; dogs in bedrooms and bar area

NETHER STOWEY
Old Cider House

25 Castle Street, Nether Stowey, Bridgwater, Somerset TA5 1LN (01278) 732228

£60; 5 individually decorated rms. Carefully restored Edwardian house in secluded garden, with own-brewed beers, big comfortable lounge, log fire, delicious breakfasts (their own bread and preserves) and imaginative, candlelit evening meals using home-grown and local produce, and a small carefully chosen wine list; resident chocolate labrador; plenty of walks and dog friendly beaches nearby; partial disabled access; dogs welcome away from dining room; welcome pack, treats, postcard; £3.50

PORLOCK
Andrews on the Weir

Porlock Weir, Minehead, Somerset TA24 8PB (01643) 863300

£130; 5 pretty rms, some with sea view. Family-run Victorian villa housing a restaurant-with-rooms overlooking Porlock Bay; country house-style décor in comfortable lounge areas, imaginative modern british cooking using first-class local produce (Exmoor hill lamb, fish freshly landed on the nearby quay, and west country cheeses are excellent), lovely puddings, a well chosen wine list, and friendly service; cl Mon and Tues, 22 Dec-22 Jan; children over 12; dogs welcome in bedrooms

Seapoint

Redway, Porlock, Minehead, Somerset TA24 8QE (01643) 862289

£76; 1 rm plus two apartments. Surrounded by the Exmoor hills and with views of Porlock Bay (plenty of fine walks), this Edwardian guesthouse has a comfortable sitting room with winter log fire, friendly and relaxing atmosphere, enjoyable home-made food in candlelit dining room, and fine breakfasts; three resident cats; cl Dec/Jan; they are kind to children; dogs welcome away from dining room

SELWORTHY
Hindon Farm

Selworthy, Minehead, Somerset TA24 8SH (01643) 705244

£70; 3 rms. Organic Exmoor hill farm of 500 acres with sheep, pigs, cattle, donkeys and ducks; lovely walks from the door to the heather moors (must be on a lead on the farm until away from stock animals); fine breakfasts using their own organic bacon, sausages, eggs and fresh baked bread; self-catering cottage with free organic produce on arrival; own organic farm shop; several resident dogs; no B&B Christmas and New Year; dogs in bedrooms if well house trained, £5

SHEPTON MALLET
Charlton House and Mulberry Restaurant

Charlton Road, Shepton Mallet, Somerset BA4 4PR (0.5 miles off A37; A361 E) (01749) 342008

£260; 26 attractive and stylish rooms with nice extras, and large bthrms. Substantial Georgian hotel in landscaped grounds (dogs must be kept on a lead), with oriental rugs and lots of old photographs and posters in bare-boarded rooms, and show-casing the owners' Mulberry style of informal furnishings; smart dining room and three-bay conservatory, restored 18th-c orangery dining room, exceptionally good modern cooking, interesting wines, and helpful, efficient uniformed staff; seats on the back terrace overlooking a big lawn, and croquet; health spa; they are kind to children; disabled access; dogs in the lodge and public areas; £10

SOMERTON
Lynch Country House

4 Behind Berry, Somerton, Somerset TA11 7PD (01458) 272316

£80; 9 prettily decorated rms, 4 in coach house. Carefully restored and homely Georgian house, with friendly welcome, books in comfortable lounge, and good breakfasts in airy, attractive dining room overlooking tranquil grounds and lake with black swans and exotic ducks; no evening meals; self-catering; resident collies; disabled access; dogs welcome away from breakfast room

STON EASTON
Ston Easton Park

Ston Easton, Bath BA3 4DF (off A37 just S of A39 junction) (01761) 241631

£285; 22 really lovely rms. Majestic Palladian mansion of Bath stone with beautifully landscaped 18th-c gardens and 26 acres of parkland; elegant day rooms with antiques and flowers, attractive restaurant with excellent food (much grown in Victorian kitchen garden), fine afternoon teas, library and billiard room, and extremely helpful, friendly and unstuffy service; walks in grounds and surrounding countryside; some disabled access; dogs in bedrooms and some other areas; £10

TAUNTON

Castle

Castle Green, Taunton, Somerset TA1 1NF (01823) 272671

£230; 44 lovely rms. Appealingly modernised partly Norman castle serving very enjoyable light meals in buzzy brasserie, fine english cooking in more formal restaurant, good breakfasts, fair value wines from thoughtful list, and efficient friendly service; pretty garden; walks in nearby park; disabled access; dogs in bedrooms, if small; £15

WELLS

Infield House

36 Portway, Wells, Somerset BA5 2BN (01749) 670989

£58; 3 comfortable rms (best view from back one). Carefully restored Victorian town house with period furnishings and family portraits, elegant lounge (lots of local guidebooks), good breakfasts in dining room with Adam-style fireplace, evening meals by arrangement, and friendly personal service; walks on nearby playing fields; resident corgi; cl two weeks beginning Dec; children over 12; dogs in bedrooms but must not be left unattended

WHEDDON CROSS

North Wheddon Farm

Wheddon Cross, Somerset TA24 7EX (01643) 841791

£70; 2 charming rms. Friendly farmhouse with open fires, attractive, comfortable sitting room with fine fabrics, bold colours and cosy sofas, lovely breakfasts and good dinner party-style meals (on request) using their own produce, and neatly kept garden and surrounding grounds; self-catering also; resident dogs; partial disabled access; dogs in bedrooms; £5

Staffordshire

DOG FRIENDLY PUBS

ALSTONEFIELD

George

Village signposted from A515 Ashbourne-Buxton; DE6 2FX

Nice old pub with good range of fairly priced food, a Peak District classic

Run by a very friendly landlady, this stone-built peak district pub has gently gone from strength to strength since she took over a couple of years ago. It's by the green in a peaceful farming hamlet and is popular with good variety of customers (including plenty of walkers) soaking up the charming atmosphere. Sitting out beneath the inn-sign and watching the world go by, or in the big sheltered stableyard behind the pub, is a real pleasure. The unchanging straightforward low-beamed bar has a collection of old peak district photographs and pictures, a warming coal fire, and a copper-topped counter with well kept Marstons Pedigree, Burtonwood and a guest such as Adnams Broadside on handpump and a dozen wines by the glass; dominoes. The menu is fairly short but it's well balanced, fairly priced, and pubby with an imaginative twist.

Marstons ~ Lease Emily Hammond ~ Real ale ~ Bar food (12-2.30, 7-9(6.30-8 Sun)) ~ Restaurant ~ (01335) 310205 ~ Children welcome ~ Dogs allowed in bar ~ Open 11-3, 6-11; 11.30-11 Sat; 12-10.30 Sun

BURTON UPON TRENT

Burton Bridge Inn

Bridge Street (A50); DE14 1SY

Straightforward cheery tap for the Burton Bridge Brewery; lunchtime snacks only

'What a gem' says one reader of this genuinely friendly down-to-earth old brick local. It's the showcase for the superbly kept beers (Bitter, Festival, Golden Delicious, Porter and XL) that are brewed by Burton Bridge Brewery who are housed across the long old-fashioned yard at the back (there's a blue-brick terrace out here, too). These are served on handpump alongside a guest such as Timothy Taylors Landlord, around 20 whiskies, an impressive 17 wines by the glass and over a dozen country wines. The simple little front area leads into an adjacent bar with wooden pews, and plain walls hung with notices, awards and brewery memorabilia. Separated from the bar by the serving counter, the little oak beamed lounge is snugly oak panelled and has a flame-effect fire and a mix of furnishings; skittle alley. Simple but hearty lunchtime bar snacks take in cheese filled oakcakes and filled giant yorkshire puddings.

Own brew ~ Licensees Kevin and Jan McDonald ~ Real ale ~ Bar food
(lunchtime only, not Sun) ~ No credit cards ~ (01283) 536596 ~ Dogs welcome
~ Open 11.30-2.15, 5-11; 12-2, 7-10.30 Sun; closed bank hol Mon lunchtime

KIDSGROVE

Blue Bell

25 Hardings Wood; off A50 NW edge of town; ST7 1EG

**Astonishing tally of thoughtfully sourced real ales on six constantly changing
pumps at simple little beer pub**

In the last ten years, over 2,500 brews have passed through the beer pumps at
this quirky double cottage at the junction of the Trent & Mersey and Macclesfield
canals. The constantly changing range is carefully selected from smaller, often
unusual brewers, such as Acorn, Castle Rock, Crouch Vale, Oakham, Townhouse
and Whim. Lagers are restricted to german or belgian brews, they've usually a
draught continental beer, at least one farm cider, around 30 bottled beers, and
various coffees and soft drinks. Service is friendly and knowledgeable. The four
small, carpeted rooms are unfussy and straightforward, with blue upholstered
benches running around ivory-painted walls, a gas effect coal fire, just a few
tables, and maybe soft piped music. There are tables in front, and more on a
little back lawn. You can get filled rolls at the weekend, and please note the
limited opening hours.

Free house ~ Licensees Dave and Kay Washbrook ~ Real ale ~ No credit cards ~
(01782) 774052 ~ Children welcome ~ Dogs welcome ~ Impromptu acoustic
Sun evenings ~ Open 7.30-11; 1-4, 7-11 Sat; 12-10.30 Sun; closed lunchtimes
and Mon except bank hols

LICHFIELD

Queens Head

*Queen Street; public car park just round corner in Swan Road, off A51
roundabout; WS13 6QD*

**Friendly with great cheese counter, bargain lunchtime hot dishes, good range of
real ales**

It's well worth making the short walk from the city centre to find this handsome
Georgian brick building, which is done up inside as an old-fashioned alehouse.
Its single long room has a mix of comfortable aged furniture on bare boards,
some stripped brick, Lichfield and other pictures on ochre walls above a panelled
dado, and big sash windows. The atmosphere is comfortably relaxed and grown-
up and staff are friendly and helpful. A highlight here is the cold cabinet of
cheeses on the left of the bar, including some interesting local ones such as
Dovedale Blue. Throughout the day (unless it gets too busy), you can make up
your own very generous ploughman's, perhaps with some pâté too, with a basket
of their good crusty granary bread, home-made pickles, onions and gherkins. At
lunchtime (not Sunday) they also have a good range of over two dozen enjoyable pubby hot dishes at amazingly low prices. The pub is a keen supporter of
local sports teams and they've a terrestrial TV for sports events. As well as a

couple of interesting guests, usually from smaller brewers, beers include Adnams, Marstons Pedigree and Timothy Taylors Landlord; small garden.

Marstons ~ Lease Denise Harvey ~ Real ale ~ Bar food (12-2.15 (cheese all day and only cheese Sun)) ~ No credit cards ~ (01543) 410932 ~ Dogs welcome ~ Open 12-11(11.30 Fri, Sat); 12-3, 7-11 Sun

WRINEHILL

Hand & Trumpet

A531 Newcastle—Nantwich; CW3 9BJ

Big attractive dining pub with good food all day, professional service, nice range of real ales and wines; pleasant garden

Cleverly open plan and stylish yet still intimate feeling, this sturdy building has been handsomely converted with top quality fixtures and fittings. At its heart, the solidly built counter has half a dozen handpumps dispensing well kept Caledonian Deuchars IPA, Thwaites Original, Timothy Taylors Landlord and three guests from brewers such as Derby, Salopian and Woodlands. They also keep a fine range of about 22 wines by the glass and about 85 whiskies. Linked open-plan areas working around the counter have a good mix of dining chairs and varying-sized tables on polished tiles or stripped oak boards, and several big oriental rugs that soften the acoustics as well as the appearance. There are lots of nicely lit prints on cream walls above the mainly dark dado and below deep red ceilings. It's all brightened up with good natural light from bow windows and in one area a big skylight. Service is relaxed and friendly; good disabled access and facilities; board games. Food here is soundly imaginative and very tasty. French windows open on to a stylish balustraded deck with teak tables and chairs looking down to ducks swimming on a big pond in the sizeable garden, which has plenty of trees.

Brunning & Price ~ Manager John Unsworth ~ Real ale ~ Bar food (12-10(9.30 Sun)) ~ (01270) 820048 ~ Children welcome till 7pm ~ Dogs allowed in bar ~ Open 12-11(10.30 Sun)

DOG FRIENDLY HOTELS, B&Bs AND FARMS

HOPWAS

Oak Tree Farm

Hints Road, Hopwas, Tamworth, Staffordshire B78 3AA (just off A51 W of Tamworth; Hints Road) (01827) 56807

£85; 9 comfortable, spacious and pretty rms. Carefully restored farmhouse with elegant little lounge, fresh flowers, attractive breakfast room, friendly atmosphere and owners, enjoyable breakfasts, and gardens overlooking the River Tame; indoor swimming pool and steam room; walks by canals and in fields; disabled access; dogs in bedrooms; £15

ROLLESTON ON DOVE

Brookhouse Hotel

Station Road, Rolleston on Dove, Burton upon Trent, Staffordshire DE13 9AA
(1.7 miles N off A38 from A5121 junction E of Stretton, via Claymills Road and
Dovecliff Road, leading into Station Road) (01283) 814188

£115; 20 comfortable rms with Victorian brass or four-poster beds. Handsome ivy-covered William & Mary brick building in five acres of lovely gardens with comfortable antiques-filled rooms, and good food using seasonal local produce in elegant little dining room; resident cat; walks on open farmland; cl Christmas-New Year; children over 12; disabled access; dogs in ground floor bedrooms only

STOKE-ON-TRENT

Haydon House

Haydon Street, Basford, Stoke-on-Trent, Staffordshire ST4 6JD (01782) 711311

£75; 17 rms, some in annexe. Family-run Victorian house with relaxed, friendly atmosphere, attractive and comfortable lounge and conservatory, good food (popular locally) in nice little restaurant, and extensive wine list; dogs in bedrooms and public areas (not restaurant)

TAMWORTH

Old Rectory

Churchside, Harlaston, Tamworth, Staffordshire B79 9HE (01827) 383583

£48; 4 attractive rms overlooking open countryside. Former Victorian rectory in large grounds in award-winning village; spacious sunny kitchen opening on to the garden with enjoyable breakfasts that include home-made preserves and local specialities; resident dog; walks all round; dogs in bedrooms; £2

DOG FRIENDLY PUBS

ALDEBURGH

Cross Keys

Crabbe Street; IP15 5BN

Seats outside near beach, chatty atmosphere, friendly licensee, and local beer

It's fun to sit with a pint of beer on the terrace outside this 16th-c pub and watch people walking down Crag Path, especially during the Aldeburgh Festival when you may hear outside events (or at least, rehearsals for those events); there are seats in the garden, too, and the hanging baskets are pretty. This is one of the few places in Suffolk where you can eat outside by the beach. Inside, there's a happy, jolly atmosphere helped along by the obliging licensee and his staff. The interconnecting bars have two inglenook fireplaces, antique and other pubby furniture, the landlord's collection of oil and Victorian watercolours, and paintings by local artists on the walls. Adnams Bitter, Broadside and Explorer on handpump, and decent wines by the glass; games machine. Simple bar food runs from sandwiches to moules frites, with daily specials such as braised oxtail. The bedrooms are elegant.

Adnams ~ Tenants Mike and Janet Clement ~ Real ale ~ Bar food (not winter Sun evening) ~ No credit cards ~ (01728) 452637 ~ Children welcome ~ Dogs welcome ~ Open 11am(12am Sun)-midnight

EARL SOHAM

Victoria

A1120 Yoxford—Stowmarket; IP13 7RL

Nice beers from brewery across the road in friendly, informal local

With the Earl Soham brewery just across the road, the beers on handpump in this unpretentious, friendly pub are, not surprisingly, very well kept: Albert Ale, Gold, Sir Roger's Porter, and Victoria Bitter. Farm cider, too. The well worn bar has an easy-going local atmosphere and is fairly basic. It's sparsely furnished with kitchen chairs and pews, plank-topped trestle sewing-machine tables and other simple scrubbed pine country tables, and there's stripped panelling, tiled or board floors, an interesting range of pictures of Queen Victoria and her reign, and open fires. Straightforward bar food such as ploughman's and an enjoyable changing curry. On a raised back lawn are some seats, with more out in front. The pub is quite close to a wild fritillary meadow at Framlingham, and a working windmill at Saxtead.

Own brew ~ Licensee Paul Hooper ~ Real ale ~ Bar food (12-2, 7-10) ~
(01728) 685758 ~ Children welcome ~ Dogs welcome ~ Open 11.30-3, 6-11;
12-3, 7-10.30 Sun

EASTBRIDGE

Eels Foot

Off B1122 N of Leiston; IP16 4SN

Handy for Minsmere bird reserve, friendly welcome, real ales, fair value food, and long-standing live Thursday evening folk music

This cheerful beamed country local is a popular spot with bird-watchers, cyclists and walkers and the freshwater marshes bordering the inn offer plenty of opportunity for watching the abundance of birds and butterflies; a footpath leads you directly to the sea. Inside, the upper and lower parts of the bar have light modern furnishings, a friendly welcome from the helpful staff, a log fire, and Adnams Bitter, Broadside, Old Ale and seasonal beers on handpump, several wines by the glass, and Aspall's cider. Darts in a side area and board games. Bar food is popular and pubby. There are seats on the terrace and in the extensive garden.

Adnams ~ Tenants Simon and Corinne Webber ~ Real ale ~ Bar food (12-2.30, 7-9 (6.30-8 Thurs evening)) ~ Restaurant ~ (01728) 830154 ~ Children welcome ~ Dogs allowed in bar ~ Live acoustic music Thurs evening and last Sun of month ~ Open 12-3, 6-11; 11am-midnight Sat; 12-10.30 Sun

GREAT GLEMHAM

Crown

Between A12 Wickham Market—Saxmundham and B1119 Saxmundham—Framlingham; IP17 2DA

Friendly, pleasant pub with log fires, fresh flowers, great real ales and enjoyable food

This is a neat, friendly pub in a particularly pretty village. There's a big entrance hall with sofas on rush matting, and an open-plan beamed lounge with wooden pews and captain's chairs around stripped and waxed kitchen tables, and local photographs and interesting paintings on cream walls; fresh flowers, some brass ornaments and log fires in two big fireplaces. Adnams Bitter, Earl Soham Victoria, and St Austell Tribute are served from old brass handpumps and they've eight wines (including sparkling) by the glass, Aspall's cider and several malt whiskies. Enjoyable bar food, including some imaginative daily specials, is available in smaller helpings, too. A tidy flower-ringed lawn, raised above the corner of the quiet village lane by a retaining wall, has some seats and tables under cocktail parasols; there's a smokers' shelter and disabled access.

Free house ~ Licensee Dave Cottle ~ Real ale ~ Bar food (12-2.30, 6.30-9; not Mon) ~ (01728) 663693 ~ Well behaved children welcome ~ Dogs welcome ~ Occasional live music ~ Open 11.30-3, 6.30-11.30; 12-3, 7-10.30 Sun; closed Mon except bank hols ~ Bedrooms: /£80B

LONG MELFORD

Black Lion

Church Walk; CO10 9DN

Civilised hotel with relaxed and comfortable bar, a couple of real ales, modern bar food, attentive uniformed staff; lovely bedrooms

Of course, this is not a straightforward pub, it's a civilised and comfortable hotel, but customers do continue to drop in for just a drink, and they do keep Adnams Bitter and Broadside on handpump; several wines by the glass and malt whiskies, too. One side of the oak serving counter is decorated in ochre and has bar stools, deeply cushioned sofas, leather wing armchairs and antique fireside settles, while the other side, decorated in shades of terracotta, has leather dining chairs around handsome tables set for the good modern food; open fires in both rooms. Big windows with swagged-back curtains have a pleasant outlook over the village green and there are large portraits of racehorses and of people. Neatly uniformed, friendly efficient staff serve delicious inventive and attractively presented (if not cheap) food. There are seats and tables under terracotta parasols on the terrace and more in the appealing Victorian walled garden.

Ravenwood Group ~ Manager Craig Jarvis ~ Real ale ~ Bar food ~ Restaurant ~ (01787) 312356 ~ Children welcome ~ Dogs allowed in bar and bedrooms ~ Open 9am-11pm ~ Bedrooms: £97.50B/£150B

SOUTHWOLD

Lord Nelson

East Street, off High Street (A1095); IP18 6EJ

Smashing town pub with lots of locals and visitors, cheerful and chatty, excellent service, home-made pubby food and good choice of drinks; seats outside

Just moments away from the seafront, this smashing town pub remains as popular as ever. It's lively and friendly (and carefully redecorated this year) with lots of locals and visitors coming and going – but even when really busy, the good-natured service remains quick and attentive. The partly panelled bar and its two small side rooms are kept spotless, with good lighting, a small but extremely hot coal fire, light wood furniture on the tiled floor, lamps in nice nooks and corners and some interesting Nelson memorabilia, including attractive nautical prints and a fine model of HMS *Victory*. Adnams Bitter, Broadside, Explorer and a seasonal guest on handpump, Aspall's cider, and several good wines by the glass. Daily papers and board games but no piped music or games machines. Traditional pubby food includes their popular beer-battered cod. There are nice seats out in front with a sidelong view down to the sea and more in a sheltered (and heated) back garden, with the brewery in sight (and often the appetising fragrance of brewing in progress). Disabled access is not perfect but is possible, and they will help.

Adnams ~ Tenant David Sanchez ~ Real ale ~ Bar food ~ (01502) 722079 ~ Children in areas to side of bar ~ Dogs welcome ~ Open 10.30am-11pm; 12-10.30 Sun

STOKE-BY-NAYLAND

Crown

Park Street (B1068); CO6 4SE

Smart dining pub with attractive modern furnishings, bistro-style food, and fantastic wine choice

Although most emphasis in this busy, smart and friendly dining pub is on the interesting, bistro-style food, those popping in for a drink and a chat are just as welcome. Most of the place is open to the three-sided bar servery, yet it's well divided, and with two or three more tucked-away areas too. The main part, with a big woodburning stove, has quite a lot of fairly closely spaced tables in a variety of shapes, styles and sizes; elsewhere, several smaller areas have just three or four tables each. Seating varies from deep armchairs and sofas to elegant dining chairs and comfortable high-backed woven rush seats – and there are plenty of bar stools. This all gives a good choice between conviviality and varying degrees of cosiness and privacy. There are cheerful wildlife and landscape paintings on the pale walls, quite a lot of attractive table lamps, low ceilings (some with a good deal of stripped old beams), and floors varying from old tiles through broad boards or dark new flagstones to beige carpet; daily papers. Adnams Bitter, Crouch Vale Brewery Gold, and Woodfordes on handpump and a fantastic choice of 37 wines by the glass from a list of around 200 kept in an unusual glass-walled wine 'cellar' in one corner. Extremely good imaginative modern food is prepared using carefully sourced local produce such as deep-fried local rabbit with watercress and aioli and condensed milk ice-cream and lemon mousse with raspberry tuiles. A sheltered back terrace, with cushioned teak chairs and tables under big canvas parasols, looks out over a neat lawn to a landscaped shrubbery. There are many more picnic-sets out on the front terrace. Disabled access is good and the car park is big.

Free house ~ Licensee Richard Sunderland ~ Real ale ~ Bar food (12-2.30, 6-9.30 (10 Fri, Sat); 12-9 Sun) ~ (01206) 262001 ~ Children allowed but no facilities for them ~ Dogs allowed in bar ~ Open 11-11; 12-10.30 Sun; closed 25 and 26 Dec

WALBERSWICK

Anchor

Village signposted off A12; The Street (B1387); IP18 6UA

Good mix of locals and visitors in well run, attractively furnished inn, fine range of drinks, appetising modern cooking, and friendly, helpful service; bedrooms

The newly renovated flint barn here is used for private dining and other meetings; they hope to renovate the bedrooms soon, and there's now a garden bar serving the flagstoned terrace that overlooks the beach and village allotments. Inside, there's a genuine mix of both locals and visitors and the big-windowed comfortable front bar has heavy stripped tables on its dark blue carpet, sturdy built-in wall seats cushioned in green leather and nicely framed black and white photographs of local fishermen and their boats on the varnished plank panelling. Log fires in the chimneybreast divide this room into two snug halves.

They have loads of bottled beers from all over the world, 23 interesting wines by the glass including champagne and a pudding one, Adnams Bitter, Broadside and a seasonal beer on handpump and good coffee; particularly good service, daily papers, darts and board games. Quite an extensive dining area stretching back from a more modern-feeling small lounge on the left is furnished much like the bar – though perhaps a bit more minimalist – and looks out on a good-sized sheltered and nicely planted garden. Using local producers (and vegetables from their allotment), imaginative food is extremely good and the menu suggests a beer to go with each dish. The pub is right by the coast path, and there's a pleasant walk across to Southwold; in summer there may be a pedestrian ferry – though you won't know if it is running until you get there.

Adnams ~ Lease Mark and Sophie Dorber ~ Real ale ~ Bar food (12-3, 6-9) ~ Restaurant ~ (01502) 722112 ~ Children welcome ~ Dogs allowed in bar and bedrooms ~ Open 11-4, 6-11; 11-11 Sun and Sat ~ Bedrooms: £75B/£90B

DOG FRIENDLY HOTELS, INNS, B&Bs AND FARMS

ALDEBURGH

Wentworth

Wentworth Road, Aldeburgh, Suffolk IP15 5BD (01728) 452312

£158; 35 rms, 7 in annexe which are more spacious. Comfortable, traditional hotel in same family for over 80 years and overlooking fishing huts and boats; plenty of comfortable seats in lounges with log fires, antiques and books, convivial bar, cheerful long-standing staff, good enjoyable lunchtime and evening meals, nice breakfasts, and sunny terrace; walks on the beach (restricted during high season); children must be well behaved; partial disabled access; dogs in bedrooms and lounges; £2

BILDESTON

Crown

High Street, Bildeston, Ipswich, Suffolk IP7 7EB (01449) 740510

£130; 13 pretty, individually furnished rms. Lovely timber-framed Tudor inn with log fires and stripped wooden floors in spacious and convivial beamed bar, comfortable, heavily beamed lounge and elegant restaurant, enjoyable modern cooking, well kept real ales, and welcoming courteous service; seats on heated terrace and in central courtyard; disabled access; dogs welcome; £5

BUNGAY

Earsham Park Farm

Old Railway Road, Earsham, Bungay, Suffolk NR35 2AQ (01986) 892180

£70; 3 lovely sunny rms. Light and airy Victorian farmhouse with attractive garden on 600 acres of working farmland; plenty of original features, super

Aga-cooked breakfasts, with their own sausages and bacon and home-made bread, taken around large family table in prettily decorated dining room; plenty of walks (dogs must be under control on farmland); dogs in bedrooms (not to be left unattended); £5

BURY ST EDMUNDS

Angel

3 Angel Hill, Bury St Edmunds, Suffolk IP33 1LT (1 mile off A14/A143/A134 junction, following town centre signs; Angel Hill) (01284) 714000

£139; 75 individually decorated rms. Thriving, family-owned 15th-c country-town hotel with particularly friendly staff, comfortable lounge and relaxed bar, log fires and fresh flowers, and very good creative food in refurbished Eaterie restaurant and downstairs medieval vaulted room (Mr Pickwick enjoyed a roast dinner here); gardens to walk in 50 metres away; disabled access; dogs in bedrooms; £10

CAMPSEY ASH

Old Rectory

Station Road, Campsey Ash, Woodbridge, Suffolk IP13 0PU (1.4 miles off A12 via B1078 E) (01728) 746524

£120; 8 comfortable, pretty rms. Very relaxed and welcoming Georgian house by church, with charming owner and staff, log fire in comfortable and restful drawing room, quite a few Victorian prints, first-class food from set menu in summer conservatory or two other dining rooms with more log fires, good honesty bar, sensational wine list with very modest mark-ups on its finest wines, and sizeable homely gardens; resident dog; walks in garden and fields; cl Christmas; dogs in some bedrooms

HADLEIGH

Edgehall

2 High Street, Hadleigh, Ipswich, Suffolk IP7 5AP (01473) 822458

£85; 4 pretty rms plus more in Lodge House. Friendly family-run Tudor house with Georgian façade and attractive walled garden where you can have afternoon tea or play croquet; comfortable, elegant lounge, personal service, and traditional english cooking using home-grown produce and good breakfasts in stately dining room; resident dog; dogs in certain rooms; £5

HINTLESHAM

Hintlesham Hall

Hintlesham, Ipswich, Suffolk IP8 3NS (01473) 652334

£150; 33 lovely rms. Magnificent mansion, mainly Georgian but dating from Elizabethan times, in 175 acres with big walled gardens, 18-hole golf course, outdoor heated swimming pool, croquet, and tennis; restful and comfortable lounges with books, antiques and open fires, relaxed bar, fine modern cooking in three elegant restaurants, marvellous wine list, and exemplary service; gym, and beauty salon; well behaved children over 12 in evening restaurant; disabled access; dogs in ground floor bedrooms

HOPTON

Old Rectory

Hopton, Hopton, Suffolk IP22 2QX (01953) 688135

£95; 3 rms. 16th-c house in walled gardens with friendly, hospitable owners, cosy snug, relaxing drawing room, TV room, winter fires, home-made cake and tea on arrival, delicious breakfasts and evening meals in elegant dining room, thoughtful choice of wines, and seats on terrace; resident labrador and border terrier; lots of nearby walks; cl Christmas; children over 12; dogs in bedrooms; £7.50

HORRINGER

Ickworth

Horringer, Bury St Edmunds, Suffolk IP29 5QE (01284) 735350

£290; 27 rms, 11 in apartments. Lovely 18th-c house in marvellous parkland on an 1,800 acre National Trust estate (formerly owned by the Marquess of Bristol), the east wing of which is a luxury hotel; elegant and traditional décor mixes with more contemporary touches, the atmosphere is relaxed and informal, and staff are friendly and helpful; excellent modern cooking in dining conservatory and more formal restaurant; they are kind to families with lots for children to do; beauty treatments, riding, tennis, and indoor swimming pool; lots of surrounding walks; disabled access; dogs in bedrooms; canine massage; £7.00

LAVENHAM

Angel

Market Place, Lavenham, Sudbury, Suffolk CO10 9QZ (01787) 247388

£85; 8 comfortable rms. 15th-c inn with original cellar and pargeted ceiling in attractive residents' lounge, several Tudor features such as a rare shuttered shop window front, civilised atmosphere, good food in bar and restaurant, lots of decent wines, several malt whiskies, well kept real ales, and thoughtful friendly service; disabled access; dogs in one ground-floor room only and in bar; £10

Great House

Market Place, Lavenham, Sudbury, Suffolk CO10 9QZ (01787) 247431

£135; 5 lovely rms, some with own sitting area. Restaurant-with-rooms in ancient house behind handsome Georgian façade, with bare boards, antiques, open fires (inc an inglenook in the restaurant itself), exceptionally good french cooking (super french cheese board), friendly staff, and attractive flower-filled courtyard for outside eating; dogs in bedrooms if well behaved (not on furniture)

LAVENHAM

Swan

High Street, Lavenham, Sudbury, Suffolk CO10 9QA (01787) 247477

£160; 46 lovely rms. Handsome and comfortable Elizabethan hotel that incorporates several fine half-timbered buildings inc an Elizabethan house and the former wool hall; lots of cosy seating areas, interesting historic prints and alcoves with beams, timbers, armchairs and settees; good food in lavishly timbered restaurant with minstrels' gallery (actually built only in 1965), afternoon teas, intriguing little bar, and friendly helpful staff; disabled access; dogs welcome away from food areas; £10

LONG MELFORD

Bull

Hall Street, Long Melford, Sudbury, Suffolk CO10 9JG (01787) 378494

£120; 25 rms, ancient or comfortably modern. Fine black and white hotel (an inn since 1580) and originally a medieval manorial hall, with handsome and interesting carved woodwork and timbering, an old weavers' gallery overlooking the courtyard, large log fire, old-fashioned and antique furnishings, enjoyable food, and friendly service; dogs (if small) in bedrooms; £5

ORFORD

Crown & Castle

Orford, Woodbridge, Suffolk IP12 2LJ (01394) 450205

£135; 18 well designed, stylish rms, 10 in garden with own terrace. Red brick and high gabled Victorian hotel by Norman castle in seaside village (and owned by cookery writer Ruth Watson); lovely relaxed informal atmosphere, cosy, deeply comfortable lounge, cheerful bar, exceptionally good modern british cooking, super wine list with lots by glass, and excellent breakfasts; resident cat; walk in garden and around castle and by sea; children over 9 in evening restaurant; dogs in some bedrooms (at one table in restaurant, too); welcome pack; £10

ROUGHAM

Ravenwood Hall

Rougham, Bury St Edmunds, Suffolk IP30 9JA (3 miles off A14 from Beyton exit, via old Bury Road E towards Blackthorpe) (01359) 270345

£165; 14 comfortable rms with antiques, some in mews. Tranquil, Tudor country house in seven acres of carefully tended gardens and woodland; log fire in comfortable lounge, cosy, convivial bar with another log fire, good food in timbered restaurant with big inglenook fireplace and in Garden Room (home-preserved fruits and veg, home-smoked meats and fish), good wine list, and helpful service; croquet and heated swimming pool; lots of animals and resident dog; walks in grounds and lots more nearby; disabled access; dogs welcome away from restaurant

SOUTHWOLD

Swan

Market Place, Southwold, Suffolk IP18 6EG (01502) 722186

£162; 42 well appointed rms, some overlooking market square. 17th-c hotel with comfortable drawing room, convivial bar, interesting enjoyable food in elegant dining room, fine wines, well kept real ales (the hotel backs on to Adnams Brewery), and polite helpful staff; disabled access; dogs in garden bedrooms; bedding, bowls and treats; £5

WESTLETON

Crown

The Street, Westleton, Saxmundham, Suffolk IP17 3AD (01728) 648777

£120; 25 cosseting, comfortable rms. Carefully refurbished old coaching inn, a particularly enjoyable place to stay, with cosy and attractive bar area, lovely log fire and plenty of original features, well kept real ales and local cider, thoughtfully chosen wine list with lots by the glass; quiet parlour, dining room and conservatory, and attentive, helpful and friendly service; charming terraced gardens with plenty of seats; plenty to do nearby and walks in paddock, on nearby common, and beach; disabled access; dogs in bedrooms and bar; bowl, treats and warm welcome; £5

WINGFIELD

Gables Farm

Earsham Street, Wingfield, Diss, Suffolk IP21 5RH (01379) 586355

£65; 3 lovely characterful rms. 16th-c timbered farmhouse in moated gardens with woodburning stove in comfortable sitting room, nice breakfasts including home-made preserves and their own eggs in beamed dining room; charming hosts; seats in garden and plenty to do nearby; cl some winter months

WOODBRIDGE

Seckford Hall

Seckford Hall Road, Great Bealings, Woodbridge, Suffolk IP13 6NU (01394) 385678

£150; 32 comfortable rms. Handsome red brick Tudor mansion in 32 acres of gardens and parkland with carp-filled lake, putting, and leisure club with indoor heated pool, beauty salon, and gym in lovely tithe barn; fine linenfold panelling, huge fireplaces, heavy beams, plush furnishings and antiques in comfortable day rooms, good food in two restaurants and bar, fine teas with home-made cakes, and helpful service; cl 24-26 Dec; disabled access; dogs in bedrooms; £8

DOG FRIENDLY PUBS

BRAMLEY

Jolly Farmer

High Street; GU5 0HB

Relaxed village inn near the Surrey hills, with very wide selection of beers, pleasant staff and daily specials

'Everything a pub should be' enthused one reader of this welcoming village inn within a few miles of Winkworth Arboretum and walks up St Martha's Hill. Its attractive interior is a mixture of brick and timbering, with an open fireplace and timbered semi-partitions, and furnished with a homely miscellany of wooden tables and chairs; various assemblages of plates, enamel advertising signs, antique bottles, prints and old tools hang from the walls; the back restaurant area is inviting, piped music, dominoes and board games. Friendly staff serve up to 20 different national and local real ales each week, typically with eight on at a time, with Badger First Gold and Hogsback HBB alongside guests from brewers such as B&T, Brentwood, Harwich, Kings, Rebellion and Rudgate; also three changing belgian draught beers and 18 wines by the glass. The pubby bar menu specials change daily.

Free house ~ Licensees Steve and Chris Hardstone ~ Real ale ~ Bar food (12-2.30, 6(7 Sun)-9.30) ~ Restaurant ~ 01483 893355 ~ Children welcome until 9.30pm ~ Dogs allowed in bar ~ live music first or second Tues ~ Open 11am-11.30pm(midnight Sat); 12-11.30 Sun

CHARLESHILL

Donkey

B3001 Milford—Farnham near Tilford; coming from Elstead, turn left as soon as you see pub sign; GU10 2AU

Beamed, cottagey dining pub with attractive garden and good local walks

Readers enjoy the warm welcome and generous portions of food here, and you might meet its two friendly donkeys, Pip and Dusty, a reminder that the pub takes its name from much earlier donkeys that were once kept to transport loads up the hill opposite. Its saloon has lots of tables for dining, polished stirrups, lamps and watering cans on the walls, and prettily cushioned built-in wall benches, while the lounge has a fine high-backed settle, highly polished horse-brasses, and swords on the walls and beams. All their wines are available by the glass (including champagne), and you'll also find two real ales on handpump, with Greene Abbot and Old Speckled Hen, or a guest such as Fullers London Pride or Harveys Sussex; piped music. Friendly staff serve lunchtime sandwiches and daily specials that take in quite a few fish dishes including crab and lobster. The attractive garden also has a terrace and plenty of seats and there's a wendy house. On the edge of woodlands, it has been a pub since 1850. Attractive local walking areas through heathlands include Crooksbury Common, and there are paths into the woods around the pub.

Greene King ~ Lease Lee and Helen Francis ~ Real ale ~ Bar food (12-2.30(4 Sun), 6-9.30(8.30 Sun)) ~ Restaurant ~ (01252) 702124 ~ Children welcome ~ Dogs welcome ~ Open 11.30-3, 6-11; 12-10.30 Sun

COBHAM

Plough

3.2 miles from M25 junction 10; A3, then right on A245 at roundabout; in Cobham, right at Downside signpost into Downside Bridge Road; Plough Lane; KT11 3LT

Great atmosphere in 16th-c pub of considerable character, with a slight french slant to its food side

Very popular, this thriving pub has a buoyant and cheerful local atmosphere in its attractive low-beamed bar. Round to the right, a cosy parquet-floored snug has cushioned seats built into nice stripped pine panelling, and horse-racing prints. The main part is carpeted, with a mix of pubby furnishings, and past some standing timbers there are a few softly padded banquettes around good-sized tables by a log fire in the ancient stone fireplace. They have Courage Best, Fullers London Pride, Hogs Back TEA and a changing guest beer on handpump, a fine choice of wines by the glass including champagne, and good coffee – served with hot milk. You order the bar food, all made here, from a separate servery. A terrace has picnic-sets sheltering beside a very high garden wall. Service is swift and good-natured, and there are disabled facilities.

Massive ~ Manager Joe Worley ~ Real ale ~ Bar food (12-2.30(3 Sat, 6 Sun), 7-9.30; not Fri, Sat evening) ~ Restaurant ~ (01932) 862514 ~ Children welcome ~ Dogs allowed in bar ~ Occasional live music ~ Open 11-11; 12-10.30 Sun

COLDHARBOUR

Plough

Village signposted in the network of small roads around Leith Hill; RH5 6HD

Good walkers' drinks stop with own-brew beers

A useful place to know about if you're walking or cycling in some of the best scenery in the Surrey hills – around Leith Hill or Friday Street for instance – this pub has its own brewery (Leith Hill) which produces the excellent Crooked Furrow, Hoppily Ever After and Tallywhacker which are served here on handpump, alongside a couple of guests such as Ringwood Best and Timothy Taylors Landlord; also Biddenden farm cider and several wines by the glass; note that they may charge for tap water, a policy on which we're not at all keen. As we went to press, the brewery was temporarily closed due to illness, but we understand it will reopen soon. Two bars (each with a lovely open fire) have stripped light beams and timbering in warm-coloured dark ochre walls, with quite unusual little chairs around the tables in the snug red-carpeted games room on the left (with darts, board games and cards), and little decorative plates on the walls; the one on the right leads through to the candlelit restaurant; at busy times it may be hard to find somewhere to sit if you're not dining; piped music, TV. Straightforward bar food includes soup and pies. The front and the terraced back gardens have picnic-sets and tubs.

Own brew ~ Licensees Richard and Anna Abrehart ~ Real ale ~ Bar food (12-2.30(3 Sat, Sun), 6-9.30(9 Sun)) ~ Restaurant ~ (01306) 711793 ~ Children welcome if dining; not in accommodation ~ Dogs welcome ~ Open 11.30-11.30; 12-10.30 Sun ~ Bedrooms: £69.50S/£79.50S(£95B)

EASHING

Stag

Lower Eashing; Eashing signposted off A3 southbound, S of Hurtmore turn-off; or pub signposted off A283 just SE of exit roundabout at N end of A3 Milford bypass; GU7 2QG

Lovely old riverside pub with gentle improvements and attractive garden

---

The Georgian brick façade masks a much older, attractively opened-up interior, including a charming old-fashioned locals' bar on the right with red and black quarry tiles by the counter. A cosy gently lit snug beyond has a low white plank ceiling, a big stag print and stag's head on dark green walls, books on shelves by the log fire, and sturdy cushioned housekeeper's chairs grouped around dark tables on the brick floor. An extensive blue-carpeted area rambles around on the left, with similar comfortable dark furniture, some smaller country prints and decorative plates on red, brown or cream walls, and round towards the back a big woodburning stove in a capacious fireplace under a long mantelbeam; piped music and daily papers. Hogs Back TEA and a couple of guests such as Fullers London Pride and Shepherd Neame Spitfire on handpump, and several wines by the glass. Bar food runs from ploughman's, hot ciabattas and steaks to a seasonally changing blackboard menu. The river room looks out on to mature trees by a millstream, and there are picnic-sets and tables under cocktail parasols set out on a terrace and in a lantern-lit arbour.

Punch ~ Lease Mark Robson ~ Real ale ~ Restaurant ~ (01483) 421568 ~ Dogs allowed in bar ~ Open 12-3, 5-11; 12-11 Sat; 12-10.30 Sun

ESHER

Marneys

Alma Road (one way only), Weston Green; heading N on A309 from A307 roundabout, after Lamb & Star pub turn left into Lime Tree Avenue (signposted to All Saints Parish Church), then left at T junction into Chestnut Avenue; KT10 8JN

Cottagey little pub with nordic influence (particularly in the food they serve), and attractive garden

---

With a pleasant location by a rural-feeling wooded common, this cottagey pub is an unexpected scandinavian enclave, whose norwegian owners put some interesting national dishes on the menu, and the norwegian national anthem and flags feature in the décor. The chatty low-beamed and black and white plank-panelled bar (it's worth arriving early as it does get full) has shelves of hens and ducks and other ornaments, small blue-curtained windows, and perhaps horse racing on the unobtrusive corner TV. On the left, past a little cast-iron woodburning stove, a dining area (somewhat roomier but still small) has big pine tables, pews and pale country kitchen chairs, with attractive goose pictures. Drinks include Courage Best, Fullers London Pride and Wells & Youngs Bombardier on handpump, about 16 wines by the glass, norwegian schnapps and good coffee. Service by friendly staff is quick and efficient; and they have daily papers on sticks. The sensibly small choice of well liked food includes some scandinavian dishes such as frikadellen (danish pork meat cake) and dill-marinated herring fillets topped with onion and apple cream. The pleasantly planted sheltered garden has a decked area, bar, black picnic-sets and tables under green and blue canvas parasols, and occasionally a spanish guitarist playing under the willow tree on summer afternoons to accompany a barbecue, weather allowing; the front terrace has dark blue cast-iron tables and chairs under matching parasols, with some more black tables too, with table lighting and views over the common and duck pond.

Free house ~ Licensee Henrik Platou ~ Real ale ~ Bar food (12-2.15(12.30-3 Sun); not evenings) ~ (020) 8398 4444 ~ Children welcome until 6pm ~ Dogs welcome ~ Open 11-11; 12-10.30 Sun

FOREST GREEN

Parrot

B2127 just W of junction with B2126, SW of Dorking; RH5 5RZ

Beamed pub with produce from the owners' farm on the menu and in attached shop, good range of drinks, and lovely garden

With truly local food and a range of five real ales, this is a well known venue yet retains its character of a village pub, too. As well as a huge inglenook fireplace, it has a fine profusion of heavy beams, timbers and flagstones, with a couple of cosy rambling areas hidden away behind the fireplace. There are some more tables opposite the long brick bar counter, which has a few unusual wooden chairs in front. Ringwood Best and Wells & Youngs Pale Ale are served alongside three guests such Timothy Taylors Landlord, Wells & Youngs Bombardier and Wychwood Hobgoblin on handpump, freshly squeezed orange juice, local farm apple juice and 15 wines by the glass; newspapers. The owners have their own farm not far away at Coldharbour and you can buy their meats, as well as cheese, cured and smoked hams, pies, bread and preserves in their farm shop at the pub. With the pork, beef and lamb on the frequently changing menu coming from their own farm, the food accent here is particularly on meat though there are tempting vegetarian dishes, such as roasted butternut squash stuffed with vegetables and goats cheese, too. Tables outside in front face the village cricket field and there are more among several attractive gardens, one with apple trees and rose beds.

Free house ~ Licensee Charles Gotto ~ Real ale ~ Bar food (12-3(5 Sun), 6-10; not Sun evening) ~ Restaurant ~ (01306) 621339 ~ No children in restaurant after 7pm ~ Dogs allowed in bar ~ Open 11(12 Sun)-11(midnight Sat)

MICKLEHAM
Running Horses
Old London Road (B2209); RH5 6DU

Upmarket pub with elegant restaurant and comfortable bar, sandwiches through to very imaginative dishes

Run with care by attentive staff, this is an accomplished all-rounder, much liked both as a drinking haunt and as a place to eat. It has two calmly relaxing bar rooms, neatly kept and spaciously open plan, with fresh flowers or a fire in an inglenook at one end, lots of race tickets hanging from a beam, some really good racing cartoons, hunting pictures and Hogarth prints, dark carpets, cushioned wall settles and other dining chairs around straightforward pubby tables and bar stools. Adnams, Fullers London Pride, Shepherd Neame Spitfire and Wells & Youngs Bitter are on handpump alongside good wines by the glass, from a serious list; piped music. There is a tempting choice of very good pubby food and you can also eat from the more creative (though not cheap) restaurant menu in the bar. There are picnic-sets on a terrace in front by lovely flowering tubs and hanging baskets, with a peaceful view of the old church with its strange stubby steeple.

Punch ~ Lease Steve and Josie Slayford ~ Real ale ~ Bar food (12-2.30(3 Sat, Sun), 7(6.30 Sun)-9.30) ~ Restaurant ~ (01372) 372279 ~ Children in function room only ~ Dogs allowed in bar ~ Open 11.30-11; 12-10.30 Sun

THURSLEY
Three Horseshoes
Dye House Road, just off A3 SW of Godalming; GU8 6QD

Appealing and civilised cottagey village pub with good bar snacks

An appealing combination of mildly upmarket country local and attractive restaurant, and run by a group of locals who rescued it from closure, this congenial tile-hung village pub is well placed for bracing heathland walks over Thursley Common. The beamed front bar has Fullers London Pride, Hogs Back TEA and a guest such as Surrey Hills Shere Drop on handpump, farm ciders, a winter log fire, and warmly welcoming service; piped music. They try hard with the food here, sourcing locally where they can, and making their own bread, ice-cream and pasta. The attractive two-acre garden has picnic-sets and a big play fort, and there are smarter comfortable chairs around terrace tables; pleasant views over the green. During summer they hold various events such as jazz evenings, barbecues and folk-dancing festivals.

Free house ~ Licensees David Alders and Sandra Proni ~ Real ale ~ Bar food (12.30-2.15, 7-9.15; 12-3 Sun; not Sun evening) ~ Restaurant ~ (01252) 703268 ~ Children welcome ~ Dogs allowed in bar ~ Open 12-3, 5.30-11; 12-11 Sat; 12-10 Sun

DOG FRIENDLY HOTELS AND B&Bs

BAGSHOT
Pennyhill Park

College Ride, Bagshot, Surrey GU19 5ET (2.3 miles off M3 junction 3; A322, left on to A30 then right into Church Road and College Ride) (01276) 471774

£305; 123 individually designed luxury rms and suites. Impressive Victorian country house in 123 acres of well kept gardens and parkland including a nine-hole golf course, tennis courts, outdoor heated swimming pool, clay pigeon shooting, archery, fishing, and an international rugby pitch; friendly courteous staff, wood-panelled bar, comfortable two-level lounge and reading room, very good imaginative food in Latymer and Brasserie restaurants, terraces overlooking golf course, and spa with gym and indoor pool; disabled access; dogs in bedrooms and some other areas; £50

CHOBHAM
Pembroke House

Valley End Road, Chobham, Surrey GU24 8TB (01276) 857654

£110; 7 rms. Lovely house surrounded by rolling fields with warm welcome from owners, rather fine entrance hall, comfortable public rooms, and good breakfasts in dining room with spreading views; three resident jack russell bitches; tennis court; walks on nearby common; children over 5; dogs welcome by arrangement

HASLEMERE
Lythe Hill Hotel & Spa

Petworth Road, Haslemere, Surrey GU27 3BQ (01428) 651251

£205; 41 individually styled rms, a few in original house. Lovely partly 15th-c building in 30 acres of parkland and bluebell woods (adjoining NT hillside) with floodlit tennis court, croquet lawn, and jogging track; plush, comfortable and elegant lounges, relaxed bar, interesting and enjoyable food in oak panelled dining room or garden room, and good attentive service; spa with swimming pool, sauna, steam and beauty rooms and gym; disabled access; dogs in some bedrooms

HORLEY
Lawn Guest House

30 Massetts Road, Horley, Surrey RH6 7DF (01293) 775751

£65; 12 attractive rms. Handsome Victorian house (very handy for Gatwick Airport) with friendly, relaxed atmosphere, helpful owners, and good breakfasts in attractive dining room; no evening meals but plenty of places nearby; dogs can walk in back garden and in nearby playing fields; dogs welcome in bedrooms

DOG FRIENDLY PUBS

CHILGROVE

Royal Oak

Off B2141 Petersfield—Chichester, signed Hooksway down steep single track; PO18 9JZ

Unchanging and peaceful country pub with welcoming landlord, decent pubby food and big pretty garden

In fine walking and riding country and close to the South Downs Way, this is an unchanging and bustling pub with friendly, long-serving licensees. It's simply furnished with plain country-kitchen tables and chairs and there are huge log fires in the two cosy rooms of the partly brick-floored beamed bar. There's also a plainer family room. Gribble Best, Hammerpot Madgwick Gold, and Hogs Back HBB and OTT on handpump; piped music, cribbage and shut-the-box. The traditional bar menu is sensibly priced. There are plenty of picnic-sets under parasols on the grass of the big, pretty garden.

Free house ~ Licensee Dave Jeffery ~ Real ale ~ Bar food (not Sun evening or Mon) ~ Restaurant ~ (01243) 535257 ~ Children in family room until 8pm ~ Dogs allowed in bar ~ Live music second Fri evening of the month ~ Open 11.30-2.30, 6-11; 12-3 Sun; closed Sun evening and all day Mon

COOLHAM

George & Dragon

Dragons Green, Dragons Lane; pub signed just off A272, about 1½ miles E of village; RH13 8GE

Pleasant little country cottage with beamed bars, and decent food and drink

The cosy bar at this tile-hung cottage has heavily timbered walls, a partly wood-block and partly polished-tile floor, unusually low and massive black beams (see if you can decide whether the date cut into one is 1677 or 1577), simple chairs and rustic stools, some brass, and a big inglenook with an early 17th-c grate. There's also a smaller back bar and restaurant. Badger K&B, Tanglefoot, and a seasonal ale on handpump, and a chatty, relaxed atmosphere. The menu includes traditional dishes such as ploughman's, steak in Guinness pie and spotted dick. The sizeable orchard garden which is neatly kept with pretty flowers and shrubs has quite a few picnic-sets; the little front garden has a poignant 19th-c memorial to the son of a previous innkeeper.

Badger ~ Tenants Peter and Anne Snelling ~ Real ale ~ Bar food ~ Restaurant ~

(01403) 741320 ~ Children welcome ~ Dogs allowed in bar ~ Open 12-3, 6-11;
12-midnight(11 Sun) Sat

DITCHLING
Bull

High Street (B2112); BN6 8TA

**Handsome old building with cosy atmosphere in rambling traditional bars, good
choice of drinks, and quite an emphasis on food; nearby walks**

At weekends particularly, this 16th-c inn is popular with walkers and cyclists
(the South Downs Way is close by) but there are plenty of staff to keep things
running smoothly. The invitingly cosy main bar on the right is quite large,
rambling and pleasantly traditional with well worn old wooden furniture, beams
and floorboards, and a blazing winter fire. To the left, the nicely furnished rooms
have a calm, restrained mellow décor and candles, and beyond that there's a
snug area with chesterfields around a low table; piped music. Harveys Best and
Timothy Taylors Landlord with a couple of changing guests on handpump and a
dozen wines by the glass. Well liked bar food includes plenty of interesting
dishes and they do a Sunday roast. Picnic-sets in the good-sized pretty downland garden which is gently lit at night look up towards Ditchling Beacon and
there are more tables on a suntrap back terrace; good wheelchair access.

Free house ~ Licensee Dominic Worrall ~ Real ale ~ Bar food (12-2.30, 7-9.30;
12-6 Sun) ~ Restaurant ~ (01273) 843147 ~ Children welcome ~ Dogs allowed
in bar ~ Live music monthly Fri ~ Open 11-11; 12-10.30 Sun

EAST ASHLING
Horse & Groom

B2178 NW of Chichester; PO18 9AX

**Busy country pub with real ales in unchanging front drinkers' bar, plenty of
dining space and decent food; bedrooms**

If it's just a drink you're after in this bustling country pub, you'd be best to head
for the front part with its old pale flagstones and woodburning stove in the big
inglenook on the right; the carpeted area is nice too, with its old wireless set,
scrubbed trestle tables, and bar stools lining the counter. Dark Star Hophead,
Harveys Hadlow, Hop Back Summer Lightning, and Wells & Youngs Bitter on
handpump, and several wines by the glass; board games. There's also a small
light flagstoned middle area with a couple of tables. The back part of the pub,
angling right round behind the bar servery, with a further extension beyond one
set of internal windows, has solid pale country-kitchen furniture on neat bare
boards, and a fresh and airy décor, with a little bleached pine panelling and long
white curtains. French windows lead out to a garden with picnic-sets under
umbrellas. Food is tasty and pubby, including sandwiches and home-cooked ham
and eggs. It does get extremely busy on Goodwood race days, and is handy for
Kingly Vale Nature Reserve.

Free house ~ Licensee Michael Martell ~ Real ale ~ Bar food ~ Restaurant ~

(01243) 575339 ~ Children welcome before 9pm ~ Dogs allowed in bar and bedrooms ~ Open 11-3, 6-11; 12-2.30 Sun; closed Sun evening ~ Bedrooms: £45B/£70B

EAST CHILTINGTON

Jolly Sportsman

2 miles N of B2116; Chapel Lane – follow sign to 13th-c church; BN7 3BA

Excellent modern food in civilised, rather smart place, small bar for drinkers, contemporary furnishings, fine wine list and huge range of malt whiskies; nice garden

Professionally run and rather civilised, this is an enjoyable dining pub with a cosy and friendly little bar. There's a roaring winter fire, a mix of furniture on the stripped wood floors, Dark Star Hophead and Whitstable Native tapped from the cask, a remarkably good wine list with nine by the glass, over 100 malt whiskies, and an extensive list of cognacs, armagnacs and grappa. The carefully sourced food, often with unusual ingredients, is very imaginative and deliciously prepared (though not cheap), and they do a two- and three-course set lunch menu. There are rustic tables and benches under gnarled trees in a pretty cottagey front garden with more on the terrace and the front bricked area, and the large back lawn with a children's play area looks out towards the South Downs; good walks nearby.

Free house ~ Licensee Bruce Wass ~ Real ale ~ Bar food (12.30-2.30, 7-9.30 (10 Fri and Sat); 12-3 Sun; not Sun evening) ~ Restaurant ~ (01273) 890400 ~ Children welcome ~ Dogs welcome ~ Open 12-11; 12-11 Sat; 12-4 Sun; 12-3, 6-11 Tues-Sat in winter; closed Sun evening, all day Mon, two days Christmas

EAST LAVANT

Royal Oak

Village signposted off A286 N of Chichester; Pook Lane; PO18 0AX

Bustling and friendly dining pub with proper drinking area, excellent food, extensive wine list and real ales

The licensee at this pretty little white house is keen that it should remain a proper village pub where you can drop in for a drink after a walk, whilst also offering fine food in relaxed surroundings. Cooking is exemplary and the imaginative menu combinations are very tempting. It's all open plan with low beams and exposed brickwork, crooked timbers, winter log fires and church candles. The well used drinking area at the front has wall seats and sofas, Arundel Gold, Badger K&B, Palmers IPA, and Skinners Betty Stogs tapped from the cask, 17 wines by the glass from an extensive list, and a friendly welcome from the attentive staff. The attached seating area is focused on dining and sensitively furnished with brown suede and leather dining chairs around scrubbed pine tables, and pictures of local scenes and of motor sport on the walls. Outside, there are cushioned seats and tables under green parasols on the flagstoned front terrace and far-reaching views to the Downs; rambling around the side and back are terraced, brick and grass areas with more seats and attractive tubs and baskets. The car park is across the road; good walks.

Free house ~ Licensee Charles Ullmann ~ Real ale ~ Bar food (12-2.30, 6-9.30) ~ (01243) 527434 ~ Children welcome ~ Dogs allowed in bar ~ Open 11-11; closed 1 Jan

ELSTED

Three Horseshoes

Village signposted from B2141 Chichester—Petersfield; also reached easily from A272 about 2 miles W of Midhurst, turning left heading W; GU29 0JY

Bustling, friendly and well run country pub, congenial little beamed rooms, enjoyable food, and good drinks; wonderful views from flower-filled garden

The snug little rooms in this much enjoyed 16th-c pub have a cosy, chatty atmosphere and the staff are helpful and friendly. There are ancient beams and flooring, antique furnishings, log fires and candlelight, fresh flowers on the tables, and attractive prints and photographs; it's best to book to be sure of a table. Racked on a stillage behind the bar counter, the real ales include a changing beer from Bowman, Ballards Best, Timothy Taylors Landlord, Youngs Bitter and a guest such as Hop Back Spring Zing or Sharps Doom Bar; summer cider; dominoes. Generous helpings of very good, popular food includes anything from ploughman's to seasonal crab and lobster, with puddings such as panna cotta with blueberries. The flower-filled garden is lovely in summer with plenty of tables and stunning views of the South Downs. Good nearby walks.

Free house ~ Licensee Sue Beavis ~ Real ale ~ Bar food ~ Restaurant ~ (01730) 825746 ~ Well behaved children allowed ~ Dogs allowed in bar ~ Open 11-2.30, 6-11; 12-3, 7-10.30 Sun

FITTLEWORTH

Swan

Lower Street (B2138, off A283 W of Pulborough); RH20 1EL

Pretty tile-hung inn with comfortable beamed bar and plenty of seats in big back garden; bedrooms

This pretty tile-hung inn is a nice place to stay and the bedrooms are newly refurbished. The beamed main bar is comfortable and relaxed with windsor armchairs and bar stools on the part-stripped wood and part-carpeted floor; there are wooden truncheons over the big inglenook fireplace (which has good winter log fires), and Fullers London Pride and Youngs on handpump; piped music. Bar food is well liked and interesting with something for most tastes. There's a big back lawn with plenty of well spaced tables and flowering shrubs and benches in front by the village lane; good nearby walks in beechwoods. They do take your credit card if you are eating in the garden.

Enterprise ~ Lease Paul and Gillian Warriner ~ Real ale ~ Bar food (12-2.30, 6-9.30) ~ Restaurant ~ (01798) 865429 ~ Children allowed until 9pm ~ Dogs allowed in bar ~ Open 11-3, 5-11; 11-4, 7-10.30 Sun

FLETCHING
Griffin

Village signposted off A272 W of Uckfield; TN22 3SS

Busy, gently upmarket inn with a fine wine list, bistro-style bar food, real ales and big garden with far-reaching views

Usually extremely busy, this rather civilised old inn is an integral part of village life but has a good mix of visitors and locals. There are beamed and quaintly panelled bar rooms with blazing log fires, old photographs and hunting prints, straightforward close-set furniture including some captain's chairs, and china on a delft shelf. There's a small bare-boarded serving area off to one side and a snug separate bar with sofas and TV. Harveys Best, Hepworths Iron Horse, and Kings Horsham Best on handpump and a fine wine list with 16 (including champagne and sweet wine) by the glass. Food here, though not cheap, is very good – you can choose from traditional pubby dishes or quite elaborate and interesting combinations. The two acres of garden behind the pub look across fine rolling countryside towards Sheffield Park and there are plenty of seats here and on the sandstone terrace with its woodburning oven. They may ask to keep your credit card while you eat.

Free house ~ Licensees J Pullan, T Erlam, M W Wright ~ Real ale ~ Bar food (12-2.30(3 weekends), 7-9.30(9 Sun)) ~ Restaurant ~ (01825) 722890 ~ Children welcome if supervised ~ Dogs allowed in bar ~ Live jazz Fri evening and Sun lunchtime ~ Open 12-11(midnight Sat); closed 25 Dec and evening 1 Jan

GRAFFHAM
Foresters Arms

Left off A285 to Graffham, left after 1 mile signed Graffham, pub on left after 1 mile; GU28 0QA

Neat 16th-c inn run by enthusiastic young couple with local beers, a fine choice of wines by the glass and good quality food from a short, seasonal menu

In good walking country, this neat and friendly 16th-c pub is run by enthusiastic young owners. There are three connected rooms with heavy beams and joists, a few large contemporary hunting photographs and sizeable mirrors on the cream walls, quiet piped jazz and church candles and fresh flowers. The main bar area has a big log fire in the huge brick fireplace, pews with cushions and pale windsor chairs around light modern tables on the dark wooden floor, a fine old butcher's block, Horsham beers and lots of good quality wines by the glass. A brick pillar with an open fireplace separates this room with an end brick-walled one furnished with chapel chairs and a nice mix of tables. To the left of the bar is a room with more wheelbacks and one long pew beside a similarly long table on the sisal flooring, what was a fireplace now filled with neatly stacked logs and a couple of large flagons on the broad windowsill. Naming their suppliers and using much local produce (the lamb is superb), the very good food is listed on a sensibly short not over-elaborate seasonally changing menu. There are some picnic-sets out at the back.

Free house ~ Licensees Robert and Clare Pearce ~ Real ale ~ Bar food (12-3,

6-9; 12-5 Sun) ~ Restaurant ~ (01798) 867202 ~ Children lunchtimes only ~
Dogs allowed in bar ~ Open 12-11; closed from 5pm Sun and all day Mon

ICKLESHAM

Queens Head

Just off A259 Rye—Hastings; TN36 4BL

Friendly, well run country pub, extremely popular with locals and visitors, with a good range of beers, proper home cooking and seats in garden with fine views

Much enjoyed by our readers, this is a particularly well run pub where the long-serving landlord and his friendly staff are certain to make you welcome. The open-plan areas work round a very big serving counter which stands under a vaulted beamed roof, the high beamed walls and ceiling of the easy-going bar are lined with shelves of bottles and covered with farming implements and animal traps, and there are well used pub tables and old pews on the brown patterned carpet. Other areas have big inglenook fireplaces, and the back room has some old bikes hanging from the ceiling and is decorated with old bicycle and motor-bike prints. Greene King IPA and Abbot, Harveys Best, Kings Red River, Ringwood Fortyniner, and Whitstable India Pale Ale on handpump, ciders and perries, and a dozen wines by the glass. The popular, reasonably priced pubby bar food is home cooked using local produce. Piped jazz or blues, board games, and darts. Picnic-sets look out over the vast, gently sloping plain of the Brede Valley from the little garden, there's a children's play area, and boules. Good local walks.

Free house ~ Licensee Ian Mitchell ~ Real ale ~ Bar food (12-2.30, 6-9.30; all day weekends) ~ (01424) 814552 ~ Well behaved children in eating area of bar until 8.30pm ~ Dogs allowed in bar ~ Live music Sun 4-6pm ~ Open 11-11; 12-10.30 Sun; closed evenings 25 and 26 Dec

PETWORTH

Welldiggers Arms

Low Heath; A283 towards Pulborough; GU28 0HG

Country pub with long-serving landlord, unassuming bar rooms and home-cooked bar food

Run by a long-serving, friendly landlord, this is a popular country pub liked by both locals and visitors. The smallish L-shaped bar has an unassuming style and appearance, low beams, a few pictures (Churchill and gun dogs are prominent) on shiny ochre walls above a panelled dado, a couple of very long rustic settles with tables to match, and some other stripped tables (many are laid for eating); a second rather lower side room has a somewhat lighter décor. No music or machines. Wells & Youngs on handpump, and decent wines by the glass. Food is tasty and served in generous helpings. Outside, screened from the road by a thick high hedge, are plenty of tables and chairs on pleasant lawns and a terrace, with nice country views.

Free house ~ Licensee Ted Whitcomb ~ Real ale ~ Bar food (12-2(3 Sun), 6.30-9 but also see opening hours) ~ Restaurant ~ (01798) 342287 ~ Children in saloon bar only ~ Dogs welcome ~ Open 11-3.30, 6-11.30; 12-4 Sun; closed Mon; closed Tues, Weds and Sun evenings

RYE

Ypres Castle

Gun Garden; steps up from A259, or down past Ypres Tower; TN31 7HH

Traditional pub with views of Ypres Castle, enjoyable bar food, lots of fish, several real ales, and friendly service; seats in sheltered garden

This is a traditional and nicely placed pub with views of Ypres Castle and the River Rother. It's furnished with a mix of old tables and chairs, and somehow, the informal almost scruffy feel adds to its character; there are comfortable seats by the winter log fire and local artwork. Adnams Broadside, Harveys Best, local Pevensey Bay White Gold, and Timothy Taylors Landlord on handpump, and friendly, helpful service. Good bar food includes lots of fish (they even have a scallop festival), traditional pub dishes, romney marsh lamb and some imaginative specials. There's a sheltered little garden.

Free house ~ Licensee Ian Fenn ~ Real ale ~ Bar food (11-3, 6-9(8 Fri); 11-9 Sat; 12-4 Sun) ~ Restaurant ~ (01797) 223248 ~ Children welcome in back bar ~ Dogs allowed in bar ~ Live music Fri evening ~ Open 11-midnight; 11-9 Sun; closed Sun evening

SALEHURST

Salehurst Halt

Village signposted from Robertsbridge bypass on A21 Tunbridge Wells—Battle; Church Lane; TN32 5PH

Pleasant little local in quiet hamlet, chatty atmosphere, and real ales; nice little back garden

To find this chatty and relaxed little local, just head for the church. It's at its busiest in the evening when there's quite a mix of customers of all ages. To the right of the door there's a small area with a big squishy black sofa, a sizeable cushioned wooden settle and just one small table on the stone floor, a TV and an open fire. To the left there's a nice long scrubbed pine table with a sofa and cushions, a mix of more ordinary pubby tables and wheelback and mates' chairs on the wood-strip floor, and maybe piped folk music; board games. Harveys Best and Dark Star Hophead on handpump and decent wines by the glass. Bar food – which can be limited at times – usually includes filled baguettes, greek salad, a large, popular fishcake, proper burgers, local cod in beer batter and ham and eggs. There's a back terrace with metal chairs and tiled tables with more seats in the little landscaped garden.

Free house ~ Licensee Andrew Augarde ~ Real ale ~ Bar food (12-3, 7-9; not Mon, not Tues evening) ~ (01580) 880620 ~ Children welcome ~ Dogs welcome ~ Live music second Sun of month 4-7pm ~ Open 12-3, 6-11; 12-11(10 Sun) Sat; closed Mon

TROTTON

Keepers Arms

A272 Midhurst—Petersfield; pub tucked up above road, on S side; GU31 5ER

Low ceilings, comfortable furnishings on polished wooden boards, open fires, real ales, contemporary food, and seats on sunny terrace

Originally a smithy, this is now an interestingly furnished pub with good modern bar food and pleasant sitting areas for those who just want a drink. The beamed L-shaped bar has timbered walls and some standing timbers, comfortable sofas and wing-backed old leather armchairs around the big log fire, and simple rustic tables on the oak flooring. Elsewhere, there are a couple of unusual adult high chairs at an oak refectory table, two huge Georgian leather high-backed chairs around another table and, in the dining room, elegant oak tables, comfortable dining chairs and a woodburning stove; there's another cosy little dining room with bench seating around all four walls and a large central table. Ballards Best, Dark Star Hophead, and Ringwood Best on handpump, and several wines from a comprehensive list. Food here is very good, using locally sourced ingredients where possible. It includes beautifully prepared traditional dishes and some very contemporary choices; Sunday roast. There are tables and seats on the south-facing terrace.

Free house ~ Licensee Nick Troth ~ Real ale ~ Bar food ~ Restaurant ~ (01730) 813724 ~ Children welcome ~ Dogs allowed in bar ~ Open 12-3.30, 6-11; 12-3.30, 7-10.30 Sun

WILMINGTON

Giants Rest

Just off A27; BN26 5SQ

Busy country pub with friendly welcome from cheerful landlord, informal atmosphere, popular bar food, and real ales.

In a peaceful village, this inviting pub has now been run by the same friendly family for ten years. It's a popular place and the long wood-floored bar and adjacent open areas have simple chairs and tables, wooden table games, Beryl Cook prints, candles on tables, an open fire and a nice informal atmosphere. Food here is reasonably priced and pubby, and as it's very popular you must book to be sure of a table, especially on Sunday lunchtimes. Harveys Best, Hop Back Summer Lightning and Timothy Taylors Landlord on handpump; piped music, and puzzles and games on the tables. Plenty of seats in the front garden. Elizabeth David the famous cookery writer is buried in the churchyard at nearby Folkington; her headstone is beautifully carved and features mediterranean vegetables and a casserole. Plenty of walks nearby on the South Downs, and the majestic chalk-carved figure of the Long Man of Wilmington is nearby.

Free house ~ Licensees Adrian and Rebecca Hillman ~ Real ale ~ Bar food (all day Sun and bank hol Mon) ~ (01323) 870207 ~ Children welcome if well behaved ~ Dogs allowed in bar ~ Open 11-3, 6-11; 11-11 Sat; 12-10.30 Sun

WINEHAM

Royal Oak

Village signposted from A272 and B2116; BN5 9AY

Splendidly old-fashioned local with interesting bric-a-brac in simple rooms, real ales and well liked food

Logs burn in an enormous inglenook fireplace with a cast-iron Royal Oak fire-back at this old-fashioned local. There's a collection of cigarette boxes, a stuffed stoat and crocodile, some jugs and ancient corkscrews on the very low beams above the serving counter, and other bits of bric-a-brac; Harveys Best and maybe a guest beer tapped from the cask in a still room, and 14 wines by the glass. There are quiet countryside views from the back parlour and some picnic-sets outside. The bearded collie is called Bella. Using local, seasonal produce, bar food is pubby, including a ploughman's that is attractively set out on big boards; popular Sunday roasts.

Punch ~ Tenants Sharon and Michael Bailey ~ Real ale ~ Bar food (12-2.30(3 Sun), 7-9.30; no food Sun evening) ~ (01444) 881252 ~ Children welcome ~ Dogs welcome ~ Open 11-2.30 (3.30 Sat), 5.30(6 Sat)-11; 12-5, 7-10.30 Sun

DOG FRIENDLY HOTELS, INNS, B&Bs AND FARMS

ALFRISTON

George

High Street, Alfriston, Polegate, East Sussex BN26 5SY (01323) 870319

£110; 7 fine rms. 14th-c timbered inn opposite intriguing Red Lion façade, with massive low beams hung with hops, appropriately soft lighting, log fire (or summer flower arrangement) in huge stone inglenook, lots of copper and brass, plenty of sturdy stripped tables, and thriving atmosphere; popular home-made food in cosy candlelit restaurant, nice breakfasts, well kept real ales, and jovial landlord; seats out in the charming flint-walled garden behind; dogs in bedrooms and bar

BATTLE

Little Hemingfold Hotel

189 Hastings Road, Battle, East Sussex TN33 0TT (2.2 miles off A21 just N of Hastings, via A2100) (01424) 774338

£98; 12 rms, 6 on ground floor in adjoining Coach House. Partly 17th-c, partly early Victorian farmhouse in 43 acres of woodland, with trout lake, tennis, gardens, and lots of walks; comfortable sitting rooms, open fires, restful atmosphere and very good food using home-grown produce in candlelit restaurant; resident labrador and cat; cl 20 Dec-1 Mar; children over 7; dogs in bedrooms only

Powder Mills

Powdermill Lane, Battle, East Sussex TN33 0SP (01424) 775511

£140; 42 rms, some in annexe. Attractive 18th-c creeper-clad manor house in 150 acres of park and woodland with four lakes and outdoor swimming pool, and next to the 1066 battlefield; country-house atmosphere, log fires and antiques in elegant day rooms, attentive service, and good modern cooking in Orangery restaurant; three resident springer spaniels; disabled access; dogs welcome away from restaurant; £10

BRIGHTON

Grand

97-99 Kings Road, Brighton, East Sussex BN1 2FW (01273) 224300

£180; 201 handsome rms, many with sea views. Famous Victorian hotel with marble columns and floors and fine moulded plasterwork in the luxurious and elegant day rooms; good service, very good food and fine wines, popular afternoon tea in sunny conservatory, bustling nightclub, and health spa with indoor swimming pool; walks for dogs on the beach (not during the summer); partial disabled access; dogs in bedrooms; £20

Granville

124 Kings Road, Brighton, East Sussex BN1 2FA (01273) 326302

£88; 24 individually decorated themed rms. Seafront boutique hotel with attentive, friendly service, traditional breakfasts and international dishes in stylish restaurant and sleek bar on lower ground floor, and seats and tables on summer terrace; resident jack russell and westie; walks in nearby parks and on South Downs; disabled access; dogs welcome in bedrooms

CHARLTON

Woodstock House

Charlton, Chichester, East Sussex PO18 0HU (01243) 811666

£118; 13 rms. 18th-c country house close to Goodwood, with suntrap inner courtyard garden, friendly, relaxed atmosphere, log fire in homely sitting room, and cocktail bar; nearby inns and restaurants for evening meals; lots to see nearby and plenty of downland walks; partial disabled access; dogs in ground floor bedrooms; £5

CHICHESTER

Spire Cottage

Church Lane, Hunston, Chichester, West Sussex PO20 1AJ (01243) 778937

£80; 4 pretty rms, one in annexe with private entrance and garden. Country cottage built built from the old spire of the Cathedral with relaxed and friendly atmosphere, comfortable lounge, and good breakfasts with home-made preserves and home squeezed juice in dining room with winter log fire; may cl Christmas week; dogs in garden bedroom; £5

Suffolk House

East Row, Chichester, West Sussex PO19 1PD (01243) 778899

£95; 11 rms, some overlooking garden. Friendly Georgian house in centre and close to cathedral, with homely comfortable lounge bar, traditional cooking in restaurant, good breakfasts, and small walled garden; park nearby for walks; disabled access; dogs in bedrooms but must not be unattended

West Stoke House

West Stoke, Chichester, West Sussex PO18 9BN (01243) 575226

£130; 8 charming rms with countryside views. Fine Georgian restaurant-with-rooms in five acres of grounds on edge of Downs; friendly, relaxed atmosphere, large reception lounge with interesting furnishings, antiques and plenty of art, and excellent modern cooking and delicious breakfasts in blue-walled intimate restaurant (and they provide picnics for race days at Goodwood); resident dog; a few minutes' walk from Kingly Vale Nature Reserve and nearby beaches; dogs in bedrooms (must be clean and dry)

CLIMPING

Bailiffscourt

Climping Street, Climping, Littlehampton, East Sussex BN17 5RW (01903) 723511

£210; 39 rms, many with four-poster beds, winter log fires and super views. Mock 13th-c manor built only 70 years ago but with tremendous character – fine old iron-studded doors, huge fireplaces, heavy beams and so forth – in 30 acres of coastal pastures and walled gardens: open fires, antiques, tapestries and fresh flowers, elegant furnishings, enjoyable modern english and french food, fine wines, relaxed atmosphere, and spa with indoor swimming pool, outdoor swimming pool, tennis and croquet; walks maps available; close to beach; disabled access; dogs in bedrooms and lounges; bowl, biscuits, mat; £12.50

CUCKFIELD

Ockenden Manor

Ockenden Lane, Cuckfield, Haywards Heath, West Sussex RH17 5LD (0.6 miles off A272, from W roundabout via B2036) (01444) 416111

£175; 22 individually decorated, pretty rms. Dating from 1520, this carefully extended manor house has antiques, fresh flowers and open fire in comfortable sitting room, good modern cooking in fine panelled restaurant, cosy bar, and super views of the South Downs from the neatly kept garden (in nine acres); dogs in four ground floor bedrooms; £10

EASTBOURNE

Grand

King Edward's Parade, Eastbourne, East Sussex BN21 4EQ (01323) 412345

£190; 152 individually designed rms, many with sea views. Gracious and very well run Victorian hotel, with spacious, comfortable lounges, lots of fine original features, lovely flower arrangements, imaginative food in elegant restaurants, and courteous helpful service; leisure club and outdoor pool and terraces; disabled access; dogs in bedrooms; £7

FAIRLIGHT

Fairlight Cottage

Warren Road, Fairlight, Hastings, East Sussex TN35 4AG (1.9 miles off A259 via Fairlight Road; in village, second right and on into Warren Road) (01424) 812545

£70; 3 rms, one with four-poster. Comfortable and very friendly house in fine countryside with views over Rye Bay and walks in 660 acres of outstanding natural beauty; big comfortable lounge (nice views), good breakfasts in elegant dining room or on balcony; three elderly resident dogs; children over 10 and must be well behaved; dogs in bedrooms

HASTINGS

Beauport Park

Hastings Road, St Leonards-on-Sea, East Sussex TN38 8EA (1 mile off A21 just N of Hastings; A2100 towards Battle) (01424) 851222

£130; 26 attractive rms. Georgian house in 38 acres of gardens and woodland with tennis, nine-hole pitch and putt, and riding (next door); relaxed, friendly atmosphere in the Georgian-style lounge, interesting modern cooking in smart restaurant and less formal conservatory, live pianist Sat evenings, and cosy bar overlooking terrace and gardens; health club with indoor swimming pool; dogs in bedrooms and bar

LEWES

Shelleys

High Street, Lewes, East Sussex BN7 1XS (1.3 miles off A27 W roundabout; the A277 takes you straight to it, on the High Street) (01273) 472361

£195; 19 pretty rms. Once owned by relatives of the poet, this stylish and spacious 17th-c town house is warm and friendly, with good food, nice breakfasts and bar lunches in elegant dining room, and seats in the quiet back garden; dogs in bedrooms if small and well behaved

MIDHURST

Spread Eagle

South Street, Midhurst, West Sussex GU29 9NH (01730) 816911

£170; 39 individually decorated panelled rms, 4 in annexe. Historic 15th-c coaching inn with log fires in inglenook fireplaces, stained glass windows, beams and sloping floors, and very good modern food in candlelit restaurant or summer conservatory; picturesque grounds, indoor swimming pool, spa, gym and beauty centre; dogs in some bedrooms; bed, bowl and food; £15

NEWICK

Newick Park Hotel

Newick, Brighton, East Sussex BN8 4SB (01825) 723633

£165; 16 individually decorated, spacious rms inc 3 suites in converted granary. Charming and carefully restored Georgian building in 250 estate of open country and woodland; organic walled kitchen garden, two lakes with fishing, pretty views, tennis, badminton, croquet, outdoor swimming pool, quad bikes, and tank driving; comfortable and spacious public rooms (log fires, books, antiques, and comfy sofas) include study, sitting room, bar/morning room, and elegant restaurant with enjoyable dinner-party food using home-grown produce and local game, and good breakfasts; resident black labrador; no children under 3 in evening restaurant; disabled access; dogs in some bedrooms; £5

PEASMARSH

Flackley Ash

London Road, Peasmarsh, Rye, East Sussex TN31 6YH (01797) 230651

£152; 45 beautifully furnished rms. Elegant red-brick Georgian house in five acres of neat gardens, with relaxed and informal atmosphere in comfortable lounge and bar areas, good breakfasts in charming dining room with inglenook fireplace and conservatory extension, and indoor swimming pool, sauna, gym, and beauty suite; croquet and putting green; walks nearby in grounds and surrounding fields; dogs in bedrooms; £8.50

RUSHLAKE GREEN

Stone House

Rushlake Green, Heathfield, East Sussex TN21 9QJ (01435) 830553

£135; 6 rms, some with four-posters. Lovely house built at end of 15th c and extended in Georgian times and set in a thousand acres of pretty countryside (with plenty of walks and country sports) and surrounded by an 18th-c walled garden; open log fires, antiques and family heirlooms in drawing room, quiet library, antique full-sized table in mahogany-panelled billiard room, dinner party-style food in panelled dining room, fine breakfasts, and cosseting atmosphere; cl Christmas/New Year; children over 9; dogs welcome in bedrooms

RYE

Jeakes House

Mermaid Street, Rye, East Sussex TN31 7ET (01797) 222828

£100; 11 lovely rms (4 with four-posters) overlooking rooftops of this medieval town or across the marsh to sea. Fine 16th-c building, well run and friendly, with good breakfasts in dining room (plenty of nearby places for evening meals), book-lined bar with honesty bar, relaxing and comfortable oak-beamed parlour, warm fire, and lovely peaceful atmosphere; two tonkinese cats; fields, beach, and marsh for walking nearby; children over 8; dogs welcome away from dining room; £5

Rye Lodge

Hilder's Cliff, Rye, East Sussex TN31 7LD (01797) 223838

£120; 18 airy, neat rms. Family run hotel close to town and with fine views across the estuary and Romney Marsh; caring, friendly service, comfortable and convivial lounge bar, enjoyable food in smart, marble-floored, candlelit restaurant, and seats under umbrellas on terrace; leisure centre with indoor swimming pool; dogs welcome away from restaurant; £8

SEAFORD

Silverdale

21 Sutton Park Road, Seaford, East Sussex BN25 1RH (01323) 491849

£60; 7 individually decorated rms with books, videos and good quality cosmetics. Extremely friendly B&B carefully run by owners who really care about their guests and their dogs; good home cooking in dining room, generous breakfasts, small bar and little shop; two resident american cocker spaniels; limited disabled access; dogs very welcome; treats, bowls, towels

SHIPLEY

Goffsland Farm

Shipley Road, Southwater, Horsham, West Sussex RH13 7BQ (1.3 miles off A24, from roundabout at S end of Southwater bypass; Mill Straight towards Southwater, then second left on to Shipley Road; handy for A272 too) (01403) 730434

£54; 2 rms inc 1 family rm. 17th-c Wealden farmhouse on 260-acre family farm with good breakfasts in lounge/dining room (evening meals by arrangement), and friendly welcome; several resident dogs and cats; plenty of surrounding walks; dogs in bedrooms

Warwickshire

MAP 4

DOG FRIENDLY PUBS

ASTON CANTLOW

Kings Head

Village signposted just off A3400 NW of Stratford; B95 6HY

Gently civilised Tudor pub with nice old interior, imaginative (if not cheap) food, and pleasant garden

The beautifully kept bar on the right of this creeper-swathed pub is charmingly old, with flagstones, low beams, and old-fashioned settles around its massive inglenook log fireplace. The chatty quarry-tiled main room has attractive window seats and big country oak tables – it's all the perfect setting for a civilised meal out. A good range of drinks includes Greene King Abbot, M&B Brew XI and a guest such as Purity Pure Gold on handpump, with ten wines by the glass from a very decent list; piped jazz. They offer several menus here, with dishes that range from sausage and mash to more imaginative dishes such as pumpkin ravioli with wild mushroom, sage, walnuts and blue cheese. A big chestnut tree graces the lovely garden, and the pub looks really pretty in summer with its colourful hanging baskets and wisteria. It's in the middle of a very pretty village, and Shakespeare's parents are said to have married in the church next door.

Enterprise ~ Lease Peter and Louise Sadler ~ Real ale ~ Bar food (12-2.30, 6.30-9.30; 12.30-3 Sun, not Sun evening) ~ Restaurant ~ (01789) 488242 ~ Children welcome ~ Dogs allowed in bar ~ Open 12-3, 5.30-11; 12-11 Sat; 12-8.30 Sun

GAYDON

Malt Shovel

M40 junction 12; Church Road; CV35 0ET

In quiet village just off M40; nice mix of pubby bar, tasty food and five real ales

The slightly unusual layout of this bustling pub sees a sort of pathway in mahogany-varnished boards running through bright carpeting to link the entrance, the bar counter on the right and the blazing log fire on the left. The central area has a high pitched ceiling, milk churns and earthenware containers in a loft above the bar. A few stools are lined up along the counter where they serve five changing real ales which might include Adnams Best, Bass, Fullers London Pride, Everards Tiger and Wadworths 6X, and most of their dozen or so wines are available by the glass. Three steps take you up to a snug little space with some comfortable sofas overlooked by a big stained-glass window and reproductions of classic posters. Cooked by the chef-landlord, food is enjoyable and pubby, with some imaginative specials. Service is friendly and efficient (though they may try to keep your credit card while you eat); piped music, darts, and games machine. The springer spaniel is called Rosie, and the jack russell is Mollie.

Enterprise ~ Lease Richard and Debi Morisot ~ Real ale ~ Bar food (12-2, 6.30-9) ~ Restaurant ~ (01926) 641221 ~ Children welcome ~ Dogs welcome ~ Open 11-3, 5-11; 11-11 Fri, Sat; 12-10.30 Sun

GREAT WOLFORD

Fox & Hounds

Village signposted on right on A3400 3 miles S of Shipston-on-Stour; CV36 5NQ

Thoughtfully prepared food at cosy old country inn

It's nice to find such good food in an atmosphere as unspoilt and pubby as this. The chef here is careful about sourcing ingredients, and cooks from fresh virtually everything (including the breads) that appear on the fairly elaborate bar and restaurant menus. The unpretentious aged bar at this handsome 16th-c stone inn has hops strung from its low beams, an appealing collection of chairs and old candlelit tables on spotless flagstones, antique hunting prints, and a roaring log fire in the inglenook fireplace with its fine old bread oven. An old-fashioned little tap room serves Hook Norton Hooky, Purity Pure UBU and a guest such as Bass on handpump and around 60 malt whiskies; piped music. A terrace has solid wood furniture and a well.

Free house ~ Licensee Gillian Tarbox ~ Real ale ~ Bar food (not Sun evening) ~ (01608) 674220 ~ Children welcome ~ Dogs welcome ~ Open 12-2.30(3 Sat), 6-11.30; 12-3, 7-11 Sun; closed Mon ~ Bedrooms: £50B/£80B

PRESTON BAGOT

Crabmill

A4189 Henley-in-Arden—Warwick; B95 5EE

Contemporary mill conversion with comfortable modern décor, relaxed atmosphere, and smart bar food

They've used strikingly unusual but pleasing colours in the stylish transformation of this rambling old cider mill. The smart two-level lounge area has soft leather settees and easy chairs, low tables, big table lamps and one or two rugs on bare boards, the elegant and roomy low-beamed dining area has candles and fresh flowers, and a beamed and flagstoned bar area has some stripped pine country tables and chairs, snug corners and a gleaming metal bar serving Greene King Abbot, Purity Pure Ubu and a guest such as Tetleys on handpump, with eight wines by the glass from a mostly new world list. The imaginative menu (with something to suit all tastes and pockets) makes tempting reading and food lives up to expectations. Piped music is well chosen and well reproduced. There are lots of tables (some of them under cover) out in a large attractive decked garden. Booking is advised, especially Sunday lunchtime when it's popular with families.

Enterprise ~ Lease Sally Coll ~ Real ale ~ Bar food (12-2.30(3.30 Sun), 6.30-9.30) ~ Restaurant ~ (01926) 843342 ~ Children welcome ~ Dogs allowed in bar ~ Open 11-11; 12-6 Sun; closed Sun evening

SHUSTOKE

Griffin

5 miles from M6 junction 4; A446 towards Tamworth, then right on to B4114 and go straight through Coleshill; pub is at Church End, a mile E of village; B46 2LB

Ten real ales and simple good value lunchtime snacks at unpretentious country local; garden and play area

Usually busy with a cheery crowd, the low-beamed L-shaped bar at this friendly place has log fires in two stone fireplaces (one's a big inglenook), fairly simple décor from cushioned café seats (some quite closely spaced) and sturdily elm-topped sewing trestles, to one nice old-fashioned settle, lots of old jugs on the beams, beer mats on the ceiling and a games machine. The smashing choice of real ales here is well kept on handpump and dispensed (by the chatty landlord) from a servery under a very low heavy beam. Beers come from an enterprising range of brewers such as Holdens, Hook Norton, Jennings, Marstons, Moorhouses, RCH and Thornbridge; also lots of english wines, farm cider, and mulled wine in winter. Straightforward but tasty bar food includes sandwiches, ploughman's, steak and ale pie and sirloin steak. Outside, old-fashioned seats and tables can be found on the back grass, and there's a play area and a large terrace with plants in raised beds.

Free house ~ Licensee Michael Pugh ~ Real ale ~ Bar food (12-2; not Sun or evenings) ~ No credit cards ~ (01675) 481205 ~ Children in conservatory ~ Dogs welcome ~ Open 12-2.30, 7-11; 12-3, 7-10.30 Sun

DOG FRIENDLY HOTELS, INNS, B&Bs AND FARMS

BUBBENHALL

Bubbenhall House

Paget's Lane, Bubbenhall, Coventry, Warwickshire CV8 3BJ (02476) 302409

£70; 3 rms. Mainly Edwardian house in five acres of mature woodland with marvellous wildlife (including one of only two Dormouse Sanctuaries in the UK); beams, fine Jacobean staircase, TV lounge plus other comfortable rooms, hearty breakfasts in elegant dining room, and friendly, family atmosphere; resident black labrador and jack russell, and one cat; tennis court; dogs in bedrooms only

PILLERTON HERSEY

Dockers Barn Farm

Oxhill Bridle Road, Pillerton Hersey, Warwick, Warwickshire CV35 0QB (01926) 640475

£58; 2 cosy rms, one with own front door. Quietly set and carefully converted 18th-c threshing barn surrounded by fields of sheep and ponies; friendly owners, flagstoned floors, beams, interesting collections, and family portraits, and 21 acres of wildlife-friendly garden and surrounding land; three resident dogs; footpaths for walking; cl Christmas; children over 8; dogs in Granary Suite only

STRATFORD-UPON-AVON

Melita

37 Shipston Road, Stratford-upon-Avon, Warwickshire CV37 7LN (01789) 292432

£75; 12 well equipped rms. Family-run Victorian hotel close to town centre and theatre; comfortable lounge with open fire, extensive breakfasts, and pretty, carefully laid-out garden; cl Christmas; children over 5; disabled access; dogs in bedrooms only; £5

Shakespeare

Chapel Street, Stratford-upon-Avon, Warwickshire CV37 6ER (0870) 400 8182

£180; 74 comfortable, well equipped rms. Smart hotel based on handsome, lavishly modernised Tudor merchants' houses, with comfortable bar, enjoyable modern cooking in smart restaurant with lighter meals in refurbished brasserie, civilised tea or coffee in peaceful chintzy armchairs by blazing log fires, and friendly staff; seats out in back courtyard; three mins' walk from theatre; disabled access; dogs in bedrooms; £10

DOG FRIENDLY PUBS

AXFORD

Red Lion

Off A4 E of Marlborough; on back road Mildenhall—Ramsbury; SN8 2HA

Pretty pub with careful service from friendly staff, locally brewed beers and wide choice of food

Most customers are here to enjoy the popular food in this flint-and-brick pub, though they do keep Cottage Durassic Bark, Ramsbury Axford Ale from the little brewery on the edge of the village, and West Berkshire Good Old Boy on hand-pump, 15 wines by the glass and 20 malt whiskies. The beamed and pine-panelled bar has a big inglenook fireplace, and a pleasant mix of comfortable sofas, cask seats and other solid chairs on the parquet floor; the pictures by local artists are for sale. There are lovely views over a valley from good hard-wood tables and chairs on the terrace outside the restaurant, and you get the same views from picture windows in the restaurant and lounge. Food here takes in a wide range from typically pubby dishes to a more elaborate menu with quite an emphasis on (more pricey) fish dishes. The sheltered garden has picnic-sets under parasols overlooking the river.

Free house ~ Licensee Seamus Lecky ~ Real ale ~ Bar food (not Sun evening or 25 Dec) ~ Restaurant ~ (01672) 520271 ~ Children welcome ~ Dogs allowed in bar ~ Open 12-2.30, 6.30-11; 12-2.30 Sun; closed Sun evening; 25 Dec

BERWICK ST JOHN

Talbot

Village signposted from A30 E of Shaftesbury; SP7 0HA

Unspoilt and friendly pub in attractive village, with simple furnishings and tasty, reasonably priced food

In a pretty village full of thatched old houses, this is an enjoyable pub with friendly locals. The heavily beamed bar has plenty of character and is simply furnished with cushioned solid wall and window seats, spindleback chairs, a high-backed built-in settle at one end, and a huge inglenook fireplace with a good iron fireback and bread ovens. Pubby food is tasty and a couple of inter-esting specials are reasonably priced and they do a Sunday roast. Bass, Ringwood Best, Wadworths 6X and a guest such as Ringwood Fortyniner on handpump; darts and cribbage. There are seats outside.

Free house ~ Licensees Pete and Marilyn Hawkins ~ Real ale ~ Bar food (not

Sun evening) ~ Restaurant ~ (01747) 828222 ~ Children welcome ~ Dogs welcome ~ Open 12-2.30, 6.30-11; 12-4 Sun; closed Sun evening, all day Mon

BREMHILL

Dumb Post

Off A4/A3102 just NW of Calne; Hazeland, just SW of village itself, OS Sheet 173 map reference 976727; SN11 9LJ

Quirky and unspoilt; a proper country local with no frills, but some real character

Not huge, this pub has something of the air of a once-grand but now rather faded hunting lodge. It isn't for those with fussier tastes, but is run by its amiable landlord for people who like their pubs unpretentious and with some genuine character. The main lounge is a glorious mix of mismatched, faded furnishings, vivid patterned wallpaper, and stuffed animal heads, its two big windows boasting an unexpectedly fine view over the surrounding countryside. There are half a dozen or so tables, a big woodburner in a brick fireplace (not always lit), a log fire on the opposite side of the room, comfortably-worn armchairs and plush banquettes, a standard lamp, mugs, bread and a sombrero hanging from the beams, and a scaled-down model house between the windows; in a cage is an occasionally vocal parrot, Oscar. The narrow bar leading to the lounge is more dimly lit, but has a few more tables, exposed stonework, and quite a collection of toby jugs around the counter; there's a plainer third room with pool, darts, and piped music. Archers Best and Wadworths 6X on hand-pump. Bar food (served lunchtimes only) is simple, hearty and well liked by locals; Sunday roasts. There are a couple of picnic-sets outside, and some wooden play equipment. Note the limited lunchtime opening times.

Free house ~ Licensee Mr Pitt ~ Real ale ~ Bar food (lunchtimes only Fri-Sun) ~ No credit cards ~ (01249) 813192 ~ Children in eating area of bar ~ Dogs allowed in bar ~ Open 12-2.30, 7-11(midnight Sat); closed Mon-Thurs lunchtimes

DEVIZES

Bear

Market Place; SN10 1HS

Comfortable coaching inn with plenty of history, beers fresh from the local brewery, pleasant terrace, and unpretentious food

This individual and pleasant old coaching inn has a great deal of character and although it has been carefully upgraded over the years, it dates from 1559 so there are plenty of reminders of the past. The big main carpeted bar has log fires, black winged wall settles and muted cloth-upholstered bucket armchairs around oak tripod tables; the classic bar counter has shiny black woodwork and small panes of glass. Separated from here by some steps, a room named after the portrait painter Thomas Lawrence (his father ran the establishment in the 1770s) has dark oak-panelled walls, a parquet floor, a big open fireplace, shining copper pans, and plates around the walls. Served by friendly staff, the well liked bar food includes a sizeable choice of filled breads, all-day breakfast, pubby lunchtime dishes and a handful of interesting evening specials. Wadworths IPA, 6X and a seasonal guest on handpump, a good choice of wines (including 16 by the glass), and quite a few malt whiskies. A mediterranean-style courtyard with olive trees, hibiscus and bougainvillea has some outside tables. The brewery is just 150 yards away – you can buy beer in splendid old-fashioned half-gallon earthenware jars. They will keep your credit card behind the bar if you wish to run a food tab.

Wadworths ~ Tenants Andrew and Angela Maclachlan ~ Real ale ~ Bar food (11.30-2.30, 7.30-9.45 Mon-Sat; 11.30-2, 7-8.45 Sun) ~ Restaurant ~ (01380) 722444 ~ Children welcome ~ Dogs allowed in bar ~ Live jazz Sat evening in cellar bar ~ Open 9.30am-11pm(10pm Sun)

DONHEAD ST ANDREW
Forester

Village signposted off A30 E of Shaftesbury, just E of Ludwell; Lower Street; SP7 9EE

Attractive old thatched pub in charming village, good food – especially fish – and fine views from very pleasant big terrace

'Everything is just right here' is how one of our readers describes this 14th-c thatched pub – and others agree with him. The appealing bar has a welcoming atmosphere, stripped tables on wooden floors, a log fire in its big inglenook fireplace, and usually a few locals chatting around the servery: Butcombe Bitter, Butts Traditional and Ringwood Best on handpump, and 12 wines (including champagne) by the glass. Off here is an alcove with a sofa and table and magazines to read. The menu is incredibly tempting, with delicious food, fresh fish from Cornwall and Devon, inventive puddings and a good cheese board. Outside, seats on a good-sized terrace have fine country views. Good walks nearby, for example to the old and 'new' Wardour castles. The neighbouring cottage used to be the pub's coach house.

Free house ~ Licensee Chris Matthew ~ Real ale ~ Bar food ~ Restaurant ~ (01747) 828038 ~ Children welcome ~ Dogs allowed in bar ~ Open 12-3, 6.30-11; closed winter Sun evenings

EAST KNOYLE
Fox & Hounds

Village signposted off A350 S of A303; The Green (named on some road atlases), a mile NW at OS Sheet 183 map reference 872313; or follow signpost off B3089, about ½ mile E of A303 junction near Little Chef; SP3 6BN

Beautiful thatched village pub with splendid views, welcoming service, good beers, and popular food

It's well worth the effort negotiating the little lanes to reach this ancient pretty pub, especially on a clear day when you can enjoy the remarkable views right over into Somerset and Dorset from picnic-sets facing the green. Inside, there's the warmly welcoming feel of a proper long-established pub (rather than a more formal pub/restaurant), and service is prompt and cheerful. Around the central horseshoe-shaped servery are three linked areas on different levels, with big log fires, plentiful oak woodwork and flagstones, comfortably padded dining chairs around big scrubbed tables with vases of flowers, and a couple of leather settees; the furnishings are all very individual and uncluttered. Food here is well liked, with something for most tastes on the interesting menu – anything from stone-baked pizzas to venison haunch steak with a port and cranberry sauce. Butcombe Bitter, Hidden Potential, Keystone Large One, Palmers 200, and Youngs Bitter on handpump, 15 wines by the glass and Thatcher's Cheddar Valley cider. Piped music and skittle alley. The nearby woods are good for a stroll.

Free house ~ Licensee Murray Seator ~ Real ale ~ Bar food (12-2.30, 6-9) ~ (01747) 830573 ~ Well-behaved children welcome ~ Dogs welcome ~ Open 11.30-3, 5.30-11 (10.30 Sun); closed 25 Dec

FONTHILL GIFFORD
Beckford Arms

Off B3089 W of Wilton at Fonthill Bishop; SP3 6PX

Civilised 18th-c country inn with smartly informal feel, and good food, especially in the evening

This civilised country house is set on the edge of a fine parkland estate with a lake and sweeping vistas. The big, light and airy rooms are smartly informal with stripped bare wood, a parquet floor and a pleasant mix of chunky tables with church candles. In winter, a big log fire burns in the lounge bar, which leads into a light back garden room with a high pitched plank ceiling and picture windows looking on to a terrace. Locals tend to gather in the straightforward games room: darts, pool, board games, and piped music. Hop Back GFB, Keystone Large One and Wadworths IPA and 6X on handpump and several wines by the glass. The pubby lunchtime menu is expanded in the evening to include quite a few imaginative dishes.

Free house ~ Licensee Feargal Powell ~ Real ale ~ Bar food (12-2, 7-9; 12-6 Sun; not Sun evening) ~ Restaurant ~ (01747) 870385 ~ Well behaved children welcome ~ Dogs welcome ~ Open 12-11(10.30 Sun) ~ Bedrooms: £60S/£90B

GREAT HINTON
Linnet

3.5 miles E of Trowbridge, village signposted off A361 opposite Lamb at Semington; BA14 6BU

Attractive dining pub, very much a place to come for a good meal rather than just a drink

Such is the reputation for the very good food in this pretty brick dining pub that you have to book some time ahead to be sure of a table. Served by efficient staff, dishes are inventive and beautifully prepared. The comfortable bar to the right of the door has Wadworths 6X on electric pump, several wines by the glass and around two dozen malt whiskies; there are bookshelves in a snug end part of the room. The restaurant is candlelit at night; piped music. In summer, the window boxes and flowering tubs with seats dotted among them, are quite a sight.

Wadworths ~ Tenant Jonathan Furby ~ Real ale ~ Bar food (not Mon) ~ Restaurant ~ (01380) 870354 ~ Children welcome ~ Dogs allowed in bar ~ Open 12-3.30, 6-11; 12-4, 7-10 Sun; closed Mon; 25-27 Dec, 1 Jan

GRITTLETON
Neeld Arms

Off A350 NW of Chippenham; The Street; SN14 6AP

Good, chatty atmosphere in bustling village pub with popular food

With friendly, cheerful staff and chatty locals, it's not surprising that our readers enjoy this 17th-c village pub so much. It's largely open plan, with stripped stone and some black beams, a log fire in the big inglenook on the right and a smaller coal-effect fire on the left, flowers on tables, and a pleasant mix of seating from windsor chairs through scatter-cushioned window seats to some nice arts and crafts chairs and a traditional settle. Food is tasty and reasonably priced; Sunday roasts. Wadworths IPA and 6X and guests like Butcombe Bitter and Sharps Cornish Coaster on handpump from the substantial central bar counter, and a good choice of reasonably priced wines by the glass; board games. There's an outdoor terrace, with pergola. The golden retriever is called Soaky.

Free house ~ Licensees Charlie and Boo West ~ Real ale ~ Bar food ~ (01249) 782470 ~ Children welcome ~ Dogs welcome ~ Open 12-3(3.30 Sat), 5.30-midnight; 12-4, 7-11 Sun ~ Bedrooms: £60B/£80B

HORTON
Bridge Inn

Signposted off A361 Beckhampton road just inside the Devizes limit; Horton Road; SN10 2JS

Well run and distinctive canalside pub, with good traditional pub food, and pleasant garden with aviary

This neatly kept canalside pub has an aviary and fantail doves in the safely-fenced garden area where there are also picnic-sets and moorings for boats. Inside, on the red walls above a high panelled dado are black and white photos of bargee families and their barges among other old photographs and country pictures. In the carpeted area on the left, all the sturdy pale pine tables may be set for food, and there's a log fire at the front; to the right of the bar is a pubbier part with similar country-kitchen furniture on reconstituted flagstones and some stripped brickwork. Wadworths IPA and 6X tapped from the cask and several decent wines by the glass. The tasty food is pubby, with a couple of daily specials. Disabled lavatories, piped music, TV, board games, table skittles and shove-ha'penny. In 1810, the building was extended to include a flour mill and bakery using grain transported along the Kennet & Avon Canal. It's handy for walks on the downs and along the canal tow path.

Wadworths ~ Tenant Adrian Softley ~ Real ale ~ Bar food (11.30-2.30, 6.30-9)

~ Restaurant ~ (01380) 860273 ~ Well behaved children welcome ~ Dogs allowed in bar ~ Open 11-2.30, 6-11; 11-11 Sat; 12-10.30 Sun; 11(12 Sun)-3, 6-11 Sat in winter

LOWER CHUTE
Hatchet

The Chutes well signposted via Appleshaw off A342, 2.5 miles W of Andover; SP11 9DX

One of the county's most attractive pubs with restful atmosphere

'A remote rural paradise' is how one reader describes this 16th-c neat and friendly thatched pub. The very low-beamed bar has a splendid 17th-c fireback in the huge fireplace (and a roaring winter log fire), a mix of captain's chairs and cushioned wheelbacks around oak tables, and a peaceful local feel. Timothy Taylors Landlord and Golden Best and Wickwar Penny Black on handpump; piped music. Thursday night is curry night and at other times food is pubby and straightforward. There are seats out on a terrace by the front car park, or on the side grass, as well as a smokers' hut, and a children's sandpit.

Free house ~ Licensee Jeremy McKay ~ Real ale ~ Bar food (12-2.15, 6.30-9.45) ~ Restaurant ~ (01264) 730229 ~ Children in restaurant and side bar only ~ Dogs allowed in bar and bedrooms ~ Open 11.30-3, 6-11; 12-3, 7-10.30 Sun ~ Bedrooms: £60S/£70S

NEWTON TONY
Malet Arms

Village signposted off A338 Swindon—Salisbury; SP4 0HF

Smashing village pub with no pretensions, a good choice of local beers and tasty home-made food

There's a lot of genuine character in this cheerful, bustling pub. The two low-beamed interconnecting rooms have nice furnishings including a mix of different-sized tables with high winged wall settles, carved pews, chapel and carver chairs, and lots of pictures, mainly from imperial days. The main front windows are said to have come from the stern of a ship, and there's a log and coal fire in a huge fireplace. As well as beers from breweries such as Hogs Back, Hop Back, Palmers, and Stonehenge, there might be Fullers London Pride and Wadworths St George's on handpump, farm cider and several malt whiskies. Chalked up on a blackboard, the very good, changing range of home-made food includes venison dishes as the landlord runs the deer management on a local estate. The small front terrace has old-fashioned garden seats and some picnic-sets on the grass, and there are more tables in the back garden, along with a wendy house. There's also a little aviary, and a horse paddock behind. Getting to the pub takes you through a ford and it may be best to use an alternative route in winter, as it can be quite deep.

Free house ~ Licensee Noel Cardew ~ Real ale ~ Bar food (12-2.30, 6.30-10 (7-9.30 Sun)) ~ (01980) 629279 ~ Children allowed but not in bar area ~ Dogs allowed in bar ~ Open 11-3, 6-11; 12-3, 7-10.30 Sun; closed 25 and 26 Dec, 1 Jan

NORTON

Vine Tree

4 miles from M4 junction 17; A429 towards Malmesbury, then left at
Hullavington, Sherston signpost, then follow Norton signposts; in village turn
right at Foxley signpost, which takes you into Honey Lane; SN16 0JP

Civilised, friendly dining pub, beams and candlelight, super food using local,
seasonal produce, fine choice of drinks, and big garden

Although the first-rate, imaginative food remains one of the main draws to this
well run and civilised place, there's always a good mix of customers and locals
do still pop in for a drink and a chat. Three neatly kept little rooms open
together, with old beams, some old settles and unvarnished wooden tables on
the flagstone floors, big cream church altar candles, a woodburning stove at one
end of the restaurant and a large open fireplace in the central bar, and limited
edition and sporting prints; look out for Clementine, the friendly and docile
black labrador. Butcombe Bitter and a couple of guest beers like Bath Ales Gem
and St Austell Tinners on handpump, around 28 wines by the glass from an
impressive list, and quite a choice of malt whiskies and armagnacs; helpful,
attentive staff. It's best to book if you want to eat here, especially at weekends.
Using local seasonal produce (and listing their suppliers), food here is highly
inventive and excellent. There are picnic-sets and a children's play area in a two-
acre garden plus a pretty suntrap terrace with teak furniture under big cream
umbrellas, a lion fountain, lots of lavender, and box hedging; there's an attractive smoking shelter, too. It's not the easiest place to find, and feels pleasantly
remote despite its proximity to the motorway.

Free house ~ Licensees Charles Walker and Tiggi Wood ~ Real ale ~ Bar food
(12-2(2.30 Sat, 3.30 Sun), 7-9.30(9.45 Fri, 10 Sat)) ~ Restaurant ~ (01666)
837654 ~ Children welcome ~ Dogs allowed in bar ~ Live jazz and blues once a
month but maybe every Sun in summer ~ Open 11.45-3-ish, 6-midnight;
11.45-midnight Sun; they try to close Sun afternoons in winter

ROWDE

George & Dragon

A342 Devizes—Chippenham; SN10 2PN

Gently upmarket coaching inn with good, varied food and nice atmosphere

Charming inside, this is an attractive 17th-c coaching inn with quite an emphasis on the interesting food – though they do keep Butcombe Bitter and Cottage
Golden Arrow on handpump; several wines by the glass. The two low-ceilinged
rooms have plenty of wood, beams, and open fireplaces and there are large
wooden tables, antique rugs, and walls covered with old pictures and portraits;
the atmosphere is pleasantly chatty; board games and piped music. Good, if not
cheap, imaginative bar food includes dishes such as baked fresh fig with goats
cheese and proscuitto and roast cod fillet with chorizo and garlic new potato
compote. A pretty garden at the back has tables and chairs; maybe summer
barbecues. The Kennet & Avon Canal is nearby.

Free house ~ Licensees Philip and Michelle Hale, Christopher Day ~ Real ale ~

Bar food (12-3, 7-10; 12-4, 6.30-10 Sat; not Sun evening) ~ Restaurant ~ (01380) 723053 ~ Children in restaurant ~ Dogs allowed in bar ~ Open 12-3, 7-11; 12-4, 6.30-11 Sat; 12-4 Sun; closed Sun evening

UPPER CHUTE

Cross Keys

Tucked-away village N of Andover, best reached off A343 via Tangley, or off A342 in Weyhill via Clanville; SP11 9ER

Peacefully set, proper country pub, welcoming and relaxed, with enjoyable food and good beer and wines

As they have two stables at the back of this country pub, customers staying overnight can now bring their horses with them; there's around 80 square miles of open countryside to explore. (We have not yet heard from readers who have stayed here, but would expect it to be good value.) The back garden has been tidied and has a children's play area, and picnic-sets under flowering cherries on the front south-facing terrace give far views over rolling wooded uplands. Inside, it's open plan and well run with a relaxed, unstuffy atmosphere, early 18th-c beams, some sofas, a cushioned pew built around the window, and a good log fire in the big hearth on the left; pubby tables and a couple of leather armchairs by the woodburning stove on the right, darts sensibly placed in an alcove, and shut-the-box, chess, TV and piped music. Deliberately unpretentious, the very good pubby food is prepared using seasonal ingredients Fullers London Pride, Discovery and Butser and a changing guest beer such as Everards Beacon on handpump, and good wines by the glass; service is welcoming and helpful, and the charming bulldogs are called Pepper, Pudding and Mouse.

Free house ~ Licensees George and Sonia Humphrey ~ Bar food (12-2(2.30 Sat and Sun), 6-9; not Sun evening) ~ Restaurant ~ (01264) 730295 ~ Children allowed until 9pm ~ Dogs allowed in bar and bedrooms ~ Open 11-2.30, 5-11; 11-midnight Sat; 12-11 Sun ~ Bedrooms: £55S/£65S

DOG FRIENDLY HOTELS, INNS, B&Bs AND FARMS

CASTLE COMBE

Manor House

Castle Combe, Chippenham, Wiltshire SN14 7HR (01249) 782206

£180; 48 lovely rms, some in mews cottages just 50 yards from the house. 14th-c manor house in 365 acres of countryside with italian garden and parkland, 18-hole golf course with full range of practice facilities, croquet, boules, and all-weather tennis court; gracious day rooms with panelling, antiques, log fires and fresh flowers, convivial bar, warm and friendly atmosphere, and very good innovative food in smart restaurants; resident cat; disabled access; dogs in some bedrooms and lounges; £50

CHICKSGROVE

Compasses

Lower Chicksgrove, Tisbury, Salisbury, Wiltshire SP3 6NB (01722) 714318

£90; 5 rms. Lovely thatched house in delightful hamlet with warm welcome from landlord and his family, convivial bar with old bottles and jugs hanging from beams above roughly timbered counter, farm tools and traps on partly stripped stone walls, wooden settles on flagstones, carefully sourced, imaginative food, well kept real ales, and peaceful farm courtyard, garden, and play area; plenty of surrounding walks; cl Christmas; dogs in all areas, but not on beds

CHITTOE

Glebe House

Chittoe, Chippenham, Wiltshire SN15 2EL (01380) 850864

£75; 3 delightful rms. Peacefully set former chapel with fine views, seats on terraces and pretty garden; welcoming owners, antiques and pictures in comfortable drawing room, and carefully cooked breakfasts and evening meals in candlelit dining room using home-grown and local produce; three resident dogs and a chatty parrot; dogs in bedrooms; £5

COLLINGBOURNE KINGSTON

Manor Farm

Collingbourne Kingston, Marlborough, Wiltshire SN8 3SD (01264) 850859

£65; 3 comfortable, very spacious rms with sofas and dining table, and country views. 17th-c farmhouse on working arable farm lived in by same family since 1885; warmly welcoming owners, excellent hearty Aga-cooked breakfasts (you can collect your eggs from their free-range chickens), packed lunches on request and several very good local pubs and restaurants; good walking on 550 acres, in forest and along canal, and cycling and riding directly from the farm; their own private airstrip with aerial adventures on offer; dogs in bedrooms; £4

CRUDWELL

Old Rectory Country House Hotel

Crudwell, Malmesbury, Wiltshire SN16 9EP (just off A429 in village) (01666) 577194

£105; 12 big homely rms overlooking gardens. Elegant, welcoming country-house hotel, formerly rectory to Saxon church next door and set in three acres of lovely landscaped Victorian gardens; airy drawing room with antiques (owner is antique dealer) and more modern art, interesting and enjoyable food in panelled restaurant, airy conservatory, relaxed atmosphere, and unpretentious service; croquet and boules, outdoor swimming pool; Potting Shed dining pub is across road and under same ownership; dogs welcome in bedrooms

EASTON GREY

Whatley Manor

Easton Grey, Malmesbury, Wiltshire SN16 0RB (01666) 822888

£340; 15 sumptuous rms and 8 suites. Very stylish Cotswold manor house in 12 acres of gardens, meadows and woodland; spacious and rather fine oak-panelled lounge, italian furniture, silk rugs and limestone floors, a cosseting atmosphere, knowledgeable staff, classical french cooking with contemporary touches in two restaurants, and well stocked wine cellars; cinema and Aquarias spa with thermal pools, gym, and hydrotherapy pool that extends outside with lovely valley views; children over 12; disabled access; dogs in bedrooms; £25

GREAT BEDWYN

Crofton Lodge

Crofton, Great Bedwyn, Marlborough, Wiltshire SN8 3DW (01672) 870328

£70; 3 rms. Welcoming house close to Kennet & Avon canal and set in two acres of gardens with croquet, tennis and heated swimming pool; fresh flowers and home-made cakes, open fire in comfortable drawing room, good breakfasts with home-made preserves and their own free-range eggs in pretty conservatory and evening meals on request; two friendly resident golden retrievers; cl Christmas and New Year; dogs welcome if well behaved

LACOCK

At the Sign of the Angel

Church Street, Lacock, Chippenham, Wiltshire SN15 2LB (0.5 miles off A350; Church Street) (01249) 730230

£120; 10 charmingly old rooms with antiques. Fine 15th-c house, full of character and in lovely NT village; heavy oak furniture, beams and big fireplaces, restful oak-panelled lounge, and good english cooking using home-grown and local produce in three medieval, candlelit restaurants; resident cat; cl Christmas period; walks in garden and around village; disabled access; dogs in bedrooms and lounge

MALMESBURY

Old Bell

Abbey Row, Malmesbury, Wiltshire SN16 0BW (0.7 miles off A429; Abbey Row, just off B4014 through town) (01666) 822344

£125; 32 unique rms. With some claim to being one of England's oldest hotels and standing in shadow of Norman abbey, this fine wisteria-clad building has traditionally furnished rooms with Edwardian pictures, early 13th-c hooded stone fireplace, four good fires and plenty of comfortable sofas, magazines and newspapers in two lounges, library and bar; cheerful helpful service, imaginative modern food and fine wines in elegant, bustling restaurant, and attractive terrace in nice, old-fashioned garden; river walk nearby and open countryside, too; disabled access; dogs in bedrooms; bedding and bowl; £10

PURTON
Pear Tree

Church End, Purton, Swindon, Wiltshire SN5 4ED (01793) 772100

£110; 17 very comfortable, pretty rms. Impeccably run former vicarage with elegant comfortable day rooms, fresh flowers, fine conservatory restaurant with good modern english cooking using home-grown herbs, helpful caring staff, and 7½ acres including a traditional Victorian garden; resident dog and two cats; walks in grounds and nearby fields and paths; cl 26-30 Dec; disabled access; dogs welcome, but not to be left unattended in room; welcome pack

SALISBURY
Rose & Crown

Harnham Road, Harnham, Salisbury, Wiltshire SP2 8JQ (0.3 miles off A338/A354 roundabout, via A3094; handy too for A36) (01722) 399955

£155; 28 rms in original building or smart modern extension. Almost worth a visit just for the view – well nigh identical to that in the most famous Constable painting of Salisbury Cathedral; elegantly restored inn with friendly beamed and timbered bar, log fire, good bar and restaurant food, and charming Avonside garden; disabled access; dogs in bedrooms; £10

TEFFONT EVIAS
Howards House

Teffont Evias, Salisbury, Wiltshire SP3 5RJ (01722) 716392

£165; 9 rms. Partly 17th-c house in two acres of pretty gardens with ancient box hedges, kitchen gardens, and croquet; fresh flowers, beams and log fire in restful sitting room, imaginative modern cooking, fine breakfasts, and attentive, helpful staff; walks all round; cl Christmas; dogs in bedrooms; £7

WARMINSTER
Bishopstrow House

Bishopstrow, Warminster, Wiltshire BA12 9HH (1.5 miles off A36 from Heytesbury roundabout at E end of bypass; B3414) (01985) 212312

£199; 32 sumptuous rms. Charming ivy-clad Georgian house in 27 acres with heated indoor and outdoor swimming pools, indoor and outdoor tennis courts, fitness centre and beauty treatment rooms, and own fishing on River Wylye; relaxed, friendly atmosphere, log fires, lovely fresh flowers, antiques and fine paintings in boldly decorated day rooms, and really impressive food using home-grown produce in restaurant and adjacent conservatory; walks in grounds and nearby; disabled access; dogs welcome away from restaurants; £10

Worcestershire

MAP 4

DOG FRIENDLY PUBS

BIRTSMORTON

Farmers Arms

Birts Street, off B4208 W; WR13 6AP

Unrushed half-timbered village local with plenty of character

Calm and relaxing, this unchanging half-timbered pubby place is quietly free of piped music or games machines, but is home to the local cribbage and darts teams – you can also play shove-ha'penny or dominoes. Chatty locals gather at the bar for Hook Norton Hooky and Old Hooky, which are on handpump alongside a changing guest from a brewer such as Wye Valley. The big flagstoned room on the right rambles away under very low dark beams, with some standing timbers, a big inglenook, and flowery-panelled cushioned settles as well as spindleback chairs. A lower-beamed room on the left seems even cosier, and in both, white walls are broken up by black timbering. Very inexpensive simple bar food typically includes sandwiches, ploughman's, cauliflower cheese, steak and kidney pie and burgers. You'll find seats and swings out on the lovely big lawn with view over the Malvern Hills – the pub is surrounded by plenty of walks.

Free house ~ Licensees Jill and Julie Moore ~ Real ale ~ Bar food (11-2, 6.30-9.30; 12-2, 7-9 Sun) ~ (01684) 833308 ~ Children welcome ~ Dogs welcome ~ Open 11-4.30, 6-midnight; 12-4.30, 7-midnight Sun

HANLEY SWAN

Swan

B4209 Malvern—Upton; WR8 0EA

Cheerful staff, stylish décor, and appealing rural setting

Clever contemporary elements contrast very successfully with original features at this well maintained country pub. Fresh cream paintwork, attractive new oak panelling, well chosen prints, and bright upholstery work well with older rough timbering and low beams, some stripped masonry, bare boards and logs heaped up by the fire. The layout comprises two main areas: the extended back part set for dining, with french windows looking out over the picnic-sets on the good-sized side lawn and its play area, and the front part, which is more conventional; each area has its own servery. Good sturdy dining tables have comfortably high-backed chairs, and one part of the bar has dark leather bucket armchairs. Bar food includes something for most tastes; piped music, TV. On handpump, are Adnams, Charles Wells Bombardier and Shepherd Neame Spitfire; disabled access and facilities. The building is set well back from the road in lovely countryside, facing a classic village green, complete with duck pond and massive oak tree. They like dogs to be on a lead and well behaved in the bar, and they are welcome in the bedrooms.

Punch ~ Lease Malcolm Heale and Julia Northover ~ Real ale ~ Bar food (12-2.30, 6.30-9) ~ Restaurant ~ (01684) 311870 ~ Children welcome ~ Dogs allowed in bar and bedrooms ~ Open 12-3, 6-11 ~ Bedrooms: /£65B

HOLY CROSS

Bell & Cross

4 miles from M5 junction 4: A491 towards Stourbridge, then follow Clent signpost off on left; DY9 9QL

Super food, staff with a can-do attitude, delightful old interior and pretty garden

This charming pub is the sort of rewarding place that works well as a dining pub and yet remains extremely welcoming if you're just popping in for a drink. Arranged in a classic unspoilt early 19th-c layout, five quaint little rooms and a kitchen open off a central corridor with a black and white tiled floor: they give a choice of carpet, bare boards, lino or nice old quarry tiles, a variety of moods from snug and chatty to bright and airy, and an individual décor in each – theatrical engravings on red walls here, nice sporting prints on pale green walls there, racing and gundog pictures above the black panelled dado in another room. Two of the rooms have small serving bars, with Timothy Taylors Landlord, Enville and Wye Valley HPA on handpump. You'll find over 50 wines (with 14 sold by the glass), a variety of coffees, daily papers, coal fires in most rooms, perhaps regulars playing cards in one of the two front ones, and piped music. Bar food is delicious, with plenty of pub classics and a few seasonal specials. You get pleasant views from the garden terrace.

Enterprise ~ Managers Roger and Jo Narbett ~ Real ale ~ Bar food (12-2,6.30-9.15(12-7 Sun)) ~ Restaurant ~ (01562) 730319 ~ Children welcome ~ Dogs allowed in bar ~ Open 12-3, 6-11; 12-10.30 Sun

KEMPSEY

Walter de Cantelupe

A38, handy for M5 junction 7 via A44 and A4440; WR5 3NA

A warmly welcoming and unpretentious roadside inn, with enjoyable food and interesting drinks

We've always been keen on this friendly informal pub so we're very pleased to relay that since a new chef was employed (thus freeing up the charming land-lord) reader reports have been full of praise, with no hint of service being over-whelmed by too many customers. It's a comfortably relaxed place, with a pleas-ant mix of well worn furniture, an old wind-up HMV gramophone and a good big fireplace. Drinks include Cannon Royall Kings Shilling, and three guests such as Jennings Cumberland, Timothy Taylors Landlord and Wye Valley Golden Ale on handpump, locally grown and pressed apple juices and a farm cider in summer, and wines from a local vineyard; piped music in the evenings, board games, cribbage, dominoes and table skittles, and there's a pretty suntrap walled garden at the back. Food is good value and increasingly popular, concentrating on traditional pubby meals at lunchtime with more elaborate dishes in the evening. They sell jars of home-made chutney and marmalade.

Free house ~ Licensee Martin Lloyd Morris ~ Real ale ~ Bar food (12-2, 7-9; 12-7 Sun and bank hols) ~ Restaurant ~ (01905) 820572 ~ Children in dining area until 8.15 ~ Dogs welcome ~ Folk music second Sun evening of month ~ Open 12-2.30(3 Sat), 6-11; 12-10.30 Sun; closed Mon except bank hols ~ Bedrooms: £50B/£65S(£80B)

KNIGHTWICK
Talbot

Knightsford Bridge; B4197 just off A44 Worcester—Bromyard; WR6 5PH

Interesting old coaching inn with good beer from its own brewery, and riverside garden

Well kept on handpump and reasonably priced, the beers This, That, T'other and the seasonal ale at this friendly 15th-c coaching inn are brewed in their own Teme Valley microbrewery using locally grown hops. Efficient and welcoming uniformed staff also serve a guest such as Hobsons Bitter, as well as several different wines by the glass and a number of malt whiskies. With a good log fire in winter, the heavily beamed and extended carpeted lounge bar opens on to a terrace and arbour with summer roses and clematis. A variety of traditional seats runs from small carved or leatherette armchairs to the winged settles by the windows, and a vast stove squats in the big central stone hearth. The well furnished back public bar has pool on a raised side area, a games machine and juke box; cribbage. Bar food is very pubby (maybe ploughman's and pork and game pie) and there is a more expensive restaurant menu. The pub has a lovely lawn across the lane by the River Teme (they serve out here, too), or you can sit out in front on old-fashioned seats. A farmers' market takes place here on the second Sunday in the month.

Own brew ~ Licensee Annie Clift ~ Real ale ~ Bar food (12-2, 6.30(7 Sun)-9) ~ Restaurant ~ (01886) 821235 ~ Children welcome ~ Dogs allowed in bar and bedrooms ~ Open 11-11; 12-10.30 Sun ~ Bedrooms: £50S/£84B

MALVERN
Nags Head

Bottom end of Bank Street, steep turn down off A449; WR14 2JG

Remarkable range of real ales, appealing layout and décor, and warmly welcoming atmosphere

This is a terrifically enjoyable little pub, with readers loving its splendid individuality. Its superb range of well kept beer and tasty bar food attract a good mix of customers, including plenty of locals, and the mood is chatty and easygoing. A series of snug individually decorated rooms, with one or two steps between, gives plenty of options on where to sit. Each is characterfully filled with all sorts of chairs including leather armchairs, pews sometimes arranged as booths, a mix of tables with sturdy ones stained different colours, bare boards here, flagstones there, carpet elsewhere, and plenty of interesting pictures and homely touches such as house plants and shelves of well thumbed books, a coal fire opposite the central servery, broadsheet newspapers, shove-ha'penny, cribbage and dominoes, and a good juke box; piped music. If you feel confused by the astonishing range of 16 beers here they will happily help you with a taster. House beers are Banks's, Bathams, Marstons Pedigree, St Georges Charger, Dragon Blood, Maidens Saviour, and Woods Shropshire Lad and their nine changing guests (last year they got through over 1,000) come from a tremendous spread of brewers far and wide. They also keep a fine range of malt whiskies, belgian beers, Barbourne farm cider and decent wines by the glass. Tasty lunchtime food includes pubby standards but in the evenings they only serve food in the extension barn dining room (no dogs here). It's worth arriving early as they don't take bookings. Outside are picnic-sets and rustic tables and benches on the front terrace (with heaters and umbrellas) and in a garden.

Free house ~ Licensee Clare Willets ~ Real ale ~ Bar food (12-2, 6.30-8.30) ~ Restaurant ~ (01684) 574373 ~ Children welcome ~ Dogs welcome ~ Open 11-11.15(11.30 Fri, Sat); 12-11 Sun

OMBERSLEY

Kings Arms

Main Road (A4133); WR9 OEW

Cosy Tudor building with tasty food and attractive courtyard

King Charles is reputed to have stopped at this striking black and white timbered inn after fleeing the Battle of Worcester in 1651 – one room has his coat of arms moulded into its decorated plaster ceiling as a trophy of the visit. The building is said to date from about the 1400s, and the various wood-floored cosy nooks and crannies, and three splendid fireplaces with good log fires, certainly show signs of great age. The charming rambling interior has fresh flowers throughout, and lots of rustic bric-a-brac. Service is warmly friendly, Marstons Best and Pedigree and a couple of guests such as Black Sheep and Jennings Cocker Hoop on handpump are well kept, and they've darts and board games. Enjoyable sensibly priced bar food includes sandwiches, tempting specials and 28-day hung ribeye steak. A tree-sheltered courtyard has tables under cocktail parasols, and colourful hanging baskets and tubs in summer, and there's another terrace.

Banks's (Marstons) ~ Lease Caroline Cassell ~ Real ale ~ Bar food (12-23.0, 6-8.30) ~ (01905) 620142 ~ Children welcome ~ Dogs allowed in bar ~ Open 12-11(midnight Sat); 12-10.30 Sun

DOG FRIENDLY HOTELS, INNS, B&Bs AND FARMS

AB LENCH

Manor Farm House

Ab Lench, Evesham, Worcestershire WR11 4UP (01386) 462226

£80; 2 rms. Comfortable 250-year-old house in rural spot with lovely fenced-in half-acre garden; relaxing reception rooms, study with TV, some interesting objects collected from around the world, enjoyable evening meals, nice breakfasts, and charming, friendly owners; plenty of surrounding fields for walks; two resident maltese dogs and one cat; children over 12; cl Dec-Jan; dogs in bedrooms, if small

BROADWAY

Broadway Hotel

The Green, Broadway, Worcestershire WR12 7AA (1 mile off A44 from B4632 roundabout; turn right on High Street) (01386) 852401

£145; 19 well kept rms. Lovely 15th-c building, once a monastic guest house, with galleried and timbered lounge, cosy beamed bar, attractively presented food served by attentive staff in airy comfortable restaurant, and seats outside on terrace; plenty of walks nearby; limited disabled access; dogs in some bedrooms

Lygon Arms

High Street, Broadway, Worcestershire WR12 7DU (01386) 852255

£140; 77 lovely rms (half in Garden and Orchard wings). Handsome hotel that has been welcoming visitors since 1532 and where Oliver Cromwell and King Charles I once stayed; interesting beamed rooms, oak panelling, antiques, log fires, fine modern cooking in Great Hall with minstrels' gallery and more informal brasserie, excellent service, and charming garden; health spa and heated indoor pool; disabled access; dogs in bedrooms and some public areas; £15

EVESHAM

Evesham Hotel

Coopers Lane, off Waterside, Evesham, Worcestershire WR11 1DA (off A44 via B4035 into centre) (01386) 765566

£117; 40 spacious rms with games and jigsaws. Comfortably modernised and cheerful family-run hotel with warmly friendly, relaxed and jokey atmosphere, popular restaurant with very good food (esp lunchtime buffet), huge wine and spirits list, and sitting room with games and toys; indoor swimming pool surrounded by table tennis and table football, and grounds with croquet, trampoline, swings and putting; can walk dogs in the garden or along the River Avon close by; cl 25-26 Dec; disabled access; dogs in bedrooms only

GREAT MALVERN

Cowleigh Park Farm

Cowleigh Park, Cradley, Malvern, Worcestershire WR13 5HJ (0.8 miles off A449; A4219 NW) (01684) 566750

£70; 3 rms. Black and white timbered, 17th-c farmhouse in own grounds and surrounded by lovely countryside, with carefully restored and furnished rooms, and good breakfasts with home-made bread and preserves; self-catering also; resident dog and two cats; cl Christmas; children over 7; dogs in bedrooms; £3

HIMBLETON

Phepson Farm

Phepson, Droitwich, Worcestershire WR9 7JZ (01905) 391205

£60; 6 rms, 4 in renovated farm buildings. Relaxed and friendly 17th-c farmhouse on small sheep farm with fishing lake, comfortable guests' lounge, and good breakfasts, with seasonal fruit compote, in separate dining room; self-catering cottages; resident labradors and cats; walks on farm and nearby Wychavon Way; cl Christmas and New Year; dogs in ground floor bedrooms; bowl, feed mat, towels and treat; £5

MALVERN WELLS

Cottage in the Wood

Holy Well Road, Malvern, Worcestershire WR14 4LG (just off A449; Holy Well Road, which is off W, just N of B4209) (01684) 575859

£135; 30 pretty rms, some in separate nearby cottages. Family-run Georgian dower house with quite splendid views across Severn Valley and marvellous walks from grounds; antiques, log fires, comfortable seats and magazines in public rooms, and modern english cooking and an extensive wine list in attractive restaurant; limited disabled access; dogs in ground-floor bedrooms; bedding, bowls and welcome treat; £7.50

DOG FRIENDLY PUBS

APPLETON-LE-MOORS

Moors

Village N of A170 just under 1.5 miles E of Kirkby Moorside; YO62 6TF

Neat and unfussy pub with a good choice of drinks, proper country cooking using own-grown produce, and plenty of nearby walks; comfortable bedrooms

The landlady of this little stone-built pub is thinking of retiring, so to be sure of her good cooking this is perhaps a place to head for sooner rather than later. Using own-grown vegetables and salads and local organic produce, food is very enjoyable, with one or two imaginative specials. The pub is strikingly neat and surprisingly bare of the usual bric-a-brac. Sparse decorations include just a few copper pans and earthenware mugs in a little alcove, a couple of plates, one or two pieces of country ironwork, and a delft shelf with miniature whiskies. The whiteness of the walls and ceiling is underlined by the black beams and joists, and the bristly grey carpet. Perfect for a cold winter evening, there's a nice built-in high-backed stripped settle next to an old kitchen fireplace, and other seating includes an unusual rustic seat for two cleverly made out of stripped cartwheels; plenty of standing space. To the left of the bar you'll probably find a few regulars chatting on the backed padded stools: Black Sheep Best on hand-pump, over 50 malt whiskies and a reasonably priced wine list. Darts and board games. There are tables in the lovely walled garden with quiet country views and walks straight from here to Rosedale Abbey or Hartoft End, as well as paths to Hutton-le-Hole, Cropton and Sinnington.

Free house ~ Licensee Janet Frank ~ Real ale ~ Bar food (see opening hours; not Mon (except for residents)) ~ Restaurant ~ No credit cards ~ (01751) 417435 ~ Children welcome ~ Dogs allowed in bar and bedrooms ~ Open 7-11; 12-3, 7-11 Sun; closed Mon; closed Tues-Sat lunchtimes ~ Bedrooms: £45B/£70B

BLAKEY RIDGE

Lion

From A171 Guisborough—Whitby follow Castleton, Hutton le Hole signposts; from A170 Kirkby Moorside—Pickering follow Keldholm, Hutton le Hole, Castleton signposts; OS Sheet 100 map reference 679996; YO62 7LQ

Extended pub in fine scenery and open all day

As this extended pub is usefully open all day and serves food until 10pm, it's popular with walkers on the nearby Coast to Coast Footpath; there are plenty of other surrounding hikes and this is the highest point of the North York Moors National Park. The views are stunning. The beamed and rambling bars have warm open fires, a few big high-backed rustic settles around cast-iron-framed tables, lots of small dining chairs, a nice leather settee, and stone walls hung with some old engravings and photographs of the pub under snow (it can easily get cut off in winter). Greene King Old Speckled Hen, John Smiths, and Theakstons Best, Old Peculier, Black Bull and XB on handpump; piped music and games machine. Pubby food is served in generous helpings. This is a regular stop-off for coach parties.

Free house ~ Licensee Barry Crossland ~ Real ale ~ Bar food (12-10) ~ Restaurant ~ (01751) 417320 ~ Children welcome ~ Dogs allowed in bar ~ Open 10am-11pm

BRADFIELD
Strines Inn

From A57 heading E of junction with A6013 (Ladybower Reservoir) take first left turn (signposted with Bradfield) then bear left; with a map can also be reached more circuitously from Strines signpost on A616 at head of Underbank Reservoir, W of Stocksbridge; S6 6JE

Friendly, bustling inn with fine surrounding scenery and good mix of customers

Although there's a 16th-c coat of arms over the door into this moorland inn, the place probably dates back 300 years before that. It's surrounded by superb scenery on the edge of the High Peak National Park and there are fine views, plenty of picnic-sets, a children's play area, and peacocks, geese and chickens. Inside, it's well run and enjoyable, and the main bar has a welcoming atmosphere, a good mix of customers, black beams liberally decked with copper kettles and so forth, quite a menagerie of stuffed animals, homely red-plush-cushioned traditional wooden wall benches and small chairs, and a coal fire in the rather grand stone fireplace. A room off on the right has another coal fire, hunting photographs and prints, and lots of brass and china, and on the left is another similarly furnished room. Good value enjoyably traditional food is served in hearty helpings. Bradfield Farmers Pale Ale, Jennings Cocker Hoop, and Marstons Pedigree on handpump and several malt whiskies; piped music.

Free house ~ Licensee Bruce Howarth ~ Real ale ~ Bar food (12-2.30, 6-9 winter weekdays; all day weekends and summer weekdays) ~ (0114) 285 1247 ~ Children welcome ~ Dogs welcome ~ Open 10.30am-11pm; 10.30-3, 6-11 in winter; closed 25 Dec ~ Bedrooms: £60B/£80B

BURN
Wheatsheaf

A19 Selby—Doncaster; Main Road; YO8 8LJ

Plenty to look at and a friendly welcome, half a dozen real ales and good value straightforward food

Most customers come to this friendly roadside pub to look at the amazing collections of memorabilia while enjoying one of the half a dozen real ales. There really is masses to see: gleaming copper kettles, black dagging shears, polished buffalo horns and the like around its good log and coal fire (and a drying rack with bunches of herbs above it), decorative mugs above one bow-window seat, and cases of model vans and lorries on the cream walls. The highly polished pub tables in the partly divided, open-plan bar have comfortable seats around them and John Smiths and Timothy Taylors Best and guests such as Brown Cow Montana Pale, Fernandes Triple O, Milestone Black Pearl, and Ossett Pale Gold on handpump at attractive prices and over 30 malt whiskies. The straightforward bar food is very fairly priced and they do a Sunday roast. A pool table is out of the way on the left, cribbage, dominoes, games machine, TV, and there may be unobtrusive piped music. A small garden behind has picnic-sets on a heated terrace.

Free house ~ Licensee Andrew Howdall ~ Real ale ~ Bar food (12-2 daily, 6.30-8.30 Thurs, Fri and Sat; no food Sun-Weds evenings) ~ (01757) 270614 ~ Children welcome ~ Dogs welcome ~ Open 12-midnight

CHAPEL LE DALE

Hill Inn

B5655 Ingleton—Hawes, 3 miles N of Ingleton; LA6 3AR

Friendly inn with fine surrounding walks, appealing food cooked by the licensees, and a fair choice of real ales

You can be sure of a warm and friendly welcome in this bustling ex-farmhouse, run by a family of chefs. With wonderful remote walks all round, many of the customers are walkers who create a relaxed and chatty atmosphere. There are beams and log fires, straightforward seats and tables on the stripped wooden floors, nice pictures on the walls, stripped-stone recesses, and Black Sheep Best, Dent Aviator, Theakstons Best, and Timothy Taylors Landlord on handpump; several wines by the glass. Food is tasty and can be imaginative.

Free house ~ Licensee Sabena Martin ~ Real ale ~ Bar food (12-2.30, 6.30-8.45; not Mon except bank hols) ~ Restaurant ~ (015242) 41256 ~ Children in dining areas if eating ~ Dogs allowed in bar ~ Open 12-3.30, 6.30-11; 12-11 Sat; 12-4, 6.30-11 Sun; closed Mon (except bank hols), 24 and 25 Dec

CONSTABLE BURTON

Wyvill Arms

A684 E of Leyburn; DL8 5LH

Well run and friendly dining pub with excellent food, a dozen wines by the glass, real ales and efficient helpful service; bedrooms

Very efficiently run, this is a spotless and friendly dining pub with particularly good, popular food, and as we went to press they were starting work on creating a kitchen that will be partly on view to diners. But drinkers are catered for too – there's a small bar area with a mix of seating, a finely worked plaster ceiling with the Wyvill family's coat of arms, and an elaborate stone fireplace. The second bar, where food is served (though they also have a sizeable restaurant), has upholstered alcoves, hunting prints, and old oak tables; the reception area of this room includes a huge chesterfield which can seat up to eight people, another carved stone fireplace, and an old leaded church stained-glass window partition. Both rooms are hung with pictures of local scenes. Copper Dragon Golden Pippin, Theakstons Best, and a couple of changing guests on handpump, a dozen wines by the glass, and some rare malt whiskies. Using seasonal produce, herbs from their own big garden and game from the estate across the road, food here is first class and deliciously imaginative; board games and darts. There are several large wooden benches under large white parasols for outdoor dining. Constable Burton Gardens are opposite and worth a visit.

Free house ~ Licensee Nigel Stevens ~ Real ale ~ Bar food ~ Restaurant ~ (01677) 450581 ~ Children welcome but must be well supervised ~ Dogs allowed in bar and bedrooms ~ Open 11-3, 5.30-11; closed Mon ~ Bedrooms: £60B/£80B

COXWOLD

Fauconberg Arms

Off A170 Thirsk—Helmsley, via Kilburn or Wass; easily found off A19, too; YO61 4AD

Friendly family running nicely updated 17th-c inn, enjoyable generous food

This lovely old place fits perfectly in mood with the relaxed style of the charming unchanging village, and quaint nearby Shandy Hall, the home of Laurence Sterne the eccentric 18th-c novelist. In summer, picnic-sets and teak benches out on the cobbles look along the village's broad tree-lined verges, bright with flower tubs. In winter, the heavily beamed and flagstoned bar welcomes you with log fires in both linked areas, one in an unusual arched fireplace in a broad low inglenook. Both generations of the family are helpful and cheerful. They have well kept Theakstons Best and Thwaites Best with a couple of guests like John Smiths and Thwaites Dark Mild on handpump, and a thoughtful choice of wines by the glass. Muted heritage colours, some attractive oak chairs by local craftsmen alongside more usual pub furnishings, and nicely chosen old local photographs and other pictures and china give a stylish feel without being at all pretentious. Generous helpings of well liked bar food ranges from snacks up to hearty dishes such as slow-roast belly pork with fresh ginger, apple and cider gravy, and they have a super cheese board.

Free house ~ Licensee Simon Rheinberg ~ Real ale ~ Bar food (12.30-2.30(3 Sat), 6.30-9.30; 12.30-6 Sun; not Sun evening or Tues) ~ Restaurant ~ (01347) 868214 ~ Children welcome ~ Dogs allowed in bar ~ Live impromptu music Sun evenings ~ Open 11-3, 6-11(midnight Fri); 11-midnight(11 Sun) Sat; closed Tues

EAST WITTON

Blue Lion

A6108 Leyburn—Ripon; DL8 4SN

Civilised dining pub with interesting rooms, daily papers and real ales, inventive food, and courteous service; comfortable bedrooms

With first class food and very comfortable bedrooms, this smart and civilised dining pub also cleverly manages to have a proper bar that welcomes drinkers, too. This big squarish bar has high-backed antique settles and old windsor chairs on the turkey rugs and flagstones, ham-hooks in the high ceiling decorated with dried wheat, teazles and so forth, a delft shelf filled with appropriate bric-a-brac, several prints, sporting caricatures and other pictures on the walls, a log fire, and daily papers; the friendly labrador is called Archie. Whilst not cheap, food from the varied and imaginative menu is excellent, with everything from sandwiches up to soft shell crab deep-fried with chilli and ginger with a fennel salad, and flash-roasted venison with red wine, chestnut and vegetable risotto. Black Sheep Best and Riggwelter, and Theakstons Best on handpump and an impressive wine list with quite a few (plus champagne) by the glass; courteous, attentive service. Picnic-sets on the gravel outside look beyond the stone houses on the far side of the village green to Witton Fell and there's a big, pretty back garden.

Free house ~ Licensee Paul Klein ~ Real ale ~ Bar food ~ Restaurant ~ (01969) 624273 ~ Children welcome ~ Dogs allowed in bar and bedrooms ~ Open 11-11 ~ Bedrooms: £67.50S/£89S(£99B)

GRINTON

Bridge Inn

B6270 W of Richmond; DL11 6HH

Bustling pub with welcoming landlord, comfortable bars, log fires, a fine choice of drinks, and good food; neat bedrooms

After enjoying one of the good walks surrounding this well run and friendly country pub, both wet walkers and their dogs are welcome in the bar. This is cheerful, gently lit and red-carpeted, with bow window seats and a pair of stripped traditional settles among more usual pub seats, all well cushioned, a good log fire, Jennings Cumberland and Cocker Hoop, and guests such as Marstons Sun Bright and York Yorkshire Terrier on handpump, nice wines by the glass, and 20 malt whiskies. On the right, a few steps take you down into a dark red room with darts, board games, a well lit pool table, ring-the-bull, and piped music. Friendly, helpful service. On the left, past leather armchairs and a sofa by a second log fire (and a glass chess set), is an extensive two-part dining room. The décor is in mint green and shades of brown, with a modicum of fishing memorabilia. The often interesting food is prepared using their own herbs and seasonal produce from local suppliers, and they make their own jams, marmalade and chutneys. There are picnic-sets outside, and the inn is right opposite a lovely church known as the Cathedral of the Dales. The bedrooms are neat and simple, and breakfasts are good. This is a pretty Swaledale village.

Jennings (Marstons) ~ Lease Andrew Atkin ~ Real ale ~ Bar food (all day) ~ Restaurant ~ (01748) 884224 ~ Children welcome ~ Dogs allowed in bar and bedrooms ~ Open 12-midnight(1am Sat) ~ Bedrooms: £46B/£72B

LITTON

Queens Arms

From B6160 N of Grassington, after Kilnsey take second left fork; can also be reached off B6479 at Stainforth N of Settle, via Halton Gill; BD23 5QJ

Friendly pub in fantastic walking area, own-brew beers, good homely food and simply furnished bars; bedrooms including a walkers' room

Hard-working, thoughtful licensees run this friendly pub. The main bar on the right has a good coal fire, stripped rough stone walls, a brown beam-and-plank ceiling, stools around cast-iron-framed tables on the stone and concrete floor, a seat built into the stone-mullioned window, and signed cricket bats. The left-hand room is an eating area with old photographs of the Dales around the walls. From their own microbrewery, they offer Litton Ale and Potts Beck Ale, and there's usually a guest such as Tetleys on handpump. Darts and board games. Bar food is heartily traditional – just the thing after a good walk. There's a safe area for children in the two-level garden and plenty of surrounding walks – a track behind the inn leads over Ackerley Moor to Buckden, and the quiet lane through the valley leads on to Pen-y-ghent.

Own brew ~ Licensees Jayne and Doug Goldie ~ Real ale ~ Bar food (12-2.30, 6.30(7 Sun)-9) ~ Restaurant ~ (01756) 770208 ~ Children welcome away from bar ~ Dogs welcome ~ Open 12-3(3.30 Sat), 6.30-11; 12-3, 7-10.30 Sun ~ Bedrooms: /£75S

MIDDLEHAM

White Swan

Market Place; DL8 4PE

Still has proper pubby bar in smartly extended inn, well liked food and real ales

If you are lucky, you can bag one of the seats in the window of the bar in this pleasant, extended coaching inn that look across the cobbled market square. There's a beamed and flagstoned entrance bar with a proper pubby atmosphere, a long dark pew built into a big window, a mix of chairs around a handful of biggish tables, and an open woodburning stove. Black Sheep Best and Ale, John Smiths and Theakstons Best on handpump from the curved counter, 12 wines by the glass, 20 malt whiskies and quite a few teas and coffees; piped music. The varied menu ranges from king prawns with sesame and ginger to various pizzas and braised lamb shank with spring onion mash. Food is popular and they offer a two- and three-course early bird menu (6.30-7.30 Sunday-Friday).

Free house ~ Licensee Kim Woodcock ~ Real ale ~ Bar food (12-2.15, 6.30-9.30) ~ Restaurant ~ (01969) 622093 ~ Children welcome ~ Dogs allowed in bar ~ Open 11-11(midnight Sat); 12-10.30 Sun

MILL BANK

Millbank

Mill Bank Road, off A58 SW of Sowerby Bridge; HX6 3DY

Imaginative food in cottagey-looking dining pub, real ales, fine wines and specialist gin list, friendly staff and interesting garden sculptures; walks nearby and good views

Although this impressive dining pub looks cottagey and traditional from the outside, once you get inside, the rooms have a clean-cut minimalist modern décor, and there are local photographs for sale. It's divided into the tap room, bar and restaurant, with Tetleys and Timothy Taylors Landlord on handpump, 20 wines by the glass including champagne, port and pudding wines, and a specialised gin list; friendly staff. Top notch food is inventive and contemporary though you can get a sandwich (available until 7pm), Outside, the terrace has a glass roof and fold-away windows that make the most of the glorious setting overlooking an old textile mill. The Calderdale Way is easily accessible from the pub.

Free house ~ Licensee Glenn Futter ~ Real ale ~ Bar food (12-2.30, 6-9.30(10 Fri and Sat); 12.30-4.30, 6-8 Sun; not Mon) ~ Restaurant ~ (01422) 825588 ~ Children welcome ~ Dogs allowed in bar ~ Open 12-3, 5.30-11; 12-10.30 Sun; closed Mon, first week Jan, first two weeks Oct

OSMOTHERLEY

Golden Lion

The Green, West End; off A19 N of Thirsk; DL6 3AA

Welcoming, busy pub with simply furnished rooms, lots of malt whiskies, real ales, interesting bar food, and fine surrounding walks

Run by a friendly landlord, this attractive old stone pub has an enjoyably bustling atmosphere. The roomy beamed bar on the left is simply furnished with old pews and just a few decorations on its white walls, candles on tables, John Smiths, Timothy Taylors Landlord and a guest from Salamander on handpump, several wines by the glass, and 50 malt whiskies. The well prepared imaginative food is very popular so it's best to book as it does get pretty packed. There's also a separate dining room, mainly open at weekends, and a covered courtyard; piped music. Benches out in front look across the village green to the market cross, and there's a new terrace. As the inn is the start of the 44-mile Lyke Wakes Walk on the Cleveland Way and quite handy for the Coast to Coast Walk, it is naturally popular with walkers.

Free house ~ Licensee Christie Connelly ~ Real ale ~ Bar food (12-2.30, 6-9) ~ Restaurant ~ (01609) 883526 ~ Children welcome ~ Dogs allowed in bar ~ Open 12-3, 6-11; 12-11(10.30 Sun) Sat; closed Mon and Tues lunchtime

SKIPTON

Narrow Boat

Victoria Street; pub signed down alley off Coach Street; BD23 1JE

Extended pub near canal with eight real ales, proper home cooking, and good mix of customers

The fine choice of eight real ales on handpump remains quite a draw to this extended pub: Black Sheep Best, Copper Dragon Best Bitter and Golden Pippin, Timothy Taylors Landlord, and four guests like Abbeydale Last Rites, Daleside Stout, Elland Dragon Hunter, and Phoenix Navvy. Several continental beers and decent wines, too. The bar has a good mix of both locals and visitors, old brewery posters and nice mirrors decorated with framed beer advertisements on the walls, church pews, dining chairs and stools around wooden tables, and an upstairs gallery area with an interesting canal mural. The pub is down a cobbled alley, with picnic-sets under a front colonnade, and the Leeds & Liverpool Canal is nearby. Popular bar food is pubby and home cooked.

Market Town Taverns ~ Manager Tim Hughes ~ Real ale ~ Bar food (12-2.30, 5.30-8.30; 12-4 Sun; not Sun evening) ~ (01756) 797922 ~ Children welcome if dining ~ Dogs welcome ~ Open 12-11

WATH IN NIDDERDALE

Sportsmans Arms

Nidderdale road off B6265 in Pateley Bridge; village and pub signposted over hump-back bridge on right after a couple of miles; HG3 5PP

Beautifully placed restaurant-with-rooms plus welcoming bar, real ales and super choice of other drinks, imaginative food

Extremely well run by the charming Mr Carter for over 30 years, this civilised and friendly 17th-c restaurant-with-rooms is consistently enjoyed by our readers. Of course, it's not a traditional inn but it does have a welcoming bar with an open fire, Black Sheep Best and Ale on handpump, and locals who do still pop in – though most customers are here to enjoy the particularly good food. The thoughtfully composed menu is imaginative and dishes are prepared using the best local produce. There's a very sensible and extensive wine list with 15 by the glass (including champagne), over 30 malt whiskies and several russian vodkas; quiet piped music. Benches and tables outside and seats in the pretty garden; croquet. As well as their own fishing on the River Nidd, this is an ideal spot for walkers, hikers and ornithologists, and there are plenty of country houses, gardens and cities to explore.

Free house ~ Licensee Ray Carter ~ Real ale ~ Bar food (during opening hours though only until 7pm Sun evening) ~ Restaurant ~ (01423) 711306 ~ Children allowed until 9pm ~ Dogs allowed in bar ~ Open 12-2.30, 6.30-11(10.30 Sun); closed 25 Dec, evening 1 Jan

WIDDOP

Pack Horse

The Ridge; from A646 on W side of Hebden Bridge, turn off at Heptonstall signpost (as it's a sharp turn, coming out of Hebden Bridge road signs direct you around a turning circle), then follow Slack and Widdop signposts; can also be reached from Nelson and Colne, on high, pretty road; OS Sheet 103 map reference 952317; HX7 7AT

Friendly pub high up on the moors and liked by walkers for generous, tasty food, five real ales, and lots of malt whiskies

A real oasis for walkers on the Pennine Way and Pennine Bridleway, this isolated pub has a good, bustling atmosphere. There's a welcome from the friendly staff, and the bar has warm winter fires, window seats cut into the partly panelled stripped stone walls that take in the moorland view, sturdy furnishings, horsey mementoes, and Black Sheep Best and Special, Greene King Old Speckled Hen, and Thwaites Bitter and Lancaster Bomber on handpump, around 130 single malt whiskies and some irish ones as well, and eight wines by the glass. The friendly golden retrievers are called Padge and Purdey, and there's another dog called Holly. Decent bar food at fair prices includes pubby meals and daily specials. Note that they do stop food service promptly. Seats outside and pretty summer hanging baskets. Leave your boots and backpacks in the porch.

Free house ~ Licensee Andrew Hollinrake ~ Real ale ~ Bar food (not Mon or Tues-Thurs winter lunchtimes) ~ (01422) 842803 ~ Children in eating area of bar until 8pm ~ Dogs allowed in bar ~ Open 12-3, 7-11; 12-11 Sun; closed lunchtimes Mon-Thurs in winter; closed Mon

DOG FRIENDLY HOTELS, INNS, B&Bs AND FARMS

BAINBRIDGE

Rose & Crown

Bainbridge, Leyburn, North Yorkshire DL8 3EE (01969) 650225

£68; 12 comfortable rms. 15th-c coaching inn overlooking lovely green, with antique settles and other old furniture in beamed and panelled front bar, open log fires, cosy residents' lounge, big wine list, and home-made traditional food in bar and restaurant; disabled access; dogs in some bedrooms

BOLTON ABBEY

Devonshire Arms

Bolton Abbey, Skipton, North Yorkshire BD23 6AJ (just off A59/B6160 roundabout) (01756) 710441

£225; 40 individually furnished rms with thoughtful extras. Close to the priory itself and in lovely countryside with plenty of walks, this civilised former coaching inn owned by the Duke of Devonshire has been carefully furnished with fine antiques and paintings from Chatsworth; log fires, impeccable service, beautifully presented imaginative food, and super breakfasts; health spa; resident chocolate labrador and spaniel; disabled access; dogs in bedrooms and some public areas; welcome pack, treats, bedding

CRAY

White Lion

Cray, Skipton, North Yorkshire BD23 5JB (01756) 760262

£70; 10 comfortable rms all with showers. Welcoming little pub spectacularly isolated 335 metres up with super views, lots of walks, traditional feel with flagstones, beams and log fires, good bar food, and decent wines; residents only 25 Dec; partial disabled access; dogs in bedrooms and other areas; £3

CRAYKE

Durham Ox

West Way, Crayke, York YO61 4TE (3.8 miles off A19 from northernmost Easingwold exit; in Easingwold bear left on Church Hill, keep on via Mill Lane) (01347) 821506

£80; 6 rms in renovated farm cottages. Bustling inn, very well run and genuinely friendly, with huge inglenook fireplace, interesting satirical carvings in panelling, and antique furniture on flagstones in bustling bar, lower bar with large framed print of famous Durham Ox (which weighed 171 stones), real ales, several wines by glass, a dozen malt whiskies, excellent food in bar and restaurant, and good breakfasts; seats on terrace and in covered courtyard; fantastic views over Vale of York

ELSLACK

Tempest Arms

Elslack, Skipton, North Yorkshire BD23 3AY (01282) 842450

£74.95; 14 chic modern rms. Friendly, bustling inn with three log fires in stylish rooms, quite a bit of exposed stone work, amusing prints on cream walls, several real ales, quite a few wines by the glass, good food, warm welcome from helpful staff, and tables outside; dogs in bedrooms

HALIFAX

Holdsworth House

Holmfield, Halifax, West Yorkshire HX2 9TG (1.2 miles off A629; heading N out of centre, fork right up Shay Lane) (01422) 240024

£125; 40 traditional, individually decorated, quiet rms. Lovely, immaculately kept 17th-c house outside Halifax and set in own neatly kept grounds; antiques, fresh flowers and fires in comfortable lounges, lots of sitting areas in two bar rooms, friendly, particularly helpful staff, and three carefully furnished dining rooms with enjoyable food and good wine list; disabled access; dogs in bedrooms and some public areas; £10

HAROME

Pheasant

Mill Street, Harome, Helmsley, North Yorkshire YO62 5JG (01439) 771241

£130; 12 rms. Family-run hotel with relaxed homely lounge, traditional bar with beams, inglenook fireplace and flagstones, good, popular food using their own eggs, vegetables and fruit, efficient service, and indoor heated swimming pool; walks along country lanes; cl Christmas, Jan and Feb; children over 7; disabled access; dogs in bedrooms (not to be left unattended)

HARROGATE

Alexa House

26 Ripon Road, Harrogate, North Yorkshire HG1 2JJ (on A61 N of centre) (01423) 501988

£85; 13 rms, some in former stable block. Attractive Georgian house with friendly staff, comfortable lounge with honesty bar, and marvellous breakfasts in dining room; walks in nearby local park; good disabled access; dogs in bedrooms only

HAWNBY

Laskill Grange

Easterside, Helmsley, York, North Yorkshire YO62 5NB (01439) 798268

£80; 3 rms, some in beamy converted outside building. Attractive and welcoming creeper-covered stone house on big sheep and cattle farm near Rievaulx Abbey and lots of nearby walks; open fire, antiques and books in comfortable lounge, conservatory overlooking the garden, good food using home-grown produce, and own natural spring water; self-catering also; cl 25 Dec; partial disabled access; dogs in bedrooms if well behaved

HELMSLEY

Black Swan

Market Place, Helmsley, North Yorkshire YO62 5BJ (on A170; Market Place) (01439) 770466

£160; 45 well equipped, comfortable rms. Striking Georgian house and adjoining Tudor rectory with beamed and panelled hotel bar, attractive carved oak settles and windsor armchairs, cosy and comfortable lounges with lots of character, and a charming sheltered garden; dogs in bedrooms and certain lounges; £10

KILBURN
Forresters Arms
Kilburn, York, North Yorkshire YO61 4AH (01347) 868386

£72; 10 clean, bright rms. Friendly old coaching inn opposite pretty village gardens; sturdy but elegant furnishings made next door at Thompson mouse furniture workshop, big log fire in cosy lower bar, interesting Henry Dee bar in what was a stable with manger and stalls still visible, and enjoyable food in restaurant and beamed bar; disabled access; dogs welcome away from dining room; £5

KNARESBOROUGH
Dower House
Bond End, Knaresborough, North Yorkshire HG5 9AL (on A59, just W of B6165; Bond End) (01423) 863302

£110; 31 clean, comfortable rms. Creeper-clad 15th-c former dower house with attractively furnished public rooms of some character, good food in Terrace Restaurant, super breakfasts, helpful service, and leisure club with indoor swimming pool, gym, spa, steam room, and sauna; two resident cats; walks along River Nidd; partial disabled access; dogs in some bedrooms; £7.50

Newton House Hotel
5-7 York Place, Knaresborough, Yorkshire HG5 0AD (A59 near centre; York Place) (01423) 863539

£90; 11 well equipped rms. Elegant family-run 18th-c house close to river and market square, with warm welcome for guests of all ages, comfortable sitting room with magazines, books, sweets and fresh fruit and good generous english breakfasts in separate dining room; no evening meals but plenty of places close by; they provide a list of local walks; resident dog; cl 1 wk Christmas; dogs welcome; bed, bowls, towels, toys, and treats available

LANGTHWAITE
Charles Bathurst
Arkengarthdale, Richmond, North Yorkshire DL11 6EN (01748) 884567

£92.50; 19 comfortable, pretty rms. Friendly well-run country pub with bustling atmosphere, good mix of customers, roaring log fire and pine furniture in bar, residents' lounge with sofas, imaginative food in wooden-floor restaurant and other dining areas, real ales, and lots of lovely surrounding walks; dogs in bedrooms

LEEDS
42 The Calls
Leeds, West Yorkshire LS2 7EW (0113) 244 0099

£129; 41 attractive rms using original features (those overlooking river have a fishing rod). Stylish modern hotel in converted riverside grain mill in peaceful spot overlooking River Aire, with genuinely friendly staff, boldy decorated public rooms, lots of original paintings and drawings, marvellous food in next-door chic but informal Brasserie Forty 4, and super breakfasts in River Room; cl four days over Christmas; disabled access; dogs welcome in bedrooms

Malmaison

Sovereign Quay, Leeds, West Yorkshire LS1 1DQ (0113) 398 1000

£187.90; 100 spacious rms with CDs and air conditioning. Stylish hotel, once a bus company office, with bold, modern furnishings, contemporary bar and brasserie, enjoyable food, decent breakfasts, popular Sunday brunch, and help-ful friendly service; disabled access; dogs in bedrooms; £10

LONG PRESTON

Maypole

Main Street, Long Preston, Skipton, North Yorkshire BD23 4PH (on A65 towards NW end of village) (01729) 840219

£60; 6 comfortable rms. Neatly kept 17th-c pub with generous helpings of enjoyable traditional food (and nice breakfasts) in spacious beamed dining room, open fires in public and lounge bars, real ales, and helpful service; walks on the moors close by; dogs in bedrooms and bar; £6

MALHAMDALE

Miresfield Farm

Malham, Skipton, North Yorkshire BD23 4DA (01729) 830414

£68; 10 rms. Spacious old farmhouse with good freshly prepared food in beamed dining room, pleasant conservatory, two lounges (one with open log fire), and lovely garden by stream and village green; resident dogs; walks along the Pennine Way; dogs in bedrooms; £5

MARKINGTON

Hob Green

Markington, Harrogate, North Yorkshire HG3 3PJ (2 miles off A61 S of Ripon; keep on through village) (01423) 770031

£115; 12 pretty rms. Lovely gardens and over 800 acres of rolling countryside surround this charming 18th-c stone hotel; comfortable and pretty lounge and garden room, log fires, antique furniture, fresh flowers, relaxed atmosphere, good interesting food, decent choice of wines, and friendly service; dogs in bedrooms

MASHAM

Swinton Park

Masham, Yorkshire HG4 4JH (01765) 680900

£160; 30 well equipped rms (inc 4 suites) with garden views and decorated on theme of a yorkshire town, garden, castle and so forth. Grand luxury castle hotel dating in part from 17th c and still an ancestral home; several sumptuously decorated day rooms (though atmosphere is relaxed and friendly), bar in family museum, private cinema, and snooker and victorian games room; imaginative food in elegant restaurant using seasonal produce from extensive walled garden and estate; 200 acres of parkland and gardens, falconry, fishing, golf, off road driving, spa, exercise room and popular cookery school, and 20,000 acre estate, too; resident labrador; disabled access; dogs in bedrooms; welcome letter from resident dog, treats, welcome, bowl, bed; £25

MIDDLETON

Cottage Leas Country Hotel

Nova Lane, Middleton, Pickering, North Yorkshire YO18 8PN (1.5 miles N off A170 just W of Pickering, via Middleton Lane/Nova Lane) (01751) 472129

£88; 17 comfortable rms. Delightful and peaceful 18th-c farmhouse in two acres of gardens, beamed ceilings, open log fire in cosy lounge, well stocked bar, enjoyable creative food in light and airy dining room, and marvellous breakfasts; partial disabled access; dogs in some bedrooms

MONK FRYSTON

Monk Fryston Hall

Main Street, Monk Fryston, Leeds, West Yorkshire LS25 5DU (01977) 682369

£115; 29 individually decorated rms, many with garden views. Benedictine manor house in 30 acres of secluded gardens with lake and woodland; public rooms with oak-panelling, log fires in inglenook fireplaces, antiques, paintings and fresh flowers, interesting modern cooking in elegant restaurant, hearty breakfasts, and friendly helpful staff; limited disabled access; dogs in bedrooms and public areas (not restaurant)

OTLEY

Chevin Country Park Hotel

Yorkgate, Otley, West Yorkshire LS21 3NU (1.8 miles off A660; up East Chevin Road then first right on York Gate) (01943) 467818

£136; 49 rms, some in log lodges deep in woods. Comfortable hotel, built of finnish logs and surrounded by 44 acres of woodlands, lakes and gardens (lots of wildlife); leather sofas in lounge, informal bar, warm and cosy lakeside restaurant (one of the biggest log buildings in Britain and now with terrace and roof balcony) with good food, friendly service, and leisure club with swimming pool, gym, sauna, and hot tub; tennis and fishing; dogs in some bedrooms; £10

PICKERING

White Swan

Market Place, Pickering, North Yorkshire YO18 7AA (01751) 472288

£145; 21 lovely rms inc 3 suites. Smart old coaching inn with log fire and panelling in properly pubby convivial bar, charming country atmosphere, real ales, second fire in handsome art nouveau iron fireplace, big bow window and bare boards in lounge bar, residents' lounge in converted beamed barn, particularly good imaginative food in flagstoned restaurant (yet another open fire), and impressive wine list; walks nearby; disabled access; dogs welcome away from restaurant; £12.50

PICKHILL

Nags Head

Pickhill, Thirsk, North Yorkshire YO7 4JG (2.1 miles off A1 Masham turnoff; village signed off B6267 in Ainderby Quernhow) (01845) 567391

£80; 15 well appointed rms. Popular, bustling inn with quite an emphasis on imaginative modern food, fine choice of carefully chosen drinks, tap room and smarter lounge with jugs, coach horns and ale-yards hanging from beams, quite a collection of ties, open fires, friendly service, library-themed restaurant, real ales and carefully chosen wines, seats on front verandah, and boules and quoits pitch, and nine-hole putting green; self-catering cottage, too; dogs in bedrooms (not to be left unattended)

RAMSGILL

Yorke Arms

Ramsgill, Harrogate, North Yorkshire HG3 5RL (01423) 755243

£180; 12 attractive rms. Enjoyable small former shooting lodge (restaurant-with-rooms) with antique furnishings, log fires, exceptionally good imaginative cooking in comfortable dining rooms (breakfasts with home-made marmalade), flagstoned sitting areas where walkers are welcome, fine wines, real ales, courteous service, and lovely surrounding walks; children over 12 in dining room; dogs in one bedroom and in bar

REETH

Arkleside Country Guest House

Reeth, Richmond, North Yorkshire DL11 6SG (01748) 884200

£75; 8 cosy rms. Country guest house in former row of 17th-c lead miners' cottages with lovely Swaledale views and plenty of nearby walks; friendly atmosphere, homely bar, comfortable lounge with log-burning stove, good breakfasts, and evening meals in traditional stone-walled restaurant; little garden; dogs in bedrooms; £5

RICHMOND
Millgate House
Millgate, Richmond, North Yorkshire DL10 4JN (01748) 823571

£95; 4 rms, 2 overlooking the garden. Georgian town house with lots of interesting antiques and lovely plants, peaceful drawing room, warm friendly owners offering meticulous attention to detail, and good breakfasts in charming dining room which also overlooks the award-winning and really lovely garden (no dogs here but riverside walks nearby); resident whippet; children over 10; dogs welcome in bedrooms

RIPLEY
Boars Head
Ripley, Harrogate, North Yorkshire HG3 3AY (just off A61 N of Harrogate)
(01423) 771888

£125; 25 charmingly decorated rms. Fine old coaching inn in delightful estate village, with relaxed, welcoming atmosphere, comfortable sofas in attractively decorated lounges (some furnishings come from attic of next door Ripley Castle where owners of this inn have lived for over 650 years), long flagstoned bar, notable wines by glass, fine food in bar and restful dining room, and unobtrusive service; disabled access; dogs welcome away from dining areas; bed, bowls, bonio on turn-down; £10

RIPON
Old Deanery
Minster Road, Ripon, North Yorkshire HG4 1QS (01765) 600003

£110; 11 stylish rms. Carefully modernised 17th-c hotel built on site of former monastery and opposite cathedral; fine old oak staircase and hand-carved panelling, comfortable leather sofas and log fire in lounge, convivial bar, good breakfasts, contemporary food in attractive, candlelit dining room with bare boards and chandeliers, attentive service and one-acre garden; walks along river and canals, both nearby; cl 25-29 Dec; dogs welcome in bedrooms

SEDBUSK
Stone House
Hawes, North Yorkshire DL8 3PT (01969) 667571

£109; 23 rms, 5 with own conservatories (and liked by dog owners). Small, warmly friendly Edwardian hotel in stunning setting with magnificent views; country-house feel and appropriate furnishings, attractive oak-panelled drawing room, billiard room, log fires, and exemplary service offering good local information; pleasant extended dining room with excellent wholesome food and super breakfasts; wonderful walks; P. G. Wodehouse stayed here as guest of original owner who employed a butler called Jeeves – it was on him that Wodehouse based his famous character; cl Jan; disabled access; dogs in bedrooms, on leads in lounges; bowls and blankets

SKIPSEA

Village Farm

Back Street, Skipsea, East Yorkshire YO25 8SW (01262) 468479

£70; 3 quiet, attractively contemporary rms. Carefully renovated traditional farmhouse and outbuildings set around a central courtyard with good breakfasts in separate annexe; three resident dogs; nearby walks along 40 miles of beach; self-catering, too; children welcome if well behaved; disabled access; dogs in bedrooms; £7.50

STUDLEY ROGER

Lawrence House

Studley Roger, Ripon, North Yorkshire HG4 3AY (2.2 miles off A61; B6265 through Ripon) (01765) 600947

£110; 2 spacious, lovely rms with peaceful views. Attractive Georgian house with two acres of lovely garden on edge of Studley Royal deer park and Fountains Abbey; fine antiques and pictures, log fire in restful drawing room, good breakfasts, and delicious evening meals; three border terriers and one black labrador; cl Christmas and New Year; children by arrangement; dogs in bedrooms

THORNTON WATLASS

Buck

Thornton Watlass, Ripon, North Yorkshire HG4 4AH (01677) 422461

£80; 7 rms, most with own bthrm. Cheerful country pub overlooking cricket green in very attractive village, with interesting beamed rooms, open fire, real ales, enjoyable food in dining room, Sun lunchtime jazz, and lots of nearby walks; resident border collie; cl 25 Dec; dogs in bedrooms and residents' lounge; £5

YORK

Grange Hotel

1 Clifton, York YO30 6AA (01904) 644744

£160; 36 individually decorated rms with antiques and chintz. Regency town house close to Minster, with elegant public rooms, deep comfortable sofas and newspapers to read in front of open fire, super breakfasts, excellent food in brasserie with black leather chairs and modern art (informal cellar bar, too), and warm friendly staff; car park; disabled access; dogs welcome in bedrooms

DOG FRIENDLY PUBS

Colton Arms

Greyhound Road; W14 9SD

Unspoilt little pub kept unchanged thanks to its dedicated landlord; it's peaceful and genuinely old-fashioned, with well kept beer

Do go out of your way for a pint at this unspoilt little gem, and when you get there, don't be deterred by its inconspicuous exterior. Thanks to the friendly, dedicated landlord (and his son) this peaceful, unassuming place has survived intact down the years – it's been exactly the same for the last 40 years. As he says, 'A pub like this is a little strange in London nowadays, but most people seem to like it'. Like an old-fashioned country pub in town, the main U-shaped front bar has a log fire blazing in winter, highly polished brasses, a fox's mask, hunting crops and plates decorated with hunting scenes on the walls, and a remarkable collection of handsomely carved antique oak furniture. That room is small enough, but the two back rooms, each with their own little serving counter with a bell to ring for service, are tiny. Well kept Adnams, Fullers London Pride and Harveys on handpump, with, in summer, Caledonian Deuchars IPA, and in winter, Greene King Old Speckled Hen. When you pay, note the old-fashioned brass-bound till. Pull the curtain aside for the door out to a charming back terrace with a neat rose arbour. Food is limited to weekday lunchtime sandwiches only. The pub is next to the Queens Club tennis courts and gardens.

Enterprise ~ Lease N J and J A Nunn ~ Real ale ~ Bar food (weekday lunchtimes only) ~ No credit cards ~ (020) 7385 6956 ~ Children over three welcome till 7pm ~ Dogs allowed in bar ~ Open 12-3, 5.30-11.30; 12-4, 7-11.30(11 Sun) weekends

Crown

Grove Road/Old Ford Road; E3 5SN

Stylish dining pub with civilised bar, interesting food and choice of moods in upstairs dining rooms

Light and airy and full of lively chat, this sizeable pub is newly refurbished. The bar is relaxed and informal, with contemporary furnishings, Greene King East Green and Endeavour and Sharps Doom Bar on handpump, and a good choice of wines by the glass. There are high bar stools covered with faux animal hides by the simple bar counter, two-person stools in the same material around chunky pine tables on the polished boards, candles in coloured glass holders, a big bay window with a comfortable built-in seated area with cushions in browns, pinks and greens, a brown leather sofa beside a couple of cream easy chairs, and a scattering of books and objects on open shelves. The food here is from a sensibly short lunchtime menu. Upstairs, the three individually decorated dining areas – again, with simple contemporary but stylish furniture on carpeted or wooden floors – overlook Victoria Park.

Geronimo Inns ~ Lease Tanya Stafford ~ Real ale ~ Bar food (12-3, 7-10; 12-5 Sun; not Sun evening) ~ Restaurant ~ (020) 8880 7261 ~ Children allowed until 3pm ~ Dogs allowed in bar ~ Open 12-11

Dove

Upper Mall; W6 9TA

One of London's best-known pubs with lovely back terrace overlooking river, and cosily traditional front bar; interesting history, and sometimes unusual specials

So many writers, actors and artists have been drawn through the doors of this famous riverside pub over the years that there's a rather fascinating framed list of them all on a wall. It's said to be where 'Rule Britannia' was composed, and it was a favourite with Turner, who painted the view of the Thames from the delightful back terrace, and Graham Greene. The street itself is associated with the foundation of the Arts and Crafts movement – William Morris's old residence (open certain afternoons) is nearby. By the entrance from the quiet alley, the front snug (said to be Britain's smallest and apparently listed in *The Guinness Book of Records* is cosy and traditional, with black panelling, and red leatherette cushioned built-in wall settles and stools around dimpled copper tables; it leads to a bigger, similarly furnished room, with old framed advertisements and photographs of the pub. That opens on to the terrace, where the main flagstoned area, down some steps, has a verandah and some highly prized tables looking over the low river wall to the Thames reach just above Hammersmith Bridge. There's a tiny exclusive area up a spiral staircase, a prime spot for watching the rowing crews out on the water. They stock the full range of Fullers beers, with Chiswick, Discovery, ESB, London Pride and seasonal beers on handpump. They make a real effort in sourcing the ingredients for the well liked pubby food which runs from lunchtime sandwiches and might include some more unexpected specials such as tuscan vegetable fritatta. The pub isn't quite so crowded at lunchtimes as it is in the evenings. A plaque marks the level of the highest-ever tide in 1928.

Fullers ~ Manager Nick Kiley ~ Real ale ~ Bar food (12-3, 6-9; 12-4, 5-9 Sat; 12-5 Sun) ~ (020) 8748 9474 ~ Dogs welcome ~ Open 11-11; 12-10.30 Sun

Fox & Hounds

Latchmere Road; SW11 2JU

Victorian local standing out for its excellent mediterranean cooking; mostly evenings only, but some lunchtimes too

There's excellent mediterranean cooking at this otherwise unremarkable big Victorian local. It's run by the two brothers who transformed the Atlas (in Seagrave Road, SW6 1RX, which also welcomes dogs), and has a very similar style and menu. The pub can fill quickly, so you may have to move fast to grab a table. It's still very much the kind of place where locals happily come to drink

– and they're a more varied bunch than you might find filling the Atlas. The spacious, straightforward bar has bare boards, mismatched tables and chairs, two narrow pillars supporting the dark red ceiling, photographs on the walls, and big windows overlooking the street (the view partially obscured by colourful window boxes). There are fresh flowers and daily papers on the bar, and a view of the kitchen behind. Two rooms lead off, one more cosy with its two red leatherette sofas. Fullers London Pride, Harveys and a guest such as Black Sheep are on handpump; the carefully chosen wine list (which includes over a dozen by the glass) is written out on a blackboard; the varied piped music fits in rather well; TV. The garden has big parasols and heaters for winter.

Free house ~ Licensees Richard and George Manners ~ Real ale ~ Bar food (12.30-3(4 Sun) Fri-Sat; 7-10.30(10 Sun); not Mon-Thurs lunchtimes) ~ (020) 7924 5483 ~ Children welcome till 7pm ~ Dogs welcome ~ Open 12-3, 5-11; 12-11 Fri, Sat; 12-10.30 Sun; closed Mon lunchtime; 24 Dec-1 Jan

Greenwich Union

Royal Hill; SE10 8RT

Enterprising refurbished pub with distinctive beers from small local Meantime Brewery, plus other unusual drinks, and good, popular food

This bustling place is the tap for the small Meantime Brewery in nearby Charlton, and is the only place with all their distinctive unpasteurised beers on draught. The range includes a traditional pale ale (served cool, under pressure) a mix of proper pilsners, lagers and wheat beers, one a deliciously refreshing raspberry flavour and a stout. The helpful, knowledgeable staff will generally offer small tasters to help you choose. They also have Adnams on handpump, and a draught cider, as well as a helpfully annotated list of unusual bottled beers including some of their own. The rest of the drinks can be unfamiliar too, as they try to avoid the more common brands, and the popular food is from a seasonally changing menu; they also offer a Saturday brunch and a Sunday roast lunch. Perhaps feeling a little more like a bar than a pub, the long, narrow stoneflagged room has several different parts: a simple area at the front with a few wooden chairs and tables, a stove and newspapers, then, past the counter with its headings recalling the branding of the brewery's first beers, several brown leather cushioned pews and armchairs under framed editions of *Picture Post* on the yellow walls; piped music. Beyond here a much lighter, more modern-feeling conservatory has comfortable brown leather wallbenches, a few original pictures and paintings, and white fairy lights under the glass roof; it leads out to an appealing back patio with green picnic sets and a couple of old-fashioned lampposts. The fence at the end is painted to resemble a poppy field, and the one at the side to represent wheat growing. Though there are plenty of tables out here, it can get busy in summer (as can the whole pub on weekday evenings). In front are a couple of tables overlooking the street.

Free house ~ Licensee Andrew Ward ~ Real ale ~ Bar food (12-4, 5.30-10; 12-9(10 Sun) Sat) ~ (020) 8692 6258 ~ Children welcome ~ Dogs welcome ~ Open 12-11; 11-11 Sat; 11.30-10.30 Sun

Old Jail

Jail Lane, Biggin Hill (first turn E off A233 S of airport and industrial estate, towards Berry's Hill and Cudham); TN16 3AX

Country pub close to the city, with big garden, interesting traditional bars with RAF memorabilia, and good daily specials

With its lovely big garden (with well spaced picnic-sets on the grass, several substantial trees, and a nicely maintained play area), it's easy to forget that this good all-rounder is only ten minutes or so from the bustle of Croydon and Bromley. Situated on a narrow leafy lane and feeling very much in the countryside, it's popular with families at the weekend. Inside, several traditional beamed and low-ceilinged rooms ramble around a central servery, the nicest parts being the two cosy little areas to the right of the front entrance; divided by dark timbers, one has a very big inglenook fireplace with lots of logs and brasses, and the other has a cabinet of Battle of Britain plates – a reference perhaps to the pub's popularity with RAF pilots based at nearby Biggin Hill. Other parts have wartime prints and plates too, especially around the edge of the dining room, up a step beyond a second, smaller fireplace. There's also a plainer, flagstoned room; discreet low piped music. Fullers London Pride, Harveys and Shepherd Neame Spitfire on handpump; friendly, efficient service. There's a standard menu with things like good value sandwiches and ploughman's, as well as a wide choice of tasty blackboard specials, and they have a choice of roasts on Sundays. With nice hanging baskets in front, the attractive building wasn't itself part of any jail, but was a beef shop until becoming a pub in 1869.

Punch ~ Lease Richard Hards ~ Real ale ~ Bar food (12-2.30(2 Sat, 3 Sun), 7-9.15(9.30 Sat); not Sun evening or bank hols) ~ (01959) 572979 ~ Children welcome ~ Dogs welcome ~ Open 11.30-3, 6-11.30; 11.30-11 Fri, Sat; 12-10.30 Sun

Prospect of Whitby

Wapping Wall; E1W 3SH

Waterside pub with colourful history and good river views – welcoming to visitors and families

Although this cheerful place rather plays upon its colourful history (which tourists love and it's a favourite with evening coach tours), this is all part of the fun. It claims to be the oldest pub on the Thames (dating back to 1543), and for a long while was better known as the Devil's Tavern, thanks to its popularity with smugglers and other ne'er-do-wells. Pepys and Dickens both regularly popped in, Turner came for weeks on end to study the scene, and in the 17th c the notorious Hanging Judge Jeffreys was able to combine two of his interests by enjoying a drink at the back while looking down over the grisly goings-on in Execution Dock. Plenty of bare beams, bare boards, panelling and flagstones in the L-shaped bar (where the long pewter counter is over 400 years old), and an unbeatable river view towards Docklands from tables in the waterfront courtyard. Adnams Best, Courage Directors, Fullers London Pride, Greene King IPA and Old Speckled Hen, and Timothy Taylors Landlord on handpump, 22 wines by the glass, and a dozen malt whiskies; very friendly, efficient staff. Bar food includes sandwiches, fish and chips, burgers, steak and mushroom pie, and puddings like chocolate fondant and treacle sponge pudding.

Spirit ~ Manager Terry Standing ~ Real ale ~ Bar food (12-9.45) ~ (020) 7481 1095 ~ Children welcome ~ Dogs welcome ~ Occasional live music ~ Open 12-11(midnight Fri and Sat); 12-10.30 Sun

Spaniards Inn

Spaniards Lane; NW3 7JJ

Very popular old pub with lots of character and history, delightful big garden, and wide range of drinks and good food

Definitely a real plus, this busy and historic former toll house has a very large and quite charming garden. It's nicely arranged in a series of areas separated by judicious planting of shrubs. A crazy-paved terrace with slatted wooden tables and chairs opens on to a flagstoned walk around a small raised area with roses and a side arbour of wisteria, clematis and hops. There are even some chickens down at the end. It's popular with families (including those with dogs) and you may need to move fast to bag a table. There's an outside bar, regular summer barbecues, and a new area for smokers. Dating back to 1585, the pub is well known for its tales of hauntings and highwaymen (some of which are best taken with a very large pinch of salt), and the low-ceilinged oak-panelled rooms are attractive and full of character, with open fires, genuinely antique winged settles, candle-shaped lamps in shades, and snug little alcoves. The atmosphere is friendly and chatty, and there's an impressive range of drinks, with half a dozen ales including Adnams, Fullers London Pride, Harveys and Marstons Old Empire with a couple of guests such as Fullers London Porter and Timothy Taylors Golden Best; they have occasional themed beer festivals – they've even show-cased beers with dog-related names. They also have a couple of ciders on hand-pump, an incredible range of continental draught lagers, and 20 wines by the glass – though in summer you might find the most popular drink is their big jug of Pimms. The well liked pubby bar food is served all day. The car park fills up fast, and other parking nearby is difficult; it's fairly handy for Kenwood.

Mitchells & Butlers ~ Manager David Nichol ~ Real ale ~ Bar food (11.30(12 Sun)-10) ~ (020) 8731 6571 ~ Children welcome ~ Dogs welcome ~ Open 11(10 Sat, Sun)-11

White Cross

Water Lane; TW9 1TH

Splendidly set Thames-side pub with paved waterside area; busy in fine weather, but comfortable in winter too – though watch out for the tides

The very pleasant paved garden in front of this perfectly set Thames-side pub enjoys terrific views of the river. It gets quite busy out here in summer, when it can even feel rather like a cosmopolitan seaside resort, and there's an outside bar to make the most of the sunshine (they may use plastic glasses for outside drinking). Boats leave from immediately outside for Kingston and Hampton Court and it's not unknown for the water to reach right up the steps into the bar and cut off the towpath at the front – if you're leaving your car by the river check tide times so as not to return to find it marooned in a rapidly swelling pool of water. Inside, the two chatty main rooms have something of the air of the hotel this once was, with local prints and photographs, a traditional wooden island servery, and a good mix of variously aged customers. Two of the three log fires have mirrors above them – unusually, the third is below a window. A bright and airy upstairs room has lots more tables, and a pretty cast-iron balcony opening off, with a splendid view down to the water; piped music, TV. Served all day from a food counter (thus eliminating a wait even when it's busy), bar food includes sandwiches, salads, sausage and mash, fish and chips, home-made pies, daily roasts, and (in summer) scones and clotted cream. Wells & Youngs Bitter and Special and a couple of guests such as Caledonian Deuchars IPA and Wells & Youngs Bombardier on handpump, and a dozen or so carefully chosen wines by the glass; welcoming service.

Youngs ~ Manager Alex Gibson ~ Real ale ~ Bar food (12-9.30(8 Sun)) ~ (020) 8940 6844 ~ Children welcome in upstairs room till 6pm ~ Dogs welcome ~ Occasional live music Thurs ~ Open 11-11; 12-10.30 Sun

DOG FRIENDLY HOTELS

22 Jermyn Street Hotel

22 Jermyn Street SW1Y 6HP (020) 7734 2353

£284.90; 5 rms and 13 suites – spacious with deeply comfortable seats and sofas, flowers, plants, and antiques. Stylish little hotel owned by the same family for over 80 years and much loved by customers; no public rooms but wonderful 24-hr service, helpful notes and suggestions from the friendly owners, in-room light meals, and warm welcome for children (with their own fact sheet listing shops, restaurants, and sights geared towards them, free video library, old-fashioned and electronic games, and own bathrobes); walks in three nearby parks; disabled access; dogs in bedrooms if small and well behaved; meals, bowls, bedding

Chesterfield

35 Charles Street W1X 8LX (020) 7491 2622

£286; 107 well equipped, pretty rms. Charming hotel just off Berkeley Square, with particularly courteous helpful staff, afternoon tea in panelled library, a relaxed club-style bar with resident pianist, and fine food in attractive restaurant or light and airy conservatory; Hyde Park for walks is close by; disabled access; dogs in bedrooms; bowls, treats, bed and toy

Malmaison

Charterhouse Square EC1 6AH (020) 7012 3700

£225; 97 stylish, modern, very well equipped rms. Large, elegant red-brick

Victorian hotel converted from a nurses' residence for St Bartholomew's hospital and set in the cobbled courtyard of leafy Charterhouse Square; imaginative modern cooking in brasserie (exceptionally good steaks and popular Sunday brunch, too), chic bar set off the spacious lobby, with comfortable sofas, and helpful, attentive service; the Thames Path for walks is close by; cl Christmas; disabled access; dogs in bedrooms; dog basket; £10

Rubens

39-41 Buckingham Palace Road SW1W 0PS (020) 7834 6600

£182; 161 well equipped, individually furnished rms inc luxurious suites in the Royal Wing. Opposite Buckingham Palace and near Victoria Station, this attractive hotel has comfortable day rooms inc lounge with views of the Royal Mews, open fire in bar, and library restaurant with fine international food; disabled access; dogs in bedrooms; bowl, toys, bed, menu and other services available

Wyndham Grand

Chelsea Harbour SW10 0XG (020) 7823 3000

£179; 154 luxury suites and 6 penthouses. Spacious hotel tucked away in the quiet modern enclave of the Chelsea Harbour development and overlooking its small marina; enjoyable mediterranean-Asian cooking in Aquasia restaurant and bar, friendly service, health club, and swimming pool; disabled access; dogs in bedrooms; £30

DOG FRIENDLY PUBS

ABOYNE

Boat

Charlestown Road (B968, just off A93); AB34 5EL

Welcoming pub by the River Dee with good food; open all day, bedrooms

The first thing you will see as you go into this pleasantly pubby inn is a model train, often chugging around just below the ceiling, making appropriate noises. The partly carpeted bar – with a counter running along through the narrower linking section – also has scottish pictures and brasses, a woodburning stove in a stone fireplace, and games in the public-bar end; piped music and games machine. Spiral stairs take you up to a roomy additional dining area. They have Timothy Taylors Landlord and a couple of guests such as Caledonian Deuchars IPA and Inveralmond Thrapplesouser on handpump, also 40 malt whiskies. Tasty food, with dishes served in a choice of sizes, is prepared using plenty of fresh local produce. The pub – right by the River Dee – used to serve the ferry that it's named for; outside there are tables and they've recently opened six bedrooms so do let us know how you find them if you stay here.

Free house ~ Licensees Wilson and Jacqui Clark ~ Real ale ~ Bar food (12-2, 5.30-9) ~ Restaurant ~ (01339) 886137 ~ Dogs welcome ~ Open 11-11(12 Sat) ~ Bedrooms: £57.50B/£57.50B

GAIRLOCH

Old Inn

Just off A832/B8021; IV21 2BD

Delightful old pub with fish and seafood from neighbouring harbour; good beers too, especially in summer

The chef at this delightfully set 18th-c inn sometimes walks down to the adjacent pier to see what's being landed in the little fishing harbour – needless to say fresh seafood is a speciality here. Manned by welcoming staff, the cheerfully relaxed public bar is popular with chatty locals, no doubt here for the decent range of drinks, which include Greene King Abbot and Isle of Skye Blind Piper (a blend of Isle of Skye ales made for the pub and named after a famed 17th-c local piper), three guests such as Adnams, An Teallach Crofters Pale Ale and Isle of Skye Blaven, quite a few fairly priced wines by the glass, a decent collection of 30 malt whiskies, and speciality coffees. It's quite traditional, with paintings and murals on exposed stone walls and stools lined up along the counter; darts,

TV, fruit machine, pool and juke box. Bouillabaisse, seared scallops and langoustines are commonly on the food board, and mussels, crabs, lobster, skate, haddock and hake often crop up, too. Otherwise, the menu usually includes a good mix of dishes. The pub is nicely tucked away from the main shoreside road, with picnic-sets prettily placed by the trees alongside a stream that flows past under the old stone bridge, and is well placed for strolls up Flowerdale valley to a waterfall – you might spot eagles over the crags above. Credit (but not debit) cards incur a surcharge of £1.75.

Free house ~ Licensees Alastair and Ute Pearson ~ Real ale ~ Bar food (12-9.30 in summer) ~ Restaurant ~ (01445) 712006 ~ Children welcome ~ Dogs welcome ~ Open 11-1(12 Sun); open only 4-12 wkdys in winter ~ Bedrooms: £40B/£75B

GATEHOUSE OF FLEET
Masonic Arms
Ann Street, off B727; DG7 2HU

Nicely transformed pub with really excellent food, and relaxed traditional bar

Though the very popular food which is prepared in very tempting ways (maybe bass fillet with tomato crust on parmesan mash or goan beef curry) is quite a draw here (it's worth booking), the comfortable two-room beamed bar is still pubby, with Caledonian Deuchars IPA and a guest such as Houston Auld Copperhead on handpump, and a good choice of whiskies and wines by the glass; traditional seating, pictures on its lightly timbered walls, and blue and white plates on a delft shelf; piped music, TV and pool. Service is friendly and efficient, and there is a relaxed warm-hearted atmosphere. The bar opens into an airily attractive conservatory, with comfortable cane bucket chairs around good tables on its terracotta tiles, pot plants, and colourful pictures on one wall. The conservatory then opens through into a contemporary restaurant, with high-backed dark leather chairs around modern tables on bare boards. There are picnic-sets under cocktail parasols out in the neatly kept sheltered garden, and seats out in front of the flower-decked black and white building; this is an appealing small town, between the Solway Firth and the Galloway Forest Park.

Challenger Inns ~ Lease Paul Shepherd ~ Real ale ~ Bar food (12-2, 6-9) ~ Restaurant ~ (01557) 814335 ~ Children welcome ~ Dogs allowed in bar ~ Open 11.30-2.30, 5.30-11.30; 11.30-11.30 Sat, Sun

INVERARAY
George
Main Street East; PA32 8TT

Well placed and attractive, with atmospheric old bar, enjoyable food and pleasant garden; comfortable bedrooms

Run by the same family since 1860, this handsome Georgian inn has plenty to offer. Its dark bustling pubby bar oozes Scottish history from its bare stone walls, and shows plenty of age in its exposed joists, old tiles and big flagstones.

It has antique settles, cushioned stone slabs along the walls, carved wooden benches, nicely grained wooden-topped cast-iron tables and four cosy log fires. The bar carries over 100 malt whiskies and a couple of beers from Fyne on hand-pump; darts. A smarter flagstoned restaurant has french windows that open to tables tucked into nice private corners on a series of well laid out terraces. You order the generously served enjoyable pubby food (including haggis, neeps and tatties) at your table. It's near Inveraray Castle, and the shore of Loch Fyne (where you may glimpse seals or even a basking shark or whale), and well placed for the great Argyll woodland gardens, best for their rhododendrons in May and early June.

Free house ~ Licensee Donald Clark ~ Real ale ~ Bar food (12-9) ~ Restaurant ~ (01499) 302111 ~ Children welcome ~ Dogs welcome ~ Live entertainment Fri/Sat ~ Open 11-midnight ~ Bedrooms: £35B/£70B

ISLE OF WHITHORN
Steam Packet

Harbour Row; DG8 8LL

Unfussy family-run inn with splendid views of working harbour from bar and some bedrooms, and good food

Big picture windows at this modernised inn have fine views out over a busy crowd of yachts and fishing boats in the harbour, and then beyond to calmer waters. Run by the same family for over 26 years, this is an unfussy but welcoming place. The comfortable low-ceilinged bar is split into two: on the right, plush button-back banquettes and boat pictures, and on the left, green leatherette stools around cast-iron-framed tables on big stone tiles, and a woodburning stove in the bare stone wall. Bar food can be served in the lower-beamed dining room, which has excellent colour wildlife photographs, rugs on its wooden floor, and a solid fuel stove, and there's also a small eating area off the lounge bar, as well as a conservatory. The menu is very tempting with inventive specials. Three guests from brewers such as Batemans and Kelburn are kept alongside the Theakstons XB on handpump, and they've quite a few malt whiskies, and a good wine list; TV, pool and board games. There are white tables and chairs in the garden. You can walk from here up to the remains of St Ninian's Kirk, on a head-land behind the village.

Free house ~ Licensee Alastair Scoular ~ Real ale ~ Bar food (12-2, 6.30-9) ~ Restaurant ~ (01988) 500334 ~ Children welcome except in bar ~ Dogs allowed in bar and bedrooms ~ Open 11(12 Sun)-11(midnight Sat); closed 2.30-6 Tues-Thurs in winter ~ Bedrooms: £30B/£60B

KILMAHOG
Lade

A84 just NW of Callander, by A821 junction; FK17 8HD

Lively and pubby, with own brew beers, and shop specialising in scottish brews; traditional scottish music at weekends, and good food

It's all family hands on deck to offer a cheery welcome at this lively inn. One of the licensees is passionate about real ale, which explains not just their own excellent beers, but also the scottish real ale shop with over 120 bottled brews from 26 microbreweries around Scotland. In the bar they always have their own WayLade, LadeBack and LadeOut on handpump, along with a guest such as Broughton Clipper, nine wines by the glass and about 30 malts. There's plenty of character in the several small beamed areas – cosy with red walls, panelling and stripped stone, and decorated with highland prints and works by local artists; piped music. The menu includes scottish dishes, such as battered haggis balls and raspberry cranachan and meals are hearty and home cooked using local ingredients. A big windowed restaurant (with a more ambitious menu) opens on to a terrace and a pleasant garden with three fish ponds.

Own brew ~ Licensees Frank and Rita Park ~ Real ale ~ Bar food (12(12.30 Sun)-9; 12-3, 5-9 Mon-Fri in winter) ~ Restaurant ~ (01877) 330152 ~ Children welcome ~ Dogs allowed in bar ~ Ceilidhs Fri and Sat evenings ~ Open 12(12.30 Sun)-11(1 Fri, Sat)

KIPPEN

Cross Keys

Main Street; village signposted off A811 W of Stirling; FK8 3DN

Cosy village inn, popular with locals and visitors

The recent addition of a few extra comforts has not detracted from the timeless local atmosphere which has always been a large part of the appeal here. The cosy bar is timelessly stylish with lovely dark panelling and subdued lighting. A straightforward lounge has a good log fire, and there's a coal fire in the attractive family dining room. They have Harviestoun Bitter & Twisted on handpump, and over 30 malt whiskies; cards, dominoes, TV in the separate public bar; piped music. Bar food might include chicken breast stuffed with haggis, battered haddock with crushed peas, and five cheese ravioli with tomato and basil sauce. Tables in the garden have good views towards the Trossachs.

Free house ~ Licensee Debby McGregorand Brian Horsburgh ~ Real ale ~ Bar food (12-9(8 Sat)) ~ Restaurant ~ (01786) 870293 ~ Children welcome ~ Dogs allowed in bar and bedrooms ~ Open 12-11(1 Fri, Sat); closed Mon ~ Bedrooms: £70S/£90S

KIRK YETHOLM

Border

Village signposted off B6352/B6401 crossroads, SE of Kelso; The Green; TD5 8PQ

Welcoming and comfortable hotel with good inventive food and a famous beer story

Run by a warmly hospitable couple, this well tended hotel has good, interesting food, comfortable bedrooms, and owing to an old tradition, a particularly good welcome for walkers (and a water bowl for dogs). Alfred Wainwright determined that anyone who walked the entire 256 miles of the Pennine Way National Trail would get a free drink. He left some money here to cover the bill, but it has long since run out, and the pub has generously continued to foot the bill. In recent times the Broughton Brewery has helped out by producing an exclusive beer, Pennine Way. They usually have another scottish beer on handpump too, such as Atlas Three Sisters, decent wines by the glass and a good range of malt whiskies. The cheerfully unpretentious bar has beams and flagstones, a log fire, a signed photograph of Wainwright and other souvenirs of the Pennine Way, and appropriate borders scenery etchings and murals; snug side rooms lead off. Using carefully sourced ingredients (including local fish, game and organic pork), food from the seasonal menu is inventive without being at all pretentious. There's a roomy pink-walled dining room, a comfortable lounge with a second log fire, and a neat conservatory; piped music, TV, darts, board games, and children's games and books. A sheltered back terrace has picnic-sets and a play area, and the colourful window boxes and floral tubs make a very attractive display outside.

Free house ~ Licensees Philip and Margaret Blackburn ~ Real ale ~ Bar food (12-2, 6-9(8.30 winter), unless booked for weddings) ~ Restaurant ~ (01573) 420237 ~ Children welcome away from public bar ~ Dogs allowed in bar and bedrooms ~ Open 11(12 Sun)-11 ~ Bedrooms: £45B/£90B

KIRKCUDBRIGHT
Selkirk Arms
High Street; DG6 4JG

Comfortable well run hotel with good service, enjoyable imaginative food and local sports bar

There's a tradition that Burns composed the Selkirk Grace while staying in this well kept and much modernised 18th-century hotel (though a rival school of thought is that he did so while staying at St Mary's Isle with Lord Daer, Selkirk's son). Either way, this place stocks a beer called The Grace, which is brewed especially for them by Sulwath, alongside a guest beer such as Timothy Taylors Landlord. The bars here range from the very simple locals' front bar which has its own street entrance, a TV for live sport, darts and dominoes, to a welcoming partitioned high-ceilinged lounge bar at the heart of the hotel, with comfortable upholstered armchairs and wall banquettes and original paintings which are for sale. Bar food is limited but the bistro meals are more elaborate. Service is thoughtful and efficient and there's a nice friendly atmosphere. A neatly set out garden has smart wooden furniture with contrasting blue umbrellas and also a 15th-c font. The hotel is in the older part of this attractive historic town at the mouth of the Dee where a handful of fishing boats land their catch on the quay.

Free house ~ Licensees Douglas McDavid and Chris Walker ~ Real ale ~ Bar food (12-2, 6-9) ~ Restaurant ~ (01557) 330402 ~ Children welcome away from public bar ~ Dogs welcome ~ Open 11-11(12 Sat)

WEEM

Ailean Chraggan

B846; PH15 2LD

Friendly family-run hotel with good food – a particularly nice place to stay

Beautifully kept, small and friendly, this family-run hotel is a lovely place to stay – as one reader put it, 'every request was promptly met and with a smile'. You're likely to find chatty locals in the bar which carries around 100 malt whiskies, a couple of beers from the local Inveralmond brewery on handpump, and a very good wine list with several by the glass; winter darts and board games. The lovely views from its two flower-filled terraces look to the mountains beyond the Tay, and up to Ben Lawers (the highest peak in this part of Scotland) and the owners can arrange fishing nearby. Thoughtfully sourced food from an inventive changing menu is served in either the comfortably carpeted modern lounge or the dining room,

Free house ~ Licensee Alastair Gillespie ~ Real ale ~ Bar food ~ Restaurant ~ (01887) 820346 ~ Children welcome ~ Dogs allowed in bar and bedrooms ~ Open 11-11 ~ Bedrooms: £57.50B/£95B

DOG FRIENDLY HOTELS, INNS, B&Bs AND FARMS

ACHILTIBUIE

Summer Isles Hotel

Achiltibuie, Ullapool, Ross-shire IV26 2YQ (01854) 622282

£140; 13 comfortable rms. Beautifully placed above the sea near end of very long and lonely road and with plenty of surrounding walks; warm, friendly, well furnished hotel with delicious set menus using wonderful fresh ingredients (in which it's largely self-sufficient), a choice of superb puddings and excellent array of uncommon cheeses; pretty watercolours and flowers; self-catering, too; cl Nov-Easter; children over 8; dogs in bedrooms but must not be left unattended

ALYTH

Tigh Na Leigh

22-24 Airlie Street, Alyth, Perthshire PH11 8AJ (01828) 632372

£80; 5 comfortably furnished, well equipped rms. Former Victorian doctor's house with friendly, helpful owners, informal and relaxing atmosphere and interesting contemporary décor; three different lounges – one with a log fire, one for TV and a reading one with books, daily papers and a computer – super breakfasts with home-made bread and preserves and good, enjoyable meals using local, seasonal produce (some is home grown) in conservatory dining room; landscaped gardens (dogs must be on lead) and nearby parks; two resident cats; cl 24 Dec-12 Feb; children over 12; dogs in bedrooms; treats and towels; £7.50

ANSTRUTHER
Spindrift

Pittenweem Road, Anstruther, Fife KY10 3DT (01333) 310573

£66; 8 comfortable, well equipped rms (the Captain's Room is a favourite). Neatly kept Victorian house with friendly owners, elegant guest lounge with honesty bar, and enjoyable breakfasts and homely evening meals (by arrangement) in attractive dining room; cl Jan; dogs by arrangement

APPLECROSS
Applecross Inn

Shore Street, Applecross, Strathcarron, Ross-shire IV54 8LR (01520) 744262

£90; 7 rms, all with breathtaking sea views over Sound of Raasay. Gloriously placed informal inn with tables out by shore, simple comfortable and friendly bar, log or peat fire in lounge, small restaurant with excellent fresh fish and seafood; plenty of walks; cl 25 Dec and 5 Jan; partial disabled access; dogs welcome

ARDEONAIG
Ardeonaig Hotel

Ardeonaig, Killin, Perthshire FK21 8SY (01567) 820400

£180; 27 rms. Extended 17th-c farmhouse on South shore of Loch Tay, with log fire in snug and lounge, library with fine views, fresh local produce for enjoyable food in new bistro; salmon fishing rights on the loch – as well as fishing for trout – a drying and rod room, and boats and outboards; shooting and stalking can be arranged, lots of surrounding walks; self-catering cottages; children over 12; partial disabled access; dogs in some bedrooms; £10

ARDUAINE
Loch Melfort Hotel

Arduaine, Oban, Argyll PA34 4XG (01852) 200233

£138; 25 rms with gorgeous sea views. Comfortable hotel, popular in summer with passing yachtsmen (hotel's own moorings), nautical charts and marine glasses in airy modern bar, comfortable lounges, own lobster pots and nets so emphasis on seafood, pleasant foreshore walks, and outstanding springtime woodland gardens; resident beagle; cl Jan-mid-Feb; disabled access; dogs in cedar wing only

AUCHENCAIRN
Balcary Bay

Auchencairn, Castle Douglas, Kirkcudbrightshire DG7 1QZ (01556) 640217

£120; 20 rms with fine views. Charming hotel, once a smugglers' haunt, with wonderful views over bay, neat grounds running down to water, comfortable public rooms (one with log fire), relaxed friendly atmosphere, good enjoyable food inc super breakfasts, and lots of walks; resident red setter; cl Dec and Jan; disabled access; dogs in bedrooms only

BALLATER
Auld Kirk

31 Braemar Road, Ballater, Aberdeenshire AB35 5RQ (01339) 755762

£90; 7 attractively refurbished rms. 19th-c church converted to hotel in 1986 and still with bell tower, stained glass and exposed rafters; now a restaurant-with-rooms with stylishly furnished bar, Minister's room (small and cosy room next to bar where breakfasts and lunches are taken), and unique Spirit Restaurant with vaulted ceilings, ornate chandeliers, and cathedral windows; two resident dogs; disabled access; dogs in bedrooms and bar

BRIDGE OF CALLY
Bridge of Cally Hotel

Bridge of Cally, Blairgowrie, Perthshire PH10 7JJ (01250) 886231

£70; 18 rms. Friendly family-run former drovers' inn set on 1,500 acres of private moorland, with good food using seasonal game in popular restaurant and convivial, chatty and comfortable bar; salmon fishing, deer stalking, shooting, golf and skiing can be provided or are within easy access; disabled access; dogs welcome in two rooms but must be well behaved

CALLANDER
Poppies

Leny Road, Callander, Perthshire FK17 8AL (on A84 (Leny Road)) (01877) 330329

£79; 9 newly refurbished rms. Small private hotel with excellent food in popular and attractive candlelit dining room, comfortable lounge, cosy bar with good choice of malt whiskies, helpful friendly owners, and seats in the garden; cl 6-11 Nov, 2-22 Jan; disabled access; dogs welcome in bedrooms

CLACHAN SEIL
Willowburn

Clachan Seil, Isle of Seil PA34 4TJ (01852) 300276

£170 inc dinner; 7 rms facing the water. Simple little white hotel on shore of Clachan Sound, with enthusiastic, welcoming owners, open fire and local guide-books in straightforward lounge and bar (both with lovely views), imaginative food using local and home-grown produce and delicious breakfasts in airy dining room overlooking water; guests' dogs get a letter from the hotel's pets (labrador, hovawart and one cat); lots of wildlife and walks; cl mid-Nov-mid-Mar; children over 8; dogs in bedrooms and residents' bar; welcome pack, towels, bedding

CROMARTY

Royal

Marine Terrace, Cromarty, Ross-shire IV11 8YN (01381) 600217

£80; 10 rms. Traditional waterfront hotel (you may see dolphins) with friendly owners and staff, attractive lounges, bars and sun lounge, and good home cooking with an emphasis on seafood; gets very busy in summer; self-catering, too; good walks on beach and nearby grassland areas; dogs welcome away from eating areas

CULLEN

Seafield Hotel

Cullen, Buckie, Banffshire AB56 4SG (01542) 840791

£90; 23 attractively furnished, spacious rms. 19th-c former coaching inn with easy-going, comfortable and friendly atmosphere, residents' lounge and convivial bar, log fires, fresh flowers and antiques, good enjoyable food using plenty of local fresh fish (and of course the famous cullen skink soup) in informal restaurant, nice breakfasts, helpful staff, and fine sandy beach just 5 minutes away; lots to do nearby; partial disabled access; dogs in bedrooms; £5

DRUMNADROCHIT

Polmaily House

Drumnadrochit, Inverness IV63 6XT (2.5 miles off A82 via A831 W)
(01456) 450343

£140; 14 light, elegant rms. Very relaxing and comfortable hotel in 18 acres of grounds, with drawing room and library, open fire and excellent food in restaurant (wonderful packed lunches, too); a happy place for families with well equipped indoor play area and lots of supervised activities, and plenty of ponies and pets; indoor heated swimming pool, tennis, croquet, fishing, boating, and riding; lots of walks; disabled access; dogs in some bedrooms; £10

DULNAIN BRIDGE

Auchendean Lodge

Dulnain Bridge, Grantown-on-Spey, Morayshire PH26 3LU (01479) 851347

£90; 2 comfortable rms. Edwardian hunting lodge with wonderful views over Spey Valley to Cairngorm mountains; two homely lounges with plenty of pictures and knick-knacks, piano for guests' use, and warm log fire; enthusiastic owners, super breakfasts with honey from own bees and organic fruit for jams, and lovely garden; Bess, the owner's dog, loves taking other dog friends for walks in the nearby woods and moors; one cat; cl mid-Oct-Easter; children over 12; dogs in bedrooms and one lounge; bedding and treats available; £5

DUNBLANE

Cromlix House

Cromlix, Dunblane, Perthshire FK15 9JT (01786) 822125

£190; 14 rms inc 8 spacious suites. Walking, loch and river fishing or shooting on 2,000 acres around rather gracious country house; relaxing day rooms with fine antiques and family portraits, informal atmosphere, very good food using local produce in two dining rooms, and courteous service; dogs in bedrooms only; £10

EAST HAUGH

East Haugh House

East Haugh, Pitlochry, Tayside PH16 5TE (1 mile off A9 just S of Pitlochry, on Old Military Road parallel to A9) (01796) 473121

£118; 12 rms, 5 in converted bothy, some with four-posters and one with open fire. Turreted stone house with lots of character, delightful bar in cream and navy with fishing theme, house-party atmosphere, and particularly good food inc local seafood and seasonal game and home-grown vegetables cooked by chef/proprietor; excellent shooting, stalking and salmon and trout fishing on surrounding local estates; two resident dogs and lots of walks; cl Christmas week; disabled access to one room; dogs in ground floor bedrooms with direct access outside; £10

EDINBURGH

Malmaison

1 Tower Place, Leith, Edinburgh EH6 7DB (0131) 468 5000

£150; 100 stylish, well equipped rms, some with harbour views. Converted baronial-style seamen's mission in fashionable docks area of Leith with very good food in downstairs brasserie (wrought iron-work, leather banquettes and candlelight), cheerful light and airy café bar with terrace, and friendly service; gym; free parking; disabled access; dogs if small; £10

ERISKA

Isle of Eriska Hotel

Ledaig, Oban, Argyll PA37 1SD (2 miles off A828 N of Connel) (01631) 720371

£300; 25 rms. Impressive baronial hotel in wonderful position on small island linked by bridge to mainland; very relaxed country house atmosphere, log fires and pretty drawing room, excellent food, exemplary service, and comprehensive wine list; leisure complex with indoor swimming pool, sauna, gym and so forth, lovely surrounding walks, and nine-hole golf course, clay pigeon shooting and golf – and plenty of wildlife inc tame badgers who come nightly to the library door for their bread and milk; resident dogs; cl Jan; disabled access; dogs welcome in bedrooms

GATEHOUSE OF FLEET
Cally Palace

Gatehouse Of Fleet, Castle Douglas, Kirkcudbrightshire DG7 2DL (2.5 miles off A75 via B727 or B796) (01557) 814341

£206 inc dinner; 56 rms. 18th-c country mansion, a hotel since 1934, with marble fireplaces and ornate ceilings in public rooms, relaxed cocktail bar and sunny conservatory, enjoyable food in elegant dining room (smart dress required), evening pianist, and helpful friendly staff; 18-hole golf course, croquet and tennis, indoor leisure complex with heated swimming pool, private fishing/boating loch, and plenty of walks; cl Jan; disabled access; dogs in bedrooms but must not be left unattended; £5

GIFFORD
Tweeddale Arms

Gifford, Haddington, East Lothian EH41 4QU (01620) 810240

£90; 13 rms. Civilised late 17th-c inn in quiet village with views across green to fine avenue of 300-year-old lime trees; tranquil lounge with comfortable sofas and chairs, public bar with real ales, open fire and chatty, relaxed atmosphere, gracious dining room with wide choice of changing food, and helpful service; walks nearby; disabled access; dogs in some bedrooms and must be well behaved

GIGHA
Gigha Hotel

Isle of Gigha PA41 7AA (01583) 505254

£87; 13 rms, most with own bthrm. Traditional family-run hotel, small and attractive with lovely views, lots of charm, bustling bar (popular with yachts-men and locals), neatly kept comfortable residents' lounge, and local seafood in restaurant; self-contained cottages, too; fields for dogs to walk in; cl Christmas; dogs welcome in bedrooms

GLASGOW
Hotel du Vin

One Devonshire Gardens, Glasgow G12 0UX (0141) 339 2001

£145; 49 luxurious rms. Boutique hotel, under new ownership, in tree-lined Victorian terrace, with new bar and bistro, modern european cooking, a carefully chosen wine list, and friendly, helpful staff; parks nearby for dogs to exercise; disabled access; dogs in bedrooms

Malmaison

278 West George Street, Glasgow G2 4LL (0141) 572 1000

£160; 72 very well equipped, individually decorated rms, some with french windows. Stylishly converted church with greek façade, striking central wrought-iron staircase, well stocked bar in vaulted basement, relaxed contemporary atmosphere, friendly staff, and enjoyable modern food in attractive brasserie; gym; disabled access; dogs if small in bedrooms, and in other rooms not serving food; £10

GLENROTHES
Balbirnie House

Markinch, Glenrothes, Fife KY7 6NE (0.5 miles off A92 N of A911, via B9130) (01592) 610066

£195; 30 rms. Fine Georgian country house in 400-acre park landscaped in Capability Brown style, with fresh flowers, open fires and antiques in gracious public rooms, extremely good inventive food, and a big wine list; disabled access; dogs in bedrooms; £20

INNERLEITHEN
Traquair Arms

Innerleithen, Peebles-shire EH44 6PD (01896) 830229

£80; 15 comfortable rms. Very friendly hotel with interesting choice of good food in attractive dining room, cosy lounge bar, friendly service, superb local Traquair ale, nice breakfasts, and quiet garden; self-catering cottages, too; ten minutes to open countryside; cl 25 and 26 Dec; dogs welcome away from restaurant

INVERNESS
Dunain Park

Inverness IV3 8JN (on A82 SW) (01463) 230512

£225; 15 spacious, attractive rms. 18th-c italianate mansion in six acres of well tended gardens and woodland, a short walk from the River Ness and Caledonian Canal; charming owners, comfortable drawing room and cosy lounge with open fires and fresh flowers, extremely good food making the best of wonderful local produce, generous breakfasts, and a fine collection of whiskies; lots of walks and horse riding, fishing, and golf courses nearby; disabled access; dogs in garden cottages; £10

ISLE ORNSAY
Eilean Iarmain

Isle Ornsay, Isle of Skye IV43 8QR (01471) 833332

£160; 16 individual rms inc 4 suites (those in main hotel best), all with fine views. Sparkling white hotel with Gaelic-speaking staff and locals, big cheerfully busy bar, two pretty dining rooms with lovely sea views, and very good food; disabled access; well behaved dogs welcome

Kinloch Lodge

Isle Ornsay, Isle of Skye IV43 8QY (01471) 833214

£175; 14 rms. Surrounded by rugged mountain scenery at the head of Loch Na Dal, this charming white stone hotel has a relaxed atmosphere in comfortable and attractive drawing rooms, antiques, portraits, flowers, log fires, and good imaginative food; cookery demonstrations; two resident whippets; plenty of surrounding walks; children by arrangement; cl 22-28 Dec; dogs in bedrooms; £5

KELSO

Ednam House

Ednam, Kelso, Roxburghshire TD5 7HT (01573) 224168

£106; 32 rms (the original ones are the nicest) inc 2 suites. Large Georgian manor house by River Tweed with three acres of gardens and owned by same family since 1928; three distinctive lounges with antiques and plenty of comfortable seating, two bars (one with fishing theme), excellent food in large candlelit dining room overlooking river, lovely informal atmosphere and particularly good, friendly service; shooting and fishing by arrangement; genuine welcome for children; two resident dogs; cl two weeks over Christmas and New Year; partial disabled access; dogs welcome away from restaurant

KILBERRY

Kilberry Inn

Kilberry, Tarbert, Argyll PA29 6YD (01880) 770223

£155 inc dinner; 3 ground-floor rms. Homely and warmly welcoming inn on west coast of Knapdale with fine sea views, old-fashioned character, very good traditional home cooking relying on fresh local ingredients; resident dog; cl Jan-mid-Mar; children over 12; partial disabled access; dogs in bedrooms; bowls and treats; £10

KILCHRENAN

Ardanaiseig

Kilchrenan, Taynuilt, Argyll PA35 1HE (01866) 833333

£248; 17 lovely big, themed rms with views of the loch or gardens. Scottish baronial mansion quietly set in its own natural gardens and woodland right on Loch Awe; antique-filled reception areas, comfortable squashy sofas, bold décor and colours, marvellous modern cooking, super afternoon tea, and very friendly young staff; open-air theatre, tennis and croquet, bathing, fishing, and rowing boat; resident jack russell; cl 2 Jan-1 Feb; children over 10 in restaurant; dogs in bedrooms; £10

Taychreggan Hotel

Kilchrenan, Taynuilt, Argyll PA35 1HQ (01866) 833211

£133; 18 rms. Civilised hotel with fine garden running down to Loch Awe and 40 acres of grounds where dogs may walk (they can arrange water sports, riding, deer stalking, fishing and golf); comfortable, elegant drawing room, convivial bar, snooker, polite, efficient staff, good freshly prepared food and carefully chosen wine list in dining room, dozens of malt whiskies, and pretty inner courtyard; cl Christmas; dogs in some bedrooms (must not be left unattended); £10

KILNINVER

Knipoch

Knipoch, Oban, Argyll PA34 4QT (01852) 316251

£168; 20 rms. Elegant very well kept Georgian hotel in lovely countryside overlooking Loch Feochan; fine family portraits, log fires, fresh flowers and polished furniture in comfortable lounges and bars, carefully chosen wines and malt whiskies, and marvellous food inc their own smoked salmon; three resident dogs; dogs welcome in bedrooms

KINCLAVEN BY STANLEY

Ballathie House

Stanley, Perth PH1 4QN (01250) 883268

£196; 42 pretty rms, some luxurious and some in newer building with river views from balconies. On vast estate with fine salmon fishing on River Tay (lodges and facilities for fishermen) and plenty of sporting opportunities, this turreted mansion has a comfortable and relaxed drawing room, separate lounge and bar, good enjoyable modern scottish cooking, croquet and putting; limited disabled access; dogs in some bedrooms (not to be left unattended); treats; £10

KINNESSWOOD

Lomond Country Inn

Main Street, Kinnesswood, Kinross KY13 9HN (3.7 miles off M90 junction 8 northbound; turn right off A90 on B919; a little further from junction 7 southbound, via A911) (01592) 840253

£70; 12 comfortable rms, 8 in an extension. Attractive little inn in village centre with views across Loch Leven (nice sunsets), open fires, informal bustling bar, well kept real ales, and good reasonably priced bar and restaurant food using local produce; walks in grounds and elsewhere; disabled access; dogs welcome away from dining room; £2

KIRKTON OF GLENISLA
Glenisla Hotel
Glenisla, Blairgowrie, Perthshire PH11 8PH (01575) 582223

£70; 6 cosy rms. Old coaching inn in lovely quiet countryside with lots of country pursuits all around; convivial, traditionally furnished beamed bar with open fire, drawing room with comfortable sofas, flowers and books, games room, enjoyable seasonal food and hearty scottish breakfasts in elegant dining room, and well kept real ales; dogs in bedrooms; £5

LOCKERBIE
Dryfesdale Hotel
Dryfebridge, Lockerbie, Dumfries-shire DG11 2SF (1 mile off A74 junction 17; B7076 N) (01576) 202427

£110; 27 fine rms with views of grounds. Relaxed and comfortable former manse in five acres of grounds, open fire in homely lounge, convivial bar, good food in pleasant airy restaurant, garden and lovely surrounding countryside, putting and croquet; good disabled access; dogs in some bedrooms; £5

MEIKLEOUR
Meikleour Hotel
Meikleour, Perth, Perthshire PH2 6EB (01250) 883206

£120; 5 comfortable, spotlessly clean rms. Attractive, early 19th-c inn, friendly and civilised, with log fires in two lounge rooms (one carpeted, one with flagstones), a modicum of fishing equipment (the River Tay is nearby), local beers, tasty pubby food and elegant panelled restaurant specialising in local game and fish, and good breakfasts; Victorian-style seats out on small colonnaded verandah and tables and picnic-sets under tall conifers on gently sloping lawn – note the nearby beech hedge planted over 250 years ago and the grandest in the world; dogs in bedrooms

MELROSE
Burts
Market Square, Melrose, Roxburghshire TD6 9PN (2.9 miles off A7 via A6091 and B6374; Market Square – handy for A68 too) (01896) 822285

£116; 20 rms. Welcoming 18th-c family-run hotel close to abbey ruins in delightfully quiet village; coal fire in bustling bar, residents' lounge, consistently popular imaginative food, and exceptional breakfasts; riverside walks for dogs; cl 26 Dec, 2-4 Jan; partial disabled access; dogs in bedrooms and bar

MINNIGAFF

Creebridge House

Creebridge, Newton Stewart, Wigtownshire DG8 6NP (01671) 402121

£100; 18 rms inc 2 with four-posters. Attractive country-house hotel in three acres of gardens with relaxed friendly atmosphere, open fire in comfortable drawing room, cheerful bar, and big choice of delicious food inc fine local fish and seafood in garden restaurant; walks in nearby woods; resident cat; cl three weeks in Jan; dogs in bedrooms; bedding, bowls, chews

MUIR OF ORD

Dower House

Highfield, Muir of Ord, Ross-shire IV6 7XN (0.8 miles off A832 from station, via A862 N) (01463) 870090

£140; 4 rms with fresh flowers and views. Gabled cottage with family home-type atmosphere and surrounded by lovely wooded garden, friendly owners, cosy lounge with log fire, ornaments, books and antiques, attractive, homely dining room, wholesome and interesting british cooking, and generous scottish break-fasts using their own eggs and local honey; high tea for small children; cl Christmas; disabled access; dogs welcome in bedrooms

NEWTONMORE

Crubenbeg House

Falls of Truim, By Newtonmore PH20 1BE (01540) 673300

£60; 4 individually decorated, well equipped rms. Carefully run guest house with wonderful views from all rooms, charming, friendly owners, lots of teddy bears (Mrs England collects them), open fire in comfortable, homely guest lounge, and marvellous breakfasts taken around large antique table in light and airy dining room; packed lunches and light suppers by arrangement; resident saluki/ alsatian; lots of surrounding outdoor activities; cl some time in Nov and Jan; children over 12; disabled access; dogs in bedrooms (not to be left unattended) and other areas (not restaurant)

PITLOCHRY

Killiecrankie House Hotel

Killiecrankie, Pitlochry, Perthshire PH16 5LG (3 miles off A9 via B8019/B8079 Killiecrankie road just N of Pitlochry) (01796) 473220

£140; 10 spotless rms. Comfortable country hotel in spacious grounds with splendid mountain views, mahogany-panelled bar with fine wildlife paintings, cosy sitting room with books and games, relaxed atmosphere, friendly owners, and excellent well presented, locally sourced food and good wine list in elegant restaurant; resident cocker spaniel bitch; fine nearby walks; cl Jan-Feb; disabled access; dogs in some bedrooms but must not be left unattended; £10

PORT APPIN

Airds Hotel

Port Appin, Appin, Argyll PA38 4DF (2 miles off A828) (01631) 730236

£295 inc dinner; 11 lovely rms. Instantly relaxing 18th-c inn with lovely views of Loch Linnhe and island of Lismore; two comfortable and elegant lounges, open log fire, conservatory, professional courteous staff, charming owners, exceptional food (as is wine list), and lots of surrounding walks, with more on Lismore (small boat every hour); croquet and putting lawn, clay pigeon shooting and riding; self-catering cottage; children over 9 for dinner (high tea at 6.30pm); dogs in some bedrooms; £10

PORT CHARLOTTE

Port Charlotte Hotel

Port Charlotte, Isle of Islay (01496) 850360

£130; 10 comfortable rms. Welcoming inn with lovely views over Loch Indaal (a sea inlet) and across to the mountains of Jura; central bar with log and peat fire and padded wall seats and pubby chairs on bare boards, comfortable and relaxed residents' lounge, nice pictures throughout, real ales, exceptional collection of around 140 Islay and rare Islay malts, roomy conservatory, lots of seafood and local lamb and beef in good restaurant, and lovely views; seats in garden; stroll down to sandy beach; dogs in bedrooms only

PORTPATRICK

Knockinaam Lodge

Portpatrick, Stranraer, Wigtownshire DG9 9AD (01776) 810471

£300 inc dinner; 9 individual rms. Lovely, very neatly kept little Victorian hotel in 30 acres of garden and woodland with own private beach; comfortable and relaxing lounges, open fire and fresh flowers, wonderful food, and friendly caring service; dramatic surroundings, with lots of fine cliff walks; resident black labrador; children over 12 in evening restaurant (high tea at 6pm); dogs in some bedrooms; £20

PORTREE

Rosedale

Quay Brae, Portree, Isle of Skye IV51 9DB (0.4 miles off A87 via A855; on Bank Street take sharp right down Quay Brae) (01478) 613131

£100; 21 rms, many with harbour views. Built from three fishermen's cottages with lots of passages and stairs, this family-run waterfront hotel has a traditional lounge, small first-floor restaurant with freshly cooked popular food, lots of whiskies in cocktail bar, helpful staff, and marvellous views; walks along shore or in forest; cl Nov–Mar; disabled access; dogs in some bedrooms and bar; must be well behaved

RAASAY

Borodale House

Isle of Raasay, Kyle, Ross-shire IV40 8PB (01478) 660222

£80; 12 comfortable, individually decorated rms. On island just 20 mins from Skye, this Victorian hotel has marvellous views over the Sound of Raasay, and is popular with walkers and bird-watchers; good lunches, afternoon teas and evening meals using venison and pork from the island, and hearty breakfasts; dogs in bedrooms; £5

SCARISTA

Scarista House

Scarista, Harris, Isle of Harris HS3 3HX (01859) 550238

£175; 5 rms, some in annexe. Marvellously wild countryside and empty beaches surround this isolated small hotel with antique-furnished rooms, open fires, warm friendly atmosphere, and plenty of books (no radio or TV); impressive wine list and good food in candlelit dining room using organic home-grown vegetables and herbs, hand-made cheeses, their own eggs, home-made bread, cakes, biscuits, yoghurt and marmalade, and lots of fish and shellfish; excellent for wildlife, walks and fishing; resident dog and two cats; cl Jan-Feb; dogs in bedrooms and library

SCONE

Murrayshall House

Perth PH2 7PH (01738) 551171

£170; 41 rms inc 16 suites, plus lodge which sleeps six. Handsome mansion in 300-acre park where dogs may walk and very popular with golfers (it has two of its own courses); comfortable elegant public rooms, warm friendly staff, relaxed atmosphere, imaginative food, and good wines; resident cat; disabled access; dogs in bedrooms

SCOURIE

Scourie Hotel

Scourie, Lairg, Sutherland IV27 4SX (01971) 502396

£90; 20 rms with views to Scourie Bay. A haven for anglers, with 36 exclusive beats on 25,000-acre estate; snug bar and cocktail bar, two comfortable lounges and good food using plenty of local game and fish in smart dining room; fine walks on the doorstep; resident springer spaniel and two cats; cl Oct-Mar; dogs in bedrooms and lounge

SHIEL BRIDGE
Kintail Lodge

Glenshiel, Kyle, Ross-shire IV40 8HL (on A87) (01599) 511275

£104; 12 big rms. Pleasantly informal and fairly simple former shooting lodge on Loch Duich, with magnificent views, four acres of walled gardens, residents' lounge bar and comfortable sitting room, good well prepared food inc local seafood in conservatory restaurant, and fine collection of malt whiskies; three resident dogs; dogs welcome away from eating areas

SHIELDAIG
Tigh an Eilean

Shieldaig, Strathcarron, Ross-shire IV54 8XN (01520) 755251

£240 inc dinner; 11 rms. Attractive hotel in outstanding position with lovely view of pine-covered island and sea – kayaks, private fishing and sea fishing arranged; within easy reach of NTS Torridon Estate, Beinn Eighe nature reserve and Applecross peninsula; pretty woodburner in one of the two comfortable residents' lounges, newly refurbished bar, library, and modern dining room with delicious food inc home-baked bread; two resident black labradors; cl end Oct-mid-Mar; dogs in bedrooms only; bedding, bowls and meals on request

SPEAN BRIDGE
Letterfinlay Lodge

Letterfinlay, Spean Bridge, Inverness-shire PH34 4DZ (on A82 7 miles N of Spean Bridge/A86 junction) (01397) 712622

£80; 14 cosy rms. Secluded and genteel family-run country house with picture window in extensive modern bar overlooking loch, comfortable reading room, elegantly panelled small cocktail bar, good popular food in sun lounge and conservatory, seats out on sundeck, and friendly attentive service; grounds run down through rhododendrons to the jetty and Loch Lochy – dogs may walk here; fishing can be arranged; disabled access; dogs in some bedrooms

SPITTAL OF GLENSHEE
Dalmunzie House

Glenshee, Blairgowrie, Perthshire PH10 7QG (01250) 885224

£140; 17 rms with fine views and named after local families. Turreted, baronial-style Victorian shooting lodge peacefully set in huge estate among spectacular mountains, plenty of walks within it, and own golf course; comfortable drawing room, open fires in two other lounges, cosy, informal bar and antiques-filled library (designed to assist guests tracing their ancestors), hearty breakfasts, enjoyable lunches and afternoon teas, and extremely good evening meals using the best local produce in candlelit restaurant; cl Dec; disabled access; dogs in bedrooms; £5

STRONTIAN

Kilcamb Lodge Hotel

Strontian, Acharacle, Argyll PH36 4HY (01967) 402257

£130, plus winter breaks; 12 rms. Warm, friendly little hotel in 22 acres by Loch Sunart, with log fires in two lounges, carefully cooked food using fresh ingredients from organic kitchen garden, fine choice of malt whiskies in small bar, and friendly, relaxed atmosphere; beach, fishing boat, four moorings and jetty; cl Jan; children over 10; dogs in bedrooms only; treats and towels (dogs love to swim in loch); £5

TARBERT

Stonefield Castle

Stonefield, Tarbert, Argyll PA29 6YJ (01880) 820836

£120; 33 rms. With wonderful views and 60 acres of surrounding wooded grounds where dogs may walk, this scottish baronial mansion has a panelled lounge bar and other comfortable sitting areas, convivial bar, good food and super views in restaurant, and snooker room; disabled access; dogs in bedrooms; £10

DOG FRIENDLY PUBS

CRICKHOWELL

Bear

Brecon Road; A40; NP8 1BW

Civilised and interesting inn with splendid old-fashioned bar area warmed by a log fire, good food and bedrooms

This comfortably traditional coaching inn, in the heart of this delightful little town, has been run by the same owners for over 30 years now, and although some things have been carefully refreshed (the dining area has been given an overhaul for instance) they remark that they don't want to change things just for change's sake, and are constantly being told to keep it just as it is. The comfortably decorated, heavily beamed lounge has fresh flowers on tables, lots of little plush-seated bentwood armchairs and handsome cushioned antique settles, and a window seat looking down on the market square. Up by the great roaring log fire, a big sofa and leather easy chairs are spread among rugs on the oak parquet floor. Other good antiques include a fine oak dresser filled with pewter mugs and brass, a longcase clock, and interesting prints. Food is usually very rewarding, anything from sandwiches to butternut squash ravioli on braised leeks and courgettes or welsh black beef sirloin, and they do a popular three-course Sunday lunch. Brains Rev James, Greene King Ruddles Best and a guest such as Skirrid on handpump, as well as 24 malt whiskies, vintage and late-bottled ports, unusual wines (with several by the glass) and liqueurs; disabled lavatories. Successfully blending its charms with efficient service, it is a welcoming place to stay – some refurbished bedrooms are in a country style, though the older rooms have antiques; more expensive rooms have jacuzzis and four-poster beds.

Free house ~ Licensee Judy Hindmarsh ~ Real ale ~ Bar food (12-2, 6-10; 12-2, 7-9.30 Sun) ~ Restaurant ~ (01873) 810408 ~ Children welcome with restrictions ~ Dogs allowed in bar and bedrooms ~ Open 11-3, 6-11; 12-3, 7-10.30 Sun ~ Bedrooms: £70S/£86S(£133B)

EAST ABERTHAW

Blue Anchor

B4265; CF62 3DD

Ancient waterside pub, loaded with character and a popular place for a beer

Flower baskets and ivy adorn the ancient stone walls of this atmospheric thatched pub, which dates back to 1380 and has been run by the same family since 1941. The building has massive walls, low-beamed rooms and tiny doorways, with open fires everywhere, including one in an inglenook with antique oak seats built into its stripped stonework. Other seats and tables are worked into a series of chatty little alcoves, and the more open front bar still has an ancient lime-ash floor. Friendly staff serve Brains Bitter, Theakstons Old Peculier, Wadworths 6X and Wye Valley Hereford Pale Ale on handpump, alongside a changing guest such as Moles Rucking Mole. Bar food includes something for most tastes. Rustic seats shelter peacefully among tubs and troughs of flowers outside, with more stone tables on a newer terrace. From here a path leads to the shingly flats of the estuary. The pub can get very full in the evenings and on summer weekends, and it's used as a base by a couple of local motorbike clubs.

Free house ~ Licensee Jeremy Coleman ~ Real ale ~ Bar food (12-2, 6-9; not Sun evening) ~ Restaurant ~ (01446) 750329 ~ Children welcome ~ Dogs allowed in bar ~ Open 11-11; 12-10.30 Sun

FELINFACH

Griffin

A470 NE of Brecon; LD3 0UB

A classy dining pub for enjoying good, unpretentious cooking featuring lots of home-grown vegetables; upbeat rustic décor, nice bedrooms

With a nice mixture of locals coming in for a drink and diners enjoying the interesting food, this friendly and stylish inn is tucked away in a hamlet on the Dulas valley just west of the Black Mountains. The back bar is quite pubby in an up-to-date way, with three leather sofas around a low table on pitted quarry tiles, by a high slate hearth with a log fire, and behind them mixed stripped seats around scrubbed kitchen tables on bare boards, and a bright blue-and-ochre colour scheme, with some modern prints. The acoustics are pretty lively, with so much bare flooring and uncurtained windows; maybe piped radio. The two smallish front dining rooms, linking through to the back bar, are attractive: on the left, mixed dining chairs around mainly stripped tables on flagstones, and white-painted rough stone walls, with a cream-coloured Aga in a big stripped-stone embrasure; on the right, similar furniture on bare boards, with big modern prints on terracotta walls, and good dark curtains. Using organic produce from the pub's own kitchen garden (from which the surplus is often for sale), food if not cheap is consistently very good and sensibly imaginative. They have a thoughtful choice of wines including 12 by the glass, welsh spirits, cocktails and Breconshire Cribyn, Tomos Watkins OSB and a guest like Tomos Watkins Cwrw Braf on handpump; local bottled ciders and apple juice, and a fine range of spirits, cocktails and sherries. Wheelchair access is good, and there are tables outside. Bedrooms are comfortable and tastefully decorated, and the hearty breakfasts nicely informal: you make your own toast on the Aga (which can be a somewhat leisurely process) and help yourself to home-made marmalade and jam.

Free house ~ Licensees Charles and Edmund Inkin ~ Real ale ~ Bar food (12.30(12 Sun)-2.30, 6.30-9.30(9 Sun); not Mon lunch (exc bank hols)) ~ Restaurant ~ (01874) 620111 ~ Children welcome ~ Dogs allowed in bar and bedrooms ~ Live music Sun night ~ Open 11-11; 11.30-10.30 Sun ~ Bedrooms: £67.50B/£110B

GLADESTRY
Royal Oak

B4594 W of Kington; HR5 3NR

A thoroughly likeable, welcoming village local on the Offa's Dyke Path

Just below the abruptly steep end of Hergest Ridge, this is an enjoyably unpre-tentious village pub well liked by locals, farmers and walkers. The simple bar is warmed by an open fire and has beams hung with tankards and lanterns, stripped stone and flagstones, and near the piano hang pictures of the Gladestry football team; there's also a cosy turkey-carpeted lounge, also with an open fire. Chatty groups gather around the tiny bar, where the staff draw Brains Rev James and Hancocks HB from handpump; walking boots are allowed in the main bar only. Very straightforward pubby food includes sandwiches, soup, sausage and chips, lasagne, three-bean chilli, rump steak, puddings; and Sunday roasts. There's a small, sheltered lawn at the back with picnic-sets and there's a camping field.

Free house ~ Licensees Brian Hall and Sharon Mallon ~ Real ale ~ Bar food (12-2.30, 7-9.30 (not Sun evening)) ~ (01544) 370669 ~ Children welcome ~ Dogs allowed in bar ~ Open 12-3, 6(7 Sun)-11

HAY-ON-WYE
Blue Boar

Castle Street/Oxford Road; HR3 5DF

Dark cosy medieval bar and generous home cooking

The irregular shape of the bar here gives cosy corners, and its candlelight or shaded table lamps, squared dark ply panelling and handsome fireplace (with a good winter fire) make for a relaxed atmosphere. There are pews, country chairs, and stools at the counter, which has Shepherd Neame Spitfire, Timothy Taylors Landlord, and a beer named for the pub on handpump, a good choice of wines by the glass and whiskies, and interesting bottled ciders including organic ones; service is good and the landlady is friendly. Food is good value, enjoyable and interesting.

Free house ~ Licensees John and Lucy Goldsworthy ~ Real ale ~ Bar food (12-2.30, 6-9(9.30 Fri and Sat); all day during school hols and festivals) ~ Restaurant ~ (01497) 820884 ~ Children welcome ~ Dogs welcome ~ Open 9.30am-11pm(11.30 Fri and Sat)

LITTLE HAVEN
St Brides Inn

St Brides Road – in village itself, not St Brides hamlet further W; SA62 3UN

Cheerful seaside inn with Anglo-Russian owners, tasty food and a log fire

The Russian landlady and English landlord here run this little pub, at the south end of St Bride's Bay on the Pembrokeshire coast, with clockwork efficiency. There's a neat stripped-stone bar and linking carpeted dining area, and a good log fire; Marstons Banks and Pedigree on handpump, and several malt whiskies. Food changes weekly and, along with sandwiches and soup and other traditional pub dishes, might include a beef stroganoff made to the landlady's family recipe – they sometimes have russian theme nights, too. A curious well in a back corner grotto is though to be partly Roman; across the road is a sheltered sunny terraced garden.

Marstons ~ Lease Graham Harrison-Jones ~ Real ale ~ Bar food (12-2, 6-9) ~ Restaurant ~ No credit cards ~ (01437) 781266 ~ Children welcome in bar until 7.30pm ~ Dogs allowed in bar ~ Open 12-11; 12.30-11.30 Sat; 11.30-10.30 Sun; closed Mon Nov-May, and first week of Jan

LLANARMON DYFFRYN CEIRIOG

Hand

On B4500 from Chirk; LL20 7LD

Comfortable rural hotel in a remote valley; cosy low-beamed bar area, good bedrooms

Well converted from an ancient farmhouse, this inn in the Ceiriog Valley is in rewarding hill-walking country not far from Pistyll Rhaeadr, the highest waterfall in Wales beneath the Berwyn Hills. The black-beamed carpeted bar on the left of the broad-flagstoned entrance hall has a good log fire in its inglenook fireplace, a mixture of chairs and settles, and old prints on its cream walls, with bar stools along the modern bar counter, which has Weetwood Eastgate on handpump, several malt whiskies, and reasonably priced wines by the glass; happy and welcoming staff help towards the warm atmosphere. Round the corner is the largely stripped stone dining room, with a woodburning stove and carpeted floor; TV, games machine, darts, pool and dominoes. This is a peaceful place to stay and they do a good country breakfast; the residents' lounge on the right is comfortable and attractive. Besides lunchtime sandwiches and ploughman's, there's a seasonally changing menu which might include grilled trout from a local trout farm in the valley. There are tables out on a crazy-paved front terrace, with more in the garden, which has flowerbeds around another sheltered terrace.

Free house ~ Licensees Gaynor and Martin de Luchi ~ Bar food (12-2.15(12.30-2.45 Sun), 6.30-8.45) ~ Restaurant ~ (01691) 600666 ~ Well supervised children welcome ~ Dogs allowed in bar and bedrooms ~ Open 11(12 Sun)-11(12.30 Sat) ~ Bedrooms: £65B/£110B

LLANBERIS

Pen-y-Gwryd

Nant Gwynant; at junction of A498 and A4086, ie across mountains from Llanberis – OS Sheet 115 map reference 660558; LL55 4NT

In the hands of the same family for decades, an illustrious favourite with the mountain fraternity

Full of climbers' mementoes, this family-run mountain inn memorably placed beneath Snowdon and the Glyders has changed remarkably little – one reader noted that everything is probably much as it was on his father's first visit in 1916. It was used as a training base for the 1953 Everest team and their fading signatures can still be made out, scrawled on the ceiling. One snug little room in the homely slate-floored log cabin bar has built-in wall benches and sturdy country chairs to let you gaze at the surrounding mountain landscapes – like Moel Siabod beyond the lake opposite. A smaller room has a worthy collection of illustrious boots from famous climbs, and a cosy panelled smoke room has more fascinating climbing mementoes and equipment; darts, pool, board games and bar billiards. There's a sociable atmosphere, and alongside Bass on handpump, they've home-made lemonade in summer, mulled wine in winter, and sherry from their own solera in Puerto Santa Maria. Your order the short choice of simple, good-value home-made lunchtime bar food through a hatch, and a gong at 7.30 signals the prompt start of service in the evening restaurant, but they don't hang around – if you're late, you'll miss it, and there's no evening bar food. Staying here can be quite an experience. The excellent, traditional breakfast is served at 8.30am; they're not generally flexible with this; comfortable but basic bedrooms, dogs £2 a night. The inn has its own chapel (built for the millennium and dedicated by the Archbishop of Wales), sauna and outdoor natural pool.

Free house ~ Licensee Jane Pullee ~ Real ale ~ Bar food (lunchtime only) ~ Restaurant (evening) ~ (01286) 870211 ~ Children welcome ~ Dogs allowed in bar and bedrooms ~ Open 11-11(10.30 Sun); closed all Nov-Dec, and midweek Jan-Feb ~ Bedrooms: £40/£80(£94B)

LLANFERRES
Druid

A494 Mold—Ruthin; CH7 5SN

17th-c inn with beams, antique settles and a log fire in the bar; wonderful views

This cosy, rambling whitewashed inn beneath the eastern side of the Clwydian Hills is in super territory for walks, with the summit of Moel Famau and Offa's Dyke Path not far away. You can enjoy the views from tables outside at the front and from the broad bay window in the civilised, smallish plush lounge. The hills are also in sight from the bigger beamed and characterful back bar, with its two handsome antique oak settles as well as a pleasant mix of more modern furnishings. There's a quarry-tiled area by the log fire, and a three-legged cat, Chu. Marstons Burton and a guest from breweries such as Hook Norton or Jennings are on handpump, and the pub stocks more than 30 malt whiskies. The wide range of bar food should suit most tastes. A games room has darts and pool, along with board games; piped music, TV.

Union Pub Company ~ Lease James Dolan ~ Real ale ~ Bar food (12-3, 6-9; 12-9.30 Sat; 12-9 Sun) ~ (01352) 810225 ~ Children welcome ~ Dogs allowed in bar and bedrooms ~ Open 12-3, 5.30-11; 12-12 Sat, Sun ~ Bedrooms: £48S/£70S

PORTH DINLLAEN
Ty Coch

Beach car park signposted from Morfa Nefyn, then 15-minute walk; LL53 6DB

Idyllic location right on the beach, far from the roads; simple fresh lunches

The coastal position of this unspoilt place is really special: you can arrive at low tide along a beach backed by low grassy hills and sand-cliffs, with gulls and curlews for company (otherwise you can walk across via the golf course). The pub is said to have been used by 17th-c smugglers and pirates, and the walls and beams are hung every inch with pewter, riding lights, navigation lamps, lanterns, small fishing nets, old miners' and railway lamps, copper utensils, an ale-yard, and lots of RNLI photographs and memorabilia; there are ships in bottles, a working barometer, a Caernarfon grandfather clock, and simple furnishings. An open coal fire burns at one end of the bar; occasional piped music. From a short menu, simple lunchtime bar food includes sandwiches, salads, local crab and mussels and pies. There are tables outside. Although there's no real ale here, there's a range of bottled beers.

Free house ~ Licensee Mrs Brione Webley ~ Bar food (12-2.30) ~ (01758) 720498 ~ Children welcome ~ Dogs welcome ~ Live music twice weekly in July and Aug ~ Open 11-11(11-3 daily, 6-11 Fri, Sat Easter to spring bank hol); 11-4 Sun; open during day in Christmas week; Sat and Sun 12-4 only in winter

RAGLAN

Clytha Arms

Clytha, off Abergavenny road – former A40, now declassified; NP7 9BW

Beautifully placed in parkland, a relaxing spot for enjoying good food and beer; comfortable bedrooms

Readers savour the position of this civilised white house with its setting on the edge of Clytha Park. With long heated verandahs and diamond-paned windows, it's comfortable, light and airy, with scrubbed wood floors, pine settles, big faux fur cushions on the window seats, a good mix of old country furniture and a couple of warming fires. Run by charming licensees, it's the sort of relaxed place where everyone feels welcome, from locals who've walked here for a pint, to diners in the contemporary linen-set restaurant. The very enjoyable food is pubby and hearty, and they have a tapas menu that's much liked by readers; there's a beer and cheese festival at the August bank holiday weekend. The restaurant menu is pricier and more elaborate, with set menus at £19.50 for two courses. An impressive choice of drinks includes well kept Evans and Evans Best Bitter, Felinfoel Double Dragon and Rhymney Bitter, three swiftly changing guest beers from brewers such as Brains, Shepherd Neame and Tring, an extensive wine list with about a dozen or so by the glass, over 20 malt whiskies, about three farm ciders and maybe their own perry. They have occasional cider and beer festivals; darts, shove-ha'penny, boules, bar billiards, draughts, large-screen TV for rugby matches, and board games. The pub has its own english setter and collie. Don't miss the murals in the lavatories (one reader felt the loos could still benefit from sprucing up). Service can be slow at busy times. The bedrooms are comfortable, with good welsh breakfasts.

Free house ~ Licensees Andrew and Beverley Canning ~ Real ale ~ Bar food (12.30-2.15, 7-9.30; not Sun evening or Mon lunch) ~ Restaurant ~ (01873) 840206 ~ Children welcome ~ Dogs allowed in bar and bedrooms ~ Open 12-12(10.30 Sun); closed Mon lunchtime; 3.30-6 Mon-Thurs ~ Bedrooms: £60B/£80B

SHIRENEWTON

Carpenters Arms

Mynydd-Bach; B4235 Chepstow—Usk, about 0.5 miles N; NP16 6BU

Pleasantly unsophisticated former smithy, with nicely timeless décor

There's an enjoyably pubby feel to this friendly former country smithy, which in summer has attractive hanging baskets. Inside are an array of chamber-pots, an attractive Victorian tiled fireplace, and a collection of chromolithographs of antique royal occasions. One of the unusual interconnecting rooms still has black-smith's bellows hanging from the planked ceiling. Furnishings run the gamut too, from one very high-backed ancient settle to pews, kitchen chairs, a nice elm table, several sewing-machine trestle tables and so forth; darts, board games and piped pop music. Straightforward bar food, written up on blackboards, takes in a wide choice of pubby dishes, including sandwiches, filled baked potatoes, pies and steaks, and they do inexpensive senior citizens' specials on weekdays. On handpump are Bass, Fullers London Pride and Shepherd Neame Spitfire and an occasional seasonal guest. There are tables outside at the front.

Punch ~ Lease Gary and Sandra Hayes ~ Real ale ~ Bar food (12-2.30, 6.30-9.30; Sun 12-8; not Mon) ~ No credit cards ~ (01291) 641231 ~ Children welcome ~ Dogs allowed in bar ~ Open 12-3, 5.30-12; 12-midnight Sat, Sun; 12-3.30, 5.30-12 (10.30 Sun) in winter

SKENFRITH

Bell

Just off B4521, NE of Abergavenny and N of Monmouth; NP7 8UH

Elegant but relaxed, generally much praised for classy though pricey food and excellent accommodation

Getting good reports for food this year, this is a relaxed but smart country inn just over the road from the substantial ruins of Skenfrith Castle and overlooking the River Monnow. The big back bare-boards dining area is very neat, light and airy, with dark country-kitchen chairs and rush-seat dining chairs, church candles and flowers on the dark tables, canary walls and a cream ceiling, and brocaded curtains on sturdy big-ring rails. The flagstoned bar on the left has a rather similar décor, with old local and school photographs, a couple of pews plus tables and café chairs; St Austell Tribute and Timothy Taylors Landlord as well as Broome Farm cider on handpump from an attractive bleached oak bar counter; board games. Food is very thoughtfully prepared, focusing on mostly simple but very effective preparations that make the most of fresh ingredients from named local suppliers, and the vegetables, soft fruit and herbs that come from their own kitchen garden (guests are welcome to look around). They have good wines by the glass and half-bottle, and make good coffee. The lounge bar on the right, opening into the dining area, has a nice Jacobean-style carved settle and a housekeeper's chair by a log fire in the big fireplace. There are good solid round picnic-sets as well as the usual rectangular ones out on the terrace, with steps up to a sloping lawn; it's a quiet spot. The bedrooms are comfortable, with thoughtful touches.

Free house ~ Licensees William and Janet Hutchings ~ Real ale ~ Bar food ~ (01600) 750235 ~ Children under 9 welcome in restaurant until 7pm ~ Dogs allowed in bar and bedrooms ~ Open 11-11(10 Sun); closed all day Mon in winter ~ Bedrooms: £95B/£105B

USK

Nags Head

The Square; NP15 1BH

Spotlessly kept by the same family for many years, traditional in style, as warm a reception as could be hoped for, with good food and drinks

The Key family, who have now been landlords here for over 40 years, generate praise from readers from one year to the next: 'a smashing pub' and 'standards never drop, warm welcome, lovely atmosphere, our favourite pub' are typical comments. With a friendly chatty atmosphere (and perhaps a knot of sociable locals), the beautifully kept traditional main bar has lots of well polished tables and chairs packed under its beams (some with farming tools), lanterns or horse-brasses and harness attached, as well as leatherette wall benches, and various sets of sporting prints and local pictures – look out for the original deeds to the pub. Tucked away at the front is an intimate little corner with some african masks, while on the other side of the room a passageway leads to a new dining area converted from the old coffee bar; piped music. The well liked food here is reasonably priced, generously served, and covers quite a range – anything from frog legs in hot provençale sauce to rabbit pie. You can book tables, some of which may be candlelit at night; nice proper linen napkins. They do several wines by the glass, along with four ales on handpump – from Brains Bitter, Bread of Heaven, Rev James or SA and Buckleys Best. The centre of Usk is full of pretty hanging baskets and flowers in summer, and the church is well worth a look.

Free house ~ Licensee the Key family ~ Real ale ~ Bar food (12-2, 5.30-9.30) ~ Restaurant ~ (01291) 672820 ~ Children welcome ~ Dogs welcome ~ Open 10.30-3, 5.30-11; 11-3, 6-10.30 Sun

DOG FRIENDLY HOTELS, INNS, B&Bs AND FARMS

ABERDOVEY

Penhelig Arms

Terrace Road, Aberdovey, Gwynedd LL35 0LT (01654) 767215

£100; 15 comfortable rms, 4 in annexe impressively furnished, with fine harbour views. In fine spot overlooking sea, with cosy bar, open fires, delicious food with emphasis on daily-delivered fresh local fish in restaurant, extensive (and fairly priced) wine list with 30 by glass (champagne, too), splendid breakfasts, and charming friendly service; lovely views of Dovey estuary and five miles of beach to walk on; cl 25-26 Dec; disabled access; dogs in bedrooms; £5

ABERSOCH

Porth Tocyn Hotel

Bwlch Tocyn, Pwllheli, Gwynedd LL53 7BU (01758) 713303

£90; 17 cottagey and attractive rms, most with sea views. On headland over-looking Cardigan Bay, this comfortable and homely place – converted from a row of lead miners' cottages – has been run by same hard-working family for over 50 years; several cosy interconnecting sitting rooms with antiques, books and fresh flowers, sunny conservatory, most enjoyable traditional cooking (lots of options such as light lunches, high teas for children as they must be over 7 for dinner in the restaurant, and imaginative Sun lunches), and helpful young staff; lots of space in pretty garden, heated swimming pool, tennis court; they are kind to children; two resident cats; cl early Nov to just before Easter; disabled access; dogs in bedrooms by prior arrangement

BARMOUTH

Lawrenny Lodge

Aberamffra Road, Barmouth, Gwynedd LL42 1SU (01341) 280466

£76; 7 comfortable rms, some with river and sea views. Small family-run hotel overlooking Cardigan Bay and close to famous Barmouth Bridge and town centre; traditionally furnished lounge and dining room, little bar, cooked welsh break-fasts and evening meals and packed lunches on request; lovely surrounding walks; resident black labrador and cat; cl Dec and Jan; children over 12; dogs welcome anywhere

BEDDGELERT

Sygun Fawr Country House

Beddgelert, Caernarfon, Gwynedd LL55 4NE (01766) 890258

£88; 11 rms. Spectacular scenery surrounds this secluded 17th-c hotel, with lots of surrounding walks; beams, stripped stone walls, inglenooks, antiques, and restful atmosphere, varied imaginative menu in restaurant and dining conserva-tory, and 20 acres of mountainside and gardens; dogs in one downstairs bedroom; £4

BETWS-Y-COED

Ty Gwyn

Betwys-y-Coed, Gwynedd LL24 0SG (on A5 (and A470)) (01690) 710383

£72; 12 pretty rms. 17th-c coaching inn, now a restaurant-with-rooms, with beamed lounge bar, ancient cooking range, easy chairs, antiques, silver, cut glass, old prints and interesting bric-a-brac; really good, interesting meals, real ales, and highly professional service; nice setting overlooking river and plenty of surrounding walks; dogs in bedrooms; £5

BROAD HAVEN

Druidstone Hotel

Broad Haven, Haverfordwest, Dyfed SA62 3NE (01437) 781221

£120; 11 rms and 5 cottages, some with sea view, shared bthrms. Alone on coast and above fine beach with exhilarating cliff walks, this roomy and informally friendly hotel, run by very nice family, has something of a folk-club and Outward Bound feel at times; it's extremely winning and relaxing if you take to its unique combination of good wholesome and often memorably inventive food, slightly fend-for-yourself approach amid elderly furniture, and glorious seaside surroundings; resident parsons terrier and eight cats; self-catering cottages; dogs welcome away from restaurant

CONWY

Sychnant Pass House

Sychnant Pass Road, Conwy, Gwynedd LL32 8BJ (2.5 miles off A55 junction 16 via Sychnant Pass Road towards Conwy through Dwygyfylchi and Capelulo) (01492) 596868

£95; 10 rms. Victorian house in two acres among foothills of Snowdonia National Park, with big comfortable sitting rooms, log fires, relaxing, friendly atmosphere, and enjoyable food (restaurant is open to non-residents, too); three resident dogs and two cats; cl Christmas and Jan; dogs in bedrooms

CRICCIETH

Mynydd Ednyfed Country House

Caernarfon Road, Criccieth, Gwynedd LL52 0PH (01766) 523269

£94; 9 individually decorated rms, some with four-posters. Beautifully set 400-year-old house in 8 acres of garden, orchard, paddock and woods with lovely views overlooking Tremadog Bay, and once home to Lloyd George's family; traditional lounge bar, enjoyable food using local produce in comfortable dining room and airy conservatory, and friendly staff; all-weather tennis court and treatment room; cl 23 Dec-5 Jan; dogs if small and well behaved in bedrooms only; £7

EGLWYSFACH

Ynyshir Hall

Eglwysfach, Machynlleth, Dyfed SY20 8TA (just off A487 SW of Machynlleth) (01654) 781209

£285; 9 individually decorated rms. Carefully run Georgian manor house in 14 acres of landscaped gardens adjoining Ynyshir coastal bird reserve; particularly good service, antiques, log fires and paintings in light and airy public rooms, extremely good food using home-grown vegetables, and delicious breakfasts; resident mountain dog; lots to do nearby; children over 9; disabled access to ground-floor rms; dogs in ground floor bedrooms; treats, ball, bedding, bowl; £3

GELLILYDAN

Tyddyn Du Farm

Gellilydan, Blaenau Ffestiniog, Gwynedd LL41 4RB (just off A470 by A487 junction) (01766) 590281

£75; 4 ground-floor, private stable and long barn suites with jacuzzi baths, one with airbath, fridges and microwaves. 400-year-old farmhouse on working farm in heart of Snowdonia, with beams and exposed stonework, and big inglenook fireplaces in lounge; children can help bottle-feed the lambs, and look at goats, ducks, sheep and shetland ponies; three dogs; fine walks, inc short one to their own Roman site; partial disabled access; dogs welcome away from dining room; £3

GILWERN

Wenallt Farm

Twyn-Wenallt, Gilwern, Abergavenny, Gwent NP7 0HP (0.6 miles off A465; turn off S just W of A4077 junction, then bear left) (01873) 830694

£56; 5 rms. Friendly and relaxing 16th-c welsh longhouse on 50 acres of farmland in Brecon Beacons National Park, with oak beams and inglenook fireplace in big drawing room, TV room, good food in dining room, packed lunches on request, and lots to do nearby; partial disabled access; dogs in some bedrooms; £3

LLANABER

Llwyndu Farmhouse

Llanaber, Barmouth, Gwynedd LL42 1RR (01341) 280144

£84; 7 charming rms, most with own bthrm, some in nicely converted 18th-c barn. Most attractive 16th-c farmhouse just above Cardigan Bay, with warm welcome from friendly owners, big inglenook fireplaces, oak beams, mullioned windows, relaxing lounge, enjoyable breakfasts, and good imaginative food in candlelit dining room; resident dog; plenty of nearby walks; cl 25-26 Dec; dogs welcome away from dining room

LLANARMON DC

West Arms

Llanarmon Dyffryn Ceiriog, Llangollen, Clwyd LL20 7LD (01691) 600665

£125; 15 rms. Charming and civilised 16th-c inn with heavy beams and timbers, log fires in inglenook fireplaces, lounge bar interestingly furnished with antique settles, sofas in old-fashioned entrance hall, comfortable locals' lounge bar, good food, and friendly quiet atmosphere; large garden where dogs may walk and the lawn runs down to the River Ceiriog (fishing for residents); disabled access; dogs welcome away from restaurant; £6

LLANDELOY

Lochmeyler Farm

Llandeloy, Haverfordwest, Dyfed SA62 6LL (01348) 837724

£60; 12 pretty rms. Attractive creeper-covered 16th-c farmhouse on 220-acre working dairy farm; open fire in neatly kept and homely beamed lounge, traditional farmhouse cooking in pleasant dining room, mature garden, and welsh cakes on arrival; resident labrador, collie, and cocker spaniel; can walk around the farm trails; no children; partial disabled access; dogs welcome in bedrooms

LLANDRILLO

Tyddyn Llan

Llandrillo, Corwen, Clwyd LL21 0ST (01490) 440264

£110; 13 pretty rms. Elegant and relaxed Georgian house with four acres of lovely gardens and surrounded by Berwyn mountains; fresh flowers in comfortable public rooms, enjoyable food using top ingredients, and impressive wine list; fine forest walks (guides available), and watersports, fishing and horse riding can be arranged; three resident cats; disabled access; dogs in bedrooms; £5

LLANDUDNO

St Tudno

15 North Parade, Llandudno, Gwynedd LL30 2LP (01492) 874411

£130; 19 individually decorated rms, some with sea view. Well run, smart seaside hotel opposite pier, with genuinely helpful and friendly staff, Victorian-style décor in restful sitting room, convivial bar lounge, relaxed coffee lounge for light lunches, and attractive italian-style restaurant; resident cat; small indoor pool; walks on beach; dogs in bedrooms (but they must not be left unattended); £10

LLANFAIR DC

Eyarth Station

Llanfair Dyffryn Clwyd, Ruthin, Clwyd LL15 2EE (0.6 miles off A494 S of Ruthin) (01824) 703643

£72; 6 pretty rms. Carefully converted old railway station with quiet gardens and wonderful views; friendly relaxed atmosphere, log fire in airy and comfortable beamed lounge, good breakfasts and enjoyable suppers in dining room (more lovely views), sun terrace, and heated swimming pool; lots of walks; resident cat; cl 25 Dec; disabled access; dogs in bedrooms by arrangement and not to be left unattended; £6

LLANGAMMARCH WELLS

Lake

Llangammarch Wells, Powys LD4 4BS (2 miles off A483 via B4519, then first right) (01591) 620202

£170; 30 charming, pretty rms with fruit and decanter of sherry. Particularly well run 1860s half-timbered hotel in 50 acres with plenty of wildlife, well stocked trout lake, and tennis and riding; deeply comfortable tranquil drawing room with antiques, paintings and log fire, wonderful afternoon teas (under chestnut tree overlooking river in summer), courteous service, fine wines and good modern british cooking in elegant candlelit dining room, and liberal breakfasts; two resident dogs; children over 8 in evening dining room; disabled access; dogs in some bedrooms; £6

LLANSANFFRAID GLAN CONWY

Old Rectory Country House

Llanrwst Road, Glan Conwy, Colwyn Bay, Clwyd LL28 5LF (1.7 miles off A55 junction 19 via A470 S) (01492) 580611

£99; 5 deeply comfortable rms. Georgian house in pleasant gardens with fine views over Conwy estuary, Conwy Castle and Snowdonia; delightful public rooms with flowers, antiques and family photos, good breakfasts (restaurants nearby for evening meals), and warmly friendly staff; walks on quiet adjoining lane and around nearby estuary; cl 15 Dec-6 Jan; children over 5; dogs in coach house only

LLANWDDYN

Lake Vyrnwy Hotel

Llanwddyn, Oswestry, Powys SY10 0LY (01691) 870692

£165; 52 individually furnished rms – some overlooking lake. Large impressive Tudor-style mansion in 26,000 acre estate – 16,000 acres are dedicated to the RSPB; conservatory looking over water, log fires and sporting prints in comfortable and elegant public rooms, convivial bar, relaxed atmosphere, and good food using their own lamb and game from estate, and home-made preserves, chutneys, mustards and vinegars; enjoyable teas too; disabled access; dogs in bedrooms; £10

LLANWRTYD WELLS

Carlton Riverside

Dolycoed Road, Llanwrtyd Wells, Powys LD5 4RA (just off A483, on Dolycoed Road) (01591) 610248

£65; 5 spacious, well equipped rms. Restaurant-with-rooms run by warmly friendly owners with comfortable and relaxing L-shaped lounge (with bar and library), attractive dining room overlooking river, exceptionally good, innovative food using top-quality local produce (delicious puddings), thoughtful wine list, and super breakfasts with home-made bread and marmalade; cl 10-29 Dec; dogs welcome in bedrooms

LLECHRYD

Castell Malgwyn

Llechryd, Cardigan, Dyfed SA43 2QA (01239) 682382

£95; 19 attractive rms. Handsome, creeper-covered 18th-c house with eight acres of woodland, half-a-mile of river frontage (fishing and shooting), and lots of walks; homely comfortable lounge, convivial bar lounge, good, enjoyable food and nice breakfasts using local produce, friendly staff, and plenty of regular guests; resident dog and cat; partial disabled access; dogs in bedrooms and library bar; £10

MONTGOMERY

Dragon

Market Square, Montgomery, Powys SY15 6PA (3 miles off A483 via B4385; Market Square) (01686) 668359

£87.50; 20 rms. 17th-c black and white timbered, family-run hotel with pleasant grey-stone tiled hall, comfortable residents' lounge, beamed bar, and restaurant using local produce; indoor swimming pool, sauna; countryside walks; dogs welcome away from drink and food areas

NANTGWYNANT

Pen-y-Gwryd

Nantgwynant, Caernarfon, Gwynedd LL55 4NT (01286) 870211

£94; 16 rms, some with own bthrm. Cheerful hotel in two acres by Llanberis Pass in Snowdonia National Park; warm log fire in simply furnished panelled residents' lounge, rugged slate-floored bar that doubles as mountain rescue post, lots of climbing mementoes and equipment, and friendly, chatty games room (plenty of walkers, climbers and fishermen); hearty enjoyable food, big breakfasts, and packed lunches; sauna, outdoor swimming pool, and table tennis; private chapel; cl Nov-New Year and only open wknds till March; disabled access; dogs in bedrooms and bar; £2

OXWICH

Oxwich Bay Hotel

Oxwich, Swansea, West Glamorgan SA3 1LS (01792) 390329

£75; 26 rms. Comfortable hotel on edge of beach in lovely area, with dedicated friendly staff, food served all day, restaurant/lounge bar with panoramic views, summer outdoor dining area, and welcome for families; dogs in cottage bedrooms; £5

PRESTEIGNE

Radnorshire Arms

High Street, Presteigne, Powys LD8 2BE (01544) 267406

£65; 19 rms. Rambling, handsomely timbered 17th-c hotel with old-fashioned charm and unchanging atmosphere, elegantly moulded beams and fine dark panelling in lounge bar, and latticed windows; enjoyable food (inc morning coffee and afternoon tea), main restaurant plus more intimate one, well kept real ales, and politely attentive service; walks nearby (or in the garden); dogs in garden lodges; £10

PWLLHELI

Plas Bodegroes

Efailnewydd, Pwllheli, Gwynedd LL53 5TH (01758) 612363

£170; 11 rms with scandinavian-style decor. Lovely Georgian manor house, aptly described as restaurant-with-rooms, in tree-filled grounds and fronted by 200-year-old beech avenue; comfortably restful rooms, enjoyable modern cooking using superb fresh local produce and good wine list in light and airy restaurant, very nice breakfasts, and genuinely friendly, helpful staff; cl mid-Nov-March; dogs in one bedroom

RHAYADER

Beili Neuadd

Rhayader, Powys LD6 5NS (2 miles off A470, via B4518 NE) (01597) 810211

£54; 3 rms with log fires. Charming 16th-c stone-built farmhouse with panoramic views and set in quiet countryside with garden, paddocks, and woodland; beams, polished oak floorboards, log fires, and nice breakfasts in garden room; walks in paddocks and garden; self-catering in converted barn; three resident dogs and one cat; dogs in bedrooms if well behaved

ST BRIDES WENTLOOG

West Usk Lighthouse

St Brides Wentloog, Newport, Gwent NP10 8SF (01633) 810126

£120; 3 rms. Unusual ex-lighthouse – squat rather than tall – that was on island in Bristol Channel (the land has since been reclaimed); modern stylish furnishings, lots of framed record sleeves (Mr Sheahan used to work for a record company), informal atmosphere, good big breakfasts, and Rolls-Royce drive to good local restaurant; flotation tank, aromatherapy, reflexology, and hypnotherapy, large roof terrace with palm and shrubs and a barbecue, and lots of nearby walks; authentic mongolian yurt and mobile home, too; resident border collie, cl 25 and 26 Dec; dogs in one bedroom; £5

ST DAVID'S

Warpool Court

St David's, Haverfordwest, Dyfed SA62 6BN (01437) 720300

£190; 25 rms. Originally built as St David's cathedral school in 1860s and bordering NT land, this popular hotel has lovely views over St Bride's Bay; Ada Williams's collection of lovely hand-painted tiles can be seen in comfortable lounges, food in elegant restaurant is imaginative, and staff are helpful; quiet gardens (walks here and in surrounding fields), heated summer swimming pool, tennis, table tennis, pool and croquet; cl Jan; dogs in bedrooms; £10

TAL-Y-BONT

Lodge

Tal-y-Bont, Conwy, Gwynedd LL32 8YX (01492) 660766

£80; 14 rms with views of garden. Friendly little modern hotel in over three acres on edge of Snowdonia, with open fire, books and magazines in comfortable lounge, friendly bar, generous helpings of popular food using lots of home-grown produce in restaurant, and good service; lots of walks; good disabled access; dogs in bedrooms; £5

TAL-Y-CAFN

Tal-y-Cafn Hotel

Tal-y-Cafn, Colwyn Bay, Clwyd LL28 5RR (01492) 650203

£69.50; 4 well appointed rms. Attractive and comfortable roadside inn in Conwy Valley and close to Bodnant Garden; terracotta walls and traditional pubby furniture in lobby, snug wood-panelled bar, and dining area, big fire in huge inglenook fireplace, real ales, efficient service, good, straightforward and sensibly priced bar food, and seats in spacious hedged garden; dogs in bedrooms

TINTERN PARVA

Parva Farmhouse

Tintern, Chepstow, Gwent NP16 6SQ (01291) 689411

£80; 8 comfortable rms. Friendly stone farmhouse built in 17th c, with leather chesterfields, woodburner and honesty bar in large beamed lounge, books (no TV downstairs), and very good food and wine (inc wine using locally grown grapes) in cosy restaurant; 50 yards from River Wye and lovely surrounding countryside; resident border terrier cross; children over 12; dogs in bedrooms and residents' lounge; £3

TY'N-Y-GROES

Groes

Ty'n-y-Groes, Conwy, Gwynedd LL32 8TN (01492) 650545

£95; 14 spacious rms, each with seating area and some with terrace or balcony. Family run and thoroughly welcoming ancient inn with rambling, low-beamed and thick-walled bars, antique settles, cheerful winter log fires, collections of stone cats and old clocks, fresh flowers, beer from family's own brewery, airy and verdant conservatory, well presented food using local game, lamb, fish and home-grown herbs, and seats in pretty back garden; well appointed wooden cabin to rent, too; dogs in bedrooms

Channel Islands

MAP 1

DOG FRIENDLY PUBS

GRÈVE DE LECQ

Moulin de Lecq

Le Mont De La Greve De Lecq; JE3 2DT

Cheerful family friendly old mill in lovely location with pubby food and four real ales

Outside this aged black-shuttered water mill, you'll find a massive restored waterwheel with its formidable dark wood gears located on the other side of a thick stone wall inside the bar – it's almost worth a visit in itself. During their occupation of the Island the Germans commandeered it to generate power for their searchlights. The pub is in a quiet spot, with a stream trickling past, lots of picnic sets with umbrellas outside on a terrace, and a good children's adventure playground. The road past here leads down to pleasant walks on one of the only north-coast beaches, and to surrounding forests. Inside, the bar is fairly traditional, with plush-cushioned black wooden seats against white-painted or stone walls, dark wood beams and a good log fire in a stone fireplace. Chatty friendly staff serve four changing beers from brewers such Ringwood and Skinners on handpump, and a farm cider. Bar food is simple and filling. Up a narrow flight of stairs, there's a popular games room with the old grain-hopper and grinding-wheel box, a fruit machine, pool, juke box and board games; piped music.

Free house ~ Licensee Kenneth Jenkins ~ Real ale ~ Bar food (12-2, 6-9) ~ Restaurant ~ (01534) 482818 ~ Children welcome ~ Dogs allowed in bar ~ Open 11-11

ROZEL

Rozel

La Vallee De Rozel; JE3 6AJ

Traditional tucked-away pub with reasonably priced food, nice hillside garden

Just out of sight of the sea, at the edge of a charming little fishing village, this friendly place has a very pleasant steeply terraced and partly covered hillside garden. Inside, the counter (with Bass, Courage Directors and Ringwood under light blanket pressure) and tables in the traditional-feeling and cosy little dark-beamed back bar are stripped to their original light wood finish, and there are dark plush wall seats and stools, with an open granite fireplace and old prints and local pictures on cream walls. Leading off is a carpeted area with flowers on big solid square tables. Fairly priced pubby food is served in generous helpings. Piped music, TV, juke box, darts, pool, cribbage and dominoes in the games room.

Free house ~ Licensee Trevor Amy ~ Real ale ~ Bar food ~ Restaurant (not Sun evening) ~ (01534) 869801 ~ Children welcome ~ Dogs allowed in bar ~ Open 11-11

ST BRELADE

Old Portelet Inn

Portelet Bay; JE3 8AJ

Family-friendly place with generous pubby food (something virtually all day), and good views; can be very busy

Families feel particularly welcome and relaxed at this well run 17th-c farmhouse. There's a supervised indoor play area (half an hour 60p), another one outside, board games in the wooden-floored loft bar, and even summer entertainments; also a games machine, pool and piped music. There are picnic-sets on the partly covered flower-bower terrace by a wishing well, and seats in the sizeable land-scaped garden, with lots of scented stocks and other flowers; it's just a short walk down a long flight of granite steps to the beach – the pub is well placed to give views across Portelet (Jersey's most southerly bay). The low-beamed downstairs bar has a stone counter (with Bass and a guest such as Courage Directors kept under light blanket pressure, and a dozen wines by the glass), a huge open fire, gas lamps, old pictures, etched glass panels from France and a nice mixture of old wooden chairs on bare oak boards and quarry tiles. It can get very busy (they do take coaches), but does have its quiet moments, too. From a short snack menu, generous helpings of straightforward food are quickly served by neatly dressed attentive staff.

Randalls ~ Manager Anthony Mulligan ~ Real ale ~ Bar food (12-9(8 Sun)) ~ (01534) 741899 ~ Children welcome ~ Dogs allowed in bar ~ Open 10(11 Sun)-11

Old Smugglers

Ouaisne Bay; OS map reference 595476; JE3 8AW

Happy unassuming place with four real ales, beer festivals and traditional food; families welcome

Every year they host two real ale and cider festivals at this nicely straightfor-ward old free house. The rest of the time you will find well kept Bass, Ringwood Best, Skinners Betty Stogs and a guest such as Greene King Abbot on handpump, as well as a farm cider. The welcoming bar here, developed just before the war from old fisherman's cottages has thick walls, low black beams, log fires in a large fireplace and cosy black built-in settles. Children are welcomed with colouring pads and crayons, and they've a TV, sensibly placed darts, cribbage and dominoes. Bar food is pretty straightforward but they do offer portuguese kebabs as a speciality. A glassed porch, running the width of the building, takes in interesting views over one of the island's many defence towers.

Free house ~ Licensee Andrew Walker ~ Real ale ~ Bar food (12-2, 6-9) ~ Restaurant ~ (01534) 741510 ~ Children welcome ~ Dogs welcome ~ Open 11-11

ST JOHN

Les Fontaines

Le Grand Mourier, Route du Nord; JE3 4AJ

Nicely traditional public bar, bigger family area, decent food, views from terrace, play area

There seems to be plenty of room for everyone at this big converted farmhouse. You'll find the cheery bustle of happy dining families in one area, and locals, perhaps communing in the true Jersey patois, in the well-hidden public bar. As you go in, look out for a worn, unmarked door at the side of the building, or as you go down the main entry lobby towards the bigger main bar go through the tiny narrow door on your right. These entrances take you into the best part, the public bar, which has very heavy beams in the low dark ochre ceiling, massively thick irregular red granite walls, cushioned settles on the quarry-tiled floor and antique prints. The big granite-columned fireplace with a log fire warming its unusual inglenook seats may date back to the 16th c, and still sports its old smoking chains and side oven. The quarry tiled main bar is a marked contrast, with plenty of wheelback chairs around neat dark tables, and a spiral staircase leading up to a wooden gallery under the high pine-raftered plank ceiling. Beers might include Bass and Wells & Youngs Bombardier; piped music and board games. A bonus for families is Pirate Pete's, a play area for children. The pub is in a pretty spot on the north coast, with good views from seats on a terrace. The very traditional bar menu is supplemented with a few interesting specials.

Randalls ~ Manager Hazel O'Gorman ~ Real ale ~ Bar food (12-2.15, 6-9) ~ (01534) 862707 ~ Children welcome ~ Dogs allowed in bar ~ Open 11.30-11

Dog Quiz Answers

1 c – source 2008 study commissioned by Butcher's dog food
2 Sir Thomas Champneys' German *pudelhund* Fidele, a poodle type of water-hound who had saved him from drowning, was buried there at his master's feet, in the 1790s. When the bishop found out, the dog had to be exhumed and reburied under a wonderful commemorative urn in his late master's park. But in 1877 church restorations showed that the dog was still there. The monument has since been moved to the graveyard, and a plaque in the church porch tells the story of this unique burial of a dog in consecrated ground.
3 Her Majesty the Queen (Sandringham Sydney).
4 Leona Helmsley, the hotels heiress who died in 2007; she also left $12 million to her own maltese, Trouble, whose security now costs $100,000 a year.
5 Booger, a pit bull terrier, who had saved his owner's life before his own death two years previously, and was cloned for $50,000, using DNA from his frozen ear.
6 Pencil.
7 Cocker spaniel.
8 Labrador.
9 Walthamstow.
10 About 45mph.
11 'The one with the waggley tail?'
11a 'I don't want a bunny or a kitty, I don't want a parrot that talks; I don't want a bowl of little fishies...'
11b 'He can't take a goldfish for walks.'
12 Never – they still keep them and in summer you can now book mountain hikes with a group of them (they are no longer used for rescue work).
13 Snoop Dogg.
14 A 2,500-year-old fable by Aesop, about a dog that wouldn't let cattle near the hay it was lying on.
15 German shepherd (from 'Genetic Structure of the Purebred Domestic Dog', H G Parker *et al*, *Science*, 304, p1160).
16 Boots.
17 Fang.
18 Eddie.
19 21,000.
20 Twice a year.
21 Only for some genuinely working dogs, only in England and Wales; for all others it has been banned by law since 2007.

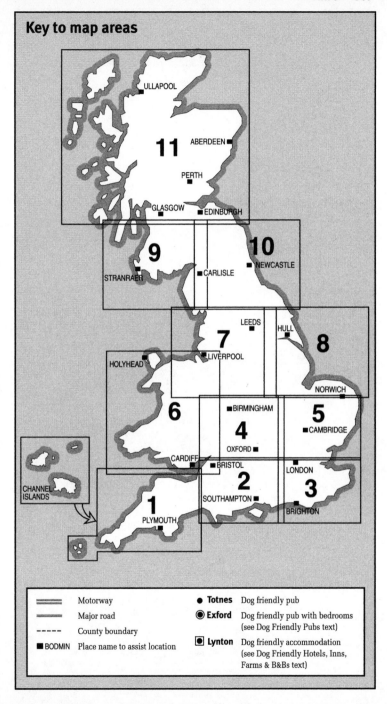

Key to map areas

ULLAPOOL

11

ABERDEEN

PERTH

GLASGOW   EDINBURGH

9   **10**

NEWCASTLE

STRANRAER   CARLISLE

LEEDS   HULL

7   **8**

HOLYHEAD   LIVERPOOL

NORWICH

6   BIRMINGHAM   **5**

4   CAMBRIDGE

CARDIFF   OXFORD

BRISTOL   LONDON

2

CHANNEL
ISLANDS   SOUTHAMPTON

BRIGHTON

1   **3**

PLYMOUTH

	Motorway	**Totnes**	Dog friendly pub
	Major road	**Exford**	Dog friendly pub with bedrooms (see Dog Friendly Pubs text)
	County boundary	**Lynton**	Dog friendly accommodation (see Dog Friendly Hotels, Inns, Farms & B&Bs text)
■ BODMIN	Place name to assist location		

1

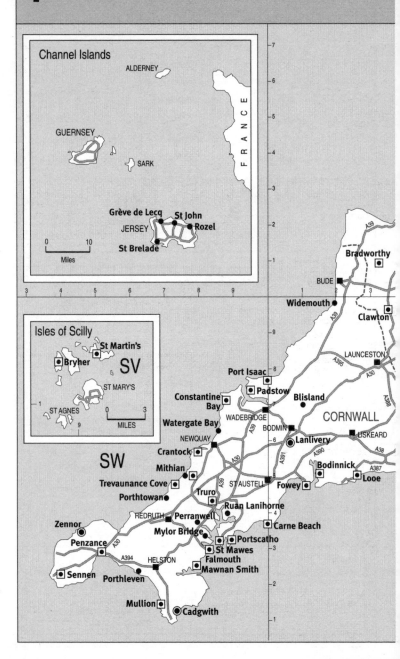

Channel Islands

ALDERNEY

FRANCE

GUERNSEY

SARK

Grève de Lecq   St John
JERSEY   Rozel
St Brelade

0   10
Miles

7

6

5

4

3

2

1

3   4   5   6   7   8   9   1

Isles of Scilly

St Martin's

Bryher   SV

ST MARY'S

ST AGNES   0   3
MILES

1

9

SW

Bradworthy

BUDE

Widemouth

Clawton

LAUNCESTON

Port Isaac

Padstow   Blisland

Constantine
Bay   WADEBRIDGE   CORNWALL

Watergate Bay   BODMIN

NEWQUAY   Lanlivery   LISKEARD

Crantock   Bodinnick

Mithian   Looe

Trevaunance Cove   ST AUSTELL   Fowey

Porthtowan   Truro

Ruan Lanihorne

REDRUTH   Perranwell   Carne Beach

Zennor   Mylor Bridge

Penzance   Portscatho

Sennen   HELSTON   St Mawes
Falmouth

Porthleven   Mawnan Smith

Mullion   Cadgwith

A39

A395

A30

A388

A390

A38

A387

A391

A39

A30

A394

1

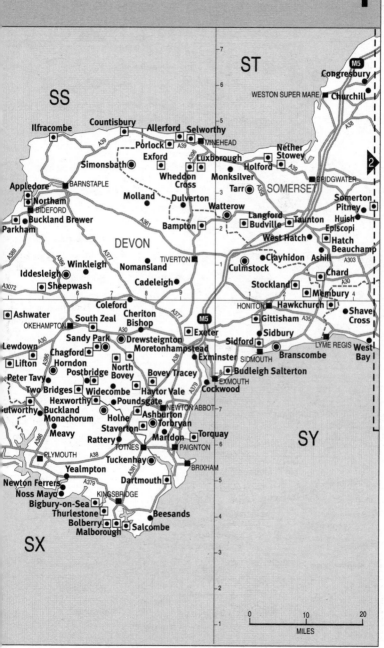

ST

SS

Congresbury

WESTON SUPER MARE ■ Churchill

Ilfracombe Countisbury Allerford Selworthy
Porlock A39 MINEHEAD
Exford Luxborough Nether
Simonsbath Wheddon Monksilver Stowey
Appledore Cross Holford BRIDGWATER
BARNSTAPLE Molland Dulverton Tarr SOMERSET Somerton
Northam BIDEFORD Watterow Pitney
Buckland Brewer Bampton Langford Taunton Huish
Parkham Budville Episcopi
West Hatch Hatch
DEVON Beauchamp
Winkleigh Nomansland TIVERTON Clayhidon Ashill
Iddesleigh Culmstock A303
Sheepwash Cadeleigh Chard
Stockland Membury
Coleford HONITON Hawkchurch
Ashwater Cheriton Gittisham A35 Shave
South Zeal Bishop Cross
OKEHAMPTON A30 Exeter Sidbury
Sandy Park Drewsteignton Sidford LYME REGIS West
Lewdown Chagford Moretonhampstead Exminster Branscombe Bay
Lifton Horndon North SIDMOUTH
Peter Tavy Postbridge Bovey Bovey Tracey Budleigh Salterton
Two Bridges Widecombe Haytor Vale EXMOUTH
Hexworthy Poundsgate Cockwood
utworthy Buckland Holne NEWTON ABBOT
Monachorum Ashburton Torbryan Torquay
Meavy Staverton Marldon SY
Rattery PAIGNTON
PLYMOUTH A38 TOTNES Torquay
Tuckenhay
Yealmpton BRIXHAM
Newton Ferrers Dartmouth
Noss Mayo KINGSBRIDGE
Bigbury-on-Sea
Thurlestone Beesands
Bolberry Salcombe
Malborough

SX

0   10   20
MILES

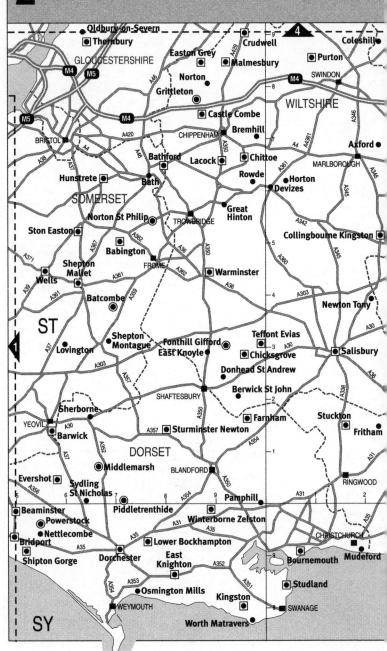

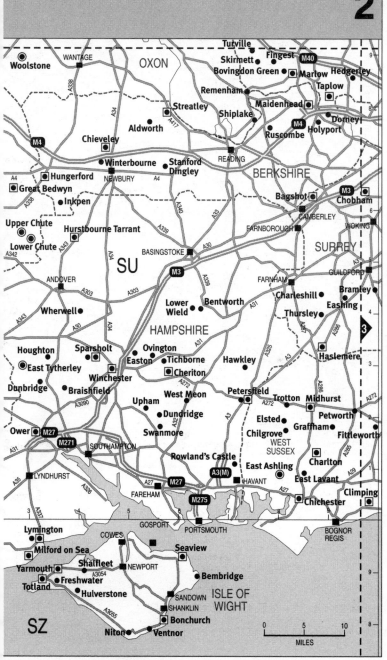

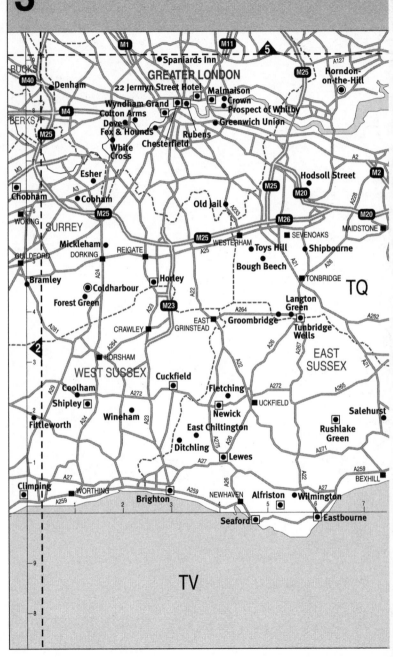

3

M1 · M11 · 5 · A127

BUCKS · M40

M25 · Denham · **GREATER LONDON** · Spaniards Inn · M25 · **Horndon-on-the-Hill**

BERKS · M4 · **22 Jermyn Street Hotel** · **Malmaison** · **Crown**

M25 · **Wyndham Grand** · **Prospect of Whitby**

Cotton Arms · **Greenwich Union**

M3 · **Dove** · **Rubens**

Fox & Hounds · **Chesterfield**

White Cross · **Hodsoll Street** · M2

Esher · M25

Chobham · A3 · **Cobham** · **Old Jail** · M20 · M20

WOKING · M25 · M26 · MAIDSTONE

SURREY · **Mickleham** · WESTERHAM · SEVENOAKS

GUILDFORD · DORKING · REIGATE · A25 · **Toys Hill** · **Shipbourne** · A26

Bramley · A24 · **Horley** · **Bough Beech** · TONBRIDGE

Coldharbour · A21 · **TQ**

Forest Green · A23 · M23 · **Langton Green**

CRAWLEY · A22 · A264 · **Groombridge** · **Tunbridge Wells** · A262

EAST GRINSTEAD · **2** · A264 · **EAST SUSSEX** · A21

HORSHAM · A26 · A267

WEST SUSSEX · **Cuckfield** · A22

Coolham · A272 · **Fletching** · A272 · A265

Shipley · **Newick** · **UCKFIELD** · **Salehurst**

Fittleworth · **Wineham** · A23 · **East Chiltington** · **Rushlake Green**

A24 · **Ditchling** · A275 · A271

Lewes · A22 · A259 BEXHILL

Climping · A27 · WORTHING · A26 · A259 · A27 · **Eastbourne**

A259 · **Brighton** · NEWHAVEN · **Alfriston** · **Wilmington**

Seaford · **Eastbourne**

TV

3

ESSEX

A127

SOUTHEND-
ON-SEA

SHEERNESS

WHITSTABLE

MARGATE

A299

A28

● **Boyden Gate**

RAMSGATE

● **Oare**

A2

FAVERSHAM

M2

A2

● **Canterbury**

A257

TR

M20

● **Thurnham**

Selling

A256

A2

● DEAL

A20

A274

KENT

A28

● **Boughton Lees**

A229

● **Pluckley**

● **Bodsham**

A258

● **St Margaret's
Bay**

● **Staplehurst**

ASHFORD

A260

● **Stowting**

● **Dover**

● **Biddenden**

M20

A20

A229

A28

A2070

FOLKESTONE

A259

Brookland

A266

A259

Peasmarsh

● **Rye**

A21

Battle

● **Icklesham**

A259

● **Fairlight**

Hastings

0   5   10
MILES

4

Wrekin
TELFORD
STAFFS
Lichfield
Hopwas
Tamworth
M54
M6
M6 Toll

SJ

Ironbridge
Norton
WOLVERHAMPTON
WALSALL
Shustoke

Longville
A454
Worfield
WEST BROMWICH
M6
M6

BRIDGNORTH

SHROPSHIRE
STOURBRIDGE
BIRMINGHAM

Hopton Wafers
M5
SOLIHULL
M42

Ludlow
KIDDERMINSTER
Holy Cross
M42
M40

Brimfield
BROMSGROVE
M5
Preston Bagot

WORCESTERSHIRE
Aston Cantlow

Ombersley
Himbleton
REDDITCH

Bringsty Common
Knightwick
Stratford-upon-Avon

LEOMINSTER
WORCESTER
A22
B439

SO
Kempsey

Malvern
Great Malvern
Ab Lench

HEREFORDSHIRE

HEREFORD
Malvern Wells
Hanley Swan
Evesham
Chipping Campden

Ledbury
Birtsmorton
Broadway

Woolhope
Great Wolford

Hoarwithy
Sellack
Corse Lawn
Stow-on-the-Wold
Kingham

St Owen's Cross
M50
Lower Slaughter
Lwr Oddington

Ross-on-Wye
GLOUCESTERSHIRE
Guiting Power
Bledington

Glewstone
Cheltenham
Nether Westcote

Symonds Yat
GLOUCESTER
Great Rissington

Blaisdon
Cowley
Little Barrington

MONMOUTH
English Bicknor
Chedworth

Newland
Cranham
North Cerney
Burford

Brimpsfield
Bibury

Clearwell
Parkend
Sheepscombe
Duntisbourne Abbots
Barnsley
Langford

STROUD
Sapperton
CIRENCESTER

Coates

North Nibley
Nailsworth
Ewen

M5
Tetbury

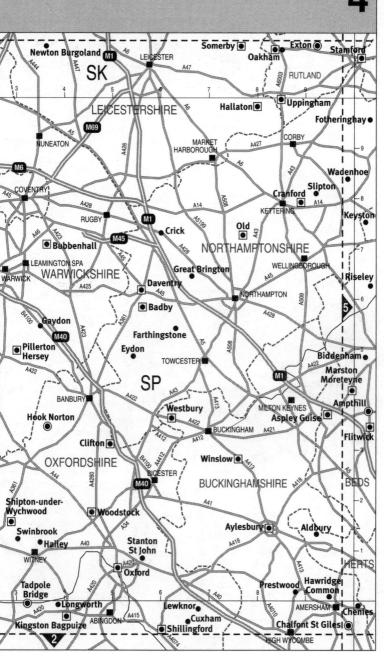

5

LINCS

WISBECH

DOWNHAM MARKET

8

A1122

A1122

Stamford

A15

Barnack

Helpston

A47

A605

A1122

A10

A101

Wansford

Peterborough

Elton

Fotheringhay

NORTHANTS

CAMBRIDGESHIRE

A1(M)

A141

A142

A11

A1065

A14

A5

Keyston

A14

Huntingdon

A141

A1123

Ely

A142

A11

Buckden

A1

B645

A14

Reach

NEWMARKET

Riseley

A428

Fen Ditton

Little Wilbraham

BEDFORDSHIRE

A1198

A10

Cambridge

TL

Six Mile
Bottom

A11

4

BEDFORD

A421

A600

A603

Sandy

A1

Northill

Broom

Old Warden

Houghton
Conquest

Ashwell

Hinxton

Great Chesterford

A505

A1092

A1017

Ampthill

Heydon

Little Walden

Flitwick

A6

A10

M11

A507

Howlett End

M1

A505

A1(M)

STEVENAGE

ESSEX

BRAINTREE

LUTON

Knebworth

A120

Bishop's Stortford

A120

A131

Batford

Chapmore End

A1060

A1081

HERTFORD

A414

HEMEL
HEMPSTEAD

Frithsden

HERTFORDSHIRE

A10

HARLOW

A414

CHELMSFORD

ST ALBANS

A41

Flaunden

A12

Chenies

M25

Stapleford Tawney

Margaretting
Tye

M25

BRENTWOOD

3

Spaniards Inn

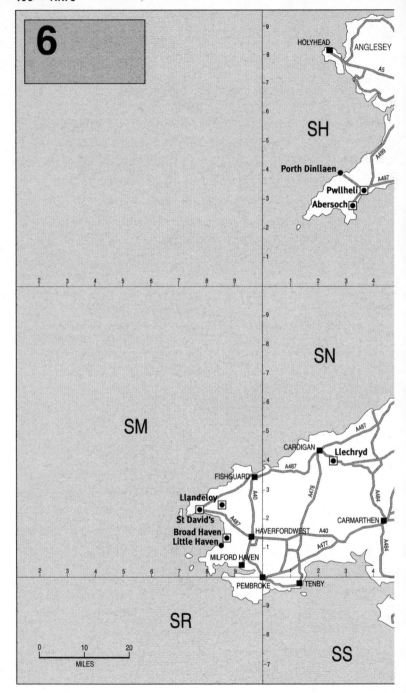

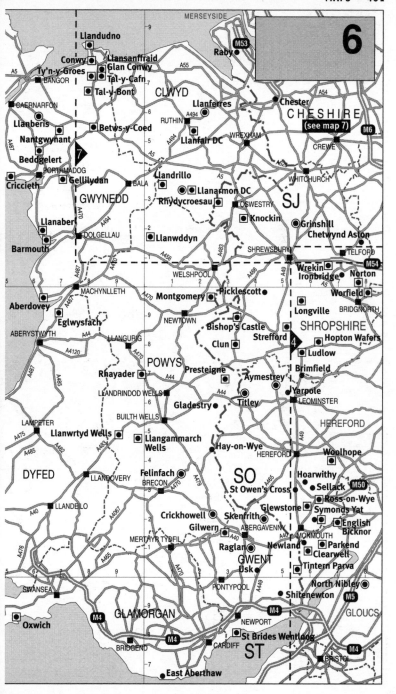

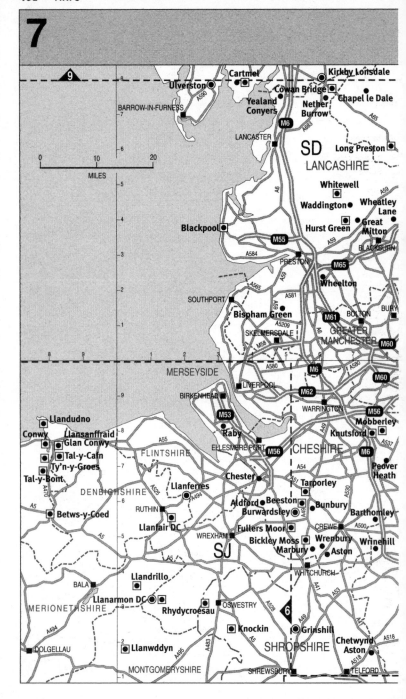

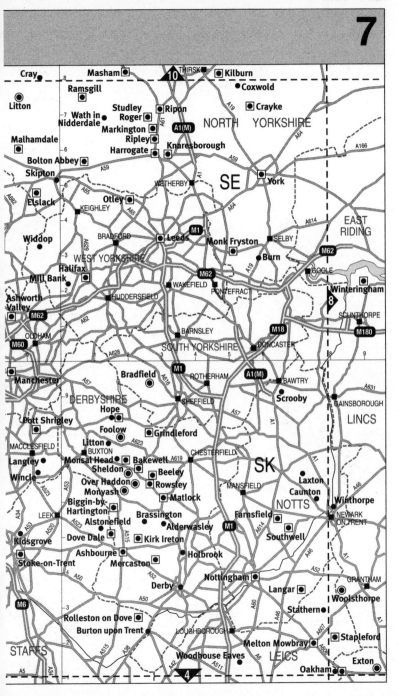

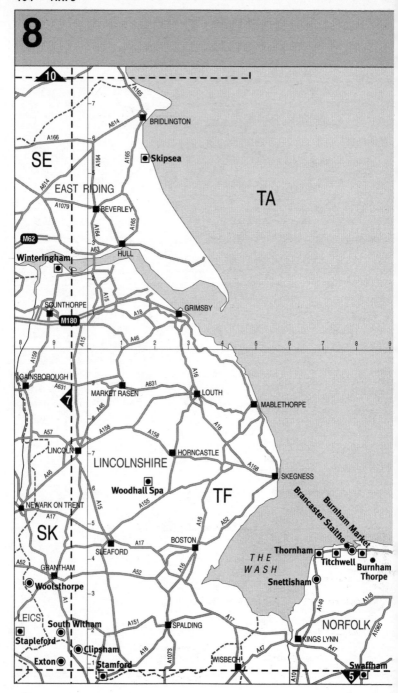

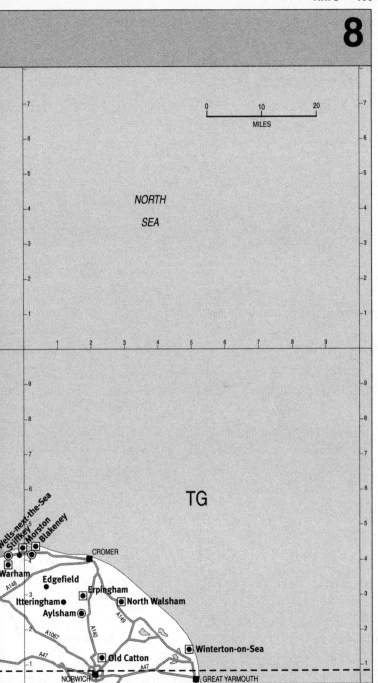

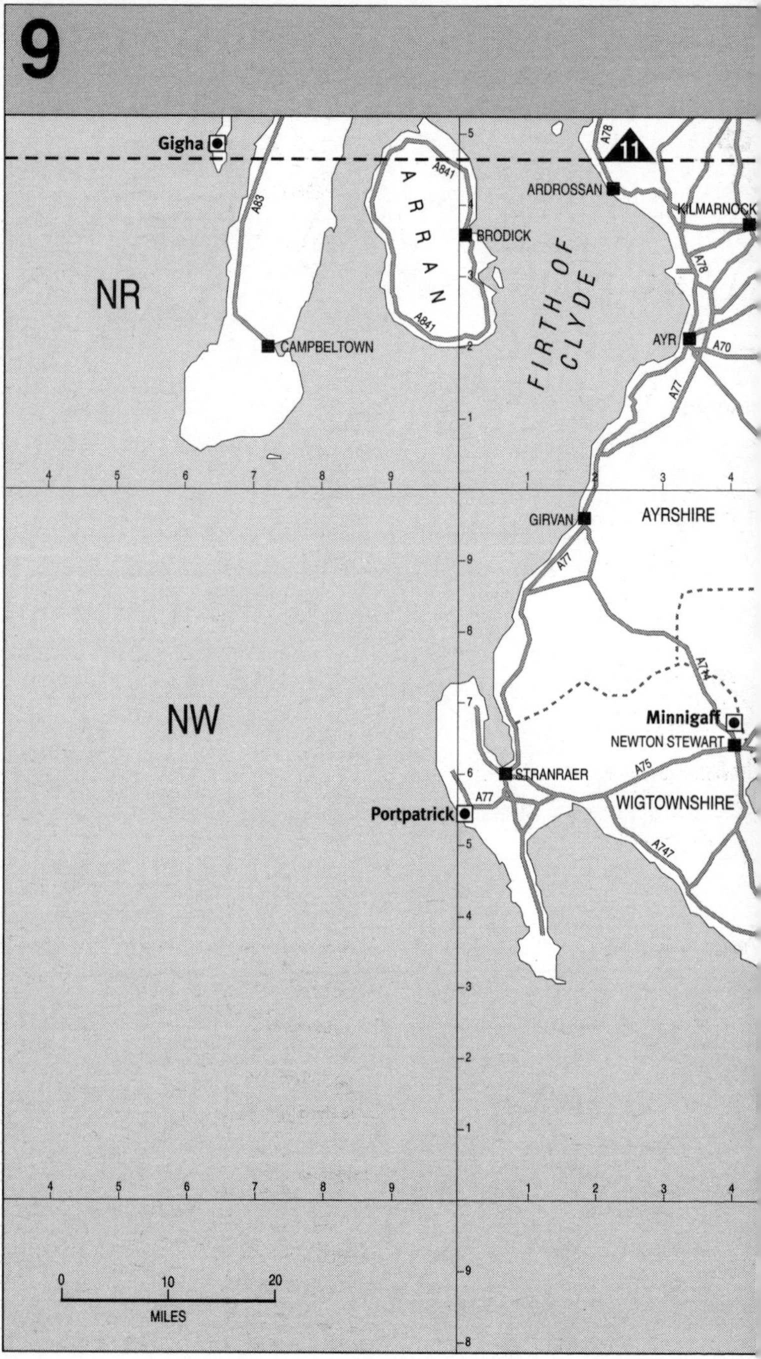

9

NR

NW

Gigha

A83

A841

A R R A N

BRODICK

A841

CAMPBELTOWN

FIRTH OF CLYDE

ARDROSSAN

KILMARNOCK

A78

A71

AYR

A70

A77

11

GIRVAN

AYRSHIRE

A77

A76

Minnigaff

NEWTON STEWART

STRANRAER

A75

A77

Portpatrick

WIGTOWNSHIRE

A747

```
0        10        20
        MILES
```

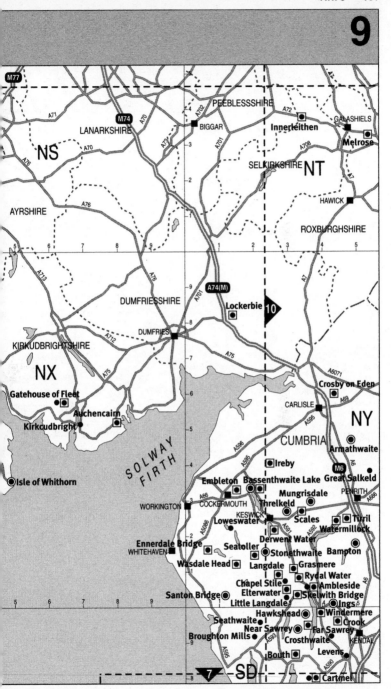

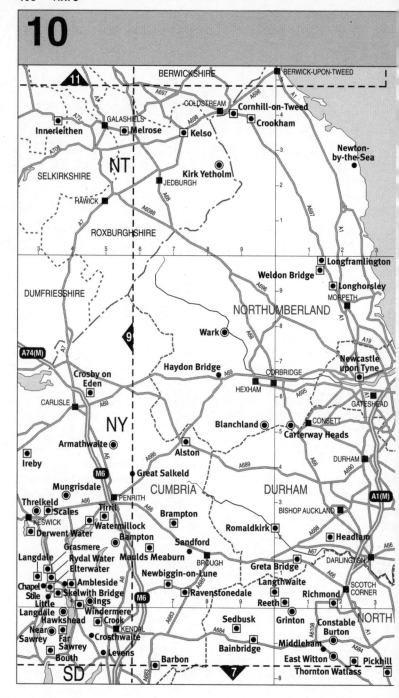

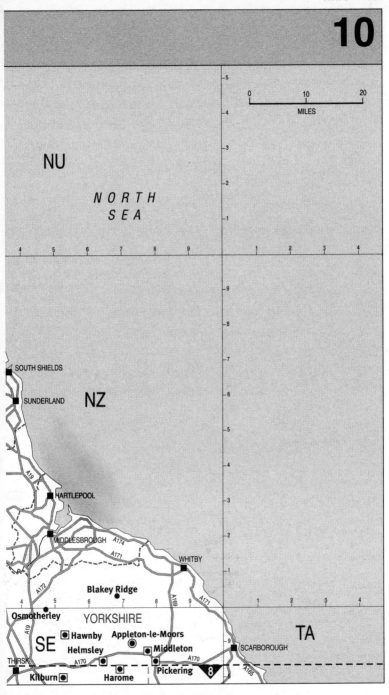

10

NU

NORTH SEA

0   10   20
MILES

NZ

■ SOUTH SHIELDS

■ SUNDERLAND

A19

■ HARTLEPOOL

■ MIDDLESBROUGH   A174

A171

■ WHITBY

A172

Blakey Ridge

A169   A171

● Osmotherley   YORKSHIRE   TA

A19   ◉ Hawnby   Appleton-le-Moors   ◉ SCARBOROUGH

SE   Helmsley ◉   ◉ Middleton

THIRSK   A170   ◉   A170   A165

◉ Kilburn   ◉ Harome   Pickering   ◢8◣

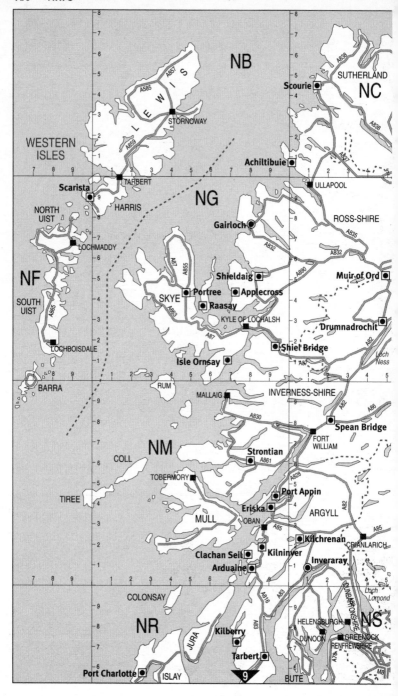

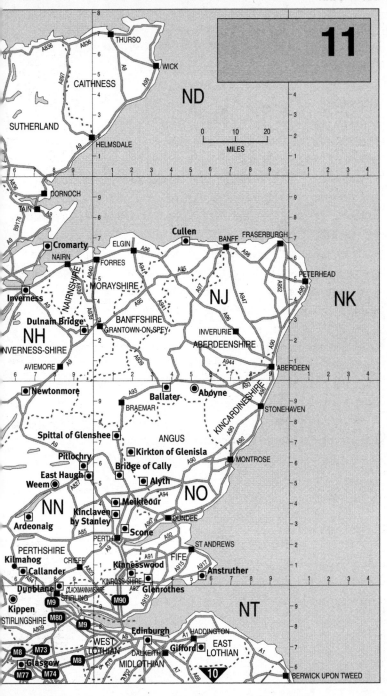

11

THURSO

WICK

CAITHNESS

ND

SUTHERLAND

A9

HELMSDALE

0   10   20

MILES

DORNOCH

TAIN

Cromarty

ELGIN

Cullen

BANFF

FRASERBURGH

NAIRN

FORRES

PETERHEAD

Inverness

NAIRNSHIRE

MORAYSHIRE

NJ

NK

Dulnain Bridge

BANFFSHIRE

GRANTOWN-ON-SPEY

INVERURIE

NH

ABERDEENSHIRE

INVERNESS-SHIRE

AVIEMORE

ABERDEEN

Newtonmore

Ballater

Aboyne

BRAEMAR

STONEHAVEN

KINCARDINESHIRE

Spittal of Glenshee

ANGUS

Pitlochry

Kirkton of Glenisla

East Haugh

Bridge of Cally

MONTROSE

Weem

Alyth

Meikleour

NO

NN

Kinclaven

by Stanley

Ardeonaig

Scone

DUNDEE

PERTH

ST ANDREWS

PERTHSHIRE

CRIEFF

FIFE

Kilmahog

Kinnesswood

Kippen

Callander

Anstruther

KINROSS-SHIRE

Dunblane

CLACKMANNANSHIRE

Glenrothes

STIRLING

NT

Kippen

M9

M90

STIRLINGSHIRE

M80

M9

Edinburgh

HADDINGTON

M8

M73

WEST

LOTHIAN

Gifford

EAST

LOTHIAN

Glasgow

M8

DALKEITH

MIDLOTHIAN

M77

M74

10

BERWICK UPON TWEED

Report Forms

Please report to us: you can use the tear-out forms in this book, or write on plain paper to our freepost address, The Good Pub Guide, FREEPOST TN1569, WADHURST, East Sussex TN5 7BR. Alternatively you can email us at **dogs@goodguides.com**

We need to know what you think of the places in this edition, and we need to know about other places you think are worthy of inclusion. It would be helpful to know about ones that should *not* be included.

Please tell us how welcome you felt with your dog, and about any special facilities or welcoming touches that were provided for your dog.

The atmosphere and character are very important features – so please try to describe what is special about a place. And we need to know about any changes in décor and furnishings, too. Food and drinks are also important, and if you have stayed overnight, please tell us about the standard of accommodation.

It helps enormously if you can give the full address for anywhere new, though just its postcode is very helpful.

Though we try to answer all letters, please understand if there's a delay (particularly in summer, our busiest period).

I have been to the following places in *The Good Guide to Dog Friendly Pubs, Hotels and B&Bs*, and found them as described, and confirm that they deserve continued inclusion:

Continued overleaf

PLEASE GIVE YOUR NAME AND ADDRESS ON THE BACK OF THIS FORM

Establishments visited continued

....

....

Your own name and address *(block capitals please)*

....

....

....

POSTCODE
....

....

Please return to:
Dog Friendly Guide
FREEPOST TN1569
WADHURST
East Sussex
TN5 7BR

> **IF YOU PREFER, YOU CAN SEND
> US REPORTS BY EMAIL:
> dogs@goodguides.com**

Report On

....**(Establishment's name)**

Establishment's address

....

....

....

POSTCODE
....

☐ YES, My dog was welcome   ☐ NO, My dog was not welcome

Please tick one of these boxes to show your verdict, and give reasons, descriptive comments, prices and the date of your visit

Continued overleaf

PLEASE GIVE YOUR NAME AND ADDRESS ON THE BACK OF THIS FORM

Report on continued

....

....

Your own name and address *(block capitals please)*

....

....

....

POSTCODE

....

....

Please return to:
Dog Friendly Guide
FREEPOST TN1569
WADHURST
East Sussex
TN5 7BR

IF YOU PREFER, YOU CAN SEND
US REPORTS BY EMAIL:
dogs@goodguides.com

Report On

....**(Establishment's name)**

Establishment's address

....

....

....
POSTCODE
....

☐ YES, My dog was welcome   ☐ NO, My dog was not welcome

Please tick one of these boxes to show your verdict, and give reasons, descriptive comments, prices and the date of your visit

Continued overleaf

PLEASE GIVE YOUR NAME AND ADDRESS ON THE BACK OF THIS FORM

Report on continued

....

....

Your own name and address *(block capitals please)*

....

....

....

....

....

Please return to:
Dog Friendly Guide
FREEPOST TN1569
WADHURST
East Sussex
TN5 7BR

IF YOU PREFER, YOU CAN SEND
US REPORTS BY EMAIL:
dogs@goodguides.com

Report On

....(Establishment's name)

Establishment's address

....

....

....
POSTCODE
....

☐ YES, My dog was welcome   ☐ NO, My dog was not welcome

Please tick one of these boxes to show your verdict, and give reasons, descriptive comments, prices and the date of your visit

Continued overleaf

PLEASE GIVE YOUR NAME AND ADDRESS ON THE BACK OF THIS FORM

Report on continued

....

By returning this form, you consent to the collection, recording and use of the information you submit, by The Random House Group Ltd. Any personal details which you provide from which we can identify you are held and processed in accordance with the Data Protection Act 1998 and will not be passed on to any third parties. The Random House Group Ltd may wish to send you further information on their associated products. Please tick box if you do not wish to receive any such information. ☐

....

Your own name and address *(block capitals please)*

....

....

....

....

In returning this form I confirm my agreement that the information I provide may be used by The Random House Group Ltd, its assignees and/or licensees in any media or medium whatsoever.

....

Please return to:
Dog Friendly Guide
FREEPOST TN1569
WADHURST
East Sussex
TN5 7BR

IF YOU PREFER, YOU CAN SEND
US REPORTS BY EMAIL:
dogs@goodguides.com

Report On

....**(Establishment's name)**

Establishment's address

....

....

....

POSTCODE
....

☐ YES, My dog was welcome   ☐ NO, My dog was not welcome

Please tick one of these boxes to show your verdict, and give reasons, descriptive comments, prices and the date of your visit

Continued overleaf

PLEASE GIVE YOUR NAME AND ADDRESS ON THE BACK OF THIS FORM

Report on continued

....

By returning this form, you consent to the collection, recording and use of the information you submit, by The Random House Group Ltd. Any personal details which you provide from which we can identify you are held and processed in accordance with the Data Protection Act 1998 and will not be passed on to any third parties. The Random House Group Ltd may wish to send you further information on their associated products. Please tick box if you do not wish to receive any such information. ☐

....

Your own name and address *(block capitals please)*

....

....

....

....

In returning this form I confirm my agreement that the information I provide may be used by The Random House Group Ltd, its assignees and/or licensees in any media or medium whatsoever.

....

Please return to:
Dog Friendly Guide
FREEPOST TN1569
WADHURST
East Sussex
TN5 7BR

IF YOU PREFER, YOU CAN SEND
US REPORTS BY EMAIL:
dogs@goodguides.com

Report On

....**(Establishment's name)**

Establishment's address

....

....

....

POSTCODE
....

☐ YES, My dog was welcome   ☐ NO, My dog was not welcome

Please tick one of these boxes to show your verdict, and give reasons, descriptive comments, prices and the date of your visit

Continued overleaf

PLEASE GIVE YOUR NAME AND ADDRESS ON THE BACK OF THIS FORM

Report on continued

....

By returning this form, you consent to the collection, recording and use of the information you submit, by The Random House Group Ltd. Any personal details which you provide from which we can identify you are held and processed in accordance with the Data Protection Act 1998 and will not be passed on to any third parties. The Random House Group Ltd may wish to send you further information on their associated products. Please tick box if you do not wish to receive any such information. ☐

....

Your own name and address *(block capitals please)*

....

....

....

....

In returning this form I confirm my agreement that the information I provide may be used by The Random House Group Ltd, its assignees and/or licensees in any media or medium whatsoever.

....

Please return to:
Dog Friendly Guide
FREEPOST TN1569
WADHURST
East Sussex
TN5 7BR

IF YOU PREFER, YOU CAN SEND
US REPORTS BY EMAIL:
dogs@goodguides.com